560

# THE
# ECONOMICS
# OF
# DEFENSE
# IN THE
# NUCLEAR
# AGE

*Originally published by Harvard University Press*

*Charles J. Hitch & Roland N. McKean*

# THE
# ECONOMICS
# OF
# DEFENSE
# IN THE
# NUCLEAR
# AGE

*With contributions by
Stephen Enke, Alain Enthoven,
Malcolm W. Hoag, C. B. McGuire,
and Albert Wohlstetter*

*Atheneum  New York*  1978

*Published by Atheneum*
*Reprinted by arrangement with Harvard University Press*

*Copyright © 1960 by The RAND Corporation*
*All rights reserved*
*Library of Congress catalog card number 60-10042*
ISBN 0-689-70094-6
*Manufactured in the United States of America by*
*The Murray Printing Company, Forge Village, Massachusetts*
*Published in Canada by McClelland & Stewart Ltd.*

*First Atheneum Printing January 1965*
*Second Printing December 1965*
*Third Printing October 1966*
*Fourth Printing September 1967*
*Fifth Printing September 1969*
*Sixth Printing November 1970*
*Seventh Printing August 1973*
*Eighth Printing April 1974*
*Ninth Printing November 1975*
*Tenth Printing November 1978*

# PREFACE

The purpose of this book is to explain *a way of looking* at military problems which we and others with whom we have been associated have found fruitful in insights and productive of solutions. Essentially we regard *all* military problems as, in one of their aspects, economic problems in the efficient allocation and use of resources. We believe that this way of looking at military problems goes far toward reconciling the apparent conflict of views between the officers and officials who are responsible for defense and the officials and Congressmen whose primary interest is economy — except in determining the over-all size of the military budget, where conflict between these points of view is inevitable.

While we have strong views (or prejudices) on the substantive solutions of many of the military-economic problems which we discuss, we have tried to subordinate them in writing this book. We are concerned more with how to look at military problems and how to go about solving them than with the substantive solutions themselves — which are, in any event, dependent on current circumstances and technologies and hence ephemeral. One of our aims has been to focus attention on the new problems which have become important as a result of the revolution in military technology since the development of atomic weapons. But we try to avoid taking sides on current controversies regarding military strategy except where the issue is too fundamental to be evaded, like the desirability of protecting our deterrent capabilities or of making preparations for localized, limited warfare. That more of our illustrative examples have been taken from Air Force than from Army or Navy problems in no way reflects our views regarding the relative importance of the three Services, but is the result of historical accidents that have given us greater familiarity with Air Force problems.

The book is in no sense a text in how to do military "operations research" or "systems analysis." The treatment is nonmathematical (except for the Appendix at the end of the volume), and problems of designing appropriate models of military reality are usually neglected. We hope, however, that operations researchers will find here the economic concepts and analysis which are essential to their craft, and that military decision-makers will find material which will enhance their understanding of operations research and their ability to use it.

We wish to thank and give credit to our other collaborators. Alain Enthoven wrote the Appendix, "The Simple Mathematics of Maximization," at the end of the volume. Chapter 14, "Logistics," was written by Stephen Enke, and Chapter 15, "The Economics of Military Alliance," by Malcolm W. Hoag. C. B. McGuire prepared Chapter 8, "An Illustrative Application of Economic Analysis," and its appendix. The author of Chapter 18, "Choosing Policies for Deterrence," was Albert Wohlstetter. We are indebted to the Harvard University Press for permission to use Chapter 14, which originally appeared in *The Review of Economics and Statistics*, to the Council on Foreign Relations for permission to use Chapter 18, which originally appeared in *Foreign Affairs*, and to John Wiley and Sons, Inc., for permission to use excerpts from R. N. McKean's *Efficiency in Government through Systems Analysis*, a RAND Corporation research study published by Wiley and Sons in 1958 as one of the series of Publications in Operations Research sponsored by the Operations Research Society of America.

Our greatest debt is to the U. S. Air Force and The RAND Corporation for making it possible to prepare the book. Without their support and the stimulus of the RAND environment, we could not have done the study. Most of it was written as a part of Project RAND, the research program conducted by The RAND Corporation for the U. S. Air Force. Thanks are due also to Yale University, where Mr. Hitch worked on the manuscript during the Spring of 1957 while he was Irving Fisher Professor of Economics.

For the development of our views and ideas, we are indebted to a great many persons, particularly to past and present colleagues at The RAND Corporation and to numerous members of the military Services. In connection with the preparation of this manuscript, we wish to thank especially Col. George A. Lincoln and his staff at the U. S. Military Academy and Col. Wesley W. Posvar of the U. S. Air Force Academy for discussions of plans for the book and for criticisms of portions of it; Bernard Brodie, F. R. Collbohm, Daniel Ellsberg, Alain Enthoven, Gene H. Fisher, Robert N. Grosse, Oleg Hoeffding, Leland L. Johnson, Joseph A. Kershaw, Burton H. Klein, Andrew W. Marshall, Richard H. Moorsteen, Richard R. Nelson, Russell T. Nichols, Henry S. Rowen, John R. Summerfield, Philip Wolfe, Charles J. Zwick (all of The RAND Corporation), Kenneth J. Arrow of Stanford University, Thomas C. Schelling of Harvard University, Robert M. Solow of the Massachusetts Institute of Technology, and Alan P. Carlin, a graduate student at the Massachusetts Institute of Technology, for criticisms and suggestions regarding parts of the manuscript; and Joseph M. Goldsen, Brownlee W. Haydon, Norman M. Kaplan, Malcolm W. Hoag, William W. Taylor (all of RAND), Wil-

liam M. Capron of Stanford University, and Paul G. Clark of Williams
College for reading and criticizing the entire manuscript.

Needless to say, the authors — not the organizations or individuals
who have helped them — are responsible for the views expressed in this
study. (McKean alone, however, is responsible for the minor changes
made in the third printing.)

C. J. HITCH

R. N. McKEAN

# CONTENTS

# TABLES

# FIGURES

# THE ECONOMICS OF DEFENSE IN THE NUCLEAR AGE

# 1. DEFENSE AS AN ECONOMIC PROBLEM

National security[1] depends upon many factors, which writers on the subject classify in different ways. Important among them are the morale of a country's soldiers, the number and ingenuity of its scientists, the character and skill of its political and military leaders, its geographic position relative to other countries, and even — in this nuclear age — the prevailing winds that blow across its expanses.

But national security also depends upon economic factors, which are variously interpreted and defined. Most speakers and writers who stress the importance of economic factors are referring to the economic strength of the nation, as contrasted with its military forces. They allege that the United States exerted a decisive influence in the later stages of World Wars I and II through its superior economic strength. Russia, it has been said, is more fearful of "Detroit" than of either the Strategic Air Command or the Divisions of NATO.

Other experts use the concept of economic factors more narrowly, to refer to the constraints on military forces imposed by the budget — the necessity to limit costs. Thus, Professor Kissinger[2] contrasts "doctrinal," "technological," and "fiscal" influences on our military strategy and concludes that the fiscal, as well as the technological, has been too influential at the expense of military doctrine. Similarly Mr. Hanson Baldwin complains that "In the Western World — though not in Russia — costs are a more decisive factor in shaping defense than is military logic." [3]

In this book we will be concerned with economics in its most general sense. Economics is not exclusively concerned, as the above interpretations imply, with certain types of activities (industrial) rather than others (military), or with the traditional points of view of budgeteers and comptrollers.[4] Being truly economical does not mean scrimping — reducing expenditures no matter how important the things to be bought. Nor does

---

[1] In most of this volume, the terms "defense" and "national security" will be used interchangeably. Wherever defense is used in a narrower sense, e.g., defense as opposed to offense, we believe the context will make this clear.

[2] Henry A. Kissinger, "Strategy and Organization," *Foreign Affairs,* April 1957, pp. 379–394.

[3] "Arms and the Atom — I," *New York Times,* May 14, 1957, p. 21.

[4] Problems of eliminating redundant overhead costs, preventing the padding of expense accounts, restricting the use of chauffeur-driven cars to top officials, etc., while important, are relatively narrow management problems, and not our concern in this book.

it mean implementing some stated doctrine regardless of cost. Rather economics is concerned with allocating resources — choosing doctrines and techniques — so as to get the most out of available resources. To economize in this sense may imply spending less on some things and more on others. But always economics or economizing means trying to make the most efficient use of the resources available in all activities in any circumstances.

In our view the problem of combining limited quantities of missiles, crews, bases, and maintenance facilities to "produce" a strategic air force that will maximize deterrence of enemy attack is just as much a problem in economics (although in some respects a harder one) as the problem of combining limited quantities of coke, iron ore, scrap, blast furnaces, and mill facilities to produce steel in such a way as to maximize profits. In both cases there is an objective, there are budgetary and other resource constraints, and there is a challenge to economize.

Economy and efficiency are two ways of looking at the same characteristic of an operation. If a manufacturer or a military commander has a fixed budget (or other fixed resources) and attempts to maximize his production or the attainment of his objective, we say that he has the problem of using his resources efficiently. But if his production goal or other objective is fixed, his problem is to economize on his use of resources, that is, to minimize his costs. These problems may sound like different problems; in fact they are logically equivalent. For any level of either budget or objective, the choices that maximize the attainment of an objective for a given budget are the same choices that minimize the cost of attaining that objective.[5] If the Bessemer process is the most economical method of producing steel from the one point of view, it is the most efficient from the other. If Missile X is the system that provides maximum deterrence with a $10 billion SAC budget, it is also the missile which most economically achieves that level of deterrence. In other words, there is no conflict of interest between the budgeteer who is supposed to be interested in economizing and the military commander who is supposed to be interested in efficiency — except in the determination of the *size* of the budget or the magnitude of the objective to be achieved. They should be able to agree on all the "subsequent" decisions.

For this reason it is misleading to imply, as do Kissinger and Baldwin in the articles just quoted, that economic or cost factors are necessarily in conflict with strategic, doctrinal, and technological considerations, and must somehow be reconciled with them, with not too much weight being assigned the economic. There *is* a conflict between defense and other goods

[5] This point is elaborated upon in Chapter 7 and in the Appendix on "The Simple Mathematics of Maximization" at the end of the book.

in deciding on the size of the military budget.[6] Economizing involves deciding how much of other things to sacrifice in the interests of military strength. But in all decisions on how to spend the military budget — on what kinds of equipment and forces, to implement what kind of strategy — there is no such conflict. Strategy, technology, and economy are not three independent "considerations" to be assigned appropriate weights, but interdependent elements of the same problem. Strategies are *ways of using* budgets or resources to achieve military objectives. Technology defines the *possible* strategies. The economic problem is to choose that strategy, including equipment and everything else necessary to implement it, which is most efficient (maximizes the attainment of the objective with the given resources) or economical (minimizes the cost of achieving the given objective) — the strategy which is most efficient also being the most economical.

Strategy and cost are as interdependent as the front and rear sights of a rifle. One cannot assign relative weights to the importance of the positions of the front and rear sights. It does not make sense to ask the correct position of the rear sight except in relation to the front sight and the target. Similarly one cannot economize except in choosing strategies (or tactics or methods) to achieve objectives. The job of economizing, which some would delegate to budgeteers and comptrollers, cannot be distinguished from the whole task of making military decisions.

### ECONOMIZING AT DIFFERENT LEVELS

The problem of national security might in theory be regarded as one big economic problem. The nation has certain resources — now and prospectively in the future — which are conventionally classified by economists as various sorts of land, labor, and capital. These resources can be used to satisfy many objectives of the nation and its individual citizens — national security, a high standard of living, social security, a rapid rate of economic growth, and so on. These are, of course, competing objectives. In general, the more resources the nation devotes to national security, the less it will have for social security and vice versa. We could (as some economists have done)[7] conceive of a "social welfare function" which we would attempt to maximize by an appropriate allocation of the nation's resources among the various activities satisfying these objectives.

In fact, for reasons which will become familiar as we proceed but are in any event obvious, this kind of approach to the problem of national

---

[6] See Chapter 4.

[7] See Kenneth J. Arrow, *Social Choice and Individual Values,* John Wiley and Sons, New York, 1951, and A. Bergson (Burk), "A Reformulation of Certain Aspects of Welfare Economics," *Quarterly Journal of Economics,* February 1938, pp. 310–334.

security is completely impractical and sterile. We have to break economic problems, like so many others, into manageable pieces before we can make a good beginning at finding solutions. And in fact, in the United States and all other countries, governments and departments of defense are organized to deal with appropriate parts of the grand problem at many different levels.

As a beginning let us consider economic problems at each of three rather gross levels. National security, from the point of view of an economist, may be said to depend on three things: (1) the quantity of national resources available, now and in the future; (2) the proportion of these resources allocated to national security purposes; and (3) the efficiency with which the resources so allocated are used.

Several parts of the government — including, for example, the Council of Economic Advisers and the Joint Congressional Committee on the Economic Report — are concerned with problems at the first and "highest" of these levels. Of course the quantity of resources existing in the present cannot be influenced by economic policy; but their full and productive employment can be, and so can their rate of growth, and therefore the quantity of resources that will be available in the future. Present resources are the consequence of past economic policies.

Problems at the second level are the special responsibility of the Bureau of the Budget and the Appropriations Committees of Congress, although all executive departments are deeply involved, and every Congressman is interested. We decide the proportion of national resources to be devoted to defense when we vote a national security budget. In effect we are then choosing between more defense and more of other things. President Eisenhower expressed this choice vividly:

> The cost of one modern heavy bomber is this: a modern brick school in more than 30 cities.
> It is two electric power plants, each serving a town of 60,000 population.
> It is two fine, fully equipped hospitals.
> It is some 50 miles of concrete highway.[8]

Problems at the third level — the efficient use of the resources allocated for defense — are primarily and in the first instance internal problems of the defense departments and agencies, although for reasons that we will have to examine, the President, other departments, and the Congress are concerned with the solutions to some of them. The problems consist in choosing efficiently, or economically, among the alternative methods of achieving military tasks or objectives. These alternative

---

[8] "The Chance for Peace," an address reprinted in *The Department of State Bulletin*, April 27, 1953, p. 600.

methods may be different strategies, different tactics, various forces, or different weapons.

It is not apparent to many who are unfamiliar with military problems how wide the range of choice really is. There is typically an infinity of ways to carry out a military mission, some much more efficient, or economical, than others. Consider the range of choice in the following three examples, taken from three different levels of decision-making within the departments of the government concerned with defense:

a. The provision of some measure of protection to the United States economy and population against atomic attack. The broad "pure" alternatives include: (1) widespread dispersal of industry and population before attack; (2) shelters and underground construction; (3) fighter and missile defenses; (4) full reliance on an atomic striking force for deterrence or, in some circumstances, to destroy the enemy striking force on the ground. There are, of course, many ways of implementing each broad alternative, as well as many "mixes" or combinations of the pure alternatives.

b. Extension of the range of bomber aircraft. Broad alternatives include the use of: (1) operating bases farther forward, fixed or floating; (2) air refueling; (3) staging bases forward for ground refueling; (4) larger aircraft with greater fuel capacity. If there is time enough for a development program, additional alternatives would include the use of: (5) high energy fuels, chemical or nuclear; (6) lighter structural materials; (7) boundary layer control; and many others.

c. The design of a new machine gun. There are many possible performance characteristics: range, accuracy, lethality of bullet, durability, reliability — some of which may have high military worth, some little. Each has its cost in money, development time, and production time; each its "trade-off" against other characteristics.

This factoring of the big economic problem into many subproblems at different levels has some disadvantages, which we will consider at appropriate places. But it makes both the analytical and the decision-making problems tractable, an advantage not to be lightly discarded. The sergeant in the *New Yorker* cartoon understands the point well when he shouts: "I'm telling you for the last time, Harwick. It's none of your business how much it costs the taxpayers. Your job is to fire that gun." [9]

## THE ORGANIZATION OF THE BOOK

The purpose of this book is not to solve military-economic problems at the various levels. We shall point out that certain policies stated in general terms, such as the protection of our deterrent forces, are ex-

[9] Cartoon by Alan Dunn in *The New Yorker War Album* [no date], originally in *The New Yorker*, August 23, 1941.

tremely important, but we will not, except in hypothetical examples, compare *specific* alternatives and indicate preferred strategies and weapon systems. This is the continuing task of responsible decision-makers and the analysts who advise and assist them. It can never be done once and for all because good solutions change with circumstances, and circumstances change constantly. Our main purpose is more modest: It is to help decision-makers, their advisers, and interested citizens in general, by showing how economic analysis — ranging from just straight thinking about alternative courses of action to systematic quantitative comparisons — can contribute to the selection of preferred (efficient, economical) policies and actions.

Part I (Chapters 3 to 6) is concerned with problems at a relatively high level, choices affecting the resources available for defense. Chapters 3 and 4 are directly concerned with the determination of the defense budget — what the constraints are, and how we should choose the size of the budget. Chapter 5 takes up the indirect effects of defense programs, considerations that bear upon the determination of the budget or of other policies affected by the national security effort. Chapter 6 attempts to measure and compare the economic strengths for war of the major powers.

Part II (Chapters 7 through 12) is concerned with problems at lower levels — the problems of efficient choice within the departments responsible for defense[10] — and with methods of analyzing various alternatives. Our primary concern, stressed in Chapters 7 and 9, is with straight thinking about military problems, especially the design of analyses and the use of appropriate economic criteria to aid in choosing preferred policies. Chapter 8, an application of economic analysis to a military problem, is intended to illustrate many of these points. Chapters 10 and 11 consider the complications associated with "incommensurables," uncertainty, the enemy, and time. Chapter 12 inquires whether better institutional arrangements can promote efficiency, or economy, in the military, either as an alternative to analysis or as a reinforcement of it.

Part III takes up some special problems and applications, looking at them as economic problems of choice. Included in this Part are discussions of research and development, logistics, alliances, economic warfare, disarmament, mobilization, civil defense, and recuperation in the event that an atomic exchange should occur. The concluding chapter presents major considerations that should be weighed in analyzing what is perhaps the most critical problem of all — that of shaping policies for deterrence.

[10] Not, strictly speaking, within the Department of Defense. A number of agencies outside the Department of Defense, including the National Security Council, the Office of Civil Defense, the Atomic Energy Commission, etc., as well as parts of the Bureau of the Budget, the Treasury, and the Departments of State and Commerce, make or participate in military decisions at these levels.

SOME ESSENTIAL BACKGROUND

First, however, we must take a careful look at the kinds of threats that a nation's defenses are required to meet. The urgency of a fresh evaluation of alternative military strategies is greatly heightened by the revolutionary weapon developments of the past decade, by drastic changes in the nature of the wars against which we must guard. Chapter 2, therefore, discusses recent crucial changes in military technology and missions, which form the background of the problems to be studied in the remainder of the book.

## 2. THE BACKGROUND: DEFENSE AGAINST WHAT?

During the last decade or so the development and accumulation of nuclear weapons — first by the United States, then by the USSR and finally by other nations — have revolutionized the problems of national security. No comparable technological revolution in weapons has ever before occurred in history. The analogy of gunpowder is frequently suggested, but the substitution of gunpowder took place gradually over a period of centuries; and, like the weapons it replaced, gunpowder was used almost exclusively in a circumscribed area known as the battlefield. Nuclear weapons, a few years after their invention, have made it feasible — indeed, cheap and easy — to destroy economies and populations. They will not necessarily be used for this purpose; but the fact that they can be so used profoundly influences the character of the security that is attainable, as well as the policies by which we must seek it. Today, or next year, or within ten years, any one of several nations can unilaterally destroy the major cities of the others, and the latter, if they are prepared and respond quickly, can make the destruction mutual. In these circumstances, problems which once dominated our thinking about defense become unimportant. And while other problems assume new importance, we have scarcely had time to learn what they are, let alone how to think about them.

Because the weapons environment critically influences choice of policy, this chapter will first describe and project the weapon developments themselves, and then attempt to trace their implications for the kinds of war that our policies should be designed to prepare for or prevent. At this point we shall be concerned with the technological possibilities in the absence of any agreement to disarm or adopt significant limitations on the use of weapons.

### WEAPON DEVELOPMENTS

Enough is known concerning the development and production of nuclear weapons and the means of delivering them — both here and in the USSR — for a general consideration of medium- and long-term policies. For this purpose we can collapse the next decade or so to the present point in time. Exact estimates of present or near-future capabilities of both the United States and the USSR in terms of thermonuclear weapons and carriers are not here required. The significant facts are plain enough to informed public opinion throughout the world. They may be summarized as follows:

1. The number of urban centers which account for most of the economic strength of a major military power like the United States or Russia is small — certainly not more than a few hundred. Fifty-four United States metropolitan areas contain sixty per cent of the nation's manufacturing industry. Their population of well over 65,000,000, while only forty per cent of the national total, includes a much larger proportion of the nation's highly skilled technical, scientific, and managerial personnel. The 170 metropolitan areas listed by the Census Bureau contain seventy-five per cent of manufacturing industry and fifty-five per cent of the nation's population.[1] The concentration of industry in Russian urban centers appears to be roughly the same as in the United States, although the centers themselves tend to be more compact and therefore easier targets. While the total Russian population is less concentrated than that of the United States (almost half live on farms), the concentration of industrial and skilled labor and management is at least as great. Britain, Germany, and other industrial countries present even fewer targets.

The elimination of fewer than 200 metropolitan areas in either the United States or the USSR (still fewer elsewhere) would therefore, as a direct effect, reduce industrial capital by 75 per cent and the most valuable human resources by about as much. This, in itself, would demote a first-class power to third class, but to the direct effects must be added indirect ones. Because of the interdependence in a modern industrial economy, the productivity of the surviving unbalanced economic resources would be reduced, perhaps disastrously. Radioactive fallout would be likely to inflict serious casualties on populations outside the target cities.

2. How many bombs would be required to "eliminate" a metropoli-

---

[1] The metropolitan area concept as defined by the Census Bureau is, unfortunately, not a perfectly satisfactory measure of urbanization — because its definition is primarily on a county unit basis. The figures above include, therefore, some capital and population which may be sufficiently far from presumed city targets as not to be vulnerable to the direct effects of urban bombing, except fallout. On the other hand, the arbitrary legal boundaries of cities are much too restricted and even less satisfactory for our purposes.

tan area? It depends, of course, upon the size and shape of the area and the size of the bomb as well as upon other factors. But we were told by the Chairman of the Atomic Energy Commission after one test in the Pacific that a thermonuclear explosion could destroy any city on earth.[2] We know that very much smaller bombs will destroy small cities, as the first primitive 20 kiloton atomic bomb destroyed Hiroshima, a city of 250,000, killing a third of its population; that thermonuclear weapons have been made in the multi-megaton "yield" range; and that the area of destruction from blast increases as the two-thirds power of the yield (thus, a ten megaton bomb would devastate an area approximately sixty times as great as that devastated by a twenty kiloton bomb). We have also been told that the area of intense radioactive fallout from the Bikini shot was 7,000 square miles — that is, an area fifteen times the size of Los Angeles or approximately equal to the total land area of New Jersey.

About the long-term radiation hazards from such fission products as strontium-90 and cesium-137 we know less. The dangers resulting from a large-scale attack would be significant, though they may not affect the number of weapons that "rational" attackers would be willing to dispatch.

In any event, we are clearly entering a one-bomb-to-one-large-city era, which means usually one, perhaps occasionally two or three, bombs per metropolitan area. Barring large-scale passive defenses, total bomb-on-target requirements to destroy urban concentrations in the United States appear to be in the low hundreds, even allowing some to be assigned to economic targets outside cities. A larger number of bombs would have to be dispatched if delivered by missiles with low accuracy or reliability. Against a very effective air defense the number dispatched might have to be several times the number required on target — but we are told that no completely effective air defense is in existence and, as we shall see, it is questionable how effective air defense can be made against surprise attack.

3. Nuclear weapons of the same kind or in their small, light, "tactical" guise[3] may revolutionize war on the ground and at sea as drastically as the strategic air war. Less is evident about "requirements" for nuclear weapons against military targets: the number needed to destroy some highly dispersed and "hardened" military forces could be very large. What is evident is (1) that tactical forces armed with even moderate numbers of nuclear weapons and the means of delivering them can easily and quickly defeat forces which do not possess them; (2) that

---

[2] *New York Times*, April 1, 1954. Mr. Strauss was not using "destroy" in a literal physical sense, and he was undoubtedly implicitly assuming no large-scale expensive passive defense measures to reduce vulnerability.

[3] The largest "strategic" thermonuclear weapons may be even more effective against some military targets, e.g., by making huge areas uninhabitable for long periods.

both the United States and Russia can use such weapons, and (3) that ground, naval, or tactical air forces that have not adapted their deployment and tactics to the new weapons will be hopelessly vulnerable to nuclear attack.

4. While Russia's weapon technology and nuclear stockpile *may* still lag behind ours, it would be rash indeed to expect any such lags to widen. As to technology, the Russians have obviously made tremendous progress in rocket engines and missiles, and quite possibly have more first-rate scientists working on their programs than the United States has in its programs. As to nuclear stockpiles, increases in production rates on both sides depend mainly on a willingness to invest in additional productive capacity. No one believes any longer that a shortage of some crucial specific resource like uranium ore will conveniently (for us) inhibit Soviet production. The Soviet Union is compelled by the strongest of motives to match or surpass the United States programs, and has not hesitated in the past to undertake very large investment programs (for example, in steel) to meet security objectives.

Several implications of these weapon developments for the relative strengths of offense and defense have become fairly clear. These implications may be summarized in the following way.

1. The game is loaded against the defense when small-scale (by World War II standards) sudden attacks can cause catastrophic and perhaps irreparable damage.

2. Responsible officials of the Air Force and of the North American Air Defense Command have told us repeatedly that a leak-proof defense is not now attainable. Under some, not too unlikely, circumstances of surprise attack, we could fare very badly.[4]

While air defenses can undoubtedly be vastly improved over the next few years, the offense is likely to improve concomitantly. Ballistic missiles present formidable problems for air defense.

3. The superiority of the offense does not necessarily imply that either side can eliminate the enemy's ability to retaliate in force; still less that either side can *guarantee* such elimination. A strategic bombing force is much easier to protect by active and passive measures and by mobility and concealment than are economic and population targets. Such developments as nuclear-powered submarines armed with Polaris and train-mobile Minuteman missiles are offensive weapons with revolutionary implications. Moreover, the development of thermonuclear weapons, by greatly reducing the number of bombs on target required to cause massive damage to economic and population targets, has enhanced

---

[4] We could of course do much better against a *small* attacking force *if we had adequate warning* than we could in less favorable circumstances.

the retaliatory capability of whatever portion of one's striking force manages to escape surprise enemy attack. Unless the attacker is extremely successful, he may fail to prevent effective retaliation.

4. Similar considerations apply to tactical engagements, on the ground and at sea. Nuclear weapons and modern delivery systems give an attacker the ability to compress a devastating attack in space and time. Again we appear to have made much greater progress in offensive missiles than in missile defenses. And here, as in the strategic war, it is hard for the attacker to insure against effective counterattack.

That the superiority of the offense will persist is, of course, not certain. Judgments about the future rarely are. The revolution in military technology which began with the atomic bomb is a continuing, even perhaps an accelerating, one and will certainly take unexpected, unpredictable turns. And the fact that the odds favor the offense by no means implies that attempts to provide any defense are a foolish waste of resources. On the contrary, some kinds of defense measures are essential and integral components of a strategy of deterrence. But the prospects are poor that we will ever again be able to rely on such defenses to prevent great destruction if deterrence fails and an attack is launched.

## IMPLICATIONS FOR KIND OF WAR

The weapon developments that have been described could conceivably influence the character of warfare in either of two directions, neither of which can be ignored in our plans. They could increase the violence of war, or they could limit it.

### ALL-OUT THERMONUCLEAR WAR AND LIMITED LOCAL CONFLICTS

Most obviously, these developments could make war "total" to a degree never before experienced. An all-out thermonuclear war involving nations like the United States and the Soviet Union could easily destroy either or both, at least as powers of any consequence, in a matter of days or perhaps even hours.

There is increasing recognition, however, that the dangers implicit in participation in all-out thermonuclear war may result in a stalemate. In the words of Sir Winston Churchill, a "balance of terror" may replace the balance of power. Nations may become too fearful and cautious to use or even threaten to use their ultimate weapons, except for direct self-protection. This would mean, assuming no change in the objectives of Russia or Red China, a continuation of the cold war, with the Russians and Chinese attempting to win uncommitted areas by political and economic warfare, by subversion, and by limited, local military aggression.

To avoid piecemeal surrender, we might determine to engage in defensive or counter-military actions also limited in character.[5]

These military actions, or limited, local wars, may flare up as a result — indeed as an extension — of international negotiation, of internal revolution, or of pawn moves by major powers to test or exploit a weakness. They are the late twentieth century "balance of terror" counterpart of the limited-scale, limited-objectives wars of the "balance of power" century between Waterloo and World War I. We have seen many of these limited wars in recent years: the contest in the Formosa Straits, the Indo-China War, the Korean War (small only in comparison with World War II), the Greek-Albanian-Yugoslav conflicts, the Chinese Civil War, the Indonesian revolutions, the Suez invasion, the Lebanon crisis, and others. While some of these were not of primary concern to the major powers, most of them were. Challenges (or opportunities) like Greece, Korea, and Suez will continue to present themselves. The recent history of restraint in the use of nuclear weapons,[6] of attempts to confine these conflicts, of negotiated armistices, of ability to swallow frustration where the outcome was completely adverse (as for us in Indo-China and for the USSR in Greece) — all these are significant indications that the war of limited scale and limited objectives is here to stay.

But so is the danger of thermonuclear war, despite its recognized suicidal threat.[7] There are many ways in which all-out war could be triggered by accident or misunderstanding. Either side may resort to a thermonuclear strike to protect some presumed vital interest (for example, on our side, Western Europe), or in frustration or desperation (for example, if the cold war appears to be going hopelessly against it), gambling upon the very great advantages accruing from a surprise first strike. Finally, the very fearsomeness of the threat is an invitation to a calculating, ruthless power to remove it by force if any happy circumstance presents itself — as, for example, the temporary impotence or vulnerability of the opposing strategic air force; or his own temporary invulnerability resulting from, say, a breakthrough in air defense technology. Moreover, in considering the prospects of some power initiating thermonuclear war, we cannot confine ourselves to the Soviet Union

[5] See Henry A. Kissinger, *Nuclear Weapons and Foreign Policy*, Harper and Bros., New York, 1957, Chapter 5 and *passim*, for an extreme but persuasive statement of this argument.

[6] We would by no means rule out the use of tactical atomic weapons in local wars; in fact, there have been numerous authoritative statements that the U.S. will so use them. But past restraint must be explained in part by the fear that their use would make it more difficult to limit the scale and objectives of the conflict.

[7] On the delicate nature of the balance of terror, see Chapter 18, "Choosing Policies for Deterrence."

and the United States. Within the next ten to twenty years (not too long a period for the weighing of some military economic policies) several nations in addition to the United States and the USSR are likely to acquire a substantial thermonuclear capability. Quite apart from specifically military atomic programs, the widespread use of reactors for power will result in stocks of nuclear materials that may find their way into weapons.

It appears then that in our national security planning we must consider at least two kinds of war — all-out thermonuclear war on the one hand, and limited, local actions of a holding or counteroffensive character on the other.

The relative probabilities of these two kinds of war occurring will depend in part on the policies we pursue. If we prepare to deal with only one, we invite defeat, indeed destruction, by the other. The number of kinds of war which we must consider cannot, therefore, be reduced below two.

### WAR CALLING FOR PROLONGED MOBILIZATION

Does the number have to be increased to three? Is there a third kind of war, besides total and local wars, for which we must prepare? It has sometimes been suggested that a third possibility is a large-scale and long war, like World War II, in which strategic bombing of cities is either withheld or, if attempted, is ineffective *on both sides*.[8] Let us call this the World War II type war, although it might differ from World War II in such important military aspects as the widespread use of atomic weapons against military targets.

The question whether this World War II type of war is likely enough or dangerous enough to justify extensive preparations is, as will be seen, a crucial one for economic mobilization policy. We will simply state our views, because to defend them would carry the discussion far beyond its intended scope.

The contingency that strategic bombing would be attempted but ineffective *on both sides* seems to be extremely unlikely, for reasons already explained.

Mutual withholding of strategic attacks on cities for fear of retaliation is a somewhat more serious possibility — but only if the withholding is combined with quite limited war objectives: If the apparent winner presses on for anything like "unconditional surrender," the apparent loser would convert the limited war to a total one. But a limited objectives war would be unlikely to be large-scale and long, like World War II. Mutual

---

[8] If ineffective on only one side, the strategic bombing would be decisive and the war short.

withholding plus limited objectives define what is essentially a local action.[9]

If a war of this kind did occur, we would have time to mobilize our industrial potential and ought to "win" eventually, just as we did in World War I and World War II, even if we were relatively unprepared at its beginning.[10]

In short, this kind of war appears so far to be the least likely (of the three) and least important in our preparations. It might become most important if atomic disarmament is achieved. But this has not looked very promising, and effectively controlled atomic disarmament (the only kind that United States policy has contemplated) may no longer be feasible unless completely new ideas for inspection and enforcement are conceived and accepted.[11]

Some British writers have suggested that the contestants might fight a lengthy "broken-back war" to a conclusion on the ground *after* successful strategic bombing on both sides. This would be Phase II of an all-out thermonuclear war. We should not completely ignore it in our planning, yet it is obviously not too important if Phase I is completely successful on both sides, or if one side falls substantially shorter of complete success than the other.

## IMPLICATIONS FOR THE IMPORTANCE
## OF ECONOMIC STRENGTH

### DECLINING IMPORTANCE OF ECONOMIC WAR POTENTIAL
### IN ITS CONVENTIONAL SENSE

The term "economic war potential" has usually meant the maximum *fully mobilized* capability of an economy to supply the men and materials required to fight a war. There are two objections to this concept. The first is its vagueness. What constitutes a "maximum" diversion of resources to war depends importantly upon (a) political and morale factors which in all countries fluctuate with circumstances, and (b) the time allowed for conversion to war production: the longer the mobilization period, the greater the peak war output. There is no single number or simple set of numbers which can represent "the" economic war potential of a nation.

Second, and more important, recent and prospective technological

[9] There are other difficulties associated with mutual withholding of city bombing in any war transcending a local action. There may be no practicable way to delimit the restriction: we know that many "strictly military" targets are separated from large centers of population by less than the lethal radius of large bombs.

[10] This is almost a *reductio ad absurdum*. Russia would not allow us to win complete victory while she possessed a nuclear stockpile.

[11] See Eugene Rabinowitch, "Living with H-Bombs," *Bulletin of the Atomic Scientists,* Vol. XI, No. 1, January 1955, pp. 5–8.

developments associated with nuclear weapons have greatly reduced the significance of economic war potential in the sense of maximum fully mobilized capacity for war production. Before the development of nuclear weapons and the means of delivering them on distant targets, the military power of the United States could be fairly well measured by its economic potential. Geography afforded us the time we needed, if pressed, to translate most of our potential into power.[12] Because we were the wealthiest nation in the world with the largest steel and machinery industries, we were also the most powerful militarily.

The development of nuclear and especially of thermonuclear weapons represents a momentous turning point in the cost of acquiring military capabilities. Destructive power has now become so cheap that wars can be won or economies destroyed before there is time for mobilization.

*In an all-out thermonuclear war the superior economic war potential of the United States is important only to the extent that it has been effectively diverted to security purposes before war starts.* This is true for all our forces, offensive or defensive. It is particularly and most obviously true for our strategic air offensive forces and air defense. For preparedness for full thermonuclear war the United States must learn to rely on forces in being — not as cadres about which much larger, newly mobilized forces will be organized, but as *the* important forces.

Economic war potential also appears to be less than decisive in fighting local wars (Viet Minh could defeat France in the jungles of Northern Indo-China), and of even less importance, as potential, in countering assaults by infiltration, subversion, civil war, and astute diplomacy. In limited wars, too, forces in being seem likely to play a crucial role, useful reserves being mainly those that can be mobilized promptly. Once hostilities have begun, industrial potential cannot be brought to bear soon enough. Even in World War II, the industrial potential of the allies did not save France or count for much in the first two or three years.[13] More recently, in the Korean War, industrial potential was not the force that saved the port of Pusan or shaped the course of the conflict. In all such actions — limited in objectives, means, and scope — full industrial mobilization is not approached, and economic war potential never comes into play.

In consequence the significance of economic war potential in its usual meaning has been degraded. The nation which can maintain the most formidable forces in being is not necessarily the wealthiest. In peacetime the proportion of national resources that can be diverted to national security purposes is by no means constant among nations. Both in peace-

[12] Even before the development of nuclear weapons, geography proved an inadequate defense for European countries against Blitzkrieg tactics based on aircraft and tanks.

[13] See C. J. Hitch, *America's Economic Strength,* Oxford University Press, London, 1941, pp. 60–73, 95–110.

time and in fighting limited wars, countries with less economic war *potential* may support larger military budgets and forces. Russia, for example, a much poorer country than the United States, has supported a larger peacetime military program.

This situation is a particularly dangerous one for the United States. Shielded by geography, we have traditionally (before the Korean War) maintained very small forces in peacetime, and have regarded them as cadres rather than as integrated fighting units in a state of readiness. There is a strong tendency for nations (like individuals) to persist in policies which have been successful long after the external conditions essential to success have vanished, especially when they are pleasant and cheap like this one. The United States will probably maintain a substantial industrial lead over possible enemies for many years, but if we rely upon it as mobilization potential as we did before World War II, we will be inviting irrevocable disaster.

THE IMPORTANCE OF ECONOMIC STRENGTH BEFORE THE OUTBREAK OF WAR

Without doubt, then, "the nostalgic idea that our industrial power is our greatest military asset could ruin our military planning." [14] This does not mean, however, that economic strength will be any less important in the pursuit of national objectives in the future than in the past. Military power is derived from economic strength, and foreign policy is based on both. Economic strength that is used for national security purposes *in time* is the embodiment of military power. Using it in time demands a new approach to national security problems — which to some extent we have already made.

The essential contribution of economic strength is that it enables us to do more of the numerous things which are desirable from the point of view of national security, but which, in their fullness, not even the wealthiest nation can afford.

What are these desirable things in a thermonuclear era — that is, things that have positive payoffs and that we would like to have if resources were unlimited?

1. Preparations for and deterrence of thermonuclear war. These would include strategic air forces, warning networks, active air defenses, and passive defenses of various kinds including perhaps dispersal, shelters, and large-scale stockpiling of both weapons and industrial commodities. It appears desirable not only to do all these things but to do them in style — to confront the Soviet Union with a variety of strategic air threats, each absolutely invulnerable to any conceivable weapon which

---

[14] Thomas K. Finletter, *Power and Policy,* Harcourt, Brace and Company, New York, 1954, p. 256.

might be used against it; to erect a continental air defense system embodying all the latest and most expensive equipment of which any scientist has dreamed; and to buy enough passive defense of all kinds to insure our survival if by any chance an enemy attack still gets through.

2. Preparations for local and limited wars also appear desirable: challenges to fight such wars are almost certain to occur, and it would be comforting to be able to accept such challenges, or to make counterchallenges, if we want to. Sometimes it is argued that limited wars can be handled without ground forces or tactical air power simply by threatening massive retaliation against any and all provocations. If this were true, conventional military forces would be superfluous. The trouble is that the enemy might not believe our threat to launch a thermonuclear attack in the event of minor provocations.[15] Moreover, he might be correct in disbelieving, for we are probably not willing to use H-bombs to cope with minor aggressions — partly to avoid inhumane destruction, partly to retain allies, but mostly to escape the H-bombs that could in turn descend on us. Consequently, without conventional forces, we might have nothing with which to counter local aggressions and be wide open to "nibbling" tactics by the enemy. The net result might also be a heightened probability of thermonuclear war.

Preparation in style also seems desirable. Local, limited wars have taken many forms and have occurred in many places in recent history; future possibilities are even more numerous. We might have to fight in Southeast Asia, the Middle East, or the Balkans, with or without atomic bombs, with native help of varying qualities. We should like to have heavy matériel stocks pre-positioned and, in addition, a large capacity for moving men and matériel rapidly by sea and by air to the theater of action. To back up our ready forces for such wars it would be desirable to have trained reserves and facilities for quickly expanding the production of matériel.

3. It would be desirable too (if resources were unlimited) to prepare to fight a World War II type of war. Even though this sort of conflict seems unlikely, it might conceivably occur. Preparations would call for ready forces to fight a holding action (these might do double duty for local wars), and measures to enlarge the mobilization base and to increase its security and the speed with which it can be converted. The accumulation of raw material stockpiles from overseas sources would be desirable, for example, in addition to securing the sea lanes. Construction of new

[15] For a discussion of these issues, see Bernard Brodie, "Unlimited Weapons and Limited War," *The Reporter*, November 18, 1954, pp. 16–21; and William Kaufmann, "Limited Warfare," in W. Kaufmann (ed.), *Military Policy and National Security*, Princeton University Press, Princeton, N.J., 1956, pp. 102–36.

capacity in industries that might "bottleneck" the expansion of war production, support of multiple sources of supply by expensive splitting of procurement contracts, and the training and maintenance of large reserve forces might be undertaken.

4. Cutting across all these areas, it would clearly be desirable to support a very large research and development effort. We are in an era in which a single technological mutation (as in the past, the development of radar and the atomic bomb) can far outweigh in military importance our substantial resource advantage. There are conceivable future mutations of equal importance — invulnerable long-range ballistic missiles, perhaps a high-confidence defense against nuclear weapons. Research and development is most obviously desirable in the context of thermonuclear wars: here certain kinds of technological slippage could break the stalemate, blunt deterrence, and place us at the mercy of the Kremlin. But it is also possible to conceive of developments which would, for example, greatly improve the capability of the United States to fight small engagements in out-of-the-way places. Development is cheap only by contrast with the procurement and maintenance of ready forces. If we tried to develop everything interesting (and possibly significant and therefore "desirable"), we could use all the potential as well as all the actual scientific and engineering resources of the country.

5. Finally, there are substantial opportunities to use economic strength in the cold war itself.[16] Economic warfare, whether waged against our enemies or for our friends, can be expensive. It is widely believed that the Marshall Plan saved Western Europe from collapsing into chaos and perhaps Communism between 1947 and 1950, but at a cost of about 10 billion dollars. The United States is now spending roughly a billion dollars a year on economic aid to friendly and neutral countries; and the Soviet Union is lending over half a billion dollars annually, partly to its satellites and partly to other countries. Britain and Western Europe might spend many billions of dollars "uneconomically" on nuclear power plants to reduce their economic dependence on Middle Eastern oil, which is vulnerable both to Arab nationalism and to Soviet power. Economic strength permits a nation to wage the cold war more effectively, to reduce its vulnerability to hostile moves, and to improve its position and power by extending its influence.

These, then, are the desirable things — the things it would be nice to do from the point of view of national security. In the aggregate they far exceed our economic capabilities, so that hard choices must be made. But the greater our economic strength, the more desirable things we can

---

[16] These opportunities will be discussed in Chapter 16.

do, and the better we can do them. We cannot prepare for all kinds of wars, but maybe we can prepare for more than one. We cannot develop every technological idea of promise, but maybe with three times Russia's economic strength we can develop enough more than she to keep ahead in the race for technological leadership. We cannot buy perfect protection against thermonuclear attack by any combination of active and passive defenses, but perhaps we can afford enough defense to reduce Russian confidence of complete success to the point where she is deterred from striking. Perhaps on top of all this, we can afford a positive economic foreign policy which will preserve our alliances and increase our influence on developments in the uncommitted parts of the world.

At the least, the possession of greater economic strength enables us to do more of these things than we otherwise could do. But it does so if, and only if, we use the strength now, during the cold war, before a hot war starts. For that reason the term "economic war potential" will not be used in the present study. The timely translation of economic strength into military power, the proportion of that strength so translated, and the efficiency of the forces in being, have become of critical importance — as opposed to some theoretical maximum potential which could be translated into military force at some later date. While the traditional concept of the mobilization base is not yet fully obsolete and may even justify a limited expenditure of budget, it is no longer the shield of the Republic.

# PART 1.  THE RESOURCES AVAILABLE FOR DEFENSE

## 3. RESOURCE LIMITATIONS

As noted earlier, Part I is devoted to problems of choice at comparatively high levels, choices among policies that affect (1) the resources at the nation's disposal and (2) the proportion of resources allocated to national defense. Our national security depends first of all upon these choices, for they determine the volume of resources available for defense.

Resource limitations are our starting point because in all problems of choice we strive to get the most out of what we have. To put it another way, we try to use the resources that are available to us so as to maximize what economists call "utility." Resources are always limited in comparison with our wants, always constraining our action. (If they did not, we could do everything, and there would be no problem of choosing preferred courses of action.) As a consequence, resource limitations are often called constraints. We try to achieve the most desirable outcome that is possible in view of these constraints.

We should therefore inquire into the nature of resource limitations as a preliminary step in selecting courses of action. In this chapter we shall discuss specific *versus* general resource constraints, the total resources that are at the nation's disposal, and policies that would influence those resources in the future. In subsequent chapters of Part I, we shall discuss how to choose the size of the defense budget and the major considerations bearing on that choice.

### SPECIFIC VERSUS GENERAL CONSTRAINTS

How should constraints be expressed if they are to be most meaningful in appraising a nation's strength and in choosing the scale of the defense effort? What are the effective limitations on what we can do? Sometimes constraints are expressed as the projected supplies of specific items such as laborers in each skill and age bracket, tons of bauxite and mica, board feet of lumber, or kilowatt-hours of electricity. The supplies of individual items like these will be called "specific constraints." Sometimes, however, resource limitations are expressed as projected amounts of money that can be spent, putting a limit on the total effort but not on quantities of specific resources that can be employed. Such an over-all limitation will be called a "general constraint." In which form should constraints be expressed in different circumstances? In which form do they more accurately reflect the real limitations imposed by the physical world?

In some problems, the constraints unquestionably ought to be expressed as definite quantities of specific products. Consider, for example, the decisions of a task force commander in a naval engagement. He must try to get the most from the particular items that are at his disposal — destroyers that are now in the force, man hours available for maintenance and operations, ammunition on hand, and so on. It is beside the point that, by allocating money in a budget differently, he could have equipped a task force with another aircraft carrier at a sacrifice of so many destroyers. The option of shifting basic resources from the production of one item to the production of another is hardly open at this stage of the game. Hence, in this situation, it is not a budget that constrains the actions of the commander. Limited stocks of specific items genuinely *are* the constraints, and they should be expressed in that fashion.

In other problems, however, the supplies of specific resources are not fixed, and the use of specific constraints is wrong. Consider the problems of the Navy in choosing next year's purchases of equipment. Of course, there will be some specific constraints — the physical impossibility, for example, of suddenly procuring an extraordinarily large quantity of some newly developed fuel or of completing an extra super carrier before a certain date. But one principal constraint will be the budget. Within the limits of this budget, it will be physically possible to acquire varying amounts of many items — more training and less electronic gear, more ammunition and less manpower. In these circumstances, it *is* chiefly the budget that constrains: the Navy's supplies of many items are not fixed, and it would be wrong to choose policies as if they were.

Let us turn from the problems of naval planning for next year to problems of national policy over, say, the next decade. At first glance, the supplies of many basic resources may appear to be fixed. Manpower seems to be limited to its present size plus annual growth. Ore and petroleum reserves can hardly be manufactured. There is only so much coal to be mined. The acreage of each type of soil is already set. And yet, upon more careful inspection, one sees that the supplies of these resources that will be available in future periods are not really fixed. Medical programs and education can affect the total supply of labor. Through retraining, one kind of manpower can acquire a different skill. More intensive mining can recover a larger proportion of given ore reserves. A shift of resources can yield more metals at the expense of textiles or more titanium and less copper. The use of fertilizers, irrigation, drainage, tractors — these and many other innovations can alter the inventory of land, both in total and in composition.

Thus except in the very short run, the nation can usually get more of one item — even of many so-called basic resources, as far as future supplies are concerned — by sacrificing something else. The more distant the future to which the problem pertains, the less applicable are specific constraints. Where time and technology permit adjustments, the nation is not constrained by fixed supplies of individual resources, and thinking in terms of specific constraints is misleading. The real constraints, the truly "basic" resources, are exceedingly complex and difficult to measure, involving the state of the technological art, stocks of ingenuity and knowledge, institutional arrangements, and incentives as well as the total supplies of capital and people. Probably the most satisfactory way to represent these constraints is by means of some aggregate dollar amount of output that is at the nation's disposal each year. Such an amount, say national income or gross national product (GNP),[1] is a general constraint similar to a budget. It is a rough indicator of the aggregate output that is available annually, an indicator having no implication that the nation must work with specific quantities of individual items.

General monetary constraints are not put forward as perfect indicators of resource limitations even in the long run. Frequently some specific constraints will be operative as well as the general one (as in the case of the Navy's super carrier). Sometimes, too, specific limitations are imposed by decree of higher authority. For instance, the branches of the service, in planning ahead, face not only the general constraint of their budgets but also the specific constraint of a manpower ceiling set by Congress. Strictly speaking, in problems of national policy as in most others, there is usually a combination of specific and general constraints.

MONEY COSTS WHEN GENERAL CONSTRAINTS APPLY

Only by counting the costs that constitute the real constraint can we determine the policies that achieve a specified task at minimum cost. If the stock of magnesium is the real constraint (and the only one), we should be interested in the cost of alternative actions in terms of magnesium. If several individual inputs are limited, we should be interested in the cost of alternative policies in terms of those inputs. If there is a general monetary constraint but specific inputs are not fixed, we should consider cost in dollars.[2]

---

[1] Gross national product will be discussed in more detail in the next section of this chapter.

[2] Only by counting costs in these terms can we determine the policies that achieve the most with the given constraints, that is, with the available resources.

To some people, dollars do not appear to reflect real resource cost, and their use has little appeal. Let us examine the justification for paying attention to monetary expense. What, in a fundamental sense, is the "cost" of a course of action? It is whatever must be given up in order to adopt that course, that is, whatever could otherwise be kept or obtained.[3] If we examine the problem of planning future programs from the standpoint of the Defense Department, it seems fairly obvious that money costs are pertinent. The Department faces a budgetary constraint. For the most part it does not face a limitation on particular weapons or supplies but can buy more of them by paying their prices. What does the Department give up in order to implement one course of action? The answer is money — or, to go one step further, the alternative weapons or supplies that could otherwise be purchased. The Department could substitute one item for another by paying the price of the one instead of paying the price of the other. Dollar costs do reflect what must be given up in order to adopt a particular policy. They reflect real sacrifices by the Department because the prices of different items show the rates at which they can be substituted for each other.

This is not to say that money costs perfectly represent resources sacrificed by the Defense Department. The prices of goods to be bought in the future are uncertain. One course of action may itself drive up the price of particular weapons or materials, and it is not possible to predict these effects with complete accuracy. The characteristics and cost of some items will change as technology advances. The quantity of some exceptional items may literally be fixed, or nearly fixed, even if we are looking several years ahead. Nonetheless, imperfect as it is, the money cost of a future program usually shows the sacrifice that would be required of the Department better than other measures of cost. While dollars do not precisely measure the real sacrifices, costs in terms of metals and manpower would be grossly misleading. Saying that airplanes cost so much aluminum and ships so much steel plate does not tell us how one may be exchanged for the other. Saying that each costs so many dollars adheres more closely to the facts, namely, that the services can, in making future plans, trade one for the other.

But even if dollars reflect resource costs fairly well from the viewpoint of the Defense Department, do they do so from the standpoint of the nation? If the economy is a reasonably competitive one, the answer is Yes. The reason is that market prices in a competitive economy reflect not only the approximate rate at which the Defense Department can exchange one item for another but also the approximate rate at

[3] That is, the cost is the sacrificed alternative *opportunity*. Hence, economists refer to these sacrificed alternatives as the "opportunity costs" of a course of action.

which the whole economy can substitute one article or material for another. Suppose that the price of a bomber is $1,000,000 and that of a destroyer $20,000,000. How can 20 bombers possibly entail the same resource cost as a destroyer? In other words, how can the construction of 20 bombers use up materials and manpower that could otherwise have produced one destroyer? Aircraft construction requires different metals, engineers with different skills, and different facilities from those required in shipbuilding. Obviously the set of inputs needed in the one case cannot be directly substituted for the other set of inputs. The specialist in aerodynamics cannot be put to work promptly and effectively on the design of destroyers. The labor force that might be used to build bombers in the Southwest cannot be shifted en masse to shipyards in Philadelphia.

Nonetheless, 20 bombers can use resources that would otherwise make it possible for the economy to produce one more destroyer. It is indirect substitution that makes this possible. If the bombers are ordered, the contractor must recruit the necessary laborers, build any newly required facilities, and buy the materials. In order to attract these resources, he will have to pay about what they could earn in their next-best use. These amounts or prices, in a competitive economy, correspond to the value of the output that the resources could otherwise produce. The sum of these amounts — the cost of the bombers — is therefore the value of civilian, or other, outputs that must be sacrificed.

As the recruitment of laborers and the purchase of materials takes place, a chain reaction is set off. The firms that begin to lose the laborers and materials try to replace them. The prices of aluminum, aeronautical engineers, and other resources used in aircraft production may rise somewhat relative to the prices of other inputs. Consumers of these scarcer resources shift to substitutes. Some workers learn that good jobs are available in aircraft plants and transfer to them, leaving vacancies in their former occupations, which in turn are attractive opportunities to still other workers. As a result of this process, the resources for the bombers are in effect released from myriad industries — perhaps coal-mining in Illinois, hair cutting in New Jersey, shrimp fishing in Louisiana — industries that are far removed from aircraft production.

Now suppose the destroyer is to be constructed instead of the airplanes. Imagine that we have a table model of the economy with figures to represent the various resources, and let us transfer the resources by hand. We do not move the men and materials directly from the aircraft industry to the shipyards. Instead we move them back to their next-best uses in the economy. The materials and men that would have replaced them in those uses are moved back in turn to their next-best uses. Simultaneously, we transfer resources into the production of destroyers, drawing them from other kinds of shipbuilding and related parts of the economy and setting off another sequence of shifts and substitutions.

If it is hard to take these roundabout substitutions seriously, remember that they happen constantly in real life. In any particular year some industries (for example, electronics or plastics) expand, and others (say, railroads or movies) decline. The growing industries, as a rule, take over few of the inputs once employed by the declining industries. Relative prices, reflecting the substitution possibilities among goods and services, lead firms to shift resources much more efficiently than transferring them directly from declining industries to expanding ones.[4]

As a consequence, money costs of *future* defense activities approximate the real alternatives that are foregone — the real sacrifices that are entailed — when one activity or weapon system is selected. This will be true for those problems in which a general monetary constraint is proper, that is, for problems pertaining to dates sufficiently in the future to permit the production and procurement of varying quantities of weapons and matériel.

### GNP AS THE CONSTRAINT ON THE NATION'S ACTIVITIES

So far we have discussed the constraints and costs that are appropriate to defense problems or even problems in general. What about the problem at hand, that of assessing the nation's strength and deciding how much should be diverted to defense? By and large, in dealing with this problem, a general limitation on our efforts, such as GNP, is more nearly accurate and more useful than specific constraints. This problem is not how best to conduct a naval engagement with given weapons — not how to assess the power of a retaliatory attack that could be launched immediately. Instead the problem is how to gauge the strength that is the source of our defense effort and how to determine the share that should go to national security. These questions pertain to the planning of defense policies in future years, not to the planning of tactics for today's mission. There is time for a great deal of adjustment, and the constraint is more appropriately described as a general monetary one. It is more nearly correct to say that a projected $560-billion GNP (1957 dollars) will constrain our defense effort in 1965 than to say that 250,000 short-tons of magnesium, 150 billion ton-miles of transport, and 8 million long tons of sulfur will limit our program.

[4] A more complete and rigorous discussion of these points can be found in most textbooks on the principles of economics, e.g., Paul Samuelson, *Economics*, 3d ed., New York, McGraw-Hill Book Co., 1955, pp. 17–21, 34–37, 49–50, 475–525.

Moreover, even if particular resources were limited, a list of specific constraints would not be as manageable and meaningful as GNP in debating the above questions. Judgment as well as analysis must play an important role in assessing the nation's strength and deciding upon the share to be devoted to defense. These are questions that must be considered and debated at the highest levels — by the voters, by the administration in power, by the Congress. An electronic computer could take a large number of specific constraints and show a variety of combinations of output that could be produced. (It is scarcely possible, however, for a computer to show *all* of the combinations of output that could be produced with limitations of particular resources. Moreover, it is doubtful that such a tremendous mass of data would help anyone to reach better decisions about the national security budget.)[5] But the selection of the "correct" combination of defense and nondefense outputs depends greatly upon the unarticulated preferences of Congressmen and voters.

That being the case, the resource limitations must be described in terms that the human mind can comprehend. It would be difficult, indeed impossible, for people to debate policy in the following manner: "In 1965 our strength will consist of 900 thousand short tons of fluorspar, 80 million man-years of labor, 15 thousand flasks of mercury (and so on). As the future situation looks to us now, the United States should plan on devoting 20 thousand tons of fluorspar, 20 million man-years of labor, and 2 thousand flasks of mercury to defense." It would surely be more meaningful to hear: "In 1965 our GNP will be 560 billion dollars. As the situation seems to shape up, the United States might plan on devoting 10 or 12 per cent of its GNP or roughly 60 to 70 billion dollars to national defense." For in the end, obligational authority and appropriations will be expressed in dollars, not in commodities. The debate about the scale of the military effort will take place mainly in terms of budgets (and the capabilities various budgets will buy), not in terms of commodities (and the weapons they can produce). Accordingly, as an aid in this debate, the constraint on the nation's activities — our economic strength — is most meaningful if it is expressed as a general monetary limitation.

Statements by government officials show that the debate usually does proceed in terms of a general monetary constraint, not only in appraising over-all strength but also specifically in deciding how many resources

[5] This is *not* to say that electronic computers are unable to help us find useful answers to lower level problems of choice. On the contrary, they can help in many instances — as will be stressed in Part II. For in many lower level problems, a suitable criterion can be made explicit, and calculations can point to the preferable courses of action.

should be devoted to defense.[6] Right after the 1955 Geneva conference, former Secretary of Defense Wilson was reported as saying that "he was considering whether more might not be spent on defense in the future if the national product and income continued to expand prosperously. To maintain the current level of defense spending in the face of a continually expanding economy, he suggested, would be tantamount to a cutback."[7] Thinking about defense expenditures in relation to GNP is not new. For example, President Truman in his 1952 Economic Report to the Congress stated, "Our total output [GNP], measured in 1951 prices, was more than 90 billion dollars higher than in 1939, and more than 100 billion above 1929. . . . The growth of production during the last few years now enables us to carry the security program without undue impairment of the rest of the economy."[8]

For other problems, to be sure, other means of describing resource constraints are more pertinent. Suppose the problem is to select policies for industrial mobilization, as in World War II, rather than to choose the scale of the defense effort for cold or limited war. In that case, specific limitations are of the greatest significance. Thus, the programming of production in World War II depended upon the projected supplies of critical materials, skilled labor, and fabricated components (small electric motors, for example).[9] Because they were primarily concerned with the problems of industrial mobilization, previous books on the economics of defense have usually emphasized these limitations on individual resources.[10] But, as stressed earlier, the crucial problem in the nuclear era is not planning how best to mobilize our reserve strength. Instead the most urgent questions have to do with the planning of our forces in being for deterrence and limited conflicts. One of these questions is how much of our strength should be turned into forces in being. And for the purpose of attacking this question, we should think mainly in terms of a general monetary constraint.

[6] See, for example, *Study of Airpower,* Hearings Before the Subcommittee on the Air Force of the Committee on Armed Services, U.S. Senate, 84th Congress, 2d Session, Part XXII, U.S. Government Printing Office, Washington, D.C., 1956, pp. 1668–72.

[7] *New York Times,* November 17, 1955, p. 11.

[8] *The Economic Report of the President,* together with a Report to the President, The Annual Economic Review, by the Council of Economic Advisers, Washington, D.C., 1952, p. 2.

[9] See D. Novick, M. Anshen, and W. C. Truppner, *Wartime Production Controls,* Columbia University Press, New York, 1949.

[10] E.g., George A. Lincoln, *Economics of National Security,* 2nd ed., Prentice-Hall, Inc., New York, 1954; J. Blackman, A. Basch, S. Fabricant, M. Gainsbrugh, and E. Stein, *War and Defense Economics,* Rinehart & Co. Inc., New York, 1952; *Economic Mobilization and Stabilization,* L. V. Chandler and D. H. Wallace (eds.), Henry Holt and Co., New York, 1951; S. E. Harris, *The Economics of Mobilization and Inflation,* W. W. Norton & Co. Inc., New York, 1951.

Gross national product, or GNP, is simply the dollar value of a nation's final output over a period of one year — about $440 billion in 1957 in the United States (1957 dollars). It is the total volume of goods and services, valued at market prices, that is at the nation's disposal over the period. Unlike net national income, GNP represents the whole of the nation's output, no portion being already set aside to allow for depreciation. Therefore any consumption, replacement of wornout or obsolete equipment, additions to the stock of capital, military outlays, or other government expenditures must come from GNP.[12] Of course, this measure is a proper constraint only if we are speaking of *full-employment* GNP. If only half the nation's resources are employed, GNP will be relatively small, but in those circumstances it is not a true indicator of the nation's capacity to produce. A larger defense program, or more of any program, can then be produced without sacrificing other things — simply by getting idle resources back to work. Thus the constraint referred to here is GNP at a high level of employment.

GNP is not the same thing as the total wealth of the nation — the value of its land, buildings, and equipment. The total wealth of the United States has been estimated to be about 800 billion dollars (as of 1948 and in 1948 prices).[13] If the value of people as producers was counted among the country's assets, the figure would be much higher. But an estimate of the country's wealth is not directly pertinent to the problem of planning the national defenses. The assets of an individual or firm can be sold or "cashed in," and the proceeds can be devoted to any purpose that is chosen. Not so with the assets of the whole nation. They cannot be liquidated in order to get resources for defense or for any other purpose. The resources that can be devoted to national security are essentially the outputs that can be obtained each year from the stock of capital and supply of labor. Those are the outputs that make up GNP. If all of GNP is consumed, the capital stock is slowly depleted. If part of it is invested, capital may be maintained or augmented. But GNP is the amount that is at our disposal over a year's time.

---

[11] For a full description of the concepts and methods used by the U.S. Government in measuring gross national product, see *National Income Supplement to the Survey of Current Business,* prepared in the Office of Business Economics of the U.S. Department of Commerce, U.S. Government Printing Office, Washington, D.C., 1954, pp. 27–158.

[12] For our present purpose, this statement is sufficiently accurate. It is not 100 per cent correct, for a nation could consume more than GNP for a time by drawing on inventories or on foreign balances, credits, or gifts.

[13] Raymond Goldsmith, "A Perpetual Inventory of National Wealth," *Studies in Income and Wealth,* Vol. 14, National Bureau of Economic Research, New York [no date], p. 18.

If each year's GNP is expressed in current prices, it will reflect changes in the general price level, that is, inflation or deflation. If it is expressed in terms of a constant price level, GNP is an index of the physical volume of final output. When talking about past years, it is often proper to refer to GNP in current dollars, since past defense budgets too are ordinarily in current dollars. When considering future national-security policies, however, there is no reason to introduce the capricious effects of changes in the general price level. Our concern is either with the relationship between the defense budget and GNP or with physical output in "constant" dollars. In discussing future GNP and future budgets, we should think of the amounts in constant dollars.[14]

It should be noted that GNP includes government expenditures for goods and services as though this amount measured accurately the value of the government's final product. Two major objections to this procedure are widely recognized: (1) This is not a satisfying measurement of the value of government output. The government's services may be worth either more or less than their cost. (2) Part of the government's output, for example, statistical services, may be regarded as intermediate products — that is, as ingredients of private output whose value is already counted. Why, then, do our national income accounts continue to use expenditures to represent the final product in government? The answer is simply that this procedure, rough as it is, appears to be better than the practicable alternatives.

There are other difficulties with the concept and measurement of GNP.[15] There are questions particularly about the extent to which such measurements can reflect ultimate national well-being. But these difficulties need not detain us. Even if it does not measure total satisfaction or welfare accurately, full-employment GNP appears to be a useful index of physical production possibilities — a useful indicator of the flow from which resources for national defense must be diverted.

There is another aspect of GNP that should be kept in mind. Earlier it was pointed out that unique outputs of specific items cannot properly be regarded as fixed constraints. GNP as observed and measured, even

[14] Whether to use GNP valued at market prices or by an "adjusted factor cost standard" depends partly upon the precise problem that is being considered. See Abram Bergson, *Soviet National Income and Product in 1937,* Columbia University Press, New York, 1953, pp. 42–54. For the United States (where indirect business taxes are small compared to their amount in, say, the USSR) it probably makes little difference which of the two is used. Unless otherwise specified, we will refer in this study to GNP valued at market prices.

[15] Examples are the difficulties in handling non-marketed outputs and changes in the quality of products. For discussions of these and other points, see *A Critique of the United States Income and Product Accounts,* Studies in Income and Wealth, Vol. 22, A Report of the National Bureau of Economic Research, Princeton University Press, Princeton, N.J., 1958.

with full employment, is not absolutely invariant either. Later in this chapter, methods of stimulating the growth of GNP will be mentioned. But quite apart from long-term growth, there is a certain amount of short-run resiliency — of quick expansion that can be achieved by taking up the slack. For example, at the outbreak of the Korean conflict, the nation was experiencing what one might call normal full employment. Yet in 1951 the 20-billion-dollar increase in annual defense expenditures was accompanied by a 20-billion-dollar increase in real national income, an amount of growth almost triple the amount that could ordinarily be expected. As a consequence, instead of the drastic price-level inflation anticipated by many persons, there was a sharp increase in real production — the military services using more output without reducing the nation's consumption or investment — and only a modest inflation. Part of this increment in output was no doubt illusory — attributable to flaws in the measurements. But not all of it. How did the increase in the defense budget produce this effect? Presumably by offering larger lures, causing people to work harder and longer, attracting additional persons into the labor force, bringing more rapid application of technological improvements, and altering the composition of output. Thus, projected full-employment GNP is not an absolutely inflexible limitation on output.[16] Nevertheless, it is a good approximate indicator of the over-all constraint on the nation's activities.

It should be noted too that while GNP is a useful index of resource limitations, it is no simple matter to divert GNP from consumption to defense, or investment. On the contrary, it is a difficult thing to do, particularly in a free democratic society. J. K. Galbraith has pointed this out very forcefully in his book, *The Affluent Society*.[17] Most of the growth of the United States, for instance, stems from increases in consumption and from private investment designed to meet consumers' demands. Interdependence makes it technically difficult for us to give up the use of certain items (even the family's second car) that may appear to be frills; and our emphasis on consumption makes it psychologically difficult for us to sacrifice such items.

Consequently, according to Galbraith, the "minimum" standard of living is always the existing one, and no Administration or Congress that is interested in being reelected is likely to propose any substantial

[16] For an attempt to allow for the extra capacity that would come to light if expanded defense spending caused the nation to produce under pressure, see Gerhard Colm and Manuel Helzner, "General Economic Feasibility of National Security Programs," National Planning Association, March 20, 1957, published in *Federal Expenditure Policy for Economic Growth and Stability*, Hearings before the Subcommittee on Fiscal Policy of the Joint Economic Committee, 85th Congress, 1st Session, U.S. Government Printing Office, Washington, D.C., 1958, pp. 359–360.

[17] J. K. Galbraith, *The Affluent Society*, Houghton Mifflin Company, Boston, 1958, pp. 161–180 (Chapter XII on "The Illusion of National Security").

reduction in that standard of living. In this connection, it may be significant that the United States devoted mainly "slack" or growth to World War II and the Korean conflict; in neither instance was the absolute level of consumption (as usually measured) reduced.

We must therefore avoid identifying GNP, or even expected growth of GNP, with economic strength for the cold war. It is an illusion to think that the United States can twist a faucet and convert its mighty GNP into deterrent capability without a change in popular value-judgments. It takes both GNP and willingness to make sacrifices to yield resources *for national defense.*

DETERMINANTS OF GNP

As mentioned earlier, the truly basic resources include not only the supplies of capital and people but also institutional arrangements, incentives, and the state of the technological art. Such factors are the underlying determinants that one may consider when trying to estimate future GNP or to figure out policies that can increase it. The principal determinants are summarized in the following list.[18]

A. Initial Stock of Basic Resources and Their Use
  1. Manpower
     a. Labor
     b. Number of hours in the work-week
     c. Level of employment
     d. Extent of skill and training
  2. Stock of capital equipment
  3. State of the art and knowledge
  4. Degree of efficiency in the use of resources
     a. Allocation of resources among uses
     b. Methods of organization to make use of our knowledge
     c. Incentives to produce
B. Growth
  1. Increase in manpower
     a. Increases in the labor force
     b. Changes in the work-week
     c. Changes in the level of employment
     d. Improvement in skills and training
  2. Growth of capital stock

[18] For other lists of growth determinants and discussions of them, see M. Abramovitz, "Economics of Growth," in *A Survey of Contemporary Economics,* Vol. II, Richard D. Irwin, Inc., Homewood, Ill., 1952, especially pp. 132–144; W. Arthur Lewis, *The Theory of Economic Growth,* George Allen & Unwin, Ltd., London, 1955; *Capital Formation and Economic Growth,* A Conference of the Universities-National Bureau Committee for Economic Research, Princeton University Press, Princeton, N.J., 1955; W. W. Rostow, *The Process of Economic Growth,* The Clarendon Press, Oxford, 1953.

3. Advances in the state of the art
   a. Amount of resources devoted to research and education
   b. Incentives to explore new ideas
4. Efficiency in taking advantage of innovations
   a. Incentives to introduce innovations
   b. Mechanism for reshuffling resources in response to innovations.

Most of these items and their relation to the nation's potential output are self-explanatory. Thus, the pertinence of manpower, capital equipment (for example, machines, buildings, and other structures), and the state of the art (for example, knowledge of hybrid corn or transistors) is probably clear. The role of efficiency in the use of these resources, however, may need to be clarified. Without suitable incentives and a reasonable allocation of its resources, a nation can fall short of getting maximum output from its manpower, capital, and "laboratory knowledge." If monopoly, governmental restrictions, tax structures, or other "institutions" impair incentives or discourage resources from moving to their best uses, the potential GNP of the nation will not be fulfilled.

Such factors can also operate to promote or retard long-run growth of GNP. The institutional framework undoubtedly has much to do with advances in the state of the art. In one environment, inventiveness flourishes; in another, it languishes. Moreover, even after new ideas are conceived, the institutional framework influences the rate at which innovations are made and diffused and the speed with which resources are subsequently reshuffled.[19] If monopolistic restrictions, financial organization, or government policies tend to shelter the status quo, known technological improvements may not spread rapidly, and resources may not shift quickly to what now become their best uses.

One wonders, naturally enough, about the quantitative significance of these various factors. Are some of them, such as incentives and institutional framework, merely high-sounding abstractions that actually exert little influence on the growth of GNP? Does it turn out, upon close inspection, that the rise of GNP is accounted for almost solely by the increase in capital equipment and the labor force? Or does it turn out that the other factors do play a major part in economic growth?

Recent studies have begun to shed light on the answers to these questions. These studies indicate that the rise of GNP in the United

[19] The effects of institutions on the growth of knowledge, the application of new ideas, and the reshuffling of resources have attracted a good deal of attention in recent years. For provocative discussions, see W. Arthur Lewis, pp. 1–200; Yale Brozen, "Business Leadership and Technological Change," *American Journal of Economics and Sociology,* Vol. 14, pp. 13–30; and Yale Brozen, "Invention, Innovation, and Imitation," *American Economic Review,* Papers and Proceedings, XLI, May 1951, pp. 239–257.

States has far outstripped the growth in the quantities of capital and labor.[20] More specifically, they suggest that half or more of the increase in national product must be attributed to rising productivity of the inputs. One researcher concludes that "Of the historic increase in GNP, about half represented the effect of increased resources, and half, the effect of increased efficiency of resource use." [21] According to another inquiry, an index of factor inputs (capital and labor combined) quadrupled between the decade of 1869–78 and that of 1944–53, while over the same period net national product grew to 13 times its original size.[22] Such results indicate that new ideas and their efficient and widespread application may be of overriding importance to growth.

This conclusion apparently applies with as much force to "under-developed" countries as it does to the United States:

The per capita output of the United States rose at a rate of about 1.9 per cent per year (compounded) of which only about one-tenth is ascribed to the rise in the stock of tangible capital, according to Fabricant.[23] The rest of this remarkable economic growth may be represented as coming from increases in output per unit of input of labor and of such capital.

Such fragmentary data as there are for Latin-American countries indicate the same pattern. In Mexico, for example, the relatively large crop producing sector increased its output 60 per cent from 1925–29 to 1945–49, using, however, only 27 per cent more input; thus output per unit of aggregate input rose by 26 per cent. Farm production in Brazil was 55 per cent larger in 1945–49 than in 1925–29. The input index rose only 30 per cent; and, accordingly, output per unit of aggregate input increased 20 per cent.[24]

Such data do not show just what influence is exerted on economic growth by each factor, but they do suggest that, to achieve rapid growth,

[20] M. Abramovitz, "Resource and Output Trends in the United States since 1870," *American Economic Review,* Papers and Proceedings, XLVI, May 1956, pp. 5–23, reprinted by the National Bureau of Economic Research as Occasional Paper No. 52; John W. Kendrick, "Productivity Trends: Capital and Labor," *Review of Economics and Statistics,* XXXVIII, August 1956, pp. 248–257, reprinted by the National Bureau as Occasional Paper No. 53; Jacob Schmookler, "The Changing Efficiency of the American Economy: 1869–1938," *Review of Economics and Statistics,* XXXIV, August 1952, pp. 214–231.

[21] Schmookler, p. 224.

[22] Abramovitz, p. 8.

[23] Solomon Fabricant, "Economic Progress and Economic Change" (a part of the 34th Annual Report of the National Bureau of Economic Research, May, 1954). Tangible capital here consists of structures, including housing, equipment, inventories and net foreign assets, but excluding consumer equipment, military assets and land and subsoil assets [footnote from passage quoted].

[24] Clarence A. Moore, "Agricultural Development in Mexico," *Journal of Farm Economics,* February, 1955; Clarence A. Moore, "Agricultural Development in Brazil" (unpublished TALA paper, No. 54–044, September 29, 1954, University of Chicago) [footnote of T. W. Schultz, author of the passage quoted]; Theodore W. Schultz, "Latin-American Economic Policy Lessons," *American Economic Review,* Papers and Proceedings, XLVI, May 1956, pp. 430–431.

an economy needs more than a growing supply of tools and labor. It needs education and investment in human beings, research, and an environment in which inventiveness is stimulated, and a framework in which the reshuffling of resources is permitted. Both new discoveries and untrammeled adjustment afterward seem to be important to rapid growth. On the one hand, inventions cannot be applied unless they are discovered, and, on the other hand, the fruits of inventions cannot be harvested unless they are widely applied and resources are efficiently reallocated. Consider the effects of a single innovation — atomic power. Suppose that atomic power made the cost of electricity $2\frac{1}{2}$ mills per kilowatt hour less than it would otherwise be. It has been estimated that our national income would be increased by no more than $\frac{2}{3}$ of 1 per cent.[25] Even this growth could occur only if there was considerable readjustment in the economy. And only if "trigger effects" (the impacts of further innovations that emerge as firms try to take advantage of atomic power)[26] were introduced — only then could the projected increase in national income become very impressive. Without the trigger effects, most great inventions — the printing press, the railroad, the internal combustion engine — would surely have made only modest contributions to total production. Hence, not only institutions that stimulate research and inventiveness but also those that facilitate full adjustment by the economy are influential factors in economic growth.

GNP, PAST AND FUTURE

So much for the meaning of GNP and its determinants. How has this index to the nation's strength read in recent years? How do recent readings compare with those of earlier years? What are the prospects that lie ahead?

In 1957, GNP amounted to $440 billion. Of this final output of $440 billion, $284 billion or 65 per cent was devoted to personal consumption, $65 billion or 15 per cent to gross private domestic investment, and $47 billion or 11 per cent to national security. (The remainder was net foreign investment and other government purchases of goods and services.)

Compare these figures with the corresponding amounts for earlier years. In 1953, when United States expenditures on the Korean conflict were at their peak, we produced a gross national product of $399 billion and devoted $60 billion or 15 per cent to national security programs.

---

[25] Herbert A. Simon, "The Effects of Atomic Power on National or Regional Economies," Chapter XIII in Sam H. Schurr and Jacob Marschak, *Economic Aspects of Atomic Power,* Princeton University Press, Princeton, N.J., 1950. For the assumptions that guided the preparation of these exploratory estimates, see that volume and particularly Chapter XIII.

[26] *Ibid.,* pp. 232–234.

In 1929, GNP was only $197 billion, and national security expenditures were less than one per cent.[27]

As for future years, the President's Materials Policy Commission has estimated that GNP can rise at a rate of about 3 per cent per year, at least for the next few decades.[28] In making the projections, the Commission's staff tried to take into consideration the determinants of GNP that were discussed above. Looking at 1975 (really "a shorthand means of denoting 'sometime in the 1970's'"), the Commission assumed a labor force of 82 million poeple. This figure rested on an estimate that there would be 146 million people 14 years of age and over, with the labor force constituting, as at present, 56 per cent of that number. Of this supply of laborers, 4 million were expected to be in the military service, $7\frac{1}{2}$ million in agriculture, and $2\frac{1}{2}$ million unemployed. Another assumption was that the average work week would decline 15 per cent by the middle 70's. Finally, with our institutional arrangements, the probable growth of the capital stock, and advances in technology, it was believed that productivity (average output per man-hour) would rise at a rate of $2\frac{1}{2}$ per cent per year. The resulting rate of growth would yield a GNP of $700 billion — over 50 per cent greater than that of 1957 — by the middle 1970's.

Figure 1 shows the past and projected growth of GNP, and the past allocations to national security, consumption, and private domestic investment. National security outlays, it might be noted, include the programs for atomic energy, stockpiling, and Mutual Defense Assistance, as well as the strictly military programs. As can be seen in the figure, GNP has increased rapidly during the past two decades, and can continue

[27] All the amounts and calculations in this section are in terms of 1957 dollars. The amounts in 1954 dollars are given in the *Survey of Current Business,* July 1958, pp. 10–11. They were converted to 1957 dollars by using the implicit deflators published in the same source. For more precise measurements, this method of putting the amounts in 1957 dollars would be too rough, but for our purposes the procedure seems to be suitable.

National security expenditures in current dollars for 1941 to 1957 (*Ibid.,* pp. 4–5) were converted to 1957 dollars by using the implicit deflators for federal purchases of goods and services. For 1929 to 1940, inclusive, national security outlays were approximated in the following way: For those years, military expenditures as a percentage of military plus civil governmental expenditures have been estimated (M. Slade Kendrick, *A Century and a Half of Federal Expenditures,* Occasional Paper No. 48, National Bureau of Economic Research, New York, 1955, p. 41). These factors were applied to "federal purchases of goods and services" (roughly equivalent to the National Bureau's "military plus civil" expenditures) in 1957 dollars.

[28] *Resources for Freedom,* A Report to the President by the President's Materials Policy Commission, Vol. II, U.S. Government Printing Office, Washington, D.C., 1952, pp. 111–12. Most efforts to project GNP have produced similar estimates; see, for example, Committee for Economic Development, *Economic Growth in the United States, Its Past and Future,* A Statement on National Policy by the Research and Policy Committee, February, 1958, pp. 42–43.

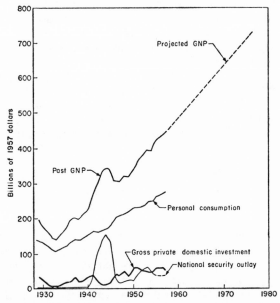

**Fig. 1. GNP and major components, 1929–1957; and GNP projected to 1975**

to grow at about the same rate. While personal consumption has not quite kept pace with this rate of growth, national security outlays have risen from nearly nothing to about 10 per cent of GNP. Note, however, that national security expenditures constituted a smaller part of the total in 1957 than they did during either the Korean War or World War II. Table 1 traces these components as percentages of gross national product.

**Table 1. Major components as percentages of GNP in selected years**

| Components | Percentages of GNP | | | | | |
| --- | --- | --- | --- | --- | --- | --- |
| | 1930 | 1940 | 1944 | 1950 | 1953 | 1957 |
| Personal consumption | 71 | 68 | 49 | 66 | 62 | 65 |
| Gross private domestic investment | 15 | 15 | 4 | 19 | 15 | 15 |
| National security | 1 | 1 | 46 | 7 | 15 | 11 |
| Other | 13 | 16 | 1 | 8 | 8 | 9 |

If we merely continue to devote 10 per cent to national security, the absolute amount could reach $70 billion in 1957 dollars by the early 1970's. And if the national security program became 15 per cent of GNP (over $100 billion in 1957 dollars), consumption and investment could still expand tremendously. In other words, production possibilities are likely to increase greatly over the next two decades, easing the constraint on these various activities. If we view this future growth from the vantage point of, say, the early 1960's, we still have considerable latitude in choosing how this extra output is to be used.

ALTERNATIVE POLICIES AFFECTING FUTURE RESOURCES

Future GNP is not irrevocably determined. It does not have to behave in accordance with projections like those shown above. Quite apart from errors of estimation, GNP may deviate from its projected path on account of either fortuitous events or deliberate policies. In this section, the possibilities of deliberately increasing future resources will be mentioned. They will not be examined in detail, for the primary concern of this study is defense, not general economic growth. But it is relevant not only to take existing resource constraints into account but also to consider at least briefly the means of influencing future constraints.

Even in the short run when the supply of resources is given, government policies can affect the level of employment and the efficiency with which the resources are employed. Monetary-fiscal policy to avoid the unemployment that comes with recession can be of enormous significance. During the thirties, to take an extreme example, the loss of GNP due to unemployment was "some 300 billion dollars — almost equal to the real economic cost of World War II." [29] Recession could severely reduce our strength without being anything like the deep depression of the 1930's. Of course, the actual GNP that occurs when there is large-scale unemployment is not properly a constraint on defense activities, for resources can then be put into defense programs without sacrificing other outputs. Nonetheless, in reducing our economic strength and pulling down the economies of our allies, recession would seriously undermine our national security. Moreover, recession would shrink investment, retard technological advance, and stunt the future growth of GNP, resulting in more confining resource limitations at a later date than would otherwise exist. We should make no mistake on this point — a sharp recession could curtail ominously the economic basis for national security planning. Therefore the government should be willing to cut taxes, expand the volume of money, and reduce interest rates if aggregate demand slumps and serious unemployment develops. We should keep up our guard against overconfidence in "new-era" psychology.

It would be wrong, however, in trying to avoid recession, to invite drastic inflation. Deficits and easy money in *all* circumstances are not the answer. For severe inflation too prevents the economy from functioning efficiently and retards its development. It frequently leads to price

[29] Samuelson, *Economics*, p. 225.

controls, which inhibit the market mechanism, because people object to its inequities. Furthermore, violent inflation (or any inflation suppressed by price controls) pushes people into inefficient activities such as barter and efforts to convert monetary receipts into goods immediately. Hyperinflation usually ends with the economy thoroughly disorganized.

Thus, among the government actions that are vitally important to GNP and its growth are monetary-fiscal efforts to guide aggregate demand for goods and services — to steer the economy between the Scylla of deflation and the Charybdis of inflation.[30]

Other government policies affect the efficiency with which given resources are used, thus influencing the size of GNP. On the one hand, restrictions on firms and individuals, though stemming from the best of intentions, may distort the allocation of resources and impair incentives. Price controls, price supports, minimum wage laws, tariffs, and subsidies often produce such distortions. On the other hand, failure to intervene in certain situations allows distortions to persist. Examples are situations in which monopolistic groups can restrict entry into occupations or industries, or situations in which firms do not bear certain costs that they inflict on others (for example, by polluting water or congesting highways). In addition to their influence on the efficiency of the private economy, public policies determine the efficiency with which the government's own activities are conducted.

It is inappropriate here to describe specific policies that would yield increased efficiency in the private and public sectors of the economy. We will, however, stress one point. In order to choose the specific actions that constitute preferred policies, policy-makers need analytical assistance wherever it can be provided. They need well-conceived estimates of the prospective gains and costs of alternative courses of action. Without such estimates, advice is bound to consist of generalities and to sound arbitrary, or like an exhortation to do good. To say anything concrete about the merits of, say, a particular subsidy, the costs and gains from alternative arrangements must be estimated. To make recommendations about a particular health program, the costs and effects have to be gauged, albeit roughly. To choose the government investments that will contribute most to future GNP, the impacts of alternative investments must be measured as best we can. Systematic effort to determine preferred courses of action is called "operations research" when applied to problems in military or industrial operations. It is called "systems analysis" when applied to certain broader or longer-range problems, particularly the comparison of weapons systems. It is called "cost-benefit analysis" when such things as water-resource developments are being considered. More and better analysis may be useful in increasing efficiency in shaping many

[30] Stabilization problems and policies will be considered in Chapter 5.

government programs and policies.[31] And increased effectiveness in shaping these policies means higher GNP and greater growth — a larger resource base for defense and all the other activities that contribute to the national well-being.

In the longer run, when the supplies of capital, labor, and knowledge can be expanded, there are additional methods of increasing future GNP. While this country would hardly attempt to control the quantity of labor, government policies may affect the evolution of the work week and will definitely influence the health, education, training, and mobility of our manpower. This form of investment, that is, in human resources, probably yields a comparatively high return.[32] National policy can also influence the volume of private investment in capital equipment and, more directly, the volume of public investment. Private capital formation depends, in part, upon monetary-fiscal policies because they affect the availability of funds, upon the size and character of the government budget because some public spending competes with private spending and other public spending stimulates it, upon the tax structure because some taxes deter investment more than others. Public capital formation, of course, is determined by the proportion of the budget that is devoted to investment.

Another means of shaping economic development is by devoting more funds to basic research and exploratory development, and, of course, by maintaining a free economy in which the fruits of discoveries can best be harvested. The government sponsors a good deal of research at present, much of it as part of the national security programs, but the payoff to the nation from still more research appears to be high. Such evidence as adding up the direct results of a few outstanding developments tends to support this conclusion.[33] Although it is extremely hard to measure the returns attributable to research, the average annual return on this form of investment has been estimated to be from 100 to 200 per cent.[34] Calculations have been made which suggest the same general range in one sector of the economy, agriculture. The savings in 1950 due to improvements in production techniques from 1940 to 1950 have been esti-

[31] Roland N. McKean, *Efficiency in Government through Systems Analysis,* John Wiley and Sons, New York, 1958.

[32] Theodore W. Schultz, *Redirecting Farm Policy,* Macmillan Co., New York, 1943, pp. 68–71.

[33] For example, see *The Mighty Force of Research* by the Editors of *Fortune,* McGraw-Hill Book Co., Inc., New York, 1956; Yale Brozen, "The Economic Future of Research and Development," *Industrial Laboratories,* Vol. 4, December 1953, pp. 5–8; Allen Abrams, "Measuring the Return from Research," Proceedings of the Fourth Annual Conference on the Administration of Research, University of Michigan, Ann Arbor, 1951; and Zvi Griliches, "Research Costs and Social Returns: Hybrid Corn and Related Innovations," *Journal of Political Economy,* October 1958, pp. 419–431.

[34] This was the estimate of Raymond Ewell of the National Science Foundation — mentioned in *The Mighty Force of Research,* p. vi.

mated at 60 to 300 per cent (lower and upper limits) of ten years' research and extension outlays at the 1950 rate of expenditure.[35]

A substantial amount of government activity in this sphere, particularly in basic research, seems to be justified. Research that is profitable to the whole economy may nonetheless be unprofitable to any individual firm, because the gains are so widely diffused. Such research must usually be sponsored by universities, foundations, or government agencies.

There are several ways in which defense policy can itself affect resources available in the future. National-security programs may have by-product effects on the determinants of GNP, for instance, on the employment level or the rate of technological advance. Also, the efficiency of defense activities can influence the resources that will be available in the future by affecting the amount that the nation can devote to investment.

## SUMMARY

In the very short run (say in a military situation in which a commander must use the specific forces at his disposal), resource constraints are properly viewed as quantities of specific inputs. In the longer run, in decisions affecting the situation several years hence, the main resource limitations are best viewed as general monetary constraints, and costs are best measured as dollar costs.

In connection with longer-run decisions, the over-all constraint on the nation's consumption, investment, defense, and other activities can be regarded as the nation's capacity to produce as measured by full-employment GNP (gross national product). Only for very sudden and drastic changes in the level and composition of such activities would it be either helpful or necessary to think in terms of specific resource constraints.

GNP in the United States is likely to increase a great deal over the coming decades, offering considerable freedom of choice in determining the amounts to be devoted to defense (and the other categories of expenditure). Moreover, national policies, including defense planning itself, can affect the growth of the nation's resources.

[35] Theodore W. Schultz, "Agricultural Research: Expenditures and Returns," in *The Economic Organization of Agriculture*, McGraw-Hill Book Co., Inc., New York, 1953, pp. 114–122. If we look at a longer period, savings in 1950 due to improvements from 1910 to 1950 are from 130 to 230 per cent of 40 years' research and extension outlays at the 1950 rate of expenditure.

## 4. DIVERTING GNP TO DEFENSE: HOW BIG A DEFENSE BUDGET?

**D**efense expenditures in recent years have set new records for peacetime, outlays for military plus other major national security activities amounting to about 50 billion dollars annually. Budgets of this size, naturally enough, are viewed with considerable concern. Have the added outlays in recent years purchased things that were worth the cost? Or has spending just become a "happy reflex?" [1] How much of GNP should be devoted to defense? Before we take up such questions, or try to show how they should be approached, let us review a few points about the formulation of the budget in the United States.

### THE BUDGETARY PROCESS [2]

The annual defense budget is part of the massive document, *The Budget of the United States,* which the President sends to Congress each January. An enormous amount of time, effort, and "bargaining" goes into its preparation.

Consider the military budget for the fiscal year 1960 (July 1959 to July 1960). Part of the work on these estimates was started about two years earlier — that is, in mid-1957. At about that time [3] the departments of the Army, Navy, and Air Force began to plan for the fiscal year 1960. They based their figures on the force requirements and long-range plans tentatively established at various levels in the Executive branch. On the basis of directives from the top levels of the Army, Navy, and Air Force, the lower levels worked up detailed programs showing the physical inputs that would be "required."

Next, in the spring and summer of 1958, these programs were modified, costed, and converted into departmental budgets. Early in this period, the Secretary of Defense issued "budget guidelines" to the indi-

[1] Senator Paul Douglas has wondered if people are now conditioned so that their mouths water when budget-time rolls around much as Dr. Pavlov's dogs began to salivate when a bell was rung.

[2] For a detailed account, see Arthur Smithies, *The Budgetary Process in the United States,* McGraw-Hill Book Company, New York, 1955, pp. 101–159 and 240–256. We are indebted to Frederick M. Sallagar of The RAND Corporation for several of the points stressed in this section.

[3] The procedures are constantly evolving, and they vary from one department to the next; the statements here depict a sort of "average" procedure that may not be one hundred per cent correct for any particular department over any particular budget cycle.

vidual Services. Then the budget offices of the departments issued their "calls for estimates," and the various commands and bureaus prepared budget estimates. During the summer the departmental budget offices sent preliminary budgets to the Secretary of Defense. At this point the Secretary discussed the figures with the President and with officials in the Bureau of the Budget. After some further revision, perhaps on the basis of Presidential ceilings, the estimates were sent to the Budget Bureau.

During the autumn of 1958, these figures were revised by the Budget Bureau and also by the Defense Department. A series of discussions involving officials in the individual departments, the Defense Department, and the Budget Bureau took place. The Secretary of Defense, after consulting with the Chief of Staff and each departmental secretary, officially transmitted the estimates to the Budget Bureau. The latter sent its recommendations to the President. In January 1959, the President, having reached final decisions, submitted the official document to Congress along with his budget message. (Sample exhibits, taken from the budget for the fiscal year 1960, are shown later in the chapter.)

Finally, the stage that we usually read about in the papers was reached. During the spring and early summer of 1959 there were the hearings before the subcommittees of the Committee on Appropriations, the Congressional debates, and the passage of appropriations bills for the fiscal year 1960 by both the House and the Senate. (At the same time, the Services were trying to adjust their programs to make them consistent with the revisions in their budgets.)

Thus, budget formulation is a long and complex process, and the results are influenced considerably by the mechanics and institutions involved. It is a process of bargaining among officials and groups having diverse strengths, aims, convictions, and responsibilities. Also, these participants naturally have various "political" considerations in mind — concerns about the impact of budgetary decisions on the success of rival departments or officials, on the attitudes of voters, on the actions of various groups. The effects, as far as reaching sound decisions is concerned, are not all bad — nor are they all good.

Other notable characteristics of the process are oppressive deadlines and inadequate opportunities for decision-makers to study exhibits. At best, officials can hardly give attention to the issues commensurate with their importance. Both civilian and military administrators have other day-to-day decisions to make, multitudes of them. If we ask ourselves how we would prepare or evaluate this thousand-page document or the hundred-page portion pertaining to the Defense Department, we can better appreciate the awesome nature of this task.

Moreover, there is often severe personal penalty for originating mistakes yet little or no penalty for perpetuating past decisions — except in time of crisis. Consequently there are strong forces against making "new" decisions (in budget formulation as well as in other governmental problems of choice) except when palpable crises occur.

In brief, deciding upon the defense budget is a tremendous task that must be performed under difficult circumstances. We cannot expect to identify or achieve "optimal" solutions; we should have no illusions on this score. Nonetheless, looking at the problem in the right way can aid us in reaching better solutions. It can help officials get better results with existing institutions — and it may point toward institutional modifications that can improve budgetary decision (see also Chapter 12).

## BUDGET-FIRSTERS VERSUS NEED-FIRSTERS

To get the most out of the nation's resources, we should devote fewer billions to national security if some defense activities are worth less to the nation than they cost, and spend still more billions if extra defenses would yield greater value than the other things that the money could buy. This way of looking at the problem is not universally accepted, however. Some persons apparently believe that the size of the national security program should be determined in the light of cost alone. They name some figure and say "That's all we'll pay, and that's that." Others apparently believe that the program should be planned on the basis of need alone. In Congressional hearings, military leaders are often asked to reveal what they "really need." For instance, Senator Chavez told General Maxwell D. Taylor, "We would like to know what you need and not what the Budget Bureau thinks you should have." [4] As another case in point, Senator Ervin deplored the Defense Department's willingness to cut purchases below our "needs." According to the Senator, this attitude smacked of the economic philosophy of an old acquaintance who used to say, "Now, good boy, if you want to get along in this world you just have to do without the things you have to have." [5]

Some simply say that the task of determining budget size has to be done one way or the other:

In general, there are two ways in which the problem of balancing defense needs against fiscal requirements can be approached. One way is to ascertain essential defense needs and then see if the funds can be made available to meet them. The other is to predetermine, as a matter of fiscal policy, a dollar limit for defense

[4] *Department of Defense Appropriations for 1957,* Hearings Before the Subcommittee of the Committee on Appropriations, U.S. Senate, 84th Congress, 2d Session, U.S. Government Printing Office, Washington, D.C., 1956, p. 93.

[5] *Study of Airpower,* Hearings Before the Subcommittee on the Air Force of the Committee on Armed Services, U.S. Senate, 84th Congress, 2d Session, Part XXII, U.S. Government Printing Office, Washington, D.C., 1956, p. 1691.

expenditures; and thereupon refuse to satisfy any defense needs that cannot be compressed within that limit.[6]

The truth is, however, that one cannot properly draw up defense plans on the basis of either cost alone or needs alone. There is no budget size or cost that is correct regardless of the payoff, and there is no need that should be met regardless of cost.

On the one hand, there is no presumption that the defense budget is now, or should be, near any immovable upper limit. As far as physical and economic feasibility is concerned, national security expenditures could be raised (within a two- or three-year transition period) by, say, $30 billion per year. With appropriate changes in tax rates and monetary policy (see Chapter 5), this could be done without causing severe inflation.

From existing levels, in other words, outlays for defense activities can be raised if we really want to raise them — if we feel that we need extra defense programs more than other things. There is, of course, a maximal amount that could be devoted to national security. It is less than total GNP, since part must go for subsistence and supporting activities in order to have any security program at all. But there is no magic number like fifty or seventy-five or one hundred billion dollars which we can stand, and above which we can't. To be sure, the larger the budget, the greater the sacrifice, but we cannot say, as some have tried to argue, that taxes amounting to more than 25 per cent of national income must inevitably bring collapse or intolerable inflation.[7] Countries in Western Europe have successfully borne taxes in excess of 30 per cent of GNP.

We shall not try to add to the evidence that much larger programs are economically feasible.[8] We believe that we can take this proposition as our point of departure. There are serious questions, of course (as noted in the preceding chapter), as to whether or not extremely large programs are politically feasible — whether or not United States consumers in the aggregate are ever willing to cut back on consumption. Even if reductions of consumption are ruled out, however, growth of the economy of the United States would by itself permit increases in defense outlays

[6] *Airpower,* Report of the Subcommittee on the Air force of the Committee on Armed Services, U.S. Senate, 84th Congress, U.S. Government Printing Office, Washington, D.C., 1957, p. 9.

[7] For example, Colin Clark took such a position, often cited, in "Public Finance and Changes in the Value of Money," *Economic Journal,* December 1945, pp. 371–389.

[8] On this subject, the writers agree with many of the general conclusions in the study by Gerhard Colm, *Can We Afford Additional Programs for National Security?,* National Planning Association, Washington, D.C., October 1953, and the subsequent paper by Gerhard Colm and Manuel Helzner, "General Economic Feasibility of National Security Programs," March 1957, published in *Federal Expenditure Policy for Economic Growth and Stability,* Hearings Before the Subcommittee on Fiscal Policy of the Joint Economic Committee, 85th Congress, 1st Session, U.S. Government Printing Office, Washington, D.C., 1958, pp. 356–364.

up to about $10 billion per year. If we wished to do so, therefore, we could raise the annual defense budget by $20 billion in two years' time without cutting aggregate consumption, investment, or civil government programs.[9] To repeat, then, the defense budget is not near any absolute upper limit.

On the other hand, there is no particular national security program that we need in an absolute sense. As mentioned in Chapter 2, a list of the "desirable" items that could strengthen our defense would be almost endless. Where does one draw the line (without reference to cost) between what is needed and what is not? There are no clear-cut "minimal" needs, either for defense as a whole or for particular programs. President Eisenhower emphasized this point:

Words like "essential" and "indispensable" and "absolute minimum" become the common coin of the realm — and they are spent with wild abandon. One military man will argue hotly for a given number of aircraft as the "absolute minimum." . . . And others will earnestly advocate the "indispensable" needs for ships or tanks or rockets or guided missiles or artillery — all totaled in numbers that are always called "minimum." All such views are argued with vigor and tenacity. But obviously all cannot be right.[10]

Outlays for various programs *can* be cut if we feel that we need other things even more. It is up to us to choose.

In brief, our national security budget is not near any physical limits — GNP minus subsistence, on the one hand, or zero expenditures, on the other. Also, because of growth, large *future* increases could be accomplished without cutting consumption. Consequently, our range of choice is wide. Making the choice should be viewed as a problem of getting the most out of resources, not as one of hunting for a tablet on which the right budget, requirement, or doctrine is inscribed. In formulating defense budgets we should not be "need- or doctrine-firsters" — those who insist upon discovering what we "need" regardless of what we have to give up. Nor should we be "budget-firsters" — those who insist upon discovering what we can give up regardless of how much we value defense activities. Instead let us be deliberate choosers, changing our budgets and reshaping our forces as long as a change appears to gain more than it costs. If taken literally, the questions, "What can we afford for defense?" and "What are our needs?" are the wrong ones to ask in deciding upon the size of the defense effort. The right question is, "How much is needed for defense *more than it is needed for other purposes?*"

[9] The hypothetical programs discussed by Colm and Helzner, *op. cit.*, do not imply reductions in aggregate consumption.
[10] "The Eisenhower Tax Program," *U.S. News and World Report*, May 29, 1953, p. 98.

## HOW MUCH FOR PROGRAMS VERSUS HOW MUCH FOR OBJECTS [11]

In trying to answer the above question, we should probably think in terms of programs — that is, combinations of activities that produce distinguishable products. A governmental program is the counterpart of an industry in the private sector of the economy — and is just as ambiguous, as hard to define, and yet as useful a concept as an industry. There is one important difference, however. In the private sector of the economy, markets reveal prices for industry outputs, even if they are intermediate products. In the governmental sector, there are no markets for most outputs, and the significance of the products, especially quantities of intermediate outputs, becomes especially hard to judge. To facilitate judgments about their value, programs should be aggregations of activities yielding products that can be at least subjectively appraised. In general, we should move toward thinking in terms of programs that perform tasks and yield end-products,[12] speaking rather loosely, rather than actions that yield objects or intermediate products.

Let us illustrate the distinction between a program and an object (we use this terminology because the *Budget of the United States* has made a similar distinction between "programs" and "objects"). Certain activities of the Air Force, the Army, and the Navy produce retaliatory striking power or deterrence, and these activities might be grouped together and called a program. In providing deterrence, the Services use missiles, manpower, food, paper clips, and transportation — intermediate items which might be called "objects of expenditure."

Several points about programs and objects should be noted. First, decisions about the size of programs and those about the things to be bought are interdependent. One would not make one of these decisions in complete ignorance of the other. If the desired striking power is increased, different types of equipment may become the most efficient means, and if some equipment innovation appears (for example, more accurate ballistic missiles), a different level of striking power may become the proper choice. But to some extent these choices have to be made separately — by different people or at different times. In making one choice we try to make reasonable assumptions about the other.

Second, just what one means by an "end-product" or a "program" is not unambiguous. The line of demarcation between programs and objects

[11] For other discussions of some of these points and of related topics, see Arthur Smithies, especially pp. 229–277, and Jesse Burkhead, *Government Budgeting*, John Wiley and Sons, New York, 1956, pp. 110–181.

[12] David Novick, "Which Program Do We Mean in 'Program Budgeting'?" The RAND Corporation, P-530, May 12, 1954.

is not clear-cut. Is the Military Air Transport Service a program or simply an activity supporting, say, the Tactical Air program? Or is even the latter merely something to be purchased for a program that might be called "deterrence and fighting of limited wars"? Even such tasks as providing nuclear striking power and providing forces for limited war have interrelationships. Neither is solely a supporting activity of the other, yet each can influence the credibility and effectiveness of the other. It may seem that one is driven to regard every military item and activity as an object purchased for and contributing to *one* program — national security.

Despite these complexities, officials do find it helpful to think in terms of several programs, and there is hope of developing categories that will be even more meaningful. After all, our only chance of pondering the gains as well as the costs of defense budgets is to think in terms of rather broad aggregations of activities. We cannot appraise the adequacy of the defense budget, either subjectively or with the aid of quantitative analysis, by thinking about the gains from such categories as paper clips, petroleum, or personnel. Nor can we go to the other extreme and think in terms of a single national security program. Such an aggregation is too broad; we have no conception of units of "national security" that could be purchased. But there are possibilities between these extremes — aggregations of activities that produce species of end-products such as capabilities for nuclear retaliation or for limited war. Complications and difficulties abound, and yet for some such programs we can make judgments about, or even develop quantitative clues to, their worth as well as their cost.

Perhaps an analogy from a consumer's budget will help clarify those points. An individual cannot judge intelligently how much he should spend on a car if he asks, "How much should I devote to fenders, to steering activities, and to carburetion?" Nor can he improve his decisions much by lumping all living into a single program and asking, "How much should I spend on life?" Yet it is often helpful to ask, "How much am I willing to spend on my car-program — on transportation to work, stores, and recreational facilities?" Although not really an end-item, an individual's transportation is closer to an end-product than fenders or carburetors. While his car program is somewhat interrelated with, say, his recreational program, the interrelationships do not dominate the outcome, and he can get some feeling for the gains from the car, making reasonable assumptions about the other program.

In determining the size of the defense budget, then, we should ask whether various broad programs should be increased or decreased, and we should keep trying to define programs about which we can make sounder judgments. To be sure, attention should also be given to the detailed objects of expenditure. They help determine the efficiency with which the programs are carried out, and much of the economics of defense pertains to increasing the efficiency with which resources are employed *within* defense programs. The way the Services use materials and manpower deserves hard scrutiny — even at the highest levels. If Congress, through the review of defense expenditures, can perceive better ways to combine objects of expenditure or discover wasteful purchases that can be eliminated, it should certainly insist upon the increased efficiency.

But the objects of expenditure already get a goodly share of attention at the Congressional level. The annual hearings on appropriations are to a considerable extent about such matters as maintenance costs, the utilization of surplus butter and cheese by the Services, the location of National Guard armories, aircraft fuel and oil, travel costs, and the location of flag officers' quarters. Attention is attracted by things like the 104-year supply of Jeep parts once held by the Services or the 11,000 dozen oyster forks owned on one occasion by the Navy.[13] Here we wish to stress that the broader problem, the selection of the scale of defense programs, also deserves careful attention. At whatever degree of efficiency can be achieved, the question remains: Should the nation buy larger or smaller national-security programs? Are the last increments to existing programs worth their cost? Would further increments to particular programs be worth more than their cost?

### HOW TO APPROACH THE CHOICE OF PROGRAM-SIZES [14]

To the preceding questions, we cannot provide definitive quantitative answers, of course. No analysis can yield solutions to the problem of choosing program-sizes that would necessarily be valid for all Congressmen and voters. Each person's answer depends upon how much value he attaches to deterrence of nuclear war, to the checking of limited aggressions, and to other products of national defense. It depends upon his attitude toward risks and uncertainty — that is, upon whether he is inclined to gamble or to hedge. It depends upon his valuation of side effects or impacts that cannot be made commensurable (in any *generally* valid way) with the main effects of the programs. Nevertheless, we can devise exhibits and analyses that facilitate weighing the gains and costs of alternative program-sizes. In deciding how much (if any) penicillin to buy, a man with pneumonia does not know precisely how much he

[13] Paul H. Douglas, *Economy in the National Government,* University of Chicago Press, Chicago, 1952, p. 150. To make matters worse, it turned out that "10,442 dozen of these oyster forks were of such a poor quality that, so the records showed, they were usable only in an emergency !"

[14] In various parts of this section the writers are indebted to David Novick of The RAND Corporation.

values good health, how to assess the risks, or precisely what the side effects will be; but it helps a lot to know how much penicillin costs and what effect it has on pneumonia.

It might be reemphasized that judgments or measurements of gains are just as important as measures of the costs (which are really the alternative gains that could be obtained if the resources were put to other uses). We cannot make intelligent decisions on the basis of either alone. In this section we turn first to exhibits of costs and then to the possibilities of appraising gains, in both instances taking the exhibits in recent budgets as points of departure. In doing this, we must regard certain changes, such as more extensive crossing of departmental lines, as being feasible. Crossing departmental boundaries could be achieved either by organizational changes or by the preparation of special exhibits separate from the main budget documents.

### BREAKDOWNS OF COST IN RECENT BUDGETS

Since 1949 the budgetary presentations in the Department of Defense have been improved. Proposed obligational authority and expenditures [15] have been collected into one document and put into somewhat more meaningful categories than had previously been used.[16] These recent compilations probably make possible more informed judgments about expenditure levels than could be made in earlier years. Nonetheless, the current presentation falls far short of being an effective program budget. Perhaps the best way to demonstrate this shortcoming is to present and discuss briefly a few sample exhibits from a recent budget. (It should be noted, however, that the format of the defense budget is constantly undergoing revision.)

*The broad functional budget.* To begin with, there is the broad functional budget in which all defense activities are put into one huge program called "major national security." [17] This is indeed an end-product program, but it is *too* comprehensive — embracing all Army, Navy, Air Force, and other national-security missions. To appreciate its cost and significance is almost impossible. Few persons have any subjective "feel" for a national-security capability — that is, for the output that would be pro-

[15] In the U.S. Budget, "obligational authority" is total authority to make commitments during the designated fiscal year, whether the cash is to be expended in that year or later on; and "expenditures" are the estimated disbursements during the fiscal year, whether the obligations were incurred in that year or previously. We shall refer mostly to obligational authority here, believing that it approximates future costs more closely than would the scheduled disbursements.

[16] For comments on the form of earlier budgets and the evolution of the current form, see Smithies, pp. 232–237.

[17] The other governmental functions are international affairs and finance, veterans' services and benefits, labor and welfare, agriculture and agricultural resources, natural resources, commerce and housing, general government, interest, and allowance for contingencies. *The Budget of the United States Government for the Fiscal Year Ending June 30, 1960,* U.S. Government Printing Office, Washington, D.C., 1959, p. M25.

vided. And there is little hope of ever devising quantitative measures that would shed much light on this mixture of capabilities. To try to sort out several less inclusive programs would seem to be a more promising approach.

*The current "performance" budgets of the individual services.* The present budget does classify expenditures into less inclusive categories that have been called programs. (In the Budget for the fiscal year 1960, they are often labeled "appropriation groups.") There are fairly detailed exhibits in terms of both programs and objects. The classification of expenditures by program, however, turns out to be a classification by organization unit (Army, Navy, and Air Force) and account title,[18] though the exhibits for each account title include a few paragraphs purporting to describe the program and its performance. Consider the summary presentation at the front of the section devoted to the Department of Defense. In order to conserve space, Table 2 omits proposed expenditures and shows only proposed new obligations.[19]

**Table 2. Budget authorizations and expenditures[a]
by major appropriation groups or "programs"
(millions of dollars)**

| | New obligational authority | | |
|---|---|---|---|
| *Appropriation groups*[b] | 1958 enacted | 1959 estimate | 1960 estimate |
| Military personnel — total | 10,982 | 11,475 | 11,625 |
| Operation and maintenance | 10,237 | 10,306 | 10,512 |
| Procurement — total | 11,054 | 14,524 | 13,348 |
| Research, development, test, and evaluation | 2,258 | 3,464 | 3,772 |
| Construction — total | 2,086 | 1,369 | 1,563 |
| Revolving and management funds | 130 | — | 30 |
| Total, Department of Defense | 36,747 | 41,138 | 40,850 |

[a] Source: *The Budget of the United States Government for the Fiscal Year Ending June 30, 1960,* p. 445.

[b] Amounts for these "appropriation groups" are further subdivided into amounts for certain subgroups and for the branches of the Service (Army, Air Force, Navy), but the groups shown here are the basic categories that have been regarded as programs.

Note the nature of these "programs." Few of the items on this list are even remotely like end-product missions, and the dollar amounts are not the costs of achieving capabilities in such missions. Instead, the items are collections of objects used in a variety of tasks; and the dollar figures are the sums of selected costs from all of them. For instance, "military personnel" covers officers and men for all military

[18] The "account titles" are the major "programs" listed in Table 2.

[19] See footnote 15 for an explanation of these terms.

functions. "Military personnel, Air Force" includes men for the Strategic Air Command, Tactical Air Command, and all other Air Force activities.

How does one choose the amount that should be spent on categories like across-the-board procurement or military personnel? Surely this choice is made by seeking the most efficient way of carrying out end-product programs such as achieving a nuclear deterrence force. And efficiency *within* programs can and should be sought more carefully than by pondering proposed expenditures for total personnel, procurement, and construction. Indeed, the use of these categories is likely to cause inefficiency. Procurement of new missiles or aircraft often has special glamor or appeal, and the Services may find that the best way to get money is to ask for increased procurement authority. Other categories such as military construction may appear to be relatively remote from operational capabilities and be neglected.[20] As a consequence, vital actions such as the dispersing and hardening of our deterrent force are postponed, and the constraints on specific objects of expenditure (like governmental allocations of specific materials to firms) bring about unbalanced inefficient operations. In short, this classification of expenditures by account titles gives little help either in choosing program levels or in seeking efficiency within programs.[21]

It was mentioned at the outset that current budgetary exhibits include breakdowns of expenditure both by programs (so-called) and by objects. To make clear what these objects are and why they do not convey useful information about end-product programs, Table 3 presents a sample breakdown of authorizations by objects — the one for Army personnel.

The amounts proposed for these object classes (such as travel or transportation of things) may aid officials in locating inefficiencies; though systematic analysis would be necessary before anyone could be reasonably sure where inefficiency existed. Such a list of amounts can scarcely assist anyone, however, in weighing alternative program levels.

IMPROVING THE BREAKDOWN OF COSTS

The first step in trying to improve our choice of program sizes is probably to put budget figures into categories that more nearly correspond

[20] A tendency to neglect construction or other investments that do not yield a quick or tangible output is sometimes suggested by the communications underlying budgetary guidelines. For instance, one assumption used in a memorandum sent to the departmental secretaries in connection with the budget for fiscal year 1955 was as follows: "Military public works programs will be limited to those items for which there is an immediate operational requirement" (*Study of Airpower,* p. 1644).

[21] The budget also contains a further breakdown of these so-called programs (classifications by account title) by "activities." For instance, obligations for Air Force Military Personnel are broken down into amounts for pay and allowances, subsistence in kind, and so on. These categories are again types of objects, and they help little in appraising program levels.

**Table 3. Object classification of obligations
for "Military personnel, Army," 1960 estimate**[a]

| Object Classification | Obligations in millions of dollars |
|---|---|
| 01 Personal services: military | 2,989 |
| 02 Travel | 172 |
| 03 Transportation of things | 49 |
| 07 Other contractual services | 13 |
| 08 Supplies and materials | 233 |
| 11 Grants, subsidies, and contributions | — |
| 12 Pensions, annuities, and insurance claims | 3 |
| 14 Interest | 1 |
| 15 Taxes and assessments | 55 |
| Total direct obligations | 3,514[b] |

[a] Source: *The Budget of the United States Government for the Fiscal Year Ending June 30, 1960*, p. 460.

[b] The individual items do not add up to this total because of rounding. For "grants, subsidies, and contributions," the amount was less than $500,000.

to end-product missions.[22] Officials can make more perceptive judgments about the importance to the nation of these missions than they can make about the worth of categories like those listed above. Moreover, as will be indicated near the end of this chapter, there is hope of devising useful quantitative clues to the importance of end-product missions.[23] Thus, for these programs, there would be both rough estimates of the costs and a chance of gauging the gains.

A budget designed to show the approximate costs of such missions would naturally have to cross departmental lines. Activities that contribute to a broad military capability are seldom confined to one branch of the Service. Air Force activities, Naval operations, and the Army's role in active defense contribute to strategic deterrence, and all three departments also contribute to limited-war capability. The sort of exhibit that might be used to set over-all program levels is illustrated by Table 4. In this presentation, there would be essentially three broad programs: (1) deterrence or fighting of all-out war, (2) deterrence or fighting of

[22] One format (using the Air Force as an example) has been suggested by G. H. Fisher in "Weapon-System Cost Analysis," *Operations Research*, October 1956, pp. 568–571.

Another "pro forma budget," also using the Air Force as an example, has been proposed in Smithies, pp. 265–277. In this format, major "programs" include forces in being, support of forces in being, force build-up, and mobilization reserves, with the first three broken down into strategic, tactical, air defense, and air transport portions.

[23] We use the term loosely. At best, as was pointed out earlier, no aggregation of defense activities yields an output that is unambiguously an independent end-product, and *some* "programs" will inevitably comprise leftovers or aggregations that are not very meaningful.

Table 4. Possible format of national security budget

| Programs and sub-programs | Proposed force composition (No. military units, where applicable) | | | | Expenditures implied by proposed programs | | | |
|---|---|---|---|---|---|---|---|---|
| | '60 | '61 … | '64 | '65 | '60 | '61 … | '64 | '65 |

*Deterrence or Fighting of All-Out War*
  Nuclear Striking Force (AF, Navy)
    B-47
    B-52
    Atlas
    Polaris
    .
    .
    etc.
  Active Defense (Army, Navy, AF)
    Early Warning
    Interceptors
      F-102
      Bomarc
      .
      .
    etc.
    Local Defense
      Nike
      .
      .
    etc.
  Passive Defense (OCDM)
    Dispersal
    Shelters, Evacuation
    Recuperation Planning

*Deterrence or Fighting of Limited Wars*
  Ground Forces (Army, Marine)
  Sea Power (Navy)
  Tactical Air (AF, Navy)
  Transport, Air and Sea (AF, Navy)
  Military Aid to Other Countries
    (Mutual Security)
  Reserves for Mobilization
    Military Units (Army, Navy, AF)
    Defense Production (OCDM)

*Research and Development (AEC, AF, Army, Navy)*
  Exploratory
  Weapon Systems

*General Administration*

*Miscellaneous*

limited war, and (3) research and development. Each of these would be divided into component missions. Many of the latter would be interdependent to a great degree (the broad programs to a lesser degree), and the costs of one would depend in part upon the sizes of the others. Some parts, such as a submarine force or a transport fleet, would contribute to both the nuclear deterrent capability and the limited-war mission.

In principle, one always likes to know the incremental or *extra* cost of whatever policy or program he is considering. If he considers two programs and a certain item is necessary for each of them, its cost cannot properly be allocated between the two. One can ask several different questions: whether Programs A + B are worth their combined cost (including any unallocable items), whether Program A is worth its incremental cost, or whether Program B is worth its incremental cost. Proper costing depends upon which of the questions is being asked. Since preparing and digesting numerous cost estimates is itself rather costly, however, it is uneconomic to insist on precise estimates. In the budgetary exhibits suggested here, the costs of programs and program-increments would be rough approximations. Joint costs might be allocated among programs according to crude rules of thumb, or sometimes assigned to one program with recognition that others were being aided. Some items used jointly, such as top administration, could be considered as a separate aggregate (called, for the sake of convenience, a program).

These particular aggregations simply represent one set of possibilities. There may be others that would be equally or more useful. It might be better if exploratory development and weapon systems development were explicitly regarded as separate programs (see Chapter 13), their proposed costs never being lumped together into a single figure. Additional programs might be formulated from the activities in the "all other" or "miscellaneous" category. In a general way, however, Table 4 does indicate the way we should approach the choice of program-sizes and the direction in which our budgetary exhibits should probably be evolving.[24]

Notice that this format would project the costs entailed by these programs, year by year, for several years ahead. This information (for example, about future operating costs, which are sometimes extremely heavy) is essential in making decisions about program levels.[25] Yet

[21] The use of the suggested exhibits would call for, or be aided by, a number of changes in current estimation procedures — for example, increased emphasis on the use of statistical cost factors and a shortened budget cycle, increased attention to costs *during* the formulation of proposed programs (i.e., prior to their translation into budgets), improved cost analysis, and perhaps a better system of accrual accounting. Some of these reforms are discussed in Smithies, pp. 237–265, and in David Novick, "Weapon-System Cost Methodology," The RAND Corporation, Report R-287, February 1, 1956. See also Fisher, pp. 558–571.

[25] Note, however, that only costs which are genuinely entailed should be so shown. R and D programs, for instance, do *not* imply the procurement and operation of the whole menu of weapon systems that are under development.

conventional budgetary documents do not reveal the future expenditures that are implied by proposed programs. Future expenditures are vitally important whether the new programs are larger or smaller, that is, whether our concern is with initiating new programs or with terminating old ones. For frequently the major impact of either will be felt not in the next year, but in the more distant future. Expenditures in the first year on a new weapon system, for example, are likely to be a small proportion of the ultimate future cost of procurement and operation. Similarly, the savings from canceling a going program are often mainly or exclusively in future years: in the current budgetary year the costs of cancellation may equal or even exceed any gross savings. The flexibility in the budget in any current year, in either direction, is small compared with the possible impact of program decisions this year on the budgets of future years. The fact that everyone is mainly concerned with the current annual budget is frustrating because that budget has so little "give," and inefficient, because it neglects the larger, hidden part of the budget iceberg.

Actually, what is needed is an exhibit similar to Table 4 for each of several program levels. Then the Administration and the Congress could choose among explicit, meaningful programs in deciding upon the size of the defense budget.[26] When only one program level is presented, either additions to the budget or cuts in it must be made blindly — and sometimes with consequences that are worse than they need be. Disproportionate cuts may be made in some budget categories, or supplements may be voted to others which will buy little in the way of military capability without corresponding increases in complementary activities. Adjustments may require frantic and inefficient reprogramming. With a range of alternative levels prepared in advance, adjustments could be made by simply turning to a level that had been consciously considered and whose elements had been balanced.

Charles Silberman and Sanford Parker, in an article entitled "The Economic Impact of Defense," [27] attempted in 1958 to calculate the costs of, and indicate the gains from, alternative supplementary defense programs proposed by the Rockefeller Brothers Fund Report,[28] the official Gaither Report,[29] and others. They conclude on costs: "The Administration's defense program now calls for a rise from $43.3 billion in fiscal 1958 to $45.5 billion in fiscal 1959, with the rate of increase slowing down thereafter. The Rockefeller program would have spending rise to

---

[26] Of course, where possible, the indicators of performance discussed below should also be estimated and presented for each of the alternative budget levels.

[27] *Fortune* Magazine, June 1958, p. 102.

[28] *International Security — The Military Aspect*, published by the Rockefeller Brothers Fund, Inc., 1958.

[29] As reported in unconfirmed press stories. The Report itself has not been made public.

$53.2 billion in fiscal 1961, while the third program, as *Fortune* has called it — a synthesis of the recommendations of experts who worked on the Gaither Report and other studies — would have spending rise to $65 billion in fiscal 1963. And still other experts urge programs that would add up to perhaps $75 billion." Unfortunately the Congress and the public must make up their minds about the right size of defense budgets with little official information of this sort about the costs or gains of either larger or smaller programs.

### INDICATORS OF PERFORMANCE IN RECENT BUDGETS

The next step toward improving our decisions about program-sizes is to get better information about the outputs of alternative programs. Budgetary presentations today do attempt to describe the product that is being purchased. At the beginning of the portion of the United States Budget pertaining to the Department of Defense, there is an informative discussion of force structure and of certain military activities.

Moreover, since 1949, when the Services were instructed to submit "performance budgets," they have classified proposed outlays into the so-called programs that were previously discussed, and have tried to indicate the output or performance that would be purchased. These indicators are not very revealing, however, chiefly because the categories into which outlays are grouped are remote from end-product programs. As an example, consider the paragraphs on the performance of the "military personnel" category — one of the programs mentioned earlier in connection with Table 2.

### MILITARY PERSONNEL[30]

The following narrative statement covers the active duty appropriations for the Army, Navy, Marine Corps, and Air Force.

1. *Pay and allowances.* — This provides for the pay and allowances of military personnel on active duty including cadets and midshipmen at the three service academies, aviation cadets, and other officer candidates.

The number of active duty military personnel provided for is shown in the following table. The personnel in the civilian components of the Defense forces are described under the pertinent appropriations below.

In addition, provision is made for payment for proficiency advancements to selected enlisted personnel in critical-skill areas. Funds are provided for advancement of 80,000 men by June 30, 1959, and 163,000 men by June 30, 1960. It also provides for the Government's contribution to the Federal old-age and survivors insurance trust fund under the Servicemen's and Veterans' Survivor Benefits Act,

---

[30] This excerpt from the narrative statement (in budgets prior to that for fiscal-year 1960, it was entitled "Program and Performance") is from *The Budget of the United States Government for the Fiscal Year Ending June 30, 1960,* p. 459. In the published statement the exhibit includes the "average number" as well as the "year-end number" of personnel.

|  | *Year-end Number* | | |
| --- | --- | --- | --- |
|  | Actual | Estimate | |
|  | 1958 | 1959 | 1960 |
| Defense total | 2,599,848 | 2,525,000 | 2,520,000 |
| | | | |
| Officers | 325,460 | 318,515 | 316,045 |
| Enlisted | 2,264,290 | 2,194,091 | 2,190,911 |
| Officer candidates | 10,098 | 12,394 | 13,044 |
| | | | |
| Army | 898,192 | 870,000 | 870,000 |
| | | | |
| Officers | 104,220 | 100,100 | 100,100 |
| Enlisted | 792,271 | 768,200 | 768,200 |
| Military Academy cadets | 1,701 | 1,700 | 1,700 |

purchase of individual clothing for initial issue to enlisted personnel, replacement of clothing issues in Korea, and for payment of clothing maintenance allowances.

2. *Subsistence in kind.* — This provides for the purchase of food supplies for issue as rations to enlisted personnel including emergency and operational rations.

3. *Movements, permanent change of station.* — This provides for. . . .

The only parts of the above passage that convey much information are the numbers, and, since personnel are ingredients rather than end-products, even they are not very helpful. Sometimes, descriptions of performance are a good deal worse, constituting merely lyrical pleas for a program. The following example, though it pertains to nondefense (and non-Federal) activities, illustrates the generalities that are sometimes used to describe performance:

Instead of thinking of money alone . . . citizens should hear children singing in the spring concert, travel with the crippled child in early morning from his home to his special unit, feel that school roofs are tight and walls are safe, see the pupils in the corridors washing their dirty hands and drying their clean ones, accompany in spirit the injured child to the hospital for treatment, and see salmon fishing in Alaska with children in the fifth grade. A top performance budget paints pictures in words that justify the expenditure.[31]

Small wonder that some officials (for example, Mr. John Taber, long of the House Appropriations Committee) prefer a budget in terms of objects to be purchased. (With the latter one can at least try to say something about the internal efficiency of programs.) The advantages of

[31] Harold E. Akerly, "For Better Public Relations Use a Performance Budget," *Nation's Schools,* February 1951, p. 37, copyright 1951, The Modern Hospital Publishing Co., Chicago; all rights reserved; cited in Jesse Burkhead, *Government Budgeting,* John Wiley and Sons, Inc., New York, 1956, p. 138.

a program budget are considerably reduced if the indicators of performance are uninformative or downright misleading.

If activities are grouped into more meaningful missions, however, it seems likely that better subjective appraisals of output can be made and also that better indicators of performance can be provided. There is no hope, of course, of measuring the ultimate "worth" of defense. It is obviously impossible to put a generally valid price tag on the output. The gains from program increments cannot therefore be expressed in the same units as the costs, and the two cannot be compared in terms of a common denominator. But there is hope of describing the product meaningfully, and some ways of describing it are more meaningful than others. Similarly, no researcher can measure the ultimate worth of a new car to a particular consumer. But there is hope of meaningfully describing this product, and what the car will do is a more meaningful description to the consumer than the car's chemical composition.

*Changes in force structure.* As a first approximation, force structure for each category in Table 4 — numbers of B-52 wings, Atlas squadrons, army and naval units of various types — would be much closer to the end-products than the numbers of personnel or pieces of equipment. To some extent, the quantity of wings and divisions in each category suggests what is being purchased. Note that this information is constantly used at present. Officials in the Services and in the Defense Department are as familiar with force structure as they are with their own names. Part of the information is published in the Budget and is fully aired in Congressional hearings on appropriations. Even so, force structure may not be considered systematically *in conjunction with costs* as in Table 4, for costs by such military units have seldom been presented. Long-range planning and also programming have been in terms of military units, but budgeting (that is, translating the programs into costs) has usually been in terms of other categories.

Numbers of wings and divisions, however, do not reveal enough about capabilities. For one thing, force structure per se may not tell much about the kind of capability that it provides. An augmentation of our forces may increase our capability to strike first, but not our ability to strike second. If so, it may help deter minor aggressions somewhat, but as far as the thermonuclear war is concerned, it may produce negative deterrence. Or, additional divisions may increase our ability to fight World War II but not our strength in more likely kinds of conflict. If so, they may produce small gains.

*The enemy's response.* For another thing, force structure per se does not tell us anything about the enemy's position or about his probable reaction to changes in the structure of our forces. Yet what our forces buy for us is clearly relative to the enemy's capability and his reaction to our decisions. This fact can hardly be emphasized enough. The pertinent question is whether or not we are buying sufficient strength, *relative to potential enemy forces* (when fairly sensible strategies are attributed to him), to deter central war and cope with limited aggressions. We need a higher national security budget if the potential enemy is Soviet Russia than if it is Argentina; higher if we have no allies than if we have reliable ones; higher if the enemy devotes 20 per cent of his national product to the military efficiently than if he devotes 10 per cent inefficiently; higher if the enemy increases his technological and industrial capability in future relative to ours, while devoting the same proportion to military purposes; higher if our strategy draws containment lines in the Eastern Hemisphere than if these are drawn at our own shores. Discussion of the appropriate size of military budgets often misses this essential point of relativity. An increase in the absolute efficiency with which we use resources ("more bang for a buck") creates no presumption that the budget can be cut when a potential enemy is correspondingly increasing his absolute efficiency ("more rubble for a ruble").

Thus when considering program increments or decrements, we must try to take into account the enemy's position and probable response. Are our forces strong enough, and properly designed, in view of his situation and his capabilities? If we add to our forces in a particular way, can he easily counter our move? What deterrent capability (or ability to fight local wars and keep them limited) will we end up with? Will our action yield a better basis for finding mutually advantageous weapon limitations or disarmament measures?

For these several reasons, most simple indicators of performance, including changes in force structure, that would be affected by program increments or decrements are not sufficiently revealing. Fortunately, it is often possible to indicate in more significant terms what program increments will buy.

*Changes in designated capabilities.* It is possible to make analyses comparing alternative ways of carrying out broad missions such as the strategic deterrence mission. Such analyses seek to answer questions like: Which combination of means yields the greatest deterrent capability for a given budget? Capability may be measured by the destruction that could be inflicted on potential enemies in selected (and not improbable) contingencies even if we received the first strike. Chapter 18 will discuss the major factors to consider in choosing policies for deterrence and indicate the quantitative nature of the problem. Part II will deal with the methods and possibilities of comparing various courses of action in planning defense. Here we wish only to point out that similar analyses can be devised to answer a different type of question: What capabilities are yielded by different program levels? What changes in capability result from program increments or decrements? The analyses would by no means point to the preferred program level — but they would give highly relevant indicators of performance.

Analysis could also provide revealing indicators of another gain from portions of the strategic deterrence mission — namely the contribution of retaliatory capability, active defenses, passive defenses, and recuperation planning to the chance of survival in the event of enemy attack. Analysis could give a rough yet informative picture of, say, capital, human beings, and emergency stocks that would survive a plausible enemy attack. These data, in conjunction with program costs, would also help in choosing among alternative program levels.

In addition, analysis of this sort might be able to reveal what different program-levels could accomplish in the limited-war mission (another of the broad programs listed in Table 4). Calculations might give clues to the scale and kinds of local aggressions that could be "handled" with alternative programs for limited-war capability. The results would constitute quantitative clues to what we could do in various plausible contingencies. Obviously the outcomes of such conflicts could not be projected with precision. Nonetheless, such clues to our capability would be more revealing than numbers of divisions, tactical air units, and so on.

These indicators of gain would not embrace all possible effects of program changes. There would be spillover effects on other programs. For instance, a change in strategic deterrence capability would have some influence on our prospects regarding limited conflicts. There would also be other impacts not reflected in the suggested indicators of performance — impacts on our relations with neutral or friendly nations, on the basis for trying to reach mutually advantageous agreements with enemy nations, and so on. There would be further indirect effects on our economy that will be discussed in the next chapter. But a budget in terms of broad programs for which such indicators of performance could be provided would help sort out the major implications of alternative budgets. It would facilitate the task of weighing the costs and gains of budget increments or decrements.

As for the research and development program, there is probably no good way of indicating the performance that would be purchased with alternative program-levels. Research and development activities are by nature explorations into an unknown and distant future. Estimating the results of research is even more uncertain than measuring the consequences of, say, future programs for limited war. We can try to estimate the potential gains *if* certain break-throughs or developments can be achieved, and such estimates are valuable clues in shaping research and development programs (see Chapter 13). Even though estimates of potential payoff are helpful, however, tremendous uncertainties must be recognized. Exploratory research and development often produces quite unpredicted payoffs. Hence, while the output of research and development is of enormous significance to future capabilities, that output is extremely uncertain in both form and magnitude, and there is no way to show what a particular year's program will produce. Judgment on the size and character of the program must be based largely on experience with similar programs in the past, taking both failures and successes into account.

It is partly for this reason that it seems to be appropriate to segregate research and development as a separate program or programs. In a sense it is a supporting activity. But we do not know to what extent it will turn out to support strategic deterrence and to what extent it will support other missions. Moreover, because the program's objective is to acquire knowledge rather than to carry out a well-defined task, research and development should be managed differently from operational missions (see Chapter 13). It is best, therefore, to regard research and development as a separate program — probably to regard exploratory research and development and what might be called weapon-systems development as separate and distinct programs. But no over-all indicator of performance in these activities (or in Administration and Miscellaneous!) can be provided.

Where meaningful indicators are feasible, they would have to be separate presentations, not just a few numbers in another column of Table 4. But they would be introduced *along with* the breakdown of costs by broad missions. Like that breakdown of costs, the indicators of performance and the underlying analyses would usually have to bear a military classification. These tools could nonetheless be valuable to military planners, to officials in the Department of Defense and the Budget Bureau, and to Congressional leaders.

One aspect of the gains — and costs, for that matter — that merits a final mention is their uncertainty (a subject which will be considered in some detail in Chapter 10). When a program increment is considered, one cannot see a particular outcome that is certain and that determines a unique set of gains. What one foresees is a number of potential outcomes, some more likely and others less likely, but all of them quite possible. This uncertainty makes the task of weighing gains and costs still more formidable. Instead of the question being, "What is the worth of this particular increase in capability?" the question is, "What is the worth of this probability distribution of increases in capability (or of this uncertain increase in capability)?" Furthermore, since steps can often be taken to hedge against contingencies, another question arises: "What is the worth of particular attempts to reduce uncertainty?"

Obviously, these questions are hard to answer. Different individuals, given the same information about prospective gains and costs, will answer differently. The main reason is that the answer depends upon one's attitude toward risk. Some people prefer a comparatively safe policy and will give up a great deal in order to reduce the chance of disaster. Others are willing to live more dangerously.

## HOW BIG A BUDGET DURING HOT WAR?

If and when local conflicts break out, certain programs are likely to seem more important to us than had previously been the case. If the conflict lasts long, it will be imperative to expand certain activities. Consequently the national-security budget is almost certain to rise. The nature of the problem, however, is still the same. In order to decide how much should be spent on national security, one should think, not just about expenditures for objects, but about the gains and costs of having higher (or lower) programs. The types of gain and cost to be considered, and the analyses that would help one weigh them, are the same.

If all-out war involving unlimited objectives should occur, the choice among alternative budget *levels* would probably not concern us greatly. In the unlikely event that atomic weapons were not exchanged, the war would be similar in many respects to World War II. The budget would probably approach its upper limit — GNP minus subsistence and "necessary" supporting activities.[32] During the first few years of such a war, physical constraints (the difficulty of shifting resources from one activity to another) rather than budgetary ones might limit the diversion of resources to defense. In any event, the considerations discussed above would probably not play much of a role in setting budget levels.

In the more likely event that unlimited war led to a thermonuclear exchange, interest in budget formulation would fall off considerably! In those circumstances, it would make little difference whether one thought in terms of programs or of objects; and the exhibits suggested above would have little bearing on the challenging problems of the day.

---

[32] As explained earlier, it is difficult to determine such an upper limit, because it is hard to define "necessities." Someone always insists (quite properly): "Give me the luxuries of life, and I'll do without the necessities." But we can say that at some budget level, the sacrifice entailed by trying to devote more to defense becomes enormous.

# 5. INDIRECT EFFECTS OF DEFENSE SPENDING

In Chapter 4, we talked about the principal direct gains and costs of defense programs. The direct gains are such desired products as deterrent and limited-war capabilities. The direct costs are simply the goods and services that might otherwise be enjoyed but which must be given up if the national security programs are to be carried out. As indicated earlier, the values of these alternative outputs are reflected in the prices of the inputs diverted to the defense programs. Thus, for the purpose of budgetary decisions, the value of the foregone output is satisfactorily measured in most instances by the money cost of the defense programs. The direct cost of a change in the programs is the change in expenditures that would be entailed.

In addition, however, there are other impacts of the defense budget which may be called "indirect effects." Some of these impacts are costs, and some are benefits. Some are consequences which should be considered in choosing the size of the defense budget, and some are consequences that should mainly affect other policies rather than defense planning itself.

## EFFECTS ON ECONOMIC STABILITY

Government expenditures — and a large proportion of them are national security outlays — have significant effects on the stability of the economy. In other words, government spending can make it easier in some circumstances, and more difficult in others, to control inflation or recession. The importance of avoiding severe fluctuations is fairly clear. Recession can shrink actual GNP far below its potential, reducing output and investment, generating frustration and disorder, undermining the strength and will of our allies. Severe inflation can divert effort into barter and uneconomic activity and result in inequities and unrest. Since these phenomena are so important, we shall examine the possible impacts of the defense budget on them rather carefully. As a preliminary step, we shall review the general nature and causes of instability.

It should be made clear at the outset, however, that the potential effects on stability should not dictate our defense policies. The scale and nature of defense expenditures should be decided on the basis of their merits as national-security measures — and should not be regarded as countercyclical tools. This is not to say that the implications of the defense budget for stability can be ignored. They should certainly be recognized. But they should be dealt with chiefly by adjusting monetary-fiscal policies rather than by capriciously changing defense programs.

### THE NATURE OF RECESSION AND INFLATION

As a point of departure, consider a period of comparative stability — say, April 1955 to April 1956 in the United States. During this time, less then 3,000,000 were unemployed[1] — a situation which we shall call "full employment" — and the consumer-price index stayed within a narrow range (between 114.2 and 115.0). For this situation to exist, aggregate money demand had to equal the amount that would buy our full-employment output during the period at the going price level. Aggregate money demand here comprises the total spending for goods and services by individuals, firms, and governmental units — in short, by all spenders.

Note that this stability of the price level did not mean that all individual prices were stable. The prices of some items were going up, the prices of others down, because of changes in taste, technology, and resource constraints. Along with the changes in particular prices, the electronics industry expanded, cinema exhibition declined, some workers left farming and some entered the construction trades, some people moved from one part of the country to another. It was only in the aggregate that employment held steady, or maintained a steady rate of growth; and it was only in an aggregate or "average" sense that prices were stable. That, of course, is what we want — flexibility for individual prices to adjust and for resources to be shifted, yet no severe fluctuations of prices in general and no drastic drop in total employment.

Consider next what happens if aggregate money spending declines. Here we mean, not just a shift in spending from automobiles to weapons or from movies to electronic gadgets, but a fall in the total volume of spending. How might such a thing happen? Maybe households cut their consumption expenditures. Maybe individuals and firms, doubtful about the profits from further expansion or modernization, reduce their investment outlays. Perhaps government expenditures drop. For present purposes, the specific reasons for the tightening of belts (in the aggregate) do not matter. The essential point is that, with the decline of spending, it becomes impossible for total output in the next period to be sold at the existing price level. Something has to give — either part of the output remains unsold or prices fall.

Actually some of each usually happens, the sequence being somewhat as follows. When aggregate expenditures begin to fall, some sellers, retailers for example, find their inventories piling up. So far there are no reductions in the prices they have to pay to workers, wholesalers, and suppliers. The retailers have to reduce their orders. Next the inventories

[1] Well under 5 per cent of the civilian labor force.

of wholesalers and manufacturers accumulate, and they reduce their orders for raw materials, labor, and supplies. Because of swollen inventories and idle resources, downward pressure is exerted on prices, including those of labor and raw materials. It should be noted, however, that many prices seem to be "sticky" as far as downward movement is concerned, especially in recent years. Besides, by this time the belt tightening has become far more severe because many persons receive lower incomes or have no jobs at all, firms make lower profits or incur losses, and everyone anticipates a continuation of this downward spiral. Thus, even if some prices move downward (they did not seem to do so in the 1957–58 recession), total demand declines more rapidly than costs, and there is widespread unemployment.

In the description just given, a decline in aggregate demand started the recessionary process, but it need not always begin in this manner. The same process could be set off if aggregate demand simply grew less rapidly than full-employment output. Or, it is perhaps conceivable that prices could be "pushed ahead" of demand by zealous labor unions and pervasive monopoly. All that is necessary to start recession is for total spending to be less than enough to buy full-employment output at the going price level.

Suppose now that total money spending is more than enough to buy the full-employment output at the existing level of prices. As before, there are numerous possible explanations for this state of affairs. Perhaps households increase consumption, firms expand investment, or government spending goes up. In any event all spending units together — families, firms, and government units — try to buy more goods than are for sale at the going price level. Again something has to give: either the shelves become bare or prices rise. Some sellers, say retailers, find their inventories getting low, some buyers encounter bare shelves. The buyers raise their bids and the retailers raise theirs in an effort to replenish their inventories. The effects percolate through the economy, raising prices of consumers' goods, raising prices of raw materials, labor, and all inputs. In this process, however, there is little change in employment. Some wives may join the labor force, a few retired persons may return to work, and there may be a slight reduction of frictional (that is, "between-jobs") unemployment. But with comparatively full employment at the outset, the excess of money demand over full-employment-output-times-existing-prices spends itself mainly in an upsurge of prices in general.[2]

---

[2] For a more complete discussion and numerous references on economic fluctuations, see William Fellner, "Employment Theory and Business Cycles," in *A Survey of Contemporary Economics,* ed. Howard S. Ellis, Blakiston Co., Philadelphia, 1948.

GOVERNMENT SPENDING: A FORCE AGAINST RECESSION, TOWARD INFLATION

Defense spending, which often amounts to 10 per cent of GNP nowadays, is a significant component of government and of total spending. When government spends such an amount for national security (or for anything else), it tends to buoy up total spending. The existence of this demand makes a deficiency of total demand less probable. Moreover it facilitates the application of other antideflationary measures, like the injection of additional money into the economy.

These statements need to be explained. First, suppose that the government's outlays are matched by taxes on the incomes of individuals and firms. The money is therefore taken away from private spenders in order to be spent on defense. Nonetheless, these outlays act to some extent as a prop against deflation. The reason is that, in the hands of the government, the money is definitely to be spent as called for by the budget, while in the hands of individuals or businesses, part of the income may be saved.[3] In other words, the defense effort is a component of total demand that will not melt away even if people decide to reduce their personal spending.

If the above assumption about tax policy is altered, the existence of government programs makes possible a stronger antideflationary effect. Suppose that the outlays are matched, not by taxes, but by borrowing from firms and individuals. The smaller tax bill leaves a larger disposable income in the hands of the public, and people are therefore inclined to spend more than they otherwise would. To be sure, some persons take a portion of their cash (the same amount that in the previous case was paid to the Treasury as taxes) and buy government bonds. In this instance, however, these persons get bonds in exchange for their money. The bonds are fairly liquid assets, and after the government disburses the borrowed cash, the public holds more liquid assets than before. This encourages and facilitates spending out of the larger disposable incomes. Hence there is an extra stimulus to total demand.

Suppose, finally, that the outlays are matched by borrowing from the Federal Reserve Banks or, what amounts to practically the same thing, by the issuance of new money.[4] This would result in a still stronger stimulus to total spending, for there would be an increase in

---

[3] The argument is more complex than this, mainly because there are "leakages" from both private and government "disposable income" (see W. J. Baumol and M. H. Peston, "More on the Multiplier Effects of a Balanced Budget," *American Economic Review,* March 1955, pp. 140–148). Also there may be secular adjustments in consumption out of income. But it is generally agreed that extra government outlays, even though matched by tax receipts, will nearly always result in *some* increase in aggregate spending.

[4] For the sake of simplicity, we omit the intermediate case of borrowing from the commercial banks. The essential point is that extra government spending (unless *more* than matched by taxes or borrowing) is almost certain to be inflationary.

the stock of money as well as a larger disposable income in the hands of the public. Thus, the existence of the defense program acts as a guard against recession by being a relatively firm component of total demand and by making it easy to implement antideflationary policies.

It would be wrong to attribute a certain increment in employment to the defense program in any and all circumstances. Whether or not the program prevents any unemployment depends upon whether or not deflation and unemployment are threats. Much of the time private spending would be ample. Moreover, even if private spending slumps, monetary-fiscal measures could stimulate it, or other forms of government spending could increase aggregate demand just as effectively as defense outlays. We do not have to have defense programs in order to avoid unemployment (or to have inflation). Nevertheless, given the existing situation, a large security budget *is* an antideflationary force. This is one of the indirect effects that should be recognized.

A corollary of the preceding argument is that a large defense effort increases the likelihood of inflation. Given the prevailing institutional arrangements, we do not argue that the defense budget acts as an automatic stabilizer. The argument is that the security program tends to buoy up total demand and make it easier (and more tempting) to run deficits and inject new money. This upward pressure on aggregate demand is felt in inflationary times as well as in periods of recession. It can lead to or aggravate inflation as well as alleviate deflation.

Perhaps some bias toward inflation is desirable. That is, we may legitimately prefer a heightened risk of inflation in order to have a lower probability of depression, since the losses encountered in moderate deflation are more serious than the losses and dangers faced in moderate inflation. Whether one considers the net effect of large defense budgets on economic stability to be good or bad depends upon one's attitude toward these risks. All that will be attempted here is to point out these indirect consequences of large defense programs.

If we were sufficiently clever at controlling fluctuations, of course, we would always have stability, and neither government spending nor anything else would deserve the label "inflationary force." But it does not appear that we have learned that much about fluctuations. We have learned some things — that government surpluses and reductions in the stock of money will counter inflations and that deficits and increases in the stock of money will work against deflations.[5] But we have learned little about when to take action or how much action to take in a

---

[5] Even this proposition is not universally accepted. Some persons, including well-known public officials, believe that large government expenditures will lead to depressions that will "curl our hair" (*New York Times,* January 17, 1957, p. 1). The argument apparently rests on the belief that large budgets and/or deficits will undermine confidence so much that their net effect is to reduce aggregate demand.

particular situation. Does a slump in housing and a modest increase in unemployment mark the beginning of a downward spiral or just another "rolling readjustment"? Should the government act or will this action convert a self-correcting "roll" into an inflation? It is not easy to answer these questions. We know little about the behavior of expectations or about the lags between events or actions and the resulting shifts in aggregate demand. In short, we cannot yet shrug off deflation (or inflation) as something that can easily be controlled. In these circumstances we can legitimately say that large defense expenditures have an inflationary (antideflationary) bias.

### SUDDEN SHIFTS IN DEFENSE SPENDING

Thus far we have thought in terms of a relatively constant, or perhaps steadily rising, defense budget. What if the budget is subject to violent shifts, to sudden increases or decreases? (Indeed such shifts have occurred several times since World War II.) What effect would these changes have on economic stability? Conceivably, defense spending could fluctuate so as to have a stabilizing influence, but it is unlikely to do so, unless the aims of national security are subordinated to those of stabilization policy. Such a distortion of defense objectives is surely undesirable. The value of national defense does not conveniently change as aggregate demand shifts. Moreover, even if we tried to subordinate security aims to stabilization policy, the defense program would be an unwieldy and unreliable tool of stabilization because of the lags between changes in appropriations and changes in cash expenditures. In all likelihood, markedly unstable defense budgets would aggravate the instability of total demand, or, looked at in another way, would aggravate the difficulty of formulating proper monetary-fiscal policies.

### STABILIZATION POLICY TO MINIMIZE ILL EFFECTS

As has been indicated, the possible effects of the defense program on economic stability should be recognized — and dealt with by adjusting stabilization policies. What kind of policies could cope best with the inflationary pressure of a large defense program or the destabilizing influence of a fluctuating effort?

*Avoid price controls in the new defense situation.* — A few words first about some measures that are *not* the most effective way to cope with fluctuations in the situation that we probably face — that is, a long period of tension and cold-war defense programs. These measures are controls over individual prices and the rationing of commodities by quotas rather than by prices. Such controls have not been proposed very seriously in the United States for several years (partly because recession has been the threat during several of those years). They deserve our attention, however, because some persons still regard controls as a sort of panacea, because they will be proposed if the defense budget rises sharply or whenever rapid inflation threatens (and because traditionally price controls have been a central topic in the economics of defense).

Price controls and rationing by quotas should usually be considered as a package. By and large, one cannot function as a stabilization measure without the other. If price controls alone are attempted, they soon lead to the rationing of consumer's goods. At the controlled prices, which are lower than those that a free market would produce, the quantities demanded exceed the amounts supplied. Shortages therefore develop, and empty shelves confront users whose needs are urgent. As a consequence, unless empty-shelves rationing is accepted, further directives for rationing the items to consumers must be devised. The same thing happens with respect to producers' goods. Even if allocations are not introduced initially, they will follow on the heels of price controls. With the prices of some inputs below the market, shortages develop. Also, productive resources flow into those uses that happen now to offer favorable price-cost relationships. For instance, inputs tend to go into the production of the "uncontrolled" items, even though they may clearly be less valuable to the nation than additional quantities of the "controlled" commodities. Further controls must then be imposed in order to allocate materials and inputs among producers.

During World War II and in other instances of all-out mobilization, keeping prices down by means of such controls was deemed to be the preferable policy. During prolonged partial mobilization, however, price controls are comparatively ineffective in checking inflation or in promoting equity during inflation and are comparatively costly in terms of lost efficiency and individual freedom. These effects of direct controls will be examined briefly.

In a period of all-out mobilization such as World War II, controls may slow down the pace of inflation, make possible the purchase of war matériel at lower prices than would otherwise prevail, enable the government to conduct the war with smaller deficits and injections of money, and reduce the ultimate extent of inflation. In a period of cold war, military budgets are relatively high, but they are not blank checks with which to buy matériel as rapidly as resources can be shifted to the production of military goods. (The higher the defense budget, the less applicable the propositions stated below. They are intended to apply when military budgets are, say, 10 to 20 per cent of GNP.) In this situation, the size of deficits and new issues of money will not be affected greatly by price ceilings. Controls will not significantly reduce the ultimate extent of inflation but will at best only postpone part of the rise in the price level. And during a sustained cold-war effort, the postponing will not be as successful as it might be during a relatively short and intensive mobilization. If there is persistent inflationary pressure, black markets and price increases will gradually prevail.

Moreover, price controls will not in these circumstances do much to relieve inequity, the consideration that often lies behind the desire for price controls. Inflationary pressures may create opportunities for the clever or lucky to gain at the expense of others, without creating any new prods to production. This is a legitimate argument against inflation but not necessarily for its suppression by means of direct controls. For this method of countering inflation does not prevent fortuitous or contrived gains. In the main, it simply makes these gains available to a different group of clever or fortunate persons.

What is perhaps more important is that direct controls themselves produce inequities. Under rent controls, for example, instead of each family weighing the urgency of its demand for an apartment and adjusting its bid, an administrator must weigh the urgency of competing claims. However good the intentions of administrators, crude rules of thumb are inevitably adopted. For instance, people who already occupy apartments stay on at below-market rents, with the result that bachelors occupy three-bedroom apartments while whole families must crowd in with their in-laws. In the handing out of valuable goods of any sort — television licenses, tobacco-acreage quotas, or airline routes — the choice is so complex that inequitable rules of thumb must prevail. Even the best of authorities cannot allocate valuable privileges in a way that is notable for "fairness."

One of the costs of controls, and over a prolonged period of preparedness it could be a heavy one, is loss of individual freedom. For direct controls reduce the extent to which people make their own choices in the light of relatively impersonal constraints. Whether or not a person gets an apartment, quota, or permit is determined in part by the personal decisions of government officials. These controls move the economy away from competition to satisfy a comparatively impersonal market toward rivalry to please particular office-holders. It may help one perceive the effects if he imagines the quarrels, bribes, and frustrations that might occur if the government controlled the weather.[6] To be confronted with a market price gives a person more choice than to be confronted with a flat prohibition or fixed quota. We may want government to guide the disposition (sale) of certain goods, but discretionary allocations proliferate a kind of power that we generally like to avoid — the power of government officials to grant or deny important favors — and lessen the scope of individual freedom.

[6] G. L. Schwartz, "Planning and Economic Privilege," *The Manchester School*, XIV, January 1946, 53–71.

This loss of freedom not only is undesirable in and of itself but also may have further undesirable impacts on incentives and growth. If freedom of choice is sufficiently hampered, it can conceivably bring widespread frustration, resentment, and loss of incentives. Giving up the flexibility of the market can generate a bias in favor of the status quo, impairing future growth. Consequences of this sort may seem rather far-fetched in the United States, but the possibility of such things happening in "small amounts" should be recognized.

Finally, one must consider the cost of direct controls in terms of their effect on the efficiency of resource allocation. During a prolonged partial mobilization, it is unlikely that allocations and quotas will work as well as freely moving prices in allocating resources among uses.[7] All prices cannot be successfully fixed, and distortions of relative prices occur. (Even if all prices were fixed simultaneously and correctly at first, they could not respond promptly to changes in circumstances, and distortions would soon develop.) The maladjusted price structure induces firms to put resources into the wrong uses. These effects of controls have been recognized to an increasing extent by Socialist economists.[8]

There is no point in exaggerating the inefficiency that direct controls bring. Democratic countries such as Great Britain and the United States have indulged in such controls and survived! The Soviet Union has applied direct controls for many years, managing nonetheless to expand heavy industry and defense production enormously. The Soviet Union has experienced the kinds of difficulties mentioned above, but has achieved its *main* ends anyway by diverting resources from consumption to defense and particular forms of investment. Thus the use of direct controls is not fatal. Indeed, for rapid and drastic mobilization, certain direct controls may be better than the practicable alternatives,[9] particularly in countries that do not have a vigorous competitive framework. But there is much support for the view that other means of dealing with price-level inflation are better in the kind of defense situation that probably lies ahead — namely, perpetual partial mobilization.[10]

[7] Of course, freely moving prices will perform this task only if purchasing power is given to the defense department. That is, if the government is unwilling to bid for weapons, freely moving prices will not lead resources into defense production.

[8] Within the U.S.S.R., for example, debates have been taking place in recent years about the defects of certain controls and about the possibilities of employing prices more effectively in the future. R. W. Davies reports on part of this debate in "Reports and Commentaries: Industrial Planning Reconsidered," *Soviet Studies,* VIII, April 1957, pp. 426–435.

[9] For a variety of views on this question, see Aaron Director (ed.), *Defense, Controls, and Inflation,* The University of Chicago Press, Chicago, 1952, especially pp. 202–253.

[10] See, for example, Bernard F. Haley, "Are Price Control and Rationing Necessary?" *American Economic Review, Papers and Proceedings,* XL, May 1950, pp. 199–208; Arthur

Nor would the regulation of individual prices and outputs be the preferred policy if there should be deflation associated with an unstable defense program. We may still encounter severe recessions, and it may be tempting to keep particular prices up by issuing edicts, by destroying output, or by restricting production through devices like the NRA of the 1930's. Such policies are ineffective in checking general deflation, inequitable in distributing aid among producers, detrimental in limiting freedom of choice, and pernicious in their effect on efficiency. To sum up, direct controls are not well suited to minimizing the possible destabilizing impacts of defense outlays during a long cold war. We shall turn next to some measures that are better suited to this task.

*Adopt a suitable monetary-fiscal framework.* Perhaps a minimum set of measures is one that would make the federal budget into an automatic stabilizer. This set of policies would not remove the possibility of wide fluctuations but would almost certainly work in the right direction, that is, toward the damping of fluctuations. These policies would comprise several parts.[11]

The first would be to set government outlays on goods and services solely on the basis of their merits in comparison with private consumption and investment. They would neither be cut as revenues fell, nor increased as a deliberate effort to counteract fluctuations. Unless tastes or technology changed considerably, the budget *for goods and services* would be relatively stable. The second policy would be to set the rules governing transfer payments. The terms under which assistance was to be granted to the needy or unemployed would be stable, but the amount paid out would increase during deflation and decrease during prosperity. These variations would occur because assistance to the unemployed, social security benefits to older persons who retire from the labor force, and payments to farmers would go up as distress due to recession increased.

The third element of this minimum program would be to set tax rates and exemptions so as to balance the budget (approximately) when high levels of employment occurred. It is assumed that the personal income tax

Smithies, "Fiscal Aspects of Preparedness for War," *American Economic Review,* XXXIX, May 1949, pp. 356-365; Tibor Scitovsky, Edward Shaw, Lorie Tarshis, *Mobilizing Resources for War,* McGraw-Hill Book Co., Inc., New York, 1951, pp. 110-133; or the Cabinet Committee on Price Stability for Economic Growth (Richard M. Nixon, Chairman), "Interim Report to the President," mimeographed release dated June 29, 1959.

[11] These measures are similar to various long-advocated suggestions for using the budget as a partially automatic stabilizer. Probably the best-known proposals were advocated by the Committee for Economic Development, originally in the policy statement, *Taxes and the Budget: A Program for Prosperity in a Free Economy,* The Committee for Economic Development, New York, 1947. See also Milton Friedman, "A Monetary and Fiscal Framework for Economic Stability," *American Economic Review,* June 1948, pp. 245-264, reprinted in *Essays in Positive Economics,* University of Chicago Press, Chicago, 1953, pp. 133-156.

would yield a major portion of the revenues and that the tax structure would be progressive. This arrangement would imply, on the one hand, an increase in tax rates if the nation decided to expand government activities (either purchases of goods and services or the *program* of transfer expenditures). On the other hand, tax rates could be reduced if government programs were cut. For any given set of programs, the tax structure would be fixed. Tax *receipts*, however, would decline in time of recession because of the fall in taxable incomes, and rise during inflation because of the rise in taxable incomes.

A fourth element of this plan might be to eliminate capricious changes in the stock of money. To do this, the monetary authorities could follow a definite rule to offset all changes in the money supply except increases corresponding to federal deficits and decreases corresponding to surpluses. If an antideflationary bias was desired, taxes could be set so that a moderate deficit would occur at a high level of employment,[12] thus providing a specified secular increase in the stock of money. In these circumstances, the supply of money would change, increasing by the amount of the deficit or decreasing by the amount of the surplus, but it would not change capriciously. The monetary authorities would issue or retire net amounts of money as indicated, engaging in open market operations so as to offset all other changes.

Notice how this arrangement (which existing institutions are beginning to approximate) would operate. It would automatically generate surpluses during periods of inflationary pressure, because tax receipts would rise and transfer payments would fall. These surpluses would siphon off part of the income stream and also reduce the stock of money in circulation, reducing aggregate demand below what it would otherwise be. During periods of recession, the arrangement would automatically generate deficits, because tax receipts would fall and transfer payments would rise. These deficits would expand the income stream and also increase the stock of money. And, the more severe the recession, the greater the deficit.

It was indicated above that monetary-fiscal policies of this automatically-stabilizing type are a minimum program for dealing with fluctuations and alleviating the possible destabilizing effects of defense budgets. Many economists believe that we can do better by supplementing

[12] As the economy grows, a gradual expansion of total spending and of the stock of money might be required just to prevent a falling price level. This should be the goal according to some, e.g., The Cabinet Committee on Price Stability for Economic Growth. Others urge that a moderate degree of inflation would be desirable, e.g., Sumner Slichter, "Thinking Ahead: On the Side of Inflation," *Harvard Business Review*, September-October 1957, p. 15 ff. All agree, however, on the desirability of avoiding severe inflation.

automatic stabilizers with discretionary adjustments in taxes and expenditures. They argue that neither method completely avoids the hazards of forecasting, because some sort of forecasting is necessary in devising either set of actions, and point out that discretionary adjustments would make possible the use of additional, later information.[13] Also most stabilizing budget schemes can by themselves only "cushion," not reverse, a change in aggregate spending — amounting thus to "built-in tranquilizers" [14] rather than built-in stabilizers. We are very likely to need additional action when severe fluctuations occur.

For instance, what if the automatic corrective influences were not strong enough, and large expenditures pushed us into a serious inflation, or a slump in aggregate demand produced a severe deflation? If deep recession or violent inflation occurred, additional measures that work in the right direction might be easy to prescribe despite our inadequate knowledge of quantitative impacts and their timing. To counteract severe deflation, larger deficits matched by larger issues of money (not the destruction of crops or restriction of output) would be called for. To counteract serious inflation, larger surpluses matched by decreases in the stock of money (not direct controls) would be the preferred means.

As we know from previous war-time experience, it is difficult to raise taxes enough to offset extremely high defense outlays. If monetary-fiscal actions could not cope with inflation, the next-best device would be "expenditure rationing." [15] Generalized purchasing power rather than particular commodities would be rationed. In effect, a new form of money or spending power would replace the old, at least temporarily. The total amount of the new purchasing power would be less than the old and might be rationed in a more desirable manner. Total demand would then be limited and channeled to the buyers whose wants were to be met, yet individual prices could guide firms to an efficient use of resources, and considerable freedom of choice would be left to individuals. Thus this device, too, is a means of manipulating aggregate demand (though it is considerably more complicated than the monetary-fiscal measures described above). And, generally speaking, the manipulation of aggregate demand is the preferred method of alleviating any destabilizing effect of cold-war budgets.

[13] See Walter W. Heller, "CED's Stabilizing Budget Policy After Ten Years," *American Economic Review,* September 1957, pp. 634–651.

[14] *Ibid.,* p. 645.

[15] One such proposal is described in M. Kalecki's article, "General Rationing," *Studies in War Economics,* prepared at the Oxford University Institute of Statistics, Basil Blackwell, Oxford, 1947, pp. 137–141. A more complete scheme for expenditure rationing was suggested by A. P. Lerner in an unpublished paper, "Design for a Streamlined War Economy." Another proposal is discussed in Scitovsky, Shaw and Tarshis, pp. 145–257.

## OTHER INDIRECT COSTS

### THE INDIRECT BURDEN OF TAXES

If the evils of price-level inflation or direct controls, or both, are to be avoided, larger military programs must bring higher taxes.[16] These extra taxes may themselves inflict some indirect costs[17] — the adverse impacts of higher taxes on incentives and on resource allocation — though such costs are likely to be less serious, as far as moderate defense budgets are concerned, than the effects of inflation or widespread controls.

Higher taxes for defense do not *necessarily* impair incentives to work and to invest. If we knew all about people's preferences and could tax in a sufficiently discriminating manner, and if the tax-paying public were fully convinced of the need for the taxes, we could prevent unfavorable impacts on incentives (as long as people have enough left to maintain their physical strength). For instance, suppose we knew that as disposable income fell, the utility of an increment to income increased, while (as one would expect) the utility of an extra amount of leisure did not increase. In those circumstances, a higher *average* rate of tax along with lower rates on incremental income (for example, in the middle and upper brackets) would actually increase the number of hours that taxpayers wish to work.[18] Presumably this same conclusion applies to their efforts in general to raise their incomes, that is, to the intensity with which they work and to their incentives to invest. Thus if we knew enough about the satisfaction that taxpayers get from extra income, extra leisure, and extra relaxation on the job, we could, within limits, design taxes that increase incentives.[19] In practice, however, we are likely to

[16] Unless there are enough unemployed resources to produce the defense outputs.

[17] Perhaps it should be repeated that the resources diverted to military purposes by tax payments (or by inflationary financing, for that matter) are *direct* costs of defense. That is, if the military has $10 billion more, the rest of the economy has about $10 billion less, unless it is possible to use unemployed or underemployed resources or to get increased production by overtime and by drawing into the labor force people who do not normally work.

[18] Certain other assumptions are also implied. For analysis of this and other cases, see Gershon Cooper, "Taxation and Incentive in Mobilization," *Quarterly Journal of Economics,* February 1952, 43–66. In some of these cases, the effects on incentives can be predicted; in others those effects are indeterminate unless still more assumptions are introduced. For further discussions and references, see *Federal Tax Policy for Economic Growth and Stability,* papers submitted by panelists appearing before the Subcommittee on Tax Policy, Joint Committee on the Economic Report, 84th Congress, 1st Session, U.S. Government Printing Office, Washington, D.C., 1956.

[19] These would probably be highly "regressive" taxes by current American standards. Someone once proposed a negative marginal rate aimed at inducing everyone to become a millionaire. In this scheme, the prevailing tax rates would apply to incomes of less than a million dollars per year, but the tax bill would drop to zero for those who had incomes of a million dollars or more!

lack the necessary knowledge. We do not know enough about people's preferences to gauge very accurately the effects of various tax structures. Also, there are conflicting objectives and ethical convictions that may make a tax policy which appears desirable from the point of view of incentives completely impractical from a political point of view.

If it is low enough, of course, almost any kind of tax is innocuous, but if it is high enough, any *practicable* tax is likely to distort and otherwise adversely affect incentives and the functioning of the economy. It seems likely, for example, that taxation on the scale and of the type retained in England after World War II had serious disincentive effects. Moreover, these indirect costs are, past a point, a sharply *increasing* function of budget size. Resolution and ingenuity can push that point far higher than anything we have experienced in peacetime — if need be. But the higher, the harder. For United States budgets in effect in the late 1950's, the indirect burden of taxes would appear to be small.[20] Budgets twice that size, however, might entail significant indirect costs.

Note that in order to design taxes so that they will not impair incentives, it may be necessary to sacrifice "equity." For example, to lower tax rates on increments in income relative to the average rate, it is necessary to make the tax structure less progressive. The majority of people apparently regard a less progressive tax system as a less equitable one. Be that as it may, we need to reexamine our concepts concerning a good tax system. Beliefs regarding the best compromise between the claims of equity and of efficiency which were formed in a period when government budgets were low may no longer be applicable in a period when budgets are consistently high. The Soviet Union has been able to minimize disincentive effects by more or less proportional taxes on consumption of a type which would be inconceivable in the United States. Western countries may nonetheless be willing to trade some progressiveness in tax rates for an extra stimulus to incentives.

Similar conclusions apply to the effect of higher taxes on the efficiency of resource allocation. It is possible to conceive of a tax structure such that higher taxes do not distort the allocation of resources. If taxes were on incomes alone or impinged to the same extent on the costs of all items, higher taxes would not lead to inefficient forms of business organization, to inefficient methods of production, or to the production of uneconomic items. Again, our knowledge (for example, of the incidence of taxes) is insufficient; political constraints greatly influence the design of tax measures, and conflicting objectives often figure in the formulation of tax policy. In practice, therefore, we should probably count on some

---

[20] Perhaps it should be noted that special treatment of capital gains *has* provided an opportunity for many persons to get increments in income taxed at relatively low rates.

distortion of resource allocation if taxes are raised drastically, even though we can certainly improve the design of our tax system.[21]

### EFFECTS OF HAVING GOVERNMENT DO OUR SHOPPING

Even without the imposition of direct controls, government purchase of a much larger proportion of the nation's output can have some undesirable consequences. The greater the extent to which government does our shopping for us, the smaller the scope left for competition and freely moving prices to guide production. As a result, producers might operate less efficiently, at least in producing nonstandard items, than when producing for private customers. More specifically, government contracting on a huge scale might becloud objectives and sap incentives in private production, not because of a lack of good intentions, but as a result of the sheer complexity of government aims and practices in procurement.[22] For example, cost-plus-fixed-fee production contracts, while they may occasionally be the best practicable arrangement, invite inefficiency. Consider also the effect of security regulations, however necessary they may be, on employee efficiency and on technical communication among military research and production contractors. Consider the effect of government personnel regulations and practices upon efficiency within government agencies and over the wide economic sectors these agencies control or influence.

Also, the manner of awarding contracts sometimes stimulates the wrong achievements. Thus, if the maintenance of a stable aircraft industry is overemphasized and contracts apportioned so as to protect each company from financial failure, the inefficient firms may be able to count on about the same rewards as the efficient ones. As for research and development, each firm can then move forward by just keeping in step — by coming up with designs that are only marginal improvements over their predecessors. Such contracting practices are unlikely to yield either efficiency in production or boldness in development. Too much emphasis on a stable industry gets our objectives mixed up. The situation is like the fox-hunt to which one hunter brought a female dog. The dogs got off to a fast pace, and it looked like a fine hunt — until someone noticed that the fox was running fifth. Over-all effectiveness, particularly in re-

---

[21] For discussions of tax policy, see *Federal Tax Policy for Economic Growth and Stability*, and U. K. Hicks, "Direct Taxation and Economic Growth," *Oxford Economic Papers* (New Series), VIII, October 1956, pp. 302–317.

[22] For a survey of these problems and possible improvements in procurement methods, see the Commission on Organization of the Executive Branch of the Government, *Task Force Report on Military Procurement*, U.S. Government Printing Office, Washington, D.C., 1955.

search and development, will be "running fifth" if contracting practices reward the wrong type of activity.[23]

Describing these indirect costs — inflationary pressures, the costs of direct controls if they are used, the indirect burden of taxes, the side effects of having government do more of our shopping — may give a misleading impression. It may convey the idea that we know the quantitative significance of these indirect costs and that they are bound to be disastrous. Neither of these things is true. There are circumstances in which quite high budgets accompanied by high taxes and some inflation have positive, or at least no deleterious, effects. No one comparing the United States economy of the thirties with that of 1945–1959 can fail to be impressed by the gain in strength and vitality. Was this gain in spite of, rather than because of, the one hundred billion dollar military budgets of World War II and the fifty billion dollar budgets following the Korean War? Doubtless in some sense the answer is Yes: still greater prosperity could have been achieved by other means involving smaller long-run economic risks. But as a practical matter, the other means were not found or applied. In any event, nations are not ruined by small doses of inflation, by the temporary use of price controls, by considerable increase in government "shopping," or by fairly heavy taxes.

We need a better understanding of these economic problems and of the implications for military budgets and for the whole complex of related domestic economic policies. In the meantime, let us not be so bemused by good but incomplete economic theory about these indirect costs that we run undue risks with national security.[24]

### OTHER INDIRECT BENEFITS

Finally we should recognize that defense programs produce some indirect gains (in addition to serving as a guard against deflation). There are numerous spillover benefits to private sectors of the economy. The construction and maintenance of certain facilities — such as highways that are built for defense purposes or sea and air navigational aids — help the transportation industry to cut costs or provide improved services.[25]

[23] For a discussion of possible improvements in the drawing and awarding of contracts, see Chapter 12 on "Institutional Arrangements to Promote Efficiency."

[24] For views similar to those expressed in this section, see *The Problem of National Security,* A Statement on National Policy by the Research and Policy Committee of the Committee for Economic Development, July, 1958.

[25] The benefits discussed here are "technological," not "pecuniary," spillovers. That is, these benefits improve private firms' physical production possibilities, enabling them to get greater outputs from given inputs (or to achieve a given output with less input). In contrast, the purchase of uniforms bestows a "pecuniary" gain on the textile industry, but it represents merely a shift of demand and profits from other industries (from whom the taxpayers would otherwise have bought goods).

The purchase of airplanes and ships, by increasing the scale of operations in these industries, makes it possible for airlines and shipping companies to get their equipment at lower cost. This happens because shipbuilding and aircraft manufacturing are "decreasing cost" industries over the relevant range of output. Within this range, the larger the output of a particular model, the lower its unit cost; and the larger the scale of operations in general, the cheaper certain inputs are for any additional models.

Education and training are parts of the defense program that yield spillover benefits to individuals and firms. The "G.I. Bill" was a major stimulus to higher education and to many types of vocational training. In all likelihood, the military Services will continue to offer similar, though less extensive, educational opportunities. Such investment in human resources probably yields a large payoff to the nation (see Chapter 3). In addition to sponsoring education in this fashion, the Services give new recruits various kinds of training that is valuable even if the men leave the service. The training and seasoning of flyers provides a pool of skilled, experienced pilots that is available to the airlines. The airlines and the users of their services are thereby benefited and national income increased. Similarly, the training and seasoning of jet aircraft mechanics, electronic specialists, and a host of other technicians yield spillover benefits to the private economy.[26]

The defense program gives a fillip to investment in education in still another way. The increased demand for scientists, engineers, electronics experts, and skilled technicians, stemming from both military operations and military research and development, is causing extra investment in scientific skills. In all likelihood, this investment will prove to be a profitable one from the standpoint of the whole economy (as well as that of the individuals). Even if the military's demand for these skills subsides, this scientific training and experience will be valuable to the nation.

Perhaps the most important of these indirect gains, however, are the spillover benefits from military research and development. Some of these benefits are obvious. The development of a good transport plane for the military can lead directly to improved civil aviation.[27] Some of the indirect benefits are less obvious. For instance, a Crane Company official has pointed out: "What were once government specials are now

---

[26] This is not to say that the provision of such training by the military Services is an optimal policy. It would probably be more efficient for the economy as a whole and less expensive to the Defense Department, if the Services hired men who were already partially trained, just as they now hire doctors and dentists who are already trained. But, *given* the present recruitment and training policies, we should recognize the spillover benefits that accrue outside the Defense Department.

[27] See Craig Lewis, "Air Force Tests Turboprop Reliability," *Aviation Week*, April 29, 1957, pp. 50–61.

standard products, such as the chlorine valves we originally developed for chemical warfare." [28] New ideas resulting from research are likely to have numerous and unforeseen applications.[29] Military research and development led to such items as silicon transitors, improved anti-motion-sickness drugs, and new flame-proofing for fabrics. Special rockets may be useful as emergency brakes for trucks. Even the immense costs incurred in the development of the atomic bomb may eventually prove worthwhile on strictly nonmilitary grounds. Knowledge of space will no doubt provide nonmilitary gains that cannot at present be foreseen.

In fact, the spillover benefits from research and development by themselves may make it economical to increase this type of defense expenditure (or to stimulate research in other ways). A well-conceived research and development program has a double payoff — better weapon systems, on the one hand, and a bigger resource base, on the other. The Russians are undoubtedly devoting a much larger proportion of their scientific and technical resources to military work than we are. Moreover, they appear to have almost as many scientists and engineers as we do and to be training new ones at a somewhat faster rate and of no lower quality. This rate may be more significant for future defense postures than the rate at which they are currently expanding their capacity in basic industries.

All this is not to say that these indirect benefits could be achieved only by means of national security programs. In a world where large defense outlays were unnecessary, other government policies or private actions could produce these extra gains (education, advances in the state of the art) more directly and effectively. It is to say, however, that in this world where large defense budgets must be considered, we should recognize the indirect benefits as well as the costs, both in deciding the size of the defense budget and in determining other relevant public policies.

[28] "Who Wants Defense Work?" *Business Week,* May 18, 1957, p. 91. Quotation reprinted by permission of publisher.

[29] For many specific examples, see Herbert E. Striner, Richard U. Sherman, Jr., Leon N. Karadbil, Alexander Sachs, Margaret H. Tupper, and Sidney G. Winter, Jr., *Defense Spending and the U.S. Economy,* ORO-SP-57, Operations Research Office, Vol. I, June 1958, pp. 16–29, and Vol. II, May 1958, Appendices B, C, and D.

# 6. THE ECONOMIC STRENGTHS
## OF THE MAJOR POWERS

In Part I we have discussed limitations on resources available to a nation and the choice of the amount to be spent on defense. We stressed how one should think about this problem of choice by trying to weigh gains against costs instead of being either a "budget-firster" or a "doctrine-firster." In this connection, interrelationships between a nation's choices and the enemy's policies, and the interdependence among defense programs (that is, the fact that the worth of one program often depends upon the size and nature of other activities) are important. Also, the possible indirect effects of defense (or other governmental) spending should be recognized. To conclude Part I, we shall call attention to a few facts about the economic strengths and potential defense budgets of some major powers.

## PROBLEMS OF INTERNATIONAL COMPARISONS

As argued earlier, gross national product (GNP) is a useful indicator of a nation's basic strength — one that is more significant, for purposes of looking several years ahead, than a long list of specific resources. Consequently, in appraising the strengths of the major powers, we shall be concerned mainly with their potential GNP's and plausible defense budgets that could come from those GNP's. In order to convey any meaning, these GNP's and budgets have to be expressed in terms of the same monetary unit. It conveys almost nothing to say that the Soviet Union's GNP was 1,194 billion rubles in 1955 while that of the United States was 390 billion dollars. Hence these amounts for the various nations have been converted to 1955 dollars.

At the same time, the uncertainties about these figures must be recognized. No formal way of taking uncertainties into account can be prescribed, but wise interpretations and decisions are not reached by ignoring them. It is advisable therefore to review some of the difficulties of international comparisons.

First of all, even though gross national product is a good indicator of a nation's strength, it cannot reflect all aspects of the resource base from which defense capability must come. Moreover, these are aspects that can vary from one nation to the next. Among the obvious examples are the possible strengths and weaknesses of political institutions. Also GNP does not reflect the advantages of certain locational and geographic features. Perhaps we should stress too that indicators of basic strength are not proportional to potential military capability. The poorer nations have greater difficulty than the richer ones in sparing a given percentage of their output for defense, and the democratic nations may have greater political difficulty than authoritarian countries in diverting resources to defense.

In addition, there are conceptual difficulties in measuring GNP that impair to some extent its significance and its comparability as among different nations. These difficulties were referred to in Chapter 3, but they deserve special emphasis when making international comparisons. There is a problem, for example, in determining just which outputs are "final" products and which are "intermediate." Are statistical services in government final outputs or merely intermediate products that are used in the production of subsequent final goods? For the appraisal of one nation's strength or growth, the answer to this question may not matter much, but when comparing the strengths of various nations, it becomes important, since all countries do not follow uniform measurement practices. There are also problems in deciding how many "do-it-yourself" activities are to be counted in the gross national product. One nation may include few housekeeping services in GNP, because they are performed at home, while another nation, in which a higher proportion of wives work outside the home and hire various tasks done, may count a large portion of such services. (In their official estimates of "gross product," Eastern European countries include only the output of material goods and "productive" services, excluding all personal and government services.)

Even after we adjust or accept the estimates expressed in domestic currencies, we face the extremely serious problem of comparing them. What we wish to do in comparing the GNP's of two countries is to compare the baskets of goods that can be produced in the two economies. The usual (and frequently the only practical) way to do this is to value the goods and services produced in each country in the prices that prevail in one of them. The resulting index of relative GNP's would be different, of course, if prices in the other country were used as weights.

It might be noted that a similar procedure is used when GNP's of one nation are compared for different years. The goods and services are valued (in other words, weighted) by using the prices that prevailed in one of the years. The indexes would be different if the prices of a different year were used as weights.

In both instances the so-called "index-number problem" confronts us. The results help show capacities to produce, given that particular set of weights, but do not reveal capacities in other circumstances. There is little assurance, moreover, that relative prices in the United States are appropriate weights to attach to the output of the Soviet Union. At minimum, therefore, it seems advisable to compare two sets of indexes for any pair of countries: one set using the prices of one country as weights, the second set using the prices of the other country as weights.

When United States GNP is the base, this procedure is tantamount to converting GNP's of other nations into dollars by using "purchasing power equivalents," that is, ratios showing the amounts of the other currencies having the same purchasing power as one dollar. The procedure is tantamount to this because it implies such purchasing power equivalents even if they are not directly used in the calculations. For example, calculating the indexes described previously for France and the United Kingdom would imply certain franc-dollar ratios and pound-dollar ratios. For the sake of convenience, therefore, we shall refer to this procedure as converting GNP's to dollars by using purchasing-power equivalents.

One study of international comparisons which will be used a good deal in this chapter followed this procedure in comparing the GNP's of the United States and selected European countries.[1] In these calculations, for example, the United Kingdom's GNP in 1955 was estimated to be from 16 per cent of United States GNP (using European relative price weights) to 20 per cent of United States GNP (using United States relative price weights).[2] Note that the results consist of two percentages, not a unique percentage. The range covered by these two does not necessarily embrace all the relevant possibilities, but it reflects some of the most important ones.

Another way of comparing GNP's is to convert them to a common currency by means of prevailing exchange rates. For the United Kingdom, this method would have indicated a 1955 GNP amounting to only 13 per cent of United States GNP (at the exchange rate of $2.80 per pound sterling). Although exchange rates have often been used for such conversions, the procedure has serious shortcomings. In order for conversion by exchange rate to reflect output correctly, the ratio of the internal purchasing powers of the currencies would have to equal the exchange rate. And for this to be true, there would have to be a state of long-run equilibrium, no trade barriers, and the same price ratios for domestic final goods as for internationally traded goods. Because these conditions are unlikely to exist, the use of exchange rates is somewhat hazardous. Even so, if used cautiously, conversion by exchange rates has some usefulness for broad appraisals of economic strengths. Later in this chapter,

[1] Milton Gilbert and associates, *Comparative National Products and Price Levels,* Organisation for European Economic Cooperation, Paris [no date].

[2] *Ibid.,* p. 86. These percentages were calculated from the comparative GNP's that are shown in the source.

GNP's will be converted to dollars by means of exchange rates in a few instances.

Probably the main thing to avoid is any notion of certainty (which the use of conventional exchange rates might foster) about GNP's that are translated into dollars. Because of the difficulties of international comparisons, there is no estimate for any country that is *the* correct one. Partly in order to keep readers aware of this fact, we make use in this chapter of ranges rather than of unique estimates. It is believed that these ranges will "bracket" the plausible possibilities and give emphasis to the extent of the uncertainties.

Similar difficulties hamper the comparison of defense budgets, most of which are also shown here as ranges. First, the amounts to be spent on defense do not embrace all aspects of a nation's military capability. Geographic and climatic features that give one nation a strategic advantage do not appear in its budget. Political institutions, which trouble the comparison of GNP's, may still further complicate the comparison of the resources devoted to national security. For instance, democratic methods are an aspect of the resource base that may be relatively conducive to general strength and well-being yet not necessarily conducive to military superiority in the nuclear era. Morale in military activities does not show up in the budget, nor do such critical items as diplomatic and bargaining skills.

Second, the amount devoted to defense may not correctly reflect the purchasing power of the defense budget. The purchasing power of a country's currency, in relation to other currencies, may be larger in defense than it is in consumption. The defense budget of the Soviet Union in comparison with that of the United States is the outstanding example. Because of pricing practices, lower wage-rates, or perhaps greater efficiency in certain activities, a ruble purchases more relative to a dollar in heavy industry and defense than it does in other sectors of the economy. While we try to make allowance for this extra purchasing power of the ruble in defense activities (see Table 10), we wish to stress that there is considerable uncertainty about the figures on comparative defense budgets as well as about those on GNP's.

## GNP AND GROWTH: SOME MAJOR POWERS

### GNP'S OF MAJOR POWERS IN 1955

Estimated 1955 gross national products of several major powers are shown in Table 5. (The sources and methods used in preparing these estimates are described in Table 10, at the end of the chapter.) The purpose of these figures is to indicate the basic economic strengths of these nations. Gross national product in the USSR was less than half,

Table 5. GNP's of some major powers, 1955
(billions of 1955 US dollars)

| Power | GNP |
|---|---|
| United States | 390 |
| USSR | 120–150 |
| United Kingdom | 60– 70 |
| West Germany | 50– 70 |
| France | 40– 60 |
| Canada | 30– 40 |
| Italy | 20– 40 |
| Japan | 20– 40 |

ᵃ All estimates have been rounded to the nearest 10 billion dollars. Currencies have been converted to dollars by means of price ratios (purchasing power equivalents) in all cases except Canada and Japan. The ranges are intended to embrace the most likely GNP figures for purposes of comparing economic strengths; the use of ranges is intended also to emphasize that there is inevitably great uncertainty about other nations' GNP's expressed in dollars. The sources and calculations pertaining to these figures are shown in Table 10 at the end of this chapter.

probably about a third, that of the United States, and GNP's in the other countries trailed well behind those of the two major powers. We have refrained from including any GNP estimate for China because such a figure appears (as of 1960) to be so speculative.[3]

As for the other nations that are omitted from Table 5, their strengths are comparatively small, and estimates would be extremely uncertain. For instance, the 1955 GNP of Yugoslavia, stated as 1,552 billion dinars,[4] can hardly be more than 3 or 4 billion 1955 dollars. Similarly, the GNP's of Poland, Eastern Germany, and numerous Western countries are certainly smaller than the GNP's of the powers listed in Table 5. For our purposes, it seems permissible to neglect them.

In most instances, we should note, it is a hazardous and misleading procedure to add GNP's of different nations to estimate the aggregate strength of some political bloc. On the one hand, it would not allow for any gains from further division of labor. For example, the United States and Great Britain acting together might have a more powerful resource base than the simple addition of GNP's would show. Also, to add GNP's

[3] Considerable attention is now being given to the Chinese national accounts, however. Tentative estimates for 1952 (in Yuan) are presented by Alexander Eckstein, with the assistance of Y. C. Yin and Helen Yin, "Communist China's National Product in 1952," *The Review of Economics and Statistics,* May 1958, pp. 127–139. Many data and estimates are' available in William W. Hollister's *China's Gross National Product and Social Accounts 1950–1957,* Free Press, Glencoe, Illinois, 1958. Ta-Chung Liu has examined China's economic growth in "Structural Changes in the Economy of the Chinese Mainland, 1933 to 1952–57," *American Economic Review, Papers and Proceedings,* May 1959, pp. 84–93.

[4] *World Economic Survey, 1956,* United Nations, New York, 1957, p. 253. The Communist concept of GNP is different from that of the Western nations, but the comparative weakness of the USSR satellite countries is obvious.

would gloss over and still further conceal the awesome index-number problems that are present in comparing GNP's. Finally, and perhaps still more importantly, combining GNP's would ignore each nation's uncertainty about the role and precise aims of the other and the difficulties therefore of working together (see Chapter 15 on "The Economics of Military Alliance").

If two nations actually gave up their individual sovereignties and merged, we would in effect add their GNP's (though changes in the division of labor would affect the results). Short of this, nations cannot be certain about each other's aims, strategy, and diplomacy. Even among countries that have a great deal in common, such as the United Kingdom, the United States, and other English-speaking nations, each has grave doubts about the others' objectives and firmness of purpose, and there are serious disagreements about the correctness of one another's strategy. Witness the sharp criticism in Britain of United States policies in the Far East and of the general defense strategy.

As for the Soviet bloc, some parts of which have in effect surrendered their sovereignty, the smouldering resentment that is often present, as in Hungary or Poland, casts doubt on the ultimate effectiveness of their cooperation. The situation at times verges on civil war. For this bloc, too, it would usually be misleading to add GNP's.

It may be useful to sum the GNP's in a certain bloc when considering *particular* contingencies. If the Soviet threat develops in such a way as to generate great solidarity in Western Europe, total GNP in Western Europe might be a useful indicator of its strentgh for cold war. If relationships within the Soviet bloc become more harmonious, perhaps the individual national products should be summed. In general, however, the summing of GNP's would not give an accurate picture of the resource-base for defense, and in the tables, therefore, we deal only with the GNP's of individual nations. In formulating its policies, each nation should recognize the role of aid and alliances, but not usually to the extent of trying to add allies' economic strengths together.

### RATES OF GROWTH OF MAJOR POWERS

The main factors that determine the growth of an economy were summarized in Chapter 3. At this point, we shall discuss briefly the working of these factors today, especially in the Soviet Union, and then compare projected growth rates.

Manpower — including education, training, and the level of employment — is one of the important determinants of growth. In this connection, at least two points deserve special attention. First, the Soviet Union now places a great deal of emphasis on education, and in many relevant courses of study already turns out about as many graduates as the

United States.[5] In other words Russia has gained considerably vis-à-vis the West in this resource, trained manpower, and will probably continue to gain. (China too appears to have ambitious plans for investing in human resources.)

Second, the Soviet Union can do better than the market economies in avoiding unemployment (though in doing so, she may experience more "under-employment," that is, misallocation of resources). The free economies are likely to have fairly sharp recessions occasionally unless they inject purchasing power liberally and accept a heightened risk of inflation. Thus, in the first quarter of 1958, industrial production changed (in comparison with the first quarter of 1957) by the same proportion in both the United States and the Soviet Union — but the changes were in opposite directions: 11 per cent up in Russia, 11 per cent down in the United States! [6] Planned economies, too, have "rolling readjustments" as long as they make or permit shifts of resources, but by accepting certain limitations on freedom, they can avoid extensive unemployment.

Investment, or change in the stock of capital equipment, is another determinant of growth. The most marked difference among the major powers is probably the comparatively high percentage of total investment, and of GNP, that the Soviet Union devotes to industry and, even more noticeably, to heavy industry. During most of the nonwar years since 1928, about 40 per cent of total investment in the Soviet Union has been in industry, the amount during 1948 rising to almost 50 per cent.[7] The corresponding percentage in the United States has been about 25. This form of investment has a high rate of return *in terms of future growth* in comparison with, say, investment in trade, residences, and recreational facilities. (This statement does not mean that the Soviet Union somehow finds more profitable investments than the United States. It does mean, however, that if returns are defined as future growth, not as the satisfaction of existing consumers, then investment in heavy industry pays off better than investment in bowling alleys.)

In addition, total investment as a percentage of GNP has been somewhat higher in the Soviet Union than in the United States. The Soviet investment program has been a remarkable achievement for a country with a larger population but a much lower GNP than the United States. As for future growth, it is now feasible for the Soviet Union to divert still

[5] *Soviet Economic Growth: A Comparison with the United States,* A Study Prepared for the Subcommittee on Foreign Economic Policy of the Joint Economic Committee by the Legislative Reference Service of the Library of Congress, U.S. Government Printing Office, Washington, D.C., 1957, pp. 90–97.

[6] See the speech by Allen W. Dulles, Director of the Central Intelligence Agency, as reported in *New York Times,* April 29, 1958, p. 8.

[7] Norman M. Kaplan, "Capital Formation and Allocation," in *Soviet Economic Growth,* ed. Abram Bergson, Row, Peterson and Co., White Plains, N.Y., 1953, pp. 50–59.

larger proportions of GNP to investment (as well as to defense, which will be discussed later in the chapter), and to continue putting much of the investment into its "growth sectors."

We should recognize the possibility of diminishing returns as more labor and man-made capital are applied to types of capital that are comparatively fixed. We doubt that this is too important, except that returns to capital increments can be expected to diminish after a nation has exploited the high-value opportunities, for example, for repairs and reconstruction, that sometimes exist at the end of a war. When forms of capital that have become relatively scarce on account of the war are applied to the other resources, incremental returns are high at first but must decline after a while. This is another reason that one cannot simply extrapolate the high postwar rates of growth in various countries. West Germany, Japan, and Russia have all experienced high returns on postwar investments, returns that can scarcely be duplicated by new capital formation over the next twenty years.

Another determinant of growth is technological advance. There is no reason to believe that either bloc will lag in research or, more particularly, in applying the results of basic research that may be undertaken elsewhere. In a planned economy like that of the Soviet Union one might expect lags or inefficiency in reshuffling resources in response to innovations — but such phenomena have not seemed to inhibit industrial development much in recent years. In summary, for a good many years to come the Soviet Union can probably maintain the average peacetime growth rates attained during the past few decades, though probably not the exceptional rates achieved in the immediate postwar years.

Table 6 on possible future rates of growth has been drawn up in the

### Table 6. Possible rates of annual growth of GNP of these powers

| Powers | Percentage of growth[a] |
|---|---|
| United States | 2½–3½ |
| USSR | 5–6 |
| United Kingdom | 2–3 |
| West Germany | 4–5 |
| France | 2–3 |
| Canada | 3–4 |
| Italy | 3–4 |
| Japan | 4–5 |

[a] These figures are based upon estimated rates of growth over approximately the past 3 decades, upon rates of growth in recent years, and upon bits of evidence concerning current institutions and circumstances. Sources and calculations are shown in Table 11 at the end of the chapter. The use of ranges, it is hoped, will stress the fact that there is necessarily considerable uncertainty about future growth rates.

light of these various considerations and of experience since the mid-twenties. (Table 11 at the end of the chapter explains the derivation of the figures that are presented in Table 6.) We shall mention a few points about past experience and the way it affects projections for the years ahead. Growth rates in "recent years," usually 1950–1956 in Table 11, play a big role in assessing future possibilities. For in many respects conditions in recent years are more closely akin to those of the future than are the circumstances of long ago. In other respects recent experience may be far from representative, so we must try to include results from some earlier years. At the same time, we should avoid stressing war years, for we want to assess, not growth or future strength during hot wars, but future strengths for cold-war defenses. One final point. There is no "right" way to estimate trends, no way to be sure about projections of future development. To emphasize the existence of uncertainty, the figures in Table 6 are shown as ranges and are labeled "possible growth rates."

In the table, the higher growth rates are those of the Soviet Union, West Germany, and Japan. Italy and Canada are next, followed by the United States and then by the United Kingdom and France. If the United States maintains a high degree of stability, or at least avoids frequent or prolonged recessions, the Western powers can probably achieve the higher rates of growth shown in the table. If the United States tolerates even moderate periods of recession, however, it will surely pull the growth rates — its own and those of the other nations with which the United States trades — down to the lower figures.

Output in France, it might be noted, has risen rapidly, over 4 per cent annually, in the period 1950–1956. But we cannot ignore the persistent tendency toward stagnation, due perhaps to French institutions and instability.[8] Over the three decades following the mid-twenties, while most of the major powers were growing at over 2 per cent per year, France grew at a rate of about $\frac{1}{3}$ of 1 per cent annually (Table 11).

It should be noted that some scholars doubt the Soviet Union's ability to maintain growth rates as high as those suggested here.[9] There is, naturally enough, considerable controversy over prospective industrial growth in the Soviet Union. And, while it would not be wise to underestimate Soviet strength in planning our defense policies, neither would it be prudent to grossly overestimate their capabilities. In connection with this controversy, we wish to note three points.

First, even those scholars who are skeptical of the progress of the

[8] See Warren C. Baum, *The French Economy and the State,* Princeton University Press, Princeton, 1958.
[9] C. Warren Nutter, "Industrial Growth in the Soviet Union," *American Economic Review, Papers and Proceedings,* May 1958, pp. 398–411.

Russians and their ability to maintain recent rates of growth concede that Soviet industrial development has been impressive.[10]

As to the shorter periods of Soviet industrial growth, it seems reasonably clear that there are no similar periods in American industrial history that fully duplicate the rapidity of Soviet growth from 1928 to 1955, although the American period 1885–1912 — when production started at about the same level — comes close. Among recent years, the American period 1939–51 is perhaps most comparable to the Soviet period 1928–40, in that it, like the Soviet period, followed a decade of depression and stagnation; here, again, the American growth rate falls short of the Soviet one, though not by a great deal. The most recent short period of rapid growth — 1950–55 — has no counterpart in normal American times; it does not appear unusual when compared with our period of wartime mobilization (1939–43), though the initial heavy unemployment in the latter case must be taken into account.[11]

Second, a moderate underestimate of an enemy's capability is more hazardous, in today's circumstances, than a modest overestimate. A slight underestimate could lower our guard enough to vitiate deterrence and bring disaster; a moderate overstatement of their strength would increase the cost of our defense program but (unless the program was designed to provoke attack) not bring catastrophe.

Third, the predominant tendency in the United States appears to be to disparage and underestimate Soviet achievements. When the Soviet Union exploded an A-bomb and later a hydrogen device, our press emphasized our lead more than their accomplishment. When they put up large satellites, we stressed, almost *ad nauseam,* our skill at "miniaturization." Also, each time the Soviet Union does something ahead of us, at least a few stories and statements give large credit to their espionage rings. We may go sometime to the opposite extreme and start thinking of the Soviets as being "ten feet tall," but so far we have pretty consistently and dangerously erred in the other direction. Soviet GNP and Soviet defense budgets have an alarming potential for future growth.

PROJECTIONS OF FUTURE GNP'S

These rates of growth in conjunction with the preceding estimates of GNP make possible the projections of future gross national products shown in Table 7. The results of course embrace rather wide ranges of GNP. Nonetheless they shed some light on comparative economic strengths in the future, and on growth of the resources that can be made available to defense.

The projections are for the years 1965 and 1975. By the latter year the growth of the whole group of nations is remarkable. But the gains of

[10] *Ibid.,* p. 410.
[11] *Ibid.,* p. 409.

### Table 7. Possible GNP's, 1965 and 1975 [a]
### (billions of 1955 US dollars)

| Power | 1965 | 1975 |
|-------|------|------|
| United States | 500–550 | 640–780 |
| USSR | 200–270 | 320–480 |
| United Kingdom | 70–100 | 90–130 |
| West Germany | 70–110 | 110–190 |
| France | 50– 80 | 60–110 |
| Canada | 40– 60 | 50– 90 |
| Italy | 30– 60 | 40– 90 |
| Japan | 30– 70 | 40–110 |

[a] These are projections based upon the GNP's for 1955 presented in Table 5 and the possible rates of growth presented in Table 6.

the Soviet Union are especially striking. West Germany catches up with the United Kingdom and in fact probably emerges as the third most powerful nation. (China, not shown in the table, is likely to have a smaller gross national product than Germany or the United Kingdom.)

The range of GNP's projected for the Soviet Union is not at all far-fetched. Mr. Allen Dulles, director of the U.S. Central Intelligence Agency, apparently credits the Soviet Union with the ability to do as well or better: "Whereas Soviet gross national product was about 33 per cent that of the United States in 1950, by 1956 it had increased to about 40 per cent, and by 1962 it may be about 50 per cent of our own." [12]

The particularly wide ranges of the projections for the smaller nations arise chiefly from the difficulties of converting the estimates to dollars. For many other "smaller" countries such as Yugoslavia, Turkey, or the Latin-American nations, the uncertainties would be as great or greater, yet it is fairly certain that none can enter the list of the eight strongest powers by 1975.

## DEFENSE BUDGETS

The difficulties of making international comparisons of defense outlays have already been emphasized. We should keep these in mind while interpreting Tables 8 and 9 on recent and projected defense budgets.

As shown in Table 8, there were no military budgets of the same order of magnitude in 1955 as those of the United States and the Soviet Union. The range and size of the estimate for the Soviet Union merits special comment.

It may seem paradoxical that the Soviets could spend only 13 per cent of a much smaller GNP than that of the United States and still produce

[12] Speech before the U.S. Chamber of Commerce as reported in *New York Times*, April 29, 1958, p. 8.

## Table 8. Defense budgets, 1955

| | Defense expenditures | | |
| Power | Domestic currency[a] (billions of units) | | As a per cent of GNP[b] | As a range in U.S. dollars[c] (rounded to nearest billion) |
|---|---|---|---|---|
| United States | 40.5 | (US dollars) | 10% | 41 |
| USSR | 153 | (rubles) | 13% | 19–31[d] |
| United Kingdom | 1.6 | (pnds. sterling) | 8% | 5– 7 |
| France | 1102 | (francs) | 7% | 2– 4 |
| West Germany | 7.4 | (D.M.) | 4% | 2– 3 |
| Canada | 1.8 | (Can. dollars) | 7% | 2– 3 |
| Italy | 551 | (lire) | 4% | 1– 3 |
| Japan | 142 | (yen) | 2% | 0– 1 |

[a] Estimates for countries other than Japan and the USSR were taken from the *NATO Letter*, North Atlantic Treaty Organization, Information Service, January 1958, p. 21.

The figure for the USSR is 13% of estimated GNP in rubles (1174 billion as shown in Table 10) or 153 billion rubles. This is the percentage (rounded to the nearest percentage point) that was estimated in *Soviet Economic Growth: A Comparison with the United States*, A Study Prepared for the Subcommittee on Foreign Policy of the Joint Economic Committee by the Legislative Reference Service of the Library of Congress, U.S. Government Printing Office, Washington, D.C., 1957, p. 127.

The estimate of defense expenditures in Japan is from *Economic Survey of Asia and the Far East 1956*, United Nations, Bangkok, 1957, Special Table L, p. 190.

The definitions of "defense expenditures" are not exactly comparable in all instances, but the figures show at least roughly the relative magnitude of various defense budgets.

[b] The percentages, except that for the USSR, are simply the defense outlays of Table 8 divided by the GNP's of Table 10, and then rounded. Regarding the defense budget of the USSR, which has been adjusted to include more than the items in the published budget, see the preceding footnote. (Note that USSR defense outlays are 15 to 20% of their GNP if our estimates of the two amounts in dollar equivalents are used.)

[c] In all instances except Canada and Japan, the range in dollars was derived by using (at least implicitly) special price ratios to reflect relative purchasing power in the defense sectors of the economies. For France, the U.K., West Germany, and Italy, the estimated defense budgets are presented in Gilbert and associates, *Comparative National Products and Price Levels*, The Organisation for European Economic Cooperation, Paris, no date, p. 86. For the USSR, defense outlays in rubles (153 billion) were converted to dollars by means of two ratios — 5 and 8 rubles per dollar. Price ratios in this range appear to be appropriate in 1950 for many industrial outputs related to defense, e.g., construction and machinery (see Norman M. Kaplan and William L. White, *A Comparison of 1950 Wholesale Prices in Soviet and American Industry*, The RAND Corporation, Research Memorandum RM-1443, May 1, 1955, p. 33. A closely related point is often made — namely, that the USSR is *comparatively* efficient in defense and heavy industry (see *Soviet Economic Growth: A Comparison with the United States*, p. 132 and Abraham S. Becker, *Prices of Producers' Durables in the United States and the USSR in 1955*, The RAND Corporation, Research Memorandum RM-2432, August 15, 1959).

For Canada and Japan, price ratios were unavailable. The ranges of their budgets in dollars were derived by applying the percentages shown in Table 8 to the dollar ranges of the GNP's in Table 5.

[d] We wish to emphasize that the USSR estimates are conservative ones in the sense that the range should probably be higher. Ruble-dollar ratios declined between 1950 and 1955. It is especially likely that the lower limit of this range, 19 billion (1955) dollars, is too low. It is based on a ruble-dollar ratio of 8 to 1, but by 1955 it appears that 5 to 1 is much more likely to approximate the real relationship in the defense sectors of the economies.

such large military capabilities. When Soviet prices of military items are taken into account,[13] however, their budgets in terms of dollars are not mysteriously small. As indicated in Table 8, Soviet defense outlays in 1955 may have been the equivalent of over 30 billion dollars. For several

[13] As noted below, special ruble-dollar ratios are used to estimate the USSR defense budget in Table 8.

possible reasons (such as cheaper labor, past investment in heavy industry, and price policies), the Soviet Union has a comparative advantage in producing military power. In terms of dollars, therefore, Soviet defense budgets amount to far more than 13 per cent of their GNP (at least 15 to 20 per cent in 1955, according to Tables 5 and 8).[14] The sacrifice entailed is better reflected by the percentage devoted to defense when the calculations are in terms of the domestic currency,[15] but comparative sizes of defense programs are better shown when they are converted to a common currency by purchasing power equivalents.

**Table 9. Possible defense budgets, 1965 and 1975** [a]
**(billions of 1955 US dollars)**

| | 1965 | | 1975 | |
| --- | --- | --- | --- | --- |
| *Power* | % of GNP | Range | % of GNP | Range |
| United States | 10% | 50–55 | 10% | 64– 78 |
| USSR | 15 | 35–65[b] | 15 | 60–115[b] |
| United Kingdom | 10 | 7–10 | 10 | 9– 13 |
| West Germany | 5 | 4– 6 | 10 | 11– 19 |
| France | 10 | 5– 8 | 10 | 6– 11 |
| Canada | 10 | 4– 6 | 10 | 5– 9 |
| Italy | 5 | 2– 3 | 5 | 2– 5 |
| Japan | 5 | 2– 4 | 5 | 2– 6 |

[a] These are not predictions of future defense budgets. The figures simply represent the potential growth of their budgets if these nations grow as suggested in Table 7 and if they increase the percentages of GNP devoted to defense as suggested in Table 9. These percentages are plausible ones. The percentage for the USSR would be compatible with rapid growth of both investment and consumption — well over a 4% annual increase in non-defense outlays if GNP grows at 5%, and over a 5% annual increase if GNP grows at 6%. (In the calculations, defense rubles were again converted to dollars at ratios of 5 and 8 rubles per dollar.)

[b] See footnote [d] of Table 8.

Table 9 presents some projections of future defense budgets. Several points about them should be stressed. First, the projections are not supposed to be "maximum" defense budgets, that is, the various nations' GNP's minus nondefense "requirements." Nations can certainly push their outlays above the amounts shown in the table. But the higher they raise military expenditures, the greater the sacrifices, and actual budgets are almost sure to fall short of hypothetical maxima. Showing plausible budgets should be more helpful to the formulation of policies affecting the distant future than showing "maximum" budgets.

Second, the projections are supposed to be plausible budgets *if* certain

[14] Allen Dulles has suggested that in the late 1950's, the proportion of GNP devoted to defense by the Soviet Union was already "about double" that of the United States (*New York Times,* April 29, 1958, p. 8).

[15] Gilbert, p. 51.

events take place; they are not intended to be predictions of what will in fact take place. (Indeed, if such projections succeed in influencing policies, they may be a cause of their own inaccuracy.) Projections of defense budgets, like those of an individual's weight, may be far from the mark because these things are determined by choice, not by natural law. If nations decide to do so, they can raise outlays far above, or hold them far below, the amounts presented here. To raise defense outlays means giving up something else, however, and governments encounter resistance — especially, sometimes, in democratic countries. It would take a highly defense-minded populace in the United States to support a military budget that persistently amounted to 15 per cent of GNP. The Soviet Union probably faces less severe political constraints, and may easily, as the economy grows, devote 20 to 25 per cent of GNP to defense.

Moreover, the "game" aspect of budget determination will have a great deal to do with future defense outlays by the various powers. In other words, each nation's budget decisions will depend upon the actions of the other countries. If the Soviet Union should devote 25 per cent of GNP to military purposes, the populace of the United States might well become "highly defense-minded" and put more than 15 per cent of United States resources to the same purpose. One can be sure that such developments would affect the budgets of other nations also. By the same token, the United Kingdom will probably base her strategy and military expenditures on those of the United States and the Soviet Union.

The figures in Table 9, therefore, simply give the potential growth of the budgets of several nations if their economies develop· as suggested earlier and if the nations divert to defense the percentages of GNP shown in the table. The projections are supposed to be plausible ones, subject to change if there are arms limitations, altered growth patterns, or altered security-mindedness in the United States or in other nations. Such figures — like projections of a person's weight *if* he eats X calories per day — should be useful in choosing courses of action. For most countries the percentages in Table 9 are only slightly higher than those that currently prevail. For West Germany 10 per cent of GNP, considerably higher than at present, is assumed to go into defense by 1975. For the Soviet Union the percentage (of GNP *in rubles*) is raised from 13 in 1955 to 15 in 1965 and 1975.

To some it may appear that no nation could possibly want such large defense budgets. If the major powers have enough thermonuclear capability now to destroy urban civilization, what is the point in spending still more on national security? Unfortunately, there may be good reason to increase defense budgets enormously. The world finds itself in one of the most dangerous situations that can be imagined (see

Chapter 18 regarding the delicate nature of the stalemate), and it could be worth a large proportion of GNP to any nation to reduce the likelihood of catastrophe. The most hopeful policy seems to be for each side to safeguard deterrence by making its deterrent force invulnerable — an expensive course of action, but one that might maintain at least a balance. Of course, the United States should strive for a preponderance of deterrent power and for a capability to deal with more than one kind of war. At the same time, some have suggested that nations may get into a costly race to protect population and some branches of industry. In short, the situation is critical, and it is entirely possible that defense budgets will soar during the coming decade or so.

THE MAIN CONCLUSIONS

The figures in Table 9 suggest at least three things. One is that the absolute amount spent on defense by the two major powers can rise enormously over the next decade and a half. Another, and perhaps the most significant, is that the Soviet Union's defense budget can overtake that of the United States by 1965 and outstrip it by 1975. The third is that the potential increases in the budgets of the smaller powers, while sharp in terms of percentages, will not (with the probable exception of China) produce major military capabilities even by 1975.[16] Consider the two that promise to be strongest in Western Europe, Germany and the United Kingdom. If anything like the pattern in Table 9 emerges, each will still spend, even in 1975, less than half the 1955 United States budget. (A "United Western Europe," of course, could be an impressive third power, though its defense outlays would probably still lag well behind the budgets of either the United States or the Soviet Union.)

With respect to economic strength in general, the over-all conclusions that stand out are fairly simple. Productive capacity will grow tremendously over the next couple of decades, and Soviet economic strength is likely to increase relative to the capacities of Western nations. To be sure, there are aspects of economic strength that are not revealed by GNP, but by and large, to discuss a host of specific resources would just clutter up the main picture.

A few special factors not reflected in either GNP's or defense budgets deserve review. They support the same general position — that Soviet Russia may gain considerably on the other powers. The relatively unfamiliar expanse of the Soviet Union and the opportunity to disperse and conceal its bases will continue to be a valuable resource. Geography makes the

---

[16] See pp. 354–356 in Chapter 18, however, concerning the $n$th country problem and the danger of accidental outbreak of war; even with relatively small capabilities, nations may be able to acquire enough nuclear weapons to aggravate these dangers seriously.

## Table 10. Estimates of GNP's, 1955

| Power | Domestic currency[a] | Billions of 1955 dollars | | | |
|---|---|---|---|---|---|
| | | Converted by means of price ratios | | | Estimated range rounded to nearest $10 billion |
| | | Exchange rate | Lower estimate | Higher estimate | |
| United States | 392 (billions 1955 dollars) | — | — | — | 390 |
| USSR | 1,202 (billions 1955 rubles[b]) | — | 120.2[c] | 150.3[c] | 120–150 |
| United Kingdom | 19 (billions 1955 pounds) | 53.1[d] | 59.6[d] | 69.9[d] | 60– 70 |
| France | 16,790 (billions 1955 francs) | 48.0[e] | 42.6[e] | 58.5[e] | 40– 60 |
| West Germany | 176 (billions 1955 D.M.) | 41.8[f] | 50.1[f] | 69.3[f] | 50– 70 |
| Canada | 27 (billions 1955 C. dol.) | 27.0[g] | — | — | 30– 40 |
| Italy | 13,639 (billions 1955 lire) | 21.8[h] | 22.5[h] | 40.5[h] | 20– 40 |
| Japan | 7,877 (billions 1955 yen) | 21.9[i] | — | — | 20– 40 |

[a] Unless otherwise noted, these figures were taken from the International Monetary Fund's *International Financial Statistics*, March 1958. This publication will hereafter be referred to as IFS.

[b] Oleg Hoeffding and Nancy Nimitz, *Soviet National Income and Product*, The RAND Corporation, Research Memorandum, RM-2101, April 6, 1959, pp. 8–9.

[c] The lower estimate is based on an average ruble-dollar ratio of 10/1 (1954) estimated for "all (consumers') commodities and services" with USSR 1952 or 1954 weights (See Norman M. Kaplan and Eleanor S. Wainstein, "A Comparison of Soviet and American Retail Prices in 1950," *Journal of Political Economy*, December 1956, p. 486, and "A Note on Ruble-Dollar Comparisons," *Journal of Political Economy*, December 1957, p. 543. The higher estimate is based on an assumed ruble-dollar ratio of 8/1. This ratio was chosen because the ruble-dollar ratio for investment goods is apparently lower than that for consumer goods (see Norman M. Kaplan and William L. White, *A Comparison of 1950 Wholesale Prices in Soviet and American Industry*, The RAND Corporation, Research Memorandum, RM-1443, May 1, 1955, p. 72). In the study just cited, the median ratio for "all (industrial) commodities and services priced" was 7.9/1.

Conversion of Soviet GNP by means of these ratios gives results that bracket the figure implied by Mr. Allen Dulles, namely a Soviet GNP one third as large as that of the U.S. or about $130 billion in 1955 (see "Russia's Growing Strength Could Be A Weakness," *U.S. News and World Report*, May 11, 1956, p. 124, cited in *Soviet Economic Growth: A Comparison with the United States*, A Study Prepared for the Subcommittee on Foreign Economic Policy of the Joint Economic Committee by the Legislative Reference Service of the Library of Congress, U.S. Government Printing Office, Washington, D.C., 1957, pp. 132–134).

[d] The exchange rate used was 2.80 dollars per pound or .358 pounds per dollar. The pound/dollar ratio used for smaller estimate of GNP was 0.319 pounds per dollar, and that used to obtain the larger GNP figure was 0.272 pounds per dollar. These were the purchasing power equivalents for 1955 as estimated by Milton Gilbert and associates in *Comparative National Products and Price Levels*, Organisation for European Economic Cooperation, Paris, no date, p. 30. The lower ratio was based on European quantity weights, the higher ratio on U.S. quantity weights.

[e] The exchange rate was 350 francs per dollar. The franc/dollar ratios based on price observations were 287 and 394 francs per dollar (see Gilbert, *op. cit.*, p. 30).

[f] The exchange rate used was 4.21 D.M. per dollar. The ratios based on price observations were 2.54 and 3.51 D.M. per dollar (Gilbert, *op. cit.*, p. 30).

[g] The exchange rate was .999 Canadian dollars per U.S. dollar. The range shown was judged to be a reasonable one in view of the fact that the exchange rate usually leads to an understatement of other countries' strengths in terms of dollars and in view of the range of the price ratios estimated for the United Kingdom (see footnote [d] above).

[h] The exchange rate was 625 lire per dollar. The ratios estimated by Gilbert were 337 and 605 lire per dollar.

[i] The exchange rate was 360 yen per dollar. The probable range was judged to be about the same as that of Italy, mainly because conversion by exchange rates yields practically the same GNP figure for the two countries.

## Table 11. Estimates of rates of growth

| | Net national product | Industrial production,[d] | | Gross national product | |
| | | Recent years | | Recent years[e] | Up to 1975[f] |
| Power | Recent decades[a] | (1928–1955) | (chiefly 1950–56) | (chiefly 1950–56) | (Guesstimates) |
|---|---|---|---|---|---|
| United States | 2¾% | 3.6% | 4.4% | 3.5% | 2½–3½% |
| USSR | 4½[b] | 7.7–9.2 | 9.9–10.9 | 7 | 5–6 |
| United Kingdom | 2½ | | 3.1 | 2.7 | 2–3 |
| France | ⅓ of 1 | | 7.4 | 4.3 | 2–3 |
| West Germany | 2½ | | 11.3 | 9.1 | 4–5 |
| Canada | 4° | | 5.3 | 5.0 | 3–4 |
| Italy | 1½ | | 8.4 | 5.2 | 3–4 |
| Japan | 2¾° | | 17.3 | | 4–5 |

*Average annual rates of growth*

a These percentages are Kuznets' "per cent changes per decade" converted to annual equivalents (see Simon Kuznets, "Quantitative Aspects of the Economic Growth of Nations," *Economic Development and Cultural Change*, October 1956, pp. 84, 54, 60, 63, 87, 77, 81, 91.) The periods covered are 1924–33 to 1950–54, for the United States and Italy; 1925–34 to 1949–53, for the United Kingdom; 1924–33 to 1949–53, for France; 1936 to 1950–54, for Germany; 1925–34 to 1950–54, for Canada; 1923–32 to 1950–54, for Japan; and 1928 to 1954, for the USSR.

b For the USSR, the "per cent change per decade" was not given for a comparable period. Growth of national income was stated, however, to be from 11.32 billion rubles in 1928 to 35.56 billion rubles in 1954 (all in 1900 prices). These data imply an average annual growth of about 4½ per cent.

c The data for Canada pertained to GNP, and those for Japan to "national income," rather than to net national product (or income). It should be remembered too that, for a variety of other reasons, the comparability of the data is far from perfect. Nonetheless it is believed that they shed light on growth rates. (See Kuznets, "Quantitative Aspects of the Economic Growth of Nations," pp. 5–9.)

d The estimates of the growth in US and USSR industrial production (1950 to 1955) are summarized in *Soviet Economic Growth: A Comparison with the United States*, A Study Prepared for the Subcommittee on Foreign Economic Policy of the Joint Economic Committee by the Legislative Reference Service of the Library of Congress, U.S. Government Printing Office, Washington, D.C., 1957, Table 2, p. 24. The higher estimates for the USSR are based on the data and methods of Donald R. Hodgman, *Soviet Industrial Production, 1928–51*, Harvard University Press, Cambridge, Massachusetts, 1954, especially pp. 89 and 134. The lower estimates for the USSR are modifications made by the staff that prepared the study for the Joint Economic Committee. The estimates for the U.S. are based on Federal Reserve Board Indexes.

The estimates for the other countries are averages of the annual percentage changes from 1950 to 1956, based on data reported in *World Economic Survey 1956*, United Nations, New York, 1957, p. 153, and *World Economic Report, 1953-54*, United Nations, New York, 1955, pp. 28, 34–35, and 45.

e The figure for the USSR is a rough estimate made for 1950–1955 in *Soviet Economic Growth: A Comparison with the United States*, pp. 136, 149. Approximately this rate of growth was indicated later (April 28, 1958) by Allen W. Dulles: "Annual growth over-all has been running between 6 and 7 per cent, annual growth of industry between 10 and 12 per cent" (*New York Times*, April 29, 1958, p. 8).

The figures for the other countries are averages of the annual percentage changes from 1950 to 1956 as given in *World Economic Survey 1956*, p. 155, and *World Economic Report, 1953-54*, pp. 24, 31.

f These "guesstimates" are based, though not according to any prescribed formula, on the growth rates shown in the other columns. In the case of the USSR, somewhat more weight is given to recent years than to earlier ones, which involved transitional difficulties that need not be repeated. Also, since we are concerned with economic strength *for* defense, not strength *during* a war, the non-war years are probably of greater significance than those of World War II.

Soviet Union less vulnerable to submarine attack than the United States. The comparative vulnerability of the United States on these counts makes it costly for the West to achieve a retaliatory deterrent force. The Soviet Union may also have advantages in attracting the support of "neutrals." It can show impressive growth rates by restricting the role of consumers' sovereignty. Central planning is more glamorous (to those who have not lived with it) than attempts to promote individualism. Moreover, freedom of movement and speech in a free nation produces a steady flow of emissaries and pronouncements, some of which are sure to be offensive to neutral nations. Finally, the process of decision-making in an authoritarian country may increase the chances of keeping its intentions secret and therefore increase the number of contingencies against which the other nations must plan.

These are some of the extra-budgetary strengths and weaknesses that should be kept in mind. They are part of the resources available for defense, and serve to reinforce the conclusion that the Soviet Union can outstrip the free nations in building military forces and upset the balance of terror — if the Western nations base their choices on wishful thinking.

# PART II.  EFFICIENCY IN USING DEFENSE RESOURCES

# 7. EFFICIENCY IN MILITARY DECISIONS[1]

In this Part we will assume that the amount of the nation's resources to be devoted to military use has been determined. Our problem is: How can we use these resources efficiently to buy military power, or more broadly, national security? Actually, the solutions to the problems of Parts I and II are interdependent to some extent, and, as noted earlier, analyses of the sort to be described in Part II are important in appraising the effectiveness of defense programs and therefore in deciding upon their size. However, we must usually tackle these choices — the size of the budget and the effective use of that budget — one at a time, making reasonable assumptions about one choice while analyzing the other.

While the efficient allocation or use of resources has always been the core problem of economic theory, economists have until recently made little attempt to apply the theory to military, or indeed any governmental, expenditure. A possible explanation is the small proportion of national resources formerly devoted to the military sector (indeed to the whole government) in the United States and other Western countries except in wartime. Now with the prospect of United States national security expenditure continuing indefinitely at 10 per cent or more of GNP and total government expenditure (including state and local) at two to three times this level,[2] the efficient use of the very large resources involved has become a matter of primary importance.

The reason the efficient use of military (and other government) resources is a special problem is the absence of any built-in mechanisms, like those in the private sector of the economy, which lead to greater efficiency. There is within government neither a price mechanism which points the way to greater efficiency, nor competitive forces which induce government units to carry out each function at minimum cost. Because of the lure of profits and the threat of bankruptcy, private firms are under pressure to seek out profitable innovations and efficient methods. In this search they have often used, and are now using to an increasing extent,

[1] See also the Appendix, "The Simple Mathematics of Maximization," at the end of this volume. Also pertinent are the articles in "Economics and Operations Research: A Symposium," *Review of Economics and Statistics,* August 1958, pp. 195–229.

[2] A great deal of what is said in this Part about the efficient use of resources by the military applies equally to many other kinds of government expenditure.

formal quantitative analysis. But even if they do not, continued progress and increased efficiency still tend to come about, though less rapidly. After all, *some* firm is likely to discover more efficient methods through trial and error even in the absence of systematic analysis. Subsequently, other firms observing the resulting profits copy the innovation; those that fail to do so (that is, those who make inferior choices of methods) begin to suffer losses, and hence tend to be eliminated by the process of "natural selection." [3]

In government, by contrast, there is no profit lure, and promotions or salary increases do not depend on profits. In most operations, an objective criterion of efficiency is not readily available, and even if it were, incentives to seek profitable innovations and efficient (least cost) methods are not strong. There is scope for "Parkinson's law," [4] personal idiosyncrasy, and uneconomic preferences of officials to take hold, because the costs of choosing inefficient policies do not impinge upon the choosers.[5]

Finally, the process of natural selection, whose working depends upon the degree and type of rivalry, operates only weakly, if at all, to eliminate wasteful governments or government departments. The federal government, for instance, competes only with the political party that is out of office, and survival in this competition depends upon many factors other than efficiency in the use of resources. Thus, there is neither an adequate price mechanism to reveal the cheapest methods of performing public functions nor any force which induces or compels the government to adopt such methods.[6]

## THREE GENERAL APPROACHES

What, in these circumstances, can be done? We want efficiency; we want to obtain the greatest possible security from a given budget, both because national security is itself of such transcendent importance, and because the more efficient the use of the military budget the more resources we can have for nonmilitary purposes. But how, in a sector containing 10 per cent of the economy (much more if we include civilian

[3] A. Alchian, "Uncertainty, Evolution, and Economic Theory," *The Journal of Political Economy*, LVIII, June 1950, pp. 211–221. The prevention of mistakes by systematic analysis would be a cheaper path to progress than their correction by natural selection — *if* the analyses always led to correct policies. On the difficulties of correct analysis we will have much to say below.

[4] C. Northcote Parkinson, *Parkinson's Law: and Other Studies in Administration,* Houghton Mifflin Co., Boston, 1957.

[5] For a provocative discussion of this matter, see the paper by A. Alchian and R. Kessel presented at the Universities-National Bureau of Economics Research Conference on Labor Economics in April, 1960.

[6] In a few government activities, e.g., the Military Sea Transport Service, simulation of the market mechanism is attempted. The possibilities and limitations of such market simulation within the government are discussed in Chapter 12.

government functions) with no adequate price mechanism and no institutions forcing natural selection of the efficient, can we achieve efficiency?

There are three possible approaches, interrelated and interdependent, which will be considered in this part of the book.

1. The improvement of institutional arrangements within the government to promote efficiency. Extreme proposals have been made which would simulate price and market mechanisms within the government. Less ambitious proposals would improve budgeting and accounting methods (see Chapter 4), attempt to provide more appropriate incentives, and reorganize the apparatus of decision making.

2. Increased reliance on systematic quantitative analysis to determine the most efficient alternative allocations and methods.

3. Increased recognition and awareness that military decisions, whether they specifically involve budgetary allocations or not, are in one of their important aspects economic decisions; and that unless the right questions are asked, the appropriate alternatives selected for comparison, and an economic criterion used for choosing the most efficient, military power and national security will suffer.

It is our conviction that something can be accomplished by the third approach alone — that is, by improved understanding of the nature of the problem — even without greater use of systematic quantitative analysis and with no changes in governmental structure. In formulating policy it does help to ask the right questions instead of the wrong ones. If the alternatives are arrayed, and a serious attempt made to apply sound criteria in choosing the most efficient ones, decisions are likely to be improved even though the considerations brought to bear are mainly qualitative and intuitive. There are enough responsible and highly motivated persons involved in the decision-making process — officers, civil servants, members of the Cabinet, Congressmen, and influential citizens — to make education in principles worthwhile for its own sake.

What may be even more important, as we shall see, is that any real improvement in the methods of quantitative analysis or in government structure to achieve economy is absolutely dependent upon a firm grasp of these principles. Quantitative analyses that are addressed to the wrong question or administrative devices that promote the wrong kind of economizing can easily do more harm than good.

The role of systematic quantitative analysis in military decisions is potentially much more important than in the private sector of the economy. It is obviously more important than in households because the problems are typically so much more complex. We all know families that manage well on their incomes, and families that manage poorly, apparently attaining a lower standard of life or running into recurrent financial difficulties despite apparently adequate incomes. Some of the good family managers may rely heavily on systematic quantitative analysis — on elaborate budget calculations, the studies of consumers' research organizations, and so on. But others do not, and in general we find little correlation between goodness of household management and reliance on systematic quantitative analysis. The overwhelmingly important factors are a firm grasp of principles and good sense or judgment. The quantitative relations are usually familiar, and simple enough for a man or woman of average intelligence to work out intuitively or in the margin of an account book.

In many military problems, however, this is not true. The quantitative relations may involve many different fields of technology as well as operational factors, and are sometimes so intricate that elaborate computations are necessary. There is almost never anyone who has an intuitive grasp of all the fields of knowledge that are relevant. For example, if we are comparing the relative merits of a high performance fighter and a cheaper fighter with somewhat lower performance, it is easy to see, qualitatively, that the more expensive aircraft will do better in a two-plane duel, but that we can have more aircraft on a billion dollar budget and thereby more interceptions and duels if we choose the plane with lower unit cost. But the problem is essentially quantitative, and depends upon fairly precise answers being developed to three questions: *How many* more of the cheaper plane can be procured and maintained on a billion dollar budget? What are the relative values of numbers and various performance characteristics in interception? *How much* better is the high performance plane in a duel? In some special cases we may be able to assemble a group of "experts," each of whom has a good intuitive grasp of the factors relevant for answering one of these subquestions, and after discussion emerge with a fairly unequivocal answer. But in general, and especially where, as is usually the case, the choice is not between two but among many, systematic quantitative analysis will help — or prove essential.

For a somewhat different reason systematic quantitative analysis is more important in military than in private business decisions. There is, as we have seen, an alternative process for achieving efficiency in private business — competition and natural selection — which would be fairly effective even if the variations in techniques were random. In government this alternative does not exist. Efficient techniques and policies have to be selected consciously; and wherever the relevant factors are diverse and complex, as they frequently are, unaided intuition is incapable of weighing them and making an efficient decision.

Sound analyses, it might be noted, can not only help identify efficient courses of action but can also improve incentives. The existence of good analyses cannot alter penalties and rewards so that "what is good for the chief of each department is also good for national security"; but their existence, in conjunction with rivalry between departments, may increase the cost to decision-makers of making uneconomic decisions. That is, the existence of sound analyses plus rival branches or departments that may make use of the arguments to get their budgets increased can cause each department to veer toward more efficient policies.

The possible utility of improved institutional arrangements for promoting the efficient use of resources by government departments has been the subject of much debate. This has in the past been the province, perhaps too exclusively, of the management efficiency experts. As economists we will not have much to say about government organization and structure.[7] We believe, however, that what we say about criteria and methods of analysis can help in judging the efficacy of alternative organizational forms and that the development of practical institutions which encourage efficiency deserves far more attention than we or other economists have yet given it. It should at least be possible to remove some of the perverse incentives injected by such factors as special constraints, the premium placed on getting budgets raised rather than using budgets more efficiently, and cost-plus-fixed-fee contracts. There must be some way to provide postmasters and depot managers with more appropriate motivations, as well as to improve the government's decision-making machinery.

## OPTIMAL, EFFICIENT, AND FEASIBLE POSITIONS

We have so far used the term "efficient" in a vague and general sense to mean "making good use" (including "making the best use") of available resources. Much of the time, though, we have in mind a more precise meaning for this term. We can best define it by contrasting "efficient," "optimal," and "feasible" positions.[8]

In order to reach an *optimal* solution to problems of choice, we must be able to value various "situations" or outputs. Then we can revise our choices and shift resources to get the maximum value that is possible in the face of whatever constraints confront us. Even if we cannot always compare the values of different outputs, however, we can find some positions that yield more of some valuable outputs without yielding less of any others. When we cannot produce more of one output without sacrificing another, we have reached an *efficient* position. Many other situations are *feasible*, of course, by using the resources inefficiently. The differences

[7] But see Chapter 12.
[8] The conditions for economic efficiency are examined more rigorously and in greater detail in the Appendix, "The Simple Mathematics of Maximization," at the end of this study.

between efficient positions and the others will be clearer if we consider a simple example.

### ONE INPUT, TWO OUTPUTS

Suppose that we are concerned with the allocation of a military budget, fixed at $B billion, between the procurement (and maintenance in a state of readiness) of two forces — say, a strategic bombing force and an air defense force. Suppose further, for the sake of simplicity in this example, that the effectiveness of the strategic bombing force can be measured by a single number — the expected number of enemy targets that it could destroy after D Day — and that the effectiveness of the air defense force can be similarly measured by its "kill potential" — the number of attacking enemy bombers it could be expected to shoot down in certain circumstances.

We can draw a production-possibility curve, as in Figure 2, representing all possible *maximum* combinations of target destruction and kill

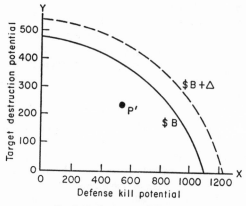

**Fig. 2. Production possibility curve**

potential which we can buy with $B billion — maximum in the sense that the fraction of the budget allocated to the strategic bombing force is spent in such a way as to maximize the target destruction potential of the force, and the fraction allocated to air defense is so spent as to maximize kill potential.[9] The Y intercept represents the target destruction potential that we could achieve by spending all $B billions on the strategic air force, the X intercept the kill potential from spending all on air defense.

[9] The estimation of the points on this curve is, of course, the job of systematic quantitative analysis. The curves in this chapter are purely hypothetical.

An efficient use of resources, in the technical sense, is one which makes it impossible to increase one valuable output without increasing a valuable input or decreasing another valuable output. It is apparent that each point on our curve represents an efficient use of resources in this sense; the curve is therefore a locus of "efficient points." At any point on the curve it is possible to increase target destruction only by moving to the left along the curve; that is, by decreasing kill potential, or by moving to a higher curve (dotted in Figure 2) representing a larger budget ($B + \triangle$ billion).

All points such as P' lying below and to the left of the curve of efficient points represent inefficient uses of resources, and are therefore called "inefficient points." They do, however, represent *feasible* uses of a budget of $B billion. We can draw up a plan to spend $B billion inefficiently to achieve a target destruction potential of only 200 and an air defense kill potential of only 500 — probably all too easily. But if we did have such a plan, we could revise it, without additional budget, to increase target destruction potential without decreasing kill potential (or vice versa). We can always find several efficient points which are unequivocally superior to an inefficient point.

Note that the points lying above and to the right of the curve on Figure 2 are simply *infeasible* on a budget of $B billion. The efficient points form a boundary between the feasible and the infeasible points.

But which of the infinity of efficient points should our military planners choose? At one extreme there is an efficient point providing no offensive capability, at the other extreme an efficient point providing no defensive capability. While both may be efficient in a technical sense, at least one and possibly both would be disastrous for the security of the United States. Technical efficiency is not a sufficient condition for economic choice.

In principle the answer is easy: We want to choose that efficient point which maximizes the "utility" or "military worth" of the combined forces. In practice, as we shall see in Chapter 9, the explicit measurement of military worth frequently presents formidable difficulties. If we abstract from these difficulties for the moment in order to clarify definitions, we can draw curves (called indifference curves) that reflect our preference for some combinations of target destruction and kill potential over others (Figure 3). Combinations represented on a curve to the right and higher (more of both goods) are obviously preferred to combinations on a curve to the left and lower (less of both). We are indifferent among combinations represented by different points on any single curve; we are willing to sacrifice some defense potential if we can obtain thereby a sufficiently enhanced offensive potential, and vice versa. Indifference curves are typically convex to the origin, which means that the more of

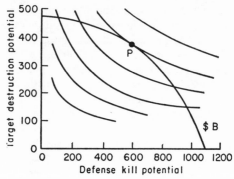

Fig. 3. Indifference curves and optimal point

one good (for example, offense) we give up, the less willing we are to sacrifice still more, and therefore the larger the increment of the other (for example, defense) we insist upon having in compensation.[10]

The *optimal* use of our $B billion budget is represented by the point of tangency of the original curve of Figure 2 with an indifference curve (Point P of Figure 3). From this point it is not possible to improve our position (that is, move to a higher indifference curve representing a preferred combination) by any change in allocation or use of resources.

If all portions of the production-possibility curve are not concave to the origin, there may be complications. The shape of this curve depends upon whether the costs of producing the goods measured on the axes are increasing or decreasing. Or, to put the matter another way, the shape depends upon whether the returns per extra dollar expended on the outputs are decreasing or increasing. Returns can usually be assumed to be decreasing, making the production-possibility curve concave to the origin. But there are troublesome counter-examples; for example, returns in terms of defense kill potential might be increasing if we consider extra outlays on plugging gaps in an almost completed radar line.[11] If there are increasing returns and part of the curve has a peculiar shape, we have to look at large reallocations as well as small ones.[12] We may find

[10] The incremental amount of Y we need to compensate for an incremental loss of X is the slope of the indifference curve at any point. It is the rate at which we are willing to trade one for the other.

[11] Many, plausible examples of "increasing returns," however, are really examples of rectifying errors, which can be done by redesigning one's proposal, not solely by expanding outlays along one axis or the other. If I forget to include a bathroom in my plans for a new house, and therefore the addition of a bathroom has a high payoff, is it correct to say that house construction is an example of increasing returns?

[12] Malcolm W. Hoag, "Some Complexities in Military Planning," *World Politics*, July 1959, pp. 553–576.

For more on these possible complications, see the Appendix at the end of this volume.

more than one point of tangency between the production-possibility curve and the indifference curves, or we may find no point of tangency and the highest indifference curve may be attained where the production-possibility curve intercepts one of the axes (that is, it may then be best to spend the entire budget on the item that yields increasing returns).

The frequent difficulty in locating *the* optimal point by systematic quantitative analysis, while unfortunate, should not be regarded as disastrous in all or even most practical problems of military choice. In the first place, decision-makers or their advisers who have thought deeply about a problem are likely to have shrewd ideas about the sector of the curve containing the optimal point, even if they cannot provide a mathematical proof of its exact location. If systematic quantitative analysis can narrow the choice to a set of efficient points, the burden placed upon intuitive judgment is reduced and the quality of judgment should be improved. Secondly, optima are characteristically flat, like the crest of Half Dome rather than the peak of the Matterhorn. It isn't usually important to find the precise peak or point of tangency. On Figure 3 one can move along the opportunity curve for some distance on either side of the point of tangency without getting far from the highest attainable indifference curve.

In the third place, *the best practical aim of systematic quantitative analysis is to demonstrate that some course of action A is better than some alternative course of action B,* when B is what is proposed, or planned, or will otherwise occur. If B is an inefficient point, systematic quantitative analysis can find several efficient points A, A', A", . . . which can be shown to be superior to B even if nothing is known about military worth except that certain capabilities, like target destruction and air defense kill potential, contribute to it (see Figure 4).

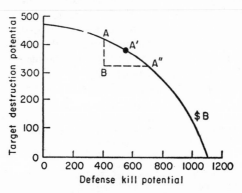

**Fig. 4. Efficient points versus inefficient points**

Let us emphasize once more that this concept of seeking efficient points is extremely important. For while we cannot usually find optimal, or second-best, or even $j$th-best, solutions, it frequently enables us to identify improvements over existing or proposed policies.[13]

## TWO INPUTS, ONE OUTPUT

In the preceding example we considered a planning problem that involved the allocation of a single valuable input (a budget) to produce two valuable outputs (target destruction potential and defense kill potential). The extension of this case to three or more outputs raises no new problems, although diagrammatic representation in two dimensions is no longer possible. If there are three outputs, the production-possibility and indifference curves become three-dimensional surfaces; if n, they are n-dimensional surfaces.

Problems involving two or more inputs do, however, require a somewhat different, although analogous, approach. Consider first the simplest of these, where there are two valuable inputs and only one valuable output. We might, as an example, take a subproblem of our first example, namely, the procurement of a strategic air force which will maximize target destruction. Suppose, for simplicity of analysis, that only two valuable inputs are required by a strategic air force — say bomber aircraft and bombs.[14] We will continue to assume, again grossly simplifying reality, that the output or objective of the strategic air force can be measured as a single dimension — expected number of targets destroyed. We may estimate by systematic quantitative analysis and plot the maximum potential destruction with varying numbers and combinations of bombs and bombers. (See Figure 5.) We estimate, say, that with 400 bombs and 400 bombers the best we can achieve, with the best tactical employment of the bomber force, is the expected destruction of 200 targets, represented by point P (that is, we estimate that 50 per cent of the bombers, each armed with a bomb, will be attrited or will miss the target). Similarly, we estimate that it would take 250 bombs and 250 bombers to destroy 100 targets (point P'): the expected attrition rate will be higher with a smaller strike force.

With what other combinations of bombs and bombers can we expect

[13] The difficulties of determining second-best policies have received some well-deserved attention in recent years. See I. M. D. Little, *A Critique of Welfare Economics,* Clarendon Press, Oxford, 1950, especially Chapter VII, pp. 110–120, and Chapter XV, pp. 267–272; J. E. Meade, *The Theory of International Economic Policy,* Vol. II, *Trade and Welfare,* Oxford University Press, London, 1955, Chapter VII, "The Marginal Conditions for the Second-Best," pp. 102–118; R. G. Lipsey and K. Lancaster, "The General Theory of Second Best," *Review of Economic Studies,* 1956–57, pp. 11–32; and M. J. Farrell, "In Defense of Public-Utility Price Theory," *Oxford Economic Papers,* February 1958, pp. 109–123.

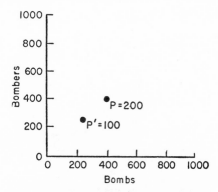

Fig. 5. Substitution between bombs and bombers

to destroy 200 targets? Of course, with many possible combinations. As is typically the case in military (and other) operations, one valuable input may be substituted for another — within broad limits. There is no necessity to plan to use the same number of bombs and bombers. If the number of bombers exceeds the number of bombs, the aircraft not carrying bombs can serve a useful function as escorts, cutting down the attrition of the bomb carriers. If the number of bombs exceeds the number of bombers, some bombers can carry more than one bomb, attacking targets in sequence; or, alternatively, bombers surviving the first strike can be sent on a second. Of course, as we continue to substitute one input for the other, substitution will become more and more difficult. It will require at least 200 bombs to destroy 200 targets, no matter how many bombers we have at our disposal. Similarly some minimum number of aircraft will be needed to penetrate enemy defenses and deliver bombs on 200 targets, no matter how plentiful the bombs.

The locus of point P, showing the combinations of bombs and bombers which, with best tactical employment, can be expected to destroy 200 targets, is therefore a curve (known in economic theory as an "isoquant") convex to the origin and more or less asymptotic, at both extremes, to lines parallel to the X and Y axes (see Figure 6). The locus of the point P' (expected destruction = 100 targets) will be a curve of similar shape closer to the origin. Other isoquants can be estimated for any given level of expected target destruction — the best tactical employment

<sup>14</sup> We will assume in this example that bombs must be paid for by the Air Force, as if the Atomic Energy Commission managed bomb production as an "industrial fund" or business. It is apparent that military forces should be planned *as if* bombs were costly inputs whether funds are actually transferred or not. See Stephen Enke, "Some Economic Aspects of Fissionable Material," *Quarterly Journal of Economics,* Vol. 68, May 1954, pp. 217–232.

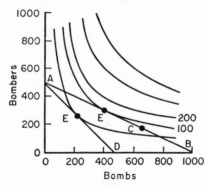

Fig. 6. Isoquants and exchange curves

being assumed for the combination of bombs and bombers represented by each point.

The use of resources is "efficient" in this case with a single valuable output or objective, where it is impossible to increase the output without increasing the use of at least one of the valuable inputs.

In Figure 6 every point on each of the isoquants represents an efficient use of resources. It is therefore possible to move to a higher isoquant (that is, destroy more targets) only by increasing the use of at least one valuable input (bombs or bombers).

But which of this infinity of efficient points is *optimal*? In order to answer this question, we must have a measure of the relative costs[15] of bombs and bombers. Suppose, again for simplicity of exposition, that the costs of both bombs and bombers are constant, that two bombs can always be exchanged for one bomber. We can now immediately determine the optimal combination of bombs and bombers for any allocation of budget to the strategic air force. If the budget is sufficient to buy 500 bombers (all spent on bombers) or 1,000 bombs (all spent on bombs), the optimal combination of bombs and bombers to procure is represented by point E on Figure 6. At this point the "exchange" curve (the straight line A-B) showing the combinations which may be procured with the given budget is tangent to a target isoquant — the highest isoquant which it can attain.

Let us go over the meaning of these curves again in order to make them clear. The exchange curve shows the way the inputs can be exchanged (in buying or producing them) while keeping the total budget constant. The isoquant shows the way the inputs can be substituted for each other while keeping the quantity of output constant. When the

[15] The problems of defining the appropriate measure of costs are postponed to Chapter 9.

two curves are tangent, as at point E on Figure 6, no further substitution of one input for the other can increase the output.[16] The only way to increase output in those circumstances would be to get a larger budget.

Other points such as C on the exchange curve would be non-optimal. For exchange curves representing different budgets, there would be other optimal points, of course. The expected target destruction so calculated for all hypothetical budget allocations to the strategic air force (the budget being divided among inputs in each case in the optimal manner) was part of the information needed for the construction of the production-possibility curve in our first example, shown in Figure 2.

A number of interesting and characteristic relations between inputs and outputs may be "read off" Figure 6. Suppose that the price of bombs is higher — one bomb exchanging, say, for one bomber as in the exchange curve AD. In that circumstance, the optimal combination will tend to contain a smaller ratio of bombs to bombers, and appropriate tactics economizing on bombs will have to be used. With a higher price for bombs, the target destruction potential at any given budget level will be reduced, but not by as much if the ratio of bombs to bombers is optimally adjusted as if this ratio is left unchanged. We can also use this diagram to see how much the budget would have to be increased to maintain the same target destruction potential with a higher price for bombs: more bombers and fewer bombs would be purchased with the larger budget.

If the quantity of one input is limited (for example, if no more than, say, 300 bombs may be obtained from the Atomic Energy Commission at any price) the exchange curves become vertical at this point, as in Figure 7. Increments of high budgets must all be spent on bombers, and tactics optimally adjusted to whatever bomb/bomber ratio results. Calculations of this kind can be used to estimate how much additional bomb production would be worth — in terms of bombers and therefore also in terms of dollars. In the hypothetical example shown in Figure 7, the target destruction that can be achieved with a maximum of 300 bombs available and a budget equivalent to 600 bombers could be achieved with a budget equivalent to 500 bombers if bombs were continuously available at half the cost of bombers. In other words, the additional bombs would be "worth" 100 bombers more than their cost.

The extension of this case to three or more valuable inputs requires nothing more than the abandonment of plane geometry. For an examination of the general case and a more rigorous discussion of economic efficiency, we refer the reader to the Appendix on "The Simple Mathe-

---

[16] The slope of the exchange curve indicates the trade-offs possible in buying the inputs. It is the ratio of their marginal or incremental costs — the latter being the extra cost of buying an additional unit of each item. The slope of the isoquant similarly indicates the trade-offs possible in using the inputs. At the point of tangency these slopes, or trade-off possibilities, are equal.

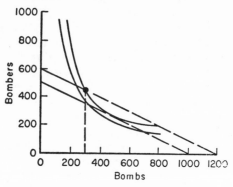

Fig. 7. Exchange curves with special constraints

matics of Maximization." Here let us turn to the use of economic analysis in the search for more efficient courses of action.

### THE ELEMENTS OF AN ECONOMIC ANALYSIS

The essence of economic choice in military planning is not quantitative analysis: calculation may or may not be necessary or useful, depending upon the problem and what is known about it. The essential thing is the comparison of all the relevant alternatives from the point of view of the objectives each can accomplish and the costs which it involves; and the selection of the best (or a "good") alternative through the use of appropriate economic criteria.

The elements of a military problem of economic choice, whether its solution requires advanced mathematics, high speed computing equipment, or just straight hard thinking, are therefore the following:[17]

1. An objective or objectives. What military (or other national) aim or aims are we trying to accomplish with the forces, equipments, projects, or tactics that the analysis is designed to compare? Choice of objectives is fundamental: if it is wrongly made, the whole analysis is addressed to the wrong question. For instance, we assumed in example 1 above that the sole objective of air defense is the slaughter of enemy aircraft: if in fact one of its major objectives is the early identification of an enemy attack and the provision of tactical warning to United States targets, the force we selected in example 1 is unlikely to be either optimal or efficient.

2. Alternatives. By what alternative forces, equipments, projects, tactics, and so on, may the objective be accomplished? The alternatives are frequently referred to as *systems*[18] because each combines all the

---

[17] These elements will be shown "in action" in the next Chapter — "An Illustrative Application of Economic Analysis."

[18] Hence "systems analysis," a term frequently applied to complex quantitative analyses.

elements — men, machines, and the tactics of their employment — needed to accomplish the objective. System A may differ from System B in only one respect (for example, in number of bombs per bomber), or in several (number of bombs per bomber, number of strikes, and so on), but both are complete systems, however many elements they have in common. The great problem in choosing alternatives to compare is to be sure that all the good alternatives have been included. Frequently we lack the imagination to do this at the beginning of an analysis; we think of better alternatives (that is, invent new systems) as the analysis proceeds and we learn more about the problem. The invention of new and better systems in this fashion is indeed one of the principal payoffs from this kind of analysis.

3. Costs or resources used. Each alternative method of accomplishing the objective, or in other words each system, involves the incurring of certain costs or the using up of certain resources (these are different phrases to describe the same phenomena). Costs are the negative values in the analysis (as the objectives are positive values). The resources required may be general (as is commonly the case in problems of long-range planning), or highly specific (as in most tactical problems), or mixed. Some of the difficult problems of which costs to include and how to measure them are considered in Chapter 9.

4. A model or models. Models are abstract representations of reality which help us to perceive significant relations in the real world, to manipulate them, and thereby predict others. They may take any of numerous forms. Some are small-scale physical representations of reality, like model aircraft in a wind tunnel. Many are simply representations on paper — like mathematical models. Or, finally, they may be simple sets of relationships that are sketched out in the mind and not formally put down on paper. In no case are models photographic reproductions of reality; if they were, they would be so complicated that they would be of no use to us. They have to abstract from a great deal of the real world — focusing upon what is relevant for the problem at hand, ignoring what is irrelevant. Whether or not one model is better than another depends not on its complexity, or its appearance of reality, but solely on whether it gives better predictions (and thereby helps us to make better decisions).[19] In systems analyses models of one type or another are required to trace the relations between inputs and outputs, resources and objectives, for each of the systems to be compared, so that we can predict the relevant consequences of choosing any system.

[19] Bombardiers once bombed visually, using simple models in their heads to estimate the bomb's trajectory in relation to the target. Modern bombsights use mathematical models, requiring high speed computers for solution, to make the same estimate. The model used by the modern bombsight is better only if its predictions are more accurate — a question of fact which has to be tested by experiment.

5. A criterion. By "criterion" we mean the test by which we choose one alternative or system rather than another. The choice of an appropriate economic criterion is frequently the central problem in designing a systems analysis. In principle, the criterion we want is clear enough: the optimal system is the one which yields the greatest excess of positive values (objectives) over negative values (resources used up, or costs). But as we have already seen, this clear-cut ideal solution is seldom a practical possibility in military problems.[20] Objectives and costs usually have no common measure: there is no generally acceptable way to subtract dollars spent or aircraft lost from enemy targets destroyed. Moreover, as in two of the cases above, there may be multiple objectives or multiple costs that are incommensurable. So in most military analyses we have to be satisfied with some approximation to the ideal criterion that will enable us to say, not that some system A is optimal, but that it is better than some other proposed systems B, C, and so on. In many cases we will have to be content with calculating efficient rather than optimal systems, relying on the intuitive judgment of well-informed people (of whom the analyst may be one) to select one of the efficient systems in the neighborhood of the optimum. The choice of criteria is the subject of Chapter 9.

It cannot be stated too frequently or emphasized enough that economic choice is *a way of looking at problems* and does not necessarily depend upon the use of any analytic aids or computational devices. Some analytic aids (mathematical models) and computing machinery are quite likely to be useful in analyzing complex military problems, but there are many military problems in which they have not proved particularly useful where, nevertheless, it is rewarding to array the alternatives and think through their implications in terms of objectives and costs. Where mathematical models and computations are useful, they are in no sense alternatives to or rivals of good intuitive judgment; they supplement and complement it. Judgment is always of critical importance in designing the analysis, choosing the alternatives to be compared, and selecting the criterion. Except where there is a completely satisfactory one-dimensional measurable objective (a rare circumstance), judgment must supplement the quantitative analysis before a choice can be recommended.

## THE REQUIREMENTS APPROACH

In the absence of systematic analysis in terms of objectives and costs, a procedure that might be called the "requirements approach" is commonly used in the military departments and throughout much of the government. Staff officers inspect a problem, say, the defense of the continental United States or the design of the next generation of heavy

[20] In private industry this "ideal" criterion is the familiar one of profit maximization.

bomber, draft a plan which seems to solve the problem, and determine requirements from the plan. Then feasibility is checked: Can the "required" performance characteristics, such as some designated speed and range, be achieved? Can the necessary budget be obtained? Does the nation have the necessary resources in total? If the program passes the feasibility tests, it is adopted; if it fails, some adjustments have to be made. But the question: What are the payoffs *and the costs* of alternative programs? may not be explicity asked during the process of setting the requirement or deciding upon the budget. In fact, officials have on occasion boasted that their stated "requirements" have been based on need alone.

This, of course, is an illusion. Some notion of cost (money, resources, time), however imprecise, is implicit in the recognition of any limitation. Military departments frequently determine "requirements" which are from 10 to 25 per cent higher than the available budget, but never ten times as high, and seldom twice as high. But this notion of cost merely rules out grossly infeasible programs. It does not help in making optimal or efficient choices.

For that purpose it is essential that alternative ways of achieving military objectives be costed, and that choices be made on the basis of payoff and cost. How *are* choices made by military planners prior to any costing of alternatives? We have never heard any satisfying explanation. As we noted in our discussion of Figure 6, a good or efficient choice depends upon the relative costs of different resources or inputs; there was no "good" bomb/bomber combination or tactic independent of cost. The derivation of requirements by any process that fails to cost alternatives can result in good solutions only by accident. Probably military planners sometimes weigh relative costs in some crude manner, at least subconsciously, even when they deny they do; or they make choices on the basis of considerations which ought to be secondary or tertiary, such as the preservation of an existing command structure, or the matching of a reported foreign accomplishment.

The defects of the requirements approach can be seen clearly if we think of applying it to our problems as a consumer. Suppose the consumer mulls over his transportation problem and decides, "on the basis of need alone," that he requires a new Cadillac. It is "the best" car he knows, and besides Jones drives one. So he buys a Cadillac, ignoring cost and ignoring therefore the sacrifices he is making in other directions by buying "the best." There are numerous alternative ways of solving the consumer's transportation problem (as there are always numerous ways of solving a military problem), and a little costing of alternatives prior to purchase might have revealed that the purchase of "the best" instrument is not *necessarily* an optimal choice. Perhaps if the consumer had purchased a Pontiac or a secondhand Cadillac he would have saved enough to maintain and operate it and take an occasional trip.[21] Or if he had purchased a Chevrolet he could have afforded to keep his old car and become head of a two-car family. One of these alternatives, properly costed and compared, might have promised a far greater amount of utility for the consumer than the purchase of a new Cadillac "on the basis of need alone." Or the exercise might have reassured the consumer that the new Cadillac was indeed optimal. While expensive unit equipment is not necessarily optimal, in some cases it can be proved to be.

### THE PRIORITIES APPROACH

Another procedure that seems to have a great deal of appeal, in both military planning and other government activities, is the "priorities approach." To facilitate a decision about how to spend a specified budget, the desirable items are ranked according to the urgency with which they are needed. The result is a list of things that might be bought, the ones that are more important being near the top and the ones that are less important being near the bottom. Lists that rank several hundred weapons and items have sometimes been generated in the military services.

At first blush, this appears to be a commendable and systematic way to tackle the problem. When one reflects a bit, however, the usefulness and significance of such a list begins to evaporate. Consider the following items ranked according to their (hypothetical) priorities: (1) Missile X, (2) Radar device Y, (3) Cargo aircraft Z. How do you use such a ranking? Does it mean that the entire budget should be spent on the first item? Probably not, for it is usually foolish to allocate all of a budget to a single weapon or object. Besides, if a budget is to be so allocated, the ranking of the items below the first one has no significance.

Does the ranking mean that the money should go to the first item until no additional amount is needed, then to the second item until no further amount is needed, and so on? Hardly, because there could be some need for more of Missile X almost without limit. Even if only a limited amount of Missile X was available, to keep buying right out to this limit would usually be a foolish rule. After quite a few Missile X's were purchased, the next dollar could better be spent on some other item. Even using lifeboats for women and children first is foolish if a sailor or doctor on each lifeboat can save many lives.

Perhaps a priority list means that we should spend more money on the higher-priority items than on those having a lower priority. But this

[21] Costing in our sense is never simply the cost of a unit of equipment; it is always the cost of a complete system including everything that must be purchased with the equipment and the cost of maintaining and operating it. See the next section below and Chapter 8, pp. 136–139.

makes little sense, since some of the items high on the list, for example, the radar device, may cost little per unit and call at most for a relatively small amount of money; while some lower-ranking purchases, such as the cargo aircraft, may call for comparatively large sums if they are to be purchased at all. In any event, the priorities reveal nothing about how much more should be spent on particular items.

Just how anyone can use such a list is not clear. Suppose a consumer lists possible items for his monthly budget in the order of their priority and he feels that in some sense they rank as follows: (1) groceries, (2) gas and oil, (3) cigarettes, (4) repairs to house, (5) liquor, and (6) steam baths. This does not mean that he will spend all of his funds on groceries, nor does it mean that he will spend nothing on liquor or steam baths. His problem is really to allocate his budget among these different objects. He would like to choose the allocation such that an extra dollar on cigarettes is just as important to him as an extra dollar on groceries. At the margin, therefore, the objects of expenditure would be equally important (except for those that are not purchased at all).

The notion of priority stems from the very sensible proposition that one should do "first things first." It makes sense, or at least the top priority does, when one considers the use of a small increment of resources or time. If one thinks about the use of an extra dollar or of the next half-hour of his time, it is sensible to ask, "What is the most urgent — the first-priority — item?" If one is deciding what to do with a budget or with the next eight hours, however, he ordinarily faces a problem of *allocation,* not of setting priorities. A list of priorities does not face the problem or help solve it.

Thus in formulating defense policy and choosing weapon systems, we have to decide how much effort or how many resources should go to each item. The "priorities approach" does not solve the allocation problem and can even trap us into adopting foolish policies.[22]

## SOME MISUNDERSTANDINGS

There is some resistance to the use of economic analysis in military problems that is based on misunderstanding.

An economically efficient solution to military problems does not imply a cheap force or a small military budget. It simply implies that whatever the military budget (or other limitation, for example, on personnel), the greatest military capabilities are developed. Since military capabilities are plural and not easily commensurate, an efficient military

[22] For a revealing discussion of priority lists, see *Military Construction Appropriations for 1958,* Hearings before the Subcommittee of the Committee on Appropriations, House of Representatives, 85th Congress, 1st Session, U.S. Government Printing Office, Washington, D.C., 1957, pp. 420–427.

establishment, in the technical sense, would merely be one in which no single capability — anti-submarine, ground warfare, offensive air, and so on — could be increased without decreasing another. An optimal establishment would in addition have the right "balance" among capabilities — a harder problem for analysis.

From the point of view of the nation, of the military establishment as a whole,[23] and of the Treasury Department, the achievement of efficiency and the approach to an optimal solution can be a common objective. There is a conflict of interest between the Treasury, the Bureau of the Budget, and economy-minded Congressmen on the one hand, and the military services on the other when the level of the budget is in question. The military services always (and properly) want more; the economizers always (and also properly) offer resistance, or try to impose reductions. But once the budget has been determined, there is no longer conflict of interest.

In fact the choices that maximize military capability for a given budget are the same choices that minimize the cost of attaining that capability. As we shall see in Chapter 9, the capability-maximizing criterion (given budget) and cost-minimizing criterion (given capability) are logically equivalent and therefore lead to the same choices and the same programs (for any given scale of operations, as determined by either budget or capability). If an Atlas missile system maximizes our strategic air power for a given SAC budget, it also minimizes the cost of providing that much strategic air power.

Some officers object to economic analysis because they think it implies cheap equipment, or the continued use of obsolescent equipment. This is by no means the case except, properly, where the use of cheap or old equipment results in lower system cost. New equipment does tend, on a unit basis, to be more expensive than old; but this does not mean that its use is uneconomic, any more than the use of modern more expensive equipment is necessarily uneconomic in industry. What counts, in the military as in industry, is not the unit cost of procurement, but the total system cost — the cost of procuring and maintaining and operating the whole system in which the new equipment is embedded — of achieving an appropriate capability or objective. This may be greater or less with new, more "expensive," higher performance equipment. In the case of the atomic bomb it was much less, although the bombs themselves are presumably much more expensive. There is no presumption that the substitution of the "expensive" B-47 for the "cheap" B-29 was uneconomic. The problem of the relative worths and costs of quality and

---

[23] There are undoubtedly sectional interests within the military — particularly commands, services, and staff units — which might suffer from increased efficiency in the establishment as a whole, and have therefore a perverse incentive to prevent efficiency.

quantity is, in the military as in private industry, an economic problem, amenable to economic calculus.

Another misunderstanding is reflected in the question, "What do dollars matter when national survival is at stake?" They matter precisely because they represent (however imperfectly in some circumstances) generalized national resources at the disposal of the military. Unless they are economically used, resources will be wasted, and the nation will have less military capability and a smaller chance of survival. If any one dimension of military power is wastefully planned, that is, at greater than minimum cost, some other dimension will, with a given total military budget, have fewer resources at its disposal and necessarily less capability. Of course waste can be compensated, within limits, by voting higher military budgets at the expense of non-military objectives, but legislatures are understandably less than willing to raise budgets for this purpose. If they vote a higher budget, they want the still greater military capability that an economic use of the higher budget would make possible.

## EFFICIENCY IN THE LARGE VERSUS EFFICIENCY IN THE SMALL

It is convenient in analyzing national security problems (and many others) to distinguish between "efficiency in the large" and "efficiency in the small." (Efficiency in this section will again be used in the general sense of "making good use" of resources — not in the technical sense defined earlier in the chapter.) Efficiency in the large, or at relatively high levels, involves getting the gross allocations right in reference to major objectives — in the case of national security, the allocation of resources between military and non-military uses, and allocations to the Services and the major military "missions" in conformity with national objectives. Efficiency in the small, or at relatively low levels, involves making good use of the resources allocated to each mission and the numerous subordinate jobs within each.

Quantitative economic analysis can be useful in both types of problems, although the type of analysis that is appropriate in the two cases is likely to differ. Typically in decisions at relatively high levels there are important qualitative or intangible factors which make it impossible to define a satisfactory criterion and therefore impossible to devise an explicit model which points the way to *the* right decision.[24] Nevertheless the explicit use of models and of quantitative analysis is not only possible in many such problems, but essential if good solutions are to be found.

Take as an example the division of the budget for the strategic air war between offense and defense. This is a comparatively high level

---

[24] Some lower level problems are in this respect precisely like the high level ones.

problem, beset by intangibles. On one side is the mystique of the offense — the conviction of military services everywhere that morale depends upon offense-mindedness, and that reliance on defensive measures is self-defeating. On the other side is the morale and resolve of the civilian nation: will it dare to threaten war if it is defenseless against enemy bombs? And in between is that most pervasive of all intangibles — the mind of the enemy. How does it function, and what will deter him?

Nevertheless, quantitative calculations are essential to a rational solution. Calculations can show that with the expenditure of a tolerable number of billions of dollars annually on an offensive force *and on the defense of the offensive force,* we can with high confidence (say, 90 per cent) guarantee effective retaliation against an aggressor and therefore that a rational aggressor will be deterred. Similar calculations can show how this total deterrent budget should be divided between the offensive force and various protective devices including warning nets, hardening of installations, and interceptor and missile defenses.

At the same time, calculations can show that much larger budgets (beyond the range of practical politics) will provide only partial and uncertain (low-confidence) protection in the event deterrence fails.

Calculations of this kind, whether made explicitly or implicitly, account for the prevalent view, undoubtedly correct as of the early 1960's, that protected offensive deterrent power has first claim on the national security budget. For what we are trying to do in allocating between offense and defense is to minimize some combination of (a) the chance that all-out thermonuclear war will occur, and (b) the amount of damage we will suffer if it does occur.[25] While we do not know precisely what combination we want to minimize, we can as a first approximation regard it as the product of (a) and (b). We would be willing to reallocate budget from deterrent forces to protective ones like Nikes or civilian shelters only if the expected damage to us if war occurs was reduced by a greater factor than the chance of war was increased.

Of course, we cannot make a complete, explicit calculation of such a product, for we do not have a direct measure of the chance of war. The final stage in allocating funds between deterrent and survival measures is a task for judgment, but judgment's task can be greatly facilitated by calculations showing how accomplishments of the proximate objectives, that is, ability to inflict damage and ability to survive attack, are related to budget expenditures.

If the technical possibilities of offense and defense, as reflected in the budget costs of buying given amounts of deterrent power and protection, were drastically altered by, say, some technological break-

---

[25] The amount of damage we will be able to inflict on the enemy is implicit in the calculation, since that *is* our means of deterring war.

through in defense, our judgment about the best allocation would also change. Suppose that, both for the Russians and ourselves, the relations were more or less reversed, so that at practical budget levels we could buy a high-confidence, virtually leak-proof defense; while the similar effectiveness of the Russian defense made the task of providing an effective retaliatory force tremendously uncertain and expensive. We are sure that in these circumstances men of good judgment would assign top priority to providing the curtain of death rays that would kill incoming bombers, missiles, and bombs. On the other hand our strategic bombing forces, in fighting for appropriations for their low-confidence mission, would find themselves in the same difficult, uncomfortable position that Continental Air Defense and the agencies responsible for civil defense now occupy.

Of course *priority* provides no clue to the proportion of the budget to be allocated to the deterrence mission — except when the total budget is small. When the budget is large, the best proportions depend upon the effects of *increments* of budget spent on deterrence and survival respectively (and these effects are calculable).

As we descend to lower levels of decision making, there is frequently a change in the proportion of quantitative and qualitative factors that affords greater scope for explicit analysis. If the problem is not how much to allocate to air defense relative to other missions, but with which of two proposed electronic gun sights to equip fighter aircraft, the relevance and necessity of quantitative analysis becomes obvious. To make a rational choice we must, at the least, have quantitative evidence on accuracy, reliability, cost and availability, weight and the consequences of added weight, and so on. Of course the great majority of problems of military choice are, like this one, lower level problems, which are decided in the first instance at levels in the departmental or military hierarchy well below the top.

The bulk of explicit quantitative analysis so far attempted in the military, chiefly by operations analysis groups, has been directed toward such lower level problems, and this will probably always be true, and it may be desirable. Not only do the lower level problems demand quantitative analysis and appear more "manageable"; they are, in the aggregate, of great importance. Experienced operations researchers report that they frequently discover that some of the systems which they compare are better by large factors — three, four or more — than others seriously proposed, sometimes with enthusiastic advocates. This should come as no surprise to economists who have studied international differences in productivity and costs, or even differences among enterprises within a nation. There are many ways to make any product or achieve any objective, and some are much more efficient than others. In the absence of an adequate economic calculus, highly inefficient ways can be and are chosen.[26]

In some of the following chapters, we try to illustrate an economic approach to problems of choice at various levels. In Chapter 8 we present an example of systematic quantitative analysis, applied in this instance to a comparatively low level problem, the choice of cargo aircraft for a military transport fleet. This analysis makes use of a fairly clear-cut criterion and relies heavily upon an explicit model. In the last chapter of the book, we consider major factors that should figure in an economic analysis of a relatively high level problem, that of shaping our policies for deterrence. In this problem, while the conclusions depend critically upon quantitative calculations, we have to find means to cope with a formidable array of intangibles and uncertainties. Other chapters in Part III discuss major considerations affecting the economic analysis of problems of choice (such as choosing policies in military alliances or shaping logistics plans) at various levels.

SUB-OPTIMIZING

The usual task of quantitative analysis is the improvement of decisions at relatively low levels in the military hierarchy — efficiency in the small. But while decisions at these levels appear more susceptible to quantitative analysis, and indeed frequently are, such analysis presents peculiar and formidable difficulties. These are associated with the choice of criteria, and will be more fully discussed in Chapter 9. What follows here is an impressionistic introduction to the nature of the problem.

In the first place, for a lower level analysis to be more manageable, it must be confined to a lower level context. Many of the things that would be treated as variables in a higher level analysis — specifically, decisions at still higher levels and at the same levels in other branches of the military — must be taken as given. The systems to be compared in the analysis, while "complete" in some sense, must be limited, with only a few elements varying from system to system.

Analyses so confined to lower level contexts, which assume decisions given at higher and collateral levels, are called "sub-optimizations."[27] They attempt to find optimal (or near optimal) solutions, but to subproblems rather than to the whole problem of the organization in whose

---

[26] We are not suggesting, of course, that *all* international or intercompany differences in productivity measure differences in the efficiency of utilization of resources. Where labor is a relatively cheap factor it will usually be efficient to choose methods which result in lower average labor productivity. But the differences do measure the wide range of alternative methods and therefore the range of possible error if economic rationale is lacking.

[27] Sub-optimizations correspond to the partial equilibrium analyses of conventional economic theory.

welfare or utility we are interested. If a consumer tries to solve his transportation problem (Cadillac *vs.* Chevrolet) more or less in isolation, taking other major decisions affecting his income and expenditure as given, he is sub-optimizing. If the Air Force tries to decide between two gun sights for fighters, taking the general organization, size and tactics of fighter defense as given, it is sub-optimizing. If we are taking a Departmental or Service point of view, we sub-optimize when we try to solve a problem at a level lower than that of the Secretary or Chief of Staff. From a national point of view, even problems at the Chief of Staff level, in a context coextensive with the responsibilities of the Service, must be regarded as sub-optimizations.

Sub-optimizations are both necessary and inevitable, and provide scope for productive quantitative analyses of important problems of choice. But they are hard to do well. While analysis appears to become more manageable as we move to lower levels, limit the context, and restrict the scope within which systems vary, three inter-related problems tend to become more formidable the further we move in this direction:

1. The first is the problem of selecting an appropriate criterion — appropriate, that is, to the level at which the decision is being studied — that is consistent with higher level criteria, and ultimately with the welfare of the organization or group in which we are really interested. It is very easy to choose some proximate criterion in a low level problem that is inconsistent with higher level criteria — to take a previous example, maximizing air defense kill potential when an equally important or more important function of air defense is to provide adequate warning.

2. The second we will call the problem of spillovers; and this too we will discuss at greater length in Chapter 9. When we confine analysis within narrow contextual limits, there is always a possibility that some of the consequences may affect — favorably or unfavorably — other parts of the larger organization or group with whose welfare we are concerned. Certain SAC deployments will facilitate, and others will make more difficult, the task of the air defense system in providing warning to and defense of SAC bases. These spillover effects would be missed in an analysis narrowly confined to SAC.

3. Third, there is the problem of choosing the context and the elements that will be permitted to vary in the systems compared. The context need not, and indeed normally should not, be as restricted as the area of immediate decision that provides the *focus* of the analysis. The broader the context the less the danger from inconsistent criteria and the less likely it is that significant spillover effects will be missed. The broader the context, too, the fewer other decisions one needs to take as given, and the greater opportunity one has to explore the interdependence of decisions at different and collateral levels. But breadth of context and

any increase in the number of variables have to be purchased by drastically increasing the complexity of the analysis,[28] with all this implies in terms of research manpower, expense, and time. So we don't want to expand context or increase variables unnecessarily.

How large should the context be? How many decisions should be analyzed simultaneously? There are no rules except — be aware of the dangers, and use good sense to reduce them. Some low level problems are "factorable," that is, good decisions don't depend much upon other decisions, and spillovers aren't too important. Where problems are relatively factorable, the context can be kept small and the variables few. One can frequently minimize the cost of one operation without much affecting others. But other problems simply aren't factorable in this sense. Their solution, even if responsibility is fixed at a low level in the hierarchy, has wide ramifications. And any optimal solution must take account of the interdependence of this problem and others. As an obvious and extreme example, an analysis of the location of SAC bases cannot be successfully sub-optimized even at the level of SAC Headquarters. Their location not only has spillovers on air defense, as we have seen, and on our ability to fight local wars in various parts of the world; but it may also affect the whole structure of our alliances. We must either optimize on a fairly grand scale (probably impossible in any explicit quantitative manner), or frankly label our sub-optimization a partial analysis, dealing only with *some* of the factors important to a decision.

Consider another hypothetical example, mentioned above, which demands, in the design of the analysis, some compromises between desirable breadth of context and the need to keep research requirements within practical limits. Suppose the analyst's assignment is to select the "best" of several proposed electronic gun sights for fighter aircraft. How large a context should he assume in the study? How many other decisions should he assume to be given?

At one extreme he might fit the sights into very small systems — say specific fighter aircraft — and "score" them by the number of hits registered in tests on tow targets. Would this give him the right answer? Not necessarily. In the first place the criterion may not be closely related to the real task of fighter aircraft. The sights (or some of them) may be heavy enough to affect the plane's range, or its speed or maneuverability. The number of tubes in the electronic system would affect the reliability and the ease of maintenance of the weapons system. Further-

---

[28] The number of cases to be computed and compared increases as the power of the number of interdependent variables. If we let each variable take four alternative values and have two variables, the number of cases is $4^2$ or $16$ — a back-of-the-envelope problem. If we increase the number of variables to 10, we have to compute $4^{10}$ cases, or more than a million, and probably need a high speed electronic computer.

more, performance in combat situations might not be taken sufficiently into account in comparing the number of hits on a tow target.

To overcome some of these shortcomings, the analyst might enlarge the context slightly and fit each gun sight into a fighter plane in combat (on paper) with an enemy aircraft. Would it be in accordance with higher level aims to put this particular emphasis on victory in individual duels? Again, not necessarily. The best gun sight in a duel of one against one would probably turn out to be an extremely expensive one, making it necessary, with a given budget, to sacrifice numbers (or perhaps the range of the fighter). The electronic gear might cause too many aborts (planes that return to base unable to complete their mission) or keep too many planes on the ground. From the standpoint of numerical superiority, number of interceptions, and other aspects of the whole fighter operation, this gun sight might be a poor choice indeed.

The analyst appears to be driven to larger and larger systems — fitting the gun sights into planes, then the planes into fighter groups, then the groups into relevant military operations. He may even want to ask what tasks or budgets make sense in view of the whole military operation and of political realities. But while larger systems analyses make his criterion problem (or one aspect of it) more manageable, they become more cumbersome and more aggregative. At some point in the process, depending on many circumstances (how much time he has, what research resources he has, what chance he or his organization has of influencing higher or collateral decisions, how important the choice among gun sights is anyway?), he must accept a limited context and a less-than-perfect proximate criterion, try to keep aware, in a general and qualitative way, of its shortcomings and biases, treat effects outside his system crudely, and get on with his inevitable job of sub-optimizing.

## KINDS OF MILITARY DECISIONS

Military decisions may be classified by kind as well as by level. For purposes of economic analysis it is frequently useful to distinguish:

> Operations decisions (strategy and tactics)
> Procurement or force composition decisions
> Research and development decisions.

The basic difference among these kinds of decisions, from the point of view of analysis, is the time at which the decision affects the capability of the military forces concerned. An operations decision (how many destroyers to use per convoy) can affect operations and capability almost immediately; in fact, analyses and decisions focused on operations are usually concerned with the near future. A decision to procure something, on the other hand, cannot affect capability until the thing procured has been produced (in the case of manpower, trained) and fitted into operational forces. If the thing is an aircraft carrier or a bomber, the time involved may be many years. Decisions to develop something tend to affect capabilities at an even later date — after the thing has been developed, and produced, and then fitted into operational forces.

An economic analysis, whether quantitative or qualitative, will usually attempt to determine the utility of alternative systems by examining the effect on military capabilities, whenever these occur.[29] The effects of a change in tactics in 1960 can perhaps be fully evaluated in the context of 1960. But to evaluate the effects of a decision in 1960 to develop (or even to procure) a new missile may require projecting the context to 1970 or later. Analyses based on long-range forecasts are, of course, highly uncertain, and this fact drastically alters the form of analysis which it is sensible and useful to make and the kind of conclusions one can draw from it. The problems involved are considered in some detail in Chapters 9, 10, and 11.

In an operations decision, the relevant resource constraints are usually specific rather than general, simply because the time horizon is so short. If the problem involves the tactics of convoying, the escort vessels that have to be used must probably be taken as given — in number, speed, armament, and so on. No budget however large can produce more in the short run. Similarly, SAC's emergency war plans for a retaliatory strike must utilize specific planes carrying specific bombs from specific bases. The fact that the appropriate resource constraints are specific by no means inhibits economic analysis. We have seen that the problem of making economic use of a number of specific resources is fundamentally the same problem as making economic use of a single general resource, although the calculations may be more complicated. In fact, the first large-scale explicit use of quantitative economic analysis in military problems by operations research groups in the Second World War was directed toward problems of tactical operations. Serious attempts to apply the same techniques to longer-range procurement and development problems, in which constraints are more appropriately one or a very few general resources, followed much later.

Analysis focused on a *procurement* decision (for example, which of two missiles to order in 1960) almost of necessity will have to study *operations* in later years — the strategy and tactics with which each missile will be used after it has been introduced into the force. For a valid comparison, each must be used in the most effective way in the context of the appropriate future year. (Similarly, an analysis focused

[29] Some qualifications have to be made in the case of analyses for research and development decisions. See Chapter 13.

on a development decision may, in order to gauge potential payoffs, study procurement and operations as well). The analysis of a procurement problem is, however, solely directed toward the procurement decision in the immediate future; its analysis of future tactics is incidental to choice of bomber; it is tentative and leads to no recommendations about tactics. The time to make analyses focused on tactical decisions in 1968 is not earlier than 1967.

# 8. AN ILLUSTRATIVE APPLICATION OF ECONOMIC ANALYSIS[1]

To exemplify the potentialities and limitations of systematic quantitative analysis, we shall apply some of these techniques to a choice faced by a military service. This application reflects the "way of looking at military problems" that has been stressed, that is, the systematic consideration of alternative policies and the gains and costs of each. The example therefore embraces the various elements discussed above — a manageable "sub-problem" of choice, a mission or objective, alternative means of achieving that objective, costs entailed by each means, models to trace out the relationships among these elements, and a criterion for choosing the preferred means. In this chapter we simply present the analysis. In subsequent chapters, we shall refer to it in order to elucidate general points about the selection of criteria, uncertainty, the treatment of time streams, and the use of analysis in planning research and development.

## THE PROBLEM

In order to exhibit both the merits and the pitfalls of quantitative analysis, we have turned to a real problem of military choice. It is a problem of procurement or force composition — that of choosing in 195x an intercontinental military air transport fleet for the decade 1958–1967. Because we wish to focus attention on method rather than on the substance of this particular analysis, the alternative policies — in this case, alternative transport fleets — are hypothetical. The assumed characterizations, such as payloads and ranges, of the aircraft considered here do not correspond to those of existing transports. The planes cannot be

[1] This chapter may be omitted or skimmed by readers with little interest in quantitative analysis. It was written by C. B. McGuire, who participated in a study of military air transport systems carried out for the U.S. Air Force in the Logistics Department of RAND's Economics Division. D. M. Fort and A. S. Manne helped in the development of the model. The *methods* used in this illustrative analysis are similar to those of the original study.

labeled "turboprops" or "turbojets"; they are simply hypothetical aircraft whose function is to help illustrate the possibilities of systematic analysis. The context, however, is sufficiently realistic and detailed to bring out many of the complexities, and the calculations have been carried out fully in order to make the illustration complete.

Deciding on the best intercontinental air transport fleet appears to be a manageable sub-optimization. Certain higher-level questions — for instance, should the United States have an intercontinental airlift capability? — are put aside. Attention is confined to the lower level question: If the United States is to have such a capability during the period 1958–1967, what is the most efficient fleet for the mission? This decision appears to have no marked repercussions on broader defense policies or on international negotiations, so we can safely "factor out" the problem for more or less separate examination. (If the choice affected the design of equipment to be transported, this effect would have to be taken into account, but the alternative aircraft do not in fact seem to have differential implications for the design of tanks, guns, gear, and so on.)

### THE MISSION OR OBJECTIVE

The assumed mission comprises two tasks, routine worldwide resupply of our military bases at *all* times and deployment in the event of a peripheral war. (Air transport needs in an all-out war are not considered, for they appear to be less than the requirements for tactical deployment in limited conflicts.) These tasks, while specified in considerable detail, are intended to be representative airlift missions. Both are stated in terms of cargo and passenger tonnages to be delivered via 20 "channels" (see Tables 14 and 15 in the appendix at the end of this chapter). A channel is specified by an origin and one or two overseas destinations. For most of the channels, several round-trip *routes* are available for delivering the required tonnage. Thus Travis Air Force Base, California, to Tokyo, Japan, is Channel 17, and five routes can be used:[2]

Route 1: Travis–Tokyo–Travis
Route 2: Travis–Midway–Tokyo–Midway–Travis
Route 3: Travis–Hickam–Midway–Tokyo–Midway–Hickam–Travis
Route 4: Travis–Hickam–Wake–Tokyo–Midway–Hickam–Travis
Route 5: Travis–Hickam–Johnston–Wake–Tokyo–Midway–Hickam–
Travis

To allow for changes in routine air resupply needs and in the availability of various aircraft, the 10-year period studied was divided into Period I, four years, 1958–1961 inclusive, and Period II, six years, 1962–

---

[2] Still other routes can be devised, of course, but the ones listed cover most of the interesting possibilities.

1967 inclusive. The magnitude of the deployment task is assumed to remain unchanged throughout the 10 years. The magnitude of the routine resupply mission is assumed to increase from about two and one-half times 1954 levels in Period I to about five times 1954 levels in Period II. This assumption of rapid growth in traffic seems justified by trends observed in the past 10 years.

The representative deployment task consists of the movement to Bangdhad, a hypothetical city in the Far East, of one infantry division (combat echelon) from Travis Air Force Base, California, one fighter-bomber wing from Travis, and two fighter-bomber wings from Tokyo. In addition, one week's supply of fuel and ammunition for the fighter-bomber wings is to be brought in from Manila. This airlift is to be accomplished in 10 days.

## THE ALTERNATIVE MEANS

The aircraft considered for the transport fleet were limited, for present purposes, to four: the C-97[3] (the currently used piston-engined aircraft), the HC-400 (HC standing for "Hypothetical Cargo" aircraft), the HC-500, and the HC-600. The last three aircraft are turbine-engined aircraft, and the higher the "HC-number," the larger the size of the aircraft.[4] Perhaps the best way to summarize the physical characteristics of these aircraft is to show their respective "payload-range" curves, which picture the combinations of cargo and range that are feasible in each aircraft (see Figure 8). These curves play a major role in the calculation of results.

Some of these aircraft are supposed to be on hand, while others are presumed to be procurable within specified production limits. Table 12 gives initial inventories and the possibilities of procurement in each of the two periods. Notice that for each of the turbine-engined aircraft, the number available increases over time, with HC-400 production ahead of HC-500 production, and the latter ahead of HC-600 production.

Since the problem pertains to a series of points in time, simplified here to two time periods, the alternatives are not just fleets, but fleet *sequences*. That is, what we seek is not actually an optimum fleet but rather the best Period I–Period II sequence of fleets. Note that what is best in Period I depends in part upon the aircraft available and most useful in Period II, and what is best in Period II depends upon the aircraft procured in Period I — a real-life complexity that cannot be shrugged off by the analyst.

---

[3] We can regard other piston-engined aircraft as being included in this category, as they can be translated into "C-97 equivalents."

[4] This statement is correct, whether size is taken to mean maximum "weight allowable cabin load," "space allowable cabin load," or "takeoff weight."

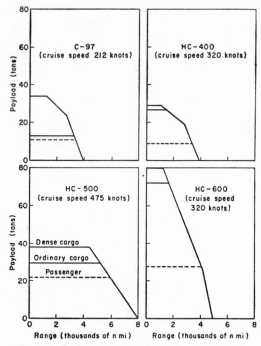

**Fig. 8. Payload-range curves of the alternative aircraft**

Since (in this chapter) we treat these aircraft as candidates for procurement, we assume that they have already been "developed," at least
as far as the prototype stage.

**Table 12. Aircraft available (illustrative analysis)**

| | | *Maximum number procurable* | |
| | *Initial inventory* | Period I 1958–1961 | Period II 1962–1968 |
| --- | --- | --- | --- |
| *Aircraft type* | | | |
| C-97   (and equivalent) | 400 | 0 | 200[a] |
| HC-400 | 100 | 400 | 700 |
| HC-500 | 0 | 50 | 100 |
| HC-600 | 0 | 0 | 125 |

[a] By 1962 the introduction of new tanker aircraft into the Air Force will presumably bring about the retirement of KC-97 tankers. If desired, these could then be modified at a nominal cost for use as C-97 transport aircraft

## THE COSTS

The costs that we wish to measure are the additional system costs
attributable to each fleet sequence. Our first step is to identify just what

it is that we are costing. We focus attention upon the wartime deployment and wartime resupply missions that each fleet must be capable of carrying out, because they appear to constitute the largest job the transport fleet will have to do. The fleet is occupied during peacetime, however, with peacetime resupply. Since large parts of the costs appropriate to the comparisons being made are operating costs, we must consider this peacetime resupply activity. If transport aircraft could be mothballed in a highly ready state (and if it were economic to prepare for war in this fashion), then the only operating costs in our comparisons would be those incurred during the conduct of the war. And since the wartime task we have postulated is short-lived, these costs would be negligible compared to the large initial costs of procuring the fleet. Quick response from a mothballed fleet, however, is difficult to obtain. Crews and maintenance personnel need practice, and the complicated aircraft of today must be operated to remain operable. In short, *practice* of the whole fleet appears to be requisite to readiness. A further important reason for operating the fleet in peacetime is that once it has been procured, it may as well be used if the benefits thereby derived exceed the operating costs. The man with a family of five who has bought a station wagon for vacations and Sunday outings will not ordinarily be averse to using it to drive to work. And if he is a careful car buyer, he will consider the operating costs of this commuting in making his selection.

We assume, therefore, that six hours daily flying for each aircraft in the fleet is necessary to a capability of immediately achieving ten hours daily flying whenever the occasion warrants. Hence, in determining fleet costs over the ten-year period, we include the operating costs of the ten years of six-hours-a-day "practice" flying. We presuppose that whatever useful work is accomplished in the course of this "practice" flying is the same for all fleets considered, so we do not bother to give any credit for this incidental (but not unimportant) accomplishment. We shall also ignore the relatively small wartime additions to the total of operating costs.

Let us turn now to the main cost components: procurement costs, installation and training costs, attrition, and annual operating costs. Here we shall simply outline the nature of these components. (For the calculations, the cost relationships had to be somewhat simplified in order to be put into "linear" equations.)

The *procurement cost* of an aircraft includes both the cost of the airframe and an initial outlay for spare parts (a by no means negligible addition). While one might argue that the latter is really an operating cost, the Air Force *does* buy spares when it buys aircraft. Procurement costs would be quite simple to calculate were it not for certain "set-up" costs and "learning" phenomena in aircraft production. Before mass production can begin, a large investment must be put into tooling (jigs, dies, fixtures, and so on) which can be used for no other aircraft. Moreover, this investment is the same whether 50 or 500 aircraft are produced.[5] And as production gets under way, the efficiency of the whole operation improves through learning. These two effects (of set-up costs and of learning) together bring about a decline in procurement cost per aircraft as the number of aircraft produced increases.

*Installations and training costs,* like procurement costs, are initial, rather than annually recurring, costs. The purchase of one particular vehicle for the fleet requires an outlay for buildings, kitchens, ground handling equipment, and so on, and for the training of crews and maintenance personnel. One of the difficult questions that must be decided is whether the resulting equipment and proficiency depreciates faster or slower than the aircraft for which it was purchased. Another is the extent to which this equipment and proficiency is of use with other types of aircraft. Must these accoutrements be retired along with their aircraft? No pat answers to these questions are possible.

*Attrition costs* result from peacetime "practice" flying operations. They differ, for present purposes, from other annual operating costs in that they must be paid for by the purchase of replacement aircraft, the cost of which, as indicated above, depends on the total number procured. Our troubles with attrition costs would end here if we were not concerned with the design of a whole fleet and with the numbers of aircraft each manufacturer can provide by certain points in time. The case of piston-engined aircraft is particularly troublesome. If, in the fleet sequence being costed, retirement of these aircraft is being carried out at a rapid rate, then attrition should be costless: an attrited aircraft constitutes a retirement. If retirement is not called for, then the attrited aircraft — no longer being produced — must be replaced by newer aircraft having an equivalent capacity. But this kind of replacement alters the composition of the fleet — the very thing we are trying to cost. For the newer aircraft that are still in production, an attrited aircraft is replaced by a new one, except when rapid retirement takes place. Whenever the number called for by a fleet sequence presses hard against the manufacturer's production limits, we must make sure that the phasing-in is not so fast as to leave no production capacity for attrition replacements.

*Annual operating cost* is the most easily dealt with of the four cost components discussed. It is almost directly proportional to the level of the peacetime "practice" flying-hour program and includes such items as wages (both crew and ground support personnel), fuel, and maintenance.

---

[5] This statement exaggerates the picture only slightly.

In order to measure the extra costs attributable to each fleet sequence, we should avoid including sunk costs, that is, expenditures already made and therefore irretrievable. Thus, we must not include in our costs the procurement expenditures for the aircraft already in the fleet. If these older aircraft cannot be sold or put to alternative uses, in effect and for present purposes, they are free. This point, which will be discussed more fully in Chapter 11, applies equally to the 100 HC-400's and to the 400 C-97's in the initial inventory.

### THE CRITERION

As in most problems, there are some considerations that we cannot successfully include in a single definitive test of preferredness. Several considerations of this sort will be pointed out in interpreting the results. The principal criterion, however, will be minimum cost over the years 1958–1967 of maintaining the specified airlift capability. That is, the system that can achieve the objective at lowest cost will be regarded as the best system (unless this test is overruled by the "outside" considerations). In applying this criterion, we have not discounted the streams of cost or gain (see Chapter 11 for a discussion of discounting). In this comparison of air transport fleets, discounting the future at plausible rates seems unlikely to affect the results; in fact, discounting the costs at as high a rate as 25 per cent leaves the ranking of the fleets unchanged.

### THE MODELS AND THE PROCEDURE

The models comprise the relationships that enable us to estimate the cost and effectiveness of alternative fleets. Details of the models and computations are shown in the appendix at the end of this chapter. Here we shall indicate only briefly the general nature of the procedure.

The technique for finding the least-cost fleet is the one described in the discussion of Figure 6 in Chapter 7 — that is, seeking points of tangency between exchange curves and output-isoquants. In other words, the models show how the transport aircraft can be traded for each other while holding total cost constant, and how they can be substituted for each other while keeping the quantity of output constant.[6] The ratio of two aircrafts' marginal costs (that is, the costs of buying and operating an additional plane) shows how they can be traded for each other while holding total cost constant. The ratio of the aircrafts' productivities (tons of cargo that can be delivered per flying hour) over each channel shows how they can be substituted while keeping the quantity of output

[6] In the language of economics, the models trace out the "marginal rates of substitution" in incurring costs and in producing transport services. These are the trade-offs referred to in Chapter 7.

constant. Finally, knowing the effects of trading one aircraft for another, we exchange them (on paper) until we determine the least-cost combination that will do the job.

The models also show the costs of certain fleets other than the least-cost one. The reason for this is that we may legitimately be interested in certain other fleets, in which case we should know their economic implications.

## RESULTS AND CONCLUSIONS

The results are presented in Table 13. The fleet that entailed the lowest cost, which we shall call the "basic least-cost" fleet, employs all three of the new aircraft in Period II (when the HC-600 becomes avail-

**Table 13. Cost and composition of alternative fleets, Periods I and II** [a]

| | Basic least-cost | | Least-cost excluding HC-600 | | Least-cost excluding HC-500 | | Least-cost excluding HC-500, HC-600 | | Least procurement | |
|---|---|---|---|---|---|---|---|---|---|---|
| | I | II | I | II | I | II | I | II | I | II |
| Composition (numbers of aircraft) | | | | | | | | | | |
| C-97 | 103 | 0 | 0 | 0 | 309 | 0 | 0 | 0 | 400 | 472 |
| HC-400 | 151 | 151 | 229 | 229 | 161 | 161 | 399 | 486 | 103 | 103 |
| HC-500 | 50 | 53 | 50 | 78 | — | — | — | — | 8 | 8 |
| HC-600 | — | 53 | — | — | — | 113 | — | — | — | 0 |
| Cost[b] (millions of 1956 dollars) | $3,986 | | $4,039 | | $4,295 | | $4,587 | | $5,129 | |

[a] A dash (—) indicates that the model is not available in that particular period. A zero (o) indicates that it is inefficient to use that aircraft even though it is available.

[b] These cost figures are the amounts as estimated by the mathematical models (see the appendix) *plus* adjustments for those elements of cost that could not be allowed for in linear relationships.

able), the C-97's being retired at the end of Period I. Least-cost fleets were also calculated with certain planes excluded. We did this for two reasons: (1) to determine the sensitivity of the costs to the presence of those planes, and (2) to identify the best fleet in case some special consideration eliminated one of the transports. It turns out that costs are not sensitive to the presence of the HC-600, for its elimination raises the expected cost negligibly. The results are more sensitive to the employment of the HC-500, for its elimination increases the cost of carrying out the mission by about 300 million dollars. Eliminating both of these aircraft raises the expected cost by about 600 million dollars.

The most striking result, however, is the marked inefficiency that would result from adopting a "least-procurement" policy — that is, a policy of buying no more new aircraft than would be necessary to carry out the task. The operating costs of the C-97 are sufficient to make this a very expensive policy, costing over a billion dollars more than the least-cost fleet. In this instance, as in many others, it is not economic to "make do" with old equipment. Economizing does *not* mean minimizing cash outlays in the current time period.

The array of results in Table 13 also brings out some interesting interrelationships between the decisions for each of the two periods. For example, if the HC-600 is excluded, it becomes efficient to use more HC-400's in Period II. This fact in turn makes it economical to procure more HC-400's in Period I. As a consequence, the exclusion of the HC-600, instead of thrusting more work on all three of the remaining aircraft, leads to the elimination of the C-97 even in Period I! That is, in these altered circumstances, it is economical to replace the C-97 immediately. The same thing happens if both the HC-500 and the HC-600 are excluded. On the other hand, if the HC-500 is excluded, it is economical to lean very heavily on the C-97 in Period I (the HC-600 being available only in Period II), and procure a comparatively large number of HC-600's (113) in Period II. The impact of these interrelationships on the composition of efficient fleets is by no means intuitively obvious.

In interpreting the results, we must recognize that there are relevant considerations outside our principal criterion. For instance, manning requirements may be an important aspect of the different fleets in addition to their effectiveness and cost (as reflected in our measures). If the military were free to adjust pay (and other policies) so as to get the personnel desired, dollar costs would fully reflect the advantages and disadvantages of various fleets with respect to manpower requirements. But since manpower ceilings and legislation on pay structure have to be considered, the Services may be unable to obtain the desired personnel at the indicated costs. In other words, heavy manpower requirements may pose some difficulties that are not reflected in costs. Another outside consideration is the effect of each fleet on base saturation. After preliminary investigations, it was assumed here that the various airbases could handle the traffic and refueling in all cases. Yet, clearly, different fleets do impose different burdens on these bases, and even if the accomplishment of the mission is not impaired in any way, the differential burdens and strains may properly bear on a final decision.

Still another consideration outside the main criterion is uncertainty. There is great strategic uncertainty. Is this mission a representative one? Is the composition of the least-cost fleet sensitive to changes in the mission? There are also uncertainties about many other matters such as technological developments, cost figures, and performance in particular instances. These tables show "best estimates" or estimates of the outcome that can be expected on the average, and other outcomes are clearly possible. In the face of these uncertainties, we may prefer, not the least-cost fleet to carry out the designated mission, but a modified version that offers insurance against very unfavorable outcomes. As a consequence, before interpreting the above results, one should make some additional calculations — to see how well the interesting fleets would perform in certain other contingencies, or to determine the least-cost fleet for altered versions of the mission.

Nonetheless, it is fairly clear, in this illustrative analysis, that an economical fleet will employ a large number of newly procured aircraft. It will employ not only the HC-400 but also at least one of the two larger transports (the HC-500 and HC-600). We cannot here compare the impacts of various fleets on such things as base saturation and manning requirements; but consideration of these factors is virtually certain to favor still further the larger turbine-engined transports, the HC-500 and the HC-600.

We wish to stress that this analysis pertains to a *relatively* low-level and uncomplicated choice. It is defined in such a way that we do not worry about spillover effects on other missions or about enemy reactions. Yet even in this analysis, there are many difficulties in selecting a criterion, spelling out the objective, measuring aircraft productivities, estimating costs, and interpreting the results. The following appendix, on the models and computations, emphasizes further the subtlety of some of these problems. For example, it makes a difference what cargo "mix" is to be moved in this mission. Also, aggregating the possible trips and routes into a manageable number of channels raises some nice questions. It is important, therefore, to be careful in preparing and appraising relatively simple analyses such as this one. In more complicated choices, it is all the more important to be clear on the methodological issues. In the following chapters we turn to a more thorough examination of several of these issues.

## APPENDIX ON THE MODELS
### AND THE COMPUTATIONS [7]

As indicated in the text, the aim of the analysis is to find the least costly fleet sequence from among all those with the required capability. How is this to be done? Once the input data — to be described below — have been gathered, it is a straightforward matter to construct a Period I fleet and a Period II fleet, each possessing at least the required capability. For comparisons to be of much use, however, these fleet sequences must

[7] We shall try to present enough information to indicate clearly the manner in which the calculations were made and to enable the reader to go over especially important computations.

have in common two further characteristics that make their construction more difficult.

First, aircraft production availabilities must not be exceeded.[8] In the case of the C-97, which is no longer being produced, the beginning inventory must not be exceeded until the retired KC-97's become available for conversion to transports in Period II.

Second, none of the fleets entering the comparisons should have *more* than the required capability. This stipulation causes more difficulty than might at first appear. While it is easy to make sure that a fleet has enough capability, it is another matter to ask that it have no more than enough, for reshufflings of the assignments of aircraft and jobs can sometimes result in unused capacity. We must be sure, in other words, that each aircraft is contributing the most it can to fleet accomplishments. Fleets that possess this characteristic of having the required capability but no excess capability, we shall refer to as *efficient* [9] fleets.

Before going on to the question of how to construct these efficient fleets, it will be useful to discuss the choice of fleet sequences to compare. Even with as few as four aircraft, the number of interesting and relevant fleets — not to mention Period I-Period II combinations of fleets — is large, so large in fact that it becomes difficult to know what comparisons to carry out. Even if production availabilities permitted, little would be learned from a comparison between, say, a "pure" fleet of HC-500's and a "pure" fleet of HC-600's. The HC-500 might be an economic aircraft to procure as a complement to, say, the HC-600, but poor as a general purpose aircraft. The HC-400 *might* be an economic procurement only as a stopgap measure prior to HC-600 production. The HC-600 might be a good Period II procurement if the HC-500 is bought in Period I, but a poor procurement if the more nearly similar[10] HC-400 serves as the stopgap.

Obviously the method of choosing the comparisons to be made should be systematic. The method described below achieves this end and at the same time ensures that the fleets chosen are *efficient* ones. The procedure consists, first of all, in using mathematical means to find the fleet sequence that costs the least among all those that meet requirements without exceeding available production. The next step is to determine the best fleet in case one of the transports is ruled out by special considerations. This fleet is determined by arbitrarily barring one of the aircraft

[8] By "production availability" is meant the number of aircraft that can be produced in a *single* facility. A second facility would lift this limitation, of course, but since the costs of additional tooling and learning make these extra aircraft substantially more expensive, this alternative has, for simplicity, been ignored.

[9] See Chapter 7 where this concept of efficiency is discussed in a more general context.

[10] Similar in the sense that the HC-400 performs relatively better on those same channels where the HC-600 performs relatively better.

in the first least-cost sequence, and solving for the least-cost fleet among those remaining. In the next step a different transport may be eliminated, and the former one restored, or both may be barred. The process continues in this fashion to form new fleet sequences — each of which, it will be noted, is the least costly in its class. The direction the procedure takes in each case is dictated partly by the analyst's interests, and partly by the outcome of the preceding calculations.

There are several reasons for our being interested in these other fleets. For one thing, our measure of the "equal capability" of the fleets being considered ignores such matters as runway requirements, cargo handling characteristics, and vulnerability. Moreover, this "equal capability" refers to only one war situation out of the many that might occur. To experienced eyes one of our fleet sequences — as capable as the others according to our crude measure — may appear to be superior in some respect, say, in vulnerability or versatility. One of the purposes of our comparisons is to show the economic implications of these other fleets that might be favored. Our procedure helps us chart a pertinent segment of the spectrum of efficient fleets.

### AIRCRAFT PRODUCTIVITIES

We shall express the productivity of a given aircraft on a given channel in terms of the number of tons of a specified cargo that can be delivered per flying hour.[11] Since several routes are usually available for each channel, we must first determine an aircraft's productivity on each route. The productivity of an aircraft on a channel will then be its productivity over its most productive route.

For the calculations, we need to know the performance of the various transports and the nature of the job to be done. As for the job, the data in Table 14 form the basis of our requirements for each of 20 channels. Channel numbers 57–61 give the tonnage requirements for the tactical deployment, and Channels 01–47 give those for routine resupply in Period I. Period II requirements are twice those of Period I for Channels 01–47, and the same as those of Period I for Channels 57–61. Table 15 gives a sample description in terms of round-trip distances and "critical legs" of representative channels.

As for the performance of the transports, their payload-range curves have already been given in Figure 8. Note that they pertain to three types of payload — passengers, ordinary cargo, and dense cargo (such as petroleum, oil, lubricants, and ammunition). When passengers are to be carried, Table 14 states this explicitly. We shall suppose that the only

---

[11] Tons delivered per *hour*, rather than per *flying hour* is a better definition of productivity, but since the same daily flying hour capability is assumed for all of our aircraft, the two definitions are equally satisfactory here.

Table 14. Ten-day cargo and passenger requirements by channel
(including routine resupply,
wartime deployment, and wartime resupply)

| Channel [a] | Passenger tons[b] | Cargo tons |
|---|---|---|
| 01 | — | — |
| 03 | — | — |
| 05 | 50 | 80 |
| 07 | 25 | 51 |
| 09 | 25 | 82 |
| 11 | 31 | 72 |
| 13 | 45 | 88 |
| 15 | — | — |
| 17 | 557 | 531 |
| 19 | — | — |
| 21 | — | — |
| 23 | 111 | 185 |
| 25 | 27 | 26 |
| 27 | 44 | 95 |
| 29 | 10 | 36 |
| 31 | 112 | 203 |
| 33 | 74 | 342 |
| 35 | 45 | 88 |
| 37 | — | — |
| 39 | — | — |
| 41 | 26 | 127 |
| 43 | 538 | 1,156 |
| 45 | 74 | 179 |
| 47 | 117 | 499 |
| 57 | 200 | 1,000 |
| 59 | 1,600 | 4,000 |
| 61 | — | 20,000 |

[a] Channels 01–47 are for routine resupply. The requirements for Channels 57–61 are for the tactical deployment in the event of peripheral war.

[b] Nine passengers to a ton. The tonnages listed (for both passengers and cargo) are hypothetical. They have been made up for the purpose of illustrating the method of analysis.

airlift of dense cargo takes place on the Clark to Bangdhad resupply run, Channel 61. When dense cargo is carried, the full weight-allowable cabin load of an aircraft can be used. However, when passengers or ordinary freight is to be airlifted, the cubic capacity of an aircraft may limit the payload. As a result, separate payload-range curves for determining allowable passenger loads are given, as well as the cubic capacity of each aircraft for cargo purposes. We assume throughout that our ordinary cargo has a uniform density of 12 pounds per cubic foot. With this information we can modify the top part of each payload-range curve to ensure that cubic capacities are not exceeded. Thus we have for each aircraft three payload-range curves — for passengers, for ordinary cargo, and for dense cargo.

**Table 15. Partial detail of MATS route structure
assumed for analysis**

| Channel [a] | Route[a] | Critical leg[b] (N. mi.) | Round-trip distance (N. mi.) | Route description[c] |
|---|---|---|---|---|
| 05 | 1 | 1280 | 2180 | Nouasseur*— Tripoli–R   (i.e., Return) |
| 07 | 1 | 3290 | 6060 | Nouasseur*— Dhahran–R |
| 07 | 2 | 2210 | 6060 | Nouasseur–Tripoli*— Dhahran–R |
| 07 | 3 | 1330 | 6240 | Nouasseur–Tripoli–Cairo*— Dhahran–R |
| 09 | 1 | 2320 | 4360 | Dover*— Lages–R |
| 09 | 2 | 1630 | 4920 | Dover–Stephenville*— Lages–R |
| 11 | 1 | 1050 | 1300 | Dover — Bermuda–R |
| 13 | 1 | 3180 | 4860 | Dover*— Keflavik–R |
| 13 | 2 | 2250 | 4940 | Dover–Stephenville*— Keflavik–R |
| 17 | 1 | 4650 | 8860 | Travis*— Tokyo–R |
| 17 | 2 | 3220 | 10120 | Travis*— Midway–Tokyo–R |
| 17 | 3 | 2460 | 11040 | Travis–Hickam–Midway*— Tokyo–R |
| 17 | 4 | 2410 | 11420 | Travis–Hickam*— Wake–Tokyo– Midway–Hickam–Travis |
| 17 | 5 | 2150 | 11520 | Travis*— Hickam–Johnston–Wake– Tokyo–Midway–Hickam–Travis |
| 19 | 1 | 4670 | 8620 | Travis*— Eniwetok–R |
| 19 | 2 | 2700 | 8980 | Travis–Hickam*— Eniwetok–R |
| 19 | 3 | 2150 | 9040 | Travis*— Hickam–Johnston–Eniwetok |
| 23 | 1 | 2150 | 4280 | |
| 25 | 1 | 1480 | 2940 | |
| 27 | 1 | 1550 | | |
| 29 | 1 | 1550 | | |
| 31 | 1 | | | |

[a] Channel and route numbers are not the same as MATS designations.
[b] Includes distance to nearest alternate.
[c] Symbols are as follows: * denotes critical leg, R denotes return.

The points in our route network where fuel is pre-positioned play a part in the determination of the critical legs in each route. We have assumed that sufficient petroleum, oil, and lubricants are available for transport purposes at all points except Bangdhad. Thus, for every route except those including a Clark-Bangdhad leg, the payloads will be determined on the basis of the customary payload-range curves and the critical legs. On routes involving Clark-Bangdhad flights, however, we must use payload-radius curves[12] *as well as* payload-range curves.[13] Whereas usually the critical leg of a route is simply the longest leg, it may or may not be the leg that limits payload on routes involving radius work.

The payload of a given aircraft on a given route is found by reading from the appropriate payload-range curve the number of tons corresponding to the length of the critical leg on this route. This means, of course, that over some of the shorter, noncritical legs of a route, an aircraft may be less than fully loaded. Transloading would be the only way to use this capacity, however, and this is probably more expensive than unused aircraft capacity.

The round-trip flight time of an aircraft on a given route is determined in two steps. We first divide the round-trip route distance by the aircraft's cruise speed. Since the resulting time estimate does not allow for delays in descents and ascents and in ground handling during intermediate fueling stops, we add 15 minutes for each landing and 15 minutes for each take-off. This sum we regard as our estimate of flight time.

The productivity of a given aircraft on a given route is now determined by dividing the appropriate payload by the appropriate round-trip flight time. For example, let us find the passenger productivity of the HC-600 on Route 2 of Channel 17. (We shall make the calculation precise so that the result will correspond with that shown in Table 16.) From Table 15 we see that the critical leg on this route is 3,220 miles. Entering Figure 8 at 3,220 miles and reading the passenger curve, we find that the HC-600 has a payload of about 28 tons — 27.8 tons, if we could read the figure accurately enough. The round-trip distance on Route 2 is 10,120 miles; dividing this figure by the cruise speed of the HC-600 (320 knots), we have 31.68 hours as the time for the round trip. Adding 15 minutes for each of the 4 landings and 4 take-offs in the round trip, we get 33.68 flying hours as our estimate of total flight time. Passenger productivity then is payload over flight time: 27.8/33.68, or 0.824 tons per flying hour.[14]

The productivity of each aircraft on each channel is shown in Table 16. Cargo and passenger productivities are given separately. Since the dense cargo appears only on Channel 61 — all of this requirement is dense cargo — it was not necessary to have a third tabulation. All of these productivities refer to "overload" or "emergency" operating conditions.

In one respect, the importance of which is difficult to judge, the

[12] A payload-radius curve shows maximum payload for any given radius, the radius being the distance to which the aircraft carries the payload when it must return without refueling at destination.

[13] Of course, where the Clark-Bangdhad leg comprises the whole channel, as in Channel 61, only the radius curves need be used.

[14] Carried out to the nearest thousandth to correspond with figures in Table 16.

### Table 16. Aircraft productivities by channel
### (tons per flying hour)

| Channel | Cargo | | | | Passengers | | | |
|---|---|---|---|---|---|---|---|---|
| | C-97 | HC-400 | HC-500 | HC-600 | C-97 | HC-400 | HC-500 | HC-600 |
| 5 | 1.337 | 3.478 | 5.321 | 9.130 | .957 | 1.202 | 3.946 | 3.550 |
| 7 | .494 | 1.207 | 2.161 | 3.169 | .365 | .471 | 1.603 | 1.390 |
| 9 | .700 | 1.481 | 2.922 | 4.123 | .500 | .642 | 2.167 | 1.895 |
| 11 | 2.115 | 5.365 | 7.968 | 14.083 | 1.513 | 1.854 | 5.909 | 5.475 |
| 13 | .593 | 1.271 | 2.649 | 3.540 | .451 | .580 | 1.964 | 1.712 |
| 17 | .274 | .559 | 1.513 | 1.544 | .217 | .279 | 1.122 | .824 |
| 19 | .340 | .728 | 0 | 0 | .243 | .312 | 0 | 0 |
| 23 | .712 | 1.583 | 2.971 | 4.417 | .509 | .653 | 2.203 | 1.928 |
| 25 | 1.015 | 2.598 | 4.139 | 7.000 | .726 | .922 | 3.069 | 2.722 |
| 27 | 1.000 | 2.536 | 4.088 | 6.912 | .717 | .910 | 3.032 | 2.687 |
| 29 | .324 | .811 | 1.292 | 2.211 | .231 | .291 | .958 | .860 |
| 31 | 1.146 | 2.896 | 4.627 | 7.863 | .819 | 1.035 | 3.432 | 3.057 |
| 33 | .662 | 1.355 | 2.772 | 3.721 | .473 | .608 | 2.056 | 1.796 |
| 35 | 1.055 | 2.360 | 4.288 | 6.633 | .755 | .956 | 3.180 | 2.824 |
| 41 | .790 | 1.844 | 3.275 | 5.025 | .565 | .722 | 2.429 | 2.132 |
| 43 | .372 | .756 | 1.591 | 2.149 | .266 | .335 | 1.180 | 1.045 |
| 45 | .219 | .467 | .959 | 1.303 | .164 | .210 | .711 | .622 |
| 47 | 1.208 | 3.094 | 4.642 | 8.123 | .864 | 1.069 | 3.442 | 3.158 |
| 57 | .494 | .968 | 2.015 | 2.594 | .353 | .448 | 1.494 | 1.324 |
| 59 | .182 | .358 | .840 | .959 | .138 | .176 | .623 | .520 |
| 61 | 1.604 | 2.135 | 5.579 | 5.720 | .780 | .988 | 3.279 | 2.919 |

measures of productivity we have been discussing are unrealistic. Notice that we always assume an aircraft to be doing one or the other — but not a mixture — of two jobs: passenger transportation and cargo transportation. Now, if it were true that when an aircraft was loaded to capacity with one of these commodities, no capacity remained for the other commodity, then only the most critical could object. Mixed loading, in this case, could always be simulated in our calculations by unmixed loading: three aircraft each with a third cargo and two-thirds passengers would for present purposes be equivalent to one aircraft of cargo and two of passengers. As aircraft engineers will be quick to point out, however, fuselage shapes spoil this nice equivalence. When an aircraft carries passengers over short or intermediate ranges, its capacity is limited by space rather than by weight. Even so, in some aircraft there remain odd-shaped spaces unsuitable for passengers but perfectly good for cargo. The belly compartment of a C-97 is an example. The reverse also holds. For structural reasons, one transport has a large bubble across the upper fuselage. Cargo can be carried in this space, but difficulty of access makes it unattractive for cargo purposes. Thus, when the aircraft is loaded with cargo to its easy-access cube capacity, there still remains space for a good many passengers.

### COST COEFFICIENTS

The complexities of the cost relationships have been described. In this section we shall outline the simplifications and approximations that make our problem a mathematically tractable one. Of course, as soon as the cost relationships are simplified for use in the minimization problem, the resulting fleets only approximate the true least-cost fleets whose name they bear, but the approximation is close enough to justify the trouble connected with the minimization procedure.

The unknowns of our problem are the numbers of aircraft (of each type) procured and the numbers (of each type) operated [15] in each period. So long as cost inputs to our problem can be used as coefficients of numbers of aircraft procured or numbers of aircraft operated, no difficulties arise, for this type of treatment yields the simple linear expressions so convenient in computing. One of the costs that can be dealt with in this manner is operating cost. Unfortunately, not all the components of cost can be represented in this convenient fashion, as is clear in the earlier discussion. The following measures were therefore taken. The total procurement cost curves, like that portrayed in Figure 9, were

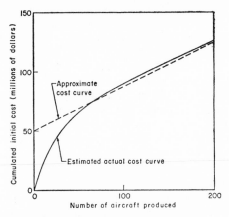

**Fig. 9. Cumulative procurement costs**

approximated by straight lines with positive intercepts, as in the dotted line in the same figure. These curves are drawn, that is, just as though the costs of tooling and learning were covered by a substantial initial investment, after which the *marginal* cost (the cost of an additional vehicle) remained exactly the same. Notice that the approximation is

---

[15] These two sets of numbers need not be the same since an aircraft may be procured at the beginning of Period I as a stopgap measure and then be retired at the beginning of Period II (i.e., not operated in Period II).

good except in the very low ranges. If it is found that this low range is critical, the approximation should be changed and the computation repeated. Obviously, foresight helps in making a good approximation at this stage.

Of the aircraft presently under consideration, only the HC-600 has a markedly curved procurement-cost function; the straight-line approximation for this aircraft resulted in a positive intercept of $50 million. Since 100 HC-400's have already been produced, the marginal procurement cost can be assumed to be constant. No HC-500's have yet been procured, but we assume that the initial tooling and learning outlay (an analytical fiction) has already been made. Both the cost of the first 100 HC-400's and the initial outlay for HC-500 production are therefore *sunk* and we do not even need to determine them; all we need here are the (constant) marginal procurement costs for these two aircraft. With these simplifications, the only mathematically troublesome aspect of procurement cost that remains is the positive intercept on the HC-600 curve. Our procedure will be to forget this intercept for the moment, proceed as if it were zero, and when we have achieved a tentative solution, check to see whether the $50 million initial outlay would affect the answer.

We shall assume that the useful life of any one of the new aircraft is ten years. It will be supposed that the C-97's are usable throughout both periods, whatever their age at the beginning of our study. Since we are only attempting to determine costs over a ten-year period, a credit will be given for the undepreciated portion of any one of the new aircraft procured midway in our period.

In our treatment of attrition, foresight again comes into play. We start the analysis with a hunch that the C-97's will be retired in favor of the newer aircraft, and charge nothing for attrition of the former. (Had this assumption turned out to be wrong, charges for attrition would then have been introduced.) Attrition of the newer vehicles is covered by further procurement at marginal procurement cost — the amount being added in with operating cost.

Installations costs we simply add in as a part of the initial cost of an aircraft. This treatment assumes that installations depreciate at the same rate as the aircraft itself, that they are specialized for use with particular aircraft, and that they cannot be inherited. Not much can be said in defense of this procedure except that it simplifies computation, and that the resulting error is probably small.

The cost numbers used explicitly in the mathematical model are costs-per-additional-aircraft and will be called *cost coefficients*. They are based on the assumptions just described. Because separate fleets are to be designed for Period I and Period II, which are four and six years long respectively, separate cost coefficients must be given for each. We will need two sets of coefficients in each period: initial cost coefficients (based on procurement and installations costs) and operating cost coefficients (based on operating and attrition costs). The complete set of coefficients, along with the initial production outlays, are presented in Table 17.

### Table 17. Cost coefficients — costs per additional airplane (millions of 1956 dollars)

|  | C-97 | HC-400 | HC-500 | HC-600[a] |
|---|---|---|---|---|
| Period I: |  |  |  |  |
| Operating Cost Coefficient | 3.69 | 3.13 | 8.13 | 7.12 |
| Initial Cost Coefficient | 0 | 1.20 | 3.00 | 2.68 |
| Total[b] | 3.69 | 4.33 | 11.13 | 9.80 |
| Period II: |  |  |  |  |
| Operating Cost Coefficient | 5.54 | 4.70 | 12.20 | 10.68 |
| Initial Cost Coefficient | 0 | 1.80 | 4.50 | 4.02 |
| Total[b] | 5.54 | 6.50 | 16.70 | 14.70 |
| Grand Total[b] | 9.23 | 10.83 | 27.83 | 24.50 |
| Initial Outlay for Production | 0 | 0 | 0 | 50 |

[a] For purposes of comparison, the HC-600 coefficients are given in Period I even though the aircraft is not available in this period.

[b] The reasons for summing these coefficients, and the conditions under which they can properly be summed, are explained in the section on "Optimizing Procedure."

### AGGREGATION OF CHANNELS

The use of an electronic computer to find the least-cost fleet sequence with the desired characteristics is perfectly feasible. Standard computing procedures exist which can be adapted to the present problem with very little alteration. Close examination of the inputs to the problem, however, indicated that moderate channel aggregation would bring the solution within reach of hand computation. This procedure, despite the more burdensome arithmetical task involved, has the advantage of allowing the analyst to see the "insides" of the problem more clearly. Those parameters and relationships on which the solution depends critically are more clearly brought to light.[16] (For these reasons hand computation of preliminary simplified models is especially helpful.)

Our object is to aggregate the 40 channels into a smaller number of groups without losing too much detail. From the standpoint of a given pair of aircraft, one channel differs from another only to the extent that the substitutability of the two aircraft on one channel is different from their substitutability on another channel. Their substitutability on a particular channel depends upon the ratio of their productivities (defined

[16] These remarks should not be construed as a *general* argument for hand computation as opposed to electronic computation, for with special measures, the latter can, of course, also answer some of the subtler questions mentioned. Too often, however, the virtues of hand computations in this respect are forgotten.

above as tonnages carried per flying hour). Therefore, the ratio of productivities for two aircraft will be called their substitution ratio. Channels with almost the same ratio can be treated as a single channel, and
their requirements can be added together.

Channels that are similar for one pair of aircraft, however, may be
quite different for another pair. One way to investigate this question is
to plot one set of such substitution ratios against another, as in Figure
10, where the ratio of HC-600 productivity to C-97 productivity is measured on the horizontal axis and the ratio of HC-400 productivity to C-97
productivity is measured on the vertical axis.

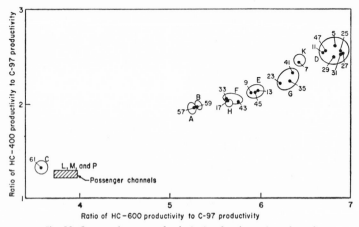

**Fig. 10. Comparative rates of substitution for the various channels**

In this first graph the points seem to fall into quite obvious clusters,
with one or two exceptions. Circles[17] have been drawn around the points
aggregated, and the new aggregate "channels" are denoted by capital
letters. In Figure 11, where the HC-500:C-97 rate of substitution is
plotted against the HC-400:C-97 rate of substitution, we see the same
aggregation. While there is nothing *necessary* about the particular
aggregation chosen, it does appear to be a reasonable one. This is true
even of Channel H, which appears to be an unlikely choice when only
Figure 10 is studied, but which is an obvious choice in Figure 11. Distinct
clustering of points is neither necessary nor sufficient for aggregation.
What is important is that the points aggregated be fairly close together
on both graphs. All of our circles have diameters sufficiently small to
avoid introducing much distortion into the problem. From this point
on, therefore, we shall deal in terms of the aggregate channels A, B, C,
D, E, F, G, H, K, L, M and P.

[17] Some of the passenger channels are not plotted separately because they fell so
close together. They all lie in the shaded rectangle.

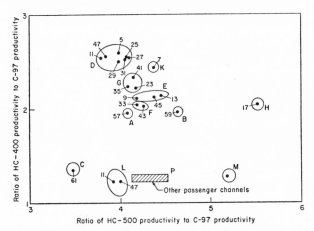

**Fig. 11. Comparative rates of substitution: another set**

### OPTIMIZING PROCEDURE

The derivation of a least-cost fleet is accomplished by trading aircraft X for Y as long as the ratio of Y's productivity to X's is in excess of the ratio of Y's marginal cost to X's marginal cost. By means of such trading, we keep finding combinations of aircraft that carry out the mission at a lower total cost.

Marginal costs[18] are somewhat complicated, in part because the procurement decisions of one period will affect the marginal costs in the other. The marginal cost of procuring an aircraft for the Period I fleet is Period I operating cost plus the Period I share of depreciation *if this vehicle is continued as a member of the Period II fleet*. In this case, the Period II marginal cost is Period II operating cost plus the Period II share of depreciation. If, alternatively, some retirement of this aircraft type takes place in Period II — that is to say, if the number of this type in the Period II fleet is less than in the Period I fleet — then the marginal cost in Period I is Period I operating cost plus the *whole* ten-year depreciation of the aircraft. The Period II marginal cost in this case is only the Period II operating cost. For the piston-engined aircraft in the beginning inventory, procurement costs are sunk, so that the marginal costs in Period I and Period II are equal to the respective operating costs in those periods. The same applies to the newer aircraft, to whose procurement the Air Force is already committed, just so long as the number of aircraft in the fleet does not exceed commitments. As soon as more than the committed number enter the fleet, then *all* of

[18] To repeat an earlier definition, "marginal cost" is the extra cost of buying and using an additional airplane.

the aircraft of this type must compete on the basis of procurement plus operating costs. In any case where production availabilities of new aircraft or beginning inventories of out-of-production aircraft are exceeded, the appropriate marginal cost figures must be increased enough to ensure that these constraints are met, just as though fictitious rental charges designed to equate demand and supply were being exacted. Notice that while a separate contest among aircraft goes on for the work on each individual channel, the local outcome depends on the global outcome because marginal costs are related to the totals of each aircraft type that appear in the fleet.

One outcome is possible which, while it appears troublesome at first sight, serves to point up some of the interesting time-phasing aspects of our problem. Suppose one of the new aircraft is a good competitor in Period I but a poor competitor in Period II, still newer types having become available in quantity. If we start by carrying out our cost-productivity comparisons on the assumption that marginal costs in the two periods include the respective shares of depreciation, then it may happen that the solution will show that the number of a certain aircraft type in the Period II fleet is smaller than the number of the same type in the Period I fleet. This is an inconsistent result, since the aircraft retired will in fact have contributed a full ten years of depreciation to total cost. But if we attempt to correct this situation by putting the full ten years of depreciation for this aircraft into Period I marginal cost, and none into Period II marginal cost, the result may turn out to be that the Period I fleet of this aircraft type is *smaller* than the Period II fleet — a *still* inconsistent result since the aircraft procured at the beginning of Period II will have contributed six years of depreciation to total fleet costs. The answer to this anomaly is that a sufficient portion of Period II depreciation must be shifted from Period II marginal cost to Period I marginal cost to bring about equality of the Period I and Period II fleets of this aircraft type. This aircraft is intermediate in its economic worth between a Period I stopgap vehicle and a full-fledged Period II competitor.

To make the calculations, we need to know the number of each aircraft type that would be required to carry out each of the 39 (unaggregated) channel jobs *alone*. This number can be computed as follows:

$$\text{Number of Aircraft Required} = \frac{\text{10-day Requirement}}{\left(\dfrac{\text{Tons per}}{\text{flying hour}}\right) \times 10 \left(\dfrac{\text{Flying hours per}}{\text{aircraft per day}^{19}}\right)}$$

When these aircraft requirement figures have been derived — one for each aircraft on each channel — they are aggregated by the channel

[19] The number of flying hours obtainable per aircraft per day is assumed to be the same for all aircraft types, ten hours.

groups defined in the last section. Since the traffic requirements change from Period I to Period II, it is necessary, of course, to determine these aircraft requirements separately for both periods. Notice the very important fact that *aircraft* requirements, not *traffic* requirements, are the numbers aggregated. The results of this computation are given in Table 18.

**Table 18. Number of aircraft of each type required to carry out each channel job alone**

| | Aircraft type | | | | | | | |
| | Period I | | | | Period II | | | |
| Channel | C-97 | HC-400 | HC-500 | HC-600 | C-97 | HC-400 | HC-500 | HC-600 |
|---|---|---|---|---|---|---|---|---|
| A | 20.2 | 10.3 | 5.0 | 3.9 | 20.2 | 10.3 | 5.0 | 3.9 |
| B | 219.9 | 111.7 | 47.6 | 41.7 | 219.8 | 111.7 | 47.6 | 41.7 |
| C | 124.7 | 93.7 | 35.8 | 35.0 | 124.7 | 93.7 | 35.8 | 35.0 |
| D | 9.2 | 3.6 | 2.3 | 1.3 | 18.3 | 7.2 | 4.7 | 2.7 |
| E | 10.8 | 5.1 | 2.5 | 1.8 | 21.7 | 10.2 | 5.0 | 3.6 |
| F | 36.2 | 17.8 | 8.5 | 6.3 | 72.5 | 35.6 | 17.0 | 12.6 |
| G | 5.0 | 2.2 | 1.2 | .8 | 10.1 | 4.5 | 2.4 | 1.6 |
| H | 19.4 | 9.5 | 3.5 | 3.4 | 38.8 | 19.0 | 7.0 | 6.9 |
| K | 1.0 | .4 | .2 | .2 | 2.1 | .8 | .5 | .3 |
| L | 1.6 | 1.3 | .4 | .4 | 3.1 | 2.5 | .8 | .9 |
| M | 25.7 | 20.0 | 5.0 | 6.8 | 51.3 | 39.9 | 9.9 | 13.5 |
| P | 156.6 | 123.0 | 35.0 | 41.4 | 191.7 | 150.7 | 43.0 | 50.4 |

Another item needed before the minimization problem can be attacked consists of the lists of productivity ratios. We can derive these ratios from the aircraft-requirement figures of Table 18, arriving at the *weighted* average for each aggregate channel of the productivity ratios of the channels aggregated. Thus, for example, on Channel C in Period I:

$$\frac{\text{C-97 Productivity}}{\text{HC-500 Productivity}} = \frac{\text{Number of HC-500's that would be needed to do the whole Channel C job in Period I}}{\text{Number of C-97's that would be needed to do the whole Channel C job in Period I}}$$

$$= \frac{35.85}{124.69} = 0.288$$

This ratio means that the C-97 is 28.8 per cent as productive as the HC-500 on Channel C. In Table 19, these ratios are given for each aggre-

#### Table 19. Productivity ratios

| | Channel | C-97 | HC-400 | HC-500 |
|---|---|---|---|---|
| HC-400 | A | 51 | | |
| | B | 51 | | |
| | C | 75 | | |
| | D | 39 | | |
| | E | 47 | | |
| | F | 49 | | |
| | G | 44 | | |
| | H | 49 | | |
| | K | 41 | | |
| | L | 81 | | |
| | M | 78 | | |
| | P | 79 | | |
| HC-500 | A | 25 | 48 | |
| | B | 22 | 43 | |
| | C | 29 | 38 | |
| | D | 25 | 65 | |
| | E | 23 | 49 | |
| | F | 23 | 48 | |
| | G | 24 | 55 | |
| | H | 18 | 37 | |
| | K | 23 | 56 | |
| | L | 25 | 31 | |
| | M | 19 | 25 | |
| | P | 22 | 28 | |
| HC-600 | A | 19 | 37 | 78 |
| | B | 19 | 37 | 88 |
| | C | 28 | 37 | 98 |
| | D | 15 | 37 | 58 |
| | E | 17 | 36 | 73 |
| | F | 17 | 35 | 74 |
| | G | 16 | 36 | 66 |
| | H | 18 | 36 | 98 |
| | K | 16 | 38 | 68 |
| | L | 27 | 34 | 109 |
| | M | 26 | 34 | 136 |
| | P | 26 | 34 | 118 |

An example of how the Table is to be read:

An HC-400 is 38% as productive as an HC-500 on Channel C.

gate channel and each pair of aircraft.[20] There is much redundancy in the table, but this makes it all the easier to compute, and separate lists for each pair of aircraft are worth the trouble.

[20] The mathematically inclined reader will notice that these productivity ratios need not be precisely the same for Period I and Period II on aggregate channels composed of both deployment and routine resupply work, such as P. Since the difference is small, however, we use the ratios from Period I throughout.

The various tables that have been presented are all that we need to solve for a series of least-cost fleets. We shall not attempt to reproduce the computational process here,[21] but will describe the optimum assignment of aircraft to channels that resulted from the Fleet 1 computation. With the aid of the cost and productivity information presented earlier, the reader will then be able to check for himself whether the conditions for an optimum hold and whether the fleet we claim to be less costly than any of the others with the required capability is *in fact* less costly. As in many other mathematical problems, obtaining the solution is rather difficult, but recognizing the solution is quite easy.

The aircraft assignment of Fleet 1 is shown in Table 20. We know

### Table 20. Aircraft channel assignment — Fleet 1

| Channel | Period I | | | | Period II | | | |
|---------|------|--------|--------|--------|------|--------|--------|--------|
|         | C-97 | HC-400 | HC-500 | HC-600 | C-97 | HC-400 | HC-500 | HC-600 |
| A |       | 10.3  |      |      |       |       |      | 3.9  |
| B |       | 111.7 |      |      |       | 111.7 |      |      |
| C | 103.4 |       | 6.1  |      |       | 31.4  |      | 23.2 |
| D |       | 3.6   |      |      |       | 7.2   |      |      |
| E |       | 5.1   |      |      |       |       |      | 3.6  |
| F |       | 17.8  |      |      |       |       |      | 12.6 |
| G |       | 2.2   |      |      |       |       |      | 1.6  |
| H |       |       | 3.5  |      |       |       |      | 6.9  |
| K |       | 0.4   |      |      |       |       |      |      |
| L |       |       | 0.4  |      |       |       |      | 0.9  |
| M |       |       | 5.0  |      |       |       |      |      |
| P |       |       | 35.0 |      |       |       | 9.9  |      |
|   |       |       |      |      |       |       | 43.0 |      |
| Total | 103.4 | 151.2 | 50.0 | — | 0 | 151.2 | 53.0 | 52.7 |

that this fleet is the least costly because it is possible to find a set of prices (that is, costs) which, for the assignment portrayed, satisfies the least-cost condition:[22] Namely, a given aircraft is in the fleet only if, on any channel where it operates, the ratio of its productivity to the productivity of any other aircraft on that channel is *at least as great* as the ratio of its marginal cost to the other aircraft's marginal cost. The set of prices consists of:

[21] The solution can be obtained by the use of a somewhat extended version of the method of Lagrange multipliers (H. W. Kuhn and A. W. Tucker, "Non-Linear Programming," in *Proceedings of the Second Berkeley Symposium on Mathematical Statistics and Probability*, Berkeley, University of California, 1951).

[22] Moreover, this is still the least-cost fleet after we take into account the $50 million initial outlay for HC-600 production (a quantity that could not be allowed for in this linear model).

$ 3.69 million for the C-97 in Period I
5.34 million for the HC-400 in Period I
12.80 million for the HC-500 in Period I
5.54 million for the C-97 in Period II
5.49 million for the HC-400 in Period II
16.70 million for the HC-500 in Period II
14.70 million for the HC-600 in Period II

We see that the C-97 price in Period I and the HC-500 and HC-600 prices in Period II are the same as the corresponding cost coefficients in Table 17. This is as it should be, for in each of these cases no production limit or inventory limit has been reached, and in the cases of the latter two aircraft no retirement takes place in Period II. In Period I the HC-500 price is somewhat higher than the corresponding cost coefficient in Table 17 because the Period I production limit of 50 aircraft is reached before the requirements have been satisfied on those channels where the HC-500 excels. In this case the fictitious rental charge referred to earlier has equated demand and supply for this aircraft.

The most interesting pricing phenomenon in this fleet concerns the HC-400. The Period I price is higher and the Period II price lower than in Table 17. Part, but not all, of the Period II share of depreciation is being charged to Period I. The reader may recall that this phenomenon is compatible only with equal numbers of HC-400's in the Period I fleet and the Period II fleet.

With these prices, the reader can check whether price and productivity ratios are consistent with the assignment presented. Perhaps the most instructive step would be to attempt to find a less costly fleet by a small change. For understanding the mechanics of the model, of course, new prices should accompany these changes, and the conditions for the solution checked.

# 9. THE CRITERION PROBLEM

In Chapter 7 we stated that the selection of an appropriate criterion is frequently the central problem in the design of an economic analysis intended to improve military decisions. Whatever the particular problem, military or civilian, it is fairly obvious that, in choosing among alternative means to our ends, we need to scan the ends themselves with a critical eye. New techniques or types of equipment may be extremely efficient in achieving certain aims, but these aims may be the wrong ones — aims that are selected almost unconsciously or at least without sufficient critical thought.

But to say that we should scrutinize our ultimate ends carefully in deciding upon the best course of action is much too vague. Suppose we wish to choose among various motorcars. Merely to name and list the things we ultimately value (such as growth, approval, security, freedom, leisure, goods) is not very helpful in solving the problem. It is wise to think about such a list, for it may prevent us from making some absurd choice that does not contribute to *any* of these things, but in most situations the list provides little counsel. One reason it fails to do so is the tremendous gap between gas consumption, wheel base, and new seat covers, on the one hand, and leisure, security, and approval, on the other. This gap has to be at least partially bridged in order to reach any conclusions about policies. Another reason is the necessity of trading part of one desideratum for some of another, sacrificing faster "pick-up" for improved fuel consumption or giving up some comforts for a little more leisure.

Similarly, the mere enumeration of objectives in choosing among weapon systems, while it may be pertinent, does not serve as a guide to specific action. The objectives may include target destruction potential, invulnerability to enemy attack, strengthening of alliances, and reliability — all to be achieved "as soon as possible." All of these things would indeed be nice to have. But while good intentions are sometimes reputed to be excellent paving materials, in themselves they do not pave the way to preferred action. In practical problems of military (or other) choice there are always constraints which prevent us from simultaneously achieving all our objectives.

## CRITERIA

Hence, in choosing among alternatives, we do more than to list things which it would be nice to have. Explicitly or implicitly we adopt criteria or tests of preferredness. One essential step in the analysis is predicting the consequences of alternative actions or systems — a step which, as indicated earlier, involves the use of sets of relationships called models. Another vital step is distinguishing preferred combinations of consequences from less desirable ones; this step entails the use of criteria. Thus, after having the features of different cars spelled out, the chooser has to decide what is the best combination of features. He may want the car that has maximum acceleration while meeting specific constraints on other aspects of performance and on cost. If so, that is his criterion. Or he may compare the features (including cost implications) of different cars subjectively and reach his decision. If so, the criterion is never made explicit, but is presumably the maximization of some function constrained by the chooser's limited resources.

There are times when the term "criterion" appears to be a misnomer. For, on occasion, as we have seen, analysis can unravel only *some* of the consequences of alternative actions and exhibit these consequences to decision-makers after the usual manner of consumers' research.[1] (By this term we mean the kind of research that is often done to help consumers choose an item such as an automobile or a refrigerator.) Insofar as this is the case, a partial criterion (comparison in terms of selected consequences) may be used. There is then no problem of devising a definitive test, but there is the closely related problem of deciding *what* consequences the decision-maker should know about. In other situations, however, the analyst may be able (or may try) to trace out all the significant effects and learn enough about the decision-maker's preferences to evaluate those effects. In these instances, quantitative analysis *per se* may be used to pick out and recommend preferred courses of action. Insofar as this is the case, a definitive test of preferredness is necessary, and the criterion problem is the devising of that test. Most of the discussion that follows will relate directly to the criterion problem faced in the latter situations, but much of it will pertain, at least indirectly, to the selection of partial criteria, that is, of selected effects that are relevant to the comparison of alternative actions.

### THE NECESSITY FOR USING "PROXIMATE" CRITERIA

Ideally we should choose that course of action which, with available resources, maximizes something like the "satisfaction" of an individual, the profits of a firm, the "military worth" of the military establishment, or the "well-being" of a group. If possible, we should like to ascertain the total amount of these magnitudes under each of various alternative policies. Then we would pick the policy that promised to yield the most satisfaction, the most profits, the most military worth, or the most well-being, depending on the identity of the person or organization whose choice we were advising. But this prescription usually helps little more than saying that we want the best. Nobody knows precisely how satisfaction and military worth are related to the observable outcomes of various courses of action. We do not have the ability to translate outcomes into such terms. In practical problem-solving, therefore, we have to look at some "proximate" criterion which serves to reflect what is happening to satisfaction or military worth. Actual criteria are the practicable sub-

[1] Consumers' research publications sometimes recommend a single "best buy," using a criterion which may or may not be acceptable to a particular subscriber. But usually they content themselves with describing features and analyzing certain consequences, letting the subscriber supply (a total or final) evaluation and make the choice.

stitutes for the maximization of whatever we would ultimately like to maximize.

In comparisons of military operations or equipment, what is desired is the course of action that would contribute most to "winning" or deterring some kind (or kinds) of war, or even more generally, to achieving national security. Since it will usually be impossible to measure achievements in any of these terms, it is necessary to adopt indirect but workable criteria that appear to be consistent with ultimate aims.

## SUB-OPTIMIZATION AND CRITERIA

The need to use proximate rather than ultimate tests opens the door to the selection of incorrect criteria. But the door is really swung wide open — in fact one might say that the welcome mat is put out — by another fact of life stressed in Chapter 7: the fact that problems of choice must be broken down into component pieces or sub-problems.

Let us examine this difficulty in somewhat greater detail. A military service (or government department or large corporation) cannot possibly have one man or one committee examine *all* its problems of choice simultaneously and pick each course of action in the light of all other decisions. It is inevitable that decision-making be broken into pieces. The division is almost necessarily along hierarchical lines, some of the broader policy choices being made by high level officials or groups, others being delegated to lower levels.[2]

Similarly, analyses must be piecemeal, since it is impossible for a single analysis to cover all problems of choice simultaneously in a large organization. Thus comparisons of alternative courses of· action always pertain to a part of the government's (or corporation's) problem. Other parts of the over-all problem are temporarily put aside, possible decisions about some matters being ignored, specific decisions about others being taken for granted. The resulting analyses are intended to provide assistance in finding optimal, or at least good, solutions to sub-problems: in the jargon of systems analysis and operations research, they are sub-optimizations.

Note again, however, that the scope of analysis does not have to, and indeed usually should not, coincide with the scope of authority in decision-making. Take the case of military decisions within the government. Analysis of a problem in antisubmarine warfare may have to be made in the context of a global war involving all services and the national economy, even though it is relevant to decisions within one bureau of the Navy

[2] We must again stress that no connotation of greater or lesser significance should be associated with these terms "higher" and "lower" levels. The lower level decisions may in some circumstances be the more important ones. Choosing the best bomber-missile systems and the means of protecting them, for example, may do more to enhance our deterrent force than allocating more funds to the Air Force to buy inferior systems.

Department. Fortunately no single authority runs the whole executive-legislative-judicial process in the United States government, but this does not mean that individual departments and subordinate units should not, on occasion, take a broad national point of view ("context" and criterion) in making decisions for which it is responsible in the hierarchy. The situation in a private corporation is precisely analogous. The individual division or department of the corporation, in making certain decisions delegated to it, will be expected to take a corporationwide point of view, tracing the full consequences of its actions on all operations of the firm.[3] The sales department is not expected to choose actions which maximize sales, or sales minus selling costs, but the total profits of the corporation — sales and other receipts minus all costs in all departments.

Piecemeal analysis and decision making have great advantages, some of which have already been stated. Small problems tend to be more "manageable" in a number of senses. As problems are broken down into smaller chunks, more detail can be taken into account by both researchers and decision-makers. In large firms a degree of decentralization greater than that which is inevitable is usually believed to be desirable so that the "man on the spot" can decide about many matters — and be held responsible for them.[4] In analysis, somewhat similarly, considerable breakdown of the problems of a corporation or a government department may be desirable so that the models used in estimating outcomes can be "on the spot," that is, less aggregative and more precise in their predictions than global or firm-wide models would be.

Finally, better hedging against uncertainty *may* result from breaking big problems into smaller ones. The difficulties that stem from inherent uncertainties will be discussed mostly in the next chapter, but a few words are in order here. If decision making is decentralized to a considerable extent, it may help against the possibility of getting stuck with lopsided views at the top. In civil government it has long been widely

[3] The exceptions in which individual divisions (e.g., those of General Motors and U.S. Steel) are instructed to act autonomously and ignore the possible repercussions of their actions on the profits of other divisions of the corporation, are instructive. In these cases the corporation has deliberately decided that the "spillover" effects on other divisions are less important in the long run than the advantages of fixing responsibility and providing strong, clear-cut incentives. There is probably also a fear that the use of corporationwide criteria in analysis may inevitably lead to an undesirable centralization of decision-making itself — a sort of "spillover" effect of a different kind. In any event, these exceptions are usually limited to certain kinds of decisions. Divisions of General Motors are supposed to be completely autonomous in buying and selling, but not in financing and therefore not in decisions requiring major capital expenditures. There are useful analogies in all this for the military.

[4] This not only takes advantage of the man-on-the-spot's familiarity with the details of a problem but also constitutes a more desirable decision-making process anyway, getting more persons in the habit of using ingenuity and taking responsibility. Indeed this is of major importance for the functioning of the economy, and probably of equal importance in the military services.

recognized that some separation of powers and dispersal of authority are important, partly as a hedging device. And in analysis, a degree of sub-optimization *may* mean, for some problems, less risk of tying all analytical results to a "bad" criterion, for instance, one involving a spuriously specific objective in which uncertainty is neglected.

On the other hand, there is a real danger in piecemeal analysis, one whose importance must be reemphasized because it is probably not as widely appreciated as are the difficulties inherent in biting off too big a chunk of the problem. The danger is that the criteria adopted in lower level problems may be unrelated to and inconsistent with higher level criteria. As mentioned before, proximate criteria have to be used in any case; but since problems must be considered one piece at a time, a whole hierarchy of proximate criteria comes into play, and potential inconsistencies are abundant.

An an example from the military sphere, suppose that the military establishes a requirement for 90 per cent reliability in the functioning of its weapon systems. Bows and arrows may pass such a test with flying colors, yet hand grenades may accomplish much more at the same cost, even if half of them are duds. Perhaps 90 per cent or 50 or 99 per cent has some intuitive appeal, but this gives little assurance that it is a sensible "requirement," criterion, or test. The point is that even plausible criteria for choosing lower level policies may not harmonize with higher level tests, that is, may not be in agreement with what we really want to do. Earlier we criticized the widespread practice in government of setting "requirements" without looking explictly at costs. Because problems must be taken up piecemeal, there is danger that requirements will be set without looking critically at payoffs either. And the achievement of a blindly selected "requirement" (even at minimum cost)[5] is likely to be inconsistent with higher level aims.

In a free enterprise economy we have a price mechanism and a system of incentives which, imperfectly but pervasively, enforce some measure of consistency between the lower level criteria used by individuals and firms in making their economic decisions and certain higher level criteria appropriate to the economy. A whole branch of economic theory, rather unfortunately labeled "welfare economics," is concerned with relations between high and low level economic criteria.[6] Under certain circum-

[5] Admittedly, if the requirement *has* to be taken as given, it is better to achieve it at minimum cost than at higher cost. Even a "bad" sub-optimization may be better than none at all. It may not make sense in the total context to raise the reliability of hand grenades to a magic 90%, but if it has to be so raised, the fewer resources we use in doing so the more will be available for sensible products.

[6] The classic work in this field is A. C. Pigou, *The Economics of Welfare*, 1st ed., Macmillan and Co., London, 1920. For an introductory and somewhat more modern exposition, see J. E. Meade and C. J. Hitch, *Introduction to Economic Analysis and Policy*, Oxford University Press, New York, 1938, especially Part II. For developments in, and

stances (the most important being absence of monopoly, free movement of factors of production, "full employment," and no external economies or diseconomies), the maximization of their own preference functions by individuals and of their own profits by firms will lead to an "efficient" use of resources in the economy — in the precisely defined senses that it will be impossible to produce more of any one good or service without producing less of some other *and* that it will be impossible to improve the satisfaction of any one individual without reducing that of another.[7] Since, in general, firms do try to maximize profits and individuals do try to maximize preference functions, there will be a tendency for resources to be efficiently used in the economy to the extent that the assumed circumstances are approximated.

This is an interesting and, within limits, a useful conclusion. It might be regarded as equally plausible, or even more plausible, that the higher level economic criterion would require firms to minimize cost per unit of output (the ratio of cost to output) or to maximize productivity per head or per man-hour (the ratio of output to some one input) instead of maximizing profits (receipts minus costs). In fact both these criteria have been widely used — in some cases appropriately, in others not — as indexes of efficiency in comparisons between firms and countries. But it can be demonstrated that maximizing either of the ratios by firms in choosing methods of production, scale of operations, and so on, would result in an inefficient use of resources in the economy.

## SOME CRITERION ERRORS

In the military (and indeed in the government generally) there is no comparable mechanism that tends to insure consistency between high level and low level criteria.[8] Since piecemeal analysis (sub-optimization) and therefore the use of low level criteria cannot be avoided, the prevention of even gross errors in the selection of criteria requires hard thought. In a very general sense all criterion errors involve inconsistency between the tests that are selected in analyzing lower level problems and the tests that are applicable at higher levels. However, some of the

qualifications to, the theory of welfare economics, see Paul A. Samuelson, *Foundations of Economic Analysis,* Harvard University Press, Cambridge, Mass., 1948, pp. 203–253; Kenneth J. Arrow, *Social Choice and Individual Values,* John Wiley and Son, New York, 1951; and R. C. Lipsey and K. Lancaster, "The General Theory of Second Best," *Review of Economic Studies,* 1956–57, pp. 11–32.

[7] Of course efficiency in this sense does not imply an "optimal" distribution of income from anyone's point of view or an "optimal" rate of growth. Efficiency is not a sufficient condition for an optimum, but it does enable us to identify improvements in many situations.

[8] There are administrative devices — committees, special staffs at higher levels, etc. — which attempt, through cooperation and "coordination," to mitigate the consequences of the absence of such a mechanism.

mistakes that occur most frequently have special characteristics and can be put into categories.

## MAXIMIZING GAIN WHILE MINIMIZING COST

The consequences of an action fall into two types — (1) those positive gains which we like to increase, or the achievement of objectives, and (2) those negative effects which we like to decrease, or the incurrence of costs. Neither type by itself can serve as an adequate criterion: the maximizing of gains without regard to cost or resource limitation is hardly a helpful test, and the minimizing of cost regardless of other consequences of the alternative actions is nonsense. Hence both gains and costs must appear in criteria but, as will be seen, they can make their appearance in various ways.

One ubiquitous source of confusion is the attempt to maximize gain while minimizing cost or, as a variant, the attempt to maximize two types of gain at once. Such efforts are made, or at least talked about, in connection with all manner of problems. It is sometimes said, for example, that we should choose new weapons "on a 'maximum effectiveness at minimum cost' basis." [9] Or consider the following criterion, which allegedly guided one military operation: "The Germans' triumphant campaign . . . was inspired by the idea of . . . achieving the unexpected in direction, time, and method, preceded by the fullest possible distraction and followed by the quickest possible exploitation along the line of least resistance to the deepest possible range." [10] In connection with civil-government choices (in India), even the London *Economist* slips. "Above all, in choosing between possible schemes, the Indian planners never admit to using the simple test: which will be more profitable? Which, in other words, will give the maximum increase in the national income for the minimum use of real resources?" [11]

Actually, of course, it is impossible to choose that policy which simultaneously maximizes gain and minimizes cost, because there is no such policy. To be sure, in a comparison of policies A and B, it may turn out occasionally that A yields greater gain, yet costs less, than B. But A will not also yield more and cost less than all other policies C through Z; and A will therefore not maximize yield while minimizing cost. Maximum gain is infinitely large, and minimum cost is zero. Seek the policy which has that outcome, and you will not find it.

It may seem that proposals to use such tests are harmless, since it is impossible to use such a criterion when the analyst buckles down to the

[9] "Organizing for the Technological War," a staff study, *Air Force,* December 1957, p. 44.

[10] B. H. Liddell Hart, *Strategy,* Frederick A. Praeger, Inc., New York, 1954, p. 240.

[11] *The Economist,* July 30, 1955, p. 400.

comparison of specific alternatives. Nonetheless, this type of criterion error should be taken seriously, for it can lead to some wild compromise criteria. If a person approaches a problem with the intention of using such a criterion, he is confused to begin with; then, when he finds that it will not work, he may fasten upon *any* sort of constraint on gain or cost that converts this impossible test into a feasible one.

OVERLOOKING ABSOLUTE SIZE OF GAIN OR COST

One common procedure is to pick that policy which has the highest ratio of "effectiveness," or achievement-of-objective, to cost. In that case, the maximizing of this ratio is the criterion. Note that the terms "effectiveness" and "achievement of objectives" mean positive gains, or the achievement of tasks that it is desirable to carry out. To examine this criterion, let us look at the comparison of alternative military weapons. These could be anything from various antitank weapons to different bombers, but suppose it is the latter. Let the ability to destroy targets, in the relevant circumstances, be the measure of effectiveness. Suppose next that a B-29 system, already on hand and relatively easy to maintain, would be able to destroy 10 targets and would entail extra costs of $1 billion — a ratio of 10 to 1 — while System X would destroy 200 targets and cost $50 billion — a ratio of 4 to 1. Does it follow that we should choose the B-29 system, the one with the higher ratio? The answer is surely No, for it might merely be a system that would invite and lose a war inexpensively. To maximize the *ratio* of effectiveness to cost may be a plausible criterion at first glance, but it allows the absolute magnitude of the achievement or the cost to roam at will. Surely it would be a mistake to tempt the decision-maker to ignore the absolute amount of damage that the bombing system could do.

Without constraints on either total level of effectiveness or total budget, the ratio of the two may point to extreme solutions, to nearly-zero or to almost infinite effectiveness and cost. Of course, common sense and empty pocketbooks prevent us from paying attention to such a ratio at the extremes. But what is its significance in the middle-ground that is not ruled out by common sense? Does the ratio take on meaning in these circumstances? The absurdity of the choice to which the ratio might lead is then bounded, and perhaps the chances that its prescription will coincide with the "correct" choice are increased, simply because the ratio is partly penned up. But still the ratio does not take on real meaning. In fact, the only way to know what such a ratio really means is to tighten the constraint until either a single budget or particular degree of effectiveness is specified. And at that juncture, the ratio reduces itself to the test of maximum effectiveness for a given budget, or a specified effectiveness at minimum cost, and might better have been put that way at the outset.

Of course, if the ratios did not alter with changes in the scale of achievement (or cost), the higher ratio would indicate the preferred system, no matter what the scale. That is, if the ratio of achievement to cost were 10 to 1 for the B-29 system and 4 to 1 for System X at *all* levels of achievement, then the B-29 system would be "dominant." For it would destroy 500 targets at the $50 billion level of cost, clearly a better performance than that of System X. But to assume that such ratios are constant is inadmissible some of the time and hazardous the rest. In the bomber illustration the assumption of constant ratios would obviously be wrong, because with larger scales of activity, it would be necessary to buy more B-29's instead of merely using the ones on hand. Moreover, whatever one's belief about the constancy of the ratio, the straightforward test of maximum effectiveness for a given budget (or, alternatively, minimum cost of achieving a specified level of effectiveness) reveals just as much as the ratio — and seems much less likely to mislead the unwary.[12]

It might be observed that ratios are sometimes handy devices for ranking a list of possible actions when (1) the scale of activity is fixed, and (2) the actions are not interdependent (more on this point later). Thus the rate of return on stocks and bonds (the ratio of annual net return to the cost of the investment) is a convenient aid in ranking securities. Then, *with a fixed investment fund,* the set of securities that yields the greatest return for that fund can be quickly determined. Note, however, the limited conditions under which this procedure can be used.

### SETTING WRONG SIZE OF GAIN OR COST

As just suggested, a criterion in which the budget or level of effectiveness is specified has the virtue of being aboveboard. The test's limitation, the fact that it relates to a particular level of cost or achievement, is perceivable with the naked eye. This fact indicates, though, that while avoidance of ratio tests is a step in the right direction, our troubles are not over. For if an incorrect or irrelevant scale of gain or cost is taken as given, the test is unlikely to result in good policy decisions.

In choosing the bombing system, let us suppose that the test is minimum cost of achieving the ability to destroy 10 targets. In these

[12] For examples of ratios used as criteria, see Charles Kittel, "The Nature and Development of Operations Research," *Science,* February 7, 1947, pp. 152–53. For more on the hazards of using ratios as criteria, see Charles Hitch, "Suboptimization in Operations Problems," *Journal of the Operations Research Society of America,* May 1953, pp. 94–95 and *passim.* See also Charles Hitch, "Economics and Military Operations Research," *Review of Economics and Statistics,* August 1958, pp. 199–209.

circumstances, the hypothetical B-29 system is better than System X. On the other hand, if the criterion is minimum cost of achieving an ability to destroy 200 targets, System X is better. Clearly it makes a difference which scale of gain (that is, effectiveness) is stipulated, and it would be possible to fix upon the wrong scale.

If the analyst has been instructed to specify a particular level of effectiveness, then someone else has, in effect, chosen this aspect of his criterion for him — for better or worse. If he has leeway, however, and chooses the scale uncritically, he is using what was described earlier as the requirements approach.[13] In other words, he is picking the desired task or level of achievement without inquiry into the sacrifices of other achievements that would be entailed. What he can do to choose the right scale will be discussed a little later. The thing to be noted here is that this sort of criterion error is always a threat in piecemeal analysis.

There is precisely the same danger if the cost (or budget, or resources) is to be stipulated instead of the task. Of course, if the budget is already definitely set by higher level decision, the analysis has to take the predetermined amount as given. But budgets for future years are never "definitely set" in a democracy, and if the analysis is concerned with development or procurement, it is usually the magnitude of future budgets that is relevant. Wherever the budget is subject to change, perhaps on the advice of the analyst, his test should not take as given a budget that is uncritically assumed or stipulated.

### NEGLECTING SPILLOVERS

In economics, impacts of one firm's action upon other firms' gains or costs are referred to as "external economies and diseconomies."[14] For example, an oil well that forces brine into the underground water supply may reduce the fertility of adjacent farmlands. Within firms or governmental units, similarly, the action of one department may affect the gains or costs of operations in other departments. (This would be the case, for instance, if the oil-producing firm owned the farmlands.) The term "spillovers"[15] will be used here, chiefly because it is short, as a general title covering all such effects.

In comparing alternative military policies, it is easy to adopt a criterion that leads to the neglect of spillover effects. For example, a

---

[13] Of course, he will presumably minimize the cost of satisfying the requirement — which is, as we have seen, better than choosing uncritically both the task and the method of accomplishing it (the "pure" requirements approach, undefiled by any cost considerations).

[14] Or sometimes "divergences between private and social product or cost."

[15] The term "spillover costs" and a helpful discussion of those that arise from congestion are contained in J. M. Buchanan's article, "The Pricing of Highway Services," *National Tax Journal,* June 1952, pp. 97–106.

classic piece of military operations research may have ignored some impacts on activities other than the one that was directly under examination. In this frequently cited example of successful analysis, alternative arrangements for washing and rinsing mess-kits were compared. As his test of preferredness, the analyst used the minimization of the number of man-hours required to do the job, given a total of four tubs. The optimal arrangement, according to this test, turned out to be the use of three tubs for washing and one tub for rinsing. A hypothetical reaction of the mess sergeant has been reported as follows:

Yeah, I remember that guy. He had some screwball idea that the mission of the Army was to eliminate waiting lines. Actually I had it all figured out that two was the right number of rinse tubs. With everyone rinsing in one tub the bacteria count would get way past the critical level. But we switched to one rinse tub while he was around because the old man says he's an important scientist or something and we got to humor him. Had damn near a third of the outfit out with the bellyache before we got the character off the reservation. Then we quick switched to three rinse tubs and really made a nice line. "Nothing like a good line to get the men's legs in condition," the old man says.[16]

The purpose of this example is not to disparage this particular piece of analysis, which may have been quite useful. The point is simply to suggest how easy it is, in the comparison of *any* policies, to neglect spillover effects.

### USING WRONG CONCEPTS OF COST OR GAIN

The manner in which cost and gain are defined may seem to be a matter of measurement. These definitions are pertinent in a discussion of criterion errors, however, because wrong concepts of cost and gain may grow out of, or be inextricably bound up with, the adoption of incorrect criteria.

Probably the most important cause of error of this sort is the exclusion of relevant costs from the computation. As we have emphasized in Chapters 4 and 7, and illustrated in Chapter 8, the costs to be compared are the full system costs of each alternative — all the costs directly or indirectly stemming from the decision. Thus, if we are trying to decide between a missile and an aircraft to accomplish a given mission, it can be completely misleading to compare the manufacturing costs of the competing major equipments. We must also count the costs (except where they are already "sunk") of all the auxiliary equipment, of the ground-handling and support equipment, of the training of personnel, and of operation for some appropriate period of time (see Chapter 11).

Our major emphasis in this volume is on peacetime preparations for

[16] From A. M. Mood's Review of P. M. Morse and C. E. Kimball, *Methods of Operations Research,* in the *Journal of the Operations Research Society of America,* November 1953, p. 307.

war and on deterring war. This means that we are interested *mainly* in peacetime, not wartime costs. We are trying to make the most of the resources available for national security in peacetime. In principle, the wartime costs are relevant. In practice, we can frequently ignore them. For in the case of general nuclear war, we expect the war to be fought with the forces in being at its outbreak. The major economic problem is to maximize the capability of these forces by using resources efficiently before the war starts — so efficiently that we hope an enemy will never dare start it. In the case of limited war there may well be significant production of weapons and expenditure of resources after the limited war begins (as in the case of Korea), but occasional wars for limited objectives will cost little compared with the year-in year-out costs of peacetime preparedness. It is estimated that the "cost of United States forces in Korea over and above the normal cost of such forces if no action was taking place" was approximately five billion dollars in the fiscal year 1951/52, about 11 per cent of total United States expenditures for major national security programs that year.[17]

Right and wrong concepts of cost and gain can, however, be illustrated by either wartime or peacetime studies. For example, in a World War II study of alternative ways to destroy enemy shipping, the criterion adopted was the ratio of enemy ships sunk (the gain) to allied man-years of effort (the cost).[18] Now our concern in this section is not with the hazards of such a ratio test,[19] but rather with the nature of these concepts of gain and cost.

*Neglect of higher level gain.* First, "ships sunk" as a measure of gain may have been an unfortunate choice (whether made by the analysts or by "higher authority"), for shipping could be effectively destroyed by actions such as mine-laying without necessarily sinking many ships. The criterion adopted would have prejudiced the case against such measures.

*Neglect of valuable inputs.* Next, let us examine the costs of these ship-sinking operations. Costs are the consequences that have negative values, or in other words they are the sacrifices that have to be made in order to conduct the operation. In the above-mentioned study, man-years of effort — which included those used in construction of vessels and equipment, training, operations, and replacements — appear to be a somewhat dubious measure of these sacrifices. One reason is that man-years, while

---

[17] *Mutual Security Act of 1952,* Hearings before the Committee on Foreign Affairs, House of Representatives, 82nd Congress, 2nd Session, U.S. Government Printing Office, Washington, D.C., 1952, p. 359.

[18] Kittel, p. 152.

[19] The operation that maximized the *ratio* of ships sunk to allied effort might be a trivial operation sinking one ship or a gigantic effort destroying vast quantities of shipping and requiring the bulk of our resources. There is little assurance that the operation picked solely on the basis of this *ratio* would contribute the most toward victory.

important in wartime (and in peacetime), were not the only items given up. Thus a method of destroying enemy shipping that used comparatively little manpower, even though it required extremely valuable equipment and skills, had a spurious advantage over a method that utilized relatively worthless equipment and much labor. In effect the test ignored inputs other than man-years as if they were free.

In extreme cases, this sort of procedure may be the correct one. Since the cost of one course of action is whatever has to be sacrificed, that cost depends upon what alternatives are genuinely possible. If, for example, the only courses of action that can be considered are different ways for unskilled laborers to use given equipment to carry out a specified task, the only input that has other uses is the labor. The analysis becomes a time-and-motion study, and a suitable test is the achievement of the specified task with the minimum expenditure of man-hours.

In general, however, the use of man-hours, a "critical material," or any other single input to represent cost is likely to be wrong. Other valuable inputs are usually involved. To ignore these other inputs is to pretend that their use involves no sacrifice, whatever the quantity employed. Another plausible procedure — putting a specific constraint on the amount of each input that is to be used — is in most cases equally misleading. Such a constraint pretends that we do not have the choice of acquiring extra amounts of the input. Sometimes the choices open to us are limited in this fashion, but placing specific constraints on all inputs usually shortens the list of alternatives that is truly admissible; hence it distorts the sacrifices entailed by taking the actions that are in fact examined.

What, then, is the right way to measure cost? As has been indicated in Chapter 3 and in Chapter 7, the answer, in principle, is that the measures in any particular problem should approximate the value of the alternatives that must be sacrificed. In long-run problems (most development and many procurement choices) the almost unlimited possibilities of substitution in the economy make dollar costs — the dollars representing general resources — a satisfactory measure in most cases, and far superior to such practical alternatives as man-hours. Dollars do, even if imperfectly, take account of the value in other uses of different skills and of factors of production other than labor. In short-run and intermediate-run problems the difficulties are greater, and one must usually impose cost or resource constraints of several kinds. In the extreme case of a field commander who has to prepare for an imminent battle with what he has on hand, the amount of each specific resource (men, tanks, ammunition, and so on) he has is fixed,[20] and no more of any one can be

---

[20] Though even here some of his resources may have value for later battles — a relevant alternative use.

secured at any price. In this case each resource must be taken as a constraint on his tactics. In less extreme cases some resources will be fixed and others variable — the latter frequently at "increasing costs" reflecting either higher incremental production costs in the short run or the withdrawal of the additional resources from increasingly valuable uses elsewhere.

The Navy, for example, may have a certain number of warships readily available for an operation in the Mediterranean (those on station there). In a very short-run problem, no more could be made available from anywhere. In an intermediate-run problem, additional ships could be obtained, but only by the very expensive method of "de-mothballing" or by transferring to the Mediterranean ships whose "outputs" are valuable in other areas (increasingly valuable the more are transferred). In a long-run problem, of course, additional ships could be procured for more dollars. Finding satisfactory cost measures and resource constraints in the intermediate-run problems will frequently tax the ingenuity of the analyst. He must try to avoid treating as free those resources that have value in other uses, or as fixed those resources that, at some cost, are variable. (Also, of course, he should avoid the opposite errors.) While perfection is unattainable, the avoidance of the grosser fallacies is not.

*"Sunk" costs and salvage values.* Consider once again the costs counted in the search for the best way to destroy enemy shipping. These costs included man-years of effort used in the construction of ships, equipment, and submarines — many of which were already built and on hand. Yet the sacrifice entailed by the use of existing equipment was really its value in other operations,[21] not the original or historical cost of constructing it. Only future sacrifices are relevant — not past. In an economic calculus "bygones are forever bygones."

This point was critical in the comparison that we made above of B-29 and X bombing systems, where the B-29's had already been produced and the X-bombers had not. Should the Air Force "be fair" to System X and insist upon costing each bomber from scratch? Never could considerations of equity be more misplaced. Any real cost associated with the production of the B-29's had already been incurred and is unaffected by what is done with them; if they have no alternative use and no scrap value, then the cost of incorporating them into the bombing system is zero. If they have a scrap value or a value in alternative uses that is sacrificed, then that value is the relevant cost. It is only the extra or incremental cost, not historical or "from scratch" cost, entailed by each alternative system that is relevant to the comparison. The analogy

---

[21] This may well be hard to measure quantitatively, but better the roughest approximation of the relevant magnitude than the most precise measure of the irrelevant.

with a business firm's view of cost is complete: in deciding whether to replace an old machine with a new one, the production cost or purchase price of the new machine enters into the calculus, but only the scrap value (or alternative use value) of the old machine, however unfair this may appear to be to the new machine.[22] Considerations of fairness, which might be appropriate in courts of equity, are an undependable basis for choosing production methods or weapon systems.

Frequently in comparing the costs and gains from alternative weapon systems during some relevant period, it will be apparent that some of the systems will be worth more than others at the end of the period. An estimate of the worth of the system at the end of the period — its probable contribution to security in following periods — is commonly referred to as the system's "salvage value." If salvage values are substantial and vary significantly from system to system, as in the case of the air transport fleets in Chapter 8, they should be subtracted from system costs (or added to system gains). If these values are small or appear to be similar for all systems, of course they can be ignored.

### ALLOCATION OF JOINT COSTS

In sub-optimizing, the analyst is frequently confronted with the necessity of computing the cost of X, when some or all of the costs of X are also costs of Y and Z. Suppose, for example, that the construction of an airbase is being considered for joint tenancy by three fighter squadrons and various Military Air Transport Service (MATS) facilities and services. Suppose that the total cost of the base is 100, of which 50 is the cost of basic or common facilities, 30 the cost of facilities required by MATS only (these might include, for example, costs of extending or strengthening runways for heavier MATS planes), and 20 the cost of facilities required by the fighter squadrons. If the base were used only by MATS its cost would be 80; if only by fighters, 70.

One way to approach the problem (it turns out to be a treacherous way) is to ask: How should the common costs be allocated among the various uses? One cabinet officer attempted to answer the question in this manner: "The Department believes that the costs of multiple-purpose . . . projects should be allocated on a basis which properly recognizes the added costs of including each separable function and a *fair*[23] share of the joint costs." [24] Again we have the unwarranted intrusion of ethical

---

[22] For examples in which business management formally compares alternative policies in terms of incremental costs and gains, see Horace C. Levinson, "Experiences in Commercial Operations Research," *Journal of the Operations Research Society of America,* August 1953, pp. 220–239.

[23] Italics ours.

[24] Former Secretary of Agriculture Brannan in *Study of Civil Works,* Part 2, Hearings before the Subcommittee to Study Civil Works of the Committee on Public Works, House of Representatives, 82nd Congress, 2nd Session, U.S. Government Printing Office, Washington, 1952, p. 198.

concepts into an economic calculus. In the Twentieth Century, it appears, we must be fair not only to people, but to weapon systems, machinery, and airbases.

If we keep firmly in mind the principle that only the *incremental* costs for which a system is responsible should be counted, problems of the type presented by the airbase offer no great difficulty. Of course which costs *are* incremental depends upon the breadth of context and the precise definition of the system. If the problem is whether to construct the airbase, and if so, whether for joint tenancy, for MATS only, or for the fighters only, we have to cost the base in three alternative systems. In the first (joint tenancy), the cost is 100; in the second (MATS only), 80; in the third (fighters only), 70. The base should be constructed if its value to MATS exceeds 80, if its value to the fighter command exceeds 70, *or if its value to both combined exceeds 100.* If its value to both combined exceeds 100, the base should be constructed for joint tenancy as long as its value to MATS exceeds 30 and its value to the fighter command 20. A businessman launching a multiproduct investment would think along precisely these same lines in maximizing his profits.[25] As long as the use values can be calculated,[26] the analyst can find a unique solution to his problem without allocating, "fairly" or otherwise, the common costs. The question simply doesn't arise.

If a formula for allocating total costs among uses is intended to show how costs respond when one use is eliminated, it can serve a very useful purpose; it is then an attempt to get better estimates of incremental costs. But a formula that is supposed to hand out "fair shares" of joint costs, the shares exactly exhausting the total, is not needed for good decisions and can lead to bad ones. Inability to allocate *all* costs meaningfully among joint products is often a fact of life, not a disgrace or a sign of laziness. The extra cost of adding on a function or a feature can be calculated, or the total cost of the combination of features — but not a meaningful total cost for one feature when undertaken jointly with the others.

## APPROPRIATE CRITERIA

So much for potential errors in the devising of tests for preferred policies. What of a constructive nature can be said about the selection of criteria? Clearly, there is no all-purpose criterion, for the appropriate test depends upon what alternatives are open to the decision-maker,

[25] George J. Stigler, *The Theory of Price,* Macmillan Co., New York, 1946, p. 307.
[26] Of course if the use values can't be calculated, the analyst may have a difficult problem on his hands and may have to be content with a "good" or "better" rather than a unique optimal solution. But allocating the common costs won't help him in this case. His fundamental difficulty is his inability to measure military worth.

upon what aspects of the situation must be taken as given, and even upon what kind of measurements are feasible. Nonetheless a few general observations about suitable criterion-forms can be made.

If gains and costs can be measured in the same unit, then to maximize gains-minus-costs is certainly an acceptable criterion-form — the equivalent of making the most out of whatever actions can be taken. Suppose the possible courses of action are to put available resources to one of three uses, to be called A, B, and C. Now the gains that could have been obtained by using the resources in B and C are what have to be given up when we use the resources in A. These sacrifices are the *costs* of devoting the inputs to use A, the costs of obtaining the gains from A. When costs are viewed in this way (that is, as gains that must be given up), it is easy to see that maximizing gains-minus-costs is the same as maximizing total gains. If A yields 100 units of gain, B yields 75 units, and C 50 units, A is the use that maximizes gains-minus-costs (100 minus 75), and it is the use that yields the greatest total gain in the circumstances. Note again that this sort of test is possible only when gains and costs are commensurable. It can be used in the comparison of the actions of business firms and certain government measures but only exceptionally in the analysis of military activities.

In any situation there are constraints. The decision-maker can borrow additional funds only at higher rates of interest, only a limited number of practical actions are open to him, and there are only twenty-four hours in his day. In many analyses, one constraint is that a particular scale of gain or cost is fixed. This constraint may be imposed when gain and cost are commensurable, as in the case of a firm comparing different ways to use a given investment budget. And it should be imposed, as a rule, for analysis in which costs and gains are incommensurable. In the latter case, naturally it is impossible to maximize gains-minus-costs; what would be the meaning of the ability to destroy ten targets minus one billion dollars? The next-best procedure[27] is to "set" either the costs or gains, seeking the way to get the most for a given cost, or to achieve a specified objective at least cost.

These two criterion-forms are equivalent, if the size of either gain or cost is the same in the two tests. If the test of maximum gain for a $5 budget points to the policy which yields a gain of 10 units, then the test of minimum cost to achieve a fixed gain of 10 will point to the same policy

[27] Equivalent to maximizing gains-minus-costs in the special case where gains and costs are commensurate and the right level of gains or costs is fixed.

— the one which achieves the gain of 10 at a cost of $5. The two tests also yield equivalent information if calculations are carried out for many different scales of cost and gain. The choice between these two criteria depends largely upon convenience of analysis and upon whether it is gain or cost that can be fixed with the greater degree of "correctness." In some cases it will be immediately apparent which way round the criterion should be stated and the analysis made. For example, the field commander (or his operations analyst), preparing for an imminent battle with a multiplicity of fixed specific resources, will obviously fix the level of resource constraints and attempt to maximize his chances of winning, rather than set some arbitrary chance of winning and calculate the combinations of resources necessary to achieve it. In other cases the preferred way round will not be apparent, and it may indeed make little difference from any point of view which is selected. For example, we can either choose some index of strategic capability we think we might be able to achieve, and calculate the necessary budget, or assume some practical budget and calculate the corresponding index of capability.

This leads us to the big question: How does one determine the right achievement or budget? If the achievement or budget is set uncritically, the procedure degenerates into the "requirements approach." For example, it might be taken as given that we "need" the Cadillac of Chapter 7 or, in the case of the bombing system, a capability of destroying ten thousand targets; and the analysis would seek the cheapest way to achieve that "requirement." What can be done to improve upon this approach?

As a starter, several tasks or scales of effectiveness can be tried, and several budget-sizes can be assumed. If the same system is preferred for all tasks or budgets, that system is dominant. In the bombing-system example, the best bomber (though not the right scale or capability) is then determined.[28] If the same course of action is not dominant, the use of several tasks or budgets is nevertheless an essential step, because it provides vital information to the decision-maker.

Note, however, that the decision-maker, if he is making a quantitative decision or if the qualitative answers vary in the scale, must then himself select the scale of the task or budget. He is presumably helped in reaching this decision by the information about the cost of achieving different tasks or the potential achievements with different budgets. But he has to draw on further information in order to set the right task or budget. He has to ask what task or budget, as the case may be, is consistent with higher-level criteria. Is a capability of destroying ten thousand targets too much or too little in view of the over-all aims of the defense program?

---

[28] This may be the decision-maker's current problem — *which* bomber to develop or procure. The decision regarding numbers may be made (and re-made) much later.

Clearly the analyst will be more helpful if he can answer these questions than if he merely estimates the results for a variety of budgets or tasks. As a matter of fact, he must try to answer these questions approximately if he is even to hit upon a reasonable range of tasks or budgets. He cannot experiment with all possible scales of achievement or cost, as the computations would be too expensive and voluminous to provide any net assistance. Hence the analyst can and should do more than try several tasks or budgets (the procedure which was labeled a "starter"). He should make some inquiry into higher level criteria and into their relationship to possible lower level tests. He may even convert the analysis into a higher level sub-optimization. At *some* higher level, of course, the criterion must be taken as given — that is, to carry out the higher level task at minimum cost, or to get the most out of the higher level budget. But this acceptance of a task or budget as given at some high level is skies apart from setting "requirements" uncritically all the way up and down the line.

### THE CRITERION FOR CHOOSING A MILITARY AIR TRANSPORT FLEET

In the hypothetical example in the preceding chapter the criterion selected was the minimum cost of maintaining a specified airlift capability over the years 1958–1967. This criterion avoids some of the elementary pitfalls of criterion selection that we have discussed. It does not try to achieve a maximum capability at minimum cost. Nor does it employ a crude ratio — like minimum cost per ton-mile — irrespective of the scale of the job to be done (the distances to be traveled and the volume of cargo to be carried). It uses system costs, omitting sunk costs and, at least in principle, allowing for the salvage value of what is left over in 1967.

It concentrates on minimizing the cost of achieving a given objective instead of maximizing the objective for a given cost, because in this particular case it seems to be easier to select a "reasonable" level for the objective than for the budget. Providing airlift is a small proportion of the total cost of preparing to fight peripheral wars, and a small part of the total cost of operating the peacetime Air Force and military establishment. To choose some arbitrary budget level for airlift and adjust all other plans to it would be to make the tail wag the dog.

The level of the objective to be achieved was not chosen arbitrarily: it was based on certain plans for fighting peripheral wars if they occur, and for supporting a planned peacetime military establishment with rapid transport. It was an objective that had to be described in considerable detail — the war had to be fought in a certain geographical location and to be of a certain magnitude, and the peacetime support had to be provided using an established network of bases involving routes of diverse specific lengths. The degree of detail in defining the objective may appear excessive (it would certainly prove to be wrong as a specific forecast). This detail was intended to illustrate representative tasks, however, and it was believed that a change in the geographical location of the war, or in the pattern of available peacetime bases, would not greatly alter the mix of short- and long-legged vehicles needed. It would be desirable, in a more complete analysis, to test this belief by trying the various fleets in achieving different tasks.

A very important side calculation was made which (assuming it to be correct) determined that any fleet that could meet the requirements of the assumed limited war and peacetime re-supply could *a fortiori* meet the requirements for air transport in a general all-out war.

Nevertheless, some doubts remain regarding this particular criterion. The calculation was a low level sub-optimization, and some of the conclusions (especially regarding the size of the task and of the fleet) might be upset by a good economic analysis at a higher level. In limited wars expensive airlift is a substitute for other expensive things we can buy, such as pre-positioned supplies, tactical air forces and troops stationed overseas, and allied military forces sustained by United States military aid. Since the study in Chapter 7 did not explore for the optimal mix of these elements, the objective chosen may have been too large or too small, perhaps influencing the composition of the optimal fleet.

There are other interdependencies (spillovers) and intangibles and uncertainties that could conceivably upset some of the assumptions or conclusions or both. For example, purchasing the more advanced types might help to promote the general state of the art of American transport aviation. A fleet which used fewer crews might make it easier for SAC to obtain the crews it needs to improve its alert status and thereby its deterrent capability. A fleet with a more flexible capability would help us deal with a variety of contingencies not included in the study — like a new Berlin airlift.

There are also complications associated with time and development uncertainties that affect the validity of the criterion. We will postpone a consideration of these to later chapters; but in general it would be indefensible to compare expenditures incurred in different years, as this example does, without applying appropriate discount rates. The advanced types require heavier expenditures now, lower expenditures in the future, compared to the types in inventory. If a sensitivity test had not shown that discount rates as high as 25 per cent failed to upset the ranking of the fleets, we would have grave doubts about the relevance of the conclusions. Since even high rates do not alter the ranking, and since many of the other omitted factors tend to reinforce the preference for the advanced types, we can safely conclude from the study that *if the pro-*

*jections of performance are correct,* the procurement of one of the newer fleets would be economical. It is interesting that the economic criterion in this instance calls for the acquisition of new, more expensive equipment even though no direct competition in performance with the enemy is involved. Of course similar economic criteria frequently lead business men to precisely the same sort of conclusion.

CRITERIA FOR DETERRENCE

Suppose that our problem (in 1959) is the design of a strategic offensive force for the middle 1960's to deter prospective enemies from attacking us. Deterrence of World War III is a frequently stated national objective. Our strategic offense force, while not the only force important for deterrence, is generally recognized to be the principal one. But "deterrence" is an elusive and qualitative concept, not too far removed from "military worth" itself. To calculate the relative contributions of alternative weapon systems, base locations, and strategies to deterrence, we require a much more precise and objective proximate criterion. What is a good criterion — one that avoids the pitfalls we have outlined and is consistent with the high level national objective of deterrence? Let us consider some possibilities (all of which have been used in similar studies), beginning with some that, while avoiding the crudest fallacies, are still clearly unsatisfactory.

a. *Numbers or weight of offense weapons (for a given budget).* Criteria of this general type are used in a surprisingly large number of cases by military correspondents, columnists, and other "experts" who should know better. Our deterrent force is held to be effective because we have more (or bigger) bombers than the Russians; or thought not to be effective because the Russians allegedly are building more long-range missiles than we. Little thought is required to dismiss such crude counting devices. What matters is not the number of aircraft or missiles on either side, or any other physical measure of their size, but in some sense the damage they are able to inflict. A missile that can carry a small bomb and deliver it within 10 miles of its target presents nothing like the deterrent threat of a missile that can carry a large bomb and deliver it within two miles.

b. *The number or value of enemy targets that can be destroyed (for a given budget).* This is a criterion that makes a little more sense. It takes into account not only the numbers of our offense bombers and missiles, but also their operational effectiveness, the yield of the bombs they can carry, their ability to penetrate enemy defenses, and the accuracy with which their bombs can be delivered. It is still, of course, an ambiguous criterion, and requires more precise definition. For example, what target system — population, industry, or military bases — should we use to keep score on alternative United States strategic forces? In principle, the one whose prospective destruction would be most likely to deter the Russians from striking. If we are not sure which target system would have this characteristic, we might have to try several, to see whether the same strategic force performed best (or well) against all. Similarly, what kind of air defenses should we assume the Russians will have in the mid-sixties? Here we will almost certainly have to assume several kinds and quantities to test the alternative forces, giving the Russians some opportunity in each instance to adjust their defenses to the composition and basing of our force. But there remains another ambiguity in this criterion — one of crucial importance. Should we count the destruction potential of the entire force (the customary procedure) or the potential of that part of the force that survives an enemy attack? In other words, are we interested in a "strike-first" or a "strike-second" capability? Which is consistent with the national objective of deterrence?

To the extent that we are concerned with deterring a direct Russian assault on us, the essence of deterrence is a strike-second capability. The Russians will be deterred, not by the damage we can do if they refrain from attacking, but by the damage we can do if and after they attack. An American force that can make a devastating first strike but is easily destroyed on the ground is more likely to invite direct attack than to deter it. (It may, however, have some utility in deterring lesser aggression, for example, against third parties.)

c. *The value of enemy targets that can be destroyed (for a given budget) after an enemy first strike.* This is much closer to what we want. It requires us, in allocating our given budget, to reduce the vulnerability of our force whenever money spent on reducing vulnerability (say, on dispersal, on increased alertness, or on underground construction) will increase our strike-second capability more than the same money spent on additional bombers or missiles and the personnel to operate them. In general, this is what deterrence demands. This criterion is probably good enough to justify extensive quantitative comparisons of our capabilities with different kinds of weapons (bombers and missiles), different base systems (continental United States *versus* overseas *versus* on or under the seas; fixed *versus* mobile), and different modes of protection (such as ground alert, airborne alert, dispersal, and underground construction). In making the comparisons we must consider a range of possible Russian attacks, with special emphasis on those that look most dangerous to us, and are therefore most likely to be preferred by the Russians.

But we should be under no illusions that this good, workable criterion is good enough to yield definitive answers. It too ignores several vital elements of this exceedingly difficult and complex problem. For example, it ignores the danger that World War III might break out as the result of an accident or misunderstanding; it would do us little good to deter a rational enemy from attacking only to stumble into hostilities by accident (and some weapons and modes of operating them are more "accident prone" than others). This criterion partly neglects the objective of deterring "minor" aggressions, such as enemy attacks on United States or free-world positions in the NATO area or the Middle East. A strike-second capability would also have a strike-first potential, but it is not obvious that the measures that are optimal for deterring a direct attack are also optimal for deterring an indirect one. This test also ignores a good many interdependencies among different military capabilities: can our strategic offensive forces be designed in such a way as to contribute to our ability to fight limited, local wars or to facilitate the task of air defense? Can it even be assumed that the best force for deterring World War III is also best for fighting it — in the event that deterrence fails?

There is, moreover, the problem of what size the "given" budget should be. The optimal mix of weapons, bases, and protective measures may or may not be similar at different budget levels (this could be tested by trying a number of different levels). But even if the mixes are similar, it is tremendously important to get the absolute level somewhere near right — to have a deterrent force that is good enough, not merely the best achievable on a budget too low to provide deterrence, or one so good that we over-deter World War III and have little left over for other vital capabilities. The fixing of this level requires, of course, a higher level study that focuses on the size of the national security budget and its allocation among the major military claimants — for strategic offense, strategic defense, limited war, and cold war. We have already indicated (Chapters 4 and 7) that while rigorous maximization at this level is silly, hard straight thinking in an economic framework can help, and can be helped by quantitative calculations. The size of the budget for the strategic offensive force must not be accepted *uncritically* as "given"; its determination is one of the most important national security decisions.

We shall return to this vital problem of deterrence in the final chapter after discussing, in intervening chapters, some additional relevant problems and techniques for dealing with them.

# 10. INCOMMENSURABLES, UNCERTAINTY, AND THE ENEMY

**W**e have seen that at best the problem of determining relevant, correct criteria is troublesome. The complications that are now to be introduced make the problem still less tractable, and indeed affect the very meaning that must be attached to the word criterion.

## INCOMMENSURABLES: MEANING, EXAMPLES, AND TREATMENT

Incommensurables, as we use the term, are certain consequences of the alternatives compared — those consequences that cannot readily be translated into the common denominator or denominators that are being used.[1] Thus, if gains are being measured in dollars (as they ordinarily are in a business problem), the effects that cannot be measured in money by any objective and generally acceptable method are incommensurables. In principle, these effects are not different from any others. They may or may not be measurable in their own appropriate quantitative terms, in a manner helpful to the decision-maker. (If not, they are "intangible" as well as incommensurable.) Moreover, an *individual* can compare them subjectively with the other effects. Indeed, implicitly the decision-maker does translate these incommensurables into the common denominator when he makes a choice. But they cannot be expressed in terms of the principal or common unit in any *generally acceptable* manner. Of course if no single unit is used extensively enough to be regarded as a common denominator, there is no basis for distinguishing between effects that are commensurable and those that are not. This is often the case in consumers' research, which we regard as the most rudimentary, least ambitious type of economic calculus.

Incommensurable objectives and costs are likely to mar the neatness of any analysis, whether it pertains to problems of business, the military, other parts of the government, or individual consumers. No matter how industriously the analyst works at devising a single quantitative test, considerations that must be measured in other units (if at all) will still be pertinent to the final decision. It is difficult to find problems of

[1] We saw in Chapter 7 that it is possible to carry out a quantitative analysis with two or more objectives or common denominators as long as we are satisfied with a set of "efficient" solutions rather than an optimal solution. We will usually assume in this section that a single common denominator is used in the explicit calculus. But see pp. 204–205 below.

military choice in which such considerations do not have to be given serious attention. We have already seen[2] that in high level military problems incommensurables may severely restrict the usefulness of quantitative analysis. They are likely to dominate any analysis of the optimum size of military budget, or its division among the military services.

Even at relatively low levels incommensurables are likely to be too important to ignore; and in some low level problems they are dominant. In other words, there are military problems at all levels in which a definitive economic calculus cannot be made because of the multiplicity, incommensurability, or nonmeasurability of the objectives or costs.

Consider the importance of such effects in military problems where quantitative analysis can be helpful. In many such problems, cost can be fairly satisfactorily measured in dollars, and the objective as the degree of achievement of some military mission. But suppose that the preferred (that is, minimum-cost) method of achieving the objective is expected to involve the loss of more lives than some alternative method that is more expensive in dollars — even when the costs of recruiting and training the additional personnel required are included, as of course they should be, in the calculations. There are at least two reasons we might be concerned about this. First, the higher casualties *may* affect the morale of our forces and degrade their efficiency in a manner not taken into account in the calculations, making the efficiency of the first method less than it appears on paper. In *principle* such reactions should be taken into account explicitly; in practice, the intangible character of a factor like morale may make this impossible. Second, we are interested in lives for their own sake. We want to win a war with no more casualties than necessary. Fewness of casualties *per se* is an objective in planning any military operation, even if a subordinate one, that is not fully allowed for by including the resource cost of replacements.

Other examples of incommensurables frequently encountered in military problems include the whole gamut of other factors influencing morale; increased capability to fight a war of type B when the major consideration is the capability to fight war A; impetus to specially promising state-of-the-art advances in choosing the next generation of some type of equipment; the maintenance of a "healthy" aircraft industry or broad mobilization base in selecting contractors (and therefore weapons); repercussions of all sorts on United States foreign relations and hence foreign policy (an extreme example is action that a potential enemy might regard as "provocative"); the effects of some methods of winning a war on the prospects for a tolerable and durable peace.

There are several ways of handling incommensurables in quantitative analysis. One way is just to ignore them: if there is no objective way

[2] Chapter 7.

to make them commensurate, have no truck with them at all. This method is not recommended; the significance of the numbers in an analysis depends upon the importance of effects not encompassed by those numbers, and the recognition of this dependence should not be left to chance. What effects are finally measured in terms of the common denominator must be made clear;[3] what major effects are *not* so measured, though perhaps initially considered as candidates for inclusion, should *at least* be described.

Sometimes it is suggested that, if the analyst works hard enough, *everything* can be put in terms of the common unit. For example, it has been suggested that the saving of a human life can be priced by consulting (1) the values implied by past decisions, (2) the average court award, or legal compensation, for accidental death, (3) the value of a person as productive capital in the economy — the sum of his expected future net earnings discounted to the present, or (4) the cost of saving a life by the cheapest alternative method. Now any of these devices may be useful in particular problems, but none provides a generally valid and appropriate measure of "the" value of human life, and the real meaning of some of them, in the absence of an organized market (like a slave market) to which governments and individuals adjust their actions, is hard to unravel.

It is possible, in some cases, to estimate the values attached to human lives implied in some World War II decisions — the amounts that were in effect traded for lives; but these values differed from one situation to the next and were not necessarily the values that should then have been, or ought now to be, assigned to lives. Court awards provide no generally appropriate value; they are notoriously influenced by adventitious factors. As for the value of a man as a productive resource, it does not reveal our valuation of a life as such. Besides, the value of a person as peacetime productive capital is almost irrelevant in war, when we are willing to sacrifice peacetime values to achieve war objectives. The costs of saving additional lives by other methods may suggest a maximum value in some circumstances, or may be useful in suggesting a reallocation of budget among various policies designed to save lives. It is inefficient, in the technical sense, to spend $10 million per life saved in the design of a bomber system when we can save lives for a small fraction of this by, say, installing seat belts in ground vehicles. Of course people may attach different worths (apart from the diverse values of persons as productive resources) to different lives — those of children, older people, military personnel, civilians, volunteers, or persons who die in particularly brutal

---

[3] For example, was the performance of the system degraded to reflect high casualty rates or not?

or painful ways. But this fact simply reinforces the original proposition, that there is no *generally acceptable* method of valuing human lives.

Suppose that the analyst's problem is the comparison of alternative strategic bombing systems that are to be maintained in a state-of-readiness to deter attack. Some of these systems will, it is estimated, result in higher casualties among crews if and when war occurs. The analyst includes in the cost of each system the expenses of recruiting and training the additional personnel required because of these higher casualties. He also estimates the degradation of each system resulting from high casualty rates. Should he *in addition* include some valuation of the crew lives lost as human lives in his cost calculations? Almost certainly not. In the first place, in an exchange of bombs, the crew lives lost will inevitably be swamped by the lives of civilians and allies lost to enemy attack: if our interest is in lives *per se*, it would be ludicrous to value the dozens in the air and neglect the millions on the ground.[4] In the second place, we are really interested not in the lives lost in any particular operation, but in the war. If we prejudice victory by selecting relatively inefficient (costly) systems because they save lives in a particular operation, we may well prolong the war and lose more lives before we win it, or even lose the war itself.

This is not to say that the attempt to "price" lives in all problems is unhelpful. Nor is it to say that it is hopeless to try to value other effects which appear at first glance to be incommensurables. In specific analyses ingenuity can often go a long way toward measuring such effects in terms of the common unit. We cannot say just where to draw the line between effects that should be measured in terms of the common denominator and those that should not. We can say, however, that insistence on the measurement of all effects in terms of a single common unit will not make for the most useful analysis. A Congressional committee was probably justified in concluding its review of an evaluation of federal resource development projects: "Some of the effort to place monetary values on indirect benefits is nothing short of ludicrous." [5]

The analyst is then frequently left, after the prudent exercise of his ingenuity in reducing everything to a common measure, with one or more important effects that defy reduction. We call them "incommensurables." What can the analyst do about them that will be helpful either to him-

[4] The expected destruction of life and property on the ground incidental to the campaign is an important incommensurable which certainly should influence the choice of weapons or strategies.

[5] It is ludicrous by our test of *general acceptability*. Each individual Congressman can decide, for example, how many millions the development of the Northwest region at the expense of the rest of the country is worth to him, but there is no reason to expect the valuations of Congressmen from Oregon and Oklahoma to coincide.

self in making recommendations based on his study, or to the decision-makers directly?

(1) A device that is frequently useful where there are two or more objectives, each of which is measurable but with no common unit of measure, is the calculation of the set of efficient solutions as explained in Chapter 7 (pp. 109–14). This may be enough in itself to identify some system that is preferred to an existing or proposed system — a good practical aim for quantitative analysis. Furthermore, by limiting the alternatives, a calculation of this kind can facilitate the exercise of judgment in selecting, from among the efficient solutions, a near-optimal one.

(2) It will frequently be possible to calculate the value one must assign the incommensurable either in dollars or in terms of the unit measuring the major objective if he is to prefer System A over System B. Thus, the analyst can tell the decision-maker: Bombing System A will give you a target destruction potential of 1,000. If you are willing to take the diplomatic trouble and risks involved in various overseas countries, System B will provide the same potential for $1 billion less (or will increase the potential to 1,500 for the same budget). For System A to be preferred, one must put a value of at least $1 billion on the avoidance of the trouble and risk. Someone must exercise judgment in deciding, but it can be helpful in making this decision to know that $1 billion is at stake rather than $100 million or $10 billion.[6]

The calculation of such break-even points or trade-offs is more difficult than, but far preferable to, the common practice of placing limiting constraints on the solution. For example, instead of trying to calculate the impact of casualty rates (through morale) on crew performance, a frequent practice is simply to rule out all solutions in which casualty rates exceed a certain arbitrary percentage. Or to take another example, some political problems of overseas basing can be swept under the rug, as far as the analysis is concerned, by simply declaring certain countries off-bounds, or by specifying in advance an "intercontinental" solution. Some such constraints on an analysis are necessary and justified. Limitations of time and cost alone prevent the consideration of every conceivable alternative and opportunity. But the selection of constraints must be made with care and discrimination and with knowledge of the havoc they can play with the analysis. Casually selected or arbitrary constraints can easily increase system cost or degrade system performance many-fold, and lead to solutions that would be unacceptable to

---

[6] If all the leading alternatives involve significant and different incommensurables, this device is not very useful. The situation would then be like that in which the little boy valued his puppy at $50,000 and, according to his story, sold it for that amount. How? By accepting a couple of $25,000 cats as payment.

the person who set the constraints in the first instance if he understood their implications.[7]

(3) In some cases where systems achieve incommensurable objectives, the analyst may be able to design another system which is better at achieving some things and as good, or almost as good, at achieving the others. Suppose for example that he is comparing the capability of a force based overseas in peacetime with that of a mobile force based in the Zone of the Interior (ZI). Suppose that quantitative analysis shows the ZI force to be markedly superior, but that the stationing of troops overseas is believed to be important for the maintenance or strengthening of our alliances. The analyst may be able to design and suggest a third solution, say, a rotation system, which has most of the advantages of the ZI based force without this incommensurable though important disadvantage. The rotation system may be almost as effective (for a given budget) as the ZI based force, and almost as acceptable to allies, while perhaps having some advantages (realistic practice in mobility) possessed by neither of the original alternatives.[8] In many cases the analyst's ingenuity may be more rewardingly exercised in trying to find ways of satisfying multiple objectives than in devising common measures for them. It can in fact be argued that the *chief* gain from systematic analysis is the stimulus that it provides for the invention of better systems.

(4) Finally, as a minimum, the incommensurables can be displayed and talked about. Quantitative or qualitative information about them may be helpful to decision-makers.[9] Although by definition they are not commensurable with the other costs and gains, clues to their impact can often be given. A very short essay on the possibilities of negotiating base rights in India might be sufficient to rule out certain alternatives that look attractive in the quantitative analysis. The annoyance to the population of sonic booms cannot be subtracted from fighter defense kill potential, but it will still be helpful to present estimates of the numbers of such booms over populated areas with different basing systems or training concepts. Such effects can be partially traced out, sometimes quantitatively, after the fashion of consumers' research, and presented in an exhibit that supplements the principal estimates. This can be helpful to the decision-maker in the same manner that consumers' research is helpful to the consumer.

---

[7] We know of studies in which an arbitrary limitation on casualties led to solutions in which, at the margin, $100 million was being spent to save a single life. Even if one regards a human life as "worth" this much, the same amount of money could be spent in ways to save many more.

[8] If the new system is better in *all* respects than any of the alternative systems it is said to be "dominant." Pure dominance is almost always unattainable, but it provides a goal for systems invention which may be approximated.

[9] For pure "intangibles" the information would have to be qualitative.

UNCERTAINTY

The estimates of costs and gains considered so far are average, predicted, or "expected" outcomes. But we know in advance that, for all sorts of reasons, these amounts may be off the mark. Actual costs of development or production of new weapons never precisely coincide with advance estimates and sometimes differ from them by factors of two to twenty. Times of availability are also very hard to estimate accurately, and as a rule greater uncertainty attaches to estimates of effects or gains than to estimates of cost and availability. The enemy never does what we expect; indeed, he always has greater or less capability than we expect. Every war is full of surprise outcomes. Now while uncertainties of these sorts are pervasive, they are likely to affect some systems in a comparison more than others. The availability of the overseas base system is more uncertain than that of the ZI base system. We can predict the performance of a weapon of which we have a prototype with much greater confidence than the performance of a rival weapon on the drawing board. As a consequence, Systems A and B may offer identical predicted outcomes, yet differ greatly with respect to other possible outcomes. These differences may be a matter of some moment if, say, A's possible results are all thought to be nearly the same as predicted, but B's range from fabulous success to utter disaster. Yet while such differences in the pattern of uncertainty — or, more precisely, in the "frequency distribution of outcomes" — are matters of great concern, it is ordinarily impossible to attach a value or price to them. A price, that is, which would have any *general* acceptability. In some situations and for some persons, to reduce the chance of a bad outcome is worth a great deal. In other situations or for other persons, even a small chance of an extremely favorable outcome carries a high premium.

TYPES OF UNCERTAINTY

It may help to put this complication in proper perspective if we see how pervasive uncertainty is. Perhaps this will also help show that uncertainty is inherent in the nature of things and is not necessarily evidence of lazy or careless estimation. One can sympathize with the general who shouts at his analyst: "Give me a number, not a range": unique numbers are easier to work with and to think about than ranges or probability distributions. But he is probably asking his analyst to falsify the real world in a manner that will make it impossible for him, as a commander, to make good decisions.

*Uncertainty about planning and cost factors.* Every model uses as inputs certain relations between its elements which are known in the military as "planning factors" — for example, the number of miles a unit can march or drive in a day over specified terrain; the radius of destruction of atomic (or other) weapons of specified power against specified objects; the circular probable error (CEP)[10] of bombing with a given bombsight as a function of, say, speed and altitude; the average number of hours a cargo plane can be used per day. It is apparent that we may attempt from time to time to determine some planning factor, for example, CEP, as a function of bomber speed and altitude, or of other parts of the system. In that case the particular planning factor would be a variable, not a given, in the analysis. But in any particular analysis many planning factors must simply be taken as given; there is never time to calculate everything from scratch. So they are borrowed from other analyses of varying quality, from books of official planning factors assembled and published by the military Services, or from other sources.

This procedure may conceal uncertainties that arise for two reasons: first, the quality of the sources from which the factors are borrowed varies from fair to bad to biased (they have seldom been estimated with the particular requirements of this analysis in mind); and second, they are almost invariably "numbers" rather than ranges or probability distributions, suppressing significant variations in the behavior of the relations in the real world.[11] Divisions do not always march the same number of miles in a day, even over "specified" terrain, for any of a thousand reasons. Even if one has the right *average* value of CEP (almost certainly an unwarranted assumption), it will be wrong for any particular strike.

Factors used to estimate costs of specified military forces and weapons systems are always uncertain, especially when they relate to the distant future. Cost estimating is an approximate art even in the most well-run businesses. Wages and material prices are subject to unforeseeable fluctuations. More important, it is impossible to predict accurately how many men, what kinds of material, and how much time will have to be paid for. On production items the range of error in cost estimates may be only 10 per cent or so — perhaps too small to be worth bothering about in view of other uncertainties inherent in the analysis. But the actual costs of developing, producing, and operating complete weapon systems have frequently exceeded cost estimates made prior to development by factors of ten or more, largely because of the technological uncertainty that existed when the costs were estimated. Necessary modifications that double system cost must be regarded as fairly normal.

*Uncertainty about strategic context.* Every war, whether all-out, limited, or cold, is fought in some "strategic context" — at a certain time and place, with certain enemies and allies, to achieve certain politi-

---

[10] The radius of the circle within which half the bombs will fall.

[11] We are arguing *not* that the use of average values is necessarily wrong, but that the uncertainty this covers up should be recognized.

cal objectives. Since the ranking of alternative forces or weapon systems may depend decisively upon the strategic context, the analyst must make assumptions about it.

In some circumstances (during a war, or in planning for an imminent outbreak of war at a particular place against a known enemy), there may be a fairly obvious "best" set of assumptions to make about the strategic context. Analysts working on North Atlantic convoy problems during World War II knew where and when the war was occurring, who the enemy was, who our allies were, the constraints under which both sides were operating, and the general political objectives and grand strategy of our side. But when the problem is to choose military forces in peacetime that will give us a capability of fighting future wars, good assumptions about the strategic context may be far from obvious.

Consider the questions that have to be answered about the strategic context in choosing among alternative future bombing systems. First, when will war occur? System A may seem far preferable if the threat occurs in two years, system B if the date is ten years away. Who will be our enemies and allies? The answer is always less obvious than it seems — if a few years are to elapse (how many could have guessed in 1942, or even in 1947, that Germany and Japan would be among our most valued allies in 1957?). Will our allies make overseas bases available for our bombers, or will they yield to "atomic blackmail"? Will the war be general or local, all-out or limited? What constraints will be imposed — say territorially, as in Korea, or on the use of nuclear weapons? It is apparent that the "best" bombing force will depend critically upon answers to questions of this kind.[12] And, curiously but perhaps fortunately, there is no *authoritative* way for the analyst to get the right answers — or any answers. Of course no single military service can provide answers; decisions about war and peace (and kind of war) are made at the highest level of government — our own and the enemy's. And just as no Congress can make decisions binding our future Congresses, neither can a President or Joint Chiefs of Staff effectively bind a future President or Joint Chiefs.[13] The analyst must face up to gross uncertainties of this strategic sort, and his recommendations may well depend upon the way he does so.

*Technological uncertainty.* Technological uncertainty may occasionally be serious in the analysis of current operational problems, but as we

---

[12] It is also apparent that the strategic context will in turn be affected by the forces and weapon systems we choose. Enemies will attempt to force us into the kind of engagements for which we are not prepared. If we prepare only for hot wars, they may choose to defeat us in cold ones.

[13] Except in a negative way. If certain forces having long lead times have not been provided, future Joint Chiefs will not be able to fight certain kinds of wars in certain ways — even if one of them then appears to be in the nation's interest.

try to peer further and further into the future it becomes more and more important and can, indeed, dominate the analysis. As we shall see in Chapter 13, technological uncertainty is the central problem in research and development decisions. There is always some technological uncertainty connected with research and development; otherwise it would not be research and development but production. But because of the interdependence of all factors in an analysis, this kind of uncertainty may influence analyses that are not focused on research and development.

For example, uncertainty regarding the A-bomb importantly (and properly) influenced our preparations for the final stages of our campaign against Japan in World War II. Uncertainty about the H-bomb — whether it would work, how soon, and how cheaply — affected not only the nuclear and missile development programs[14] but our strategic concepts and plans for future military forces of all types. Uncertainty about the progress of various missile programs inevitably and grossly influences not only missile development but bomb development, aircraft development, aircraft procurement, the composition of our air defense forces, and plans for civil defense. Expert guesses about the dates of operational readiness of important missile systems vary by as much as a decade: no one can be sure which guess is right.

*Uncertainty about the enemy and his reactions.* Two kinds of uncertainty stem from the fact that the object of miltary forces is to oppose other military forces — those of enemy (or potentially enemy) countries. A military tactic, strategy, force, or development program is never good-in-itself, but only good-in-relation-to the tactics, strategy, forces, and future weapon systems of an enemy.

First, our factual "intelligence" about an enemy is always less than perfect, and when the enemy country is a dictatorship that ruthlessly and efficiently suppresses information and restricts travel, our ignorance of its military capabilities may be gross. The practice of military intelligence agencies of presenting numbers ("best guesses") rather than ranges in their estimates obscures but does nothing to remedy the incompleteness and unreliability of most of the information on which the estimates are based. As is characteristic of uncertainty, the probable errors of intelligence estimates increase as we look further into the future. How can *we* predict when a Russian missile system will be ready when we know that the Russians, with far more knowledge of their program than we have, cannot make such a prediction with any accuracy themselves? It is unfortunate that our choice of weapon systems usually depends as critically upon enemy parameters as upon our own.

---

[14] It is widely reported that the intercontinental ballistic missile development program suffered from lack of support in the early years because the guidance problems seemed so intractable. Then the unexpected development of the H-bomb made even very inaccurate ICBM's useful.

Second, and even more fundamental than our ignorance of his capabilities, is our ignorance of the enemy's "intentions" (in the vocabulary of the intelligence agencies) or "strategy" (in the language of the theory of games). Military forces are used, wars are fought, against human beings exercising human intelligence. The best way for us to fight a war, or to prepare to fight one, is likely to depend decisively upon decisions that have been or will be made in, for example, the Kremlin. But no one has ever devised a good method of predicting the decisions of other human beings — even of human beings with whose psychological conditioning and drives we are fairly familiar. With what confidence can we expect the men in the Kremlin to be "deterred" by promises of "massive retaliation"? In what circumstances would they, or anyone else, start a thermonuclear war? What kinds of limitations (for example, territorial or in the use of nuclear weapons) might we be able to impose upon them in limited wars? What are their territorial targets likely to be in cold and limited wars? If they start a war, will they rely on mass or surprise attack (our "best" defense is likely to be very different in the two cases)?

It is easy to spend billions preparing for a kind of war or strategy that the enemy would never choose. Some individuals have special insight into the behavior of the Russian (and other) élites, but it is difficult enough to tell in advance which ones really have insight and which merely have confidence — let alone to assess the confidence that we can place in their predictions.

*Statistical uncertainty.* Finally, there is "statistical" uncertainty, the uncertainty resulting from the *chance* element in recurring events. This is the kind of uncertainty that would persist even if we could predict enemy strategies and the central values of all important parameters. We know that if we flip a penny a thousand times, it will come down "heads" approximately half the time; but that if we flip it only ten, the proportion of heads may be much higher or much lower. Similarly, we may have a radar sensing system that we expect to identify enemy planes 90 per cent of the time; it will still be possible for the planes to slip through undetected on the one day that counts. In most long-range problems, statistical uncertainties are the least of our worries; they are swamped by uncertainties regarding central values and states of the world. In some problems, however, we cannot rely exclusively on average or expected values.

### THE TREATMENT OF UNCERTAINTY

What can the analyst do to take account of the proliferation of uncertainties resulting from our ignorance of the future? As with incommensurables, the most important advice is: Don't ignore them.[15] To base an analysis and decision on some single set of best guesses could be disastrous. For example, suppose that there is uncertainty about ten factors (such as, will overseas bases be available? Will the enemy have interceptors effective at 60,000 feet?) and we make a best guess on all ten. If the probability that each best guess is right is 60 per cent (a very high batting average for best guesses from most sources), the probability that *all ten* are right is one-half of one per cent. If we confined the analysis to this best-guess case, we would be ignoring a set of futures with a 99.5 per cent probability of occurring.

So we must design the analysis to reflect the major uncertainties, and this usually means computing results for a number (sometimes a large number) of contingencies. If overseas bases may or may not be available, and some of our systems depend upon them more than others, we must test the systems assuming we have them, and again assuming we do not. If future missile CEP's (that is, accuracies) are grossly uncertain, we must make the computations with at least a high and a low value, and possibly one or two intermediate ones. If our strategic bombers may be required in local wars in the Middle East or Far East as well as for general war, we must test them in all theaters and circumstances that appear likely and important.

The trouble with computing "all interesting contingencies" is a practical one. The number of cases to analyze and compute increases as the power of the factors that are permitted to vary.[16] Unless discretion is used in restricting the cases to combinations that are really significant, we are likely to formulate a problem that is too big to solve — or at least too costly or time consuming to be worth solving. Developments in high-speed electronic computers in recent years are making it possible to compute solutions to more and more complex problems. Nevertheless it is still necessary to cut problems down to manageable size on computational grounds alone, and usually far more important is the effort required on the part of the analyst to assemble the data and structure the models for each of numerous cases. Testing systems in a different kind of war or even a different theater may double the work of analysis — and therefore either the manpower or the time required to complete the study.

So the practical problem is to design the analysis to reflect the truly

[15] Ignoring uncertainties is a chronic disease of military planners and analysts. There is a great temptation and frequently great pressure to use official planning factors, official intelligence estimates, and the best guesses of higher military authorities.

[16] As noted earlier, if there are two uncertain factors (say, kind of war and CEP) and each is permitted to take four values, the number of cases is only $4^2$ or 16. But if ten uncertain factors are permitted to take four values each, the number of cases soars to $4^{10}$, which is over 1,000,000.

significant contingencies but, in order to keep it manageable, only these. This requires practical judgment of a high order; the analyst must know a great deal about his problem — in effect, what is likely to be important and what unimportant in influencing the solution — before he structures it. Sometimes he can cut down on the number of cases that have to be computed by constructing an *a fortiori* argument; that is, if he is lucky as well as skillful, he may be able to show that his preferred system is best (or better than some alternative) when he makes unfavorable assumptions regarding many of the uncertainties, and therefore does not have to bother with computations involving favorable assumptions. But at best he will have to show how things can be expected to turn out under a number of different future circumstances, and usually one of his systems will look best in some contingencies, another in others. How does the analyst then choose the preferred system? What decision does he recommend?

MAKING DECISIONS IN THE FACE OF UNCERTAINTY

Suppose that we are considering the choice of an anti-ICBM system and are weighing the relative merits of three proposals — 1, 2 and 3 — in what appear to be the three most interesting contingencies — A, B and C (Table 21). Contingency A is very favorable to the United States —

**Table 21. Illustrative payoff matrix**

| System | Contingency | | |
|---|---|---|---|
| | A | B | C |
| 1 | 100 | 20 | 0 |
| 2 | 60 | 40 | 0 |
| 3 | 20 | 10 | 10 |

perhaps the contingency in which we strike first against the enemy's offensive force, so that its attack on us is disrupted and our defenses against it are fully alerted. Contingency B is much less favorable; here the enemy starts with a massive, coordinated attack. Finally, C is a catastrophic contingency — one, say, in which the enemy discovers a way to make a simultaneous attack without any warning against all our defended targets. We "score" the three systems for performance in each contingency by the utility or worth of what is left — 100 representing everything, and zero representing nothing.

System 1 is obviously a fair-weather system, which works splendidly if everything is just right, but is almost worthless when the going is rough. In particular, it is easily saturated. System 2, on the other hand, while leaky, is not rate-of-fire limited, and does almost as well (or badly) in case B as in case A. Both 1 and 2 are useless against a C attack. System 3 is a desperate sort of system, which uses all the funds available for burrowing underground. In consequence, even the light attack assumed in A practically destroys the country, while even the heavy, warningless attack of C leaves a little to rise from the ashes.

Which of these three systems do we choose if our choice really is restricted to these three? There is no completely satisfactory and generally accepted theory either of how people *do* make such choices or of how they *should* make such choices.

*Maximize expected value. If* it is possible to estimate the utilities (that is, the worths) of the various outcomes (as we assumed in the above table), and *if* we can also, at least roughly, calculate the probability of each contingency, it would appear reasonable to choose that course of action or system that maximized expected utility.[17] Thus, in our example, if we attached equal probability to the three contingencies, we should choose system 1. If we believed B to be four times as likely as A, and C to be wholly unlikely, we should choose system 2.

This principle is, within limits, a valid and useful guide in some situations. While attaching utilities and probabilities to outcomes is difficult, we can frequently do it in a rough fashion — yet well enough to narrow the field of choice to good alternatives. Of course there may not be agreement about the utilities and probabilities of the various outcomes. The customer may insist that the analyst let him make his own estimates and draw his own conclusion. But the theory directs our attention to the relevant questions.

*Minimax.* There is, however, an important circumstance in which it is inappropriate to ask questions about the probability of outcomes. If the contingency depends not upon "nature" or luck but upon the choice of a malevolent enemy, we are not concerned with probabilities. The rational man, it is argued, should assume that the enemy will do his worst and therefore choose the system that will minimize the maximum (worst) the enemy can do.[18] The shorthand expression "minimax" can be used to refer to this strategy. If in our example we assume that the enemy can choose the contingency, it appears that he would choose C, and that the

[17] L. J. Savage, *The Foundations of Statistics,* John Wiley and Sons, New York, 1954, pp. 1–104 (Chapters 1–5).

[18] The term "minimax" and the general flavor of this argument are borrowed from the theory of games, but we are *not* using the term minimax in the technical sense in which it is used in the theory of games. We are thinking of situations in which we have to choose a system in advance, and the enemy knows of our choice. The classical work on games is John von Neumann and Oskar Morgenstern, *Theory of Games and Economic Behavior,* Princeton University Press, Princeton, N.J., 1944 (2d ed., 1947). For a brief and highly readable volume, see J. D. Williams, *The Compleat Strategyst,* McGraw-Hill Book Co., Inc., New York, 1954.

"best" we can do in consequence is to opt for system 3 and guarantee ourselves a survival utility of 10.

There is much in this view that is relevant and important in the analysis of military problems. Where the enemy controls the choice, it is not meaningful to compute probabilities. We should focus our attention instead, as this view does, on the freedom of the enemy to choose, and the likelihood that he will choose something pretty unpleasant, if not the worst. Moreover, the enemy's worst — or "reasonable" worst — is a case on which the analyst should concentrate — not exclusively but heavily. Wishful or lazy thinking too often causes the analyst to dwell on threats that he thinks we can counter, rather than the more dangerous ones that will appeal to the enemy.

Nevertheless, these concepts and rules borrowed from game theory must be applied to actual military problems with a good deal of discretion. War, especially of the modern nuclear variety, is not a two-person zero-sum game; that is, a game in which only two players are involved, the gain of one being exactly equal to the loss of the other. And it is only in such a two-person zero-sum game that even a very intelligent enemy can "reasonably" be expected to choose the course that is worst for us. In non-zero-sum games, what is best for the enemy is not necessarily what is worst for us. To take an extreme case (although not very extreme any longer): if the enemy has an end-of-the-world machine, the worst thing he can do to us is to use it, but this also happens to be the worst — not the best — from his point of view too. We would be foolish to adapt our whole strategy to this contingency, which will have little appeal to him.

In much less extreme cases, minimax (as we are using this term) is unduly conservative. If we choose our systems solely for their ability to shore up our defense in the worst case, (a) we may not be able to shore it up enough to matter much (as in contingency C in the example), and (b) we may be sacrificing opportunities for major improvements in our capabilities to deal with other contingencies that have some substantial likelihood of occurring. For even if the situation approximates a two-person zero-sum game, the enemy may not act as game theory assumes. A minimax solution is motivated by the idea that the enemy is completely rational, perfectly intelligent, can read minds, never makes mistakes, and so on. Enemies, especially enemy countries, are seldom like that. They are run by bureaucracies that make mistakes like our own. Their intelligence has blind spots. Their leaders are full of prejudices. There is a vast amount of irrational inertia in the determination of policy. Probably no great military leader in history except the conservative Ulysses S. Grant ever worked on minimax assumptions, and Grant had such superiority in resources that he could afford to be (it made sense for him to be) conservative. Great profit can be derived in many circumstances from anticipating enemy mistakes and being prepared to take advantage of them. Minimax forfeits such opportunities.

Any departure from the two-person zero-sum assumptions accentuates the conservative bias of the solution. The contingencies in this kind of analysis are seldom under the complete control of the enemy. In our example the enemy can obviously influence who strikes first, but he can no more decide it than we can (he can decide to strike first, but that is a different matter: we may learn of the decision and preempt him). Nor can the enemy simply will the massive, simultaneous warningless strike that we feared could be so devastating in contingency C. He can will a research and development program in the hope that such a capability will prove feasible; but nature will determine whether the program is a success. In mixed cases of this sort, and *a fortiori* where there is no game at all (that is, where the only "other player" is "nature," as when the uncertainty is statistical), the bias of a solution that assumes a malevolent intelligence at work may be extreme.[19]

So we are left with no generally satisfactory answer. *If* we can estimate the probabilities and the utilities of outcomes even roughly, as sometimes in "playing against nature," expected value seems satisfactory; but if we have to use physical outcomes in lieu of their utilities, or are confronted by an intelligent enemy, we must beware of a bias toward recklessness in applying this technique. *If* circumstances approximate those assumed in the two-person zero-sum game, we can compute the minimax solution, keeping in mind its conservative bias.[20]

This reference to conservative and reckless biases in various solutions provides some clue to the basic difficulty in generalizing about the behavior of rational men in the face of uncertainty. For while rational men do act in the face of uncertainty, they act differently. There are audacious commanders like Napoleon, and conservative ones like Grant — both successful in the right circumstances. Different people simply take different views of risks — in their own lives and as decision-makers for the nation. Some "insure" and others "gamble." It is therefore most important, whether the analyst calculates a general solution or not, that he present responsible decision-makers with the kind of information provided in Table 21, and let them use their own risk-preferences in making the final choice. The risk-preferences of responsible decision-makers may be very different from those of the analyst.

[19] Some find more intuitive appeal in a variant of the minimax solution variously called minimizing the maximum "regret" or "loss." It at least gives less conservative solutions in many instances (including our example, where it would opt, not too convincingly, for system 1!). See L. J. Savage, pp. 163–171.

[20] In some circumstances, e.g., if the intelligent opposition aspect is unimportant but we cannot estimate probabilities, we may want to minimize the maximum regret.

DESIGNING FOR CONTINGENCIES

But the most important part of the answer to the pervasive uncertainty facing the analyst or the military planner is not greater subtlety in making difficult choices, but *the design of systems to cope with more of the critical contingencies.*[21] A situation like that represented in our example, where each of three proposed systems is good in one contingency and bad in the others, covering only one best, should be a challenge to the analyst and the decision-maker to invent a better system — one that looks good in more than one contingency. Truly dominant systems — those that are better in all circumstances — are hard to find, and require luck, too, but it is rare that a resourceful analyst cannot get closer to dominance than the systems in the example (Table 21).

The first thing to try in designing a system capable of coping with several contingencies is to mix ideas, concepts, or hardware from the systems designed for each contingency. Mixed systems usually involve extra costs, which can be estimated, but are frequently worth it (we have rarely relied on pure weapon systems). Multiplicity is more frequently justified in development than in procurement and operations (both because uncertainties are greater at the development stage and because the extra costs of mixing or "duplicating" are less). In other cases mere mixing may be an inadequate or inferior solution. It may be better, for example, to redesign the hardware to serve more than one purpose, combining some of the characteristics of the special purpose hardware previously compared. Or drastic redesign of operational concepts, or the invention of new ones, may be indicated. Protection against warningless attack, for example, may be better secured by concealing some of our targets, or making them mobile, than by burrowing underground. Or there may be superior concepts for burrowing. Whatever the device, the analyst's responsibility is to come up if he can with a system that has no critical soft spots and that still looks very good in the favorable contingencies.

Sometimes the redesign of systems will have a different objective from dominance. Suppose that an apparently dominant system — one that is best against some contingencies and as good as its rivals against the others — is still alarmingly ineffective in the most probable situation. Suppose, in other words, that it is still only the best of a bad lot as far as the principal contingency is concerned. We may wish in this instance to invent a system that is better against this contingency even if it is worse in other less probable situations.

Thus one reason for inventing new alternatives is to find a dominant one, enabling us to choose regardless of the probabilities that particular

[21] In this respect the problem of dealing with uncertainty is like that of dealing with incommensurables.

contingencies will occur. Another reason may be to improve upon the present poor set of alternatives.

HEDGING AND INSURANCE

Despite the ingenuity of the analyst, there may remain in an otherwise preferred system some chance of an extremely unfavorable outcome. Sometimes the best he can do (a very useful best) is to calculate the least-cost method of providing some hedge or insurance (complete or more usually partial) against this contingency. This is necessary information for a rational decision whether or not the hedge is worth making.

Hedging in business operations is frequently a highly organized activity supporting special markets. Hedging is also a typical reaction to uncertainty by individuals. A family planning an automobile trip may buy a new set of tires even though it estimates the chance of a blowout as less than 50 per cent. A hedge against even a slight possibility of a fatal accident (or major inconvenience) may be worth the price. Any purchase of insurance is an example of hedging.

The military does not have a futures market in which it can hedge, nor can it eliminate uncertainty by the purchase of insurance from commercial companies. But there are innumerable ways in which it can hedge against loss or disaster, and analysis can define and cost them. Mixed systems can be regarded as one kind of hedge; general purpose systems, another. A hedge against ECM (electronic counter-measures) may be some kind of electronic *counter* counter-measure. The extra cost can be computed in money and resources, or in the degradation of performance in more favorable contingencies.

It is not necessary that the hedge be complete and certain in its operation. We may, indeed, be able to deter the enemy from taking certain actions by what are called "low-confidence" measures — measures with only a moderate (50 per cent or less) chance of succeeding. If the enemy action is one that he would not undertake without high confidence, we can sometimes deny him this confidence by a cheap low-confidence measure of our own (if its chances of success are only 30 per cent, the enemy's cannot be higher than 70 per cent). There are occasions when intermittent patrols make sense — for the military as well as for the police. Fair-weather fighters may be useful even in defense: the enemy may be unable to plan an attack for a time when bad weather is predicted, or the weather may turn out to be good in spite of the predictions of enemy weather forecasters. Low-confidence measures are no general substitute for high-confidence measures, but they are useful hedges in some circumstances — when they are cheap and we have reason to think that the enemy is likely to insist on high confidence from his standpoint.

REDUCING UNCERTAINTY

Sometimes an important, or even the most important, conclusion of the analyst is that measures should be taken to reduce some of the uncertainties and that some decisions should be postponed until more is known with confidence.

Knowing when to make decisions may be as important as knowing what decision to make. The costs and dangers of "indecisiveness," of postponing decisions too long, are obvious and widely appreciated. But there are also costs and dangers in making decisions on the basis of incomplete and uncertain information. In recent years we have wasted billions by making premature decisions to produce operational equipment with trivial improvements in capability, when what was needed was a broad program of research and development to buy knowledge of markedly improved hardware. We simply did not know how to design equipment with a capability that would be worth the high costs.

So if the question is what to procure, the best answer may be: nothing but a research and development program, or a test program, at this stage. Do not try to decide until you know more, until you know enough about costs and performance to make useful cost-effectiveness studies. This does not mean doing nothing. One important job of the analyst is to spot the critical areas in which more knowledge is needed, and to devise proposals for getting it.

And if the question is what to develop, the answer may well be in terms of a strategy for buying information rather than a detailed blueprint of some futuristic operational weapon. With technological uncertainty layered on top of strategic uncertainty, it is rarely possible to specify an advanced weapon system far in advance and schedule a development program for it. And it may be a mistake to try. The first step is to determine the critical uncertainties and to undertake a research and development program to resolve them. Only then will we be in a position to schedule the next steps.[22]

DEALING WITH THE ENEMY

As we have seen, many of the crucial uncertainties in any military analysis stem from our ignorance of the enemy and his intentions. Analysis makes two very common mistakes in dealing with the enemy — the first is to regard him as stupid, inflexible, and devoid of initiative; the second is to attribute to him diabolical cunning, unlimited flexibility, and boundless initiative. In the cliché of the Pentagon, we insist on picturing him as either 2 feet tall or 10 feet tall. The first kind of

[22] We will return to this problem in Chapter 13.

blunder is the more frequent, but either one can ruin an otherwise excellent analysis.

How much capability and flexibility, for example, should we attribute to the Soviet Union? We have a fairly firm knowledge of her current industrial capacity and output and of her industrial growth rates. But how many ICBM's, or atomic submarines, or nuclear weapons, or defense radars can we expect them to have by 196-? These are important questions. The design, procurement, and deployment of our own weapons are obviously sensitive to the answers.

The first thing to realize is that we do not and cannot know the answers with certainty. No one can. The Russians do not know themselves. We cannot answer similar questions about our own strength in the 1960's. We should not take the best guesses of the intelligence community as gospel. The best guesses may be wrong, and even if right today, the Russian leaders can change their plans and make them wrong tomorrow. Another common error is to assume that the Russians will put all their potential for expansion into the one capability (say, atomic submarines) that happens to be critical to our analysis. The best thing we can do is to project Russian industrial capacity and the Russian military budget — with margins of error — and then face up to the Russian allocation problem in much the same way we face up to our own.

The recognition of the extreme importance of enemy intentions and enemy reactions in most military problems has led to much work in recent years on techniques to improve our ability to predict enemy reactions (that is, reduce the uncertainty from this source) and to deal with them more effectively. The most important of these are (a) game theory, and (b) "gaming" — sometimes called "war gaming" or "operational gaming."

(a) Game theory has contributed a conceptual framework for thinking about situations of conflict that has proved extremely valuable in many problems. The preceding discussion would have been impossible without constant use of concepts derived from the theory of games — like "strategy," "solution," "dominance," and "minimax." Game theory has been effectively applied to a number of tactical problems in which a conflict or "game" occurs repeatedly (as in the case of duels between fighter aircraft). It has also provided useful insights that have aided in the solution of more complex problems. But for broader military problems, formal game theory solutions have two serious deficiencies. First, most military problems are too complex to permit of practical game theory solution (even simple games like checkers are too complex for practical solution by the theory). Second, and more fundamentally, as we have seen, wars are not two-person zero-sum games — and little progress has been made in solving other kinds of games. Two-person means that there are only two sides, each with a consistent and unambiguous set of values: there is no room for "third forces" or for imperfect and shifting coalitions. Zero-sum means that the gain of one side corresponds exactly to the loss of the other; each side is playing the same game with the same rules and the same understanding of the scoring. But in war there may be no "victor"; the total losses may far exceed the total gains; the two sides may fight for objectives that are qualitatively different, not mere mirror images of each other. When the game theory solution is computed for a problem in which the circumstances do not correspond to the two-person zero-sum assumptions, its relevance depends more upon its intuitive appeal to "rational" men than on the rigorous proofs of the theory. The solution is likely, as we have seen, to be an unduly conservative one.

Game theorists have probably concentrated too much, however, on *solving* games. More emphasis should be placed, not on finding formal solutions, but on simply exploring and studying game situations — particularly, of course, those pertaining to non-zero-sum games.[23] New variants on these actions, possible gambits in tacit bargaining, the manner in which specific steps do influence payoffs, and the probable enemy reactions to specific policies — all these matters deserve intensive study, and game theory is one framework for studying them.

(b) Another means of exploring such questions is experimentation with various gaming techniques. Gaming has almost nothing in common with game theory, which it long antedates. Gaming is an exercise engaged in by human beings (individuals or teams) on two (or occasionally more) "sides"; whereas game theory has so far been a branch of mathematics. Gaming is an extremely flexible device, and can take numerous very dissimilar forms. There are war games that allow great freedom to the participants in making moves, and others that are highly "structured," with rules almost as precise as those of chess.

War games have long been used by military staffs, and were perhaps most highly developed in the nineteenth century by the German General Staff (*Kriegsspiel*). They have been used by the military, however, primarily as training devices, to teach junior officers principles that others have previously learned in actual combat. The possibility of solving problems of strategy by gaming has been considered by military authorities, but usually dismissed as unpromising. Not only is it difficult to reproduce reality adequately on a sand table, but the time and manpower required for a single play of an elaborate war game preclude the numerous plays that are needed to test out several strategies on both sides in

[23] Thomas C. Schelling, "The Strategy of Conflict: Prospectus for a Reorientation of Game Theory," *Journal of Conflict Resolution*, September 1958, pp. 203–264.

various contingencies — the sort of test that could point the way to optimal, or at least good, strategies for blue.[24]

Recent developments have concentrated on speeding up play, a necessary condition for the effective use of gaming as a problem solving device. High-speed computers have been used both to assist players in making moves and to help the umpires trace the consequences of moves.

There is little doubt that gaming activities of this kind are worthwhile. In particular, there is no doubt at all that the players learn from the game, that they acquire insights that are valid and useful to the extent that the game has been well designed. But there is some doubt that games of this kind are very effective as problem-solving devices. Rapidity of play, which permits numerous plays, is a necessary but not a sufficient condition of a game that will solve problems; and the number of plays is, in any event, still grossly inadequate by analytic standards.

Operational gaming has never really solved the criterion problem, and its attempts to evade it by substituting human beings for explicit objectives have merely obscured the issue. Game theory at least faces up to the problem, although its solution, minimax, appears too conservative except in repetitive zero-sum games. Gaming, while it frees itself from this specific and unsatisfactory criterion, has none to take its place. The blue player is usually told to behave as if he were a blue commander or the blue government; the red player, as if he were a real red. The extent to which the players are rightly motivated is unknown and unknowable.

For this and other reasons the results of repeated war games are difficult to interpret in most cases. One knows the outcomes of the plays, but one cannot determine analytically the relative importance in determining the outcomes of (1) the skill of the players, (2) their motivations, (3) the structure of the game, (4) the assumed values of various parameters, and (5) chance elements. One is left essentially with the intuitive insights that the players and observers believe they have derived from playing.

These insights, however, should not be belittled. While less than totally satisfactory (what alternative approach would give results passing this test?), they can be provocative and suggestive of good solutions which can be tested by more analytic methods. It is terribly important, no matter how it is done, to look at things from the enemy's point of view. Games provide a good stimulus and setting for doing so.

The importance of keeping the enemy's viewpoint in mind was brought out in the discussion of criteria for deterrence (Chapter 9). Many persons,

[24] For an historical account see Clayton J. Thomas and Walter L. Deemer, Jr., "The Role of Operational Gaming in Operations Research," *Operations Research,* February 1957, pp. 1–27.

leaving enemy viewpoints and responses out of account, have assumed that a large offensive force automatically provides deterrence. If we look at the matter from the enemy's point of view, a large *but vulnerable* Western striking force provides *negative* deterrence (at least as far as thermonuclear attack is concerned). In general, the analyst who looks at problems too exclusively from his own country's point of view, like some conventional military planners, is likely to forget how ingenious and resourceful the enemy may be. The war gamer whose force has been destroyed by enemy initiative is much less likely to make this dangerous kind of mistake.

THE MEANING OF CRITERIA

Earlier it was convenient to discuss criteria as though the term referred to definitive tests of preferredness. These reflections on incommensurables and uncertainty, however, make it clear that the word "criterion" sometimes means a partial test — one that provides a significant rather than a nonsensical basis for the comparison of policies and yet not a basis that embraces all the relevant considerations. In many problems, the precise relationship between proximate criteria and the ultimate test will not be known, and hence the former must be incomplete tests.

This is true in business as well as in military and other governmental problems. Consider, for example, an attempt by the managers of a firm to apply the test of "maximum profits from available resources." [25] Let us assume that when the managers consider several alternative courses of action, they can predict expected profits, and also something about the variability of profits, under each alternative policy. In other words, they can say to themselves, "Under Policy 1, profits would be $1 million, plus or minus $200,000. Under Policy 2, expected profits would be $2 million, though there is a chance that they might run as high as $3 million or that losses of $1 million would be incurred." What *is* "maximum profit from available resources" in this situation? It may be defined as maximum *average* profit, but in any event, it will be an incomplete criterion, because its relationship to the ultimate test will not be fully traced out. The ultimate criterion is to maximize something — it is usually labeled "utility" — which *depends upon* expected profits, upon the other possible profit figures, and upon the management's attitude toward risk and uncertainty. But the precise nature of this relationship is not ordinarily known. Hence to show which course of action yields maximum expected

[25] See G. Tintner, "The Theory of Choice under Subjective Risk and Uncertainty," *Econometrica*, IX, 1941, pp. 298–304; A. Alchian, "Uncertainty, Evolution, and Economic Theory," *The Journal of Political Economy*, XVIII, June 1950, pp. 211–221, or S. Enke, "On Maximizing Profits," *American Economic Review*, XLI, September 1951, pp. 556–578.

profit is to compare the policies in terms of one selected policy-consequence, that is, to apply a partial or incomplete criterion. To compare the policies with respect to other possible outcomes or to variability of outcome is to use other incomplete or partial criteria.

In military problems utility has frequently been labeled "military worth." Let us assume, for the moment, that the military worth we wish to maximize in a particular military problem is a function of the retaliatory power of SAC, the frequency distribution of results, the size of the federal budget, various diplomatic impacts, and the number of lives saved. We do not know how important some of these effects are in relation to others. Consequently we can devise no complete criterion which points to the "correct" force composition of SAC; the determination of such a force involves value judgments by several of the Executive departments and of Congress. However, we can show what would happen to a measure of SAC's retaliatory power with different force compositions. If possible, we should show data related to some of the other effects (for example, the frequency distribution of results). In any event, it is plain that maximum expected offensive power for a given SAC budget is an incomplete test, and it should be understood that the term "criterion," when it is used in connection with the economic analysis of military problems, often refers to such an incomplete test.

## 11. PROBLEMS ASSOCIATED WITH TIME

Much of the discussion so far has had a static dimension. We have usually spoken of costs and of benefits (or achievements or capabilities) as if they were timeless or, perhaps, concurrent. In fact, every cost is incurred and every benefit is realized at a particular point in time, and we are far from indifferent to the dates of these points. Next year seems far more significant to most of us than a date ten years distant. In our illustrative example in Chapter 8 we had to face up to some of the difficulties associated with time because we were dealing with a real problem. We did so in that example by constructing a simple artifice, dividing the relevant future into three periods — Period I, Period II, and "beyond the horizon" — and ignoring time differences within each period. In this chapter we will consider, in a quite general manner, some of the principal difficulties associated with time and some of the methods of dealing with them. We will discover that, as with other difficulties of systematic analysis, simplifications and compromises with the ideal are inevitable, but that there are better and worse ways to simplify.

In any economic analysis we are likely to begin with certain assets inherited from the past. In a business firm these usually include buildings, machinery, and inventories. In the airlift example in Chapter 8 they included not only the 400 C-97 cargo aircraft, but airbases, cargo handling equipment, maintenance depots, spare parts, trained crews, and so on. The production or "initial" costs involved in creating these assets have been incurred in the past; they are "sunk" costs[1] — bygones that are irrelevant in any comparison of the economic merits of alternative means of accomplishing future objectives. The use of some of these inherited assets to achieve any particular future objective may involve "opportunity" costs; that is, the use of these assets may make it necessary to forego valuable opportunities of using them to reach some other future objective. Thus, the 400 C-97's might have some use (after conversion) as tankers to refuel bombers; if they have, their net value as tankers is a legitimate cost — an opportunity cost — of providing airlift. But their value as tankers (if any) bears no necessary relation to their historical cost of production: it could be considerably greater or much less. In our example it was assumed that their marginal value as tankers (or in any other alternative use) was zero. While this may not have been literally true (they would bring something if sold for scrap), it was probably a close enough approximation for the kind of analysis we were making. The alternative-use value of specifically military equipment is frequently (although by no means always) small enough in relation to other costs that the analyst is justified in ignoring it.

The only costs and benefits in which we are interested in economic comparisons of alternatives are future costs and benefits. The opportunity costs associated with using inherited assets are one category of future costs. Far more important, in most cases, are future production costs, installation costs, maintenance costs, and operating costs.[2] These future costs are incurred at different times in the future. Some of the production costs may be incurred this year; some of the operating costs, ten years from now. We may think of the prospective costs associated with any one of the alternative means of achieving a military objective as a stream in time, whose width at any particular moment is proportional to the costs to be incurred at that date. Similarly, we may think of the benefits or capabilities associated with each alternative system as a stream in time, with width proportional to the capability expected on each date.

[1] Sunk costs and salvage values were also discussed in Chapter 7. Because of their importance and their pertinence to the treatment of time streams, we review these topics briefly here.

[2] These are also, of course, opportunity costs. All significant economic costs are opportunity costs. The reason production costs, for example, are significant, is that the productive resources used (or used up) could have been used to produce something else of value.

Now not only are the total *areas* of the cost streams (or benefit streams) associated with different alternatives likely to differ; their *shapes* are also likely to differ, and significantly. For example, if one compares the cost streams associated with the least-cost fleet and the least-procurement fleet in Chapter 8, he will discover that the least-cost stream is broader (that is, costs are greater) in the early years, when new, more efficient equipment is being procured, and narrower in the later years, after it has come into use. The savings in later years more than counterbalance the additional expenditure in the early years if no discount rate is used, that is, if costs incurred in any year are assigned the same weight or significance. But, in principle, this procedure is obviously wrong. The shapes of the streams do matter. We attach greater significance to costs and benefits this year than to prospective costs and benefits in future years, and in general we attach less significance the more distant the future year. In other words, we discount the future. The method used in Chapter 8 appears to prejudice the case in favor of the new and against the old equipment. Fortunately, it turned out that the simplification made no difference in that instance, so it was permissible.

## WHY DISCOUNT?

Individuals, firms, and governments borrow and lend in markets in which interest (or discount) rates are invariably positive. Consider first the individual or firm. If I have control over funds today I can invest them and obtain 3 or 4 per cent more every year. To me $100 today is the equivalent of at least $103 or $104 a year from now or perhaps $150 ten years from now. The government is in an analogous position. Tax income today can pay today's bills. Tax income a year from today is less useful. Today's bills must be paid by borrowing at 3 per cent (unless the government prints or otherwise creates money), and next year's tax income used to repay the loan plus interest. So $103 next year is the equivalent of $100 this year.

The principal reason interest rates are positive is that control over funds makes possible capital investments (in factories, machinery, inventories, and so on), and capital investment can be productive. This creates a large demand for present funds, and the demanders are willing to pay for the limited supply that is available. Each borrower must be willing at least to match what the marginal borrower is willing to pay. Each saver can get (at least) that price for the use of his funds.[3] As a result, the price for funds measures their opportunity cost or, in the language of economics, the marginal productivity of capital.

At the same time, this rate on funds measures our marginal time

[3] There is no need for any saver to accept less, even though some people would be willing to save and lend to industrial borrowers at lower — even zero — interest rates.

preferences — that is, the rate that we are willing to pay for consumption now rather than consumption later. The reason for this is that each person is free to adjust his savings until another dollar spent on current consumption is as important to him as another dollar saved for future consumption. If the prevailing rate of interest is 3 per cent, each of us values the marginal dollar put into consumption now as much as $1.03 for consumption next year. If this were not true, additional dollars would be shifted from consumption to savings. Hence the prevailing rate of interest measures the opportunity cost of funds diverted from either consumption or production.

In most instances, there is an additional factor that affects discounting and makes for a whole structure of rates rather than a unique interest rate. This important factor is the risk and uncertainty associated with different ventures. Risky business enterprises must pay much more than the "pure" rate of interest to obtain control of funds — and it is right that they should. If the risky enterprise does not have a prospect of a higher return than the safe one, the funds should go to the safe one. Or, to view the matter in another way, the future net gains (or gains and costs) of risky ventures should be more heavily discounted than the estimated net gains from relatively safe enterprises.

In comparisons of alternative military systems, the reasons for discounting are precisely the same as they are in the private economy. A $150 cost (or gain) that will occur ten years hence is the equivalent of only, say, $100 now, first of all because resources can be made to grow that much if put to alternative uses. The least-cost fleet in our example uses funds *now* which, if we had opted for the least-procurement fleet, could have been used to finance productive private investment. It should be charged at least a rate representing the market's evaluation of the marginal productivity of such investment.

In fact, it should be charged more than this. That market rate is the *minimum* rate appropriate in comparing military systems. There is the second, and in the typical military case quantitatively more important, reason for discounting future costs and benefits, namely, the existence of risk and uncertainty about the gains and costs. First, the war for which we are preparing may occur before the date at which the cost would be incurred or the capability realized. Second (less likely but conceivably), peace might break out, or disarmament be achieved, before the date in question. More generally, all sorts of things can happen that will completely alter the need for airlift of the type envisaged, and they are more likely to happen the more distant the year. The future costs and benefits are prospective rather than real, and may never become real. We live in an uncertain world, and its military aspects are more plagued by uncertainty than most others. Military technology is passing through a revolution — apparently an accelerating one. Concepts, tactics, strategies and alliances are all in ferment. Future weapon capabilities that look attractive today may be useless tomorrow.

## WHAT RATE?

The straightforward (but not necessarily the easiest or preferred) way to make costs and benefits at different times commensurate is simply to apply an appropriate discount rate to future costs and benefits, so that all are stated in terms of "present value." [4] This is what a business firm does, at least implicitly, in comparing present and future amounts, preparatory to choosing policies that maximize present value.[5] But what is the "appropriate" rate for this discount calculation? In general terms, the rate should be the marginal rate of return that could otherwise be earned — that is, the rate that reflects the productivity of the next-best opportunity. If the investor can borrow and lend freely, the marginal opportunity will turn out to yield approximately the market rate of interest. If he faces a fixed budget, the marginal opportunity may yield some other rate.[6] If legal or other constraints close off certain opportunities, those investments are simply not relevant and have no bearing on the selection of the rate of discount.

It is often argued that governments should not discount future amounts at as high a rate as do individuals and firms, because governments should take a longer-run view and endeavor to provide more for posterity than the decisions of private individuals would provide. We may indeed want governments to take a long view and to make extra provision for later generations — by increasing *total* public investment (in either defense or other forms) or by stimulating private investment. But, having settled this issue, governments should presumably try to channel the investment funds into those activities that have the highest

---

[4] The present value of any future cost or benefit is

$$\frac{a_n}{(1 + r_1)(1 + r_2) \cdots (1 + r_i) \cdots (1 + r_n)}$$

where $a_n$ represents the future value in year (or period) $n$, and $r_1$, $r_2$, $r_i$, $r_n$ the appropriate discount rate during the $i$th year (or period). If the $r$'s are equal, the present value $= \dfrac{a_n}{(1 + r)^n}$.

[5] It is usually assumed that businessmen attempt to maximize the present value of anticipated future income streams, costs counting as negative income. Present value maximization is the equivalent in economic dynamics of profit maximization in economic statics.

[6] This brief discussion is greatly oversimplified, but in our judgment, the finer theoretical points do not affect the main conclusions that can be drawn about comparing military systems. For more details and complexities, see Roland N. McKean, *Efficiency in Government through Systems Analysis, With Emphasis on Water Resource Development,* John Wiley and Sons, New York, 1958, pp. 74–95, and Jack Hirshleifer, "On The Theory of Optimal Investment Decision," *Journal of Political Economy,* August 1958, pp. 329–352.

rates of return. Similarly, an individual who wishes to provide more for his heirs should cut his consumption and raise his total investment, but should channel his capital into its most productive uses. In either instance, this means discounting streams of cost and gain at the marginal rate of return, not at some artificially low rate.

In government, the marginal opportunity depends upon the problem of choice that is being considered. Usually, when we look several years ahead, leaving the resources in the private economy is a pertinent alternative, one that may be taken to be the marginal opportunity. In other words, the government can repay debt or refrain from borrowing or taxing instead of making the purchase under consideration. As a consequence, the rate the government has to pay to borrow funds — on the order of 3 per cent — is a suitable minimum rate. If leaving the resources in the private economy is not an admissible alternative — if the problem is to allocate a given budget — the marginal opportunity and yield may be something else.

As suggested previously, however, we usually have to add an appropriate risk premium to this minimum rate. We should allow to some extent for the chances that the future benefits we expect may never be realized, that the costs may not have to be incurred, and that the estimated amounts may turn out to be wrong. But we do not know and cannot hope to learn precisely how risky any particular military investment is.

Some investments are certainly riskier than others. The probability of war (or peace) breaking out before realization of the anticipated benefit or cost is probably similar for all military systems; but some systems will be more vulnerable than others to uncertainties about technological advances, future strategic situations, and enemy capabilities and intentions. Advanced weapon systems, such as a future hypersonic long range bomber, appear to be among the riskiest enterprises of the modern world. Airlift systems like those compared in Chapter 8 appear to be much less risky. Technological advances in economical air transportation occur more slowly than in offensive and defensive weapon systems, and it seems likely that we will be able to use a lot of economical air transportation for something important through the 1960's even if technological or political developments rule out the danger of limited warfare in the vicinity of Bangdhad.

Perhaps, therefore, an appropriate discount rate (pure interest plus risk premium) for a military investment like that in airlift capacity would be similar to a rough average in private enterprise — say 6 to 8 per cent per annum; while the appropriate rate for an advanced weapon system might be higher — say 10 per cent or more. Twenty per cent would be an extremely high discount rate to use: it reduces a cost or benefit anticipated 5 years hence to almost a third its nominal value, and one anticipated 10 years in the future to about a sixth. If risks are *really* high enough to justify a 20 per cent discount rate, investments whose payoffs are in the distant future can rarely be justified unless the nominal payoffs are spectacular.[7] The appropriate discount rate during World War II appeared to be even higher than 20 per cent because immediate results were so much more important than distant payoffs; so we required that development and procurement be justified on the basis of payoff during a very short period.

It is clear that a rate as high as 20 or even 15 per cent per annum could not be justified in typical cold-war circumstances by the probability that war will intervene. If we really thought that war was sufficiently imminent to warrant discount rates of 15 to 20 per cent, we would be spending much more than 50 billion dollars annually on military programs. Discount rates as high as these are appropriate only for systems with high risks of obsolescence. Of course *if* our assessment of the probability of war increases, we should both increase military expenditures and use a higher discount rate in choosing *among* alternative purchases.

### WHAT VALUE FOR FUTURE INPUTS AND OUTPUTS?

We have said that future gains and costs should be discounted — that distant amounts should be weighted less heavily than present ones. Whatever the prices of individual inputs and outputs, a hundred dollars now is worth more than a hundred dollars ten years from now because (1) it can produce something, or "grow," in the meantime, and (2) we prefer a unit of satisfaction now to one ten years later. All this is not to say, however, that the price or value of *particular* objects will be lower in the future than at present. We may well expect the cost of certain inputs or the value of certain outputs to rise.

Thus, in addition to discounting cost and gain streams, a private investor must also do his best to estimate the future prices of inputs and output. He may reason that the cost of petroleum will be higher in 1970 than in 1965 because the more easily accessible supplies will be exhausted. Or he may expect the worth of an "advertising capability" to go up because of the growth of his competitors. Clearly, the future values of such items and therefore the *undiscounted* amounts of future costs and gains, are extremely important. We must not fancy that proper discounting can make up for their neglect.

Similarly in the comparison of military systems, we should discount future amounts, but the undiscounted gains and costs of certain defense

---

[7] Expenditures on research and exploratory development projects, however, which are cheap and may lead to spectacular payoffs in a decade or two, can be justified at 20 per cent or even higher discount rates. However, we are not arguing that all uncertainties can or ought to be reflected in discount rates. See Chapter 13 for a fuller discussion of the problems of choosing and planning risky research and development projects.

capabilities may be greater in 1970 than in 1965. Careful discounting does not by itself assure that the streams of costs and accomplishments are being handled properly.

This fact becomes especially important when we start taking into account the interdependence between our policies and the enemy's future actions. Suppose that an enemy is expected to have no ballistic missile capability in the early 1960's, a gradually increasing but less than decisive capability until 1965, and, after 1965, the ability to annihilate us if we have no defense. In these circumstances, anti-missile capabilities are clearly worth more to us in 1965 than in 1960. In fact, the appropriate value in the current year is zero — if the enemy cannot attack with missiles and if there are no by-products from an immediate capability like effective training for next year. On the other hand, some anti-missile capability in 1965 and later would be, on this supposition, of enormous value.

Consider a hypothetical comparison of two weapon systems. Suppose that our expected budget for defense against ballistic missiles is "given" during the next few years, and that we want to develop and procure anti-missile defense systems that will optimize, in some sense, our capability over time to shoot down incoming missiles. System A, adapted from a system developed primarily for defense against bombers, promises to give us some immediate capability but has little growth potential. System B cannot possibly provide a defense for several years, but promises a comparatively effective defense beginning, say, four years hence when it becomes operational. In choosing between the systems, we must assign reasonable values to capabilities in different years before we discount. Or it might be more practical to reformulate the problem, stipulating a reasonable time-path for our capabilities and discounting only the cost stream to seek the most efficient system for achieving the stipulated capability.

Thus, when we urge the discounting of future amounts, we mean that command over general resources now is worth more than command over the same amount of resources next year — not that specific objects are worth more now than in the future. We emphasize this fact because we do *not* wish to encourage the built-in tendency of governments to undervalue future outputs (see the concluding section of this chapter). To repeat, before discounting streams of cost or gain, one must take pains to assign realistic values to future inputs and outputs.

## SOME PRACTICAL DODGES

As a practical matter, we must abstract from some of these complexities. It is impossibly difficult in most comparisons to determine the appropriate future budgetary constraints, the proper list of alternatives and the yield of the marginal opportunity, the degrees of riskiness of various opportunities, and finally the appropriate discount rates. In these matters, as in others, we must simplify reality to a considerable extent. We seek to simplify reality enough to make systematic thought and calculation feasible yet not so much as to make the results inapplicable. Some crude approximations are usually justified, if we are careful to avoid distortion and bias. Needless to say, judgment must enter into this procedure of devising "practical dodges."

### THE TIME HORIZON

In comparing alternative weapon systems, it is never practical or desirable to estimate benefits and costs for all eternity and to determine and apply appropriate discount rates to these streams. It is always necessary to cut off the analysis at some point, ignoring or crudely lumping costs and benefits thereafter. Our ability to foresee the future becomes so limited after, say, ten or fifteen years, that for purposes of comparing weapon systems it seldom pays to try. If we did use appropriate discount rates, with appropriate allowance for risks, the comparisons would, in any event, be little affected by the distant years. The simple and straightforward thing to do is to omit them.

If a fairly early date is taken for the time horizon of the analysis, it may be desirable to lump net benefits beyond the horizon by crediting each system with some crudely calculated "salvage value" instead of simply ignoring them. This was done in our illustrative example, in which some of the cargo fleets at the end of Period II included many new high-performance planes and others consisted almost exclusively of old and obsolescent types. Clearly *some* allowance should have been made for the greater utility of fleets of the first type after the end of Period II, and this was done by valuing the various fleets (for "salvage") at initial cost minus an arbitrary straight-line depreciation allowance.

### THE RATE OF DISCOUNT

Because of uncertainties about future costs and capabilities, it is not worthwhile to devote an inordinate amount of time to refining one's estimate of "the" proper discount rate. Historical studies show that projections of cost and performance of weapon systems, particularly those made at early stages of development, have often been wide of the mark. For systems analysts to put great effort into determining "the" discount rate would probably be less productive than other uses of their time.

Moreover, because of uncertainties about future budgetary constraints and hence about marginal opportunities and their yields, the discount rate that may later be appropriate is inevitably in doubt at the time choices must be made. The best estimate may simply be a rough average rate of return in the private economy, like 6 or 8 per cent. This rate would include an average allowance for risk. Special degrees of risk associated with particular weapon systems should be pointed out by the analyst but would have to be allowed for subjectively by the final decision-makers.

Indeed, for certain classes of problems, we can make a stronger case for using an average rate of return from the private economy. At the time many weapon systems are being compared, future budgetary constraints have not been set, and we can reasonably argue that the relevant options are to buy the weapons or to leave the resources in the private economy. This choice being open, the marginal opportunity is simply investment in the private economy. Hence the rate of discount that reflects what could otherwise be earned by the resources is the rate of return that could be obtained in private investment.

We can also assume, with some justification, that this rate is consistent with time preferences in the economy — with the rate of return in consumption, so to speak. That is, we can assume that future budgets fixed by the government will be consistent with time preferences as reflected by interest rates in the private sector. Individually we do not have the opportunity to adjust government outlays so that another dollar spent on government activities is as important as another dollar saved for future consumption. But the task of our governing officials is to act for us in determining budgets, and they are able to do so in the light of prevailing interest rates. For this reason, too, we might well use an average discount rate from the private sector in analyzing long-range problems of choice.

### SENSITIVITY AND BREAK-EVEN POINTS

In short-range problems of choice — those in which narrower resource constraints exist — the average rate of discount from the private sector is less satisfactory, even if it is the best estimate that we can make. Also in many problems, whether long-run or short-run, the risk premium may be especially troublesome. The preferred procedure may then be to regard the discount rate as "variable" and test the results for sensitivity to the rates of discount. In the illustrative example in Chapter 8 the basic calculations were first made with a zero rate of discount, and the conclusions were then tested at discount rates up to 25 per cent per annum. The order of preference among the various systems was found not to be affected, although, of course, the degree of superiority was altered.

This procedure also yields a "break-even rate of discount" — that is, a rate of discount that makes the two leading systems equally attractive.

Below this rate, one system is preferred. Above this rate, another system is best. To show such break-even points is often a useful device, especially when uncertainties are great and judgment must play a major role in reaching final recommendations. By means of this device, the analyst or policy maker can see the range of discount rates within which one policy is clearly preferred and may be able to judge that the proper rate lies within that range.

### THE STIPULATED CAPABILITY

In view of the uncertainties, it may appear to be more straight-forward and appropriate in many problems to stipulate a desired capability over future time than to do any discounting of capabilities. Indeed in many instances it may appear to be the only feasible method of handling time paths for gains or capabilities. If the enemy threat were an increasing one, so usually would be our desired capability to counter it. The stipulated capability would presumably avoid "soft spots" if our intentions were defensive; it might point toward a maximum at some particular point of time if our intentions were to take the initiative. The general considerations which cause us to discount the future might be taken into account partly by attaching little or no weight to capabilities after some arbitrary cut-off point or horizon. Also, of course, the cost streams would still be discounted to seek the lowest-cost means of achieving the stipulated capability.

### PERIOD COSTING

The most common technique for comparing the costs over time of alternative systems is to add to the initial or investment costs the costs of operating each system for some fixed period, usually four or five years. Thus, one speaks of the "four-year system cost" or "five-year system cost." An end-of-period salvage value may or may not be sub-tracted. This is obviously a crude approximation to discounting. In effect, the discount rate is assumed to be zero during the period, rising abruptly to 100 per cent at the end. But in many problems such crude devices may be completely adequate. If we are merely interested in choosing a best or better system, we can test the sensitivity of the choice to the length of the period (lengthening the period is equivalent to reducing the discount rate). If there are no great differences in the ratio of initial to annual operating cost among the various systems being compared, choice will not in fact be sensitive to the length of the period or the discount rate. Frequently, however, such differences are important — especially where, as in Chapter 8, some of the systems make much more extensive use of inherited assets.

MULTIPLE PERIOD COSTING

A variant of period costing that was used in Chapter 8 is costing over two or more periods. This increases the flexibility of the method and makes it possible to deal with more complex problems. If we are interested in an extensive future period, over which the "stipulated capability" is increasing substantially, or new systems become available to satisfy it at later dates, or both of these complications confront us simultaneously, we *may* be able, as in Chapter 8, to divide the future into a conveniently small number of periods, each approximately homogenous, and aggregate stipulated capabilities and costs by periods. Of course, we still have the problem of applying appropriate discount rates to the more distant future periods *as a whole*.

In Chapter 8 the capabilities and costs are aggregated in just two periods, during the later of which some systems become available that are not available in the first period. The method demonstrates the inter-relations of choice of fleets in the two periods. For example, if the advanced HC-600 is to be procured for Period II, it pays to use some inherited C-97's during Period I and to purchase fewer of the earlier generation HC-400. If the HC-600 is not to be procured for Period II, the best procurement strategy is to invest heavily now in HC-400's.

LOWERING ONE'S SIGHTS

Some of the difficulties associated with time simply cannot be resolved by any kind of quantitative economic analysis. This does not mean that quantitative economic analysis has no useful role to play in connection with such problems, but it does mean that its role is subsidiary and that it must address itself to the practical problem of finding a better alternative rather than the best.

Consider, for example, the vexing question of whether to skip a generation of weapons. Sometimes vast savings in resources are possible if one skips — but at the cost of a lessened capability during the inter-mediate years. In the case of the cargo fleets compared in Chapter 8, it was always possible to shore up the capability in the near future by using more of the obsolescent aircraft, so this complication did not arise. But if we are interested in offensive or defensive weapons, there are cases where greater numbers cannot be made available or where no degree of quantitative superiority can compensate for inferiority in crucial weapon characteristics (for example if the enemy has an effective electronic counter-measure against which existing weapons possess no counter counter-measure).

At the end of World War II, the British government took a calculated (?) risk and decided to skip a generation of bombers, concentrating its resources on the development of the then advanced V-Bombers. This enabled it to cut its military budget substantially in the early post-war years, but would have left it without a modern bomber force if another war had occurred. It justified this course of action by arguing that the probability of war was low in the immediately following years. The United States Air Force was faced with a decision in the early post-war years whether to develop air-breathing missiles (like the Navajo and Snark) or whether to skip immediately to long-range ballistic missiles (Atlas). It decided to develop the air breathers. The Russians, faced by a similar choice, apparently made the opposite decision, putting their effort into the more advanced system.

Quantitative economic analysis could not have determined an optimum in a generally acceptable way in any of these cases. It could not have predicted the probability of war in the "soft" years; or the extent to which that probability would itself be affected by the softness; or the way in which the government or nation should value enhanced risk for a few years as compared with budgetary savings. But it might have been able to facilitate choice. At the very least it could have estimated quantitatively how much our capability would have been reduced for how long, and how much money would "really" have been saved. It might have been able to do something even more useful — to show how capability might have been shored up inexpensively during any soft period. Some cheap modifications of wartime bombers, for example, might have made them an effective fighting force for an unexpected emergency. Alternatively, surplus B-29's or B-50's might have been turned over to our allies as military aid and kept operational during the soft years (in fact, some were). In the missile case, air-to-surface missiles might have been a more attractive alternative than the long-range air-breathing surface-to-surface missile. Or quantitative analysis might have demonstrated that the lack of the air-breathing missiles would have had only a marginal effect on our capability, given the improved bombing aircraft that were to be operational during the soft years. Frequently, we can demonstrate that system A is better than system B even when we cannot show that system A is optimal. At a minimum, we can produce evidence relevant to the choice between A and B. And with a little ingenuity, we can often suggest a modification of A, system A', that is demonstrably better than A.

## UNDERVALUING FUTURE OUTPUTS

We conclude with a final warning about the valuation of future outputs. There is a marked tendency on the part of the military services, the government, and the Congress to undervalue future capabilities. The primary responsibility of the military services is the operation of today's forces. Perhaps significantly, they always have emergency war plans, but seldom long-range war plans. Moreover, the policy of rotating service personnel at short intervals (usually three years or less) means that officials are always trying to make a recognizable mark in the very near future — later someone else will be in their jobs and responsible. Governments, similarly, have short tenure in most democracies, and many political officials have even shorter tenure. The next election always appears much more significant than the election 12 years hence — when, in any event, no rewards will be showered by the electorate on a party responsible for prescient decisions 12 years earlier. Congress (as well as an administration) is notoriously interested only in *this year's* budget and its relation to possible tax relief. The result is that within research and development almost all the resources are used in developing weapon systems with a predicted combat capability in the relatively near future; that measures that promise significant savings over a period of years (like the least-cost fleet in Chapter 8) are rejected because they involve somewhat higher expenditures the following year.[8] In fact, it has for this reason been almost impossible to get approval for the purchase of high performance cargo aircraft. We will consider in Chapter 12 whether some institutional reforms (like a capital budget) might not help in reducing this inordinate undervaluation of the future. Here let us simply point out that this bias in past and current decisions presents opportunities for quantitative economic analysis to demonstrate large gains in efficiency. In many cases, unfortunately, they will be easier to demonstrate than to sell.

# 12. INSTITUTIONAL ARRANGEMENTS TO PROMOTE EFFICIENCY

As we saw in Chapter 7, there are at least three ways to promote economic efficiency in the military use of resources: better understanding of the nature of the problem, systematic quantitative analysis of problems of military choice, and improved institutional arrangements. So far in Part II we have dealt almost exclusively with the first two: understanding and systematic analysis. The question in this chapter is what role, if any, improved institutional arrangements can play either as a substitute for systematic economic analysis of the type we have been describing, or as a reinforcement of it. Economics may be able to help answer this question,

---

[8] Interesting exceptions are many water and other natural resource projects which are approved in spite of the fact that they promise rates of return as low as 2½ per cent. This is the opposite error: they should be required to earn at least 6 per cent. In this case local benefits and log-rolling play an important role in reversing usual attitudes.

not because it offers any special understanding of communications, psychology, or organization charts, but because of its traditional concern with criteria and the harnessing of decision making at different levels in the private economy.[1] Organization is *one* of the choices to be made in the light of economic criteria.

### INSTITUTIONAL ARRANGEMENTS IN THE PRIVATE ECONOMY

It is instructive to reflect that in the private sector of a free-enterprise economy we rely almost exclusively on institutional arrangements for the promotion of efficiency. The United States government does not directly concern itself with such problems as the optimal rate of output of radios or radio vacuum tubes, or the optimal rate of substitution of aluminum and copper for steel in the manufacture of automobile parts.[2] There are no grand systems analyses to determine how the nation's investment resources should be allocated either among industries or among regions.[3] The output of civilian radios and the rate of construction of retail supermarkets are results of the decisions of large numbers of individual consumers and business men, each acting on the basis of his own particular motivations and the incomplete information available to him.

As we have seen, welfare economics[4] tells us that, *in certain circumstances,* if business men attempt to maximize their profits, their decisions will tend to result in an "efficient" organization of production in the sense that no more of one good or service can be produced without producing less of another. If consumers also attempt to maximize their "satisfaction" or "utility," there is a tendency for production to be efficient in a stronger sense: no one consumer can be made better off without making another worse off.

The "certain circumstances" required for an efficient solution, like

[1] On the role of economics, see again Chapter 7 and also Charles Hitch, "Economics and Military Operations Research," *Review of Economics and Statistics,* August 1958, pp. 199–209.

[2] This is, of course, an exaggeration. There are decisions of this type with which even free enterprise governments become concerned, some more than others. Almost all governments attempt to modify particular market decisions (or their effects) for "political" (usually distributional) reasons.

[3] Again, this is an exaggeration. It is now pretty generally accepted that the aggregate level of the nation's investment activity is a legitimate concern of government even in a free enterprise country: economic analyses to estimate optimal levels are made in the U.S. by the Council of Economic Advisors. Moreover, governments have, for various reasons, attempted to influence rates of investment in particular industries — because they would be useful in a wartime mobilization, for example, or for distributional reasons (subsidized low-cost housing). The general proposition stands, however: the role of government in such decisions is secondary and usually indirect.

[4] See footnote 6 in Chapter 9.

the assumptions of all abstract "models," are never precisely realized in the real world. They include absence of fraud and coercion in profit-seeking activities, security of contract and property rights, absence of monopoly, an aggregate demand for goods and services adequate to insure full employment, and absence of spillover effects (that is, external economies and diseconomies).[5] Similarly the assumed criterion of business men — maximum profits — only approximately corresponds to the criterion of real business men, whose interests may not be identical with profits earned for stockholders. Indeed, as we have seen,[6] there is an ambiguity in the very concept of "maximum profits" in the real, uncertain world.

The efforts of governments to improve the efficiency of free-enterprise economies are appropriately, and in practice usually, devoted to making circumstances and motivations in the real world correspond somewhat more closely to those in the theoretical model, rather than to direct attempts at the center to compute efficient allocations, outputs, and methods of production. They are devoted, in the terminology that we will use in this chapter, to improving the institutional environment within which decentralized decisions are made.

For example, a major function of criminal and civil law is the prevention of fraud and coercion in business transactions and the protection of contract and property rights. These laws have an economic as well as a moral justification. There are many laws and ordinances designed to prevent or compensate for such spillover effects as smog creation by the chemical industry or the flooding of neighboring farms by a utility company's dam. The antitrust activities of the federal government are an attempt to reduce monopolistic elements and practices. There has been little attempt to reinforce the profit motive, apart from legal moves to protect the interests of stockholders from those managers who are inclined to ignore them, but there has been great concern to prevent taxes from so distorting profit incentives that they cease to provide the drive toward efficient solutions.

Our point is not that these efforts of government have been wholly successful, either in the United States or anywhere else. Obviously they have not and never will be. The assumptions of the economist's model, like those of any abstract model, are unrealizable as well as unrealized in the real world. On the contrary, our point here is that decentralized decisions work well only if the decision-makers at various levels can be given appropriate incentives and criteria — and that in the civilian economy our efforts to promote efficiency are almost wholly concentrated on the institutional environment.

[5] See p. 163–164 above.
[6] See Chapter 10, p. 204.

INSTITUTIONAL ARRANGEMENTS IN THE MILITARY SECTOR

The problem of achieving military efficiency by manipulation of the institutional framework is harder and different in character.

In the first place, because we do not start with a network of markets to determine the values of military goods and services, it is extremely difficult to apply the standard form of economic theory to tell us which institutional arrangements are and which are not conducive to efficiency. Most fundamental is the lack of markets to determine the values of final military goods — that is, various sorts of military capability. (If we had valuations for final goods, markets for such *intermediate* goods as bases, skilled manpower, and weapon systems might be developed.) The economics of welfare is dependent on markets and market-determined prices both as the source of *information* about the economy needed by businessmen and consumers, and as the *mechanism* for profit-maximizing activity. A world without markets is a different sort of world and requires a different, or at least a more general, economic theory.

We must therefore expect that we will not be able to identify optimal institutions, any more than we were able to identify optima in many other situations. The best we can hope to do, with an incomplete theory, is to identify some institutional arrangements that would be an improvement on those now existing. But this, rather than optimizing, is always the important practical problem.

We will consider in this chapter only those proposals for institutional change on which economic analysis can throw some light. For the most part these are proposals for arrangements which would either substitute for or reinforce the kind of economic calculus we have discussed in the preceding chapters. Our interest is in institutional arrangements designed to promote economic efficiency in the military sector, not in administrative or management efficiency in a broad sense.[7]

### PROPOSALS TO SIMULATE MARKETS WITHIN THE GOVERNMENT

The first group of proposals that we shall consider, recognizing the fundamental deficiency in economic institutions within the government, advocate remedying it directly by creating markets on which government-produced goods and services would be bought and sold and their values or quantities, or both, determined.

#### THE LERNER PROPOSAL

Most proposals of this kind are limited and partial, suggesting the creation of some particular market, or institutional arrangement with

---

[7] Thus most of the Hoover Commission recommendations fall outside the scope of our inquiry. But we have similar interests in improved budgeting and accounting procedures (see Chapter 5) and in increased contracting (see below, pp. 226–233).

some market characteristics. One eminent economist, however — Professor Abba Lerner — has proposed that the whole military establishment be organized in a network of markets and that it operate, by means of decentralized decision making, much as the private American economy does. We shall discuss this proposal at some length, not because it is a practicable solution to defense problems of choice, but because it is frequently instructive to press good ideas to their extreme logical conclusions.[8] To indicate some of the merits and limitations of such a scheme may help us in designing practicable policies.

In this bold and original proposal, made by Professor Lerner during World War II, he suggested that "sums of money" or budgets be placed at the disposal of the various theater commanders, who would use them in bidding for various kinds of matériel (from the supply commands) and men (presumably from the training commands), "husbanding his limited dollars so as to get the most out of them for his purpose." The prices of the various kinds of matériel and of men with various skills[9] "would be raised and lowered to make the demand for each of them equal to the supply."

The assessment of the "military worth" of marginal operations in each of the theaters would be the responsibility (indeed, under this plan almost the only responsibility) of the Joint Chiefs of Staff. They would attempt to allocate the national security budget among theater commanders in such proportions that the last million dollars given to the European Command was neither more nor less useful in the over-all war effort than the last million given to the Far Eastern Command or to defense of the Zone of the Interior.

A theater commander, in Professor Lerner's plan, would be permitted in turn to make allocations of budget to his subordinate commanders "whenever he has sufficient confidence in the judgment of his subordinates and where their knowledge of the detailed needs of their particular problems was greater than his own." The subordinate commanders would then use their budgets to bid for men and matériel.

Professor Lerner claimed a number of advantages for his proposal. Subordinate commanders would be able to make full use of their specialized knowledge (as businessmen are). The network of markets for men and matériel would provide exactly the information needed by the supply, procurement, and training commands regarding the relative use-

---

[8] Abba P. Lerner, "Design for a Streamlined War Economy," written at Amherst College, 1942. Another reason for paraphrasing this paper at some length is that unfortunately it has never been published, although it has circulated among professional economists.

[9] Professor Lerner did not propose that the pay of officers and men be determined in real markets: the prices equaling demand and supply would simply signal the training commands to produce more of some skills, less of others.

fulness of various instruments and skills. The budgeting and pricing procedures (given certain institutional assumptions not made explicit in this paper[10]) would indeed tend to produce an efficient use of military resources in which it would be impossible to increase military capability in one theater without decreasing it in another.[11] Professor Lerner adds hopefully that it would also mean "a tremendous saving of paper work."

This proposal is certainly not a practical one in the sense that there is the slightest chance of its being adopted in anything like its original form in the foreseeable future. It is far too unconventional for that, and Service traditions far too strong. Also there are serious objections to such a scheme, other than those arising out of administrative difficulties. On the level of principle, Professor Lerner's proposal does not come to grips with the fundamental objection to giving subordinate military units a completely free hand in making decisions and spending budgets. He does not ask: How will commanders and subordinate commanders be motivated? Will their motivations be consistent with the national interest? Are there important spillover effects that they will ignore? As we have seen, these are terribly difficult questions.

In this scheme, the Joint Chiefs would allocate the total budget in the first instance to the various theater commanders — the military equivalent of the final consumers. This was a natural kind of devolution in the circumstances of World War II, and might be regarded as, in principle, reasonably satisfactory. Fighting during World War II did take place in widely separated theaters against different enemies, and spillover effects might have been minimal. But in peacetime or cold war, it is by no means obvious how one should go about dividing a total national security budget among subordinate military organizations. Overseas theater commanders during cold war are not equivalent to wartime theater commanders, and in any event would account for minor slices of the pie, since most of our forces are based in the Zone of the Interior. With great uncertainty when or whether there will be war, against whom, where, and what kind, there is corresponding uncertainty how to aggregate military forces for purposes of autonomous budgeting, planning, and decision-making.

In particular, the "natural" solution of allocating budgets to the three uniformed Services, and letting them allocate in turn to subordinate intra-Service commanders, giving each full autonomy in spending, appears to be far from ideal. Each Service has not one mission but many, most of which have to be achieved in collaboration with other Services. The

---

[10] But discussed at length by Professor Lerner elsewhere. See *The Economics of Control*, Macmillan Co., New York, 1944, especially pp. 72–78.

[11] See p. 164 above. The marginal rates of substitution or trade-offs between different military resources would tend toward equality in all theaters and uses — the condition of efficient allocation.

activities of each subordinate Service command have important spillover effects on other commands within the Service, on other Services, on other Departments, especially the State Department, and on our economy and society generally. The Commander of Tactical Air Command, for example, cannot be given a completely free hand in buying and deploying forces and equipment. Tactical Air Command exists primarily to supply the air component of combined tactical operations, which ought to be designed to promote the foreign policy of the United States. And should operational commanders be given the funds to develop radically new equipment? There is much experience to suggest that this would be a mistaken policy. Operational commanders have their major responsibility in the present; they can be expected to place a heavy discount on the new, the untried, and the different. It is apparent that complete autonomy in spending on the part of subordinate commands as they exist today is undesirable as well as impractical. If something akin to the Lerner proposal were adopted, spending and related decisions of the commands would have to be controlled and constrained either by rules and orders from higher levels in the government hierarchy, or as now by the necessity to bargain with other commands to prevent them from appealing to higher authority. In other words, the proposal would have to be made much less revolutionary than it appears at first reading.

Many of the more recent proposals that we will consider in this chapter may be regarded as partial, halting steps in the direction of the Lerner solution. The fact that they are partial does not mean that they are inferior. It may make sense to take some steps in this direction, but only when advantages pretty clearly outweigh disadvantages. Even in the private economy we do not rely exclusively upon price and market mechanisms, and there are good reasons for thinking that the optimal degree of reliance upon them in the military (and the government generally) is less.

### STOCK AND INDUSTRIAL FUNDS [12]

Among these interesting piecemeal approaches are stock and industrial funds, which attempt to set up a price-and-market mechanism within the government at whatever particular points this seems feasible and desirable. Stock and industrial funds are set up by Congress; the "funds" are the working capital appropriated to finance certain defined activities, which are conducted much as though they were private businesses. Stock funds finance stock-handling activities (such as the retailing of petroleum products), and industrial funds finance industrial-type establishments (such as the operation of printing plants). The "firms" operating both

---

[12] An excellent discussion of these funds is given in Norman V. Breckner's "Government Efficiency and the Military 'Buyer-Seller' Device," *Journal of Political Economy*, October 1960, pp. 469–486.

kinds of funds purchase their inputs, adopt businesslike accounting systems, charge prices to the military units or others who buy their outputs, submit profit-and-loss statements, and try to maximize "profits." (It is frequently thought desirable to place some constraints on their autonomy that private firms do not encounter. That is, the range of decisions left up to the managers is not so wide as it is in private enterprise.) The military units who are customers are then given larger budgets to enable them to buy from these enterprises.

The funds are expected to bring about three types of improvement. First, their managers will be motivated to conduct them more efficiently, because there will be a more appropriate indicator of efficiency than would otherwise exist. There will be a mark, the amount of profit or loss, to shoot at — and to be shot at by critics or superior officers. Second, customers will be motivated to find cheaper substitutes and ways of using less of these products. These customers will not be able to get, as a free good, whatever they requisition; rather, they will have to sacrifice something in order to obtain items from these fund-enterprises. Third, the outputs of these establishments will be allocated more efficiently — that is, put to their most valuable uses — because they will be rationed by "market prices" rather than by bare shelves or semi-arbitrary quotas.

This is the way it is hoped that the funds will work. By and large, experience to date is said to be encouraging. Perhaps the best-known "stock fund" is the one used to finance the merchandising of enlisted men's clothing. This retail operation is set up as a business, and servicemen, instead of being issued new clothing to replace worn-out articles, are given a monthly allowance for the purchase of clothing. Servicemen take better care of their clothes as they try to save from their allowance, and managers take better care of the retail operation as they try to make their profit-and-loss statements look good. Medical-dental supplies and petroleum, oil, and lubricants are among the other items that are merchandised in this fashion.

Among the "industrial funds," the one that finances the Military Sea Transport Service is perhaps the most widely publicized. Under the new arrangement, space is sold, not issued upon requisition. If space that is purchased is not used, it is of consequence to the purchaser, for he must pay a penalty. If ships are not unloaded promptly, demurrage is charged. Savings have been estimated at roughly a hundred million dollars a year. Other industrial funds finance the operation of such activities as the Military Air Transport Service, printing establishments, laundries, maintenance of tanks, and testing services.

However, it is clear that these funds are no panacea and that they cannot be used indiscriminately. In the first place, the amount of stimulus to incentives depends upon the way in which funds are implemented.

The management of these enterprises will be anxious to have better profit-and-loss statements if (a) their superiors are anxious to have better statements, or (b) their remuneration is directly related to profits. Otherwise, their incentives are not likely to be sharpened. As far as the customers are concerned, they will be anxious to economize in their use of the enterprise's output if they must genuinely give up something in order to buy this output. But in order for that condition to be fulfilled, they must (a) be unable to pad the new allowance that is allotted to them, *and* (b) be able to get some gain or credit from the saving. The latter requirement will be met if customers are allowed to keep some of the saving (as in the case of soldiers who take better care of their clothing), to use some for improving their military units and enhancing their reputations, or to get recognition for savings that are turned over to higher commands or to the Treasury. Unless customers really sacrifice something if they do not economize, the signing of "checks" may not motivate them more intensely than the signing of requisitions.

In the second place, the *appropriateness* of the motivation under funded enterprises also depends upon the way in which this device is used. In some situations, prices and customers' budgets can respond rapidly and appropriately, and harness individual efforts so as to achieve over-all objectives. In other situations, they cannot. Soldiers are properly motivated when they use their allowance to buy clothing — provided constraints on the type and condition of the uniform are imposed. Motivation might not be appropriate if those constraints were removed, or if soldiers were to buy their hand grenades from the same allowance, or if each division were free to buy different weapons. For interdependencies — resulting in spillover effects — abound in military operations. Furthermore, in order for both managers and customers of funded enterprises to be motivated appropriately, costs of inputs must be measured so as to reflect their value in other uses, prices of outputs must be set (and reset) properly to reflect incremental cost, and last but not least difficult, the customers' budgets must not be "padded."

It should be noted, however, that the functioning of funds, like that of private enterprise, does not have to be perfect in order to be more efficient than alternative arrangements. There are many opportunities for the use of funded "businesses." With thoughtful screening of such opportunities and improved implementation, stock and industrial funds may contribute importantly to efficiency in the small.

### PROPOSALS FOR INCREASED RELIANCE ON THE PRIVATE MARKET ECONOMY

If it is so difficult to reap the advantages of a market economy by creating one within the military Services, an alternative possibility is to turn over to private businesses and the private market economy some tasks and functions now performed within the government. The argument for this policy is frequently put in terms of equity or principle: It is "unfair" for the government to compete with private enterprise or even to perform functions that might be performed by private enterprise. We are concerned in this chapter not with fairness but with efficiency. In what cases and circumstances can private replace public enterprise with a net gain in efficiency?

Let us say at once that in business-type activities there is a presumption that private enterprise can operate more efficiently than governments — at least more efficiently than the military Services as they are organized today. (1) In the private economy there is, and in government there is not, an imperfect but pervasive and persistent competitive mechanism for promoting efficient managements and methods and getting rid of inefficient ones. (2) Military and civil service pay scales and other conditions of employment make it impossible for the government to compete effectively with private industry for high-quality technical and management personnel. This may appear an adventitious shortcoming of a particular government at a particular time, one that could easily be remedied by legislation. Unfortunately, this is not so. Almost all democratic governments suffer from this kind of disability. In the case of military personnel there is a special problem: certain features of military life are particularly unattractive to ambitious, technically trained men, making it necessary to pay more to keep such men in the Service (in the numbers required) than a private firm has to pay for the same quality of personnel. (3) Legislative constraints and bureaucratic rules and regulations rob the military Services, as well as other departments of the government, of the flexibility needed for efficient adjustment of operations and effective competition with private industry.[13] These again are not adventitious; similar constraints are required by and are characteristic of all very large organizations.

But this presumption that private enterprise can operate more efficiently than governments applies only to "business activities," and even there can easily be upset and reversed in particular cases. The government, including perhaps especially the military Services, has numerous responsibilities and functions (not similar to those of businesses) that could not possibly be delegated to private firms; and there are many other cases where delegation, while conceivable, raises formidable difficulties. (For example, can vital military functions be entrusted to private firms against which employees may strike?) Moreover, the part of the private economy that provides goods and services to the government on contract may function less efficiently than the rest — a problem to which we will

---

[13] The damaging rigidity of military and civil service pay scales is but one example.

return in the following section. It is evident, in any event, that proposals under this heading must be piecemeal and partial.

The obvious way to transfer business-type activities to private enterprise is to buy on the market, or contract for, goods and services which have been or would otherwise be produced by a government department or agency.

It is worth noting how far the United States military Services have already moved in this direction. Before World War II a substantial proportion of military equipment was produced in army arsenals and navy shipyards; the proportion is now almost trifling. Similarly the bulk of research and development is now undertaken on contract — to some extent by universities and other nonprofit research organizations, but mainly by private business firms. There are a few government research laboratories, but the role of government is largely confined to providing common test facilities.

The most ambitious proposals for extension of this practice are in the field of maintenance. Contractor maintenance is now common for some highly specialized and intricate equipments, particularly in electronics;[14] and the Air Force has made extensive use of contract maintenance for aircraft overseas (Project Native Son). It has been proposed that major prime contractors might take over responsibility for the maintenance of complete weapon systems, including provisioning of spares, just as they now take responsibility for production, relieving the Services of this function. It is argued that the private firm could do this more efficiently and also that the prime contractor would then have reason to give due emphasis to maintainability when designing weapons. In its extreme form this does not appear to be a desirable or even a feasible arrangement. The Services must be prepared to provide certain maintenance facilities at all times and places, in all emergencies, and under combat conditions. It is difficult to see how this capability could be insured except by men under military discipline — which contractor personnel presumably would not be. But certainly the delegation of much major maintenance activity to contractors may be feasible, and the increasing complexity of military equipment in all Services is exerting heavy pressure for greater reliance on the contractors who have the required technical expertise.

---

[14] Over 50 per cent of the maintenance workload on aircraft, aircraft engines, and related equipment, and about 70 per cent of the work on electronic equipment, is performed by contractors, *Department of Defense Appropriations for 1959, Overall Policy Statements,* Hearings before the Subcommittee of the Committee on Appropriations, House of Representatives, 85th Congress, 2d Session, U.S. Government Printing Office, Washington, D.C., 1958, p. 150.

INCREASED RELIANCE ON PRIME CONTRACTORS

It has been argued, particularly by industrialists, that a great deal of the work performed by Service organizations responsible for procurement and the later stages of development (prototype production) is strictly a management function that many large industrial firms are uniquely equipped to perform well and that should be delegated to them as prime contractors. This work consists in coordinating the supply of thousands of parts and components of major items of equipment, and of the auxiliary equipment needed in functioning weapon systems — finding appropriate suppliers, writing contracts with them, monitoring the design of components to insure compatibility, and scheduling and expediting deliveries of components.

Moreover, sometimes the armed services draw up detailed specifications ("specs") even for relatively simple or unimportant items. Once, for example, the "specs" for a parachute pull-ring were five pages long, and those for pingpong balls took up 18 pages. On an order for furniture from an old established producer, even the type of sandpaper to be used on the unseen surfaces was specified. The cost of such purchasing practices probably outweighs the possible gains.

Delegation of these various management functions is entirely a matter of degree, and a large amount of delegation is current practice. Almost all prime contractors do a great deal of subcontracting. But many would like to do more, and to have a freer hand than they now have in the selection of subcontractors and in controlling specifications.

There is no doubt that many large industrial firms have demonstrated great proficiency in performing this type of management function; and that the Services, for all sorts of reasons, have difficulty recruiting, training, and holding officers with similar technical or managerial competence. On the other hand, the design of components and auxiliary equipment is frequently critical in the performance of weapon systems. The Services rather than the prime contractors know what performance characteristics are most valuable in combat; and the producers of the specialized components, rather than the prime contractors who assemble them, know the range of design possibilities and the "trade-offs" among performance characteristics and between performance and cost. Moreover, in contracts of a cost-plus nature, many management functions can hardly be delegated to the contractor. It is difficult to escape the conclusion that considerable direct contact between the Services and the producers of specialized components and equipment is desirable, and that whatever the formal contract arrangements, the Services must to a considerable extent control component design.

An ingenious and interesting variant of Service control of a weapon system has been extensively reported in the press. The Air Force entrusted the management of the ICBM and IRBM development program to a special office of the Air Research and Development Command headed by an Air Force Major General and staffed, at the top, with Service officers. This office contracted directly for major components as well as for final assembly. But the technical staff of the office was supplied on contract by an industrial company — the Ramo-Wooldridge Corporation of Los Angeles (now Space Technology Laboratories, Inc.). Whether compromise arrangements of this kind (or some other) are capable of securing the best of both worlds, or will prove to be short-lived and abortive, will have to be determined by experimentation and observation.

### PROPOSALS TO INCREASE THE EFFICIENCY OF CONTRACTORS

It is not enough to entrust production, development, and management functions to private contractors. When goods and services are purchased by government agencies on the basis of full and free competitive bidding, there is a presumption that competitive forces, working through the price and market mechanism, will provide the same spur to efficiency and low-cost supply that they do elsewhere in the private economy. But only a rather minor portion of Service purchases are made, or can be made, on the basis of competitive bidding. The expensive items of major equipment like aircraft, submarines, and tanks and their expensive major components can be produced by very few companies, and their production costs are seldom accurately estimated in advance. Moreover, frequent and extensive modifications of the original design are the rule rather than the exception both in development and in production. In these circumstances "negotiated" contracts of the "cost-plus" type are widely used.[15]

As we have seen, the Services frequently place constraints on management prerogatives that are not customary in the private economy. Some of these stem from their insistence that they control performance characteristics and therefore design. It is not unusual for prime contracts to specify not only *what* is to be supplied, but *how* — with what materials, how much subcontracting, which subcontractors, and so on. Others stem from the cost-plus character of the contract, which makes it necessary for the Services, prodded by the General Accounting Office, to see that all costs incurred are "legitimate." A "contracting officer" forces compliance with innumerable rules designed to prevent waste or fraud, and

---

[15] Cost plus a percentage of cost has been outlawed, but cost-plus-fixed-fee and cost-plus-incentive-fee contracts are extensively used. Also, many of the fixed-price contracts turn out in practice to be of a cost-plus nature because of provisions for "redetermination."

approves (or disapproves) every item of expenditure by both prime contractors and sub-contractors. He even controls, at least in theory, the wages and salaries paid all employees.

All this takes us pretty far from "free enterprise" as the term is usually understood and as it is practiced elsewhere in the economy. Certainly the departures appear to sacrifice many of the advantages of free enterprise, which these delegations of production and management functions to private firms are designed to reap. First, there would appear to be little competition when contracts are negotiated. Second, there would appear to be little incentive to produce efficiently or cheaply when all allowable costs are reimbursed and fees (allowed profits) are fixed in advance.[16] Third, there would appear to be little scope for business initiative when firms are told not only what to produce, but how, and when their expenditures (even their salary structure) are under the control of government contracting officers.

One school of thought regards the cost-plus contract as the root of all evil. Recognizing that competitive bidding is impossible or inappropriate in many cases involving the bulk of Service expenditure, it has attempted to develop so-called "incentive" contracts which retain some measure of incentive for contractors to reduce costs.[17] The most extreme form is the negotiated fixed-price contract, which fixes the final price to be paid in advance (sometimes subject to escalator clauses for wages and material costs, and always subject to design changes required by the Service). One difficulty with the fixed price contract is that, where uncertainties regarding cost are extreme, the fixed price can be far off the mark. If it is much too low, a single large contract could force a major contractor into bankruptcy; if much too high, it could result in profits that would appear exorbitant.

There has therefore been experimentation with more moderate forms of incentive contracts — their common feature being that the contractor is permitted to keep some part (determined by formula) of any cost savings, relative to some "target" cost named in the contract, but not enough to cause public outcry; and he is penalized by some part of any costs in excess of the target, but not enough to ruin him.[18] In principle,

[16] Or if they aren't completely fixed in advance, contract renegotiation is likely to sop them up after they are made. The desire of the Air Force to maintain "a healthy aircraft industry," of the Navy to maintain "a healthy shipbuilding industry," etc., still further reduces incentives to produce efficiently; there is a widespread (doubtless exaggerated) belief that the Services can be relied on not to let a major supplier fail.

[17] Incentive contracts are only possible when the product can be specified. In most research contracts it cannot be.

[18] For details on the various types of contracts, see *Department of Defense Appropriations for 1957, Procurement Policies and Practices of the Department of Defense,* Hearings before the Subcommittee of the Committee on Appropriations, House of Representatives, 84th Congress, 2nd Session, U.S. Government Printing Office, Washington, 1956.

almost everyone approves incentive contracts; the great practical difficulty is in defining an appropriate target cost, and in redefining it every time a modification is made in design. The contractor has a tremendous incentive to have the target set high, and to have it moved higher with every change order — perhaps a greater incentive than to reduce costs. Much time, effort, and ingenuity is spent in negotiating target cost figures, that must be set off against any savings from improved incentives.

In fact, the real opportunity for savings and strengthening of incentives may lie in improving the procedure for the setting of cost targets. Too often, at present, the process takes on the following pattern. The contractor prepares his estimate of the target cost, anticipating that the military service will "ruthlessly" bargain for a (familiar) percentage adjustment downward. As expected, the military service does hold out firmly for that adjustment. But analytical assistance during this process is so meager that the military bargainers have little feeling for the reasonableness of any of the estimates.[19] Despite the uncertainties that plague cost estimation, better cost analysis for the military Services during negotiation is one important way to improve incentives of contractors and increase their efficiency.[20]

Another promising general approach (although in no sense an alternative) is some intensification and redirection of competition among contractors. Competitive bidding is a useful device only in special cases, but other forms of competition can be stimulated. The Services do get to know which producers are high cost and which are lost cost.[21] They learn which can be relied upon to deliver on schedule and which cannot. They learn which are ingenious and cooperative and which dead and ingrown. They could do more than they now do to reward efficient and satisfactory contractors (say, by giving them desirable contracts) and to penalize inefficient and unsatisfactory ones — perhaps occasionally letting one of the latter fail. They can also find ways of encouraging promising new firms, and of promoting them, if they prove worthy competitors, into the charmed circle of recognized major suppliers. Imaginative, tough-minded management of this kind might help more than the most ingenious incentive-type contract.

In special cases other methods may be used to stimulate competition. Some of these will be discussed in the chapter on research and development. In research there may be opportunities for competitions with prizes. Frequently in the early stages of development it may pay to contract with two or more suppliers. In some cases this may be desirable in the later

---

[19] *Ibid.*, especially pp. 22–35, where considerable emphasis is placed on the desirability of improved cost analysis.

[20] Harold Asher, *Cost-Quantity Relationships in the Airframe Industry*, The RAND Corporation, Report R-291, July 1, 1956, pp. 129–141.

[21] Again, however, additional resources put into careful cost analysis would help.

stages (prototype production), and it may pay to contract with several producers. Nothing spurs a contractor as effectively as knowledge that his performance will be compared directly with that of a rival or rivals, with appropriate rewards and penalties — either in the short run (by the terms of the current contract) or the somewhat longer run (in the next or later contracts).

The relaxation of contractual constraints, while highly desirable in itself, depends upon the development of satisfactory substitutes for "cost-plus." Rightly or wrongly (we think rightly) the Congress and the public are determined that contractors be kept from cheating on cost-plus,[22] even to the point of being willing to sacrifice some efficiency to prevent fraud (or just excessive pocket-lining). An adequate incentive plan or adequate competition would be far more effective in preventing abuses than rules and contracting officers (no contracting officers are needed to police firms engaged in competitive bidding), but until we develop such a substitute we are stuck with the rules.

### PROPOSALS TO FACILITATE AN ECONOMIC CALCULUS WITHIN THE SERVICES

The ability of the Services to make useful economic analysis of problems of military choice itself depends upon certain institutional arrangements.

#### BETTER BUDGETING AND ACCOUNTING TECHNIQUES

The desirability of improving budgeting and accounting techniques has already been discussed in Chapter 4 as a means of improving decisions on the size of the national security budget. Precisely the same kinds of budgeting and accounting reforms are needed to generate the cost information needed for good managerial decisions at all levels within the military Services.

The following are some directions of change in budgeting and accounting techniques that would facilitate the economic analysis of military problems:

1. By far the most important reform is the recasting of budgets and accounts to reveal the costs of meaningful end-product missions or programs (like "active air defense"), rather than the costs of classes of objects (like "personnel — military"). Economic analysis is concerned with objectives, not objects; it can identify efficient programs for achieving objectives only if it can relate costs to such programs.

2. Quick budget estimating procedures must be developed. The present two-year budget cycle is completely inconsistent with the require-

---

[22] Another national prejudice, against high profits for "munitions makers," is a less defensible and indeed quite damaging hangover from the outgrown pacifism of the inter-war period.

ments of quantitative economic analysis. Economic efficiency demands that alternative programs, of different sizes and using qualitatively different weapon systems, be costed *prior* to the selection of the preferred program. Present estimating procedures are so time-consuming that the costing of a single program takes much too long, and the costing of alternative programs of any kind is out of the question. It is important to remember that all advance cost estimating is highly uncertain, particularly that which has to be done two or more years in advance of actual expenditure. Using time-consuming methods in an effort to achieve great accuracy in budget estimates makes no sense on any count.

3. Efficient choice of programs, as we have seen in Chapter 11, depends on total program costs over a period of years, not on expenditures in some particular budget year. If, as is highly desirable, long-range program planning and budget making are to be done together, budget estimates must extend over a number of years. Of course, only the estimates of costs of the preferred program in the first year become the basis of a firm request for appropriations; but which program is preferred cannot be determined without similar cost estimates for later years, always subject to reexamination and revision before they in turn become requests for appropriations.

4. Carrying out economic improvements — investments that would cut total, though not immediate, costs of achieving desired capabilities — might be encouraged by a form of "capital budget," segregating certain investments from operating expenditures. There are conceptual difficulties in assigning some outlays to the proper category, and a true capital budget for federal government activities in general may not be worth the trouble of preparation.[23] But segregating certain cost-cutting investments (say, the replacement of obsolete equipment like the inefficient transports in Chapter 8) might help officials and citizens see that those outlays are intended to reduce future burdens from the levels that would otherwise prevail. Such segregation, perhaps simply in special supplementary exhibits, might reduce the existing emphasis on *current* disbursements and facilitate the installation of efficient cost-cutting capital improvements.

We are not here arguing that quantitative economic analysis within the military should be carried out only in connection with the preparation of budgets. On the contrary, this kind of analysis can be useful at all times and levels within all organizational units. In general, the range of choice must be greatly narrowed by numerous qualitative decisions before serious budget-preparation can begin. But the choices among some

[23] Jesse Burkhead, *Government Budgeting,* John Wiley and Sons, New York, 1955, pp. 203–210, and Arthur Smithies, *The Budgetary Process in the United States,* McGraw-Hill Book Co., New York, 1955, pp. 459–461.

major alternative programs, as well as final determination of their levels, are almost inevitably incidental to the budgeting process, and require costing prior to choice. Moreover, the generation of reliable cost data in the form needed for quantitative economic analysis requires that accounts be kept in a form that permits their ready consolidation into meaningful end-product program categories.[24]

### SPECIALIZED OPERATIONS RESEARCH GROUPS

Economic efficiency in the military Services, as in households and business firms, is the responsibility of everyone, not of some specialized official or group. All staffs, at all levels, are (or ought to be) concerned with getting the most out of the resources placed at their disposal. Sometimes this requires nothing more than straight hard thinking about objectives, and the arraying and intuitive judging of alternative means of accomplishing the objectives using an appropriate economic criterion. These are always the most important ingredients of an economic calculus.

Frequently, however, special skills are necessary, or highly desirable, to make the requisite analysis. The systems to be compared may require expert scientific knowledge in a highly specialized field (or several such fields); or they may be so complex that considerable mathematical skill or high-speed computers are needed to find solutions. In any event, the designing of complex studies that combine with expert military judgment the knowledge and judgment of scientists, engineers, economists, and other social scientists is a difficult art, for which some people have much more talent than others and which requires training in scientific method and long apprenticeship. It is, in other words, the kind of function that is likely to be performed better by specialists.

The Services have, in fact, assigned it to specialized operations research groups, which have grown in number, size, and breadth of capability since their modest beginnings in World War II. Interestingly enough, in view of our discussion above (pp. 228–230), most of the operations research is now performed under contract with universities, nonprofit research organizations, and industrial companies.[25]

The definition of the precise role of these specialized groups and their best relation to the Services that employ them raises many interesting

[24] Past and current accounts of course seldom provide all (or nearly all) the cost data required in systems analyses, which are usually concerned with new weapon systems in future years; but they can provide the necessary firm base for extrapolation as well as a highly desirable check on the accuracy of past estimates.

[25] The Department of Defense contracts with the Institute for Defense Analysis, a joint project of a number of major universities; the Navy with the Operations Evaluation Group, part of a non-profit organization; the Army with the Research Analysis Corporation, and the Air Force with RAND, both being non-profit corporations. In addition all the services contract with private firms for specialized studies.

and important questions, which we can do no more than mention here. One is the degree of independence the group should be accorded. A considerable degree of freedom from control (including freedom to define the problem) is essential for the health and productivity of any scientific organization or inquiry. On the other hand, too much independence can lead to loss of rapport between the group and the decision-makers who must use its research results if they are to have practical effect.

Another important question is the level at which operations research groups should report. The answer in principle appears to be — at any and all levels at which decisions are made that might be improved by systematic quantitative analysis. In practice all the Services have attempted to supply operations research services to subordinate commands as well as to major operating commands and headquarters staffs.[26] In many cases responsibility for a major decision is so diffuse that the operations researchers making a single analysis require access to several commands and at different levels in the hierarchy.

Closely related to the reporting level are all the problems of criterion selection we discussed earlier in this Part. Should the operations research group attached to the Tactical Air Command, USAF, optimize on TAC objectives narrowly conceived? Or should it regard TAC as an arm of the Air Force, and consider spillover effects on other Air Force commands and objectives? Or should it regard the Air Force itself as simply an agent of the United States, and attempt to optimize on the broadest national objectives? Operations researchers and staff officers of Tactical Air Command to whom they report will not necessarily take the same view on all practical problems arising out of possible conflicts among possible criteria. It is one of the more awkward advantages of systematic quantitative analysis that objectives and criteria must be made clear and explicit for all to see and criticize. The possible use at lower levels of parochial criteria, which neglect spillovers, makes it important to have qualified operations research groups at the higher levels as well; that is, at the headquarters of the Services and at the level of the Department of Defense or Joint Chiefs of Staff.

### DECENTRALIZATION AND INCENTIVES IN DEFENSE DEPARTMENTS

Decentralization of the decision-making function is an extremely attractive administrative objective — in the military as elsewhere. The man on the spot can act quickly and flexibly. He has intimate first-hand knowledge of many factors relevant to his decisions. Large hierarchical

[26] In the Air Force, Operations Analysis groups at Headquarters, USAF, and at the various subordinate commands are — unlike RAND, which usually makes broader and longer range studies, and unlike similar groups who work for the Army and Navy — an integral part of the Department of the Air Force and the civil service.

organizations, by contrast, tend to be sluggish and hidebound by rules and regulations. Much of their time and energies are consumed in attempting to assemble, at the center, the information so readily available "on the firing line"; and since these efforts are never successful, their decisions have to be made on the basis of information that is both incomplete and stale. Decentralization of decision-making responsibility has the further advantage of providing training, experience, and a testing ground for junior officers. The best way to develop qualities of responsibility, ingenuity, judgment, and so on, and to identify them is to provide genuine opportunities for their exercise.

From an administrative point of view the price-and-market mechanism of the private economy can be regarded as a highly ingenious device for exploiting these advantages of decentralization, without sacrificing the major apparent advantage of centralization, which is operation in the interests of the whole rather than of the parts. Effective administrative decentralization in the military appears much more difficult to achieve. Nevertheless, the potential advantages of decentralization are so great that it would be worth a great expenditure of thought and administrative ingenuity to find partial solutions to these problems. The solutions do not have to be perfect or optimal, just better than the centralized solution, which is very imperfect indeed. We can live with *some* conflict between low level and high level criteria, as General Motors and United States Steel have deliberately decided to do.[27] If United States industrial corporations, with a market test available, consider themselves too large for centralized decisions, there is at least some presumption that the Department of Defense and the three Services are much too large to be making detailed operational decisions.

Decentralization in decision making is the counterpart, on the administrative side, of sub-optimizing in analysis, and raises issues that are strictly analogous.[28] Should Strategic Air Command (SAC) problems be delegated entirely to SAC, even though their solution affects air defense, atom bomb requirements, United States foreign policy, and so on, for which other parts of the Air Force and the government are responsible? And if so, should SAC be required to take these spillover effects into account? How can any such requirements be enforced, or even defined, and how can SAC obtain the information necessary to permit it to take the spillover effects into account, even if it wants to do so?

The fact that these are hard questions with no very satisfying answers should lead no one to jump to the conclusion that all decisions should be made hierarchically at a level high enough to include all the responsible

[27] See page 162.

[28] The issues are analogous even though the degree of sub-optimizing need not coincide with the responsibility of the decision-maker. See Chapter 9.

organizations that might be affected — for instance, in the case of many SAC problems, by the National Security Council or the President. The burden on our highest officials is already too great for them to function efficiently as decision-makers. If any such "solution" were attempted, our governmental organization would become muscle-bound, rather than merely sluggish. Unfortunately the superficial illogicalities of decentralization are more strikingly obvious than the deadening consequences of extreme centralization.[29]

In fact the United States government and the military Services are much less highly centralized than many outsiders tend to think. Departments are largely autonomous, and so are the major Commands. The President possesses some rather shadowy authority over the Departments, and the Secretary of Defense rather more over the military Services. But problems that intimately concern more than one Department are usually discussed and agreed upon in the Cabinet, the National Security Council, Cabinet Committees, or (even more frequently) in less formal direct bargaining between the Departments. Similarly, within the military, a very high premium is placed on reaching agreement in the Joint Chiefs of Staff and its Committees, and within each Service, in bargaining among various Commands and staffs.

The intense dislike on the part of all officials for authoritarian decisions by higher officials is responsible for the pervasiveness of bargaining, which distinguishes other governments as well as our own, and indeed all large organizations. The dislike is based not only on egocentrism and envy (few people enjoy taking orders) but also on a shrewd recognition of the inevitable shortcomings of centralized decision making.

Intragovernmental bargaining of this kind is a poor substitute for the price-and-market mechanism of the private economy. It occasionally leads to agreements (of a log-rolling sort) which are conspiracies against the public interest rather than a broader, less parochial interpretation of it.[30] But bargaining does achieve some of the desirable effects in government that markets and prices achieve in the private economy. It goes some way towards reconciling the autonomy of lower-level organizations with higher-level (or at least more broadly based) criteria. SAC is unlikely to make a purely unilateral decision that adversely affects another Service for fear that the decision will be appealed to higher authority; it is unlikely to make a decision impinging on United States foreign policy with-

---

[29] Recall the storms kicked up by well-intentioned economy-minded people who discover from time to time that the Marines are paying more for toilet paper than the Air Force; or that the Navy is buying typewriters in San Diego while the Army is declaring others surplus in Detroit. The bureaucratic regulations and the paper work needed to prevent such occurrences would undoubtedly be far more costly and far more damaging to efficiency than any conceivable gains from coordination.

[30] So occasionally does the market mechanism.

out full discussion with the State Department, for the same reason. There is here at least an incipient mechanism for insuring that decision-makers take spillover effects into account in making their decisions, and for providing them with some of the information they need in order to take them into account.[31]

Always, however, governmental decisions involve *some* sort of bargaining. The significant problem, therefore, is the difficult one of choosing particular bargaining arrangements that are better than others. At present, there are surely opportunities for improvement. With existing institutions, for example, the bargainers are often given the perverse incentive of trying to maximize their budgets (their costs) instead of maximizing capability for whatever budget they receive. A subordinate official may well feel that effort devoted to getting his budget increased is more rewarding than analysis and effort devoted to getting greater capability from a given budget.

This tendency might be countered by some device for permitting units to keep a part of any cost savings. An extreme form of correction, which admittedly has certain disadvantages, would be to give each unit a budget fixed in amount for two (or even more) years in advance. Commanders would then have more time and stronger reason for trying to use their budgets efficiently. Another step might be to give commands greater freedom to reallocate funds among appropriation-categories (such as construction, maintenance and operation, and personnel). If this were done, the commands would not fight a running battle over each appropriation-category, pressing hardest for those items that have the most glamour and in the end finding themselves hamstrung by constraints on the amounts of specific items that they can use. Again, commanders would have more time and reason to seek efficient combinations of the inputs, as well as greater freedom to do so. These and other ways of improving the institutional framework — of trying to remove perverse incentives, cause the costs of decisions to impinge on the decision-makers, and make criteria at various levels consistent with national aims — deserve careful study and some experimentation. Some such changes may be essential if many of the improved choices suggested by analysis or better economic understanding, or both, are to be implemented.

[31] This view of bargaining was originally presented by Charles E. Lindblom in "Bargaining: The Hidden Hand in Government," The RAND Corporation, Research Memorandum RM-1434-RC, 1955.

# PART III.   SPECIAL PROBLEMS
AND APPLICATIONS

# 13. MILITARY RESEARCH AND DEVELOPMENT[1]

In economics we distinguish between the problem of allocating resources efficiently with a given technology and the problem of advancing technology. In some circumstances and periods one of these problems seems more important; in different circumstances and periods, the other. Economic theory has a great deal more to say about the static allocation problem than about the promotion of technological progress, which is, for reasons we will explore, less tractable to analysis.

Technological progress in the field of national security now depends mainly upon the success of research and development activities sponsored by the military services and such closely related agencies of government as the Atomic Energy Commission and the National Aeronautics and Space Administration. There are other sources of useful ideas, of course. It is in the nature of research that the researcher does not know what he will discover; and many ideas developed in university or industrial laboratories or by civilian inventors have turned out to have military applications that were neither sought, anticipated, nor in some cases welcomed by their originators (for instance, Nobel's dynamite, the Wright brothers' airplane, and the concept of atomic fission). Also, the miltary Services include inventive persons who think of ingenious new devices or techniques for accomplishing military tasks outside the formal research and development establishment. But in the main the Services have to buy progress within that establishment; and their success depends upon (a) how much they spend, and (b) how efficiently they spend it.

There can be no question regarding the crucial importance of promoting military technology in the nuclear era. Any power that lags significantly in military technology, no matter how large its military budget or how efficiently it allocates resources, is likely to be at the mercy of a more progressive enemy. Both weapons and systems for delivering them have gone through several revolutions in the few years since the end of the Second World War. Individual bombs are now 1,000 times as powerful as those dropped on Hiroshima and Nagasaki, which were themselves 1,000 times as powerful as the largest dropped on Germany. Breakthroughs

[1] In this chapter we are especially indebted to Burton H. Klein and William H. Meckling (see their "Application of Operations Research to Development Decisions," *Operations Research*, May–June 1958, pp. 352–363, and see Klein's "A Radical Proposal for R. and D.," *Fortune*, May 1958, pp. 112 ff.).

in missile technology are continually threatening the whole offensive or defensive apparatus of one side or the other. Keeping ahead in the technological race is not in itself a guarantee of security in these circumstances; it remains essential to incorporate the technology in operational hardware ("forces in being") and to deploy them and use them with skill and intelligence. But no amount of production, skill, and intelligent use can compensate for significant technological inferiority. Our atomic monopoly in 1945 would have insured victory over Japan even if the ratio of our conventional forces to theirs had been reversed. Clever operations research can in exceptional cases improve some capability of a force by a factor of 3 to 10. Inventions can frequently change the same sort of capability by factors of 10 to 1,000.

Of course any particular nation will borrow much of its scientific knowledge and even its military technology from other countries. Science is international. Once a scientific discovery is made, it quickly becomes the property of scientists everywhere; frequently the same discovery is made nearly simultaneously in two or more widely separated research centers. Scientists in all leading countries (certainly including Russia) were familiar at the beginning of the Second World War with the basic scientific ideas that prompted us to initiate the Manhattan District Project. Few if any of these ideas were American in origin.

To a lesser extent the same is true of developments in military hardware. Despite military secrecy, the news of a new development leaks, and this leads to frantic copying on the part of potential enemies. The British "invented" the tank in World War I, but they disclosed it prematurely, and the most effective use of the tank in that war was made by the Germans. It is only a question of time before many additional countries perfect advanced nuclear weapons. Espionage is responsible for some of the transmission of new technological ideas from country to country, but espionage rarely does more than speed an inevitable process. New military hardware can usually be observed without too much difficulty when it becomes operational. In the United States and most Western countries full accounts are usually made available earlier than that to anyone who can read the public and technical press and the advertisements of contractors. Even if technical details are not revealed, the mere knowledge that a research objective has been achieved is an enormous help and stimulus. It means that the objective is achievable — that there is a treasure to be found and that a search (for that is what research is) is therefore definitely worthwhile. Other countries might not be developing atomic weapons today if we had not demonstrated their feasibility.

Therefore the net gains from a successful military development can only be counted on for a few years at most. If a nation's civilian economy is made more productive by research, the nation continues to gain from the increased productivity even if other countries do copy (as of course they will). But military strength is in its very essence relative. Accretions to our absolute strength are offset if potentially unfriendly nations make equivalent additions to theirs. And we must, in general, expect them to do so when a new scientific idea is responsible for our gain.[2]

Nevertheless, those few years of superiority may be decisive. Consider how our security would be prejudiced if the Russians had the technological initiative and we were reduced to copying their successes with a lag of several years (a by no means inconceivable circumstance since their launching of the first satellite). Suppose the Russians had had a four-year lead with the A-bomb. Imagine them with a similar lead in operational intercontinental ballistic missiles. Or in effective anti-ICBM's. It is misleading to say that primacy in military research and development can give us *only* lead time. This may be enough to prevent or "win" a war, and, for a nation on the strategic defensive, is essential to avoid defeat.

### KINDS OF MILITARY RESEARCH AND DEVELOPMENT

Nomenclature in the field of research and development is thoroughly confused, partly because the processes by which new scientific and technical knowledge is wrested from nature are not well understood and are anything but neat and orderly. It is customary to use some such classification as the following in discussing problems of military research and development policy management:[3]

1. *Weapon system development,* directed toward the fabrication for testing of prototypes of operational weapons. In the case of missiles (and some other systems), this may mean the fabrication of rather large test inventories. The term "weapon system" in this context is used in a narrower sense than we have used it in discussing systems analysis. The system being developed typically includes the major equipment (say a bomber aircraft) and such auxiliary equipment as power plant, bombing-navigation system, other electronics gear, and armament, but would not necessarily include an operational concept, or base system, or personnel training program.

---

[2] This by no means implies that all scientific ideas are "neutral" as between nations. The question whether the development of A- and H-bombs is on balance favorable to the West (because it enables us to offset the alleged Russian superiority in manpower) or to the Russians (because it robs us of our previously decisive advantage in mobilization potential), or unfavorable to both (because it threatens mutual destruction) is still being ardently debated. There may be aspects of national geographies, economies, or psychologies which make any given invention more useful to one country than to another.

[3] This classification is not necessarily identical with that of the National Science Foundation or of other Agencies. Also, it might be noted that there are not sharp lines of demarcation between these categories. Nonetheless, the use of such a classification is essential to the understanding of R and D problems.

2. *Component development,* that is, the more or less independent development of items of military hardware which are not themselves "weapon systems" or "major equipment," but parts or sub-systems of such major equipment. The distinction between systems and sub-systems is, of course, arbitrary. The important thing is that the Services can and do spend money productively developing engines for aircraft, guidance systems for missiles, gyroscopes for guidance systems, communication systems for armored vehicles, gear for landing aircraft on carriers, and so on, without knowing precisely the type or model of the major equipment of which the component will be a part.

3. In *exploratory development, or applied research* the objective is advancing the state of the technological art rather than obtaining immediately operational hardware. Someone has had a promising idea for a new type of vacuum tube or a new fuel or a new design to reduce drag in an aircraft wing. The idea may have emerged from paper research or may simply have been someone's inspiration. Whatever its origin it requires some sort of testing or verifying before it can be accepted as valid and incorporated in the state of the art. This may involve a laboratory experiment, a wind tunnel test, or the construction of a working model, depending upon the nature of the idea. Test models are typically very much cheaper than operational models, although there are some exceptions.

4. *Basic research* is the deliberate search for knowledge. The military Services, AEC, NASA, and so on, support a good deal of basic research in areas of special interest to them, such as aerodynamics, atomic physics, and some branches of mathematics. Basic research is typically the cheapest type of research and development if we think of something like "cost per idea explored." It frequently requires no equipment except paper, and with some exceptions (betatrons, for example) even the scientific laboratories and computing equipment that are needed cost less than a single operational prototype of a new aircraft or missile.

We estimate that, using generally accepted definitions, military research and development in the late 1950's was costing about $6 billions per annum. This estimate is both arbitrary (the boundary between "development" and "production" is hard to draw)[4] and misleading, since by far the largest part of this total is at the weapon system end of the research and development spectrum and includes large costs of fabricating operational prototypes. Expenditure really devoted to advancing science and technology in areas of special military interest is much less — perhaps $1 to $2 billions. This would include basic research (on the order of

---

[4] For example, when the Air Force (or Navy) contracts for a new model of aircraft, making the first "prototype" batch is regarded as development. But when the Navy contracts for a new model of submarine, constructing the very first is regarded as production.

$150 to $200 million), what we have called exploratory development, and some genuine state-of-the-art advancement undertaken in connection with component and weapon system development.

Most weapon system and component development is undertaken by industrial firms on contract with one of the Services, although the Navy and Army still do some in their yards and arsenals. All three Services support extensive test facilities as well as administrative staffs to determine requirements, to let contracts, and to supervise performance under contracts. Research and exploratory development is divided between internal and external research centers and laboratories. A major share of the basic research is performed on contract by laboratories and individual scientists in universities.

### PROBLEMS OF RESEARCH AND DEVELOPMENT

It is apparent that many of the problems of managing a research and development program have important economic aspects.

For example, the most fundamental problem of all, how much to spend on the program, is an allocation problem. Economic theory tells us that we "should" spend on research and development until the marginal gain from the expenditures, properly discounted, is just equal to the gain from expenditures elsewhere. But in the case of research and development, whether it is performed for a military Service or a business firm, this formula is peculiarly difficult to interpret or apply. The gain is much more uncertain — much harder to predict with accuracy — than the gain from, say, an additional fighter defense squadron with aircraft of known performance. This is particularly true of basic research and exploratory development, where the product, if any, will be knowledge — and knowledge usually far removed from any practical end use. Calculating gains from research and development is further complicated by the need for discounting. Typically the payoffs from research and development are expected in a more distant future than payoffs from procurement, since there is no enhancement of military capability until the results have been incorporated in operational hardware, procured, and deployed in operational units. This means that the discounted values of the payoff are highly sensitive to rates of discount — and as we have seen, there is great uncertainty about which discount rates are most appropriate.

These uncertainties make it difficult or, in many cases, impossible to use an explicit economic calculus to determine how much of total resources should be allocated to research and development; how these resources should be divided among the various kinds of research and development; and which specific projects should be selected. At the end of this chapter we will return to the question of what role economic calculations can play in answering such questions. Short of such calculations, however, general economic reasoning and analysis of the institutional factors affecting the research and development process can throw some light on the way these problems should be approached, and on some common pitfalls and mistakes in research and development policies and management.

It is our opinion that the three main root causes of error in the management of military research and development are: (1) a failure to appreciate the degree of uncertainty involved in research and development or, what has the same effect, a tendency to ignore uncertainties and act as if they were certainties; (2) a pervasive tendency, discussed in Chapter 11, to undervalue future outputs relative to current ones; and (3) certain characteristic tendencies of bureaucracy, particularly the strength of centripetal (centralizing) forces.

Of these the most serious and destructive is the first. *The* important thing to appreciate in making good decisions with respect to research and development is the dominant role played by uncertainty. Research and development are uncertain by definition. Research is a search, and one rarely knows in advance whether the search will be successful at all, let alone how long it will take or which route will lead to the treasure. The military Services have all too frequently tried to command the research and development community to invent new weapons to specification, just as they would command a platoon of infantry to march by the right flank. One of the Service manuals attempts to prescribe research and development planning procedures as follows:

Planning for research and development is broadly similar to planning for a military operation. . . . The objective must be clearly identified, the operation or job must be divided into component parts, units or organizations must be assigned to accomplish each part, the time and resources required for each part must be estimated, and all efforts must be time-phased in proper relationship to each other.[5]

But the essence of research and development is that it is *not* like the military operations for which this kind of planning and scheduling is appropriate.[6] Among research and development activities, this type of planning is least inappropriate for weapon system development — al-

[5] *ARDC Program Management Procedures,* ARDC Manual No. 80–4, Headquarters, Air Research and Development Command, United States Air Force, Baltimore, Maryland, September 1, 1956, p. 11.

This is not to say that R and D planning is the same in 1960, or will be the same in the future, as in the past. In the U.S. Air Force, for example, some recent changes in procedures indicate a greater recognition of the crucial role of uncertainties in R and D planning.

[6] This kind of planning is equally inappropriate for a good many classes of military operations, where uncertainties demand flexibility, probing techniques to gain information, improvisation on the battlefield, etc., rather than neat, orderly scheduling in advance to achieve a clearly identified objective.

though even there, as we shall see, it has limited usefulness and great dangers. In exploratory development and research the precise identification of objectives and scheduling are less important than trying to cover all good bets, selecting first-rate scientists and productive laboratories, promoting competition, and preserving flexibility to follow up vigorously on break-throughs.

## SOME COMMON PITFALLS

### TOO LITTLE "DUPLICATION"

One of the most important and obvious corollaries of the uncertain character of research and development is the desirability of some duplication. (Here, as is common in discussions of research and development, "duplication" means diversification or pursuit along several routes.) If, as is typically the case, there are two, three, or a dozen possible paths to some research and development objective, each with supporters and detractors, it will frequently pay to try two or more, not just one, which may fail or take an inordinately long time. In any rationally conducted program there should be duplication in this sense, and there will inevitably occur what appears with the aid of hindsight to be waste — the effort devoted to the unsuccessful (or less successful) paths.[7]

But how much diversification and where? No one knows enough to give precise answers. Some original and suggestive theoretical analysis indicates that in many circumstances there are great gains from pursuing two, three, or four paths, but rapidly diminishing returns from further duplication. Not only does the use of several routes buy time; it also, up to a point, actually saves money! The optimal amount of duplication in any particular situation is sensitive to the following factors:[8]

1. There should be more duplication, the greater the expected payoff from the research. In the Manhattan District Project, six completely distinct and independent methods of separating fissile material were under development concurrently; if the expected payoff had been less, fewer of these expensive "duplicating" projects could have been justified. Incidentally, the method that succeeded in producing the material for the first bomb was regarded at first as among the least promising. There is a strong case for some duplication in the development of critical weapon systems, despite their great cost, because of the disastrous consequences if the one horse that we back runs last.

[7] For an excellent description of the uncertainties in R and D and the importance of "duplication," see Ely Devons, "The Aircraft Industry," in Duncan Burn (ed.), *The Structure of British Industry,* Vol. 2, Cambridge University Press, Cambridge, England, 1958, pp. 54–69.

[8] For an ingenious attempt to quantify the role of these factors, see Richard R. Nelson, "The Economics of Parallel R and D Efforts: A Sequential-Decision Analysis," The RAND Corporation, RM-2482, November 12, 1959.

2. There should be more duplication, the greater the uncertainties. If, in developing a missile, the airframe is straightforward engineering, while there appear to be great uncertainties in developing the guidance, the important thing is to try several approaches to the guidance problem — perhaps completely independent approaches using competing contractors.

3. There should be more duplication, the cheaper it is to duplicate. More weapon systems should be developed than are ultimately procured (it may have made sense to develop two intermediate-range ballistic missiles — Thor by the Air Force and Jupiter by the Army — yet not to buy quantities of both for operational use). There should be more duplication in the development of difficult or critical components than in the development of whole weapon systems. And there should be most duplication in exploratory development and research, where the cost of trying another path or testing it is usually a tiny fraction of prototype fabrication costs.

As a result of factors (2) and (3), we want a great deal of "temporary" duplication. Later, as we get more information and reach more expensive stages of development, we want to decrease the number of routes to be followed.

4. There is a stronger case for duplication if the alternatives are qualitatively different, and if the factors that will determine their success or failure are independent.

### TOO LITTLE COMPETITION

This is not quite the same thing as too little duplication, although the two are closely related in practice. Duplication is possible without competition — for example, if the multiple paths are explored by the same organization or individual. And competition is possible without duplication. (The Army and Navy would compete for budget even if they never developed similar kinds of hardware.) Competition provides a spur that is frequently lacking in the research and development world of cost-plus contracts and scheduled progress. Some dedicated individual researchers do not require it, but there is nothing so stimulating to most people and organizations engaged in research and development as the fear that another company or laboratory will beat it to the objective.[9] Even competition among the military Services has proved highly beneficial. Robert Schlaifer concluded as follows from his study of the development of aircraft engines:

The American system of administering development did, however, have one feature greatly superior to both the British and the German systems. This was

[9] It helps significantly if some real monetary prize is awarded the winner — like a production contract.

the sponsorship of development by two separate agencies, the Army and the Navy. The first and most obvious result of a separate organization for naval aviation was, of course, that development specially directed at the needs of naval aviation was not slighted in the United States as it was abroad. In addition, however, the existence of two independent agencies meant that the mistakes or omissions of one were corrected in a surprisingly large number of instances by the actions of the other. Whatever may be the merits of the case for unification of the military services in other respects, there can be no doubt that the sponsorship and direction of development by two separate agencies brought results worth very much more than the cost.[10]

Unfortunately much of the competition between companies engaged in research and development is now concentrated at the stage of preliminary design. It has become a common practice for the military Services to invite industry to submit proposals (in the form of preliminary designs on paper) for the development of new weapon systems, and then to select one (or at most two) of these proposals for further support. As a result, there is intense competition among the companies involved in producing the most glamorous and promising drawings. But too often this kind of competition is a competition in optimism and exaggeration. The company that exaggerates more gets the contract. Competition is effective in promoting progress only if the consumers are well enough informed to make rational selections; and there is abundant evidence that no one — administrator or scientist — is good at picking winners at the preliminary design stage. On the other hand, judging the performance of actual hardware — even test models — is *relatively* easy and reliable. Exaggerated claims can be debunked on the test stand. Few things would have a more salutary effect on the efficiency of research and development than shifting some of the competition that now takes place at paper stages forward to early hardware stages. There are problems in doing this at reasonable cost, but longer-run savings justify a major effort to solve them.

### PREMATURE, OPTIMISTIC, AND TOO DETAILED REQUIREMENTS FOR ADVANCED SYSTEMS

Wishful thinking stimulated by the claims of contractors and enthusiasts, neglect of the uncertainties, and a natural desire on the part of responsible military officials to have the research and development establishment produce on order what they consider necessary for defense, have sometimes resulted in a tendency for the Services to specify their requirements for advanced weapon systems prematurely, optimistically, and in too great detail. Typically this kind of overspecification is

[10] Robert Schlaifer, *Development of Aircraft Engines,* in R. Schlaifer and S. D. Heron, *Development of Aircraft Engines and Fuels* (Boston, Division of Research, Harvard Business School, 1950), p. 11.

attempted following the submission of preliminary designs — or even earlier.

Studies have been made of the reliability of early estimates of (1) cost, (2) development time, and (3) physical and performance characteristics of new, advanced weapon systems. The results are striking. In the case of estimates made at the preliminary design stage, costs are typically underestimated by factors of 2, 5, 10, or in some cases substantially more. Development time is typically underestimated by 1 to 5 years. And the final system usually differs markedly from the predicted system both in physical and performance characteristics.[11] Usually, although not quite always, the estimates are optimistic — a bias one could expect from the premium on exaggeration by contractors in design competitions. But more serious than the bias (which could be discounted if it were systematic) is the wide range and scatter of the estimates. Choices at this stage must recognize these uncertainties. Precise technical and performance specifications at this stage involve self-delusion.

Premature specification makes it inevitable that many changes in specifications will have to be made as the system is developed. Detail also multiplies the number of changes in specifications that will be required, and obstructs the objective of getting a working model quickly into test. Excessive optimism in drawing up performance specifications can make the development so difficult that it must fail, or take much longer and cost much more than planned, or require a downgrading of the requirements.[12] It is not unusual for weapon system requirements to be so optimistic that several inventions or advances in the state of the art are needed on schedule if the development is to succeed. Prior to the successful test of the H-bomb, the development of the Air Force's first ICBM had been thwarted by requirements for payload and accuracy that proved infeasible. Only when these requirements were substantially relaxed after the successful H-bomb test could development proceed to the point where vehicles could be tested.

The need for changes in specifications would not matter so much if

[11] For example, more than half the aircraft developed since World War II ended up using different engines from those envisaged at the preliminary design stage. Aircraft expected to be supersonic turn out to be subsonic. Nuclear weapons expected to have a "yield" of x in fact have yields of $3x$ — or $.1x$, and so on. See A. W. Marshall and W. H. Meckling, "Predictability of the Costs, Time, and Success of Development," The RAND Corporation, P-1821, December 11, 1959.

[12] We will suggest later that instead of trying to specify all performance characteristics well in advance (x miles per hour, y C.E.P., z range, etc.), which places an intolerable strain on the art of prediction, the military Services would be well advised to indicate limiting values of such characteristics and acceptable trade-offs between them (in short, their "preference surfaces").

they could be made quickly and easily as the need became apparent. But it is a fact of life in large bureaucracies that decisions are difficult to unmake and remake and that the process is time consuming. The military research and development establishments are not an exception to this general rule. As a result much time is lost in obtaining authorization for changes in specifications through all the echelons of authority. Even more time is lost in attempting to find a way around obsolete or excessively optimistic specifications to obviate the necessity of appealing through the echelons of the hierarchy for new decisions.

An important reason for early, fairly detailed specification of weapon systems is the need to match the various components under development — for example, in the case of a missile, the airframe, power plant, warhead, and guidance. This need is real, and must be achieved at the appropriate stage. Where a system is being put together from previously developed and tested components (as was the Air Force's Thor), matching and the detailed specifications required by matching may be imposed without too much risk at the preliminary design stage. But where a new system is really advanced, where the components have yet to be developed and tested for feasibility and performance, premature concern over physical matching can delay development by years. The urgent thing is usually to get the critical components developed to the point where they can be tested (having "duplicate" efforts on the most critical ones to gain quality, time, or both). When it is known that they work is early enough to worry about matching configurations *in detail*.

### PREMATURE COMMITMENT OF LARGE FUNDS

The illusion that the future can be foreseen with something approaching certainty, plus pressure from the contractor, plus a desire by the military Services to save time and to guarantee the availability of a budget to complete the development, produce a tendency to commit large funds prematurely to highly uncertain weapon system developments. Because of the great uncertainties that affect technological development, and the equally great uncertainties regarding the military usefulness of particular developments, it is desirable to retain the flexibility to terminate developments at short notice and low cost.

One type of premature commitment is the commitment to production tooling at an early stage of the development. There are exceptional cases where some commitment may be justified at an early stage, but most of the tooling ordered before the testing of prototypes has to be scrapped because of changes in specifications. This appears to be the sort of gamble where you gain little if you win (six months of lead time at most except in periods of heavy pressure on the capacity of tool producers) ; lose a great deal if you lose (up to your total investment plus confusion and time) ; and, in view of the great uncertainties and typical drastic changes in specifications, have little chance of winning.

EXCESSIVE CENTRALIZATION OF DECISION-MAKING

There seems to be an inevitable tendency in bureaucracies for decisions to be made at higher and higher levels. The forces in this direction are simple and easy to understand, but so powerful that they are almost irresistible even when understood. There are some good reasons for making decisions at high levels. The high level official can take a broader, less parochial view; he perhaps has a better conception of over-all Service or national requirements; the fact that he is at a high level suggests that he may be an abler person. On the other hand, there are excellent reasons for making most decisions at lower levels. Officials on the spot have far better technical information; they can act more quickly; giving them authority will utilize and develop the reservoir of ingenuity and initiative in the whole organization. Moreover, if large numbers of detailed decisions are attempted at a high level, or if decisions first made at lower levels may readily be appealed to be remade, the higher levels will become swamped in detail, decisions will be delayed, the organization will become muscle-bound, and the higher levels will have neither time nor energy for their essential function of policy-making.

Nevertheless, the high level official is acutely conscious of his advantages in making any particular decision; and while the lower level official is at least equally conscious of his advantages, the higher level official is in a position of authority, and decides who is to make the decision — too frequently, of course, himself. The result is a constant tendency for the center of gravity of decision making to shift to higher echelons. New higher echelons, in fact, get invented from time to time to facilitate this movement.

The implications are serious for the kind of flexible research and development management that will capitalize on the ingenuity and initiative of science and industry. The problem is not confined to the military Services or to the government. Industry and universities have their bureaucracies too. One very perceptive administrator of industrial research, C. E. K. Mees, described the problem in industry as follows:

The best person to decide what research work shall be done is the man who is doing the research. The next best is the head of the department. After that you leave the field of best persons and meet increasingly worse groups. The first of these is the research director, who is probably wrong more than half the time. Then comes a committee, which is wrong most of the time. Finally, there is a committee of company vice-presidents which is wrong all the time.[13]

[13] As quoted by John Jewkes, David Sawers, and Richard Stillerman, *The Sources of Invention,* Macmillan & Company, Ltd., London, 1958, p. 138.

But in industry, and especially in universities, there are strong centrifugal forces to match the centripetal ones.

TOO LITTLE EMPHASIS ON EARLY STAGES OF RESEARCH AND DEVELOPMENT

It is very difficult to say whether too little or too much is being spent on military research and development as compared with the procurement and operation of forces in being. Some general considerations — the undervaluation of future outputs in government and the tendency of all bureaucracies to avoid risky ventures — would lead us to expect that too little is being spent. But there are some countervailing factors — the fascination of high performance hardware, and the very general tendency (for reasons we have examined) for the Services to be excessively confident and optimistic about the prospects of uncertain weapon system developments. On this issue of the total research and development budget no confident conclusion is possible.

It does, however, appear extremely probable that precisely the same tendencies — to undervalue distant gains and to shun projects that are risky or have no direct or obvious military payoff — have led to an excessive concentration within the research and development budget on the final stage of research and development, weapon system development, at the expense of earlier stages. Here there seem to be no countervailing tendencies of any importance. Fascination with high performance hardware reinforces the emphasis on weapon systems. So does optimism about the prospects of advanced weapon systems. It is allegedly much easier to get money from Congress for the development of impressive weapon systems with undoubted military utility if they succeed, than to get it for components with no highly specific end use in mind, or for basic or applied research that is even further from practical military applications.

But it is in research and exploratory development that spectacular advances in the state of the art are discovered; and it is there that we can afford not to stint. In most instances, we could develop weapon systems more cheaply and in less time if we placed more emphasis on the more or less independent development of critical components, and on getting them quickly to test; and, as a general rule, did not try to "marry" them in a weapon system until a set had been tested.[14] If we shifted our emphasis in this direction (from our present development practices), making a stricter separation between "inventing" and "marrying," we could probably release substantial resources for inventing.

[14] There would certainly be exceptional cases where the utility of a new advanced system and its time urgency are so great that it would be worth early matching — at high cost — to have some chance of getting the system a little sooner *if* the required inventing did proceed on schedule.

### REORGANIZING RESEARCH AND DEVELOPMENT

Since the Russians so spectacularly demonstrated their progress in advanced technology by launching the Sputniks, there has been much critical evaluation of the United States research and development program and policies. In our opinion most of the criticisms have been wide of the mark. With amazing unanimity the critics have pointed to the uncoordinated character of research and development, the lack of adequate planning, the absence of strong central direction, and the alleged duplication, competition, and waste. They demand strong central direction and coordination, review of programs and projects, elimination of competition (especially inter-Service competition), and the weeding out of duplicating projects.[15] In response to these criticisms a new, echelon of research and development planners and managers is being added to the Pentagon at the Department of Defense (DOD) level to direct all lower echelons.

These criticisms, we think, are based on a fundamental misunderstanding of the nature of research and development. They treat as certain what is highly uncertain. They try to strengthen control at the top when what is needed is initiative and spontaneity at the bottom. They try to suppress competition and diversification because particular duplications are obviously wasteful from the vantage point of hindsight, apparently unaware that duplication is a rational necessity when we are confronted with uncertainty and that competition is our best protection against bureaucratic inertia.

The popularity of these criticisms is a little surprising when one reflects that military research and development is being pilloried for

[15] As an example, the following is an excerpt from an article entitled "How Ike Answers Critics of Shake-up in the Military," in the *U.S. News and World Report* dated April 25, 1958, p. 122:

"In another area — defense research and development programs — the need for central direction is especially acute.

"This area, more than any other, invites costly rivalries. The programs are critically important. They involve the weapons of tomorrow. In these programs we cannot afford the slightest waste motion. Nor can we afford to devote three sets of scientists and laboratories and costly facilities to overlapping weapons systems and research projects.

"Recently we have been spending something more than 5 billion dollars a year for research and development programs dispersed among the several services. This great sum is used to maintain our weapon potential but does not procure one single weapon or piece of equipment for the operating forces. Not one. Eminent scientists report to me that centralization of direction over this program will surely cut costs markedly and improve efficiency.

"I have recommended that the supervision of this entire activity — and, to the extent deemed necessary, its direction — be centralized in the Defense Department under a top civilian who will be a national leader in science and technology — the actual work being done largely by the military departments, as is the case today. The Congress willing, we will substantially increase the efficiency of this multibillion-dollar research and development effort, reduce its cost, and strike at one of the roots of service rivalries."

precisely those characteristics that it has in common with research and development in the free enterprise economy. Research and development in the American economy is uncoordinated. There is no central planning or direction. There is a great deal of duplication, rivalry, and of course, viewed with the aid of hindsight, apparent waste. And yet the American economy is, in most industrial and technological areas, the most progressive and advanced in the world — certainly more progressive in those areas than the economies of countries that place much greater emphasis upon central planning and less upon competition.

We would not argue that all is perfect with research and development in the American competitive economy. There are persuasive reasons for believing that, from the point of view of national economic growth, the American economy spends too little in total on research and development and that, like the military it spends relatively too much at the quick-payoff, prototype end of the spectrum and too little at the basic and applied research end.[16]

Nor would we argue that the government could simply copy aspects of the competitive economy even if these were perfect in their own environment. There are at least two fundamental differences. In the economy the consumers are king; there are millions of them for firms to satisfy — with varied wants and in all sorts of circumstances. But military research and development has a much narrower purpose — the promotion of national security. And while national security is exceedingly complex, the government has a special capability as well as a special responsibility to define its objectives and means. This demands a kind and degree of planning and control that would serve no function in the private economy. And there is a second difference, which is of even greater practical importance. In the competitive economy, firms risk their own money; they therefore police themselves. In military research and development contractors risk public money, and some fairly effective controls against malfeasance, carelessness, and irresponsibility are needed and demanded — even at the cost of some efficiency.

Nevertheless, despite the imperfections of the competitive market solution and despite the differences in circumstances, the government could learn a great deal from observing how the private economy manages research and development. The private economy does, in effect, recognize the essential characteristic of research and development — uncertainty

---

[16] The most important reason for such underemphasis on basic research is the difficulty the private competitive firm has in latching onto property rights in the results of R and D. Patents provide partial and undependable protection in most areas. The obstacles to reaping the reward from one's own discoveries are greater the further removed the discoveries are from immediate practical application. (See Kenneth J. Arrow, "Economic Welfare and the Allocation of Resources for Invention," The RAND Corporation, P-1856, December 15, 1959.)

— and responds to it in a comparatively effective manner. The private economy is not afraid to follow multiple paths in research, and it duplicates more, the greater the payoff, and more, the less the cost. Instead of striving for an extreme form of monopolistic bureaucracy in the management of research and development, we would do well to consider emulating part of the practices of our more progressive industries.

### SOME REAL PROBLEMS OF RESEARCH AND DEVELOPMENT

The real problems of research and development policy and management in the government are not the elimination of competition and duplication. Neither, although some planning and control are essential, are those problems adequately described as the need for "strong central direction," "better planning and coordination," and similar clichés of our contemporary centralizers. But there are real and challenging problems:

1. *How can we effectively decentralize,* to promote initiative and spontaneity in industry, the laboratories, and throughout the military, while maintaining control of policy and preventing recklessness and malfeasance in the spending of public funds?

This is a general problem, by no means confined to the management of research and development, as we saw in the preceding chapter. One of the keys to its solution is an adroit use of competition. The Services can use competition among contractors to make their control of policy effective. If there are several competitors striving for future favors, they are highly sensitive to the requirements of the customer. But if there is only one source of supply, the customer is at his mercy.

Where contractors are sensitive to the customer's requirements, it is not necessary to spell out the required specifications in such damaging detail. A general indication of preferences and trade-offs — some indication of the relative worth of improvements in accuracy, reliability, and so on — will suffice. This leaves more scope for the exercise of ingenuity by the contractor, obviating some of the frustrations and delays resulting from the necessity for frequent changes in specifications.

2. At a higher level, *how can we make good use of inter-Service and inter-agency competition* while curbing its undesirable features? There is, in our view, no question that inter-Service competition serves a valuable role — particularly with respect to research and development. Like other competition, it provides a powerful stimulus to thought and action, and a safeguard against bureaucratic rigidities. It provides a number of alternative sources of support for scientists, inventors, and firms with new and unpopular ideas to be tested (and almost all great ideas were unpopular when new). If inter-Service rivalry did not exist, we would be forced to invent something very like it.

But there is also no doubt regarding the undesirable consequences of some aspects of inter-Service rivalry. Perhaps the least desirable consequence for research and development is the use of exaggerated claims, on paper, for future weapon systems in the struggles for budget, roles, and missions. This is the counterpart, at a higher level, of the use of inflated claims in the struggle for contracts at the preliminary design stage — and the two are of course closely related. If we could learn to avoid heavy commitments of money until performance has been demonstrated by prototypes or test models, we could put competition at both levels to a useful purpose.

3. *How can we judge and choose contractors and laboratories?* Successful research and development requires skill and genius. There is no substitute for talented people — and effective organizations. But how can performance be judged in a field where objective standards are lacking? And how, when competitive bidding is impossible, can the best contractors be selected?

We have no neat and simple solution, and doubt that one can be found. But we are persuaded that the Services should attempt to exercise control over contractors *mainly* by judging and rewarding performance rather than by detailed supervision. In the case of laboratories and research organizations the important thing is the successes of the whole organization over a number of years, rather than the prospects of any particular projects. If officials reoriented their thinking in this direction, instead of attempting project-by-project reviews, they would exercise more effective and meaningful control and save much valuable time of research scientists that now goes into the preparation of justifications. It is hard to judge an organization by its record, but usually easier than judging the prospects of a proposed or on-going project.

4. *How should research and development be planned?* We are convinced that the focus of research and development planning is wrong. There is too much and too early emphasis on the selection of "optimal" weapon systems — a tendency to treat the research and development problem as if it were a procurement problem. Choosing a weapon system or systems for the fabrication of prototypes is a vital function — but only one of several, and the last in time. It is at least as important to make sure that there are good prospective systems among which a choice can be made.

The appropriate function of research and development planning is to develop a strategy for broadly advancing the state of the technological art in areas of relevance to national security. This involves:

a. Determining what the areas are, and the relative emphasis to place on each. This is by no means easy: Few would have guessed in 1930 or even 1938 that atomic physics would soon become of the greatest importance. It was not apparent to many as late as 1955 that protective construction had become a vital area for military research. The relevant areas change as we make progress, and one of the most important tasks of research and development management is to spot the new areas and to get good work in them started promptly.

b. Dividing the budget among what we have called weapon system development, component development, exploratory development, and basic research. The division between the last two and the first two depends to a large extent on our time preferences. If we attach importance to future decades, we had better allocate substantial sums to basic research and exploratory development and protect them as well as we can from raids by officials who have pressing and immediate operational responsibilities.

c. Selecting the critical components — the gyroscopes, the computing equipment, the nose cones, the infra-red sensors, the rocket engines, and so on — on which the success of future weapon systems is likely to depend, and making sure that there is an adequate program for the development of each — with plenty of duplication and competition — either within weapon system development projects or independent of them.

d. Finally, selecting good weapon systems for the fabrication of prototypes.

### ECONOMIC CALCULUS IN PLANNING RESEARCH AND DEVELOPMENT

We have already indicated that the kind of explicit economic calculus illustrated in Chapter 8, at least in its present state, is of only limited use in planning research and development. Uncertainties, incommensurables, and intangibles dominate many problems. Nevertheless, economic analysis can serve a useful function both in selecting development projects and in planning them.

1. *In estimating the utility of developments.* In military problems we can sometimes place an approximate valuation on the worth of research in relation to expenditures on procurement and operations. As an example from the past, how much was it worth to develop the B-52? As a first approximation, the amount we would have had to spend on additional B-47's, tankers, bases, and so on, to give us the same strategic offensive capability without B-52's in the force that we would have with them. A calculation of precisely this kind was made in Chapter 8, where it was estimated that the development of the hypothetical HC-500 and HC-600 aircraft had been worth about $600 millions. How much would it be worth to develop a lighter-weight structural material for aircraft and missiles? In only one use, strategic air, it would be worth the savings in tankers and overseas bases now needed to extend the range of our

bombers in other ways. Calculations of this kind frequently reveal spectacular potential gains from research or development, out of all proportion to the costs of the research. And the calculations can serve a useful purpose even though they are merely first approximations, and sometimes require radical modification.[17] Even where they fall far short of coming up with a specific value of a specific development, they may indicate areas of critical need where the value of any successful research is likely to be high. They can, in short, provide some guidance for the formulation of requirements for research and development — specific or general.

2. At a more detailed level, *in planning specific development projects*. Any complex development project must be undertaken in steps or stages, the later stages depending upon the results of the earlier ones. It is therefore a problem in sequential decision making. At each stage it is possible to make use of economic calculus in comparing the costs and gains from various alternative ways of proceeding. The costs in this case are the costs of the next stages of development, not the costs of procuring and operating the developed system. For example, should we try one or two or three suggested methods of making beryllium ductile? If one, which? If two, which two? An analysis of the expected costs, times, and chances of success of the three methods may help in making a rational decision. Also, this analytical process may result in designing new tests of components and new sequences of "breadboard" models to be considered.

AN EXAMPLE FROM CHAPTER 8

Explicit quantitative analysis has been used most frequently for the first of these purposes — to provide some clue to the value or utility of a development project. *If* the development is successful, how much would it be worth to us? This usually involves comparing the cost of attaining some desired capability by procuring and operating the newly developed hardware with the cost of attaining it by some alternative program — for instance, by procuring and operating hardware already developed. If the difference in cost is large in relation to the estimated cost of development, a case exists for a detailed examination of possible development programs.

It is important to realize that this kind of quantitative analysis — the kind used to compare *procurement decisions* — while of some use in making development choices, is incomplete and inadequate as a guide to such choices. Assume that the HC-500 and HC-600 aircraft in the Chapter 8 example had not been developed, and that the question had been: Should we develop one or both; if one, which; and by what development procedures or techniques? This is a far more complicated

---

[17] They raise all the familiar difficulties associated with criteria, uncertainty, suboptimizing, time, and enemy reactions.

problem than the one actually posed there: Which transport aircraft already developed should we procure for our fleet? And while the quantitative analysis used for the latter problem gives information that is needed for good development decisions, it does not by itself point to the best choice.

All that the Chapter 8 analysis does is to estimate that the HC-500, if successfully developed, promises gains (that is, savings) of about $300 million (aside from the worth of advances in the state of the technological art that may accrue to other military or industrial activities); and that the HC-600, if successfully developed, promises savings of about $500 million. These estimates are themselves, of course, subject to great uncertainty. The uncertainties are inevitably greater at the time development decisions must be made than at the time the procurement decision is made, for the period covered by the analysis must lie further ahead of the development decision than of the procurement decision.

But quite apart from these uncertainties, with the general character of which we are by now familiar, there are other relevant uncertainties and gaps in the information provided by the analysis. What we need to know are the potential payoffs and the costs *of the development decisions under consideration.* Let us concentrate for the moment on the first of these questions: Which aircraft should we develop?

The analysis does not even give us the expected payoff from development, because it simply assumes that the development will be successful. In fact the probability that any particular development will be successful is never unity, and usually much less. It has been estimated that half the aircraft developed in the United States since the war — military and civilian — have been, in the vernacular of the industry, "dogs" — not merely somewhat inferior to some other aircraft, but wrongly conceived, technically unsatisfactory, failures. The *expected* value of a development will always be less than the potential value as calculated in Chapter 8, and sometimes much less.

Even if the aircraft is not a dog, its performance characteristics may well be less than predicted and its production costs greater, particularly if the predictions are based, as they usually have to be, on the claims of the company bidding for a development contract. Occasionally performance characteristics are better than predicted, but this is much less common;[18] costs are always greater. An optimistic bias is general. To the extent that performance is disappointing or estimated costs are exceeded, the payoff will be less than estimated in Chapter 8.

The corrected estimate of payoff must then be compared with the estimated costs of development, which were properly ignored as bygones

---

[18] Sometimes, however, there turn out to be unforeseen *applications* which make a development more valuable than anticipated.

in the procurement analysis of Chapter 8. The estimation of development costs is particularly subject to uncertainty and to optimistic bias against which the analyst must be on his guard. We will postpone the complication that the development may take any of several routes with different costs and different probabilities of success, assuming here that one route has been (or will be) selected.

If there is only one development under consideration (the question being, say, should we develop or not develop the HC-500), the criterion is, in principle, simple — as long as we are satisfied with expected values. If the expected value (discounted and adjusted somehow for uncertainties, biases, and chance of failure) exceeds the expected cost, the development should proceed.[19] In realistic cases, however, the criterion problem is more complex. Should we, for example, develop both the HC-500 and the HC-600? The analysis of Chapter 8 tells us that *if* both developments are successful, they will be worth only $100 million more than if HC-600 alone is successfully undertaken. But this does not necessarily mean that we should refrain from developing HC-500 if we expect its development to cost a little more than $100 million. For the development of the HC-500 is worth $300 million.

**Table 22. Cost and payoff of developing the HC-500 and HC-600 (millions of dollars)**

| | Estimated payoff if successful[a] | Expected payoff if probability of success = 50% | Expected cost of development | Net worth of development |
|---|---|---|---|---|
| HC-500 | 300 | 150 | 50 | 100 |
| HC-600 | 500 | 250 | 100 | 150 |
| HC-500 and -600 | 600 | 350[b] | 150 | 200 |

[a] It is assumed for simplicity that this payoff "if successful" has already been appropriately discounted.

[b] ¼ × 600 (both successful) + ¼ × 0 (neither successful) + ¼ × 500 (HC-600 succeeds, HC-500 fails) + ¼ × 300 (HC-500 succeeds, HC-600 fails). Note that we assume here, again for the sake of simplicity, that the probability of success in one development is independent of efforts on the other one.

Table 22 indicates how — in principle — we should set about determining whether to proceed with two (or more) developments rather than with one. Still assuming that we are satisfied with "expected" values, we calculate the expected net worth (expected payoff minus expected cost) of each alternative course of action. In this particular problem the three possibilities are to develop the HC-500 only, the HC-600 only, and both. The estimated payoffs if all developments are successful are 300, 500,

[19] If there is an arbitrary ceiling on the total amount that can be spent on R and D, projects that qualify by this rule may more than exhaust the budget. If transfers from other sources (the preferred alternative) are not permitted, R and D projects should be chosen to maximize the excess of payoff over cost.

and 600 respectively. The chance of success is estimated to be 50 per cent for both the HC-500 and HC-600 developments, so that the expected pay-offs, if each is developed alone, are 150 and 250 respectively. The expected payoff for developing both, however, is more than half the estimated payoff if both developments are successful. With the assumed probabilities there is one chance in four that both will be successful (payoff 600), one in four that neither will succeed (payoff 0), one in four that only the HC-500 (payoff 300), and one in four that only the HC-600 (payoff 500) will be successful. The average expectancy is 350. In the example the preferred alternative is to develop both, which promises an expected net return worth 200 — 50 more than if only the HC-600 is developed.

Two points must be stressed in connection with this example. First, there is a spurious air of precision about the figures in the table. All are the roughest kind of estimates. The uncertainties clouding the estimated payoffs have been discussed in Chapters 8, 10, and 11. There are similar uncertainties regarding development costs, which frequently exceed estimates by factors of two, three, or more. And the 50 per cent estimate of chance of success is obviously a shot in the dark; clearly there are degrees of success, and also clearly the chance of success is a function of the cost of development — of how much we are willing to pay to insure success. Most developments can be made successful if we are willing to spend enough time and money on them. Moreover, entries in the table will usually be more uncertain, not less, when we are concerned with weapon systems rather than cargo transports. The HC-500 and HC-600 are apparently fairly straightforward advances on earlier transports. Their payoffs are essentially of the cost-saving variety. If the physical and performance characteristics of the transports are about as predicted, there is little doubt that these economies (payoffs) will in fact be realized. The weapon system, however, may well represent a considerably greater advance in the state of the art, which will make the outcome as well as time and cost highly unpredictable. Moreover, there is likely to be great uncertainty regarding the military worth of the performance characteristics even if these turn out as predicted — for reasons elaborated in Chapter 10. We cannot really know in 1960 how much it will be worth in a bombing campaign in 1970 to have bombers that will fly at Mach 4 rather than at Mach 2. The worth will depend upon the character of, say, Soviet air defenses in 1970, which will depend in part upon the success of Soviet developments not yet undertaken. Mach 4 might make the difference between being able to penetrate and not being able to penetrate; or it might have trivial or even negative[20] value.

---

[20] Infra-red devices are *more* effective in detecting the higher speed power plants and in directing defense missiles into them.

Nevertheless, development decisions regarding bombers to be operational in 1970 have to be made in 1960 — or earlier. Calculations of the kind reflected in Table 22 are worth making as an aid in the decision process provided the uncertainties and biases in the data are recognized. In many realistic complex cases the problem will be more closely analogous to choosing a strategy that leaves no soft spots than it will be to a simple optimizing calculation.[21] We want something in development to cover the contingency that the Russians will be strikingly successful in developing infra-red, and something else to take advantage of opportunities if they are not. What is a "good" way of providing both, and at the same time of taking care of other "important" contingencies?

The same kind of economic calculus can sometimes be helpful in estimating the utility of developing components, or improved materials, fuels, and so on. One assumes successful development, and then compares weapon systems using the new component or material with weapon systems not using it. What, for example, is the worth of a new higher energy fuel for jet aircraft? As a first approximation, it is the difference between the cost of achieving objectives without the high energy fuel, and the cost of achieving the same objectives with it. If the fuel can be used in existing engines, the calculations involved are, of course, simple — although greater savings may be achievable later in engines specially designed to take advantage of the new fuel. If the new fuel can be used only in specially designed engines, and the engines only in specially designed aircraft, the benefits can only be realized in the more distant future, which means that the calculations may be difficult and the uncertainties large, but no new principle is involved.

If several alternative developments are capable of achieving the same military objective — as lighter-weight structural materials, higher-energy fuels, and boundary layer control can extend the range of bomber aircraft — economic calculations of a similar type can indicate how great an improvement in each case is necessary to save the extra billion dollars that would have to be spent to extend the range by simply building larger, heavier, more expensive bombers. Expert technical opinion might consider some of these improvements much cheaper or easier or more certain of development than others. Despite the unreliability of this kind of expert opinion, hard choices among development alternatives sometimes have to be made, and a rational choice has a better chance of being right than a blind one. The important thing is to avoid the naive assumption that the problem is to choose the *one* best alternative. The simultaneous development of two or more of the possible choices is frequently preferable to developing only one — no matter how superior it appears to the experts.

[21] See Chapter 10, pp. 198–199.

# 14. LOGISTICS[1]

The United States Air Force is currently flying about 150 different aircraft *models* and about 300 different aircraft *series*. The total number of supported aircraft (excluding NATO aircraft, and so on) exceeds 25,000 and roughly 35 per cent of these are combat aircraft. The Air Force has active squadrons at about 265 main bases, of which roughly 90 are overseas, and these bases must be supplied with serviceable parts. The Air Force has supply responsibility for approximately 1,300,000 different parts, and stocks various fractions of these line items at its operating bases or at its depots. Within the Zone of the Interior there are 15 depots, most of them specializing in the support of specific aircraft models, and many of them have extensive aircraft overhaul and parts repair facilities. There are also some large depots overseas. Altogether, in the Zone of the Interior and overseas, the Air Force employs about one million people. The depot system is run by the Air Materiel Command (AMC). The principal "operating" Commands are the Strategic Air Command (SAC), the Air Defense Command (ADC), the Tactical Air Command (TAC), the Air Training Command (ATC), and the Military Air Transport Service (MATS). These largely independent operating Commands practically comprise the flying Air Force. And this vast enterprise of almost a million people, occasioning resource costs of about 18 billion dollars a year, must provide in some sense the greatest possible military capability.[2]

Any analysis and further improvement of Air Force logistics must obviously wait for the definition of tractable sub-problems; one possible way of doing this, within one area of Air Force operations, is described in this Chapter.

Fortunately, at any given time, most of the Air Force, in terms of active squadrons, is flying a relatively small number of aircraft models.

---

[1] This chapter was written by Stephen Enke. It is a slightly modified version of the article "An Economist Looks at Air Force Logistics" published in the *Review of Economics and Statistics*, August 1958, pp. 230–239. Copyright, 1958, by the President and Fellows of Harvard College. Reprinted by permission. On the subject of logistics, see also Horst Mendershausen, "Economic Problems in Air Force Logistics," *American Economic Review*, September 1958, pp. 632–648, and various references cited in that article.

[2] These, and most of the following estimates of magnitude, were provided by Annette Weifenbach. They are necessarily rough approximations. Any precise statistics, if available, would require a long category definition. Recently announced cuts in budget and manning will tend to lower these estimates.

(Thus B-52's replaced B-36's as the latter were phased out.) And even more important, most bases are operated by a single Command and have only one or two aircraft models maintained on them in squadron strength. Thus, much of the problem of Air Force support breaks down into a number of smaller problems, such as how to support B-47's on SAC bases, F-100's at TAC bases, or F-102's at ADC bases. And this is the scheme of this discussion. Henceforth we shall be thinking about the logistics of a single base, within the Zone of the Interior, which has several squadrons of the same model aircraft.

The general nature of the major logistical alternatives — that is, economic tradeoffs — is shown in Figure 12. These are briefly described now. Later they will be examined more carefully.

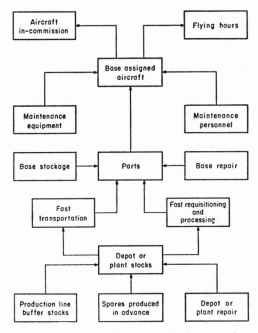

**Fig. 12. Major tradeoffs in supporting base aircraft**

First, there is a base production function, analogous to others encountered by economists in industry. The two primary outputs in this case are aircraft-in-commission (AIC) and flying hours. The main input is the number of assigned combat aircraft, there normally being 25 fighters in ADC squadrons, and 15 bombers in SAC squadrons. The subsidiary inputs can be categorized into (1) maintenance equipment — including hangars, docks, specialized test equipment, and so on; (2) maintenance personnel — radar, engine, airframe mechanics, and so on; and (3) spare parts.

Second, there is an entire base parts supply function, embracing various alternatives. Thus an F-100 series fighter may include some 70,000 listed parts (excluding the engine parts). However over 50 per cent of these may never be used at an operating base. And the base demand for over half of the remainder will be very low indeed. Most of the parts that might be base stocked are expendable and a small fraction are base reparable. So the broad alternative sources of supply at a base are (1) stock at the base, (2) repair at the base, and (3) requisitioning on the depot or factory system. The economic dilemma is that it would be most expensive to stock at a base enough different kinds of parts in sufficient quantity to ensure no "stockouts" that may ground aircraft; on the other hand, the requisitioning cycle normally takes several days, even for priority items, during which time an expensive combat aircraft may be rendered useless if the base lacks a needed and critical part.

Third, the requisitioning cycle, of base upon depot or factory and back to base, may be shortened, and in different ways. The requisition can be passed by some means of electric communication, rather than in some paper form that is physically transported from the base to the specialized depot stocking the part in question. Requisitions can be processed more expeditiously, through the use perhaps of new electronic data-processing equipment. Warehouse locating and stock picking and packaging can be altered to obtain quicker service, but at higher cost. Transportation to the requesting base from the supplying depot can be by such varied means as railroad freight, parcel post, railway express, truck, or, more rapidly, by direct airlift. The economic worth of a faster requisitioning cycle, and the most economical combination of communication, processing, and transport providing any given total-cycle time, are large and worthwhile questions in themselves.

Lastly, for this analysis, there are procurement alternatives for the supply managers of AMC. They can buy spare parts from the manufacturers and stock them at AMC depots. A small but costly fraction of these parts are assemblies that can be economically repaired, either at depots or by private contractors. Or, if parts needed as spares are also used on an aircraft currently in production, they may be obtained from special buffer stocks held by the airframe manufacturer, or his subcontractors, the parts not being used as spares being assembled into whole aircraft. The advantage of this latter procedure is that a final "buy" of spares can be deferred until more is known about base demands for spares and early engineering modifications have occurred.

## THE BASE PRODUCTION FUNCTION

The base production function provides a nice example of the principle of variable proportions, for there are many opportunities to change the proportions of aircraft, spares, and maintenance facilities, and the usual marginal physical productivity relations exist.[3]

### DEFINITION OF OUTPUTS

An initial need is to consider and define the outputs of the base. In peacetime the base squadrons must provide a certain number of flying hours for the flight crews to acquire and maintain proficiency. These practice flights generate or reveal various malfunctions in the aircraft and its equipment that may render it temporarily out of commission. Modern combat aircraft include extremely complicated electronic, hydraulic, and pneumatic systems, not to mention the engine, airframe, and instruments, so a high flying-hour output can soon develop a queue of aircraft awaiting unscheduled maintenance. (In addition, from time to time, aircraft undergo periodic or scheduled maintenance, possibly at base but usually at a special depot facility.)

In wartime, for an ADC or SAC squadron, the important requirement is to have the largest number of aircraft combat-ready and on alert, fueled, and armed, and prepared to take off. It is not enough to have aircraft that can fly if they cannot be sent on their missions. An aircraft not fully equipped (ANFE) can be as immediately useless in the event of an impending Soviet nuclear attack as an aircraft out of commission for maintenance (AOCM) or for lack of a part (AOCP).

It is apparent that flying hours and combat-ready aircraft are substitutes, in the sense of being alternative outputs. Given a normal squadron table of organization for personnel and a unit authorization list for equipment, it is possible, over a period of time, almost to ground an entire squadron by requiring it to attempt to fly far more hours each week than its maintenance facilities can provide. Determination of the shape of this substitute output relation is important, not only in the short run to squadron commanders who can schedule more or fewer flying hours, but also in the long run to those who are responsible for the prescription of tables of organization and unit authorization lists and who decide the number of aircraft that shall constitute a squadron. One contribution of econometricians has been to "model" an ADC airbase, with its squadrons of interceptors, and to combine existing Air Force data and mathematical queuing theory into estimated flying-hour versus aircraft-in-commission curves.

[3] The principle of variable proportions states that as one adds more of one input, holding the amounts of the others constant, the marginal physical product will (after a time) decline.

USE OF INPUTS

Combat aircraft, even without their spares, are so expensive a resource that they must be used rather intensively, "use" meaning practice flying or being at least in-commission. Inevitably, though, such an aircraft must spend some of its life undergoing periodic overhauls, probably at a depot. Also, especially if it has a low airframe number for its model and series, it will almost inevitably go through depot modification at some time. The remaining 85 per cent or so of its first-line life is with a squadron on home base, either in or out of commission.

If one follows a given aircraft on base from day to day, through its changing status, its non-useful life consists largely of waiting. On landing from a flight it awaits post-flight inspection. If this reveals a malfunction, or one has been reported by the flight crew, it may wait for special test equipment and an expert to diagnose the fault. It may then have to wait for specialized maintenance personnel and facilities in order to be fixed. On northern bases in the winter, it may have to wait for space in a warm hangar before work can be finished. More often than not, repair cannot be completed without some parts on the aircraft being replaced, and this may occasion a further wait while the part is obtained from base supply (perhaps a mile away) or from a depot (perhaps a thousand miles away). And when the malfunction has been remedied, the aircraft may have to await a pilot and suitable weather for a test flight before it can be declared in-commission.

On the other hand, on some days, various maintenance facilities and personnel await aircraft; hangars or docks are partially empty; and there are no calls upon over 99 per cent of the aircraft spares stocked in base supply. Because of the extreme specialization of all these inputs — there are about 25 *kinds* of maintenance skills available at a large base — some maintenance resource will always be waiting for employment. Malfunctions and parts failures are so unpredictable that equipment and personnel capacities just adequate to handle an *average* maintenance workload can be expected to develop queues of out-of-commission aircraft.[4]

ECONOMICAL BASE OPERATIONS

Here then is a complex instance of the principle of variable proportions. A larger monthly payroll for maintenance personnel of all kinds

[4] Research has already indicated the undesirability of certain "obvious" management decisions. If 50 per cent of the engine mechanics at a base are unemployed on an average, while only 20 per cent of some other specialized skill are, it might appear obvious that having fewer of the former and more of the latter mechanics would provide more AIC for a given payroll. However, if engine repairs on an average take twice as long, this is not obvious at all, as greater manning insurance is needed against the longer-time engine repair jobs having to be done occasionally.

will reduce the number of aircraft out-of-commission, at a cost, but the marginal physical return on such expenditures will decrease; aircraft out-of-commission may concurrently be waiting for various resources other than personnel, so that as delays for personnel become shorter and less frequent, other delays, for maintenance facilities perhaps, are uncovered, as it were. Thus, given the input mix, the measurement of the marginal physical product of a particular input is difficult in practice. Conceptually, it is clear however that expenditures for a given input should be continued until equal in value to the dollar worth of the fractional reduction in aircraft out-of-commission yielded by these expenditures.

Linear programming, and other modern mathematical techniques, may aid in the short run by scheduling out-of-commission aircraft and available maintenance resources of all kinds more efficiently. The problem is complicated because certain maintenance resources (human and material) can be used concurrently, others cannot, and some are best employed without interruption until a job is finished. The potentialities of sophisticated scheduling depend however upon the ability to estimate the kind and quantity of maintenance resources that will be required to return a given aircraft to commission, and the extent to which these vary among aircraft.

The longer-run problem is to prescribe the proper mix of resources, including combat aircraft, that should be assigned to a base to produce the two outputs described. Could the Air Force, by rearranging its expenditures among these resources, obtain a greater number of flying hours and ready aircraft if it assigned fewer aircraft to a squadron and base, but acquired more base maintenance facilities and personnel? These are large and important questions, and yet, because they involve decisions at a high level and involve different budget classifications, they are the kind of problem that ordinarily is not subjected to operations research and economic analysis.[5]

## BASE PARTS SUPPLY FUNCTION

The Air Force appears far more conscious of the deleterious nature of an AOCP — having an aircraft out-of-commission for lack of a part —

[5] For example, would a base produce more flying hours and/or aircraft in-commission if it had either one more whole aircraft assigned to it or the same aircraft completely disassembled as parts added to its stocks? As a whole aircraft, it might add two-thirds of an aircraft to the total of those in-commission. As an addition to the base's ordinary stock of parts, it might satisfy nearly all the spares demands now causing AOCP's, and hence contribute more in this way to an increase in aircraft in-commission. Its value as a contribution to parts will be more important if the number of whole aircraft assigned to the base is already quite large relative to the investment in base spares stocks. At some bases, contrary to policy, mechanics sometimes avoid an AOCP by robbing parts from another aircraft which, for some reason, may be out of commission for some

than of an AOCM (aircraft out-of-commission for maintenance). And yet both cost the Air Force a usable aircraft. The explanation of this attitude may be that maintenance seems inevitable, whereas lack of a needed part at a base superficially appears to be avoidable without undue cost.

ALLOCATION OF BUDGET AMONG SPARES AT BASE

Before considering the larger question of how much should be spent to avoid AOCP's, the smaller question of how best to spend a given sum of money on base stocks of spares is considered now. Conceptually, expenses should be incurred so that the probability of the $i$th unit of the $j$th part causing a crippling stockout is proportional to the cost of stocking it at base. This simple idea, analogous to the familiar rule of how to maximize satisfaction from a consumer's given budget, is of course difficult to apply.

First, of the 100,000 odd kinds of parts listed for a modern bomber, only about 50 per cent may be used at all and 10 per cent may be used only at depots. They may be bits and pieces, components of some assembly that cannot be repaired at base level; when the assembly is found not to be working it is normally replaced with a serviceable assembly, the removed carcass being sent to a factory or depot for repair.

Second, demand for parts at one base is not necessarily predictable from experience at other bases. About 10 to 30 per cent of the parts on a modern combat aircraft are peculiar to that number and letter aircraft, so that, if a new aircraft is being phased into the Air Force, there is little experience with the demand for many of its stock numbered parts. To some extent demands for parts at one base will differ from those at another having supposedly the same kind of aircraft; one base may be on a New England coastline, and another in the California desert; one may have been activated earlier and have older aircraft that are beginning to experience a different pattern of parts failures; and squadrons at some bases may be flying different kinds of practice missions.

Third, at a two-wing bomber base, about half the part line items that might be demanded may have been needed at a rate lower than 10 a year, and on smaller and more typical bases the demands for parts are lower. The actual variations in demand for a part from month to month are usually much greater relatively when the average demand per month is low. Such a high dispersion leaves the mean with only a formal significance. The old military concept of measuring stocks in so many "weeks of supply," while suitable for, say, the cavalry with horses to

---

time. Such "cannibalization" tends to be concentrated on some one aircraft, which becomes a so-called "hangar queen," and this unofficial practice supports the suspicion that some bases are "long" on aircraft and "short" on spare parts.

feed, can be most dangerous when applied to spare parts for modern aircraft.[6]

Fourth, when does a stockout ground an aircraft, causing an AOCP? Some parts are not essential to safety of flight or performance of a combat mission, although "nice to have"; for example, some of the navigational equipment duplicates functions and is installed as a precaution lest other equipment fail. Also, a temporary stockout at base of a specific part, even though essential to flight, may not be responsible for grounding an aircraft if it is also awaiting maintenance resources or *other* essential parts.

Fifth, the cost of stocking the $i$th unit of the $j$th part at a base is not necessarily its procurement cost plus transport cost to the base. For one thing, it depends on whether this results in the Air Force procuring an extra unit of this part, or whether the Air Force will simply transfer some of its worldwide stock of the part from a depot to the base. It also depends on whether the part is peculiar to one aircraft model or series, and whether this kind of aircraft will soon be retired. Moreover, the stocking of the $j$th part at a base — even though only one unit is carried — occasions certain fixed "housekeeping" costs for warehousing, record keeping, and the like. Over a period of years, a base may support different aircraft models — and even be transferred from one Command to another — and these redeployments incur transport costs if parts that were base stocked are peculiar to the departing aircraft series. Finally, many of the more expensive parts are subject to engineering change orders, and compliance with these can often be effected only at certain depots. All these factors, some of them rather intangible, affect any estimate of what it costs to stock an extra $i$th unit or an extra $j$th part at a base.

## DISTRIBUTION OF SPARES BETWEEN BASES AND DEPOTS

A larger question is to what extent the Air Force should keep its worldwide stocks of different catalogued parts at operating bases or at some of its specialized depots and supporting storage sites. Most of the considerations enumerated in the preceding paragraph tend to reduce the number of line items stocked at a base, and to some extent the quantity of a part stocked there. On the other hand, there is the feeling — exemplified in the "for want of a nail the kingdom was lost" sort of reasoning — that a multi-million-dollar aircraft should not be grounded for lack of a one-dollar part. A further factor is that, until the recent advent of some of the new large-capacity electronic data-processing ma-

---

[6] A more modern practice, of estimating parts consumption per aircraft flying hour, while clearly valid for fuel and lubricants, also has serious limitations when applied to spare parts, although there is no other obviously better coefficient of demand.

chines, it was impossible for a prime depot to keep close control over parts it supposedly "managed" once these were distributed among numerous bases.

An examination of the demand for and prices of aircraft parts is most significant for management. In general, though, of all 1.3 million line items stocked by the Air Force, 75 per cent are priced under $10 (Category III), 22 per cent between $10 and $500 (Category II) and 3 per cent over $500 (Category I).[7] World-wide monthly issues for about 400,000 aircraft support items are roughly 60 per cent under 1, 25 per cent from 1 to 10, and 15 per cent over 10; the *demand* at any *one* base per month is, of course, many times smaller. If demand and price are combined into a matrix, it is discovered that about 45 per cent of aircraft part line items are very cheap (under $10) *and* in very low demand (under 1 a month worldwide). There is a small minority of rather cheap items in fairly strong demand. The Category I parts (over $500) can usually be repaired and are slow to wear out.

One moral for management is that the high value items, because they are so few, can justifiably be procured and distributed under close controls, even when these are more costly to administer.

Another moral for management is that cheap parts can economically be stocked in greater number and quantity at base level than has been the case under Air Force regulations. Various statistics confirm this view. About 25 per cent of all aircraft parts demanded at a base during a month are not now normally stocked at a base or are not stocked in sufficient quantities. Roughly 30 per cent of AOCP's are occasioned by parts costing under $10. The average routine reorder of a base for a Category III item was for two units having a total value of $0.50; the fixed cost of processing this *routine* resupply order and shipment has been estimated at no less than $5, or about ten times the value of the order. It is not very hard to prove that it would be economical for the Air Force to keep larger stocks of cheap aircraft spares at its bases and to reorder in larger quantities than in the past. This need not mean an equivalent increase in Air Force worldwide stocks — far from it — but it does involve some shift of funds away from depot supply operations.

The rapidly advancing state of electronic data-processing has made it possible, for the first time in history, to distribute hundreds of thousands of spare parts in greater quantity to more bases, and without markedly increasing the total quantity and value of the matériel that the Air Force must stock. Within AMC each part has been managed by a prime depot (sometimes with a "zonal opposite" depot), but until recently it was impractical for the prime depot to keep up-to-date inven-

[7] As this price frequency distribution is very J-shaped, the median value for Category III items (the under $10 class) is under $1.

tory data on any of "its" parts, except those stored at the same depot facility. On Category III items an annual worldwide stock balance was kept, but this information on an average would be at least six months out of date for other bases. As a result, the prime depot tended to consider distributed matériel as "lost" to the Air Force supply system, because it could not order a base to transfer a prescribed part to another base with any assurance that the part was there to be shipped.

It is now technologically possible for the Air Force to maintain a number of data-processing centers that can execute the policies of the prime depot supply managers. Up-to-date inventory information for every storage location and part-number combination in the Air Force can be kept at such a center, so that distributed stock is as much under the control of an AMC, or using Command, supply manager as if it were at the prime depot. Also, the data-processing center, applying formulas approved by AMC or the using Command, or both, can effect automatic routine resupply of bases, because it knows when stocks at base fall to their approved reorder points. Data-processing centers of this kind, because they can instantaneously bring to bear so much more information regarding a single part and reach a programmed decision, are able to execute more reasonable and less crude management policies.

Of course, the distribution of spares among bases and depots should not be independent of the Air Force worldwide stock position. If a part has clearly been "over bought" already, it makes little sense under normal circumstances to keep only a few "weeks of supply" at using bases. On the other hand, if a part is becoming scarce worldwide, the decision whether to keep available stocks at the prime depot (as a sort of strategic reserve) or to distribute them all among some using bases (there not being enough perhaps for all bases), will depend primarily upon whether close control of distributed parts has been achieved through some of the new procedures and recently available electronic equipment.

## THE REQUISITIONING CYCLE

The cost and duration of the requisitioning cycle — which starts with a base requisitioning something it wants and ends with the receipt of the matériel at the base — is, of course, one factor in determining what parts to stock at using bases. If priority requisitions are costly, and nevertheless involve a long wait, there is much to be said for wider and deeper base stocks.[8] However, in the case of really high value items, pre-

[8] Priority requisitions are those for which there is an immediate need, in contrast to those that are for routine resupply. Priority requisitions on an average take about three to five days within the Zone of the Interior, and they are considerably more expensive, as regards transportation, communication, and processing, than routine requisitions. There is considerable dispersion around the mean elapsed time of the requisition cycle, and this "tail" of the distributed times causes as much concern among base supply

positioning of stock at numerous using bases may be less economical than having a prompt although costly means of distributing a smaller amount of centrally located stock on demand.

How much the Air Force can properly afford to pay for a shorter requisitioning cycle — neglecting considerations of military worth — depends largely upon the penalty cost to the Air Force of an AOCP at base. This is hard but not impossible to estimate within an order of magnitude. It involves consideration of the cost of an extra combat aircraft, its expected useful service life, and the normal in-commission rate for that aircraft model and series. The dollar worth (or aircraft cost) of an in-commission aircraft day, obtained in this way, gives some idea of what can sensibly be spent on base stock or a short requisitioning cycle, or both, in order to avoid an AOCP day. (A complicating factor is that some AOCP's overlap on the same aircraft, and a reduction in AOCP days on a particular aircraft may not lessen its out-of-commission time, because of other waits, as for example for some maintenance skill.) Knowing the daily demand pattern for aircraft spares, one can estimate the sort of *extra* investment in base stock that is required to reduce one kind of AOCP on an average by one day. A key question then is whether this extra investment in spares is less or greater than the penalty cost to the Air Force of one less aircraft in-commission a day.

However, increasing a base stock of aircraft spares is only one way of reducing AOCP aircraft-days at a base. Another is reducing the time of the requisitioning cycle. And this, in turn, can be reduced in various ways, as for example shortening the times taken to communicate the requisition, to process it at the depot, to pick and pack the stock, and to transport it. The logical ideal is to invest resources in shortening the time normally spent on each of these segments of the cycle in such a way that the last unit investment on each segment buys the same reduction in time.

Some of the most promising opportunities for economically reducing the length of the requisitioning cycle are in the communication and processing of requisitions. The handling of the orders can usually be expedited far less expensively than can the shipment of the merchandise. Teletyping a requisition may save a day or two as against airmailing it, and yet the difference in absolute cost may be far less than that occasioned by sending the matériel by another transportation medium that saves about the same amount of time.[9]

managers as the mean duration itself. "Wide" base stockage refers to many line items stocked; "deep" base stockage refers to the quantity stocked of a given line item.

[9] In the case of routine requisitions by bases, for which the cycle time may be 30 days, ten pounds' weight of requisitions may cause the movement of several tons of matériel, with its packaging; a policy of sending these requisitions by air rather than surface may accomplish as much, at far less cost, as a policy of airlifting the matériel instead of sending it by surface.

The substitution of electronic equipment for clerical labor can eventually save a considerable amount of time now devoted to processing requisitions and arranging shipments. This is partly because people make more errors, and every clerical mistake creates confusion and delay. Another reason is that any set of clerical procedures tends to be sequential, with the "paper" moving from person to person, at any or all of which points there may be a wait. An electronic data-processor can store more information regarding each stock numbered part than can readily be made available to one clerk, and so the computer can make what are in effect a great many simultaneous evaluations and choices, embodied in a final and more considered decision. (Of course, a considerable clerical force is needed to provide the computer with up-to-date input data, and machine programmers are needed when there is a change of supply policy.)

Shortening the requisitioning cycle — important and complicated a matter though it may be — involves at most a fairly limited sub-optimization. The costs incurred to attain this contraction must be balanced against the present possibilities of increasing aircraft in-commission by improved policies and practices at bases. In some cases increased stocking of parts — especially of the cheaper aircraft parts — may be the answer. In others it may be increased maintenance facilities or a better mix of maintenance skills and equipment.

## SOME PROCUREMENT ALTERNATIVES

In the past, the Air Force has spent on aircraft spares as much as 40 per cent or more of the purchase cost of the complete combat aircraft themselves. About half of these aircraft parts — both as regards number and value — are peculiar to only one model aircraft, and so these become obsolete when the aircraft using them is phased out. The situation is now improving.

The tendency in the past to over-buy aircraft spares — and especially peculiar parts — is attributable to several factors. Because of various institutional pressures — and the supposedly long lead times of the manufacturers — spares provisioning conferences have often been held for new model aircraft before a single production aircraft of the series has been flown. Direct demand experience is therefore almost zero. The provisioners are more likely to be blamed for providing inadequate spares support — and thereby grounding a new first-line aircraft series — than for overbuying: hence they tend to "play it safe." There are many engineering changes during the first year or so that a new model aircraft is being phased-in, and these changes may render already purchased spares obsolete before they have even been placed in a warehouse at an Air Force facility. The provisioners also cannot be at all sure of the programmed flying hours for more than a few years into the future, and to some extent spares consumption can be considered a function of flying hours.[10]

Many of these uncertainties are inevitable. Provisioners will never be able accurately to predict flying hours, demand rates per flying hour, and technological obsolescence of parts. Fortunately there is a partial remedy that is now being tried. This is to defer the initial AMC purchase of high-value parts until a number of bases have been assigned squadrons of the new aircraft and, more important, until some of these uncertainties are less obscure. In the interim, these initial squadrons can be supported directly from extra "buffer stocks" maintained by the manufacturer of the aircraft. One or two years after the first production aircraft has flown, AMC may make its first "buy" for depot stocks. The essential idea is to gain time, and to recognize that an aircraft part does not have to be irrevocably designated either a spare or a part for assembly at the time of its production. AMC is moving in this direction.

This innovation is possible because of a special set of favorable circumstances. One is that high-value Category I parts account for 45 per cent of the provisioning dollars and only 3 per cent of the spare parts line items; hence manufacturers can accord these relatively few parts special treatment. Another is that high-value parts tend, with a short lead, to be produced at about the same rate as the complete aircraft, unlike cheap bits and pieces that are often made in a few days for several years of scheduled aircraft production; thus the extra cost of a special buffer stock, geared to the aircraft production line, is small, and the risk of serious loss due to engineering change orders is slight. Finally, production of a new model aircraft tends to be comparatively slow during the first year to eighteen months, and not so many operating squadrons have to be supported from the manufacturer's special buffer stocks during this initial period.

High-value parts are nearly all assemblies, and hence reparable and subject to modification. The wearout rate of the assembly as a whole is usually very low indeed. When it malfunctions on an aircraft, it is usually because a constituent part has failed, and the assembly carcass, unless repaired at the base, will be sent to a specialized parts repair depot. (Engines are a special and extreme example of a high-value reparable item.) Consequently there are two sources of supply, the parts repair depot and the manufacturer of new units. Normally it is more economical to repair carcasses than to buy replacements, and so provisioners normally need to buy not much more than is required to fill the pipeline of

---

[10] Some people in the past have held that it was easier to obtain "100 money" (for initial procurement) than "400 money" (for maintenance and operations) from Congress, and so have tried to buy more spares for concurrent delivery with newly procured aircraft, rather than later for maintenance and operations.

the repair cycle, that is from base to repair facility and back to base. During the phase-in of a new aircraft, and for the same reasons advanced above, it may be best to defer purchases for this pipeline and instead to cycle the higher-valued carcasses through the manufacturer for repair, drawing upon his buffer stock of serviceables in the interim.

This special management of the relatively few high-value items requires detailed, timely, and accurate records of the status, location, and quantity of matériel, by part number. Full realization of the potentialities of these institutional changes, especially if they are applied to Category II depot reparables, may have to wait for further introduction of electronic data-processing equipment and related procedures. These innovations also imply an even closer relation between the aircraft industry and AMC supply and maintenance organizations.

Spares provisioning and distribution policies — as mentioned before — are not independent of one another. How essential different aircraft spares are for the flying and fighting of aircraft is barely correlated with their differences in price. Accordingly, in the case of high-value items, there is more of a willingness to adopt special procedures and use direct airlift from factory to base, because this may save many dollars on balance. Conversely, in the case of the numerous parts costing only a few dollars or less, the fear of AOCP's becomes paramount. Stated differently, distribution policies for cheap parts are likely to determine the purchases, whereas provisioning policies for high-value parts are likely to determine their distribution.

Another procurement problem in which economic analysis can be helpful is that of choosing among alternative flyaway kits. Under certain eventualities bomber and fighter squadrons must deploy to barely stocked bases far away, and so cargo aircraft must follow them with kits containing spares. The size of these kits is essentially limited by the weight that these cargo aircraft can carry. What spares should be included in the kits? These kits might be prescribed by experienced people relying only on judgment, as has sometimes been done, but this is risky. They might be designed, making explicit use of demand data, to minimize the number of subsequently unused spares in the kit, but this is clearly a fallacious criterion. To an economist, the obvious approach is to add units of each kind of usable and critical spare, up to the aggregate weight limit, so that, as nearly as possible, the probability that the marginal unit will be demanded after deployment is proportional to its weight. Flyaway kits, designed according to this principle, have been paper-tested and found superior.[11]

[11] That is, the experienced demands of deployed squadrons have been carefully collected. These have been set against both the actual squadron kit and the "equal-marginal-protection" kit described above. There would have been markedly fewer stockouts had the latter kit been available instead.

INTERDEPENDENCE OF THE LOGISTICS SYSTEM

The interactions of the Air Force logistics system are so numerous and complex that they tax human comprehension. Moreover, these interacting operations are performed by many different organizations; in addition to the AMC depots, there are all the bases of the various using Commands, not to mention the competing private companies that produce and repair for the Air Force. Thus, functional interdependence is often obscured by organizational schism.

Under these circumstances it is not surprising that the effectiveness of these Commands, and especially of their suborganizations, is occasionally viewed somewhat parochially. Zealous officers sometimes increase the efficiency of their own operation in ways that may lessen the over-all performance of the logistics system. The Air Force is probably no better or worse in this respect than other very large organizations. A few random examples follow.

Depot maintenance managers try to minimize the cost of repairs on parts. To this end they may hold up reparable carcasses until they have a large "batch" that can be run through repair at a lower unit cost. As a result, supply officials may have to procure more serviceable stock from the manufacturer, causing a net increase in cost for the system.

Similarly, the periodic overhaul of aircraft at depots can be performed at a lower cost per aircraft if only one shift is worked; however, from the point of view of an over-all system, it may be economical to work two or even three shifts in order to shorten the time valuable aircraft are out of use at depots.

Transportation officers, who have some discretion in selecting the media by which matériel will be shipped from depots to bases, may give too much consideration to minimizing transportation costs and too little to the impact of using cheaper carload and truckload shipments on base AOCP's and spares procurement.

Packaging officials are primarily anxious to minimize breakage, and have limited means for assessing the impact of heavy tare on transportation costs, particularly in the case of airlift.

Squadrons can, on occasion, undertake preventive and other kinds of maintenance that will lessen the work that must be done when the aircraft goes to an overhaul depot, but they have little incentive to do so under some circumstances.

These kinds of anomalies are only apparent if one views the logistics system as a whole. This is very difficult to do. It would take a model-builder of almost superhuman competence to represent the bare outlines of the over-all system so that it could be programmed for a computer.

One recourse is to attempt a simulation that uses both people and computers. This is especially appropriate when viewing the logistics system as a whole, because lines of authority among the various Commands and suborganizations are not always clear. Decisions are often "coordinated" compromises. Complications of this kind cannot be programmed into a computer and so analytic solutions have to be supplemented by human beings, in a laboratory, who can represent the conflicting attitudes and interests of different organizations.[12]

### ECONOMIC ANALYSIS AND LOGISTICS RESEARCH

This chapter has described some of the problems of choice pertaining to Air Force logistics. To help predict the consequences of alternative policies and practices, we may use models on paper, models in our heads, models in the form of games, or simulation laboratories to represent the functioning of logistics systems. In any event, the alternatives should be considered in terms of an economic criterion. We should look at these choices as problems of maximization in the face of constraints or, in less technical language, as problems of getting the greatest capability from our limited resources. Again, the way of looking at these problems is what we wish to stress most of all. In addition, quantitative analyses of the sort discussed in Part II can often help us reach better decisions about these issues in logistics.

# 15. THE ECONOMICS OF MILITARY ALLIANCE[1]

The existence of alliances and the possibilities of improving their effectiveness introduce another set of special problems in defense planning. This set of problems includes allocating defense tasks among the allied nations so as to realize economies of specialization, sharing defense burdens in an equitable fashion, and adjusting a nation's domestic plans to the constraints and opportunities presented by the alliances.

---

[12] For example, the Logistics Systems Laboratory at The RAND Corporation, under the immediate management of Mr. Murray A. Geisler, has completed a fairly detailed representation of much of the Air Force logistics system in order to test the feasibility and compare the effectiveness of various ideas for improvement that have been described in this Chapter. This particular simulation has employed about 50 people and an IBM 704 computer. Procedural manuals totaling 400 pages had to be prepared, with the help of AMC civilians, for the "subjects" to follow; and about 30,000 new machine instructions had to be written for the computer. About four years of experience, including the impacts of two wars, were enacted within a few months. The quantitative results alone, representing the daily activities of the numerous organizations being simulated, would stretch almost 20 miles if arranged contiguously, page by page.

[1] This chapter was written by Malcolm W. Hoag of The RAND Corporation.

### THE FEDERAL ANALOGY

To visualize the fundamental economic problems of alliance, it is helpful as a starting point, although unfortunately only as a starting point, to consider federal union as an analogy. We can conceive of the roles played by nations in an international alliance as similar to those played by the American states in fulfillment of the national military program. In either case we can ask, which political unit does what military tasks, where and why, and at what economic cost?

It is instructive to note, however, that these questions are seldom if ever raised within our federal union. We should be hard-pressed to answer them if they were. In military matters, the sovereignty of the national government is virtually complete. The allocation of military tasks, the determination of the scale of effort, and the provision of finance are federal functions. We are interested in the impact of these functions not upon individual states, but upon individual persons and business firms throughout the economy. Moreover, the control of military matters is not the only function monopolized by the central government. Rather it exists among and in some respects is subsumed under a number of other and broader federal functions. In these and other vital respects, our current international military alliances fall far short of union.

Nonetheless, the analogy is suggestive. Consider the extreme alternative. Imagine fifty sovereign military establishments within the United States, with separate currencies and independent budgetary control for each state. Add a disposition to avoid dependence upon unpredictable foreigners, so that "balanced forces" and indigenous sources of military supplies tend to be sought for each. Even if the same resources in total were devoted to military purposes, is it at all likely that the sum total of military capability from the fifty units could come close to that attainable within an integrated federal union?

The main argument for a defensive alliance is that the prospect of a united military response may deter a potential aggressor. In joining an alliance, a nation presumably values the addition of allied strength more than it fears the risk of being drawn into "other people's wars." This main argument is reinforced by the possibility of more effective military preparedness achieved through international specialization and division of labor. Within the United States we find it efficient to concentrate tank production predominantly in one or two states and to have but one Strategic Air Command. Perhaps we sometimes pursue centralization too far, but certainly we achieve far more efficient use of our resources than we would if forced to divide our effort among fifty uncoordinated military establishments. Among nations, as among the different parts of a single nation, the factors of production are unevenly distributed, and there are important economies of scale attached to many military tasks. The age-old case for enhanced efficiency by extension of specialization beyond national boundaries is a persuasive one for military as well as for other categories of production, although probably not to the same extent.

The fundamental economic problem for any alliance is that of achieving greater efficiency. How can advantage be taken of the unequal facilities for military performance among member nations? But to the very extent that the efficiency problem is solved in practice, associated problems become prominent. One of these is the problem of equity in national contributions. Imagine for the moment an alliance in which authority is retained at the level of member nations except for the assignment of military tasks, that assignment being made by an international body charged only with the pursuit of efficiency subject to over-all resource constraints. The implications are sweeping. The international body would determine what a country was to do, and therefore the resource burden to be imposed upon it. National management would be left only with the choice among means to meet that burden, nominally the matter of finance.

It is possible that the resulting distribution of burdens among nations would accidentally correspond to the distribution associated with completely national management; that is, any reallocation of tasks by the international military body would merely substitute, within each country, one job of equal resource drain for another. But it would be an extremely unusual coincidence if it did so. In all probability, the result would be a reallocation of tasks which incidentally reapportioned resource burdens among countries. Problems of "fair shares" in burdens among the members of the alliance, intimately associated and coordinated in importance with the problems of efficiency, would immediately become prominent.

Within our federal union, the issues of military efficiency and fair shares arise in quite a different way. It is exceedingly unlikely that an equal percentage of the resources lying within the boundaries of each of the states is used for federal government purposes, or that any systematic ordered relationship between federal utilization and total state resources is observed. What are the facts? We do not know, nor do we need to know. They would not be relevant to issues of fairness in contributions to federal programs. An altogether different set of facts is needed to answer the basic question of fairness. Do the benefits from and burdens of government programs bear equally upon individuals whose situations, apart from their location within the nation, are similar? If so, no issue of geographical discrimination arises.

Issues of fairness among individuals involve more than the test of impartiality in the treatment of equals. For example, it may be held that individuals with higher incomes should contribute a greater proportion of their incomes to the support of government programs, even if the per capita benefits are taken to be equal. If some states have higher average incomes per capita than others, while within states the pattern of distribution of relative incomes is the same, a progressive pattern of taxation will absorb a higher proportion of the incomes of the residents of the richer states. In this sense residents of New York may contribute more on the average to the support of federal programs than do those of Mississippi. In a discussion of fair shares among members of an alliance the federal analogy tends naturally to be stressed by the poorer nations. Poor nations argue that they should contribute lower proportions of national product for military purposes than rich nations.

Within a federal union, however, it is possible that one of the poorer states is an "arsenal state," one whose resources are disproportionately devoted to military and other types of production for federal programs because they are best adapted to that use. No "unfair" burden upon the residents of that state need result. The proportion of state resources used directly for federal purposes, including the production of military goods and services, may diverge markedly from the proportion of the incomes of state residents taken by federal taxes. Residents of the poor state pay little in federal taxes. In such a case, the flow of federal funds inward to that state as payment for production exceeds the outward flow of federal tax funds. The excess of inward flow makes it possible for arsenal-state residents to spend upon imports from other states in excess of their exports, an excess that can continue without accumulation of indebtedness to residents of other states. Conversely, other states as a whole find the spending power of their residents depleted more by federal taxation than it is reinforced by federal spending, but a continuing export surplus to the arsenal state can offset that imbalance. In other words, the operations of federal finance tend to result automatically in a continuing *transfer* of the fruits of part of the resources of other states to the arsenal state through the channels of commercial trade. Residents of the arsenal state use more civilian products than they produce, and in this way are compensated in real terms for the productive resources expended upon federal programs. The transfer of resources helps to reconcile the conflicting demands of efficiency and equity in federal programs.

The issues of military efficiency and equity or "fair shares" among countries arise in any alliance where pooling of national resources in a common effort is appreciable. It may be efficient to concentrate more production of military goods and services in a country than it would willingly support alone, and the desired concentration may be achieved by arrangements for transfer of resources from other members. But in the absence of a common international budget, transfers could not result automatically from the separate processes of taxation on the one hand

and government spending on the other. They would require financial grants between nations. Such an arrangement, which is well-established but little noticed in our federal union, would be novel in an alliance between nations and certain to receive prominent and hostile attention.

## DIVERGENT NATIONAL INTERESTS

The federal analogy serves to raise some general questions for alliance economics. How can military efficiency and equity in national contributions be defined? Are resource transfers among members necessary, and if so how are they to be implemented? All of these questions, for example, have arisen in NATO.[2]

But the federal union, of course, provides the limiting case of maximum mutual gain through division of military labor. Alliance falls short of union, and realizable mutual gain of this sort will accordingly be less, perhaps far less. Member countries will be inhibited from specializing in the military duties that each does best. One ally cannot put complete trust in military support by another even in the event of the major war whose threat brought the alliance into being. Hence each ally will have some reason to avoid specialization so extreme that it could not operate independently in military operations. And each member is likely to have, in addition, some special military objectives unshared or imperfectly shared with its allies. Although one member may be deemed an inefficient (high-cost) provider of one type of military force by other members who wish it would specialize in other types, the inefficient type may be precisely the one the particular member wishes to retain for prestige or because it is the type best suited to policing its colonies. Its allies may view these subsidiary military purposes with little or no sympathy.

Thus potential mutual gain from military specialization varies directly with the growth of confidence that foreign-policy objectives are shared throughout the alliance and that allies will be resolute in facing up to any major aggressive threats. At one extreme, lack of confidence can obviously destroy an alliance; at the other extreme, complete confidence makes it possible for a genuine merger to replace alliance. We deal here with the intermediate case. Confidence in support by allies is never perfect, but it nonetheless makes possible attaining a higher level of national security without increasing the national military budget. An allied division can rarely if ever contribute as much to national security as a division of one's own, but it can still contribute. Although the prospective contributions of allied forces are discounted appreciably because

---

[2] See the standard reference, Lord Ismay, *NATO, The First Five Years,* Paris, North Atlantic Treaty Organization, 1955; and L. Gordon, "Economic Aspects of Coalition Diplomacy — The NATO Experience," *International Organization,* X, No. 4, 1956, pp. 529–543.

they cannot be counted upon completely, their aggregate contribution may far outweigh that of the national forces that it is realistic to raise on one's own.

Even for the United States, far and away the major power in the alliances of the free world, anything approaching assured security is simply unprocurable, as we have seen.[3] We are driven to making hard budgetary choices involving less security in one aspect of military preparedness in order to attain more in another. These choices would probably become far harder if we sought military self-sufficiency, walling ourselves off from allied contributions as well as their associated risks. The most prominent example is supplied by military manpower itself. The American soldier, sailor, or airman is notoriously expensive compared to his counterpart abroad, especially when he must be transported to and maintained in distant locations. The opportunity cost of diverting a man from productive civilian employment to military employment is typically much higher in the United States than in the economies of our allies. Consequently if we replaced allied troops with additional troops of our own, our military costs would soar. Conversely, if we did not replace allied troops, but simply reduced our overseas commitments instead, we would probably increase the probability of enemy aggression. In this case we would incur a great risk to our own security. An attempt at self-sufficiency in military affairs could well result in less security in the end despite appreciably higher costs. Or consider another prominent example, that of foreign bases made available by our allies to United States forces, say, for the refueling of bombers. By permitting close-in refueling of our bombers to gain more speed or range, and compelling the Soviets to spread their air defenses far more widely, these bases gave us during the 1950's a great geographical advantage over the Soviet Union for strategic air warfare.[4] The loss of these bases could have been compensated for by building bigger bombers or missiles, more air tankers, or some other alternative, but again only at very sizable cost.

If the major power in free world alliances can strive for military self-sufficiency only at the cost of extreme inefficiencies, the minor powers can much less afford it. For many of them, replacing allied military strength fully with additional strength of their own would be completely out of the question. Their aggregate resources are far too limited. They would have to accept a marked decline in their military strength, hoping that their retreat into avowed neutrality would propitiate potential aggressors.

Thus although partially divergent military purposes among members

---

[3] Chapter 2.

[4] For some disadvantages of U.S. bases near Soviet borders (e.g., for Intermediate Range Ballistic Missiles), see Chapter 18.

of an alliance limit the extent of mutual gain possible from some pooling of their military efforts, great gain may still be possible. This is especially likely to be the case if joint military preparations are keyed to a major aggressive threat that all fear in common, leaving to separate national preparations the problems of meeting various threats that are minor by comparison. Suppose Country A estimates that ten divisions and supporting forces would be optimal for fighting its own "brushfire" wars. However, Country A agrees to raise twenty divisions as its contribution to collective defense against the major threat. These twenty divisions would presumably be designed primarily for meeting the major war contingency. Consequently they might be ill-designed for extinguishing brushfires. But given twenty divisions in readiness to be drawn upon rather than ten, Country A might regard itself as better prepared on balance to handle its own national military purposes, and this without compromising seriously the availability of its forces for the major emergency that the alliance is designed to meet. Both purposes would be met, and there would be some sizable economies realized because the same forces would serve joint purposes.

The above argument clearly must not be driven too far. If military preparations to deter the major enemy are very different in kind from those designed to handle peripheral troubles on a national basis, the argument of joint product economies loses its force. Suppose, varying our example, that the primary contribution desired from Country A is guided missiles and launching sites. This equipment might be of little or no use in dealing with national military contingencies where not much allied support is expected. Then there are no substantial joint product economies in supplying the missiles, and the problem posed by partly divergent national military purposes in an alliance can be seen most sharply. The problem can then be put this way. Should Country A be entitled to credit for contributing to collective defense only to the extent that it supplies missiles and associated installations, or should it be entitled to credit, whole or partial, for the divisions it also chooses to maintain? This question is bound to be central in a consideration of burden-sharing.

In principle, neither extreme position is tenable. Since whatever divisions Country A may choose to raise are likely to be of some positive value to its allies, it can lay claim to making some contribution with them to the alliance. On the other hand, to allow it to claim a full contribution is, from the collective point of view, doubly wrong. To do so would be to condone inefficiency, first, because the divisions, being designed and deployed for national military purposes unshared by its allies, would be ill-suited for alternative collective action. Second, the desire to have Country A specialize in missiles would presumably reflect a judgment that it would be inefficient for it to divert effort to supplying divisions, even if they were designed primarily for collective action. The wrong kind of divisions would compound the inefficiency of their being supplied by the wrong country. So, in principle, Country A should be credited with only a partial contribution for the divisions it supplies. It gets full credit for whatever missile contribution it makes, plus a discounted credit for the divisions it raises. Suppose it maintains ten divisions at an annual cost of $100 million each. For an assessment of the resource burden with which it should be credited, the total cost of $1 billion annually might first be reduced to $600 million because six divisions optimally designed and deployed for collective action are deemed as effective as the ill-designed ten; and the $600 million might then be knocked down to $500 million because other allies could alternatively supply an equivalent fighting strength that much more cheaply.

If some such procedure for discounting contributions were practicable in burden-sharing negotiations, and if resource transfers among members depended on the outcome of such negotiations, an especially powerful incentive could operate for members to tailor their military preparations toward shared alliance purposes. For every dollar Country A puts into missile preparations it would get full credit, compared with half credit for dollars put into divisions. Diverting more of its military spending from divisions to missiles would strengthen the claim that it was doing its share, and hence its right to transfers from other members. Country A might still choose to retain some divisions at the expense of missiles because of her special military purposes, but not as many. Such a burden-sharing scheme would act as a strong spur toward collective efficiency.

But to state the case for seeking international agreement about the costs of alternative hypothetical forces for members is perhaps enough to argue its impracticability. Are Country A's ten divisions really equivalent to only six divisions designed for a different purpose, or are they more nearly equivalent to four or nine? Army planners in Country A might well differ in their private opinions over this range. The experts of other countries might differ still more. The bargaining position that member countries would take on this question would naturally tend to be biased, because their own standings in the assessment of military burdens would vary according to the answer. At the next stage there would also be ample room for honest disagreement complicated by vested interests in the result. Could Country X really supply equivalent divisional fighting power one-sixth cheaper? The relative quality of different national forces would obviously raise some of the most stubborn problems of all. Finally, and most important, the distinction between the military purposes that are truly shared and those that are not is very elusive. Some military objectives may be defined on which all allies agree, say, defense of specified territories against invasion, but the intensity of member interest is likely to vary even for these objectives. And there are likely to be many other objectives shared with various intensities, as well as many other objectives about which allies disagree. For all these reasons, defining the portion of a member's military establishment that is relevant for truly shared purposes is impractical. Consequently negotiations over burden-sharing cannot begin by discounting the military expenditures of allies to correspond with assured common benefit from the results of those expenditures.

The prominent illustration is supplied by NATO. In its narrowest interpretation, the NATO military objective is to protect western Europe against Soviet invasion. Certainly it is the most explicit objective.[5] To this end, a common command has been created in Europe, with some forces of member countries formally "NATO-committed" by assignment to this command. But military contributions are not confined to these earmarked forces, which in any case have been diverted from time to time to special national purposes, for example, French troops in North Africa. The association of particular forces with NATO purposes is doubly blurred in practice because NATO-committed forces serve some national as well as international purposes while ostensibly non-NATO forces are relied upon heavily for common defense. Far and away the most prominent example of the latter is the United States Strategic Air Command (SAC). Uncommitted in any formal sense to a common allied command, and obviously serving a global defense purpose for the United States that is not confined to the North Atlantic Area, SAC is nonetheless regarded by the Supreme Allied Commander in Europe as the main deterrent to Soviet aggression in Western Europe.[6] Therefore it would not make sense to calculate collective military contributions in terms of NATO-committed forces alone. Discussions in NATO have perforce dealt with the total military burdens upon members, and it appears that no attempt has ever been made to isolate the portion of member's military expenditure deemed relevant for common ends.[7] Military burdens are discussed as if all were incurred for commonly shared benefits, an unrealistic but necessary assumption because anything approaching a precise imputation of military benefit country-by-country is manifestly impossible. The restraints upon a military division of labor in an alliance that are imposed by partly divergent national interests are thus treated as if the blame was about equal, with no nation being singled out as a special culprit.

[5] Ismay, *NATO*, p. 32. Cf. Supreme Allied Commander, Europe, *Second Annual Report*, Paris, 1953, pp. 7–8.

[6] *The NATO Letter*, February 1, 1957, p. 28.

[7] Ismay, *NATO*, never mentions the possibility, and his references to member defense expenditures and economic capabilities always refer to total expenditures and resources. See pp. 94, 110.

## MATERIEL SPECIALIZATION

Because the purposes served by national forces can typically only imperfectly be served by allied forces, and nations are all the more reluctant to trust others to serve these purposes when they are so ill-defined and changing, there is a natural tendency to emphasize the opportunities for military specialization that stop short of the forces level. These opportunities probably offer considerably less potential mutual gain, but such gain as they offer can be realized more readily. The obvious case is specialization in producing military equipment. Country A may be determined to supply many divisions of her own despite high manpower costs, but may be willing to rely on Country B for the supply of low-cost artillery. The externally supplied artillery pieces can presumably go anywhere that Country A's forces go, and can be employed for unilateral as well as collective defense. Hence lack of trust in allied support in some military contingencies need not impede matériel specialization to nearly the same extent as it does forces specialization.[8]

This reasoning is reinforced as mobilization base considerations come to play less of a role in rational military planning. If all-out wars must be fought quickly with the stocks of weapons on hand, and if peripheral national wars can be fought with but small additional drains on such stocks, the risk of relying upon outside supplies becomes small for the most likely kinds of possible wars.[9] As this risk diminishes in relative importance in national military planning, one inhibition upon inter-allied specialization in matériel supply becomes less restrictive. An associated consideration, however, is not affected in so clear-cut a fashion. When the image of another war like World War II dominates military planning, the consideration of comparative vulnerability of production sites induces one kind of inter-allied specialization. The ally most distant from the feared enemy has a special advantage in producing arms. It tends to be less vulnerable to enemy bombing or occupation, so its production is more secure. This one consideration alone may tend to lead to its specializing prominently in matériel. But as fears of another World War II subside relative to fears of other military contingencies, especially of the all-out atomic war, this consideration loses much of its force. For the worst contingency, production everywhere is vulnerable and mobilization potential is unlikely to be realized. Consequently one

[8] A special problem is created if the equipment is given away by an ally who stipulates that it be used only for self- or collective-defense. Grant military aid by the United States under the Mutual Defense Assistance Program (MDAP) carries such a stipulation, which sounds innocuous. However, does it preclude recipients from using the MDAP-supplied equipment in military ventures like the Anglo-French conflict with Egypt of which we formally disapprove? If it does, it weakens the value of the aid in allies' eyes. If it does not, it weakens U.S. incentives to supply aid.

[9] Chapter 2, pp. 11-14.

factor operating in the past to expand one kind of arms specialization should operate less strongly now.

When these two effects of diminishing emphasis upon World War II-type planning and mobilization bases are combined, the net effect upon the extent of inter-allied arms specialization is unclear. The volume of inter-allied arms trade should tend to grow as the importance of continuing and increasing flows of matériel in wartime declines relative to the importance of stocks in being. On the other hand, its volume should decline to the extent it had been motivated by special vulnerability considerations that now apply less strongly. But while the change in the volume of trade is uncertain, the change in the kind of trade that should take place is clear. Specialization should be governed more than formerly by the straightforward consideration of who can produce given items most cheaply in peacetime.

Besides the lesser complications posed for matériel than for forces specialization by divergent national interests, another reason for emphasizing mutual gain through arms trade is that tests for mutual gain are less difficult to implement. In the extreme case where more than one member is prepared to produce an identical piece of military equipment, the first test is simply which can deliver the item most cheaply. Progress toward arms standardization is notoriously slow, so the simple test is unlikely to be widely applicable. Typical problems will involve significant qualitative differences in the items compared and variance in delivery dates, and so on, as well as differences in price. Thus the Germans had to decide between buying British Centurion tanks or American M-48 tanks, not a simple comparison. But it nonetheless involves far fewer of the near-intangible political complications besetting a comparison of forces, especially a comparison of one's own forces with those of an ally. The Germans may consider one foreign tank inferior to another, but they should be able to judge reasonably well whether there is enough of a compensating cheapness in price: which tank yields the greatest combat potential for a given budget?

Going one step further, it is surely less visionary to hope that international teams of experts might appraise various sorts of matériel in terms of such a criterion than that they could ever appraise the substitutability of allied forces one for the other. In a voluntary association a nation obviously remains the final judge of where its interests lie and how well they can be served by others. But with military forces securely under its own control, it may be persuaded to accept the advice of international teams about economic sources of arms supply provided that its associates can also be persuaded. The probable mutual gain from arms specialization is easier to identify, and for this reason may be achieved to a greater extent.

So far we have discussed only why the obstacles to concentrating arms production with low-cost suppliers may not be insuperable, and why they should be regarded as less formidable than formerly. But the first question, of course, is how strong the incentives are to overcome these obstacles. Is the potential for mutual gain great or small? Arms production today covers an extremely wide variety of manufactured products. Producing one of them may call upon vastly different skills and materials than another. Consequently one ally, abundantly endowed with the special resources relevant for one kind of arms production, may be much more efficient than another whose special resources lend themselves better to producing another kind. There is a great and growing volume of trade in civilian manufactures among industrialized countries, despite trade barriers, to prove that one country does not dominate the others for all manufactures. On the contrary, the usual pattern is a comparative advantage for one kind, a comparative disadvantage for another. Some tend to think of the United States as the "natural" supplier of military matériel, for example. For many arms it undoubtedly is the "natural" in the sense of efficient supplier. But one need only mention the production of ships and much of their associated equipment for a contrasting example. The American industry requires heavy subsidies to be competitive at all with foreign shipyards in producing civilian ships, and even then it is outpaced in volume by the industries of several smaller countries. There is consequently a presumption of gross inefficiency in centering so much naval production in the United States, a heavy price to offset against any mobilization base gains.

Thus the potential for mutual gain through arms specialization is probably great, first, because nations can pursue their comparative advantages in different lines of production. Second, there are reinforcing possibilities of gain from concentration itself. Economies of scale may be realized by concentrating production with one or a few suppliers, and there is good reason to believe that such economies are likely to be much more prominent for military than for civilian production. The expensive matériel items are typically extremely complex in their technology, and production runs are typically low before extensive or revolutionary model changes occur. There are obvious exceptions. Artillery shells may be fairly simple and cheap to produce in quantity, they may remain fairly well standardized, and production runs may extend into the millions. If shipping them adds considerably to their unit cost, there is good reason accordingly for many members of an alliance to produce their own, each on a scale big enough to realize most or all of any mass-production economies. Circumstances are obviously greatly different in producing modern airplanes or large missiles. To produce such an item one has to learn a lot, one learns mostly by doing, and, if only a few hundred or thousand are to be produced in total, one is still learning how to produce them better when production ceases. As a result unit costs can be expected to decline appreciably the more of the item that is produced in one place. The phenomenon known as the "learning curve" applies.

There is considerable uncertainty about the likely shape of the learning curve in producing various items — that is, about precisely how unit costs will change as the total number produced increases. And there is even some outright confusion in the literature concerning it. But about its existence and importance there is no doubt. Early formulations applied to airframe manufacture that predicted a 20 per cent reduction in unit cost with each doubling of cumulative output have been shown to be unduly simple, but for small production runs cost-savings of this sort are realistic.[10] In an illustrative calculation based on 1954 prices, Asher has estimated that the cost per airframe pound for producing post-World War II fighter aircraft in the United States might be expected to decline from about $25 to about $15 if production were increased from 100 to 1,000 airframes.[11] Such a 40 per cent saving in costs would be a handsome payoff if ten allies concentrated their production of 1,000 airframes rather than splitting it evenly among them. And this payoff would be enhanced to the extent, probably considerable, that their airframe industries were of various efficiencies and they had chosen to concentrate upon the most efficient one.

### THE PAYMENTS PROBLEM

But how is the payoff to be divided among allies? Clearly, in the hypothetical example, this depends upon who pays for the airframes. If one nation produces all the airframes and pays for the lot, giving the equipment away, the gain of its allies is at a maximum. If, in contrast, the producing nation sells the airframes at prices just barely under the competing cost of small-lot production abroad, the gain of its allies is driven to a minimum. There are obvious possibilities for many intermediate solutions that would divide the payoff from more efficient production in varying proportions.

One simple solution to the problem of who pays for matériel is having the nation that uses the matériel pay. This solution is appealing because it is widely regarded as conventional as well as being simple. It corresponds to commercial trade. And it fits a loose alliance whose members trust one another so little that they retain much the same national forces that they would if there were no alliance. But these virtues cannot

[10] For an amplification of all of these points and a careful examination of one industry, see Harold Asher, *Cost-Quantity Relationships in the Airframe Industry*, The RAND Corporation, Report R-291, July 1, 1956.

[11] Asher, pp. 120–121.

conceal the arbitrariness of this solution when applied to a tighter alliance. From the point of view of a member especially proficient at supplying matériel, this solution is fine. It gets paid for its contribution to collective defense the more it specializes in supplying matériel for others and the less it provides forces of its own and matériel for them. The more it does so, the more onerous become the burdens upon other members who specialize in providing forces. The others cannot and should not be expected to welcome an arrangement that so obviously penalizes them. Their objections would probably be aggravated by other factors. Their prospective contribution of blood rather than treasure may seem to them especially meritorious in a way difficult to evaluate in terms of money. And if they have to pay for foreign arms, the added burden upon their balance of payments may confront them with a special economic problem.

The unacceptable arbitrariness of the simple solution to the payments problem lies in confining possible compensation to one kind of military contribution to the exclusion of other kinds. Yet the other kinds, especially troop supply, are if anything more directly tied to truly common defense. Arms, after all, can easily be sold to neutrals, but the commitment to collective defense action is the essence of alliance. Whether arms supply to allies should be compensated for can in principle only be determined by looking at total contributions. And, as we have seen,[12] this means that the total military effort of each ally has to be computed, because the part to be attributed to truly common defense cannot be isolated in practice. In principle, some test of total burdens must be applied to determine whether compensations are in order, and any restriction of the test to particular kinds of burdens is likely to compound arbitrariness in their measurement.[13] If such a total test is supplied, one result is certain. An ally whose contribution consists wholly of supplying arms to its allies will find itself paying for all or a good part of them.

Thus in principle the only "fair" way to solve the payments problem in an alliance is to weigh aggregate contributions in relation to resources, so determining any net resource transfers required to equalize burdens. But defining "fair shares" raises formidable problems and measuring them

---

[12] See pp. 288–289 above.

[13] In practice the conspicuous example of such compounding is to be found in NATO negotiations about financing the "infrastructure," i.e., installations like airfields and pipelines in Europe designed to be used in common by allied forces. Here the allies must agree on cost shares, and they do so in protracted negotiations that end up assigning shares roughly proportionate to the total economic resources of members. Consequently a country gets little credit or discredit in these negotiations for doing much or little in the way of non-infrastructure contributions.

raises still more,[14] not to mention getting international agreement among all parties — a successful outcome for a negotiation in which the measure of one's gain is precisely the loss of others, unlike associated alliance matters where there is the possibility of mutual gain. "Fairness" alone can certainly not be expected to carry enough appeal to overcome these formidable problems. The case for attempting to overcome them must be reinforced by another compelling, if less noble, consideration. In the absence of any burden-sharing agreement, the question of who pays must be answered presumably by *ad hoc* bargaining in each case, bilateral or multilateral as the case may be. Wherever such bargaining results in external support for an ally's military effort, whether in the form of grants of equipment or money, the grantor must be troubled by one doubt above all: In the absence of his support, could and should the recipient have borne the military burden at issue itself? Giving grant support to allies is designed to encourage them to undertake greater military efforts where they are efficient. But in one way it discourages them. The prospect of external support encourages countries to reduce their future domestic military budgets, especially in support of the very military specialties they know their allies are most interested in, in order to generate a claim for outside support: "You wish us to provide X because we are especially good at that specialty? Splendid; our military leaders quite agree. Unfortunately it lies beyond our means." Potential recipients have a natural incentive to strengthen their bargaining position in this way, but this incentive is perverse from the point of view of the grantor.

This perverse incentive problem can obviously be solved if it is demonstrated that an ally is doing all it can. No question of shirking can then arise. If it is efficient for such an ally to assume additional military burdens, their cost must be borne by someone else. But demonstrating that a nation is supporting a military effort up to the limits of its economic capacity is singularly hard to do. In some cases it might easily be convincingly argued that an ally could not possibly support all its military effort alone, including payment for matériel, for example, South Korea or Formosa. Yet even in these cases the question of the proportion of military effort that can and should be self-supported is an open one. In a particular case is it 40 or 50 per cent? This difference may be large in money terms, yet well within the margins of error in any calculation of economic capacity. And when one turns to much more highly developed and richer countries, especially to those that, like the United States and the United Kingdom, have devoted more than four times as great a

---

[14] For a discussion of the technical problems, see M. W. Hoag, "Economic Problems of Alliance," *Journal of Political Economy*, December 1957, pp. 530–532.

proportion of their output to defense during World War II as they are now doing, calculation of economic capacity becomes at once more elusive and more likely to result in estimates that are so high as to be irrelevant for cold war preparedness.[15]

One must then turn from the inapplicable absolute limits to relative burdens. Where it cannot be convincingly demonstrated that an ally is doing all it can, external support of allied military efforts must be defended because the ally is doing all that it should. If it is, suspicions are allayed that external support perversely encouraged the ally to slacken its own efforts. The self-interest of the grantor should impel it to apply a "burden-sharing" test of a sort even if no formal multilateral tests exist. Only by doing so can the grantor be assured that the military effort abroad made possible by its support is genuinely additive. Once assured that it is additive, an efficiency test of comparative cost can establish mutual gain from the external support — the added allied military capabilities are provided so much more cheaply than could be done directly by the grantor nation that any lack of substitutability between an ally's and one's own capability is more than offset. The grantor then generates enough more military capabilities in the form of allied forces to warrant diverting resources from providing capabilities of his own.

For a major power like the United States, overwhelmingly the grantor rather than recipient in its alliances, there are some political advantages in applying such tests bilaterally and informally. Its arrangements are then less hampered by publicity and formal precedents than would be the case if they were derived in multilateral negotiations. At the same time flexible bilateral arrangements have equally obvious disadvantages. All the onus of insisting that an ally is capable of a certain effort is thrown upon the United States, which is put in the invidious position of a big power coercing a small power without any appeal to multilaterally determined standards that would be formally nondiscriminatory. For the United States, leading its allies in the proportion of resources devoted to defense, the bargaining flexibility lost in agreeing to multilateral standards may be compensated for by using those standards to support its bargaining strength and make that strength less resented. In any case, it is clear that any formal burden-sharing scheme must command the support of the major powers, especially of the United States. And if it should command such support, a means of implementing it lies ready at hand. Where such a scheme would call for aid from Ally A to B, aid can move directly or it may be approximated indirectly by less aid from the United States to A and more to B.

[15] See Chapter 4.

## FORCES SPECIALIZATION: SOME OPEN ISSUES

How great the drive is toward any general burden-sharing obviously depends upon how truly collective defense matters become. The more interdependent the military effort of allies, the stronger this drive. The cementing forces are a shared fear of major aggression, roughly agreed objectives of foreign policy, and mutual gain from division of military labor. All of these bear upon the vital choices of the eventualities that military forces are to be designed for, and how wars are to be fought if these eventualities occur — in a word, upon strategy. A strategy may be brought into question for any one of a variety of reasons. In one member country, for example, a different political party may come into power that does not fear aggression from the nation against which the military plans of the alliance had been directed. Or there may be other disrupting political changes. But we want to concentrate here upon possible disruptions arising from technological or economic changes. Because of such changes, what was once a sensible division of military labor among allies promising great mutual gain may be challenged by a new strategy implying much less pooling of effort, less dependence, and accordingly a disinclination to treat the burdens of defense as common.

Again the pertinent case is NATO. In defending Europe, early NATO planning sought double protection. From the outset it was hoped that the retaliatory threat of the American Strategic Air Command would deter the Soviets from attacking. But army and associated forces were sought in sufficient numbers to protect Europe against invasion even if the Soviets were not deterred. In NATO jargon, the main Deterrent was to be supplemented by a sizable Shield. The associated division of military labor was, in some senses, a "natural." Primary but not exclusive responsibility for supplying troops fell to European members. For most of them this responsibility fitted their military traditions, and land armies could presumably be organized more quickly by them than other forces. Their ample manpower, deployed at or close to home, would be far cheaper to maintain than additional American troops. The United States, with its temporary monopoly of atomic weapons and long-range bombers, by default supplied all the relevant strategic airpower at the start. But over the longer run, there were powerful arguments that the United States would remain the efficient supplier of strategic atomic airpower. By the time other NATO members could produce such forces of their own, the Russians also could. The dominant consideration in a deterrent strategy would then become, as it already has, the ability to protect one's striking force so well that effective retaliation against enemy attack is virtually assured. Basing one's striking force far from the enemy and behind a deep radar screen greatly enhances this ability. It drives the enemy to using expensive long-range bombers or missiles while affording one much better possibilities of protection by getting enough warning to launch missiles and bombers or to evacuate bombers. Home-basing strategic airpower for NATO in the interior of the United States offers these tremendous advantages, plus a pooling of some of the costs of air defense (radar especially) with civilian protection, while the great geographic advantage that NATO possesses over the Russians can be exploited by using bases close to and around the perimeter of the Soviet Union for quick refueling.

Thus the NATO strategy was compatible with great gains from radical forces specialization within the alliance, as well as more modest if more easily identifiable gains from matériel specialization. But the very growth of a Soviet air-atomic threat that provides a longer-run efficiency rationale for the old division of military labor in NATO also creates doubts about the continuing desirability of the underlying NATO strategy. It creates doubts, first, because the enormous growth of Soviet military power drastically reduces the security that a dollar spent on Western defense can bring — in effect, it makes the West poorer, because even their growing resources can now buy less security. Hence, their military choices become harder, and NATO powers are naturally more inclined to question whether some capabilities can now be afforded. Specifically, should the double protection of a primarily airpower Deterrent and a primarily land-force Shield continue to be sought? The growing Soviet air-atomic power creates doubt about the NATO strategy, second, because it weakens the credibility of a massive American strategic airpower response to Soviet provocations in Europe. European NATO members may naturally have less confidence in SAC protection when invoking it would be likely to bring massive retaliatory destruction to the United States itself, the power that controls SAC employment.

These considerations give European members reason to ponder the merits of drastically different military preparation for themselves. The alternative that would depart most from the old NATO division of labor, and its rationale, may be briefly sketched as follows:

1. Fearing that SAC employment cannot be relied upon, secure a retaliatory air-atomic capability under one's own control and rely upon it to deter the Russians from attack.

2. Abandon troop and supporting contributions to the Shield because war in Europe would probably bring horrible devastation from the air even if the Shield held for a while and prevented quick Soviet occupation.

3. Raise only such conventional land, naval, and tactical air forces as seem required to take care of one's own colonial and other "brushfire" responsibilities.

In this extreme form, of course, such an alternative implies no national contribution to collective defense whatsoever, rendering irrelevant all talk of burden-sharing and division of labor. This alternative epitomizes the "chain-reaction" feared by NATO commanders as a result of British moves[16] in these directions.

Appraising this and other drastic military alternatives raises the most important issues in defense policy and the ones most difficult to assess. The issues turn critically upon chancy estimates of subjective probabilities and require that very disparate objectives be compared.[17] Should the deterrent be strengthened at the expense of a reduced ability to mitigate disaster if deterrence fails? How much in any event do specific competing measures promise to contribute toward one or both of these objectives? Anyone must necessarily be somewhat uncertain about the wisdom of a major change in defense policy, especially as drastic a change as the one sketched above, although some of its attractions and difficulties are apparent. Its main attraction lies in the possibility of so capitalizing upon modern technology that a quite small strategic air force suffices to pose a severe retaliatory threat to even a major power, say a small force of ballistic missiles that might be expected to penetrate Soviet air defenses by virtue of phenomenal speed and altitude rather than by saturating those defenses with many near-simultaneous arrivals. Consequently the force and its costs might be small enough to be commensurate with the resources of small powers, and self-defense against the worst contingency might become feasible without the encumbrances of alliance. If a nation believes that such a force can be created effectively at reasonable cost, it may stake nearly everything upon deterring war by the retaliatory threat of this force securely under its own control. Because the probability of major aggression is thought to be very low, it may spend far less upon land forces that would be needed to play its part in warding off surface invasion should aggression occur, and may give up the job of defending civilians against air attack. Budgetary economies in these spheres may appear to compensate for the cost of its own little SAC.

However, even little SAC forces can be very expensive. And for European countries, doubts about the payoff of such forces should give them greater pause than the certainty of sizable expense. First, would such forces really give them an independent capability to retaliate, and hence an objective basis for deterring Russia? Second, even if such a basis is provided, would it be translated into a greater subjective apprehension on the part of the Soviets, which it must be if it is to deter them? Doubts on the first score arise partly because European-based

[16] Great Britain, Minister of Defence, *Defence: Outline of Future Policy,* Cmd. 124. Her Majesty's Stationery Office, London, April 1957.

[17] Cf. Chapter 10.

strategic air forces are so close to Soviet air power that protecting these forces remains a formidable problem, while not protecting them subverts a strategy of deterrence by inviting all-out attack. European-based forces are but minutes of jet flying time away from Soviet medium as well as heavy bombers, and thus are exposed to very heavy and accurate bomber attack with warning times little greater than America might receive for ballistic missile attacks. Exposure to Soviet IRBM's would even reduce this warning time. Protecting European-based forces against massive surprise air assault in the face of this geographical disadvantage may be difficult and extremely expensive.

Doubts on the second score should compound those on the first. Assume that some objective basis for an independent deterrent policy is attainable at reasonable cost. One doubt then succeeds another. The evident independent power to retaliate may generate this logic in the Kremlin: "The probability of European Country X's retaliating with a nuclear attack now rises, which influences us not to provoke her. On the other hand, now that they have an independent capability, the probability that the United States SAC will respond to this provocation is lower because the Americans have an excuse for 'contracting out' of any alliance obligation. On balance, the small decline in probability of the enormous American threat being made good outweighs even a sizable increase in the threat posed by Country X with her much smaller SAC. Conclusion: We can feel freer to provoke." In brief, little SAC's in Europe may not enhance European deterrent power either because they are vulnerable or because their existence weakens the bonds of alliance by making an American SAC response less likely.

If a European member is pessimistic about securing an independently effective deterrent for these or other reasons, it may drift toward another drastic alternative that is also incompatible with the old aspirations for an alliance division of labor. It may simply neglect to raise troops for the Shield or to contribute in other ways while relying on the American SAC to deter war, an obviously risky course but an appealingly cheap one. Here there would not be contributions by all, and the burden-sharing question would appear in its nastiest form: Are some members entitled to a free ride?

What should European members contribute primarily — more capabilities in general, highly specialized forces, or a combination of capabilities? [18] Various alternatives will deserve explicit consideration as defense techniques and military positions evolve. At best, however, provision for the security of Western Europe is likely to be expensive.

---

[18] For one possible answer stressing the usefulness of limited-war forces in Europe, and for an elaboration of the NATO argument, see M. W. Hoag, "NATO: Deterrent or Shield?" *Foreign Affairs*, January 1958, pp. 278–292.

In spite of the problems and risks inherent in dependence upon allies, we should include in our consideration alternatives that try to take advantage of a fairly radical division of military labor among the Western nations.

# 16. ECONOMIC WARFARE AND DISARMAMENT

**T**wo more special problem areas are the waging of economic warfare (here including the use of military and economic aid) and the search for ways to achieve weapon limitations or disarmament. Traditionally, economic warfare has been a major topic in discussions of the economics of defense, and disarmament obviously has economic aspects. We shall not present calculations that point toward specific policies for dealing with these problems. We shall simply describe the choices to be made, and discuss some of the considerations that are important in our "way of looking at" the problems.

## ECONOMIC WARFARE AND AID

In the past, major aims of economic warfare were often to reduce the enemy's mobilization base and to bolster one's own. It was hoped that the various actions would deny critical materials to the enemy and impair his strength for war production. There were, of course, other motives for engaging in economic warfare. Sometimes the intent was merely to make a face-saving or disapproving gesture. Besides, "it seems to be a matter of simple good taste not to permit trade with an enemy while a war is going on." [1] But, by and large, the aim was said to be the impairment of the enemy's ability to mobilize or to produce military items. Partly because of the change in the significance of mobilization potential, the emphasis has shifted somewhat in recent years. Economic warfare is perhaps more than ever a gambit in negotiation, aimed at registering disapproval, rallying the support of allies or of one's own people, encouraging the resistance of small countries to subtle aggressions, or gaining friends in uncommitted countries.

In a sense, the reason for having an economic warfare capability is like the reason for having limited-war forces: The ability to counter minor aggressions with force yet without the threat of all-out war has great apparent advantages. Similarly, the ability to counter more subtle threats with something less than the threat of limited war has its attrac-

[1] Thomas C. Schelling, *International Economics,* Allyn and Bacon, Inc., Boston, 1958, p. 489.

tions. Economic warfare, including aid programs, may prevent some nibbling that would otherwise occur; it may prevent or check some threats less expensively than a credible threat of limited war; and it may reduce the over-all likelihood of war. Of course, many of these measures, particularly steps to provide economic assistance, have even more complex aims, and they should not be judged solely in terms of their probable impact on national security. Nonetheless, defense in its broadest sense is one of the major objectives of military and economic aid programs. Certainly it is the objective with which we shall be primarily concerned here.

The traditional measures of economic warfare are probably of little value to the West as far as impairing the enemy's strength is concerned. These measures consist of restrictions on trade that are intended to deny particular materials or avenues of trade to the enemy, achieved by import controls, shipping controls, export controls, and efforts to get other countries to limit certain shipments to the enemy or purchases from him. The possibilities of regulating one's own trade are fairly obvious. Other countries' trade can be influenced by trade agreements, diplomatic efforts, and the blacklisting of neutral traders. Preclusive buying, that is, buying of materials simply to prevent them from reaching enemy hands, is another (usually expensive) device.[2] A traditional counter to these measures is to encourage the building up of stocks and industries that would make one's economy more nearly self-sufficient.

These trade restrictions are difficult to administer and are "among the worst headaches of a defense program."[3] Yet the employment of such measures by the West probably does little to decrease the resources of the Communist bloc relative to those of the West. For during a prolonged cold war these measures, striking at specific resources, make only a trifling dent in the over-all economic strength of a nation. Besides this, they deny to both sides, not just to the enemy, part of the advantages of specialization and trade.

This is not to say that economic warfare cannot affect the strength of a single small country largely dependent on foreign trade. For the Soviet Union to cease buying rubber from Ceylon, or for the West to prevent Ceylon from exporting rubber, would hurt the economy of the smaller country severely. The Soviet Union could threaten considerable damage to the Icelandic economy if it became the sole buyer of Iceland's fish catch. Either the United States or the Soviet Union could injure

---

[2] For more complete discussions of various devices, see Schelling, pp. 487–532, and George A. Lincoln, *Economics of National Security*, Prentice-Hall, Inc., New York, 1954, pp. 521–544.

[3] Lincoln, p. 534.

small countries by "dumping" goods. Our economic isolation of Red China may have significantly retarded its rate of industrial development. Control over Middle East oil by any single power or bloc would be a comparatively potent weapon because it could upset the Middle East and European economies sharply, particularly during an initial period before adjustments could be made. In most instances, nonetheless, the net impact of trade restrictions on the relative strength of major powers is not great. Often their main force and significance is similar to that of a slap in the face. They are part of the process of bluffing and challenging.

Aside from the fact that economic warfare does not do much *economic* damage to the large power blocs, it has its disadvantages to the *West* as a means of probing and bargaining, for it employs a technique, restriction of international trade, that does not show the free world in its best light. In fact, there is much to be said for the opposite tactic of encouraging trade and travel between the two blocs. Unrestricted trade might make possible some economic "penetration" by the Communist nations — for example, strategic placement of personnel or gains of prestige from dumping "loss-leaders" — but freedom is the West's most important product, and it should be displayed prominently. In particular cases, it may seem advisable for Western nations to engage in state trading, partly to offset the impacts of Communist bulk trades on smaller nations. In general, however, freer trade and more extensive travel between the Communist world and the West may redound to the advantage of the free world: the Communist bloc probably has more to lose as a result of interchange than we have.

According to one economist, Albert Hirschman, it may be to the advantage of the West for the smaller countries to have some trade with the Communist bloc.[4] Substantial dependence of smaller nations on trade with authoritarian countries would be undesirable, but zero trade with them is not necessarily optimal. Influence is acquired not only through the possibility of withdrawing existing trade but also through the possibility of launching new trade relationships. Therefore United States monopoly of trade with a smaller country may not deprive the Soviet Union of *all* such influence in that country. The hope for favorable deals with the Soviet bloc may influence a nation as much as the desire to maintain existing trade with the West. Moreover, if the United States dominates this exchange of goods, it gets blamed whenever anything

[4] Professor Hirschman has presented some of his ideas on gaining influence through trade in his book, *National Power and the Structure of Foreign Trade,* University of California Press, Berkeley, California, 1945, and has developed his ideas further in unpublished papers.

goes wrong. Finally, United States monopoly of trade with a smaller nation, and efforts to prevent it from trading with the Soviet bloc, are likely to generate resentment toward the United States. For these reasons, Hirschman believes that for us to dominate trade with smaller nations and for Russia to remain an untried "greener pasture on the other side of the fence" may not make the West as influential as would some intermediate situation in which the smaller nations have some exchange and experience with both blocs.

There is an especially strong case for freer trade among the non-Communist nations. The United States loses many of the gains from its aid programs by denying the recipients a chance to earn something through honest trade. Early in 1957 the United States induced Japan to limit its exports of cotton textiles to the United States. As a part of this agreement, subquotas for particular textiles were set to protect such United States industries as velveteen (3 companies) and gingham (14 companies). Said one Japanese official:

I do not think that Japan stands alone in feeling apprehension over the growing intensity of import restriction in the U.S. It is our sincere desire that the American people take full cognizance of the fact that their every action, however slight or unpremeditated, casts an influence on all the free nations out of all proportion to their original intent.[5]

This sort of policy may appease certain vociferous pressure groups, but it does so at a high cost: An ally sacrifices an opportunity to raise its income by following the tenets of a competitive private-enterprise system; the United States consumer gives up a chance to hire people to work for him at 15½ cents an hour; and, still more important, the free world loses part of its cohesiveness and strength. At the same time, the Soviet Union is beginning to promote trade aggressively.[6]

Let us turn now to a form of economic rivalry that has come to play an increasingly prominent role in the nuclear age — that is, rivalry in dispensing economic assistance. In recent years, United States activities of this sort have cost, very roughly, a billion dollars a year. This amount includes outlays for Point-Four technical assistance, assistance to economic development, the disposition of agricultural surpluses, and a component of defense-support assistance that serves to aid development. The amount does not include private investment abroad or loans by the Export-Import Bank or the International Bank for Reconstruction and

[5] Japanese Government Economist Morio Yukawa, quoted in *Time,* January 28, 1957, p. 91.

[6] The Council for Economic and Industry Research, Inc., *Foreign Assistance Activities of the Communist Bloc and Their Implications for the United States,* a study prepared at the request of the special committee to study the Foreign Aid Program, United States Senate, U.S. Government Printing Office, Washington, D.C., 1957, p. xiii.

Development. Nor does it include military assistance, a substantial portion of which should be counted too, because military aid usually enables the recipient to shift some resources to investment and other uses. (Military aid, of course, directly contributes to the West's security to the extent that it increases the internal security of the recipient, increases collective capability against aggression, and improves the warning system. Here, however, we shall confine ourselves to those aspects of aid that figure in "economic warfare.")

Russian economic assistance has taken the form mainly of loans on attractive terms. By the end of 1956, the Communist bloc arranged to make loans to "underdeveloped" countries amounting to about $1.4 billion, chiefly to finance purchases of capital goods.[7] Interest rates are from 2 to 2.5 per cent, and the credit is granted for periods as long as 30 years. In addition to extending these loans, the Communist bloc provides technical assistance to the underdeveloped countries and trains technicians for them, mainly in the Soviet Union. Several indications, such as recent Soviet propaganda and loans in the process of negotiation, suggest that the Communist bloc may expand these economic-assistance activities.

The free world must continue to include economic aid among the alternative national security measures that merit serious consideration. These measures, like certain other defense activities, have spillover effects on the achievement of other objectives, and these effects should be recognized when decisions about the budget are being made. As far as the improvement of our defense posture is concerned, economic assistance to underdeveloped countries is a rather low-confidence measure. That is, while it may offer valuable gains,[8] we cannot be very sure of even moderate gains. Little is known about answers to the following questions. What effects do various aid programs have on the recipients' investment? What effects on private investment from abroad? What does such investment really do to the recipients' economic development?[9] What impacts would various rates of economic progress have on political development and on political allegiances? What other impacts do aid programs have on political alignments and free-world resources for defense? Certainly we should not expect miracles. After all, "For underdeveloped countries (other than 'defense support' countries) in Asia and Africa with about

[7] *Ibid.*

[8] For a strong statement of possible gains, see Max F. Millikan and W. W. Rostow, *A Proposal, Key to an Effective Foreign Policy,* Harper and Bros., New York, 1957.

[9] Some economists doubt that aid benefits the West at all. Milton Friedman argues that continued aid programs would impair the functioning of competitive private enterprise in the recipient countries, ultimately retarding their growth and weakening the free world ("Foreign Economic Aid," *The Yale Review,* Summer 1958, pp. 500–516).

three-quarters of a billion people, the inflow of American capital and technical assistance in all forms . . . is probably at an annual rate at the present time of between $1 and $2 per capita." [10]

In the face of such uncertainties, we cannot draw up a foreign-aid program that is "required." Yet here, as in so many other cases, there is a tendency to ask, "What program is 'needed' or 'required'?" and "Is it feasible?" as though this were the way to decide upon our foreign-aid activities. As for our capability, if enough other things are sacrificed, it is certainly *feasible* for the United States to devote 50 or 100 billion dollars per year to foreign aid. As for the "requirement," no particular amount of assistance is "necessary," but it may be that the larger the amount of aid (up to a point, and if it is wisely spent), the greater the gain to the free world. The question we need to answer is, "What are the costs and the gains from alternative foreign-aid programs?" The answer, however imprecise and difficult to get, is the kind of information that helps us choose among possible sizes of a program, allocations of aid among countries, mixes of military and economic aid, conditions or "strings" to be attached to loans or grants, and so on. Even here, quantitative economic analysis may be helpful. As in most instances, definitive solutions to these problems cannot be produced by such analysis, but certain relevant effects of alternative courses of action can be traced out. According to one study,[11] data on changes in voting may reflect the impacts of aid on the political vulnerability of the recipient nations. Finally, analysis can compare the cost of military aid with the cost of building similar (though more flexible) United States forces.

In conclusion, a few less conventional means of waging economic warfare may be mentioned. One way of damaging an enemy's economy is to inject great quantities of counterfeit currency. Such action is not unprecedented. Shortly after World War II, the Soviet Union, which had the printing plates, issued enough German occupation marks to cause considerable confusion and concern. Another more subtle policy might be directed against the free world — a policy of inducing instability by being alternately "peace-loving" and "tough." This policy might induce sharply fluctuating defense budgets, price levels, and employment levels in democratic nations, with debilitating effects. Against such a tactic, there is no dramatic counter-measure, but we can hope that voters and policy-makers will not *capriciously* change the size of defense programs and that they

---

[10] Thomas Schelling, "American Aid and Economic Development: Some Critical Issues," in *International Stability and Progress: United States Interests and Instruments,* The American Assembly, Columbia University, New York, June 1957, p. 130.

[11] An application of economic analysis to certain of the alternatives, and an elaboration of some of the above points, are presented by Charles Wolf, Jr., in *Foreign Aid: Theory and Practice in Southern Asia,* Princeton University Press, Princeton, N.J., 1960.

will adopt monetary-fiscal arrangements to alleviate inflations and deflations (see Chapter 5).

### WEAPON CONTROL MEASURES AND DISARMAMENT [12]

Another special problem in defense planning is designing and choosing policies in the light of possible mutually advantageous weapon control and disarmament measures. At best, there are too many ways in which a balance of terror can be unbalanced unless nations can work out effective types of agreements. Perceptive proponents of a strong, well-protected retaliatory force believe that agreement on weapon limitations can supplement that force in maintaining stable and effective deterrence.[13]

Throughout this section, it might be noted, we are thinking primarily of weapon control measures that would reduce the likelihood, or the severity, of all-out war. In this context, the word "disarmament" is something of a misnomer, for it has come to include proposals for observation and exchange of information, for reducing the chance of accidental war, for diminishing the dangers of mischievous acts by small nations, for decreasing the temptation to surprise attack, for mediating between contestants in limited wars, and for cooperating in any situation where the rival powers may have some common interest.

Thus, paradoxically, disarmament has come to mean agreements and measures that often imply the expenditure of *additional* sums on defense or the purchase of extra conventional armaments. (In this nuclear age, disarmament sometimes means armament.) These proposals deserve our most serious attention, not only because some of them might yield huge gains to the United States and the whole world, but also because some proposals could lead more surely than ever to disaster.

What are some of the things that might be done? A few persons urge the traditional pacifist line: let us give up our weapons and trust that the enemy will do likewise. Unfortunately, the situation is much too desperate for anyone to rely on wishes. If we are to preserve the free world — indeed save civilization itself — we must do something more than hope.

More practical (or perhaps more deeply worried) persons urge us to seek major agreements based on mutual advantage, not merely the minor bargains that can rest solely on faith or hope. They observe, quite correctly, that there may be forms of disarmament that would be mutually advantageous. We have to do more, however, than reiterate the urgency of seeking agreements. We must try to trace out specific steps that the

---

[12] In parts of this section, we are greatly indebted to Thomas C. Schelling. Some of the ideas are presented in his paper, "Surprise Attack and Disarmament," in *NATO and American Security,* ed. Klaus Knorr, Princeton University Press, Princeton, N.J., 1959.

[13] For instance, see Thomas K. Finletter, *Power and Policy,* Harcourt, Brace and Co., New York, 1954, pp. 367–402. See also Chapter 18 of the present volume.

United States or other Western nations could take in an effort to achieve weapon control measures.

One of the most important steps is to reexamine our military posture and ask: Are there changes that would give us greater security and a better basis for reaching agreements? Chapters 17 and 18 will discuss some crucial points to be considered in getting a better defense posture for our money.[14] Here we shall mention only briefly a few things that might be done.

We can take various precautionary measures to lower the probability of having war breaking out accidentally. We can reduce the vulnerability of our striking force to insure a strike-second capability. We might also provide larger and more mobile forces for limited war, a visible token of our ability to counter certain aggressions by means other than massive thermonuclear attack on the Soviet Union. Even without explicit agreement, the enemy might find it to his self-interest to use similar forces, eschewing the use of thermonuclear weapons in the resolution of most conflicts. The basis is then laid for both sides to search for ways to limit specific conflicts — to look for conspicuous boundaries and rules that both may tacitly agree to observe. In some circumstances, it may be worthwhile to *announce* that we will observe certain limitations provided that the enemy also does so. Such an announcement might lead to tacit agreement, not because the enemy is a good sport, but because it is really in his self-interest to observe limitations, and these have been made "conspicuous." [15] These things are feasible, however, only if our forces are properly designed.

It should be realized that forces for limited war may make the use of the big deterrent against minor aggressions somewhat less credible. Hence, while this military posture may reduce the chances that peripheral war will turn into all-out war, it may increase the frequency of local conflicts, which always have some potentiality of becoming a thermonuclear exchange. On balance, however, it seems likely that more effective forces to counter local aggressions would reduce the likelihood of an all-out war, clarify the circumstances in which the big deterrent would be used, and provide a more stable basis for negotiations.

[14] See also the excellent treatment of these issues in Henry Rowen's *National Security and the American Economy in the 1960's,* Study Paper for the Joint Economic Committee, 86th Congress, 2d Session, U.S. Government Printing Office, Washington, D.C., 1960.

[15] For a discussion of this and other provocative points concerning tacit bargaining, see Thomas C. Schelling, "Bargaining, Communication, and Limited War," *The Journal of Conflict Resolution,* March 1957, pp. 19–36.

INSPECTION AND CONTROL MEASURES

When crises arise, one nation may attack another to save itself from the other nation's attack to save itself (and so on). At least this danger exists as long as a surprise attack has a chance of destroying the other nation's retaliatory force. Consequently, the rival nations fear each other's thermonuclear force, and neither can trust the assertions of the other. In these circumstances, the significance of inspection is obvious. Neither can afford to disarm, or tie his hands in any way, unless assured that the other is carrying out his part of the agreement. Let us examine some possible control measures in this light.

Consider first an agreement to eliminate all nuclear and thermonuclear capabilities. Suppose each nation prefers no bombs at all to the present situation. Yet each nation knows that if one country cheated, that country could take command. Each nation knows, therefore, that there are powerful incentives to cheat. To prevent any cheating, moreover, would require an extremely effective inspection system, say, mobile teams of inspectors who were free to explore all regions of a country. Unfortunately, it is probably too late for assurance that a nation has *no* hidden nuclear bombs or that there are no sites for launching ballistic missiles. Moreover, it would be very difficult to maintain arrangements for freely roving teams during peripheral conflicts.

Consider next more modest attempts at disarmament — agreements to increase the stability of mutual deterrence. In this case we would accept reliance on deterrence, but would seek ways to damp other destabilizing influences. Agreements that would work in this direction include possible arrangements to limit striking forces, to make them less vulnerable, and to reduce the chances of surprise attack.

Both sides could find moves in these directions advantageous. Each has an interest in making *both* striking forces less provocative to reduce the chances of accidentally triggering a thermonuclear war. Each has an interest in making both striking forces less vulnerable to increase the certainty of retaliation. If we leave our force relatively soft, the enemy may reason that we do not really intend striking second and that he must therefore beat us to the punch. We in turn may figure that he must be planning to strike. The interaction relentlessly increases the penalty for holding back; or, to look at the other side of the coin, it increases the payoff from striking, even though some retaliation would take place.

Since each side should have an interest in reducing the vulnerability *of deterrent forces,* perhaps negotiations along these lines hold promise. In connection with such agreements, Thomas C. Schelling has pointed out another paradox: the larger the initial striking forces permitted, the easier it may be to maintain stability. With each side possessing only a small striking force, a small amount of cheating would give one side dominance over the other, and the incentive to cheat and prepare a preventive attack would be strong. Prevention would again require a highly effective inspection system. And, even if politically acceptable, extremely effective inspection might actually be destabilizing, for it might discover temporary weaknesses in the enemy's retaliatory force and thus give the discoverer an inducement to launch a preventive attack.[16]

With each side possessing, say, several thousand missiles, however, a vast amount of cheating would be necessary to give one side the ability to wipe out the other's striking capability. Consequently, such a thorough, foolproof, and hard-to-achieve inspection system might not be prerequisite to agreements.

Another suggestion of Schelling's is that nations might also seek arrangements to prevent either one from starting a war through misinterpretation of ambiguous reports about the other's actions. At minimum, we might establish a way for either nation to clear up ambiguity *if it wishes to do so*. Suppose there is an accidental nuclear explosion in one country or, during a local war, a large group of bombers is sent out to deliver small nuclear or conventional bombs. Each side will be fearful of a preemptive strike by the other and for that reason may itself consider a preemptive strike. Anxiety will mount rapidly. A quick decision will have to be made. In this situation each side may desperately want to convey to the other that it had, or has, no intention of attacking. We need some means for the nation initiating the provocative incident to prove quickly that it is not planning a surprise attack. Or a way for both nations to prove simultaneously that they are not launching attacks. Mere assertions will not be enough, but parading corroborative evidence before inspectors or radar or television cameras may be reassuring. To be sure, proof will become increasingly difficult when striking forces consist largely of missiles, but this is all the more reason for hard thinking about a *modus operandi* for situations of this sort.

We should also be thinking *in advance* about alternative stands to be taken in the event of likely contingencies (such as the crises over Lebanon, Suez, Berlin, and Quemoy) : steps to reduce commitments when they serve little purpose; unilateral announcements of positions that might be bases for tacit agreement in emergencies; advance plans to make dramatic proposals ("meet you any time any place") if certain situations occur; threats to be made in certain contingencies; and actions to make threats credible.

To elaborate on the last point, a nation can take steps to make its

---

[16] As an example of such a temporary weakness, Schelling mentions the occasion when a hurricane crippled our force of B-36's ("Surprise Attack and Disarmament").

threats or offers believable. A threat can be made more credible mainly by proving that the nation has the ability to carry it out. Or a threat can be rendered more convincing by making commitments or otherwise increasing the costs of *not* carrying it out, or even by showing that the decision is partly out of one's control. This is an old tactic — burning one's bridges behind him — that has many variants. When to use which variant in the course of bargaining is a most serious choice nowadays, for the consequences can be grave indeed.

With respect to each proposal or possibility, we should examine our ability to enforce it, its efficacy, and its other effects (if any). We should consider the validity of the purpose of a scheme (say, to reduce the danger of war by false alarm or to reduce the temptation to sneak attack), how well it meets the purpose, how it affects United States force requirements and operations, how it complements or interferes with unilateral security measures, how it affects the likelihood of deterring peripheral aggressions, what intelligence it provides to the participants in the scheme, and what problems of security arise in discussing the proposal with allies or with potential enemies. We should also check thoroughly the possibilities of enforcing the agreement, with particular reference to problems of inspection, communication, and the interpretation of evidence.

Consider a scheme that permits inspection of each side's strategic air operations, with aerial reconnaissance and ground observers. The scheme might be designed to yield advance warning of an attack, hence to make a deliberate surprise attack less likely to succeed, and hence to deter it. We have to look at the purpose of the scheme (warning) and ask whether we could in fact use the warning if we got it, and what operational changes permit us to make better use of such warning. With respect to the efficacy of the scheme, we would consider just how likely it is that the scheme, if put in effect, would in fact yield evidence of preparation of an attack, and how ambiguous that evidence would be, assuming that the enemy adapted to the scheme in a way that minimized the warning it would yield. As to enforcement, we would have to consider the problem of keeping the inspectors alert and in instant communication with governmental and military officials through some means that had minimal proclivity toward false alarm or susceptibility to enemy counterfeit.

With respect to breaches of the agreement, we would have to consider what kinds of spoofing the system might be vulnerable to, and whether such spoofing would be recognizable as such and therefore be interpreted as evidence of bad faith. And since perpetual inspection inevitably provides information that might be useful in planning an attack, we would have to adapt our air operations to the fact that they were being continuously watched. This might mean the elimination of flying schedules that, if closely observed, yielded predictable periods or areas of vulnerability, and this in turn might mean higher operating costs. The question of whether the scheme can tolerate the occurrence of limited war — for example, Soviet inspectors on SAC Far Eastern bases during an invasion of Quemoy — is another complication that must be investigated.

Thus there are several types of effort that would help us explore the possibilities of weapon control measures and disarmament. First of all, we need a relatively stable situation of mutual deterrence to give nations a chance to bargain. In the West, this calls for improved limited-war capabilities and especially the protection of the deterrent force (see Chapter 18). The latter is particularly crucial at this stage in the search for disarmament. Second, we should have more emphasis than ever before on the skillful and thoughtful design of alternatives in bargaining. This may mean allocating more resources and personnel to this task. It means thinking harder than ever before about agreements that might be mutually advantageous — searching carefully for first steps, "conspicuous focal points," rules upon which bargainers might agree. And third, we need untiring negotiation. The possible gains from these measures may be considerable. The possible losses from bad bargains can be disastrous. An economical allocation of our resources surely calls for sizable and efficient efforts devoted to this defense mission.

# 17. MOBILIZATION, CIVIL DEFENSE, AND RECUPERATION

**O**ther special aspects of defense planning are steps to facilitate mobilization and recuperation (the latter in the event that all-out war should occur). This chapter, like the others in Part III, outlines some of the choices that confront us and emphasizes the major factors to consider in comparing the alternatives.

## "WORLD WAR II" MOBILIZATION

One option that deserves our attention, since the United States has continued to spend money on it, is to maintain a base for the kind of mobilization that occurred in World War II. In the United States, much emphasis has been given to measures for this purpose, including the provision of a stockpile of raw materials, standby facilities or equipment, and plans for wartime economic organization and controls. Capacity targets for specific industries have been set and subsidies or other inducements, such as accelerated amortization, offered to insure their being met. In addition, extensive stockpiling of tools and critical materials whose overseas sources might be cut off in wartime has been undertaken to round out the base for production.

This emphasis is understandable. After all, in the past a mobilization base was almost the sole defense preparation that appeared to be called for prior to the outbreak of war. Moreover, only yesterday (or so it seems) this sort of mobilization proved its worth in the Second World War. It is only natural to ask: How could we do better next time? To work out better mobilization plans after the war is as hard to resist as working out better repartee after the party.

Unfortunately, preoccupation with this kind of mobilization base in the nuclear era is dangerous. It can not only lead to the diversion of resources into activities that have become useless. It can also obscure the issues and prevent consideration of appropriate ideas and measures. The basic difficulty is that mobilization is visualized as a one- to two-year conversion of the total economy. Future conflicts, however, are not likely to give us time for conversion. We will probably have recurrent crises, like those in Korea, Quemoy, Lebanon, and Berlin, but these should not call for massive response of the *total* economy. In short, plans to mobilize our industrial power are appropriate only for the kind of war that is least likely. For that unlikely case our economic position is strong enough that we hardly need insurance in the form of two-year raw material stockpiles and the like.

For the catastrophic contingency of thermonuclear war, we cannot contemplate plans for any large-scale war production. We must contemplate disaster and plan to prevent it or, if it occurs, to preserve a basis for recuperation. For limited wars, we need forces-in-being and flexible reserves that can be called up quickly — not a base for mobilization on a massive scale. To repeat, the World War II mobilization base constitutes preparation for the kind of war that is now least likely. To be sure, that kind of war is not inconceivable. But to insure the nation against it is like insuring oneself against being run over by a horse and buggy. Most sensible people apply their insurance premiums against more likely contingencies.

On the surface, it has apparently been accepted for some time that we should put our resources into other kinds of preparations. This view has pervaded congressional hearings for several years.[1] During the second half of the 1950's, the press mentioned repeatedly that mobilization plans were losing favor,[2] noting (in 1956) that two thousand plants

[1] For example see *Department of Defense Appropriations for 1958,* Hearings before the Subcommittee of the Committee on Appropriations, U.S. Senate, 85th Congress, 1st Session, U.S. Government Printing Office, Washington, D.C., 1957.

[2] For instance, see "U.S. Strategy Takes a New Turn," *Business Week,* August 18, 1956, pp. 149–156; "No More 'War Conversion' for Industry," *Business Week,* March 30, 1957, p. 43.

had been removed from the Pentagon's Register of Planned Mobilization Producers. What was then the Office of Defense Mobilization gradually became concerned about what kind of stockpile is most important in the nuclear age.[3] Officials considered the conversion of "some stockpiling programs that are really price-support schemes into new, separate programs that will recognize them for what they really are." [4] Under the Office of Civil and Defense Mobilization, which combined the functions of the Office of Defense Mobilization and the Federal Civil Defense Administration, purchases of strategic materials for the stockpile dwindled and were finally scheduled to cease.

Unfortunately, this recognition that mobilization-base planning is out of date [5] emerged too late and influenced policy too slowly. As late as 1957–58, the United States was still spending resources to add to a $6.5 billion stockpile of "strategic materials" such as bauxite, rubber, tin, and many other items that would be useful for full industrial mobilization but would be abundant (in the form of scrap) in the event of nuclear war. In addition, under the Defense Production Act of 1950 (as amended), the General Services Administration was subsidizing in various ways the expansion of our capacity to produce "critical materials." The General Services Administration fixed incentive prices for mica, mercury, beryl, and manganese. It guaranteed markets for copper, aluminum, fluorspar, molybdenum, titanium, and zinc. It stimulated the expansion of our machine-tool capacity by stockpiling special tools, and expanded government-owned facilities for producing nickel. Under the same Act, other agencies purchased certain agricultural products, such as castor beans, industrial oils, hemp, and Egyptian cotton, and subsidized exploration for "strategic" minerals and metals. Also, the United States devoted resources to refining plans for economic stabilization, direct controls, and the other trappings of full mobilization.

Even as we moved into the 1960's, our stockpiling policy reflected the old ideas to a considerable extent. We stopped purchasing critical materials on the grounds (officially) that our "requirement" for these items was only for a three-year war — not for a five-year war. We still maintained the stockpile. There is too much truth in the facetious remark (made in another connection) of the former Secretary of Defense:

[3] *The Economist*, "Stocktaking at the Stockpile," November 9, 1957, p. 494.

[4] *Wall Street Journal*, September 26, 1957, p. 1.

[5] In the Soviet Union, this recognition has been equally laggard among military commentators (though evidently not among policy-makers). A book recently published in Moscow gives major emphasis to the importance of economic war potential in the traditional sense (A. N. Lagovskii, *Strategiia i ekonomika*, Voennoe Izdatel'stvo Ministerstva Oborony Soiuza SSR, Moscow, 1957, reviewed by Oleg Hoeffding in "Strategy and Economics: A Soviet View," *World Politics*, January 1959, pp. 316–324).

*Mr. Scrivner.* Has any of the old equipment, any of the old conventional stuff, been kicked out?

*Secretary Wilson.* We finally got rid of the carrier pigeons. We finally made that one.[6]

A further cost to the nation is incurred when we restrict imports (such as oil) allegedly to maintain domestic production of basic materials and an industrial mobilization base. In addition we sometimes award contracts in such a manner as to keep contractors tooled up for expanded rates of output and to have standby capacity in "war industries." This excess capacity is not designed to get troops overseas quickly if a limited war breaks out, nor is it protected from nuclear attack. It is unlikely therefore to be useful in limited war, all-out war, or recuperation. The costs of this policy are extremely difficult to estimate because they are mingled inextricably with procurement and development costs. They probably added up in the 1950's to at least a billion dollars a year. It has been suggested that developing the DC-8 would have cost twice as much had it been developed as a defense item — chiefly because of extra tooling to maintain a mobilization base.

Many of our moves toward "readiness" turn out, upon close examination, to be moves toward a mobilization base that would be "faster" yet still of dubious value. It is argued, for example, that the draft machinery must be maintained because we will not have the time that was available for mobilization in previous wars. This sounds like a new strategy of readiness — of having our manpower on an alert status. Actually, however, keeping the draft machinery is far from holding manpower in a state of readiness.[7] On the contrary it points explicitly toward a time-consuming form of mobilization rather than toward the use of forces-in-being or calling up of trained reserves.

Much of our personnel reserve program turns out to be virtually old-style mobilization planning. We have a ready reserve that has weekly training sessions and two weeks of field training each year. In addition there is the standby reserve that does not meet at all. In the hearings pertaining to this legislation and in subsequent hearings on appropriations, the need for readiness rather than mere numbers in a modern reserve force was clearly recognized. Moreover, the services have *tried* to work toward a truly ready reserve. Yet, to a considerable extent, the presently planned reserves would contribute little to the more probable kinds of war.

This fact is indicated first of all by the composition of the reserve

[6] *Department of Defense Appropriations for 1958,* Hearings before the Subcommittee, House of Representatives, 85th Congress, 1st Session, Part 1, U.S. Government Printing Office, Washington, D.C., 1957, p. 242.

[7] The remarks here pertain only to this *one* argument for the draft, namely that it produces a state of "readiness."

force (including the National Guard). Some of the reserves have skills that would be useful in deterring nuclear attack. Only forces-in-being, however, are likely to serve this purpose. On the one hand, if a surprise attack occurred, reserve personnel might be decimated and disorganized by the first enemy strike, and would in any event not have served to deter the attack. On the other hand, if the uneasy balance of terror persisted, such reserves would again be of doubtful utility. They would provide no deterrence unless called up long before warning of enemy attack. Advance calling up of such reserves, however, like advance evacuation of our cities, might invite a preemptive attack by the enemy.

Reserves might be invaluable for recuperation, but plans for this contingency have not been made, and the men are not being trained for this task. Part of the reserves have been fighter-interceptor units (25 wings flying F-86D's) that might be able to carry out their function — *if* enough warning is received, *if* the threat consists of bombers, and *if* the units have up-to-date equipment. Part of the reserves might be valuable in limited wars except that few of them could be mobilized quickly enough. It took 7 to 9 months, on the average, to get National Guard Divisions ready for Korea, and the reserves under the new program will probably have no better advance preparation. Many "ready" reservists will have had only 6 months' active duty, and many will actually get little periodic training.[8] Moreover, while the need for *quick* action has increased since Korea, we are not scheduling much more mobility than we had at that time. We have little airlift even for regular forces, let alone for the reserves.

In short, for these more probable kinds of war, the reserves as currently planned do not have as much to offer as they might. What they seem to be suited for mainly is another World War II mobilization; but if this is called for, the creation of new forces at the time would serve the purpose almost as well. In just the right circumstances, of course, it is conceivable that these reserves would be valuable — say if a large-scale but limited war lasted a long time yet not long enough for the introduction of newly created forces. The possibilities of this occurring depend a good deal upon the preparations and tactics of the enemy. Unfortunately, he does not appear to be tailoring his plans to fit our reserve program.

To sum up, the nation has been devoting several billion dollars a year to preparations for an outmoded kind of mobilization. These preparations constitute insurance against the kind of war that is least likely to occur and in which the United States would have an advantage anyway. Even though this mistaken emphasis on World War II techniques

---

[8] S. L. A. Marshall, "How Ready Is Our Ready Reserve?", *The Reporter*, October 3, 1957, pp. 16–18.

has been partly corrected, there is still cause for concern. For this emphasis is a symptom of a disability that could be disastrous — namely, a dim and erratic recognition of the implications of new developments. Too often we see, and act on the basis of, only the superficial implications of changed circumstances. We draw the type of conclusion that the director of the United States satellite program reached in the fall of 1957: When asked what the implications of the second Soviet satellite were, he replied, "The launching of the second Soviet satellite indicates . . . that the Soviet Union has a capability of launching satellites at a rate of one a month." [9]

## ECONOMIC STRENGTH AS A DETERRENT
## OF LESSER AGGRESSIONS

In one sense of the term, mobilization potential may still serve as a powerful deterrent — not of thermonuclear attack but of lesser aggressions and limited wars. That is, potential aggressors may sometimes restrain themselves when tempted to start peripheral conflicts because their actions might provoke the United States or other Western nations into increasing their national security budgets and expanding their forces of all varieties. The Korean War caused the United States to get its guard up in this fashion and was surely a mistake therefore from the standpoint of the Communist bloc. Again it should be noted, however, that this deterrent of peripheral actions is really the capacity to increase the defense budget and thereby improve our posture for dealing with all cold and hot war challenges rather than the capacity for industrial mobilization during a conflict like World War II.

### RAPID MOBILIZATION FOR LIMITED WARS

There is a kind of mobilization for which the nation should prepare, but the preparations are different from those described above. This mobilization comprises the rapid calling up, equipping, and transporting of reserve units when peripheral conflicts occur. The importance of forces for limited war has been widely discussed. [10] The ability to counter certain aggressions without threatening total war could probably prevent some nibbling that would otherwise take place. In maintaining such a limited-war capability, reserve forces and their mobilization may have a critical role.

Let us consider personnel reserves first. The kind of personnel that would probably be most useful are those that could be employed in

[9] *New York Times,* November 4, 1957, p. 10.
[10] See Chapter 2 and the references cited there. The difficulties of relying solely on massive retaliation are brought out well in Finletter's discussion of the situation in Southeast Asia (*Power and Policy,* Harcourt, Brace and Company, New York, 1954, pp. 141–168). See also Chapter 18, pp. 350–354.

peripheral conflicts in a few months' time.[11] Reserves for this purpose can be kept in a state of readiness, for their missions would make use of fairly simple conventional skills that would not be rendered obsolete every couple of years. If the techniques of fighting limited wars are revolutionized, previously existing reserves will have to be retrained or replaced. (Or perhaps reserves will be utterly useless.)

These men would differ from customary reserves, however. They would have to be genuinely ready — constantly undergoing some training, and always available for being called up immediately. Otherwise they would be of little more use than freshly drafted troops. Money would have to be made available for training, drills would have to be more than meetings, and periodically there would have to be realistic dry runs of the mobilization and deployment of these reservists.

In connection with deployment, some special reservists might be mentioned, namely, those trained to operate transport vessels and aircraft. The possibilities of "Dunkirk" [12] troop and supply movements need a good deal of exploration. The Air Force has run "live" exercises such as Operations Pine Cone and Sixteen Tons[13] to test the use of reserve troop carrier units. The right kind of mobilization planning calls for many more experiments and dry runs. It may be possible to effect a Dunkirk partly by air with reserve pilots and aircraft borrowed from airline companies or diverted from other uses. If it is, however, it will require much experimentation, planning for pre-positioned supplies, and so on.

Without these activities, the value of the reserve forces will be sharply reduced. Mobility is almost as important for these reserves as for the regular forces-in-being. Experience in recent years suggests that prompt deployment of both will become increasingly vital to national security.

The fundamental lesson [of Oman] is the need for speed and mobility, and for well-trained, specially equipped ground troops as a "fire brigade" to put out little fires before they can become big conflagrations. The power and speed of modern communications and the effectiveness of modern propaganda is such that a little conflict anywhere in the world can become a major political issue and perhaps a big war unless it is quickly ended.

First news of the Oman revolt was revealed on July 19; it was not until Aug.

[11] We are referring to true reserves whose civilian activities are non-military, not to members of a "Reserve Technician System" who perform military tasks as civilians but have reserve status so that they can be put into uniform and kept on the job in emergencies. Members of this "technician system" form part of the forces-in-being to be retained, not part of a reserve to be tapped, on mobilization day.

[12] We have in mind the emergency deployment of troops, not merely their rescue and withdrawal!

[13] *Department of Defense Appropriations for 1958,* House of Representatives, Part 1, p. 238.

11 that a British-supported column, after having toiled for ninety-six miles across a barren, hot desert, captured Nizwa, capital of the Imam of Oman.[14]

This is not to argue, as some do, that naval transport of limited-war forces, including reserves, is too slow to be of any use. To be sure, forces delivered during the first few days will be of crucial significance, but those delivered up to several months after the start of hostilities will also play a vital role in many situations. (Unless this is true, *any* reserve program will be virtually worthless.) It should be recalled that the enemy, too, at least in many trouble spots, will have to move troops slowly. Reserves transported by sea can therefore be valuable. We should be exploring the use of reserves in fast mobilizations and deployments by both sea and air, weighing their respective costs against their possible usefulness.

Let us turn next to equipment reserves for this kind of mobilization. The same general principles apply. Weapons and supplies should be relatively simple to use so that they can be handled by reservists who are not spending 8 hours a day in training. Whatever their equipment, it should be ready to go by the time the reserves are mobilized. In other words, it should be possible in about a month's time to demothball, or complete the production of, any items that the reserve units do not already have. And some reserve units should be fully equipped in advance for almost immediate deployment. In the case of troop carrier units, as noted before, the transport aircraft might come from the Civil Reserve Air Fleet (planes of the commercial airlines that are earmarked for such purposes) and from other uses.

To provide certain items of equipment, it might be economic to adopt plans similar to the Air Force's "industrial production readiness policy." In order to meet requirements for extra weapons or for spare assemblies in the event of a contingency, the Air Force often arranges for contractors to hold extra inventories of materials and major parts.[15] To hold these inventories is cheaper than fabricating and storing the end-items, yet these end-products can, in an emergency, be produced within 30 days. One reason this policy is cheaper is that if the end-items are never required, the materials and subassemblies can be shifted directly to other uses, while the end-items, being more highly specialized, have less salvage value.

This arrangement should not, of course, apply to weapons for the

[14] Hanson W. Baldwin, "The Lessons of Oman . . .", *New York Times,* August 15, 1957, p. 4. See also Edward L. Katzenbach, Jr., "The Military Lessons of Suez," *The Reporter,* November 29, 1956, pp. 11–13.

[15] This arrangement appears to be economic only in contracting with "first tier vendors" for selected high-cost items.

desired capability in being. It should apply only to spares and requirements for contingencies. Equipment for reserves are in the last-named category, and major items for some units might therefore be held as bulges in the pipeline rather than as mothballed end-items. Note that this kind of "production readiness" is skies apart from standby capacity for industrial mobilization.

Once again, the importance of taking into account the enemy's response to one's policies is worth emphasizing. The value of different types of reserves and degrees of mobility depends upon the enemy's capabilities and counter-policies. If the enemy has or acquires airlift for large forces-in-being, the value of mobile regular forces to the West is high relative to reserves. If the enemy relies on reserves and slow transportation, the value of ready reserves to the West is higher than it would otherwise be. As for the Soviet Union, it has large forces-in-being and apparently plans for considerable airlift capability; but so far it relies to a great extent on slower transport and is said to maintain a tremendous reserve force that can be mobilized in 30 days. In evaluating its reserves and plans for quick mobilization, the West should consider carefully the likely responses by the Soviet Union and other nations.

## MOBILIZATION PLANNING AFTER A DISARMAMENT AGREEMENT

Another kind of mobilization that may become important is the post-disarmament type. Suppose the major powers do reach agreement on some form of weapon limitation or even of disarmament. Like an altered enemy response, agreement on almost any point will affect the types of reserve and mobilization programs that make sense — indeed the types that are permissible — and their worth. The West, and also its enemies, would find forces-in-being cut or limited, probably increasing the worth of ready mobile reserves.

Moreover, if an agreement were reached, we (both sides, in fact) would have to prepare for possible revocation of the bargain. That is, we would have to be prepared for the sudden deportation of our inspectors or sudden word that the ban was being violated. We would have to be prepared to resume the atomic race immediately in order to re-establish an effective deterrent.[16] Otherwise the enemy, facing no deterrent, might dispose of the free world once and for all. More generally speaking, we would have to keep a springboard from which to resume tests, build up missile capabilities, or take whatever steps had been banned.[17] In

---

[16] Many of these considerations were noted a decade ago by Ansley J. Coale in "The Nature of a Post-Agreement War," *The Problem of Reducing Vulnerability to Atomic Bombs,* Princeton University Press, Princeton, N.J., 1947, pp. 10–38.

[17] In this connection the West must be careful not to enter into agreements that would give the U.S.S.R. a superior springboard from which to leap if the bargain were renounced.

other words, we would have to maintain a kind of mobilization base. But note that in this case too the preparations would be radically different from keeping the old-style base for full industrial mobilization.

## CIVIL DEFENSE AND RECUPERATION [18]

Still another kind of "build-up" or rather "build-back" that may call for advance preparation is recovery from an all-out nuclear war. This process of recuperation, though in some ways related to mobilization, would be vastly different from the process of expanding munitions output and would require a very different sort of preparation. A few years ago, it is true, the aim of protective measures was conceived of as the preservation of a base for mobilization. After absorbing the enemy's atomic bombs, we were supposed to rally around our stockpile of machine tools and Chinese hog bristles (essential for paint brushes) and overwhelm the enemy with our munitions output. Fortunately, this notion is losing its grip on our thinking.[19] There are occasions when mobilization is in order, but the period following a thermonuclear attack is not likely to be one of them. It seems to be sensible, therefore, to think of providing a base for survival — a "recuperation base" rather than a "mobilization base."

There are several circumstances in which we would wish to take steps to protect civilian society. (1) We might decide to play the game very boldly, using a menacing SAC to deter lesser aggressions than attacks on Europe or the United States. In order to have a greater chance of deterring lesser aggressions, we would accept a smaller chance of deterring a surprise nuclear attack. In this circumstance, we would certainly want to expand civil defense (which might then be labeled "civil offense") and try to protect the population and the economy. (2) The Soviet Union might adopt a "civil-offense" posture, and we might find ourselves, whether we like it or not, in a civil-defense race.[20] (3) Even if the rival powers do decide to rely on mutual deterrence — even if they should decide not to protect cities on a *massive* scale — each would surely wish to take some steps toward a recuperation base as an insurance policy against total disaster. Thus there are circumstances in which substantial civil-defense measures would be called for. Before we consider civil-

[18] In this section we are particularly indebted to Herman Kahn of the RAND Corporation and Paul Clark, formerly with RAND and now at Williams College. A valuable general reference is *Civil Defense,* Hearings before a Subcommittee of the Committee on Government Operations, House of Representatives, 85th Congress, 2d Session, U.S. Government Printing Office, Washington, D.C., 1958.

[19] This is not in the least to imply that *all* stockpiling is unwise. Stockpiles designed to help us survive an attack, or stockpiles of end-items to assist rapid mobilization for limited wars, may be of great value.

[20] Although the Soviet Union has not done much to date, its civil-defense activities have been increasing, with emphasis so far on civil-defense educational programs and reinforced construction in new buildings (giving shelter against moderate blast).

defense policies, however, let us examine recuperation possibilities in general.

### RECUPERATION POSSIBILITIES [21]

If we try to visualize future weapons, types of attack, and scales of attack — say in the late 1960's or the 1970's — the outlook for a post-attack civilization is indeed bleak. It is especially bleak when we consider the likelihood of still further weapon developments. If one projects the recent trend in military technology, he foresees that weapons in great numbers with tremendous blast, thermal, and radiological effects will be possible. Missile attacks and new tactics that give little warning will be feasible. In addition, there will be technological developments that we cannot yet imagine. Recuperation may be as impossible in real life as it is in Nevil Shute's vivid fictional account of "the war that *really* ended war." [22]

It is not certain, however, that things will turn out this way, and we should not act as if it were certain. Suppose the United States was attacked. Our protected retaliatory force would divert to itself many enemy missiles that would otherwise destroy cities. In fact, the enemy might deliberately adopt a strategy of minimizing damage to cities in his first strike. Our retaliatory force might in return destroy enough of the enemy's power and organization to thwart subsequent salvos. In this way, damage to us (or to both economies) might be held down to levels that permitted survival. Or, suppose that we had enough unambiguous warning of impending attack to get our strike in first, receiving only the enemy's retaliatory attack (still a frightful blow, probably, but not as heavy as his originally scheduled strike). Furthermore, there could conceivably be startling developments in active defenses that would keep damage within finite limits.

Once such contingencies are envisaged, one can see that protective measures for the economy and recuperation planning have possibilities. Such measures might in fact make a big difference in our chances of survival and in the rate of recuperation.

Let us review some quantities similar to the ones mentioned in Chapter 2. In the United States, about 70 per cent of manufacturing[23] is carried on

---

[21] More details and additional considerations are discussed in *Report on a Study of Non-Military Defense*, Report R-322-RC, The RAND Corporation, July 1, 1958, pp. 23–31. See also Herman Kahn's article, "How Many Can Be Saved?" *Bulletin of the Atomic Scientists*, January 1959, pp. 30–31.

[22] This is the title of S. L. A. Marshall's review in *The Reporter*, August 8, 1957, pp. 50, 52. Shute's book is *On the Beach*, William Morrow, New York, 1957.

[23] The percentage is higher for some aggregates other than manufacturing, e.g., finance, insurance, and real estate; and is lower for others (such as mining). For narrower categories the percentage may be close to 100, but it is usually possible to find reasonable substitutes for items in these categories.

within the 150 most populous Standard Metropolitan Areas. The situation will be roughly the same in 1970. Hence the delivery of perhaps two hundred very large warheads could destroy 70 per cent of our manufacturing capital. To destroy much more than that percentage, however — say 80 per cent — would require the delivery of several hundred additional weapons. When allowances are made for defective and inaccurate missiles, it is clear that to demolish 80 per cent of United States capital would require a large attack. It goes without saying that this level of destruction would be catastrophic. And yet, if the initial period of disorganization and hysteria could be bridged, the survivors could probably get an economy going again.[24]

"CIVIL OFFENSE"

Since there *are* possibilities of recuperating, it is sometimes urged that we put tremendous resources into protecting the economy in order to engage in "civil offense." An enemy can scarcely doubt our determination to strike back against direct attack. But he may not believe that the United States would really punish other aggressions by launching a nuclear blow, risking (or perhaps insuring) a counterblow against the United States — *if the economy is unprotected*. Massive retaliation in these circumstances is not a very credible threat and therefore may fail to deter the enemy from aggressions short of direct attack on the United States. Steps to protect the civilian economy might steel our nerve and, more importantly, convince the enemy that we would risk a nuclear counterattack in order to punish major aggressions. In bargaining with an enemy or issuing ultimata, we would evacuate cities or proceed to deep shelters as a "show of force" to convince the enemy that we meant business.[25]

An argument that may be pertinent is that Britain and France did not resist German aggression in 1938 because — given their deficiencies in active and passive defenses — they doubted their ability to survive attacks from the air.[26] After Munich they resolved

that never again would they be put in the position of having to surrender to a similar threat. It is significant to remember that the measures suggested to avoid a recurrence of the debacle were almost exclusively concerned with the provision

[24] For some rough estimates of the time required for recuperation in different circumstances and with alternative policies, see *Report on a Study of Non-Military Defense,* pp. 26–30.

[25] There is a good discussion of this strategy in Kahn, pp. 31–32.

[26] Edward M. Earle, "The Influence of Air Power Upon History," *The Yale Review,* Summer, 1946, reprinted in Gordon B. Turner (ed.), *A History of Military Affairs Since the Eighteenth Century,* rev. ed., Harcourt, Brace and Company, New York, 1956, pp. 603–604.

of planes and more planes, anti-aircraft batteries, air-raid shelters, and civilian defenses.[27]

Of course, today's threat may be so huge that protective measures will not appreciably stiffen the backbone or increase the credibility of massive retaliation. Suppose certain "hardening" measures would only reduce mortalities from 60 million to 40 million and preserve the basis for "near-poverty" instead of "utter destitution." Would these brighter prospects reinforce our resolution in the event, say, of aggressions in the Middle East?

Even if these protective measures do steel our resolve, the policy has grave disadvantages. To the extent that it made use of time-consuming movements of the population, it would give no protection or insurance in case of a surprise attack. Moreover, the populace might well force our leaders not to use the tactic after all — when the chips were down and they could plainly see the implications. Worst of all, this policy could appear to be provocative and thereby reduce our deterrence of all-out war. The enemy could interpret preparations of this sort as steps toward a strike-first posture that would leave us vulnerable for several hours whenever brought into play. Instead of deterring the enemy, this policy might make a preemptive attack by him more likely. What conclusions would we draw if the Russians initiated a really large-scale effort in the construction of deep shelters?

A civil-defense race with both sides adopting policies of "civil offense" could be still more inflammatory. Each side would be toughening its economy and protecting its population so that it would be less reluctant to receive a retaliatory strike. These moves would take the world further from stable mutual deterrence toward an unstable form of "brinkmanship."

### CIVIL DEFENSE AS INSURANCE

But suppose that one does not advocate a policy of "civil offense." He may still want a fairly large civil-defense program as insurance in case deterrence should fail. That is, he may desire civil defenses, not to steel our resolve and show the enemy that we mean business, but purely to alleviate the catastrophe should a thermonuclear exchange occur.

There is no sharp line of demarcation between this policy and one of "civil offense," because steps to alleviate the disaster presumably make people a little more willing to risk one. Nonetheless, the design of a civil-defense program intended mainly as insurance could be less provocative than measures for "civil offense." The emphasis would be on protection from surprise attack, with minutes rather than hours of warning,

[27] *Ibid.*, p. 604.

or none at all. There would be less reliance on time-consuming shifts of population (say, to distant shelters). There might be heavy emphasis instead on protection from fallout to insure the survival of people distant from any point of bomb detonation (without fallout protection, we might lose most of the population as a by-product of an attack against our retaliatory forces). Insurance measures might also include some easily accessible blast shelters, protective construction (the value of which is not sensitive to warning time), dispersal of industry and population, improved warning facilities, and protected stockpiles for survival and recuperation.

### UNCERTAINTIES AFFECTING CIVIL-DEFENSE MEASURES

There are great uncertainties about the effectiveness of civil-defense measures. Let us consider the major forms of passive defense and our knowledge of their effectiveness.

A worthwhile package of protective measures would have to save not only people, but also other resources, including food, medicine, communications, transportation facilities, and certain governmental functions. There would be little point in preserving peope in order for them to enjoy a slightly delayed extermination. Hence, although particular measures will be reviewed singly, the most pertinent alternatives are, as usual, different *combinations* of these actions.[28]

One means of trying to protect the economy is dispersal, altering the locational pattern of capital and people. Whatever protection it offers would be insensitive to warning time, which is a great advantage in the missile age. The dangers of fallout, however, dilute considerably the possible saving of lives that dispersal by itself might yield. Moreover, a dispersal program of sufficient magnitude to offer much protection would take a long time to achieve or be very costly. Dispersal that is cheap, the shifting of capital to smaller cities when facilities wear out, takes a long time. Since total depreciation runs about $20–25 billion annually in the United States, it is sometimes suggested that $20–25 billion worth of capital could be relocated each year at little cost. The trouble is that independent conglomerations of capital do not wear out simultaneously like the one-horse shay. Suppose a roof wears out this year. Can we economically put a new roof out in the desert, leaving the undepreciated facilities in the city? Maybe a blast furnace goes out the next year. Is it cheap to construct its replacement in Pismo Beach while the rest of the steel mill is in Pittsburgh? On account of these considerations, much of the allowance for depreciation in the United States does not offer an opportunity for low-cost dispersal.

[28] For a more complete discussion of civil-defense measures, see *Report on a Study of Non-Military Defense.*

It might be possible to induce many new firms and new plants to be located in smaller cities. If the result were a gradual proliferation of cities with say 50,000 population, however, it might not give much protection. A modest increase in the scale of attack could destroy the economy as effectively as ever. The point was well put over a decade ago.

Suppose that, as a protective measure, a wholesale redistribution of population were able to relocate the 50,000,000 at present in the 200 largest cities into more than 1,000 cities, none with a population in excess of 50,000. . . . Unfortunately . . . it seems a plausible conjecture that an increase in number of bombs would be much more easily effected by other nations than a drastic alteration in the distribution of people by this country.[29]

To be much more effective, dispersal would have to be more drastic, relocating people and facilities in still smaller cities, perhaps in "ribbon" communities. But this would be tremendously expensive, sacrificing the economies of urban clustering and a good deal of the freedom we are trying to preserve. In sum, the encouragement of "costless" dispersal is surely all to the good, but it is doubtful that industrial and residential dispersal — unless we refer to an almost prohibitively expensive program — could really give much protection in our generation.

If we can count on having 10 or 15 minutes' warning, a well-designed program of blast shelters might save millions of lives. Naturally the program would have to be combined with steps to preserve other resources that would be essential to survival. There are, however, uncertainties about our ability to get and transmit warning. There are also some doubts about the ability of various kinds of shelters to shield their contents from high overpressures and ground shocks. We have much to learn about ingenious shelter designs, about resilient doors or structures, about design for multiple purposes, about the mix of supplies that is necessary for lengthy occupancy of shelters, and about the cost of shelter programs.

Another possibility is the evacuation of cities after receipt of warning, once the official policy of the United States Federal Civil Defense Administration. Unless used for "civil offense," or in conjunction with ample "strategic warning," it appears to hold little promise with the advent of ballistic missiles. Wherever warheads are delivered with less than several hours' warning, evacuation after receipt of the warning could result in more mortalities than merely doing nothing.

Protective construction, ranging from stronger support for a few ordinary structures to the building of a "national redoubt" underground, is another means of buying protection. As in the case of dispersal, the gains would be sensitive to the scale of the enemy attack (though not as

[29] Ansley J. Coale, p. 62.

much as the gains from dispersal). It should go without saying that, in considering these alternatives, time is of the essence. A sizable program of protective construction would take several years. Should we sacrifice capability in the early years in order to have a greater one later on? Would such preparations be almost obsolete by the date of completion on account of increases in offensive power?

Underground installations illustrate other uncertainties that are likely to confront us. It is often said that new manufacturing plants (of an uncomplicated type) could be put into rock mines at a low cost. These would be limestone, sandstone, granite, or in a few instances salt mines, and the space would be sheltered within a rock stratum. No man-made ceilings or walls would be necessary, except perhaps for a light film of cement that could be sprayed on inexpensively. Air conditioning could dispose of carbon monoxide from internal combustion engines (if any). The entrances might be downward-sloping tunnels 2,000 feet in length. Despite the extras, it is sometimes argued that the space could be provided at a *negative* net cost — that is, at a lower cost per square foot than it would take to build the plants above ground. Moreover, it is pointed out that the limestone from excavations, being valuable in the production of steel shapes, cement, and coarse aggregate for the recuperation stockpile, would help pay for the installations. This smacks of pulling ourselves down by our own bootstraps, but nevertheless the possibilities are interesting.

The main point here is to emphasize the uncertainty that exists about underground installations. Costs might conceivably be negative. Or they might be huge, for we really know little about the implications of deviating from conventional plant designs and structures. How much would it cost to operate more complicated plants in these mines — plants using processes that generate considerable heat or consume large quantities of water, plants that use bulky raw materials or produce bulky outputs? What would it cost to build tunnel entrances in different geological formations? How much would one have to raise wages to attract workers to underground plants? to plants without parking lots? How much would one have to subsidize businessmen to attract them to locations where expansion might be extremely expensive? What would be the impact of the unorthodox locational pattern on transportation and other operating costs? Also, what mix of plants would be most valuable to recuperation and most important therefore to protect?

In the design and protection of stockpiles, too, there is vast uncertainty. It is easy to think of many items that would be important to survival — items such as bandages, medicines, surgical instruments, food, fuel, clothing, equipment for treating sewage and purifying water, radiation meters, and decontamination equipment. Have we experimented enough to recognize other items that may be necessary? Our past policies have implied that rather specialized machine tools (part of the old stockpile for a mobilization base) would be valuable for recuperation. Yet for reconstruction in Western Europe toward the end of World War II, simpler general-purpose tools were the ones most urgently needed. And what military occupational specialty was in greatest demand for recuperative activities engaged in by our armed forces? Not skilled machinists, but blacksmiths! Along this same line, it is not clear whether bulldozers or shovels are the tools needed, at least during the first few years after an attack. Also, despite advances in techniques of mothballing we still know too little about preserving stockpiles — for example, about packaging medical supplies to prevent deterioration or even about long-term storage of farm surpluses.

Measures to obtain warning of an attack would be important in employing several of the protective steps that have been mentioned. Clearly, for instance, the effectiveness of both shelters and evacuation depends upon warning time. (Detection and warning would also be invaluable to active defenses and to the protection of military capability. Last minute, yet crucial, actions to protect our retaliatory force — for example, getting all personnel at missile sites into shelters — would be facilitated by extra seconds of warning.)

The possibilities of getting warning range from "bomb alarms" (similar to burglar alarms, which would instantly communicate to other locations the fact that a warhead had exploded in one, giving the other localities perhaps a few minutes' notice) to reconnaissance, perhaps by satellites (which might give ambiguous warning of final preparations several days in advance of an attack). In general, the longer the advance notice, the greater its worth. At the same time, however, longer warning is likely to be equivocal, and false alarms can become expensive. The enemy can engage in "spoofing," resulting in repeated alerts and protective actions that turn out to be "unwarranted." The greatest cost that might ensue is the gradual erosion of the nation's alertness and a growing indifference to warning. These possibilities suggest the importance of developing various warning systems and of devising automatic "graduated" responses. It should be mentioned incidentally that extra passive defenses (like active defenses and protection for the retaliatory force) can have a feedback on warning time. If we can force the enemy to mount a larger and more complicated attack, we can increase the likelihood of relatively early detection.

At best, however, we are uncertain about the potentialities of warning systems. Is it at all feasible to provide several minutes' warning to small cities? In 1956 exercises, it took 8 minutes for the center of the network to communicate with the 200 key point warning centers. This did not allow for indecision or delay in getting the warning to the Federal Civil Defense Administration or for communication from the key points to the 3500 sub-key-point centers. Of course, certain ways in which a war might get started or be conducted would result in considerable advance warning, at least to many parts of the country. But the fact remains that there is much uncertainty about the extent to which warning can be made more rapid or automatic.

It should be noted that even if any or all of these measures are deemed uneconomic for protecting comparatively low-value targets, they may be economic for protecting high-value targets. To take an extreme example, even if all measures appeared to cost more than they were worth to protect cities, every one of them appears to belong in the package of steps used to protect the retaliatory force. That is, it is certainly economical to put some resources into dispersal, personnel shelters, evacuation planning, underground construction, and warning devices in protecting SAC's might (whether it consists of manned bombers or ballistic missiles). It must be understood, therefore, that the gains and costs of applying a protective measure to one target (say cities) are not identical with those of applying it to other targets, such as portions of government, stockpiles for survival, or means of communication.

### A MINIMAL POLICY [30]

So much for the uncertainties. At present they make recuperation planning a low-confidence measure. Even if one rejects a large civil-defense construction program on account of such factors, however, he should consider buying a somewhat different program as a hedge against total disaster. This program would consist of intensified research and development to buy information, and a few measures that would provide modest protection in the near future.

Experiments and dry runs could help resolve many of the uncertainties previously described. Innovations in communications and warning could be brought to the test stage. New designs for shelters could be devised and tested, and more forethought could influence the testing. In a few cities, proposals for shelters or underground installations could be carried through the preliminary design stage to working drawings to get improved cost estimates. The costs of providing for dual use and for later modifications could be estimated. We could construct a few shelters of different types and get volunteers to live in them for a period of time.

A few underground plants in this country would help answer questions that cannot be answered by studying Swedish installations. More thorough study of existing and potential mine-space, particularly under

[30] See also *Report on a Study of Non-Military Defense,* pp. 33–38 and 43–47, or Kahn, pp. 33–34.

cities and with *experiments* in using such space, would be revealing. We could find out how much it would cost to induce a mining firm to extract limestone at a designated depth, at least for selected situations. Development efforts on components of underground installations — such as utilities, pipes, communications, storage, ventilation — could be undertaken.

Further research on and development of techniques of dealing with radiological effects is in order. We need to know more about "shine down" (the permeation of houses by fallout on roofs), decontamination possibilities, and trade-offs between alternative ways of coping with fallout. We need to know more about the cleansing of Strontium 90, and other materials with long half-lives, from croplands. Other methods of dealing with Strontium 90, such as long-term stockpiling of food and discriminating against Strontium 90 in the production and consumption of food, might be explored. With more information, the cost and effectiveness of these measures could be estimated.

As for other kinds of stockpiling, there is hope of learning a good deal from further investigation. If the post-attack economy is not severely damaged, cannibalization of machines and structures can provide almost everything. If there is severe damage, it may be an economy without spare parts, spark plugs, or special skills. What kind of a hedge should the stockpile constitute? Should the equipment and steel shapes be special purpose or general patch-up? We ought to do more work on these questions before we do much buying.

The small-scale program could include other forms of "advance planning." They too are partly research and development, in the sense that they consist in forming plans and finding out what is wrong with them. Exercises such as Operation Alert have indicated that a great deal of such exploration is needed. Major problems to be examined further include the restoration of government functioning after an attack; the maintenance of institutions or controls to allocate surviving resources; the provision of pure water supplies; the preservation and reallocation of medical facilities, supplies, and personnel; pre-positioning of stocks (fuel, food, power-line repair equipment, mobile communications and power-generating equipment, and so on); the protection of any above-ground stocks from thermal effects; and the reestablishment of a monetary system.

Some of these, such as the planning of post-attack monetary institutions or direct controls, sound like the traditional problems of industrial mobilization, but again the problems are different because the environments would be different. The circumstances during recuperation after a thermonuclear blow would differ drastically in many significant ways from those attending an old-fashioned mobilization. Reexamination of all the old ideas (and experimentation, wherever feasible) is needed. Another sort of plan that would merit further exploration is war damage insurance.[31] As a research and development program clarified what steps individuals should be induced to take, an insurance plan might be designed to provide some appropriate incentives.

A research and development and planning program along these lines might cost a few hundred million dollars annually instead of the many billions that a civil-defense construction program would cost. What gains, in general terms, would it offer? It would provide a good deal more information (though there is no way to clear up *all* the uncertainties about civil defense or any other mission). At the same time more information would become available about the alternative activities to which resources might be devoted. Better comparisons of the alternatives, and better decisions, would become possible. Moreover, the research and development would advance the state of the art in civil-defense activities, making possible a more effective or cheaper program, if one was later adopted. For such a later program, the research, development, and planning would have reduced lead times, making possible its faster completion.

In addition to these measures, we should consider the provision of fallout shelters to provide protection in areas that are not destroyed by blast or heat. We have enough knowledge at present to design good fallout shelters and to put them where they would make sense. Like the other measures just mentioned, fallout shelters and radiation meters would be relatively inexpensive ways to take out some insurance. They could save tens of millions of lives in some possible attacks. Furthermore, these measures would hardly incite an international civil-defense race or cause adverse reactions. An enemy would scarcely interpret this insurance policy as a currently vulnerable yet menacing "draw."

CIVIL-DEFENSE VERSUS LIMITED-WAR CAPABILITIES

There is an obvious and generally recognized trade-off between civil-defense and active-defense measures. While they interact and to some extent complement each other (each tends to make the other's job "manageable"), both serve the purpose of protecting the civilian population and economy, and the total funds we allocate for this purpose must be divided between them. This requires an economic analysis at a level sufficiently high to include active and passive, military and civil, defense possibilities and their interactions.

The trade-off between survival measures and a capability to fight lesser wars is not generally recognized, but it is none the less real, and the allocation between the two capabilities is one of the most crucial affecting national security.

[31] Jack Hirshleifer, "War Damage Insurance," *Review of Economics and Statistics,* May 1953, pp. 144–153.

This choice depends mainly upon the role we assign to strategic bombing ("massive retaliation"). If we rely upon it only to deter a direct thermonuclear attack on this country, we probably can and possibly should be content with minimum survival expenditure. If, at the other "civil-offense" extreme,[32] we propose to use the threat of strategic bombing as a major instrument of foreign policy and a substitute for tactical forces to deal with local conflicts, then we probably need a defensive survival program of major proportions.[33] For the effectiveness of the threat to use massive retaliation in this role depends upon its credibility. As noted previously, the threat is credible to deter a direct attack on the United States; it is perhaps credible to deter an all-out invasion of Western Europe. But the less serious and the less direct the challenge, the less credible becomes a threat to retaliate by starting thermonuclear war.

We might make the threat credible, or at least somewhat more credible in the more serious cases, if we spent a great deal more on active and passive defense measures. These expenditures would improve our chances of surviving as a nation and eventually recovering even after heavy thermonuclear attack (made either in retaliation for our attack, or in anticipation of it). We could finance some such measures without higher total security budgets because we would no longer have the same need for tactical forces for "graduated deterrence."

But if we are not planning to use the threat of massive retaliation to deal with the lesser challenges, the development of a spectrum of capabilities to fight limited wars would seem to have a greater claim on the budget than large-scale passive or active defenses designed to save the population. For without such capabilities we would surrender to the enemy the initiative (which the Soviets could be counted upon to seize) of forcing us to choose with every incident between appeasement and catastrophe. The strictly partial and relative security afforded by the most ambitious survival program conceivable could not be counted upon to make massive retaliation an effective general purpose instrument of foreign policy. Our national strategy could be paralyzed by its inflexibility.[34]

Indeed, large-scale measures to defend the population may have negative deterrence value, and if we provide an adequate spectrum of capabilities for fighting less-than-total wars, we may be in less danger with a modest survival program than with a large one. Perhaps our greatest danger is from an anticipatory strike. An enemy will be more fearful of attack by us if we are well prepared to absorb the counterattack. Such

---

[32] Both of these extreme positions are probably untenable, but we will have to choose a role for massive retaliation somewhere between them.

[33] Malcolm Hoag, "Is 'Dual' Preparedness More Expensive?" *Bulletin of the Atomic Scientists,* February 1957, pp. 48–51.

[34] See Kissinger, *Nuclear Weapons and Foreign Policy,* especially Chapters 4, 5 and 6.

measures as constructing widely separated deep shelters or instituting an evacuation program, which require long advance warning to be effective, are the most likely to provoke attack.

We wish to repeat, however, that this is no argument against a minimal survival program. A responsible government must buy insurance against catastrophe to the extent that this can be done with reasonable premiums. Moreover, even participation in limited wars requires that we be resolute, since any war threatens to explode into a thermonuclear exchange; and we may be more resolute if we are not completely vulnerable. To attain enough resoluteness to use limited-war capabilities is presumably worth some slight reduction in the chance of deterring direct nuclear attacks.

# 18. CHOOSING POLICIES FOR DETERRENCE[1]

Of the many problems that confront defense planners in the nuclear age, the most crucial one is choosing policies for deterrence. Choices here will determine the likelihood of premeditated attack, the possibilities of accidental outbreak of war, and the chances for disarmament or agreement on weapon limitations. The decisions of the United States may be crucial to the whole world's future as well as its own. It is perhaps more important in making these choices than in making any others that we get the most — or at least get a great deal — out of our resources. And looking at these choices in terms of an economic criterion, plus quantitative analysis in many instances, can help us get more from our resources.

We cannot here present a quantitative comparison of alternative policies for deterrence. What we can and shall do in this concluding chapter is to discuss the major considerations in looking at these choices as an economic problem or in constructing an economic analysis of the alternative policies. In addition, this chapter should suggest the quantitative nature of some of these considerations.

* * *

The first shock administered by the Soviet launching of Sputnik has almost dissipated. The flurry of statements and investigations and im-

---

[1] This chapter (other than the two introductory paragraphs) was written by Albert Wohlstetter of The RAND Corporation. The chapter appeared originally in the January, 1959, issue of *Foreign Affairs* under the title, "The Delicate Balance of Terror," and is reprinted with permission. Copyright is held by the Council on Foreign Relations, Inc., New York, N.Y. By special arrangement the section entitled "The Inadequacy of Strategic Deterrence, and Its Necessity" (with the exception of the first paragraph and the last two paragraphs in the section) has been added to the original text, and a few minor stylistic changes have been made.

provised responses has died down, leaving a small residue: a slight increase in the schedule of bomber and ballistic missile production, with a resulting small increment in our defense expenditures for the current fiscal year; a considerable enthusiasm for space travel; and some stirrings of interest in the teaching of mathematics and physics in the secondary schools. Western defense policy has almost returned to the level of activity and the emphasis suited to the basic assumptions which were controlling before Sputnik.

One of the most important of these assumptions — that a general thermonuclear war is extremely unlikely — is held in common by most of the critics of our defense policy as well as by its proponents. Because of its crucial role in the Western strategy of defense, we should like to examine the stability of the thermonuclear balance which, it is generally supposed, would make aggression irrational or even insane. The balance, we believe, is in fact precarious, and this fact has critical implications for policy. Deterrence in the 1960's is neither assured nor impossible but will be the product of sustained intelligent effort and hard choices, responsibly made. As a major illustration important both for defense and foreign policy, we shall treat the particularly stringent conditions for deterrence that affect forces based close to the enemy, whether they are United States forces or those of our allies, under single or joint control. We shall comment also on the inadequacy as well as the necessity of deterrence, on the problem of accidental outbreak of war, and on disarmament.

### THE PRESUMED AUTOMATIC BALANCE

We emphasize that requirements for deterrence are stringent. We have heard so much about the atomic stalemate and the receding probability of war which it has produced that this may strike the reader as something of an exaggeration. Is deterrence a necessary consequence of both sides having a nuclear delivery capability, and is all-out war nearly obsolete? Is mutual extinction the only outcome of a general war? This belief, frequently expressed by references to Mr. Oppenheimer's simile of the two scorpions in a bottle, is perhaps the prevalent one. It is held by a very eminent and diverse group of people — in England by Sir Winston Churchill, P. M. S. Blackett, Sir John Slessor, Admiral Buzzard and many others; in France by such figures as Raymond Aron, General Gallois and General Gazin; in this country by the titular heads of both parties as well as almost all writers on military and foreign affairs, by both Henry Kissinger and his critic, James E. King, Jr., and by George Kennan as well as Dean Acheson. Mr. Kennan refers to American concern about surprise attack as simply obsessive;[2] and many people have

---

[2] George F. Kennan, "A Chance to Withdraw Our Troops in Europe," *Harper's Magazine*, February 1958, p. 41.

drawn the consequence of the stalemate as has Blackett, who states: "If it is in fact true, as most current opinion holds, that strategic air power has abolished global war, then an urgent problem for the West is to assess how little effort must be put into it to keep global war abolished." [3] If peace were founded firmly on mutual terror, and mutual terror on symmetrical nuclear capabilities, this would be, as Churchill has said, "a melancholy paradox"; none the less a most comforting one.

Deterrence, however, is not automatic. While feasible, it will be much harder to achieve in the 1960's than is generally believed. One of the most disturbing features of current opinion is the underestimation of this difficulty. This is due partly to a misconstruction of the technological race as a problem in matching striking forces, partly to a wishful analysis of the Soviet ability to strike first.

Since Sputnik, the United States has made several moves to assure the world (that is, the enemy, but more especially our allies and ourselves) that we will match or overmatch Soviet technology and, specifically, Soviet offense technology. We have, for example, accelerated the bomber and ballistic missile programs, in particular the intermediate-range ballistic missiles. The problem has been conceived as more or better bombers — or rockets; or sputniks; or engineers. This has meant confusing deterrence with matching or exceeding the enemy's ability to strike first. Matching weapons, however, misconstrues the nature of the technological race. Not, as is frequently said, because only a few bombs owned by the defender can make aggression fruitless, but because even many might not. One outmoded A-bomb dropped from an obsolete bomber might destroy a great many supersonic jets and ballistic missiles. To deter an attack means to be able to strike back in spite of it. It means, in other words, a capability to strike second. In the last year or two there has been a growing awareness of the importance of the distinction between a "strike-first" and a "strike-second" capability, but little, if any recognition of the implications of this distinction for the balance of terror theory.

Where the published writings have not simply underestimated Soviet capabilities and the advantages of a first strike, they have in general placed artificial constraints on the Soviet use of the capabilities attributed to them. They assume, for example, that the enemy will attack in mass over the Arctic through our Distant Early Warning line, with bombers refueled over Canada — all resulting in plenty of warning. Most hopefully, it is sometimes assumed that such attacks will be preceded by days of visible preparations for moving ground troops. Such assumptions suggest that the Soviet leaders will be rather bumbling or, better, cooperative. However attractive it may be for us to narrow Soviet alternatives to

[3] P. M. S. Blackett, "Atomic Weapons and East-West Relations" (New York: Cambridge University Press, 1956), p. 32.

these, they would be low in the order of preference of any reasonable Russians planning war.

### THE QUANTITATIVE NATURE OF THE PROBLEM AND THE UNCERTAINTIES

In treating Soviet strategies it is important to consider Soviet rather than Western advantage and to consider the strategy of both sides quantitatively. The effectiveness of our own choices will depend on a most complex numerical interaction of Soviet and Western plans. Unfortunately, both the privileged and unprivileged information on these matters is precarious. As a result, competent people have been led into critical error in evaluating the prospects for deterrence. Western journalists have greatly overestimated the difficulties of a Soviet surprise attack with thermonuclear weapons and vastly underestimated the complexity of the Western problem of retaliation.

One intelligent commentator, Richard Rovere, recently expressed the common view: "If the Russians had ten thousand warheads and a missile for each, and we had ten hydrogen bombs and ten obsolete bombers, . . . aggression would still be a folly that would appeal only to an insane adventurer." Mr. Rovere's example is plausible because it assumes implicitly that the defender's hydrogen bombs will with certainty be visited on the aggressor; then the damage done by the ten bombs seems terrible enough for deterrence, and any more would be simply redundant. This is the basis for the common view. The example raises questions, even assuming the delivery of the ten weapons. For instance, the targets aimed at in retaliation might be sheltered and a quite modest civil defense could hold within tolerable limits the damage done to such city targets by ten delivered bombs. But the essential point is that the weapons would not be very likely to reach their targets. Even if the bombers were dispersed at ten different points, and protected by shelters so blast resistant as to stand up anywhere outside the lip of the bomb crater — even inside the fire ball itself — the chances of one of these bombers surviving the huge attack directed at it would be on the order of one in a million. (This calculation takes account of the unreliability and inaccuracy of the missile.) And the damage done by the small minority of these ten planes that might be in the air at the time of the attack, armed and ready to run the gauntlet of an alert air defense system, if not zero, would be very small indeed compared to damage that Russia has suffered in the past. For Mr. Rovere, like many other writers on this subject, numerical superiority is not important at all.

For Joseph Alsop, on the other hand, it is important, but the superiority is on our side. Mr. Alsop recently enunciated as one of the four rules of nuclear war: "The aggressor's problem is astronomically difficult; and the aggressor requires an overwhelming superiority of force." [4] There are, he believes, no fewer than 400 SAC bases in the NATO nations alone and many more elsewhere, all of which would have to be attacked in a very short space of time. The "thousands of coordinated air sorties and/or missile firings," he concludes, are not feasible. Mr. Alsop's argument is numerical and has the virtue of demonstrating that at least the relative numbers are important. But the numbers he uses are very wide of the mark. He overestimates the number of such bases by a factor of more than ten,[5] and in any case, missile firings on the scale of a thousand or more involve costs that are by no means out of proportion, given the strategic budgets of the great powers. Whether or not thousands are needed depends on the yield and the accuracy of the enemy missiles, something about which it would be a great mistake for us to display confidence.

Perhaps the first step in dispelling the nearly universal optimism about the stability of deterrence would be to recognize the difficulties in analyzing the uncertainties and interactions between our own wide range of choices and the moves open to the Soviets. On our side we must consider an enormous variety of strategic weapons which might compose our force, and for each of these several alternative methods of basing and operation. These are the choices that determine whether a weapons system will have any genuine capability in the realistic circumstances of a war. Besides the B-47E and the B-52 bombers that are in the United States strategic force now, alternatives will include the B-52G (a longer-range version of the B-52); the Mach 2 B-58A bomber and a "growth" version of it; the Mach 3 B-70 bomber; a nuclear-powered bomber possibly carrying long-range air-to-surface missiles; the Dynasoar, a manned glide-rocket; the Thor and the Jupiter, liquid-fueled intermediate-range ballistic missiles; the Snark intercontinental cruise missile; the Atlas and the Titan intercontinental ballistic missiles; the submarine-launched Polaris and Atlantis rockets; and Minuteman, one potential solid-fueled successor to the Thor and Titan; possibly unmanned bombardment satellites; and many others which are not yet gleams in anyone's eye and some that are just that.

The difficulty of describing in brief the best mixture of weapons for the long-term future beginning in 1960, their base requirements, their potentiality for stabilizing or upsetting the balance among the great powers, and their implications for the alliance, is not just a matter of space or the constraint of security. The difficulty in fact stems from some rather basic insecurities. These matters are wildly uncertain; we are

[4] Joseph Alsop, "The New Balance of Power," *Encounter,* May 1958, p. 4. It should be added that, since these lines were written, Mr. Alsop's views have altered.
[5] *The New York Times,* September 6, 1958, p. 2.

talking about weapons and vehicles that are some time off and, even if the precise performance currently hoped for and claimed by contractors were in the public domain, it would be a good idea to doubt them.

Recently some of our colleagues picked their way through the grave-yard of early claims about various missiles and aircraft: their dates of availability, costs and performance. These claims are seldom revisited or talked about: *de mortuis nil nisi bonum.* The errors were large and almost always in one direction. And the less we knew, the more hopeful we were. Accordingly the missiles benefited in particular. For example, the estimated cost of one missile increased by a factor of over 50 — from about $35,000 in 1949 to some $2 million in 1957. This uncertainty is critical. Some but not all of the systems listed can be chosen and the problem of choice is essentially quantitative. The complexities of the problem, if they were more widely understood, would discourage the oracular confidence of writers on the subject of deterrence.

Some of the complexities can be suggested by referring to the successive obstacles to be hurdled by any system providing a capability to strike second, that is, to strike back. Such deterrent systems must have (a) a stable, "steady-state" peacetime operation within feasible budgets (besides the logistic and operational costs there are, for example, problems of false alarms and accidents). They must have also the ability (b) to survive enemy attacks, (c) to make and communicate the decision to retaliate, (d) to reach enemy territory with fuel enough to complete their mission, (e) to penetrate enemy active defenses, that is, fighters and surface-to-air missiles, and (f) to destroy the target in spite of any "passive" civil defense in the form of dispersal or protective construction or evacuation of the target itself.

Within limits the enemy is free to use his offensive and defensive forces so as to exploit the weaknesses of each of our systems. He will also be free, within limits, in the 1960's to choose the composition of forces that will make life as difficult as possible for the various systems we might select. It would be quite wrong to assume that we have the same degree of flexibility or that the uncertainties affect a totalitarian aggressor and the party attacked equally. A totalitarian country can preserve secrecy about the capabilities and disposition of his forces very much better than a Western democracy. And the aggressor has, among other enormous advantages of the first strike, the ability to weigh continually our performance at each of the six barriers and to choose the precise time and circumstance for attack that will reduce uncertainty. It is important not to confuse our uncertainty with his. Strangely enough, some military commentators have not made this distinction and have founded their certainty of deterrence on the fact simply that there are uncertainties.

Unwarranted optimism is displayed not only in the writings of journalists but in the more analytic writings of professionals. The recent writings of General Gallois[6] parallel rather closely Mr. Alsop's faulty numerical proof that surprise attack is astronomically difficult — except that Gallois's "simple arithmetic," to borrow his own phrase, turns essentially on some assumptions which are at once inexplicit and extremely optimistic with respect to the blast resistance of dispersed missile sites subjected to attack from relatively close range.[7] Mr. Blackett's recent book, *Atomic Weapons and East-West Relations,* illustrates the hazards confronting a most able analyst in dealing with the piecemeal information available to the general public. Mr. Blackett, a Nobel prize-winning physicist with wartime experience in military operations research, lucidly summarized the public information available when he was writing in 1956 on weapons for all-out war. But much of his analysis was based on the assumption that H-bombs could not be made small enough to be carried in an intercontinental missile. It is now widely known that intercontinental ballistic missiles will have hydrogen warheads, and this fact, a secret at the time, invalidates Mr. Blackett's calculations and much of his optimism on the stability of the balance of terror. In sum, one of the serious obstacles to any widespread rational judgment on these matters of high policy is that critical elements of the problem *have* to be protected by secrecy. However, some of the principal conclusions about deterrence in the early 1960's can be fairly firmly based, and based on public information.

## THE DELICACY OF THE BALANCE OF TERROR

The most important conclusion is that we must expect a vast increase in the weight of attack which the Soviets can deliver with little warning, and the growth of a significant Russian capability for an essentially warningless attack. As a result, strategic deterrence, while feasible, will be extremely difficult to achieve, and at critical junctures in the 1960's, we may not have the power to deter attack. Whether we have it or not will depend on some difficult strategic choices as to the future composition of the deterrent forces as well as hard choices on its basing, operations and defense.

Manned bombers will continue to make up the predominant part of our striking force in the early 1960's. None of the popular remedies for their defense will suffice — not, for example, mere increase of alertness (which will be offset by the Soviet's increasing capability for attack without significant warning), nor simple dispersal or sheltering alone or mobil-

---

[6] General Pierre M. Gallois, "A French General Analyzes Nuclear-Age Strategy," *Réalités,* Nov. 1958, p. 19; "Nuclear Aggression and National Suicide," *The Reporter,* Sept. 18, 1958, p. 23.

[7] See footnote 9.

ity taken by itself, nor a mere piling up of interceptors and defense missiles around SAC bases. Especially extravagant expectations have been placed on the airborne alert — an extreme form of defense by mobility. The impression is rather widespread that one-third of the SAC bombers are in the air and ready for combat at all times.[8] This belief is belied by the public record. According to the Symington Committee Hearings in 1956, our bombers averaged 31 hours of flying per month, which is about 4 per cent of the average 732-hour month. An Air Force representative expressed the hope that within a couple of years, with an increase in the ratio of crews to aircraft, the bombers would reach 45 hours of flight per month — which is 6 per cent. This 4 to 6 per cent of the force includes bombers partially fueled and without bombs. It is, moreover, only an average, admitting variance down as well as up. Some increase in the number of armed bombers aloft is to be expected. However, for the current generation of bombers, which have been designed for speed and range rather than endurance, a continuous air patrol for one-third of the force would be extremely expensive.

On the other hand, it would be unwise to look for miracles in the new weapons systems, which by the mid-1960's may constitute a considerable portion of the United States force. After the Thor, Atlas and Titan there are a number of promising developments. The solid-fueled rockets, Minuteman and Polaris, promise in particular to be extremely significant components of the deterrent force. Today they are being touted as making the problem of deterrence easy to solve and, in fact, guaranteeing its solution. But none of the new developments in vehicles is likely to do that. For the complex job of deterrence, they all have limitations. The unvaryingly immoderate claims for each new weapons system should make us wary of the latest "technological breakthroughs." Only a very short time ago the ballistic missile itself was supposed to be intrinsically invulnerable on the ground. It is now more generally understood that its survival is likely to depend on a variety of choices in its defense.

It is hard to talk with confidence about the middle and late 1960's. A systematic study of an optimal or a good deterrent force which considered all the major factors affecting choice and dealt adequately with the uncertainties would be a formidable task. In lieu of this, we shall mention briefly why none of the many systems available or projected dominates the others in any obvious way. Our comments will take the form of a swift runthrough of the characteristic advantages and disadvantages

---

[8] See, for example, "NATO, A Critical Appraisal," by Gardner Patterson and Edgar S. Furniss, Jr., Princeton University Conference on NATO, Princeton, June 1957, p. 32: "Although no one pretended to know, the hypothesis that one-third of the striking force of the United States Strategic Air Command was in the air at all times was regarded by most as reasonable."

of various strategic systems at each of the six successive hurdles mentioned earlier.

The first hurdle to be surmounted is the attainment of a stable, steady-state peacetime operation. Systems that depend for their survival on extreme decentralization of controls, as may be the case with large-scale dispersal and some of the mobile weapons, raise problems of accidents and over a long period of peacetime operation this leads in turn to serious political problems. Systems relying on extensive movement by land, perhaps by truck caravan, are an obvious example; the introduction of these on European roads, as is sometimes suggested, would raise grave questions for the governments of some of our allies. Any extensive increase in the armed air alert will increase the hazard of accident and intensify the concern already expressed among our allies. Some of the proposals for bombardment satellites may involve such hazards of unintended bomb release as to make them out of the question.

The cost to buy and operate various weapons systems must be seriously considered. Some systems buy their ability to negotiate a given hurdle — say, surviving the enemy attack — only at prohibitive cost. Then the number that can be bought out of a given budget will be small and this will affect the relative performance of competing systems at various other hurdles, for example penetrating enemy defenses. Some of the relevant cost comparisons, then, are between competing systems; others concern the extra costs to the enemy of canceling an additional expenditure of our own. For example, some dispersal is essential, though usually it is expensive; if the dispersed bases are within a warning net, dispersal can help to provide warning against some sorts of attack, since it forces the attacker to increase the size of his raid and so makes it more liable to detection as well as somewhat harder to coordinate. But as the sole or principal defense of our offensive force, dispersal has only a brief useful life and can be justified financially only up to a point. For against our costs of construction, maintenance and operation of an additional base must be set the enemy's much lower costs of delivering one extra weapon. And, in general, any feasible degree of dispersal leaves a considerable concentration of value at a single target point. For example, a squadron of heavy bombers costing, with their associated tankers and penetration aids, perhaps $500,000,000 over five years, might be eliminated, if it were otherwise unprotected, by an enemy intercontinental ballistic missile costing perhaps $16,000,000. After making allowance for the unreliability and inaccuracy of the missile, this means a ratio of ten to one or better. To achieve safety by *brute* numbers in so unfavorable a competition is not likely to be viable economically or politically. However, a viable peacetime operation is only the first hurdle to be surmounted.

At the second hurdle — surviving the enemy offense — ground alert systems placed deep within a warning net look good against a manned bomber attack, much less good against intercontinental ballistic missiles, and not good at all against ballistic missiles launched from the sea. In the last case, systems such as the Minuteman, which may be sheltered and dispersed as well as alert, would do well. Systems involving launching platforms that are mobile and concealed, such as Polaris submarines, have particular advantage for surviving an enemy offense.

However, there is a third hurdle to be surmounted — namely that of making the decision to retaliate and communicating it. Here, Polaris, the combat air patrol of B-52's, and in fact all of the mobile platforms — under water, on the surface, in the air and above the air — have severe problems. Long distance communication may be jammed and, most important, communication centers may be destroyed.

At the fourth hurdle — ability to reach enemy territory with fuel enough to complete the mission — several of our short-legged systems have operational problems such as coordinating with tankers and using bases close to the enemy. For a good many years to come, up to the mid-1960's in fact, this will be a formidable hurdle for the greater part of our deterrent force. The next section of this chapter deals with this problem at some length.

The fifth hurdle is the aggressor's long-range interceptors and close-in missile defenses. To get past these might require large numbers of planes and missiles. (If the high cost of overcoming an earlier obstacle — using extreme dispersal or airborne alert or the like — limits the number of planes or missiles bought, our capability is likely to be penalized disproportionately here.) Or getting through may involve carrying heavy loads of radar decoys, electronic jammers and other aids to defense penetration. For example, vehicles like Minuteman and Polaris, which were made small to facilitate dispersal or mobility, may suffer here because they can carry fewer penetration aids.

At the final hurdle — destroying the target in spite of the passive defenses that may protect it — low-payload and low-accuracy systems, such as Minuteman and Polaris, may be frustrated by blast-resistant shelters. For example, five half-megaton weapons with an average inaccuracy of two miles might be expected to destroy half the population of a city of 900,000, spread over 40 square miles, provided the inhabitants are without shelters. But if they are provided with shelters capable of resisting over-pressures of 100 pounds per square inch, approximately 60 such weapons would be required; and deep rock shelters might force the total up to over a thousand.

Prizes for a retaliatory capability are not distributed for getting over one of these jumps. A system must get over all six. We hope these illustrations will suggest that assuring ourselves the power to strike back after a massive thermonuclear surprise attack is by no means as automatic as is widely believed.

In counteracting the general optimism as to the ease and, in fact, the inevitability of deterrence, we should like to avoid creating the extreme opposite impression. Deterrence demands hard, continuing, intelligent work, but it can be achieved. The job of deterring rational attack by guaranteeing great damage to an aggressor is, for example, very much less difficult than erecting a nearly airtight defense of cities in the face of full-scale thermonuclear surprise attack. Protecting manned bombers and missiles is much easier because they may be dispersed, sheltered or kept mobile, and they can respond to warning with greater speed. Mixtures of these and other defenses with complementary strengths can preserve a powerful remainder after attack. Obviously not all our bombers and missiles need to survive in order to fulfill their mission. To preserve the majority of our cities intact in the face of surprise attack is immensely more difficult, if not impossible. (This does not mean that the aggressor has the same problem in preserving his cities from retaliation by a poorly protected, badly-damaged force. And it does not mean that *we* should not do more to limit the extent of the catastrophe to our cities in case deterrence fails. We believe we should.) Deterrence, however, provided we work at it, is feasible, and, what is more, it is a crucial objective of national policy.

What can be said, then, as to whether general war is unlikely? Would not a general thermonuclear war mean "extinction" for the aggressor as well as the defender? "Extinction" is a state that badly needs analysis. Russian casualties in World War II were more than 20,000,000. Yet Russia recovered extremely well from this catastrophe. There are several quite plausible circumstances in the future when the Russians might be quite confident of being able to limit damage to considerably less than this number — if they make sensible strategic choices and we do not. On the other hand, the risks of not striking might at some juncture appear very great to the Soviets, involving, for example, disastrous defeat in peripheral war, loss of key satellites with danger of revolt spreading — possibly to Russia itself — or fear of an attack by ourselves. Then, striking first, by surprise, would be the sensible choice for them, and from their point of view the smaller risk.

It should be clear that it is not fruitful to talk about the likelihood of general war without specifying the range of alternatives that are pressing on the aggressor and the strategic postures of both the Soviet bloc and the West. Deterrence is a matter of comparative risks. The balance is not automatic. First, since thermonuclear weapons give an enormous advantage to the aggressor, it takes great ingenuity and realism at any given level of nuclear technology to devise a stable equilibrium. And second, this technology itself is changing with fantastic speed. Deterrence will require an urgent and continuing effort.

### THE USES AND RISKS OF BASES CLOSE TO THE SOVIETS

It may now be useful to focus attention on the special problems of deterrent forces close to the Soviet Union. First, overseas areas have played an important role in the past and have a continuing though less certain role today. Second, the recent acceleration of production of inter-mediate-range ballistic missiles and the negotiation of agreements with various NATO powers for their basing and operation have given our overseas bases a renewed importance in deterring attack on the United States — or so it would appear at first blush. Third, an analysis can throw some light on the problems faced by our allies in developing an independent ability to deter all-out attack on themselves, and in this way it can clarify the much agitated question of nuclear sharing. Finally, overseas bases affect in many critical ways, political and economic as well as military, the status of the alliance.

At the end of the last decade, overseas bases appeared to be an advantageous means of achieving the radius extension needed by our short-legged bombers, of permitting them to use several axes of attack, and of increasing the number of sorties possible in the course of an extended campaign. With the growth of our own thermonuclear stockpile, it became apparent that a long campaign involving many reuses of a large proportion of our bombers was not likely to be necessary. With the growth of a Russian nuclear-delivery capability, it became clear that this was most unlikely to be feasible.

Our overseas bases now have the disadvantage of high vulnerability. Because they are closer than the United States to the Soviet Union, they are subject to a vastly greater attack by a larger variety as well as number of vehicles. With given resources, the Soviets might deliver on nearby bases a freight of bombs with something like 50 to 100 times the yield that they could muster at intercontinental range. Missile accuracy would more than double. Because there is not much space for obtaining warning — in any case, there are no deep-warning radar nets — and, since most of our overseas bases are close to deep water from which submarines might launch missiles, the warning problem is very much more severe than for bases in the interior of the United States.

As a result, early in the 1950's the United States Air Force decided to recall many of our bombers to the continental United States and to use the overseas bases chiefly for refueling, particularly post-strike ground refueling. This reduced drastically the vulnerability of United States bombers and at the same time retained many of the advantages of overseas operation. For some years now SAC has been reducing the number of aircraft usually deployed overseas. The purpose is to reduce vulnerability and has little to do with any increasing radius of SAC aircraft. The early B-52 radius is roughly that of the B-36; the B-47, roughly that of the B-50 or B-29. In fact the radius limitation and therefore the basing requirements we have discussed will not change substantially for some time to come. We can talk with comparative confidence here, because the United States strategic force is itself largely determined for this period. Such a force changes more slowly than is generally realized. The vast majority of the force will consist of manned bombers, and most of these will be of medium range. *Some* United States bombers will be able to reach *some* targets from *some* United States bases within the 50 states without landing on the way back. On the other hand, some bomber-target combinations are not feasible without pre-target landing (and are therefore doubtful). The Atlas, Titan, and Polaris rockets, when available, can of course do without overseas bases (though the proportion of Polaris submarines kept at sea can be made larger by the use of submarine tenders based overseas). But even with the projected force of aerial tankers, the greater part of our force, which will be manned bombers, cannot be used at all in attacks on the Soviet Union without at least some use of overseas areas.

What of the bases for Thor and Jupiter, our first intermediate-range ballistic missiles? These have to be close to the enemy, and they must of course be operating bases, not merely refueling stations. The Thors and Jupiters will be continuously in range of an enormous Soviet potential for surprise attack. These installations therefore reopen, in a most acute form, some of the serious questions of ground vulnerability that were raised about six years ago in connection with our overseas bomber bases. The decision to station the Thor and Jupiter missiles overseas has been our principal public response to the Russian advances in rocketry, and perhaps our most plausible response. Because it involves our ballistic missiles it appears directly to answer the Russian rockets. Because it involves using European bases, it appears to make up for the range superiority of the Russian intercontinental missile. And most important, it directly involves the NATO powers and gives them an element of control.

There is no question that it was genuinely urgent not only to meet the Russian threat but to do so visibly, in order to save the loosening NATO alliance. Our allies were fearful that the Soviet ballistic missiles might mean that we were no longer able or willing to retaliate against the Soviet Union in case of an attack on them. We hastened to make public a reaction which would restore their confidence. This move surely appears to increase our own power to strike back, and also to give our allies a deterrent of their own, independent of our decision. It has also been argued that in this respect it merely advances the inevitable date at which our allies will acquire "modern" weapons of their own, and that it widens the range of Soviet challenges that Europe can meet. But we must face seriously the question whether this move will in fact assure either the ability to retaliate or the decision to attempt it, on the part of our allies or ourselves. And we should ask at the very least whether further expansion of this policy will buy as much retaliatory power as other ways of spending the considerable sums involved. Finally, it is important to be clear whether the Thor and Jupiter actually increase the flexibility or range of response available to our allies.

One justification for this move is that it disperses retaliatory weapons and that this is the most effective sanction against the thermonuclear aggressor. The limitations of dispersal have already been discussed, but it remains to examine the argument that overseas bases provide *widespread* dispersal, which imposes on the aggressor insoluble problems of coordination.

There is of course something in the notion that forcing the enemy to attack many political entities increases the seriousness of his decision, but there is very little in the notion that dispersal in several countries makes the problem of destruction more difficult in the military sense. Dispersal does not require separation by the distance of oceans — just by the lethal diameters of enemy bombs. And the task of coordinating bomber attacks on Europe and the eastern coast of the United States, say, is not appreciably more difficult than coordinating attacks on our east and west coasts. In the case of ballistic missiles, the elapsed time from firing to impact on the target can be calculated with high accuracy. Although there will be some failures and delays, times of firing can be arranged so that impact on many dispersed points is almost simultaneous — on Okinawa and the United Kingdom, for instance, as well as on California and Ohio. Moreover, it is important to keep in mind that these far-flung bases, while distant from each other and from the United States, are on the whole close to the enemy. To eliminate them, therefore, requires a smaller expenditure of resources on his part than targets at intercontinental range. For close-in targets he can use a wider variety of weapons carrying larger payloads and with higher accuracy.

The seeming appositeness of an overseas-based Thor and Jupiter as an answer to a Russian intercontinental ballistic missile stems not so much from any careful analysis of their retaliatory power under attack as from the directness of the comparison they suggest: a rocket equals a rocket, an intercontinental missile equals an intermediate-range missile based at closer range to the target. But this again mistakes the nature of the technological race. It conceives the problem of deterrence as that of simply matching or exceeding the aggressor's capability to strike first. A surprising proportion of the debate on defense policy has betrayed this confusion. Matching technological developments are useful for prestige, and such demonstrations have a vital function in preserving the alliance and in reassuring the neutral powers. But propaganda is not enough. The only reasonably certain way of maintaining a reputation for strength is to display an actual power to our friends as well as our enemies. We should ask, then, whether further expansion of the current programs for basing Thor and Jupiter is an efficient way to increase American retaliatory power. If overseas bases are considered too vulnerable for manned bombers, will not the same be true for missiles?

The basis for the hopeful impression that they will not is rather vague, including a mixture of hypothetical properties of ballistic missiles in which perhaps the dominant element is their supposedly much more rapid, "push-button" response. What needs to be considered here are the response time of such missiles (including decision, preparation and launch times), and how they are to be defended.

The decision to fire a missile with a thermonuclear warhead is much harder to make than a decision simply to start a manned aircraft on its way, with orders to return to base unless instructed to continue to its assigned target. This is the "fail-safe" procedure practiced by the United States Air Force. In contrast, once a missile is launched, there is no method of recall or deflection that is not subject to risks of electronic or mechanical failure. Therefore such a decision must wait for much more unambiguous evidence of enemy intentions. It must and will take a longer time to make and is less likely to be made at all. Where more than one country is involved, the joint decision is harder still, since there is opportunity to disagree about the ambiguity of the evidence, as well as to reach quite different interpretations of national interest. On much less momentous matters the process of making decisions in NATO is complicated, and it should be recognized that such complexity has much to do with the genuine concern of the various NATO powers about the danger of accidentally starting World War III. Such fears will not be diminished with the advent of IRBM's. In fact, widespread dispersion of nuclear armed missiles raises measurably the possibility of accidental war.

Second, it is quite erroneous to suppose that by contrast with manned bombers the first IRBM's can be launched almost as simply as pressing a button. Count-down procedures for early missiles are liable to interruption, and the characteristics of the liquid oxygen fuel limit the readiness of their response. Unlike JP-4, the fuel used in jet bombers, liquid oxygen cannot be held for long periods of time in these vehicles. In this respect such missiles will be *less* ready than alert bombers. Third, the smaller warning time available overseas makes more difficult any response. This includes, in particular, any active defense, not only against ballistic missile attacks but, for example, against low altitude or various circuitous attacks by manned aircraft.

Finally, passive defense by means of shelter is more difficult, given the larger bomb yields, better accuracies and larger forces available to the Russians at such close range. And if the press reports are correct, the plans for IRBM installations do not call for bomb-resistant shelters. If this is so, it should be taken into account in measuring the actual contribution of these installations to the West's retaliatory power. Viewed as a contribution to deterring all-out attack on the United States, the Thor and Jupiter bases seem unlikely to compare favorably with other alternatives. If newspaper references to hard bargaining by some of our future hosts are to be believed, it would seem that such negotiations have been conducted under misapprehensions on both sides as to the benefits to the United States.

But many proponents of the distribution of Thor and Jupiter — and possibly some of our allies — have in mind not an increase in United States deterrence but the development of an independent capability in several of the NATO countries to deter all-out attack against themselves. This would be a useful thing if it can be managed at supportable cost and if it does not entail the sacrifice of even more critical measures of protection. But aside from the special problems of joint control, which would affect the certainty of response adversely, precisely who their legal owner is will not affect the retaliatory power of the Thors and Jupiters one way or the other. They would not be able to deter an attack that they could not survive. It is curious that many who question the utility of American overseas bases (for example, our bomber bases in the United Kingdom) simply assume that, for our allies, possession of strategic nuclear weapons is one with deterrence.

There remains the view that provision of these weapons will broaden the range of response open to our allies. In so far as this view rests on the belief that the intermediate-range ballistic missile is adapted to limited war, it is wide of the mark. The inaccuracy of an IRBM requires high-yield warheads, and such a combination of inaccuracy and high yield, while quite appropriate and adequate against unprotected targets in a general war, would scarcely come within even the most lax, in fact reckless, definition of limited war. Such a weapon is inappropriate for even the nuclear variety of limited war, and it is totally useless for meeting the wide variety of provocation that is well below the threshold of nuclear response. In so far as these missiles will be costly for our allies to install, operate, and support, they are likely to displace a conventional capability that might be genuinely useful in limited engagements. More important, they are likely to be used as an excuse for budget-cutting. In this way they will accelerate the general trend toward dependence on all-out response and so will have the opposite effect to the one claimed.

Nevertheless, if the Thor and Jupiter have these defects, might not some future weapon be free of them? Some of these defects, of course, will be overcome in time. Solid fuels or storable liquids will eventually replace liquid oxygen, reliabilities will increase, various forms of mobility or portability will become feasible, accuracies may even be so improved that such weapons can be used in limited wars. But these developments are all years away. In consequence, the discussion will be advanced if a little more precision is given such terms as "missiles" or "modern" or "advanced" weapons. We are not distributing a generic "modern" weapon with all the virtues of flexibility in varying circumstances and of invulnerability in all-out war. But even with advances in the state of the art on our side, it will remain difficult to maintain a deterrent, especially close in under the enemy's guns.

It follows that, though a wider distribution of nuclear weapons may be inevitable, or at any rate likely, and though some countries in addition to the Soviet Union and the United States may even develop an independent deterrent, it is by no means inevitable or even very likely that the power to deter all-out thermonuclear attack will be widespread. This is true even though a minor power would not need to guarantee as large a retaliation as we in order to deter attack on itself. Unfortunately, the minor powers have smaller resources as well as poorer strategic locations.[9] Mere membership in the nuclear club might carry with it prestige,

[9] General Gallois argues that, while alliances will offer no guarantee, "a small number of bombs and a small number of carriers suffice for a threatened power to protect itself against atomic destruction." (*Réalités, op. cit.,* p. 71.) His numerical illustrations give the defender some 400 underground launching sites (*ibid.,* p. 22, and *The Reporter, op. cit.,* p. 25) and suggest that their elimination would require between 5,000 and 25,000 missiles — which is "more or less impossible" — and that in any case the aggressor would not survive the fallout from his own weapons. Whether these are large numbers of targets from the standpoint of the aggressor will depend on the accuracy, yield and reliability of offense weapons as well as the resistance of the defender's shelters and a number of other matters not specified in the argument. General Gallois is aware that the expectation of survival depends on distance even in the ballistic missile age and that our allies are not so fortunate in this respect. Close-in missiles have better bomb yields and accuracies. Moreover, manned aircraft — with still better yields and accuracies — can be used by an aggressor here since warning of their approach is very short. Suffice it to say that the numerical advantage General Gallois cites is greatly exaggerated. Furthermore, he exaggerates the destructiveness of the retaliatory blow against the aggressor's cities by the remnants of the defender's missile force — even assuming the aggressor would take no special measures to protect his cities. But particularly for the aggresssor — who does not lack warning — a civil defense program can moderate the damage done by a poorly organized attack. Finally, the suggestion that the aggressor would not survive the fallout from his own weapons is simply in error. The rapid-decay fission products which are the major lethal problem in the locality of a surface burst are not a serious difficulty for the aggressor. The amount of the slow-decay products, Strontium-90 and Cesium-137,

as the applicants and nominees expect, but it will be rather expensive, and in time it will be clear that it does not necessarily confer any of the expected privileges enjoyed by the two charter members. The burden of deterring a general war as distinct from limited wars is still likely to be on the United States and therefore, so far as our allies are concerned, on the military alliance.

There is one final consideration. Missiles placed near the enemy, even if they could not retaliate, would have a potent capability for striking first by surprise. And it might not be easy for the enemy to discern their purpose. The existence of such a force might be a considerable provocation and in fact a dangerous one in the sense that it would place a great burden on our deterrent force which more than ever would have to guarantee extreme risks to the attacker — worse than the risks of waiting in the face of this danger. When not coupled with the ability to strike in retaliation, such a capability might suggest — erroneously, to be sure, in the case of the democracies — an intention to strike first. If so, it would tend to provoke rather than to deter general war.

We have dealt here with only one of the functions of overseas bases: their use as a support for the strategic deterrent force. They have a variety of important military, political, and economic roles that are beyond our scope here. Expenditures in connection with the construction or operation of our bases, for example, are a form of economic aid and, moreover, a form that is rather palatable to the Congress. There are other functions in a central war where their importance may be very considerable and their usefulness in a limited war might be substantial.

### THE INADEQUACY OF STRATEGIC DETERRENCE
### AND ITS NECESSITY

Indeed nothing said here should suggest that deterrence is in itself an adequate strategy. The complementary requirements of a sufficient military policy cannot be discussed in detail here. Certainly they include a more serious development of power to meet limited aggression, especially with more advanced conventional weapons than those now available. They also include more energetic provision for active and passive defenses to limit the dimensions of the catastrophe in case deterrence should fail. For example, an economically feasible shelter program might make the difference between 50,000,000 survivors and 120,000,000 survivors.

---

in the atmosphere would rise considerably. If nothing were done to counter it, this might, for example, increase by many times the incidence of such relatively rare diseases as bone cancer and leukemia. However, such a calamity, implying an increase of, say, 20,000 deaths per year for a nation of 200,000,000, is of an entirely different order from the catastrophe involving tens of millions of deaths, which General Gallois contemplates elsewhere. And there are measures that might reduce even this effect drastically. (See The RAND Corporation Report R-322-RC, *Report on a Study of Non-Military Defense*, July 1, 1958.)

At the end of the war, perhaps deterrence did appear to be enough. Western forces were larger than those of the Soviet Union and its satellites. We demobilized much more extensively, relying on nuclear weapons to maintain the balance of East-West military power. This was plausible then because nuclear power was all on our side. It was *our* bomb. It seemed only to complete the preponderance of American power provided by our enormous industrial mobilization base and to dispense with the need to keep it mobilized. It would compensate for the extra men kept under arms by the East.

But the notion of massive retaliation as a responsible retort to peripheral provocations vanished in the harsh light of a better understanding here and abroad that the Soviet nuclear delivery capability meant tremendous losses to the United States if we attacked them. And now Europe has begun to doubt that we would make the sacrifice involved in using SAC to answer an attack directed at it but not at ourselves.

The many critics of the massive retaliation policy who advocate a capability to meet limited aggression with a limited response are on firm ground in suggesting that a massive response on such an occasion would be unlikely and the threat to use it therefore not believed. Moreover this argument is quite enough to make clear the critical need for more serious development of the power to meet limited aggressions. Another argument, which will not hold water and which is in fact dangerous, is sometimes used: Little wars are likely, general war improbable. We have seen that this mistakes a possibility for its fulfillment. The likelihood of both general and little wars is contingent on what we do. Moreover, these probabilities are not independent. A limited war involving the major powers is explosive. In this circumstance the likelihood of general war increases palpably. The danger of general war can be felt in every local skirmish involving the great powers. But because the balance of terror is supposed, almost universally, to assure us that all-out war will not occur, advocates of graduated deterrence have proposed to fix the limits of limited conflict in ways which neglect this danger. A few of the proposals seem in fact quite reckless.

The emphasis of the advocates of limitation has been on the high rather than on the low end of the spectrum of weapons. They have talked in particular of nuclear limited wars on the assumption that nuclear weapons will favor the defender rather than the aggressor and that the West can depend on these to compensate for men and conventional arms. Perhaps this will sound reminiscent to the reader. These are, evidently, *our* tactical nuclear bombs. We are afraid that this belief will not long stand the harsh light of analysis and that it will vanish like its predecessor, the comfortable notion that we had a monopoly of strategic nuclear weapons and that these only completed the Western and, specifically, the

American preponderance. We know of no convincing evidence that tactical nuclear weapons favor the defender rather than the aggressor if both sides use such weapons. The argument runs that the offense requires concentration and so the aggressor necessarily provides the defender with a lucrative atomic target. This ignores the fact that, in a delivered nuclear weapon itself, the offense has an enormous concentration of force. The use of nuclear weapons in limited wars might make it possible for the aggressor to eliminate the existing forces of the defender and to get the war over, reaching his limited objective before the defender or his allies can mobilize new forces. Like all-out nuclear war, it puts a premium on surprise and forces in being rather than on mobilization potential, which is the area in which the West has an advantage.

We are inclined to believe that most of those who rely on tactical nuclear weapons as a substitute for disparities in conventional forces have in general presupposed a cooperative Soviet attacker, one who did not use atomic weapons himself. Here again is an instance of Western-preferred Soviet strategies, this time applied to limited war. Ironically, according to reports of Soviet tactical exercises described in the last few years in the military newspaper, *The Red Star,* atomic weapons are in general employed only by the Russians, the West apparently employing Soviet-preferred Western strategies.[10] The symmetry of the optimism of East and West here could be quite deadly.

Whether or not nuclear weapons favor the West in limited war, there still remains the question of whether such limitations could be made stable. Korea illustrated the possibility of a conventional limited war which did not become nuclear, though fought in the era of nuclear weapons. It remains to be seen whether there are any equilibrium points between the use of conventional and all-out weapons. In fact the emphasis on the gradualness of the graduated deterrents may be misplaced. The important thing would be to find some discontinuities if these steps are not to lead too smoothly to general war. Nuclear limited war, simply because of the extreme swiftness and unpredictability of its moves, the necessity of delegating authority to local commanders, and the possibility of sharp and sudden desperate reversals of fortune, would put the greatest strain on the deterrent to all-out thermonuclear war.

For this reason we believe that it would be appropriate to emphasize the importance of expanding a conventional capability realistically and, in particular, research and development in non-nuclear modes of warfare. These have been financed by pitifully small budgets. Yet we would conjecture that if one considers the implications of modern surface-to-air missiles in the context of conventional war, in which the attacker has to make many sorties and expose himself to recurring attrition, these

---

[10] We are indebted to an unpublished paper of Mr. Constantin Melnik for this reference.

weapons would look ever so much better than they do when faced, for example, with the heroic task of knocking down 99 per cent of a wave of, say, one thousand nuclear bombers. Similarly, advances in anti-tank wire-guided missiles and antipersonnel fragmentation weapons, which have been mentioned from time to time in the press, might help redress the current balance of East-West conventional forces without, however, removing the necessity for spending more money in procurement as well as research and development.

The interdependence of limited and total war decisions makes it clear that the development of any powerful limited war capability, and in particular a nuclear one, only underlines the need, at the same time, for insuring retaliation against all-out attack. An aggressor must constantly weigh the dangers of all-out attack against the dangers of waiting, of not striking "all-out." Sharp reversals in a limited war can increase the dangers of waiting. But finally there is no question at this late date that strategic deterrence is inadequate to answer limited provocation.

Strategic deterrence has other inadequacies besides its limitations in connection with limited war. Some of these concern air defense. The power to deter a rational all-out attack does not relieve us of the responsibility for defending our cities in case deterrence fails. It should be said at once that such a defense is not a satisfactory substitute for deterring a carefully planned surprise attack since defense against such an attack is extraordinarily difficult. We know in fact of no high confidence way of avoiding enormous damage to our cities in a war initiated by an aggressor with a surprise thermonuclear attack. The only way of preventing such damage with high confidence is to prevent the war. But if we could obtain a leakproof air defense, many things would change. A limited-war capability, for example, would be unimportant. Massive retaliation against even minor threats, since it exposed us to no danger, might be credible. Deterring attack would also not be very important. Of course if both sides had such defenses, deterrence would not be feasible either, but this again would be insignificant since strategic war would be relatively harmless — at least to the targets on both sides if not to the attacking vehicles. It is a curious paradox of our recent intellectual history that, among the pioneers of both the balance of terror theory of automatic deterrence and the small nuclear weapon theory of limited or tactical war were the last true believers in the possibility of near perfect defense — which would have made deterrence infeasible and both it and the ability to fight limited war unimportant. However, in spite of the periodic announcements of "technological breakthroughs," the goal of emerging unscathed from a surprise thermonuclear attack has gotten steadily more remote.

On the other hand, this does not mean that we can dispense with the defense of cities. In spite of deterrence a thermonuclear war could be tripped by accident or miscalculation. In this case, particularly since the attack might be less well planned, a combination of spoiling counter-attacks and active and passive defenses might limit the size of the catastrophe.

But it would be a fatal mistake to suppose that because strategic deterrence is inadequate by itself it can be dispensed with. Deterrence is not dispensable. If the picture of the world we have drawn is rather bleak, it could none the less be cataclysmically worse. Suppose both the United States and the Soviet Union had the power to destroy each other's retaliatory forces and society, given the opportunity to administer the opening blow. The situation would then be something like the old-fashioned Western gun duel. It would be extraordinarily risky for one side *not* to attempt to destroy the other, or to delay doing so, since it not only can emerge unscathed by striking first but this is the sole way it can reasonably hope to emerge at all. Evidently such a situation is extremely unstable. On the other hand, if it is clear that the aggressor too will suffer catastrophic damage in the event of his aggression, he then has strong reason not to attack, even though he can administer great damage. A protected retaliatory capability has a stabilizing influence not only in deterring rational attack, but also in offering every inducement to both powers to reduce the chance of accidental war.

The critics who feel that deterrence is "bankrupt" sometimes say that we stress deterrence too much. We believe this is quite wrong if it means that we are devoting too much effort to protect our power to retaliate; but we think it is quite right if it means that we have talked too much of a strategic threat as a substitute for many things it cannot replace.

## DETERRENCE, ACCIDENTS AND DISARMAMENT

Up to now we have talked mainly about the problem of deterring general war, of making it improbable that an act of war will be under-taken deliberately, with a clear understanding of the consequences, that is, rationally. That such deterrence will not be easy to maintain in the 1960's simply expresses the proposition that a surprise thermonuclear attack might *not* be an irrational or insane act on the part of the aggressor. A deterrent strategy is aimed at a rational enemy. Without a deterrent, general war is likely. With it, however, war might still occur.

In order to reduce the risk of a rational act of aggression, we are being forced to undertake measures (increased alertness, dispersal, mobility) which, to a significant extent, increase the risk of an irrational or unintentional act of war. The accident problem is serious, and it would be a great mistake to dismiss the recent Soviet charges on this subject as simply part of the war of nerves. In a clear sense the great multiplication and spread of nuclear arms throughout the world, the drastic increase in the degree of readiness of these weapons, and the decrease in the time available for the decision on their use must inevitably raise the risk of accident. The B-47 accidents at Sidi Slimane and at Florence, South Carolina, and the recent Nike explosion are just a beginning. Though incidents of this sort are not themselves likely to trigger misunderstanding, they suggest the nature of the problem.

There are many sorts of accidents that could happen. There can be electronic or mechanical failures of the sort illustrated by the B-47 and Nike mishaps; there can be aberrations of individuals, perhaps quite low in the echelon of command; there can be miscalculations on the part of governments as to enemy intent and the meaning of ambiguous signals. Not all deterrent strategies will involve the risk of accident equally. One of the principles of selecting a strategy should be to reduce the chance of accident, wherever we can, without a corresponding increase in vulnerability to a rational surprise attack. This is the purpose of the "failsafe" procedures for launching SAC.

These problems are also relevant to the disarmament question. The Russians, exploiting an inaccurate United Press report that suggested that SAC started en masse toward Russia in response to frequent radar "ghosts," cried out against these supposed Arctic flights. The United States response, and its sequels, stated correctly that such flights had never been undertaken except in planned exercises and would not be undertaken in response to such unreliable warning. We pointed out the importance of quick response and a high degree of readiness in the protection of the deterrent force. The nature of the fail-safe precaution was also described.

We added, however, to cap the argument, that if the Russians were really worried about surprise attack they would accept the President's "open skies" proposal. But this addition conceals an absurdity. Aerial photography would have its uses in a disarmament plan — for example, to check an exchange of information on the location of ground bases. However, so far as surprise is concerned, an "open skies" plan would have direct use only to discover attacks requiring much more lengthy, visible and unambiguous preparations than are likely today.[11] The very readiness of our own strategic force suggests a state of technology that outmodes the "open skies" plan as a counter to surprise attack. Not even the most advanced reconnaissance equipment can disclose an intention from 40,000 feet. Who can say what the men in the blockhouse of an ICBM base have in mind? Or, for that matter, what is the final

[11] Aerial reconnaissance, of course, could have an *indirect* utility here for surveying large areas to determine the number and location of observation posts needed to provide more timely warning.

destination of training flights or fail-safe flights starting over the Pacific or North Atlantic from staging areas?

The actions that we need to take on our own to deter attack might usefully be complemented by bilateral agreements for inspection and reporting and, possibly, limitation of arms and of methods of operating strategic and naval air forces. But the protection of our retaliatory power remains essential; and the better the protection, the smaller the burden placed on the agreement to limit arms and modes of operation and to make them subject to inspection. Reliance on "open skies" alone to prevent surprise would invite catastrophe and the loss of power to retaliate. Such a plan is worthless for discovering a well-prepared attack with ICBM's or submarine-launched missiles or a routine mass training flight whose destination could be kept ambiguous. A tremendous weight of weapons could be delivered in spite of it.

Although it is quite hopeless to look for an inspection scheme that would permit abandonment of the deterrent, this does not mean that some partial agreement on inspection and limitation might not help to reduce the chance of any sizable surprise attack. We should explore the possibilities of agreements involving limitation and inspection. But how we go about this will be conditioned by our appreciation of the problem of deterrence itself.

The critics of current policy who perceive the inadequacy of the strategy of deterrence are prominent among those urging disarmament negotiations, an end to the arms race and a reduction of tension. This is of paramount interest to some of our allies. The balance of terror theory is the basis for some of the more light-hearted suggestions: if deterrence is automatic, strategic weapons on one side cancel those of the other, and it should be easy for both sides to give them up. So James E. King, Jr., one of the most sensible writers on the subject of limited war, suggests that weapons needed for "unlimited" war are those which both sides can most easily agree to abolish, simply because "neither side can anticipate anything but disaster" from their use. "Isn't there enough stability in the 'balance of terror,'" he asks, "to justify our believing that the Russians can be trusted — within acceptable limits — to abandon the weapons whose 'utility is confined to the threat or conduct of a war of annihilation'?" [12]

Indeed, if there were no real danger of a rational attack, then accidents and the $n$th country problem would be the only problems. As we have indicated, they are serious problems and some sorts of limitation and inspection agreement might diminish them. But if there is to be any prospect of realistic and useful agreement, we must reject the theory of

[12] James E. King, Jr., "Arms and Man in the Nuclear-Rocket Era," *The New Republic,* September 1, 1958.

automatic deterrence. And we must bear in mind that the more extensive a disarmament agreement is, the smaller the force that a violator would have to hide in order to achieve complete domination. Most obviously, "*the abolition* of the weapons necessary in a general or 'unlimited' war" would offer the most insuperable obstacles to an inspection plan, since the violator could gain an overwhelming advantage from the concealment of even a few weapons. The need for a deterrent, in this connection too, is ineradicable.

### SUMMARY

Almost everyone seems concerned with the need to relax tension. However, relaxation of tension, which everyone thinks is good, is not easily distinguished from relaxing one's guard, which almost everyone thinks is bad. Relaxation, like Miltown, is not an end in itself. Not all danger comes from tension. To be tense where there is danger is only rational.

What can we say then, in sum, on the balance of terror theory of automatic deterrence? It is a contribution to the rhetoric rather than the logic of war in the thermonuclear age. The notion that a carefully planned surprise attack can be checkmated almost effortlessly, that, in short, we may resume our deep pre-Sputnik sleep, is wrong and its nearly universal acceptance is terribly dangerous. Though deterrence is not enough in itself, it is vital. There are two principal points.

First, deterring general war in both the early and late 1960's will be hard at best, and hardest both for ourselves and our allies wherever we use forces based near the enemy.

Second, even if we can deter general war by a strenuous and continuing effort, this will by no means be the whole of a military, much less a foreign policy. Such a policy would not of itself remove the danger of accidental outbreak or limit the damage in case deterrence failed; nor would it be at all adequate for crises on the periphery.

A generally useful way of concluding a grim argument of this kind would be to affirm that we have the resources, intelligence and courage to make the correct decisions. That is, of course, the case. And there is a good chance that we will do so. But perhaps, as a small aid toward making such decisions more likely, we should contemplate the possibility that they may *not* be made. They *are* hard, *do* involve sacrifice, *are* affected by great uncertainties and concern matters in which much is altogether unknown and much else must be hedged by secrecy; and, above all, they entail a new image of ourselves in a world of persistent danger. It is by no means certain that we shall meet the test.

**APPENDIX**
**BIBLIOGRAPHY**
**INDEX**

# APPENDIX: THE SIMPLE MATHEMATICS
# OF MAXIMIZATION*

This appendix is intended for operations researchers and other readers interested in a mathematical presentation of the material presented in Part II, "Efficiency in Using Defense Resources." It is written for readers who have an elementary knowledge of differential calculus. The appendix presents necessary and sufficient conditions for the maximum and minimum of a broad class of functions. It also includes a brief discussion of methods for finding the maximum. This discussion provides the mathematical background for computations like those in the illustrative example (Chapter 8). The appendix deals only with the mathematics of maximization and does not attempt to deal with risk, uncertainty, and criterion selection, nor, except for a brief section on game theory, does it take enemy reactions into account.

## I. INTRODUCTION

Military choice can be a very subtle and complex matter. At its heart one generally finds crucial issues of criterion selection, values and intangibles, and of risk and uncertainty about nature, technology, and enemy reactions. No simple formal model of choice is likely to be sufficient for a satisfactory analysis of most real military problems. But it is often enlightening to formulate parts of the problems of choice in economic terms, that is, in terms of discovering the most effective uses of limited resources. Formulated in these terms, a problem often can be reduced to that of determining the maximum or the minimum of a function of variables that are constrained to lie within a limited region. The function is an index of the extent to which some objective or set of objectives has been achieved. It provides a ranking of all possible combinations of the variables on which it depends, at least in the region of interest. The variables represent the extent to which various resources are employed in the achievement of the objective. Their values are constrained to lie within a limited region corresponding to the resources available because the resources are limited.

Consider, for example, the problem of an analyst whose job it is to recommend an allocation of a fixed budget among alternative strategic weapon systems. His task can be interpreted as one of finding the maximum of some relevant measure of strategic air power, given the limitation of a fixed budget. The problem of finding a good criterion or measure is

* This appendix was prepared by Alain C. Enthoven of The RAND Corporation.

very important in its own right. Many analyses of defense problems founder on this issue. However, for present purposes, we must assume that the criterion problem has been solved.

Represent the extent to which each weapon system is employed, for example the number of bomber wings or missile squadrons, by a variable, $x_i$. If there are $n$ such systems, there will be $n$ variables designated by the subscripts $x_1, \ldots, x_n$. Let the index of over-all strategic power or effectiveness be $E$, whence the problem is to determine the maximum of

$$(1.1) \qquad\qquad E(x_1, \ldots, x_n)$$

subject to the budget limitation. The contribution of one *extra* unit of $x_i$ to $E$, holding all other variables constant, is known as the *marginal product* of $x_i$. In the limit, if the units in which $x_i$ is measured are chosen small enough, this will be equal to the partial derivative of $E$ with respect to $x_i$. Let this derivative be written $E_i$. Generally it will be positive; that is, for example, an extra missile increases our strategic air power.

The budget limits the permissible combinations of the variables $x_i, \ldots, x_n$. Some combinations are too expensive. Suppose, for simplicity, that the cost per unit of $x_i$, in dollars, is a constant, $p_i$. Then, the budget limitation can be expressed by the inequality

$$(1.2) \qquad\qquad B - \sum_{i=1}^{n} p_i x_i \geqq 0,$$

where $B$ is the budget, measured in dollars.

If no further restrictions are placed on the form of $E$, there is not a great deal that can be said *a priori* about its maximum when constrained by (1.2). The constrained maximum must be found by systematic search over all combinations of $x_i, \ldots, x_n$ consistent with (1.2). The fact that one particular combination is the maximizing one must be established by comparison with all other possibilities. There are no *completely* general necessary and sufficient conditions for identifying a maximum applicable to all functions, and no generally reliable way of finding one other than by comparison with all possible values.

However, the lack of completely general necessary and sufficient conditions is not of very great importance because in so many problems of allocation the function to be maximized obeys the *general law of diminishing marginal returns*. This law states that as one system or input is substituted for another, with all other inputs and $E$ held constant, the terms on which the substitution can be made will become less and less favorable. Suppose, for example, that we were to fix the value of $E$ and all but two of the inputs, say $x_1$ and $x_2$. Starting with any pair of values of $x_1$ and $x_2$ that are consistent with the value of $E$, we might inquire how the increment of $x_2$ required to keep $E$ constant varies as $x_1$ is reduced, a unit at a time. If $E$ obeys the law of diminishing marginal returns, ever increasing increments in $x_2$ will be required to offset the successive reductions in $x_1$. To illustrate, suppose that we have a force of 100 bombers and 100 missiles, and that the effect on $E$ of reducing the bomber force by 10 is just offset by increasing the missile force by 8. If $E$ obeys the law of diminishing marginal returns, more than 8 missiles will be required to offset a second reduction in the bomber force by 10. The existence of this property should not be surprising. There are some missions performed better by bombers, others performed better by missiles, still others in which the two are good substitutes for each other. As the number of bombers is reduced, the extra missiles must be used in tasks that are successively more and more suited to bombers. One would expect many missiles to be required to offset the loss of the last few bombers.[1]

Alternative combinations of $x_1$ and $x_2$ consistent with the assumed value of $E$, with $E$ and all other variables constant, are shown in Figure a.

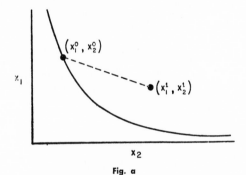

**Fig. a**

This curve is a contour line of $E$. It is called an *equal output line* or *isoquant* of $E$. There is a whole family of isoquants corresponding to different values of $E$. The slope of an isoquant can be derived from its definition. Holding $E$ and all other variables constant, we have

$$(1.3) \qquad dE = E_1\, dx_1 + E_2\, dx_2 = 0,$$

whence

$$(1.4) \qquad \frac{dx_1}{dx_2} = -\frac{E_2}{E_1}.$$

Thus, the slope of the isoquant is equal to the negative of the ratio of the marginal products. This ratio, that is $E_2/E_1$, is known as the *marginal rate of substitution* between $x_1$ and $x_2$. It indicates the rate at which $x_1$

---

[1] Of course, the relative costs may be such that the substitution is nevertheless worth making.

can be substituted for $x_2$ with $E$ constant. The law of diminishing marginal returns implies that this ratio decreases as $x_2$ increases, or, alternatively, that the isoquants must have the curvature shown in Figure a, if $E_1$ and $E_2$ are positive.

The mathematical name for the law of diminishing marginal returns is *quasi-concavity*. There are several equivalent ways of representing this property. First, if $E$ is quasi-concave, the set of values of $x_1, \ldots, x_n$ for which

$$(1.5) \qquad E(x_1, \ldots, x_n) \geqq z$$

will be convex for each real number $z$. It is convenient, at this point, to adopt the shorthand notation $x$ for the point $x_1, \ldots x_n$, $x^0$ for the point $x_1^0, \ldots, x_n^0$, and so on. The number of variables indicated will be clear from the context in which the notation appears. A convex set is a set that has the property that if it includes any pair of points, say $x^0$ and $x^1$, then it also includes any third point that lies on a straight line between them. Put alternatively, let the isoquant in Figure a correspond to $E(x^0)$ and let $x^1$ be any other point such that

$$(1.6) \qquad E(x^1) > E(x^0).$$

Then both points are in the set $x$ defined by the inequality $E(x) \geqq E(x^0)$. If $E$ is quasi-concave, any point that is an internal average of $x^0$ and $x^1$, that is, $\theta x^0 + (1 - \theta)x^1$ for any value of $\theta$ between 0 and 1, will have the property

$$(1.7) \qquad E[\theta x^0 + (1 - \theta)x^1] \geqq E(x^0).$$

This inequality can be taken to be a definition of quasi-concavity. $E$ is said to be *strictly quasi-concave* if the strict inequality holds in $(1.7)$ everywhere except at the end points $\theta = 0$ and $\theta = 1$.

An important subset of the class of quasi-concave functions is the class of *concave* functions. A concave function has the same properties of diminishing marginal returns with respect to the substitution between inputs as all quasi-concave functions, and it exhibits diminishing marginal returns as some inputs are increased, singly or in groups, while the rest are held constant. That is, if a function is concave, the marginal product of each input, $E_i$, diminishes as the amount of the input employed increases, and the marginal product of any group of inputs diminishes as the employment of the group is increased, all other variables being held constant in both cases. For example, if $E$ is concave, then the addition of 1 bomber to a force of 100 will increase $E$ less than the addition of 1 bomber to a force of 10. Similarly, the addition of 2 missiles and 2 bombers to a force of 50 missiles and 100 bombers will increase $E$ less than the same addition to a force of 5 missiles and 5 bombers. The difference between concavity and quasi-concavity is that the former is a more restrictive condition. If a function is concave, marginal returns to any combination of inputs must be constant or diminish as the combination is increased; if all inputs are doubled, output must increase by at most a factor of two. On the other hand, the quasi-concavity of a function does not indicate anything about its behavior as some inputs are increased while the others are held constant. The difference is important because it is possible to say more, especially with respect to computation, about maximization of concave functions.

There are several equivalent ways of representing concavity mathematically. Let $E$ be continuous and twice differentiable, and let $E_{ij}$ be the partial derivative of $E_i$ with respect to $x_j$. Then $E$ is concave if and only if

$$(1.8) \qquad d^2E = \sum_{i=1}^{n} \sum_{j=1}^{n} E_{ij}\, dx_i\, dx_j \leqq 0$$

for all $dx_i$ and $dx_j$, that is, if the second differential of $E$ is negative semi-definite. Alternatively, $E$ is said to be concave if the chord joining any two points on any plane profile of its graph lies on or below the graph.

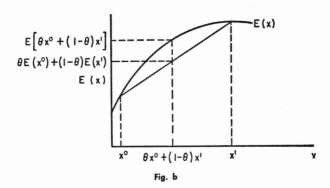

**Fig. b**

This is illustrated for a function of one variable in Figure b. Algebraically, this can be expressed by the inequality

$$(1.9) \qquad E[\theta x^0 + (1 - \theta)x] \geqq \theta E(x^0) + (1 - \theta)E(x) \qquad (0 \leqq \theta \leqq 1)$$

for all points $x^0$ and $x$.

A third definition may be more satisfying intuitively. A concave function lies everywhere on or below all of its tangent planes. Let $E_i^0$ represent the partial derivative evaluated at the point $x^0$. Then the equation of the plane tangent to $E$ at $x^0$, say $T(x)$, is

$$(1.10) \qquad T(x) = E(x_1^0, \ldots, x_n^0) + \sum_{i=1}^{n} E_i^0(x_i - x_i^0),$$

and, if $E$ is concave,

$$(1.11) \qquad E(x_1, \ldots, x_n) \leqq E(x_1^0, \ldots, x_n^0) + \sum_{i=1}^{n} E_i^0(x_i - x_i^0)$$

for all points $x^0$. This relation is shown in Figure c. $E$ is said to be *strictly* concave if the inequalities (1.8), (1.9), and (1.11) hold strictly, that is, if they do not include the possibility of equality except in the

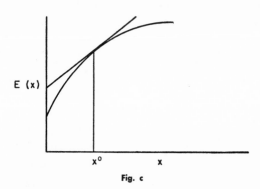

**Fig. c**

case of $dx_i = dx_j = 0$ in (1.8), in the case of the end points in (1.9), and in the case of the point of tangency in (1.11). A linear function is concave, but not strictly concave. $E$ may be concave *globally* or *locally:* it is globally concave if it is concave everywhere; it is locally concave if it is concave within a given interval.

All concave functions are quasi-concave. Moreover, all monotonically increasing functions of concave functions are quasi-concave.[2] To demonstrate the second proposition, consider any increasing function of $E$, say $\psi\{E\}$ which has the properties

$$(1.12) \qquad \begin{aligned} E(x^0) &> E(x) \text{ implies } \psi\{E(x^0)\} > \psi\{E(x)\}, \\ E(x^0) &= E(x) \text{ implies } \psi\{E(x^0)\} = \psi\{E(x)\}. \end{aligned}$$

Let $E$ be concave. Then, from (1.9),

$$(1.13) \qquad \psi\{E[\theta x^0 + (1 - \theta)x]\} \geqq \psi\{\theta E(x^0) + (1 - \theta)E(x)\},$$

or

$$(1.14) \qquad \psi\{E[\theta x^0 + (1 - \theta)x]\} \geqq \psi\{E(x) + \theta[E(x^0) - E(x)]\},$$

[2] It is not true, however, that all quasi-concave functions can be expressed as increasing functions of concave functions.

for $0 \leq \theta \leq 1$ and for all $x$ and $x^0$, from which it follows that if $E(x^0) \geq E(x)$,

$$(1.15) \qquad \psi\{E[\theta x^0 + (1 - \theta)x]\} \geq \psi\{E(x)\},$$

or $\psi\{E\}$ is quasi-concave.

By way of illustration, the function

$$(1.16) \qquad E(x_1, x_2) = (x_1 x_2)^{1/2}$$

is concave, though not strictly. The function

$$(1.17) \qquad E(x_1, x_2) = x_1 x_2$$

is strictly quasi-concave.

After a point, many weapon systems display constant or increasing average costs.[3] The constraint (1.2) was written on the assumption of constant unit costs. Suppose, however, that the cost per unit increases as the number of units purchased increases, and that the rate of increase is constant or increasing. This is the relation described by a normal supply curve, shown in Figure d.

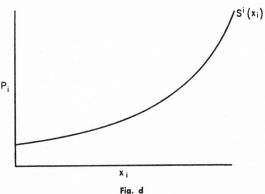

Fig. d

The presence of this property should not be surprising. Consider, for example, a market for labor. Although only a very moderate increase in the wage rate may be required to induce a worker to work 9 instead of 8 hours a day, one would expect a much larger increase to be required to induce him to work 15 instead of 14 hours. Let the average cost per unit for the $i^{\text{th}}$ input, as a function of the amount of the input employed, be

$$(1.18) \qquad p_i = S_i(x_i).$$

[3] In fact, if the prices of the original inputs are constant, a system that exhibits diminishing marginal returns will also have increasing marginal costs. See Section VI, below.

The cost of one extra unit of the $i^{th}$ input is equal to $p_i$, the average cost, plus the change in average cost or price multiplied by the number of units for which it must be paid. This cost is called the *marginal cost*. It can be written

$$(1.19) \qquad MC(x_i) = p_i + x_i \frac{dS_i}{dx_i}.$$

If marginal cost increases with $x_i$, the supply curve is *convex*. A convex function is one that obeys (1.8), (1.9), and (1.11) with the inequalities reversed. That is, a convex function has a second differential that is positive semi-definite, that lies below any chord joining two points of any plane profile of its graph, and that lies above any of its tangent planes. Just as in the case of concavity, a function may be convex or *strictly convex* (in the latter case, the inequalities are all strict) and convex globally or locally. The function shown in Figure e is convex

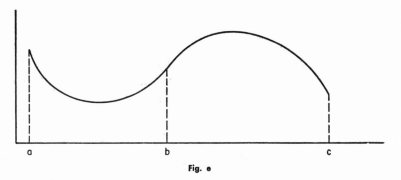

**Fig. e**

locally between $a$ and $b$ and concave locally between $b$ and $c$. A linear function is both concave and convex.

Most of the discussion that follows will be concerned with the maximization of quasi-concave and concave functions of variables constrained to lie within a convex region.[4] Most of the allocation problems that arise in practice fall into these classes. General mathematical methods are available for the solution of these problems. Other problems that do not have the appropriate convexity-concavity properties must be dealt with by special methods appropriate to the particular problem.

The fundamental principle of the theory of constrained maxima is the *marginal comparison*. Speaking loosely, an increase in the use of the $i^{th}$ system or input by one unit will increase $E$ by the marginal product of that input. But the existence of constraints means that there is a limit to

[4] A minimum problem can be converted to a maximum problem by a simple change of signs.

"free" increases in any input. After a point, an increase in any $x_i$ will have to be accompanied by a reduction in the use of other inputs. This reduction will mean a reduction in $E$. Thus, we can impute a marginal cost to each input, that is, the minimum reduction in $E$ made necessary by an increase of one unit in the use of that input. As long as it is possible to find inputs whose marginal products exceed their imputed marginal costs in this sense, it will be possible to increase $E$ by increasing their use. A relative maximum will be achieved when no further increases are possible, that is, when the marginal product of each input used is just equal to its marginal cost.

## II. CONSTRAINED MAXIMA

If $E$ obeys the law of diminishing returns, and if the unit costs or prices of the inputs are constant, how can a constrained maximum be identified? Consider the problem with just two inputs. The budget limitation can be expressed

$$(2.1) \qquad B - (p_1x_1 + p_2x_2) \geqq 0.$$

The requirement that neither input be used in a negative amount can be written

$$(2.2) \qquad x_i \geqq 0. \qquad (i = 1, 2)$$

These inequalities define a triangular area in the $x_1$, $x_2$ plane that contains all nonnegative combinations of $x_1$ and $x_2$ that satisfy the restriction that their cost does not exceed $B$. This is shown as the shaded area in Figure f.

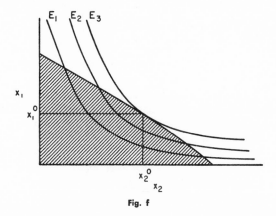

**Fig. f**

The sides of the triangle are the $x_1$ and $x_2$ axes and the line defined by (2.1) with an equality sign. The slope of this line, which will be referred to as the "budget line," is equal to $- p_2/p_1$.[5]

[5] All prices are assumed to be positive.

A whole family of isoquants of $E$, like the one shown in Figure a, can be drawn on this graph, with isoquants upward and toward the right corresponding to successively higher values of $E$, as long as $E$ is an increasing function of $x_1$ and $x_2$. Of all the points in or on the edge of the triangle, the point corresponding to the highest value of $E$ will be the point just on the highest isoquant. Superimposing the map of isoquants on the same $x_1$, $x_2$ plane, one obtains Figures f and g. These two figures correspond to two different possibilities. Either the maximizing values of $x_1$ and $x_2$ are both positive, as in Figure f, in which case the budget line is just tangent to the highest isoquant touching the triangle of feasible combinations; or, alternatively, one or the other of the maximizing values is equal to zero, as in Figure g. Let the maximizing values be $x_1^0$ and $x_2^0$

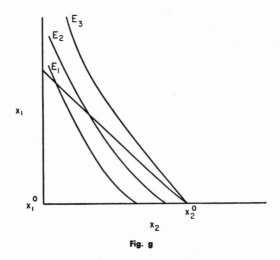

**Fig. g**

and suppose that both are positive, as in Figure f. The tangency of the highest isoquant and the budget line implies that the slopes of the line and the curve must be equal at the maximizing point. That is, writing $E_i^0$ for the value of $E_i$ at the maximum,

$$(2.3a) \qquad -\frac{p_2}{p_1} = -\frac{E_2^0}{E_1^0}$$

or

$$(2.3b) \qquad \frac{E_1^0}{p_1} = \frac{E_2^0}{p_2}.$$

At a maximum, the marginal product of the first input must be in the same proportion to its price as the marginal product of the second is to its price. Alternatively, the rate at which $x_1$ can be exchanged for $x_2$

(that is, the slope of the budget line) must equal the negative of the marginal rate of substitution. By inspection of Figure f, it is possible to verify that any departure from $(x_1^0, x_2^0)$ into or along the edge of the triangle will be a move to a lower level of $E$.

Alternatively, suppose that the slope of the budget line everywhere exceeds the slope of the isoquants at the budget line (is less, therefore, in absolute value) except possibly where the isoquants meet the $x_2$ axis. In this case, the proportionality condition (2.3a) cannot hold, and $x_1^0 = 0$, for as one moves down the budget line in Figure g, one reaches successively higher isoquants, until the highest one touching the triangle is reached, where $x_1 = 0$. Thus we have the condition that if

(2.4a) $$-\frac{p_2}{p_1} > -\frac{E_2}{E_1}$$

or

(2.4b) $$\frac{E_2}{p_2} > \frac{E_1}{p_1}$$

everywhere at the budget line, $x_1^0 = 0$. This condition states that if the marginal product of one dollar's worth of $x_1$ is always less than the marginal product of one dollar's worth of $x_2$, there is no room for $x_1$ to be included in the maximizing combination.

This maximum problem suggests a corresponding minimum problem. Suppose that one wishes to fix the value of $E$, say at $E^0$, and seek that combination of $x_1$ and $x_2$ that minimizes the total cost of attaining it. Budgets or total costs higher and lower than $B$ can be represented by budget lines parallel to $B$ and to its right and left, respectively. The lines are parallel because they all have the same slope, that is, $-p_2/p_1$. These are shown in Figures h and i. By inspection it can be seen that the same

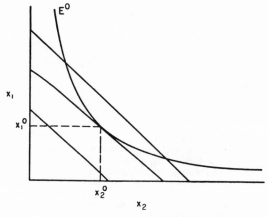

**Fig. h**

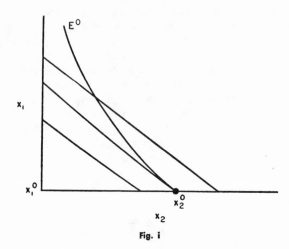

**Fig. i**

conditions apply as in the maximum problem. In fact, if $x_1^0$, $x_2^0$ maximizes $E$ given the budget $B$, then it also minimizes the cost of attaining $E(x_1^0, x_2^0)$, and the minimum cost is equal to $B$.

With the help of some algebra, these conditions can be generalized and stated rigorously for many inputs. The proofs are not difficult and they are valuable in that they illustrate the kind of mathematical reasoning involved.[6] First of all, if $x_1^0 \ldots, x_n^0$ maximizes any differentiable function $E(x_1, \ldots, x_n)$, subject to the constraints

$$(2.5) \qquad \qquad x_i \geqq 0, \qquad \qquad (i = 1, \ldots, n)$$

and

$$(2.6) \qquad \qquad B - \sum_{i=1}^{n} p_i x_i \geqq 0,$$

then

$$(2.7) \qquad \qquad E_i^0 - \lambda^0 p_i \leqq 0,$$

$$(2.8) \qquad \qquad x_i^0 (E_i^0 - \lambda^0 p_i) = 0,$$

and

$$(2.9) \qquad \qquad \lambda^0 \left( B - \sum_{i=1}^{n} p_i x_i^0 \right) = 0,$$

[6] The first two of the following proofs are essentially simplifications of the proofs contained in H. W. Kuhn and A. W. Tucker, "Nonlinear Programming," J. Neyman (ed.), *Proceedings of the Second Berkeley Symposium on Mathematical Statistics and Probability,* University of California Press, Berkeley, California, 1951, and R. Dorfman, P. A. Samuelson, and R. M. Solow, *Linear Programming and Economic Analysis,* Mc-Graw-Hill, New York, 1958, Chapter 8. The paper by Kuhn and Tucker is mathematically advanced, and unlikely to be accessible to readers with less than the equivalent of a B.A. in Mathematics. The Dorfman, Samuelson, Solow book has a very clear exposition only slightly more advanced mathematically than this one.

for some constant factor of proportionality, $\lambda \geqq 0$. That is, (2.7), (2.8), and (2.9) are necessary conditions for a maximum. Equation (2.8) implies that either $x_i^0 = 0$, in which case $E_i^0$ can be less than $\lambda^0 p_i$, or $E_i^0 = \lambda^0 p_i$, in which case $x_i^0$ can be positive. Similarly, equation (2.9) implies that if the constraint is not binding, $\lambda^0 = 0$. If the constraint is binding, $\lambda^0$ can be positive.

In order to show that these conditions are necessary, suppose that $x^0$ is a maximizing point. Then, it must be the case that no small departure from $x^0$ which does not violate the constraints, can increase $E$, or

$$(2.10) \qquad dE^0 = \sum_{i=1}^n E_i^0 \, dx_i \leqq 0$$

for all permissible variations $dx_i$, that is, small changes in the $x_i$ which are not inconsistent with the constraints.

First suppose that the constraint is not binding. In this case, the problem becomes an unconstrained maximum problem; the necessary and sufficient conditions become (2.7), (2.8), and (2.9) with $\lambda^0 = 0$. The fact that the constraint is not binding implies that permissible small positive and negative variations, $dx_i$, exist in all cases except when $x_i^0 = 0$, in which case negative variations are not permissible. In turn, let each $dx_i = k$, with all other variations equal to zero, where $k$ is a small positive number. Applying each of these variations successively to (2.10), we obtain

$$(2.11) \qquad E_i^0 \leqq 0. \qquad\qquad (i = 1, \ldots, n)$$

If $x_i^0 > 0$, let $dx_i = -k$, and make the same set of substitutions in (2.10). This implies

$$(2.12) \qquad E_i^0 \geqq 0, \qquad\qquad (x_i^0 > 0)$$

whence

$$(2.13) \qquad E_i^0 = 0$$

for $x_i^0 > 0$. If $x_i^0 = 0$, (2.11) holds. This establishes the necessity of (2.7), (2.8), and (2.9) for the case in which $\lambda^0 = 0$.

Now suppose that the constraint is binding. In this case, the permissible variations are limited by the constraint, that is,

$$(2.14) \qquad \sum_{i=1}^n p_i \, dx_i \leqq 0$$

as well as by the nonnegativity of the $x_i^0$. Assume that at least one of the maximizing input levels is positive, say the first, that is, $x_1^0 > 0$. Then the variation $dx_1 = -k$, with all other variations equal to zero, is permissible for some small positive $k$. This variation applied to (2.10) implies that $E_1^0 \geqq 0$. Now, for any other input whose maximizing value is positive, say, $x_i^0 > 0$, let $dx_i = kp_1$ and $dx_1 = -kp_i$, where $k$ is positive but small enough that the variations do not violate the nonnegativity constraints, and let all other variations equal zero. This is consistent with (2.14) whence, by (2.10),

$$(2.15a) \qquad -E_1^0 p_i + E_i^0 p_1 \leqq 0.$$

Reverse the signs of the variations. The new pair is also consistent with (2.14) whence

$$(2.15b) \qquad E_1^0 p_i - E_i^0 p_1 \leqq 0$$

and therefore,

$$(2.15c) \qquad E_1^0 p_i - E_i^0 p_1 = 0$$

for all $x_i^0 > 0$. The last equation can be written

$$(2.16a) \qquad \frac{E_1^0}{p_1} = \frac{E_i^0}{p_i} = \lambda^0,$$

where $\lambda^0$, the common factor of proportionality, must be nonnegative.[7] Alternatively, equation (2.16a) can be written

$$(2.16b) \qquad E_i^0 - \lambda^0 p_i = 0. \qquad (x_i^0 > 0)$$

For a variable whose maximizing value is equal to zero, say, $x_j^0 = 0$, let $dx_j = kp_1$ and $dx_1 = -kp_j$, all other variations being equal to zero. Applying this to (2.10), we have

$$(2.17a) \qquad -E_1^0 p_j + E_j^0 p_1 \leqq 0,$$

whence

$$(2.17b) \qquad E_j^0 - \lambda^0 p_j \leqq 0. \qquad (x_j^0 = 0)$$

This establishes the necessity of (2.7), (2.8), and (2.9) for the case in which the budget constraint is binding.

Next, it can be shown that if $E$ is a differentiable concave function and if (2.7), (2.8), and (2.9) hold for some point, $x^0$, then that point maximizes $E$ subject to the constraints (2.5) and (2.6). That is, if $E$ is concave, (2.7), (2.8), and (2.9) are sufficient conditions for a constrained maximum. The property of concavity is a substitute for the ordinary second order maximum conditions. If $E$ is concave within a specified region, then these conditions are sufficient for a maximum within that region; if $E$ is concave everywhere, these conditions are sufficient for a constrained maximum globally. To demonstrate this, assume that the

---

[7] The nonnegativity of $\lambda^0$ can be established independently of the sign of the $E_i$ and $p_i$, in the following way. Pick a variable whose maximizing value is positive, say, $x_i^0 > 0$, and let $dx_i = -kp_i < 0$ with all other $dx_i = 0$. This is consistent with (2.14) and the nonnegativity constraints if $k$ is small enough. By (2.10) this implies $-E_i^0 k p_i \leqq 0$ or $E_i^0 p_i \geqq 0$. However, since $E_i^0 = \lambda^0 p_i$, $E_i^0 p_i = p_i^2 \lambda^0 \geqq 0$; therefore $\lambda^0 \geqq 0$.

point $x^0$ satisfies conditions (2.5) to (2.9) and that $E$ is concave. The concavity of $E$ implies

$$(2.18) \qquad E(x) \leqq E(x^0) + \sum_{i=1}^{n} E_i^0(x_i - x_i^0).$$

Summing (2.8) over all $i$, we have

$$(2.19) \qquad \sum_{i=1}^{n} E_i^0 x_i^0 = \lambda^0 \sum_{i=1}^{n} p_i x_i^0.$$

Multiplying (2.7) by $x_i \geqq 0$ and adding, we have

$$(2.20) \qquad \sum_{i=1}^{n} E_i^0 x_i \leqq \lambda^0 \sum_{i=1}^{n} p_i x_i.$$

Applying (2.19) and (2.20) to (2.18), we obtain

$$(2.21) \qquad E(x) \leqq E(x^0) + \lambda^0 \sum_{i=1}^{n} p_i x_i - \lambda^0 \sum_{i=1}^{n} p_i x_i^0.$$

Now consider the set of all nonnegative $x$ that satisfy (2.6). For them, (2.21) and (2.6) imply

$$(2.22) \qquad E(x) \leqq E(x^0) + \lambda^0 (B - \Sigma p_i x_i^0);$$

therefore, by (2.9)

$$(2.23) \qquad E(x) \leqq E(x^0)$$

for all $x \geqq 0$ satisfying (2.6).

Next, it can be shown that if $E$ is a continuously differentiable quasi-concave function, and if (2.7), (2.8) and (2.9) hold for some $x^0$ with $\lambda^0 > 0$, then $x^0$ maximizes $E$, subject to the constraints (2.5) and (2.6). That is, (2.7), (2.8), and (2.9) are sufficient for a constrained maximum.[8] The requirement that $\lambda$ be positive is equivalent to there being at least one value of $i$ for which $E_i^0 > 0$; that is, at the point $x^0$ there is at least one input whose expanded use would increase $E$; therefore the budget constraint is binding.[9] In order to demonstrate that the conditions are sufficient, suppose that the theorem is false. Then there must exist a point, say $x^1$, which satisfies the constraints (2.5) and (2.6) for which

$$(2.24) \qquad E(x^1) > E(x^0).$$

Because of the continuity of $E$, it follows from (2.24) that it must be

[8] For a proof of the more general theorem of which this is a special case, see Kenneth J. Arrow and Alain C. Enthoven, "Quasi-Concave Programming," *Econometrica*, October 1961, pp. 779–800.

[9] It is clear from (2.7) that $E_i^0 > 0$ implies $\lambda^0 > 0$. Alternatively, $\lambda^0 > 0$ implies that at least one $x_i^0 > 0$ by (2.9); therefore, by (2.8), the corresponding $E_i^0 = \lambda^0 p_i > 0$.

possible to choose another point on the line between the origin and $x^1$, say, $x^2 = rx^1$ where $0 < r < 1$, so that

$$(2.25) \qquad\qquad E(x^2) \geqq E(x^0).$$

That is, since (2.24) is a strict inequality, there must be some values of $E$ between $E(x^1)$ and $E(x^0)$, one of which is $E(x^2)$. By the definition of $x^2$,

$$\sum_{i=1}^{n} p_i x_i^2 < \sum_{i=1}^{n} p_i x_i^1$$

unless all $x_i^1 = 0$. In either case, since, by hypothesis

$$B \geqq \Sigma p_i x_i^1,$$

that is, $x^1$ is assumed to satisfy the budget constraint, and

$$B > 0,$$

we have

$$(2.26) \qquad\qquad B > \Sigma p_i x_i^2.$$

Moreover, since by hypothesis $x^1$ satisfies (2.5), $x^2$ must also satisfy (2.5).

Thus far we have shown that if there exists a combination of inputs that yields a value of $E$ greater than $E(x^0)$ at the same cost as $x^0$, then there must exist another set of inputs that yields a value of $E$ at least equal to $E(x^0)$ at a lower cost.

Now, define

$$(2.27) \qquad\qquad F(\theta) = E[(1 - \theta)x^0 + \theta x^2].$$

The quasi-concavity of $E$ and (2.25) imply

$$(2.28) \qquad\qquad F(\theta) \geqq E(x^0) = F(0).^{[10]} \qquad\qquad (0 \leqq \theta \leqq 1)$$

Thus, $F$ cannot be a decreasing function of $\theta$ in the neighborhood of 0, or

$$(2.29) \qquad\qquad F'(0) \geqq 0.^{[11]}$$

However, differentiating (2.27) with respect to $\theta$, and setting $\theta = 0$, we have

$$(2.30) \quad F'(0) = \sum_{i=1}^{n} E_i^0 (x_i^2 - x_i^0)$$

$$= \sum_{i=1}^{n} x_i^2 (E_i^0 - \lambda^0 p_i) - \sum_{i=1}^{n} x_i^0 (E_i^0 - \lambda^0 p_i) + \lambda^0 \sum_{i=1}^{n} p_i (x_i^2 - x_i^0).$$

The first expression on the right-hand side must be less than or equal to zero because of (2.5) and (2.7); (2.8) implies that the second term vanishes; that the third term is definitely negative follows from (2.9)

---

[10] Recall (1.6) and (1.7).
[11] The prime indicates the first derivative of $F$ with respect to $\theta$.

and (2.26). Therefore, $F'(0)$ is negative. But this contradicts (2.29). Since the supposition that the theorem is false leads to a contradiction, the theorem must be true.

The significance of $\lambda^0$, the factor of proportionality between marginal products and prices, deserves some explanation. It is a relative measure of the force of the budget constraint, or the marginal cost, in terms of $E$, of a reduction in the budget. As the constraint is tightened, resources must be used less, and therefore their marginal products and $\lambda^0$ must increase. As the constraint is relaxed, resources can be used to a point at which their marginal products are lower than before and $\lambda^0$ decreases. Suppose the budget constraint is binding and remains so through small changes in the budget. Then permissible changes in the $x_i$ will obey the rule

$$(2.31) \qquad dB = \sum_{i=1}^{n} p_i \, dx_i.$$

If an input is used in a positive amount, then (2.16b) holds for the corresponding variable, and small positive or negative variations, $dx_i$, are permissible. If an input is not being used, then (2.17b) holds at the maximum for the corresponding variable and only nonnegative variations are permissible in that variable. Multiply each equation (2.16b) and inequality (2.17b) by any permissible variation in the corresponding variable, and add the products to obtain

$$(2.32) \qquad \sum_{i=1}^{n} E_i^0 \, dx_i \leqq \lambda^0 \sum_{i=1}^{n} p_i \, dx_i.$$

Now, if the variations in (2.32) are restricted to values satisfying (2.31), we have

$$(2.33) \qquad dE \leqq \lambda^0 \, dB.$$

Thus, $\lambda^0$ can be said to measure the minimum reduction in $E$ made necessary by a reduction of one unit in the budget. In this sense, then, $\lambda^0$ might be said to be a measure of the *marginal imputed value of the constraint*.

If any input is increased by one unit, $E$ will be increased directly by the marginal product of the input. However, assuming the budget constraint is binding, the use of other inputs will have to be curtailed if the use of one is increased, and this curtailment will mean an indirect reduction in $E$. The minimum indirect reduction in $E$ made necessary by an increase of one unit in the use of the $i^{\text{th}}$ input can be called the *marginal imputed cost of the input*. How is this cost found? The cost of increasing $x_i$ by one unit is $p_i$. Thus, the indirect $E$-reducing effect of a unit increase in $x_i$ must be the same as that of reducing the budget by $p_i$. Letting $dB$ equal $-p_i$ in (2.33), we have

$$(2.34) \qquad\qquad dE \leqq -\lambda^0 p_i.$$

In other words, $\lambda^0 p_i$ is the marginal imputed cost of the $i^{\text{th}}$ input. It is equal to the marginal cost of the input itself, that is, $p_i$, multiplied by the marginal imputed value of the constraint.

An important aspect of the theory of constrained maxima is that it is the set of rankings of all points $x$ that is implied by $E$ and not the function $E$ itself that is significant. Any other function that implies the same rankings of all points as $E$ does will yield the same results. Thus, one does not need an index or criterion that *measures* the effectiveness of alternative combinations of weapon systems; one needs only a criterion that will *rank* them. In other words, one does not need to know whether $x^0$ is *twice as* effective as $x^1$. The important thing is to be able to decide whether it is *more* effective.

Corresponding to the problem of maximizing $E$ subject to the constraint of a limited budget is the problem of minimizing the cost of attaining a specified value of $E$. It can be shown that if $E$ is differentiable and quasi-concave, the point $x^0$ that maximizes $E$ subject to (2.5) and (2.6) also minimizes the cost of attaining $E(x^0)$. That is, if $x^0$ satisfies the conditions (2.7) and (2.8), then it minimizes $\Sigma p_i x_i$ subject to the constraints

$$(2.35) \qquad\qquad E(x) - E(x^0) \geqq 0$$

and (2.5), the nonnegativity of the $x_i$.[12]

Let $x$ be any point satisfying (2.35). Then since $E$ is quasi-concave, we have, as in (2.27) and (2.28),

$$(2.36) \qquad F(\theta) = E[(1 - \theta)x^0 + \theta x] \geqq E(x^0) = F(0). \qquad (0 \leqq \theta \leqq 1)$$

Therefore, $F'(0) \geqq 0$, or

$$(2.37) \qquad\qquad \sum_{i=1}^{n} E_i^0(x_1 - x_i^0) \geqq 0.$$

The following equation is an identity:

$$(2.38) \qquad \lambda^0 \sum_{i=1}^{n} p_i(x_i - x_i^0) = \sum_{i=1}^{n} E_i^0(x_i - x_i^0) + \sum_{i=1}^{n} x_i(\lambda^0 p_i - E_i^0)$$
$$- \sum_{i=1}^{n} x_i^0(\lambda^0 p_i - E_i^0).$$

The first expression on the right-hand side is nonnegative by (2.37); the second is nonnegative because of (2.5) and (2.7); (2.8) implies that the third expression vanishes. Therefore the left-hand side must be nonnegative, or, for $\lambda > 0$

---

[12] See Arrow and Enthoven, Part IV.

(2.39)                              $\Sigma p_i x_i \geqq \Sigma p_i x_i^0$

for all $x$ satisfying (2.35).

Thus, if $x^0$ maximizes $E$ subject to a limited budget, it also minimizes the cost of attaining $E(x^0)$.

### III. ECONOMIC EFFICIENCY

In Section II, we considered the problem of determining the maximum of one function, corresponding to a single criterion for ranking alternative combinations of the inputs employed. This is the form in which many allocation problems appear. But in some circumstances it is very difficult, if not impossible, to define a single criterion which reflects adequately all of the relevant objectives. We may find ourselves confronted by two or more distinct objectives which we want to accomplish with the same budget. Do the results of Section II tell us anything useful in such circumstances? We can make relevant observations about the allocation problem even when we have no over-all criterion for ranking alternative combinations of achievement of the various objectives. We can inquire about *efficient* allocations, that is, allocations that maximize the achievement of one objective given the budget and some fixed level of achievement of the other objective. If allocation is efficient, then it will not be possible to increase the achievement of one objective without reducing the achievement of the other. There is some efficient allocation that is unambiguously better than any given inefficient allocation, and the over-all optimum allocation will be a member of the set of efficient ones.

Consider the problem of maximizing two independent criteria, say, $y^1(x_1^1, x_2^1)$ and $y^2(x_1^2, x_2^2)$, each of which is a quasi-concave function of the amounts of the two inputs $x_1$ and $x_2$ used for that purpose (the superscript 1 denotes the fact that the input is used to produce $y^1$), subject to an over-all budget constraint of the form

(3.1)                    $B - [(x_1^1 + x_1^2)p_1 + (x_2^1 + x_2^2)p_2] \geqq 0.$

There are several ways in which one might proceed to deduce conditions for an efficient allocation. For example, one might maximize $y^1$ subject to the budget constraint and the constraint that $y^2$ be at least equal to a specified amount. Or one might arbitrarily divide the budget between $y^1$ and $y^2$ and maximize each one separately. Yet another way would be to assume the existence of an unspecified quasi-concave increasing function of $y^1$ and $y^2$, maximize it, subject to the budget constraint, and then see what, if any, implications maximization has that are independent of the form of this function.

Let such a function be $E(y^1, y^2)$ and maximize it subject to the constraint (3.1). Applying the results of Section II, we have

$$E_i y_j^i - \lambda^0 p_j \leqq 0, \qquad (i = 1, 2; j = 1, 2)$$

(3.2)
$$x_j^i (E_i y_j^i - \lambda^0 p_j) = 0, \qquad (i = 1, 2; j = 1, 2)$$

$$\lambda^0 \{B - [(x_1^1 + x_1^2)p_1 + (x_2^1 + x_2^2)p_2]\} = 0,$$

where the subscripts after $E$ and $y^1$ indicate partial differentiation with respect to the indicated argument, as before. If the constraint is binding and the inputs are all used in positive amounts, these conditions imply

(3.3)
$$\frac{y_1^1}{y_2^1} = \frac{y_1^2}{y_2^2} = \frac{p_1}{p_2}$$

independently of the form of $E$. Of course these conditions are necessary for the independent maximum of $y^1$ and of $y^2$. In this simple case, allocation will be efficient if, whatever the division of the total budget between expenditure on $y^1$ and $y^2$, each is maximized subject to its own budget limitation. In order to determine the over-all optimum allocation between $y^1$ and $y^2$, one must know more about $E$.

More complicated cases arise. In the simple example discussed above, all inputs were *specific* to one or the other purpose, that is to $y^1$ or to $y^2$. The employment of an input in the pursuit of one objective precluded its having a direct effect on the attainment of the other objective. For example, manpower is used in all weapon systems, but the employment of a man in a bomber wing precludes his simultaneous employment in a fighter squadron. By way of contrast, some resources may be described as *joint* inputs.[13] A joint input is one whose employment has an impact on performance in terms of more than one objective. That is, although it may be used primarily for the achievement of one objective, a joint input has a direct effect on the achievement of others. For example, a warning system, though possibly operated by and for the air defense system, aids in the protection of our bombers and missiles and the civilian population. Joint inputs are shared, in some sense, while specific inputs have the character of exclusiveness in their employment.

Suppose, as before, that we know that it is desirable to maximize indices of the performance of two systems, $y^1$ and $y^2$, within the limitation of a fixed total budget, but that we are not able to rank alternative combinations of them. Assume that each function is quasi-concave and depends on a joint input, $x_1$, and a specific input, $x_2$. The fact that $x_1$ is a joint input means that whatever amount is used by one system is thereby available to the other also. The problem can be illustrated graphically.

[13] The distinction between joint and specific inputs corresponds to Professor Samuelson's distinction between public and private goods. It was Samuelson's analysis that suggested the following discussion. See P. A. Samuelson, "The Pure Theory of Public Expenditure," *The Review of Economics and Statistics*, Vol. XXXVI, No. 4, November 1954, pp. 387–389; "Diagrammatic Exposition of a Theory of Public Expenditure," *The Review of Economics and Statistics*, Vol. XXXVII, No. 4, November 1955, pp. 350–356.

First, the alternative combinations of $x_1$ and $x_2$ that can be purchased with a given budget are represented by the triangle in Figure j. An isoquant of $y^1$, corresponding to $\bar{y}^1$, is drawn on the same diagram. The fact that $x_2$ is a specific input means that whatever is used for $y^1$ is not available for $y^2$. Thus, given $\bar{y}^1$, alternative amounts of $x_2$ left over are given by the vertical distance between the isoquant and the budget line. For example,

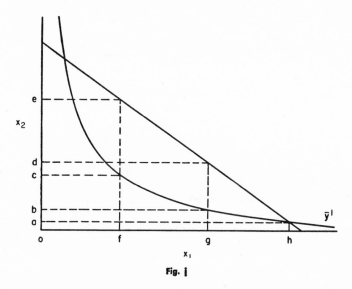

**Fig. j**

$\bar{y}^1$ of $y^1$ can be produced by $oh$ of $x_1$ and $oa$ of $x_2$, in which case there is no $x_2$ left over for $y^2$; by $og$ of $x_1$ and $ob$ of $x_2$, in which case, $bd$ of $x_2$ is left over for $y^2$; or by $of$ of $x_1$ and $oc$ of $x_2$, in which case, $ce$ of $x_2$ is left over for $y^2$.

Thus, the budget and the isoquant $y^1$ specify a set of alternative combinations of $x_1$ and $x_2$ available for $y^2$. The points corresponding to those in Figure j are graphed in Figure k, and the points are connected in a curve representing the maximal amounts available. The curve reaches a maximum at the point, in Figure j, at which the isoquant and the budget line are parallel. The units measured on the axes of Figure k are amounts of $x_1$ and $x_2$ available for $y^2$. Hence, the isoquants of $y_2$ can be plotted on the same figure. Also, more curves, like the one shown in Figure k can be drawn corresponding to higher and lower levels of $y^1$. A family of such curves, together with a family of $y^2$ isoquants is shown in Figure 1.

Given any level of $y^1$, and hence a corresponding curve representing amounts of $x_1$ and $x_2$ available for $y^2$, the level of $y^2$ will be maximized by the combination of $x_1$ and $x_2$ corresponding to the point at which the

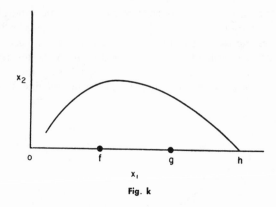

**Fig. k**

curve is just tangent to the highest $y^2$ isoquant it touches. The reasoning used to establish this is the same as that used in Section II. Suppose, for example, that the division of $x_1$ and $x_2$ corresponds to the point $P$ in Figure 1. Then, holding $y^1$ constant, that is, moving along the curve corresponding to constant $y^1$, it is clearly possible to increase $y^2$ by increasing $x_1$ and moving to the point $P^1$. Once such a point of tangency is reached, however, no further improvements in $y^2$ are possible without reducing $y^1$. Each such point of tangency is known as an *efficient point*.

Figure 1 shows that there is not one but a whole set of efficient points, indicated by the dotted line. In order to make a rational choice from among these points, one must have a criterion that ranks alternative combinations of $y^1$ and $y^2$. But without such a criterion, it is still possible

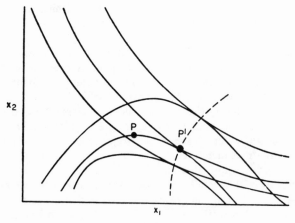

**Fig. l**

to say that an unambiguous improvement can be made if the allocation does not correspond to an efficient point, and therefore, that the over-all optimum will be found among the efficient points.

The slope of the $y^2$ isoquant, that is, $dx_2/dx_1$, is equal to $-y_1^2/y_2^{2}$.[14] Writing the budget constraint

$$(3.4) \qquad B - x_1 p_1 + x_2 p_2 \geqq 0,$$

the line relating maximal amounts of $x_2$ to $x_1$ has the equation

$$(3.5) \qquad x_2 = \frac{B}{p_2} - x_1 \frac{p_1}{p_2},$$

with slope $-p_1/p_2$. The slope of the $y^1$ isoquant is $-y_1^1/y_2^1$. Now, the curve shown in Figure k is the vertical difference between the budget line and the $\bar{y}^1$ isoquant, as a function of $x_1$. Its slope is equal to the difference between the slopes of these two functions, or $-(p_1/p_2) - (-y_1^1/y_2^1)$. The necessary tangency condition for efficient allocation, pictured in Figure l, is equivalent to the equality of this slope and the slope of the $y^2$ isoquant. Setting the two slopes equal to each other, one obtains the necessary condition for efficient allocation between a joint input, $x_1$, and a specific input, $x_2$.

$$(3.6) \qquad \frac{y_1^1}{y_2^1} + \frac{y_1^2}{y_2^2} = \frac{p_1}{p_2}.$$

The significant point is this. In Section II, we saw that for a maximum of $E$, it was necessary that the marginal rate of substitution between $x_1$ and $x_2$ in $E$ be equal to the ratio of the prices of $x_1$ and $x_2$. In the case of a joint good, it is the *sum* of the marginal rates of substitution that must be equal to the ratio of the prices, if allocation is to be efficient.[15]

These results can be stated in a unified way with the help of the technique introduced at the beginning of this section. That is, assume that alternative combinations of $y^1$ and $y^2$ can be ranked by a criterion, $E(y^1, y^2)$, that is a quasi-concave increasing function of the two variables. Then maximize $E$ subject to the over-all budget constraint.

Let $y^1$ and $y^2$ each be functions of two joint inputs $x_1$ and $x_2$, and two specific inputs, $x_3$ and $x_4$. The amounts of $x_1$ and $x_2$ used by either system, that is for either $y^1$ or $y^2$, are equal to the total amounts used. This is not the case with the specific inputs, for which it is the sum of the amounts used for $y^1$ and $y^2$ that is equal to the total amount used. For this reason, we must label $x_3$ and $x_4$ according to their uses. Let $x_3^1$ be the amount of $x_3$ used for $y^1$, $x_4^2$ the amount of $x_4$ used for $y^2$. Then the over-all budget constraint can be written

---

[14] See equation (1.4) and related discussion in Section I above.
[15] See Samuelson, "The Pure Theory of Public Expenditure," pp. 387–389.

(3.7)          $B - [x_1 p_1 + x_2 p_2 + (x_3^1 + x_3^2)p_3 + (x_4^1 + x_4^2)p_4] \geqq 0.$

Assume that the budget constraint is binding and, for simplicity, that all of the inputs are used in both $y^1$ and $y^2$ in positive amounts. Then, the constrained maximum of

$$E[y^1(x_1, x_2, x_3^1, x_4^1), \, y^2(x_1, x_2, x_3^2, x_4^2)]$$

is defined by the conditions

$$E_1 y_1^1 + E_2 y_1^2 - \lambda^0 p_1 = 0,$$
$$E_1 y_2^1 + E_2 y_2^2 - \lambda^0 p_2 = 0,$$
(3.8)          $$E_1 y_3^1 - \lambda^0 p_3 = 0,$$
$$E_1 y_4^1 - \lambda^0 p_4 = 0,$$
$$E_2 y_3^2 - \lambda^0 p_3 = 0,$$
$$E_2 y_4^2 - \lambda^0 p_4 = 0.$$

Equations (3.8) in turn imply the following conditions for efficient allocation:

(3.9)

$$\frac{y_1^1}{y_3^1} + \frac{y_1^2}{y_3^2} = \frac{p_1}{p_3}, \qquad \frac{y_1^1}{y_4^1} + \frac{y_1^2}{y_4^2} = \frac{p_1}{p_4},$$

$$\frac{y_2^1}{y_3^1} + \frac{y_2^2}{y_3^2} = \frac{p_2}{p_3}, \qquad \frac{y_2^1}{y_4^1} + \frac{y_2^2}{y_4^2} = \frac{p_2}{p_4}$$

between joint and specific inputs (as in equation 3.6) ;

(3.10)          $$\frac{y_3^1}{y_4^1} = \frac{y_3^2}{y_4^2} = \frac{p_3}{p_4}$$

between specific inputs (as in equation 3.3) ; and

(3.11)          $$\frac{E_1 y_1^1 + E_2 y_1^2}{E_1 y_2^1 + E_2 y_2^2} = \frac{p_1}{p_2}$$

between joint inputs. One of the conditions (3.9) is redundant in the sense that if the other three and (3.10) are satisfied, it must also be satisfied. If (3.9) and (3.10) are satisfied, allocation is efficient in the sense that $y^1$ cannot be increased without reducing $y^2$. The over-all optimum requires that (3.11) be satisfied also. But this condition cannot be stated independently of the weights $E_1$ and $E_2$.

If $y^1$ and $y^2$ are alternative criteria applied to the same systems, all of the inputs involved may prove to be joint ones. In this case, there is much less that can be said in the absence of a higher criterion for ranking alternative combinations of $y^1$ and $y^2$. The problem is one of evaluating the allocation of the same set of resources from two different points of view. The triangle of alternative combinations of $x_1$ and $x_2$ consistent with the budget limitation is shown in Figure m. In general, there will be one allocation along the border that maximizes $y^1$, another that maximizes $y^2$. If both objectives are desirable, the over-all optimum will be an internal average of the two allocations, that is, a weighted average with nonnegative weights whose sum is equal to unity. A set of illustrative isoquants is

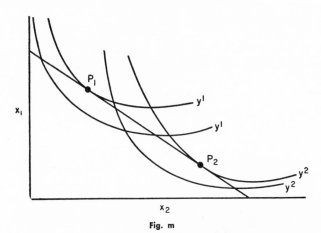

**Fig. m**

shown in Figure m. The allocation corresponding to a maximum of $y_1$ is $P_1$, that maximizing $y_2$ is $P_2$. The only thing that can be said in the absence of a higher level criterion is that the over-all optimum will be $P_1$, $P_2$, or some point in between. Points on the edge of the triangle to the left of $P_1$ or to the right of $P_2$ correspond to lower levels of *both* $y^1$ and $y^2$ than the levels attained at $P_1$ and $P_2$. Hence, such points correspond to inefficient allocations.

### IV. GENERALIZATIONS: NONLINEAR PROGRAMMING

The discussion of Section II was limited to finding the maximum of a quasi-concave function subject to one linear constraint. In practice, problems often arise involving several constraints that may not be linear. For example, the military services face specific manpower constraints as well as a budget constraint. However, the theorem of Section II, in its general form, covers these cases.[16] Suppose, for example, that $E$ depends upon two weapon systems, $x_1$ and $x_2$, and that each has a constant unit cost in dollars, $p_1$ and $p_2$, and a constant manpower requirement per

---

[16] As well as in the article by Kuhn and Tucker and the book by Dorfman, Samuelson, and Solow already mentioned, the reader can find a general statement of the theorem, for linear constraints, in A. W. Tucker, "Linear and Nonlinear Programming," *Operations Research*, Vol. 5, No. 2, April 1957, pp. 244–257.

unit, $m_1$ and $m_2$. Let the total budget be $B$, the manpower ceiling, $M$. The problem, then, is to maximize

(4.1)
$$E(x_1, x_2)$$

subject to the constraints

(4.2a)
$$B - p_1x_1 + p_2x_2 \geqq 0,$$

(4.2b)
$$M - m_1x_1 + m_2x_2 \geqq 0,$$

and, of course, $x_1 \geqq 0$ and $x_2 \geqq 0$. The region of combinations of $x_1$ and $x_2$ satisfying these constraints will, in general, have four sides (unless every combination satisfying one constraint satisfies the other, in which case the latter constraint is redundant). It is illustrated, for the case of two effective constraints, by the shaded area in Figure n. There are several

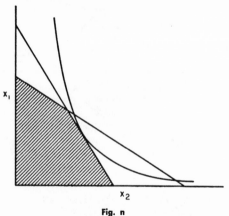

**Fig. n**

possibilities that may arise. Neither constraint may be binding. This is an uninteresting case. Alternatively, the optimal combination of $x_1$ and $x_2$ when only the budget constraint is considered may be feasible from the point of view of the manpower constraint, or vice versa. In this case, one constraint is binding and the other is not. Finally, both constraints may be binding. Examples of one and both constraints binding are illustrated in Figures n and o.

The necessary and sufficient conditions for a constrained maximum are analogous to those in the case of one constraint. However, when there are two constraints, each constraint has its own imputed marginal value. The conditions are

(4.3)
$$E_1^0 - \lambda_1^0 p_1 - \lambda_2^0 m_1 \leqq 0,$$
$$E_2^0 - \lambda_1^0 p_2 - \lambda_2^0 m_2 \leqq 0,$$

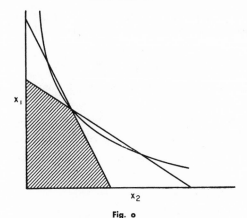

**Fig. o**

with the equalities holding when the inputs are used in positive amounts, or

$$(4.4) \quad \begin{aligned} x_1^0(E_1^0 - \lambda_1^0 p_1 - \lambda_2^0 m_1) &= 0, \\ x_2^0(E_2^0 - \lambda_1^0 p_2 - \lambda_2^0 m_2) &= 0. \end{aligned}$$

Similarly, for the constraints,

$$(4.5) \quad \begin{aligned} \lambda_1^0(B - p_1 x_1^0 - p_2 x_2^0) &= 0, \\ \lambda_2^0(M - m_1 x_1^0 - m_2 x_2^0) &= 0. \end{aligned}$$

The sense of these results is the same as the sense of the single constraint case. Each constraint has its own marginal imputed value. If a constraint is not binding, its marginal imputed value is zero. The marginal imputed cost of each input is equal to the sum of its marginal costs in terms of each constraint, weighted by the marginal imputed value of the constraint. The marginal product of each input must be less than or equal to its marginal imputed cost. If the input is used at all, its marginal product and marginal imputed cost must be equal.[17]

Strictly concave constraints do not raise any fundamentally new problems.[18] Suppose, for example, that there is a specified budget limitation

---

[17] The reader can test these results on a simple numerical example. Maximize $x_1 x_2$ subject to the constraints $1 - 2x_1 - x_2 \geqq 0$, $1 - x_1 - 2x_2 \geqq 0$, $x_1 \geqq 0$ and $x_2 \geqq 0$. The reader should be able to verify the fact that the maximizing values of $x_1$ and $x_2$ are $\frac{1}{3}$, that both constraints are binding, and that their marginal imputed values are $\frac{1}{3}$.

[18] The same constraint will be concave or convex depending upon a simple choice of sign. For example, $g(x) \geqq 0$ and $-g(x) \leqq 0$ represent the same set of points $x$. Yet, if $g(x)$ is concave, $-g(x)$ is convex. There are two important points. First, the set of points defined by the constraints must be convex. Second, by convention, inequality constraints are written in the greater-than-or-equal-to-zero form. Written this way, the constraint functions must be concave for the theorems to apply to the maximization of a quasi-concave function.

but that the prices of the resources increase with the amount purchased. Let each price be related to the quantity purchased by a supply curve

(4.6) $$p_i = S_i(x_i)$$

with the curvature shown in Figure d.[19]

Assuming two inputs, as before, the budget constraint (4.2a) can be written

(4.7) $$B - [x_1 S_1(x_1) + x_2 S_2(x_2)] \geqq 0.$$

The slope of the boundary of the area described by (4.7) is

(4.8) $$\frac{dx_1}{dx_2} = \frac{-(x_2 S_2' + S_2)}{-(x_1 S_1' + S_1)} < 0.$$

This curve becomes steeper as $x_2$ increases. That is,

(4.9) $$\frac{d^2 x_1}{dx_2^2} = -\frac{(x_1 S_1' + S_1)^2 (x_2 S_2'' + 2 S_2') + (x_2 S_2' + S_2)^2 (x_1 S_1'' + 2 S_1')}{(x_1 S_1' + S_1)^3} < 0.$$

Thus it has the curvature shown in Figure p.

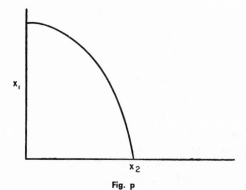

**Fig. p**

The slope of this curve has another interpretation. The total amount spent on $x_1$ is $x_1 S_1(x_1)$, that is, quantity times price. Differentiating this expression with respect to $x_1$, we get the amount by which the total cost of $x_1$ units increases as we increase $x_1$, or the marginal cost of $x_1$. The marginal cost has two components: the price of a unit of $x_1$, which must be paid for the extra unit, and the increase in the price multiplied by the number of units for which it must be paid. That is,

(4.10) $$\frac{d}{dx_1} [x_1 S_1(x_1)] = S_1(x_1) + x_1 S_1'(x_1) = MC(x_1).$$

[19] That is, $\frac{dp_i}{dx_i} = S_i' \geqq 0$ and $\frac{d^2 p_i}{dx_i^2} = S_i'' \geqq 0$.

Thus, the formula for the slope of the budget restriction curve (4.8) can be rewritten

$$(4.11) \qquad \frac{dx_1}{dx_2} = -\frac{MC(x_2)}{MC(x_1)}.$$

Superimposing the isoquants of $E$ on Figure p, one finds the familiar tangency condition for a constrained maximum. If $x_1$ and $x_2$ are used in positive amounts,

$$(4.12) \qquad \frac{MC(x_1)}{MC(x_2)} = \frac{E_1}{E_2}.$$

If $x_2$ is not used in the maximizing combination, it must be that the slope of the isoquant at the budget curve always exceeds the slope of the budget curve, or

$$(4.13) \qquad -\frac{E_2}{E_1} > -\frac{MC(x_2)}{MC(x_1)}.$$

This is the same thing as saying that the marginal product of $x_2$ is never great enough, in relation to its marginal cost, to make it worth buying any of it in preference to $x_1$.[20]

In general, a constraint limits the admissible values of the variables $x_i$ because some resource is limited in total supply. In the examples used so far the resource has been money or manpower, but it could be anything. If we write the surplus or unused amount of some resource as a function of the $x_i$ in the form $C(x_1, \ldots, x_n)$, then the constraint $C(x_1, \ldots, x_n) \geqq 0$ indicates that positive or zero unused amounts are permissible, but negative ones are not. That is, we cannot use more than the total available. If increasing the extent to which one input is used, that is, increasing $x_i$, requires the use of more of the limited resource, the unused amount will be a decreasing function of $x_i$. That is, $\partial C/\partial x_i = C_i$ will be negative. The negative of $C_i$ can be thought of as the marginal cost of the $i$th input in terms of the resource whose limitation is expressed by the constraint. If the marginal costs of all resources are constant, $C(x_1, \ldots, x_n)$ will be linear; if the marginal costs are either constant or increasing functions of $x_i$, the constraint will be concave; if all are increasing, the constraint will be strictly concave.

The necessary and sufficient conditions for a maximum with two constraints and with concave constraints are special cases of a more general theorem. Suppose that we wish to maximize $E(x)$ subject to the constraints

---

[20] That is, (4.13) can be rewritten $\dfrac{E_2}{MC(x_2)} < \dfrac{E_1}{MC(x_1)}$.

(4.14)                        $C^j(x_1, \ldots, x_n) \geqq 0$                    $(j = 1, \ldots, h)$

and

(4.15)                              $x_i \geqq 0.$                              $(i = 1, \ldots, n)$

*Let $E(x)$ and $C^j(x)$ be continuously differentiable functions. Then the following conditions are necessary for $x^0$ to maximize $E(x)$ subject to (4.14) and (4.15):* [21]

(4.16)                   $E_i^0 + \sum_{j=1}^{h} \lambda_j^0 C_i^{j0} \leqq 0,$               $(i = 1, \ldots, n)$

(4.17)                   $x_i^0 [E_i^0 + \sum_{j=1}^{h} \lambda_j^0 C_i^{j0}] = 0,$

*that is, either the equality is satisfied in (4.16) or $x_i^0 = 0$, and*

(4.18)                   $\lambda_j^0 C^j(x_1^0, \ldots, x_n^0) = 0$

*that is, either each constraint is binding, or its marginal imputed value is zero.*

Now, let a *relevant variable* be one that can take on a positive value without necessarily violating the constraints. That is, $x_{i_r}$ is a relevant variable if there is some point $x^*$ in the set of points defined by the constraints for which $x_{i_r}{}^* > 0$. *Then (4.16), (4.17), and (4.18) will be sufficient conditions for a constrained maximum if $E(x)$ and $C^j(x)$ are continuously differentiable quasi-concave functions and if at least one of the following conditions is satisfied: (a) $E_i^0 < 0$ for some $x_i$; (b) $E_i^0 > 0$ for some relevant variable $x_{i_r}$; (c) $E(x)$ is twice continuously differentiable and $E_i^0 \neq 0$; (d) $E(x)$ is concave.* [22] The conditions (4.16), (4.17), and (4.18) are a natural generalization of the conditions explained earlier in this section for the case in which there are two constraints.

---

[21] The necessity part of the theorem has been proved by Kuhn and Tucker, pp. 483–485. They point out the possibility of certain pathological cases in which no $\lambda^0$ exists that will satisfy the conditions (4.16), (4.17), and (4.18) because of the existence of singularities on the boundary of the constraint set. For example, maximize $E(x) = x_1 x_2$ subject to the constraints $x_1 \geqq 0, x_2 \geqq 0, C(x) = (1 - x_1 - x_2)^3 \geqq 0$. The constrained maximum occurs at $x_1^0 = x_2^0 = \frac{1}{2}$, but at that point (and at all points at which $x_1 + x_2 = 1$) $C_i^0 = 0$, so there can be no value of $\lambda$ that satisfies (4.16) at $x^0$. Kuhn and Tucker rule out this possibility by imposing a regularity condition on the constraints which they call the *Constraint Qualification*. This condition will be satisfied, for example, if each constraint $C^j(x)$ satisfies one of the following conditions. (1) $C^j(x)$ is linear. (2) $C^j(x)$ is a concave function, and there exists some point, $x^* \geqq 0$, at which $C^j(x^*) > 0$ for all $j = 1, \ldots, h$. (3) $C^j(x)$ is a quasi-concave function with the property that at every point $x^0$ in the set of points defined by the constraints, $C_i^{j0} \neq 0$ for some $i$, and there exists some point, $x^* \geqq 0$, at which $C^j(x^*) > 0$ for all $j = 1, \ldots, h$. These conditions should cover most cases of practical interest. For a discussion of the Constraint Qualification, for references, and for a proof of conditions (2) and (3), see Arrow and Enthoven, Part III.

[22] For the proof of this theorem, see Arrow and Enthoven.

## V. HOW TO FIND THE MAXIMUM: THE GRADIENT METHOD

The necessary and sufficient conditions for a constrained maximum enable us to *identify* the maximum but they do not tell us how to *find* it. That is, although there are exceptions, ordinarily the necessary and sufficient conditions cannot be readily solved for the maximizing values. Even in the favorable cases in which they are linear, as they would be if the maximand were a quadratic form, and therefore apparently amenable to standard techniques of solution, such techniques may fail because of the nonnegativity constraints on the $x_i$ and $x_j$. Moreover, the conditions themselves do not tell us how to make *improvements* in the allocation of the budget, improvements which may be valuable even if we fall short of the maximum. Of course, one might attempt to exhaust the alternatives. If there are not too many alternatives, this procedure may not be unsatisfactory. If the function to be maximized is not concave, one may be forced to adopt it. However, if the objective function is concave, including the possibility of linearity, there are short cut methods for finding the maximum. These methods, which are systems of successive approximations, are designed to exploit the property of concavity by using it to rule out a whole set of alternatives instead of just one each time a step is taken. Since these methods proceed by making successive improvements, they are valuable because of the improvements even if not pursued to the maximum.

If both $E$ and the constraints are linear, the problem is handled most efficiently by the methods of linear programming.[23] If $E$ is the sum of a linear function and a concave quadratic form, that is, expressible as a sum of the form

$$(5.1) \qquad E(x) = \sum_{i=1}^{n} a_i x_i + \sum_{i=1}^{n} \sum_{j=1}^{n} a_{ij} x_i x_j, \qquad (a_{ij} = a_{ji})$$

where $a_i$ and $a_{ij}$ are constants, the special methods of quadratic programming can be applied.[24] These methods, which are tailored especially to particular classes of problems, are more efficient than the more general methods described below, in the sense that they converge to the maximum with less computation. However, the more general method has the advantage of being more readily understandable. Indeed, it is a natural extension of our earlier results.

[23] See, for example, Dorfman, Samuelson, and Solow, which has a good bibliography as well as a lucid exposition of the subject. For a brief self-contained elementary exposition of the computational approach, see Harvey M. Wagner, "The Simplex Method for Beginners," *Operations Research*, Vol. 6, No. 2, March–April, 1958, pp. 190–199.

[24] For (5.1) to be concave, $\sum_{i=1}^{n} \sum_{j=1}^{n} a_{ij} x_i x_j$ must be negative semi-definite. See Philip Wolfe, "The Simplex Method for Quadratic Programming," *Econometrica*, Vol. 27, No. 3, July 1959, pp. 382–398; also, The RAND Corporation, P-1205, 25 October 1957.

The proof used in Section II to establish the necessary conditions for a constrained maximum suggests a method for finding potential improvements when $E$ is not at a constrained maximum. There it was shown that if $x^0$ maximizes $E$ subject to the constraints, it must be the case that

$$(5.2) \qquad dE^0 = \sum_{i=1}^{n} E_i^0 \, dx_i \leqq 0$$

for all variations in the $x_i$ which do not violate the constraints. If $E$ is not at a maximum, then, it should be possible to find a permissible set of variations in the $x_i$ that increases $E$.

Suppose that there is one constraint,

$$(5.3) \qquad C(x_i, \ldots, x_n) \geqq 0.$$

If the constraint is binding, the permissible variations in the variables $x_i$ are limited by the inequality

$$(5.4) \qquad \sum_{i=1}^{n} C_i \, dx_i \geqq 0.$$

Suppose that the existing combination of inputs, if there is one, or some arbitrarily chosen combination, is not known to be the maximizing one. Pick some pair of inputs, say $x_i$ and $x_j$, at least one of which, say $x_i$, is being used in a positive amount. Let $dx_i$ equal $-kC_j$ and let $dx_j$ equal $kC_i$, where $k$ is a positive constant not large enough that the variations will conflict with the nonnegativity constraints, and let all other variations be equal to zero. Clearly this satisfies (5.4). Then, we have

$$(5.5) \qquad dE = k(E_j C_i - E_i C_j).$$

If $dE$ is positive, that is if $E_i/-C_i > E_j/-C_j$, this pair of variations will lead to an improvement in $E$. If the opposite inequality holds, then the same pair of variations with signs reversed will lead to an improvement in $E$. The latter pair of variations also satisfies the constraint. The same holds true for activity or input levels that are equal to zero, except that in this case, negative variations are not permitted. Thus, in general, a reallocation away from any input with a lower ratio of marginal product to marginal cost to one with a higher ratio, and which does not violate the constraints, will lead to an increase in $E$. The process of reallocation and improvement can continue until a maximum has been reached.[25]

One important aspect of this rule for obtaining improvements in $E$ is that it does not require a full specification of the $E$ function. All that is required for successful application is the ability to compare the ratios of marginal products to marginal costs at the point in question.

---

[25] However, there is no general guarantee that this process will converge onto the maximum.

There is no reason, however, why reallocations must be carried out in pairs. Consider the following set of rules. Beginning with any set of values of $x$ and with an arbitrarily selected positive value for each $\lambda_j$, examine the marginal product and the marginal imputed cost of each input. If the marginal product exceeds marginal cost for an input, it is profitable to increase the employment of that input. Hence, if (in the notation of Section IV)

$$(5.6) \qquad E_i + \sum_{j=1}^{h} \lambda_j C_i^j$$

is positive, increase $x_i$ in proportion to (5.6). If (5.6) is negative, decrease $x_i$ in the same proportion, unless it is already equal to zero. If $x_i$ is equal to zero, and (5.6) is negative, leave $x_i$ unchanged. Similarly, if

$$(5.7) \qquad C^i(x_1, \ldots, x_n)$$

is positive, that is, if the constraint is not binding, reduce $\lambda_j$, unless $\lambda_j$ is already equal to zero. In that case, leave it unchanged. If the constraint is just satisfied, do not change $\lambda_j$. If (5.7) is negative, so that the constraint is being violated, increase $\lambda_j$.

Consider a round of adjustment to be completed each time all of the marginal products and costs have been compared and the $x_i$ adjusted accordingly, and all the constraints examined and the $\lambda_j$ adjusted appropriately. Then, if we identify each round with a unit of "time," we can construct a continuous model of this set of rules. Let the variable $t$ measure the number of units of computational time that have elapsed since the beginning of the process. Then, let

$$(5.8) \qquad \frac{dx_i}{dt} = \begin{cases} 0 & \text{if } x_i = 0 \text{ and } E_i + \sum_{j=1}^{h} \lambda_j C_i^j < 0 \\ E_i + \sum_{j=1}^{h} \lambda_j C_i^j & \text{otherwise.} \end{cases}$$

$$\frac{d\lambda_j}{dt} = \begin{cases} 0 & \text{if } \lambda_j = 0 \text{ and } C^i > 0 \\ -C^i & \text{otherwise.} \end{cases}$$

Uzawa has shown that if $E$ is strictly concave and continuously differentiable, and if the constraints are concave (not necessarily strictly) and continuously differentiable,[26] there will be a unique solution to the

[20] Most, though not all, quasi-concave functions can be transformed into strictly concave functions by some monotonic transformation that preserves the same rankings and therefore that has the same constrained maximum, or which defines the same convex set. By finding an appropriate set of transformations, then, one can extend the application of the theorem. For example, $E(x_1, x_2) = x_1 x_2$ is quasi-concave; $(x_1 x_2)^{1/3}$ is strictly concave.

constrained maximum problem, and the variables $x_i$ and $\lambda_j$ will converge to their maximizing values.[27]

As a practical matter of computation, the continuous derivatives of (5.8) must be approximated by finite differences, unless the computation is being done with a continuous analogue device. The approximating equations are known as difference equations. They relate the values of the variables $x_i$ and $\lambda_j$ in the interval of time $t$ to their values in the immediately preceding interval, $t - 1$. Let the variable $t$ take on only integral values. Then (5.8) can be approximated by the equations

$$x_i(t) = \text{the larger of} \begin{cases} 0 \\ x_i(t-1) + q\{E_i[x(t-1)] + \sum_{j=1}^{h} \lambda_j(t-1)C_i^j[x(t-1)]\} \end{cases}$$

(5.9)

$$\lambda_i(t) = \text{the larger of} \begin{cases} 0 \\ \lambda_i(t-1) - qC^i[x(t-1)], \end{cases}$$

where $q$ is a positive constant which determines the size of each step. Unless a sufficiently small value of $q$ is chosen, however, there is a danger that when the true path of a variable $x_i(t)$, determined by (5.8), undergoes a sharp change in slope between $t - 1$ and $t$, the approximating path, determined by (5.9), between $t$ and $t + 1$ (which is based on the approximating path at $t - 1$) will be an extrapolation of the true path as it was before the change in slope. In this event, the approximating path may deviate further and further from the true one.[28] This danger can be excluded by choice of a sufficiently small value of $q$,[29] but this value may be so small that convergence will be very slow. For this reason, it is desirable as a practical matter to use specially designed computational methods more efficient for the problem at hand, when they exist.

However, to illustrate the gradient method, suppose that we wish to maximize

[27] See "Gradient Method for Concave Programming, II; Global Stability in the Strictly Concave Case," Kenneth J. Arrow, Leonid Hurwicz, and Hirofumi Uzawa, *Studies in Linear and Non-Linear Programming,* Stanford University Press, Stanford, California, 1958, pp. 127–132. Arrow and Hurwicz present a method for generalizing this result to include all concave continuously differentiable functions. See "Gradient Method for Concave Programming, III; Further Global Results and Applications to Resource Allocation," Arrow, Hurwicz, and Uzawa, pp. 133–145.

[28] For a discussion of the computational problems that arise when the gradient method is applied, see Thomas Marschak, "An Example of a Modified Gradient Method for Linear Programming," Arrow, Hurwicz, and Uzawa, pp. 146–153.

[29] Uzawa has shown that if the other conditions for the gradient method are satisfied, there must be some value of $q$ small enough to make the difference equations converge. See "Iterative Methods for Concave Programming," Arrow, Hurwicz, and Uzawa, pp. 154–165.

$$(5.10) \qquad E(x_1, x_2) = 7x_1 + 6x_2 - 2x_1^2 - 2x_2^2$$

subject to the constraints

$$(5.11) \qquad 1 - \tfrac{1}{2}x_1 - \tfrac{1}{2}x_2 \geqq 0$$

and

$$(5.12) \qquad x_1 \geqq 0, \qquad x_2 \geqq 0.$$

The partial derivatives of (5.10) are

$$(5.13) \qquad \begin{aligned} E_1 &= 7 - 4x_1 \\ E_2 &= 6 - 4x_2. \end{aligned}$$

The equations corresponding to (5.9) for this problem with $q$ chosen to be .2 are

$$(5.14) \qquad \begin{aligned} x_1(t) &= x_1(t-1) + .2[7 - 4x_1(t-1) - \tfrac{1}{2}\lambda(t-1)] \\ x_2(t) &= x_2(t-1) + .2[6 - 4x_2(t-1) - \tfrac{1}{2}\lambda(t-1)] \\ \lambda(t) &= \lambda(t-1) - .2[1 - \tfrac{1}{2}x_1(t-1) - \tfrac{1}{2}x_2(t-1)] \end{aligned}$$

unless the right-hand side of one of the equations becomes negative in which case the corresponding variable is set equal to zero for that round. Select any arbitrary set of initial values such as $x_1(0) = 2$, $x_2(0) = 2$, $\lambda(0) = 2$. The results of the iteration are shown below.

| $t$ | 0 | 1 | 2 | 3 | 4 | 15 | $\infty$ |
|---|---|---|---|---|---|---|---|
| $x_1(t)$ | 2 | 1.60 | 1.50 | 1.47 | 1.46 | 1.37 | 1.125 |
| $x_2(t)$ | 2 | 1.40 | 1.26 | 1.22 | 1.21 | 1.12 | .875 |
| $\lambda(t)$ | 2 | 2.20 | 2.30 | 2.38 | 2.50 | 3.09 | 5.0 |

In this simple example, it is possible to solve the necessary and sufficient conditions to obtain the maximum directly. That is, for (5.10), (5.11), and (5.12), the necessary and sufficient conditions (4.16), (4.17), and (4.18) become

$$(5.15) \qquad \begin{aligned} 7 - 4x_1 - \tfrac{1}{2}\lambda &\leqq 0, \\ 6 - 4x_2 - \tfrac{1}{2}\lambda &\leqq 0, \end{aligned}$$

$$(5.16) \qquad \begin{aligned} x_1(7 - 4x_1 - \tfrac{1}{2}\lambda) &= 0, \\ x_2(6 - 4x_2 - \tfrac{1}{2}\lambda) &= 0, \end{aligned}$$

and

$$(5.17) \qquad \lambda(1 - \tfrac{1}{2}x_1 - \tfrac{1}{2}x_2) = 0.$$

To satisfy (5.16) and (5.17), either $x_1$, $x_2$ and $\lambda$, or the expressions in parentheses, must be equal to zero. Clearly the former possibility would not satisfy (5.15); therefore the maximizing values must be those that make the expressions in parentheses equal to zero. Solving the simultaneous equations, one obtains $x_1^0 = 1.125$, $x_2^0 = .875$, $\lambda^0 = 5$.

## VI. DECENTRALIZATION AND SUB-OPTIMIZATION

An organization the size of a military service or the Department of Defense employs a very great variety of resources, many of which have at most a very indirect relationship to its over-all objectives. If they had to be made centrally and simultaneously, the number of detailed decisions that must be made in the Department of Defense would defeat even the most effective staff. How to compare a few extra maintenance men in a bomber wing with extra ammunition in the infantry, from the point of view of national security? Fortunately, such direct comparisons do not have to be made. At least to some extent, the total problem can be organized in terms of higher and lower level criteria, although it would be a mistake to suppose that a simple comprehensive hierarchy is possible. The maintenance men are significant, for example, because they affect the combat readiness of our bomber forces. The extra ammunition is one of the factors determining the combat effectiveness of the infantry. And the effectiveness of our bomber forces and infantry bear a closer and more intelligible relationship to over-all national security than do the maintenance men and the ammunition themselves. In general, the basic inputs that the organization buys are significant because of their effects on what might be called weapon systems — which are aggregates of men and equipment whose performance can be measured in terms of definable criteria. The original resources, then, can be aggregated in terms of proximate criteria that are relevant to higher objectives.

In this sense, then, one can speak of "higher" and "lower" level decisions. One might divide our Military Establishment into total war or strategic forces and limited war or tactical forces. The former might then be divided into bomber systems, ICBM's, active air defenses, and the like. The high level decision would be the determination of the division of the total defense budget between total war and limited war capabilities. At a lower level, another organization would be concerned with dividing up the budget for strategic forces into sub-budgets for bombers, various missile systems, air defense, and so forth. At a still lower level, those responsible for bomber operation would decide how to base the bombers, how to maintain them, in what state of readiness, and the like. What is significant for present purposes is not the decentralization of decision-making authority so much as the structure of the problem in terms of higher and lower level criteria.

At the highest level, the decision-makers seek a grand optimum. At lower levels, they *sub-optimize*.[30] It is interesting to inquire into the

---

[30] See Charles Hitch, "Sub-Optimization in Operations Problems," *Operations Research*, Vol. 1, No. 3, May 1953, pp. 87–99; also "Economics and Military Operations Research," *The Review of Economics and Statistics*, Vol. XL, No. 3, August 1958, pp. 199–209.

circumstances in which the over-all problem can be factored into a hierarchy of independent sub-optimization problems.

Assume, to begin with, that the basic or elementary inputs available to the organization are used in amounts $x_1, \ldots, x_n$, and that they can be aggregated, with criteria that must be found in terms of the problem itself, into systems whose performance is measured by the variables $y^1, \ldots, y^m$, where

$$
\begin{aligned}
y^1 &= y^1(x_1^1, \ldots, x_n^1), \\
(6.1) \qquad y^2 &= y^2(x_1^2, \ldots, x_n^2), \\
&\ldots\ldots\ldots\ldots\ldots\ldots \\
y^m &= y^m(x_1^m, \ldots, x_n^m).
\end{aligned}
$$

The superscripts have the same meaning as in Section III. The form of (6.1) is based on the assumption that all inputs are specific to the systems in which they are employed. The high level problem is to maximize

$$(6.2) \qquad\qquad E(y_1, \ldots, y_m)$$

subject to the budget limitation,

$$(6.3) \qquad\qquad B - \sum_{i=1}^{n} x_i p_i \geqq 0,$$

where

$$(6.4) \qquad\qquad x_i = \sum_{j=1}^{m} x_i^j.$$

If the complete task of allocation is performed centrally, the necessary conditions for a grand optimum can be found by a direct application of the theorem of Section II. Assuming, for simplicity, that all inputs are used in all systems in positive amounts, the maximum of (6.2) subject to (6.3) is defined by the equations[31]

$$(6.5) \qquad\qquad E_j y_i^j - \lambda p_i = 0. \qquad\qquad \begin{aligned}(j &= 1, \ldots, m) \\ (i &= 1, \ldots, n)\end{aligned}$$

This maximization can be factored into the problem of determining the optimum division of the budget between the $m$ systems, and the maximization of the performance of each system subject to its own budget limitation. If each $y^j$ is maximized subject to its own sub-budget constraint, and if, for simplicity, we assume that all inputs are used in all systems in positive amounts, then it will be the case that

[31] The adjustment for "corner maxima" in which some inputs are not used in some systems does not change the content of the analysis. It is assumed, as before, that $E$ and $y^1, \ldots, y^m$ are quasi-concave functions and that the budget constraint is binding. As before, $E_j = \partial E/\partial y^j$ and $y_i^j = \partial y^j/\partial x_i^j$.

(6.6)                       $y_i^j - \lambda_j p_i = 0.$                    $(i = 1, \ldots, n)$
$(j = 1, \ldots, m)$

These conditions will be equivalent to (6.5) when

(6.7)                    $E_1\lambda_1 = E_2\lambda_2 = \cdots = E_m\lambda_m = \lambda.$

The lower level problem, then, is to satisfy (6.6) for each system by appropriate allocation of its sub-budget. The high level problem is to adjust the sub-budget constraints until the marginal imputed value of each one, multiplied by the marginal product of the corresponding system, is equal to the same magnitude for every other system, and the total budget is exhausted. The significant point is that computation can be carried out independently at the two levels, each taking into consideration, of course, the decisions of the other. This does not mean that the job of maximizing $E$ is necessarily easier than it would be if the entire problem were solved centrally. But it does mean that decentralization is possible and relatively simple, and that the various managers can concentrate their efforts on maximizing the performance of their own systems, taking the decisions of the other managers as parameters determined externally.

This high level problem can be viewed in another way. Associated with each level of $y^j$ is a minimum cost of attaining it, say, $C_j(y^j)$. The high level problem is to maximize $E$ subject to the constraint

(6.8)                       $B - \sum_{j=1}^{m} C_j(y^j) \geqq 0,$

that is, the total cost of all the systems must not exceed the budget. If $y^j$ is concave, $-C_j(y^j)$ is also. That is, if the marginal returns to added inputs in $y^j$ diminish, the marginal costs of $y^j$ increase.[32] Therefore, (6.8) is concave, and the conditions for the application of the theorem of Section IV are satisfied. The high level decision makers solve the problem of maximizing $E$ subject to (6.8). The lowel level organizations take the total costs or sub-budgets assigned to them and maximize their respective criteria. Applying the theorem of Section IV, the over-all optimum is defined by the conditions

[32] The proof of this intuitively satisfying statement is not difficult to follow. If $y(x)$ is concave, (i) $y[\theta x^0 + (1 - \theta)x^1] \geqq \theta y(x^0) + (1 - \theta)y(x^1)$. Let $C(y^*)$ be equal to the minimum cost of attaining any amount of $y$ greater than or equal to $y^*$. That is, $C(y^*) = \Sigma p_i x_i$ for the cost minimizing combination of $x_i$. By the definition of $C$, (ii) if $y^* \geqq y$, it must be the case that $C(y^*) \geqq C(y)$. Let $C(y^0) = \Sigma p_i x_i^0$ and let $C(y^1) = \Sigma p_i x_i^1$. Then (iii) $\theta \Sigma p_i x_i^0 + (1 - \theta)\Sigma p_i x_i^1 = \Sigma p_i[\theta x_i^0 + (1 - \theta)x_i^1]$. Now, $[\theta x_i^0 + (1 - \theta)x_i^1]$ is one way of attaining $y[\theta x_i^0 + (1 - \theta)x_i^1]$, but it is not necessarily the lowest cost way of doing so. Let $C\{y[\theta x^0 + (1 - \theta)x^1]\}$ be the lowest cost way. Then (iv) $\Sigma p_i[\theta x_i^0 + (1 - \theta)x_i^1] \geqq C\{y[\theta x^0 + (1 - \theta)x^1]\}$. Apply (ii) to (i) to obtain (v) $C\{y[\theta x^0 + (1 - \theta)x^1]\} \geqq C[\theta y(x^0) + (1 - \theta)y(x^1)]$. Now, (iii), (iv), and (v) taken together imply (vi) $\theta C(y^0) + (1 - \theta)C(y^1) \geqq C[\theta y(x^0) + (1 - \theta)y(x^1)]$. That is, $C$ is convex and therefore $-C$ is concave. Moreover, if a number of functions, $-C^j$, are concave, so is their sum, $-\Sigma C_j$.

$$(6.9) \qquad E_j - \lambda \frac{dC_j}{dy^j} = 0, \qquad (j = 1, \ldots, m)$$

and the exhaustion of the budget. Equation (6.9) merely states that at a maximum, marginal products are proportional to marginal costs.

Given the assumptions that have been made so far, any improvement in the effectiveness of any of the systems, given its sub-budget, will unambiguously lead to an improvement in $E$. This statement, which requires no formal proof, means that if decision-making is decentralized, the high-level authority can instruct each lower level organization to maximize the value of its appropriate criterion, and this will be consistent with the over-all optimum.

However, the assumptions underlying (6.1) and the subsequent discussion are particularly favorable to decentralization and sub-optimization. In fact, it may not be possible to break down the problem in this way because of the force of certain interactions between the various systems. For example, the effectiveness of one system may influence the effectiveness of others. To illustrate, an effective air defense system contributes to the protection of our strategic offensive forces and thereby enhances their value as a deterrent. In case of war, our strategic offensive forces would be able to inflict damage on those of the enemy, thereby easing the job of the air defense system. Such interactions, if they involve only the levels of performance of the different systems, and not allocations within the systems, do not give rise to any major problems from the point of view of decentralization.

Suppose, for example, that there are just two specific inputs, measured by $x_1$ and $x_2$, and two systems whose performance is measured by $y^1$ and $y^2$. Let $y^1$ depend only upon $x_1^1$ and $x_2^1$, but let $y^2$ depend directly on $y^1$ as well as on $x_1^2$ and $x_2^2$.[33] Assuming that both inputs are used in both activities in positive amounts, the constrained maximum of $E$ is defined by the conditions

$$\left[ \frac{\partial E}{\partial y^1} + \frac{\partial E}{\partial y^2} \frac{\partial y^2}{\partial y^1} \right] \frac{\partial y^1}{\partial x_1^1} - \lambda p_1 = 0$$

$$\left[ \frac{\partial E}{\partial y^1} + \frac{\partial E}{\partial y^2} \frac{\partial y^2}{\partial y^1} \right] \frac{\partial y^1}{\partial x_2^1} - \lambda p_2 = 0$$

$$(6.10) \qquad \frac{\partial E}{\partial y^2} \frac{\partial y^2}{\partial x_1^2} - \lambda p_1 = 0$$

$$\frac{\partial E}{\partial y^2} \frac{\partial y^2}{\partial x_2^2} - \lambda p_2 = 0.$$

[33] In the language of economic theory, this situation is known as external technological economies. See Francis Bator, "The Anatomy of Market Failure," *Quarterly Journal of Economics,* Vol. LXXII, August 1958, pp. 351–379.

Again the marginal products of $y^1$ and $y^2$ in $E$ can be factored out of the problem of maximizing $y^1$ and $y^2$ independently. But in the case of simple interactions of this kind, the marginal product of $y^1$ in $E$ is the sum of a "direct effect," $\partial E/\partial y^1$, and an "indirect effect" via $y^2$, that is $\partial E/\partial y^2 \times \partial y^2/\partial y^1$. The task of maximizing the system performance indices $y^1$ and $y^2$ remains unchanged. The information requirements at the higher level are somewhat greater than before as the indirect as well as the direct benefits of each system must now be evaluated. If the interactions are all positive, that is, in this case, if $\partial y^2/\partial y^1$ is positive, any improvement in either $y^1$ or $y^2$, with sub-budgets constant, implies unambiguously an improvement in $E$.[34]

If there are joint inputs, decentralization and sub-optimization are more difficult. Independent maximization problems cannot easily be factored out of the over-all allocation problem. For example, the joint input might be a warning system that contributes to the effectiveness of both the air defense system and the strategic offensive forces.

Suppose that there are three inputs, the first two specific, the third, joint. If $x_3$ is the joint input, the constrained maximum of $E$ will be defined by the equations[35]

$$E_1 y_1^1 - \lambda p_1 = 0, \qquad E_2 y_1^2 - \lambda p_1 = 0,$$

(6.11)
$$E_1 y_2^1 - \lambda p_2 = 0, \qquad E_2 y_2^2 - \lambda p_2 = 0,$$

$$E_1 y_3^1 + E_2 y_3^2 - \lambda p_3 = 0.$$

If each organization maximizes the effectiveness of its system, subject to its own budget restriction, and if the $y^1$ organization buys the joint input for its own use, paying for it itself and disregarding its effect on $y^2$, while the $y^2$ organization accepts the value of $x_3$ decided upon by the $y^1$ organization, the resulting set of allocations will be described by the conditions

$$y_1^1 - \lambda_1 p_1 = 0, \qquad y_1^2 - \lambda_2 p_1 = 0,$$

(6.12)
$$y_2^1 - \lambda_1 p_2 = 0, \qquad y_2^2 - \lambda_2 p_2 = 0,$$

$$y_3^1 - \lambda_1 p_3 = 0,$$

where $\lambda_1$ and $\lambda_2$ are the respective marginal imputed values of the sub-budget constraints.[35] If the central authority adjusts the sub-budget constraints to make the marginal imputed value of each one, multiplied by the marginal product of the corresponding system, equal to the same

---

[34] Can the interactions be negative? Can an improvement in one system mean a lessening in the effectiveness of another? The answer is yes. For example, an improvement in strategic air power can cause the enemy to shift his emphasis to limited wars, causing a deterioration of our position there.

[35] Again this assumes that all inputs are used in all systems in positive amounts.

magnitude for every other system, it will bring about an allocation described by

$$(6.13) \quad \begin{array}{ll} E_1y_1^1 - \lambda p_1 = 0, & E_2y_1^2 - \lambda p_1 = 0, \\ E_1y_2^1 - \lambda p_2 = 0, & E_2y_2^2 - \lambda p_2 = 0, \\ E_1y_3^1 - \lambda p_3 = 0. \end{array}$$

But the conditions (6.13) are not the same as those describing the over-all optimum, (6.11). Moreover, it is not difficult to show that in the allocation described by (6.13), if $E_2y_3^2$ is positive, not enough $x_3$ is brought.[36]

Perhaps the least promising circumstance, from the point of view of decentralization and sub-optimization, arises when the performance of one system depends not upon the aggregate performance of another system, but rather upon the *kind* of system it is, that is, upon the specific allocation of the sub-budget assigned to the other system.[37] Unfortunately, organizational structures that appear to be natural ones may not avoid this kind of interaction. For example, suppose that the effectiveness of the air defense system is measured by the total number of attacking bombers and missiles it can shoot down. The effectiveness of our strategic offensive forces, and civil defenses, depend upon the balance between area and point defenses and on which points (cities or SAC bases) are being defended. Thus, an improvement in the efficiency of the allocation of the air defense budget may have adverse effects on the performance of the offensive forces or civil defenses.

Suppose, for example, that there are two systems with performance measured by $y^1$ and $y^2$, and two specific inputs, $x_1$ and $x_2$, and that whereas $y^1$ depends only on $x_1^1$ and $x_2^1$, $y^2$ depends on $x_1^2$ and $x_2^2$ and on $x_1^1$ and $x_2^1$. That is, $y^2$ depends on the choice of inputs for $y^1$. Then we have

$$(6.14) \quad \begin{array}{l} y^1 = y^1(x_1^1, x_2^1), \\ y^2 = y^2(x_1^2, x_2^2, x_1^1, x_2^1). \end{array}$$

The necessary conditions for a constrained maximum of $E(y_1, y_2)$ are

$$(6.15) \quad \begin{array}{l} E_1y_1^1 + E_2y_3^2 - \lambda p_1 = 0, \\ E_1y_2^1 + E_2y_4^2 - \lambda p_2 = 0, \\ E_2y_1^2 - \lambda p_1 = 0, \\ E_2y_2^2 - \lambda p_2 = 0.^{38} \end{array}$$

In effect, all of the inputs to $y^1$ are joint inputs between $y^1$ and $y^2$.

---

[36] The total differential of $E$ is $dE = E_1y_1^1\,dx_1^1 + E_1y_2^1\,dx_2^1 + (E_1y_3^1 + E_2y_3^2)\,dx_3 + E_2y_1^2\,dx_1^2 + E_2y_2^2\,dx_2^2$. Let $x_1^1 + x_1^2 = x_1$ whence $dx_1^1 + dx_1^2 = dx_1$, and similarly for $x_2$. Considering only allocations that use the entire budget, $p_1\,dx_1 + p_2\,dx_2 + p_3\,dx_3 = 0$. Substituting (6.13) into $dE$ and simplifying with the help of these relationships, one obtains $dE = E_2y_3^2\,dx_3$. Therefore, staying within the constraint, an increase in $E$ can be brought about by increasing $x_3$ if $E_2y_3^2$ is positive.

[37] For a good illustration of this, see Charles Hitch, "Sub-Optimization in Operations Problems."

[38] $y_3^2 = \partial y^2/\partial x_1^1$ and $y_4^2 = \partial y^2/\partial x_2^1$. The rest of the notation is as before.

If the interactions are neglected, and each organization is given a share of the budget and ordered to maximize its system's performance, and if the shares of the budget are adjusted to make the marginal product of each input proportional to its price, the resulting allocation will be defined by the conditions

(6.16)

$$E_1 y_1^1 - \lambda p_1 = 0,$$
$$E_1 y_2^1 - \lambda p_2 = 0,$$
$$E_2 y_1^2 - \lambda p_1 = 0,$$
$$E_2 y_2^2 - \lambda p_2 = 0.$$

Suppose, now, that $y_3^2$ is positive and $y_4^2$ is negative. Then the value of $E_1 y_1^1 / p_1$ is greater in relation to, say, $E_2 y_1^2 / p_1$ or $E_2 y_2^2 / p_2$, in (6.16) than in (6.15). It is therefore too high. By similar reasoning, it can be shown that $E_1 y_2^1$ is too low. Therefore, if the interactions are ignored, too little $x_1$ and too much $x_2$ are employed in the first system. This, of course, is what one would expect. Starting with the allocation that maximizes $y_1$, one would adjust for the interactions with $y_2$ by increasing $x_1^1$ and decreasing $x_2^1$.

If there are very many interactions of this sort, the simple form of decentralization and sub-optimization described above may not be possible. Independent maximization of the performance of the first system will not produce optimal results. This does not mean that there are no possibilities for decentralization, however. For example, systems that interact strongly may be treated as one system that is to be evaluated in terms of two criteria. The organization charged with responsibility for the amalgamated system might be ordered to seek efficient combinations of $y_1$ and $y_2$, while the selection of the optimum combination is left to the high-level decision-makers. As a general matter, it is important to remember that the existence and strength of interactions is a function of the way the total problem is factored into sub-problems. A clever choice of method of decomposition can minimize the interactions and may restrict them to the simpler kinds.[39]

## VII. MAXIMIZATION AGAINST AN OPPONENT

Unfortunately for the peace of mind of the military planner, the outcome, or extent to which an objective is achieved, in a situation involving conflict depends upon the choices of the opponent as well as upon one's own choice. This raises a new criterion problem. Maximization of some index of success on the assumption that the opponent makes no changes

[39] For a discussion of interactions in defense planning, see Alain C. Enthoven and Harry S. Rowen, "Defense Planning and Organization," *Public Finances: Needs, Sources, and Utilization*, A Conference of the Universities-National Bureau Committee for Economic Research, Princeton University Press, Princeton, N.J., 1961, pp. 365–417.

in his own position in response to changes in ours is likely to lead to poor strategic choices. But if it is a mistake to assume that he will remain in the same position as we change our strategy, what should we assume about his responses?

Suppose that the desirability of the outcome from our point of view is measured by a function $E$ which depends on a set of variables, $x$, which we control and a set of variables $z$, which he controls. That is, we have

$$(7.1) \qquad\qquad E(x_1, \ldots, x_n, z_1, \ldots, z_m).$$

We wish to choose from the set, $x$, the combination that maximizes $E$ subject to the budget constraint and given the combination of variables $z$ that he chooses. But which combination of variables $z$ should we assume he chooses? This is a problem in the theory of games.[40] If his ranking of the desirability of different outcomes depends upon our choices, as well as his own, he will change $z$ as we change $x$. That is, his choice of $z$ depends upon the relative attractiveness of the different outcomes to him, and we should assume that he varies $z$ to suit his objectives. It might seem natural to assume that he always varies $z$ to minimize $E$, since he is our opponent. But this is not necessarily the case. His interests may not be directly opposed to ours. In fact, there may be outcomes that are very good or very bad for both sides. If the problem is strategic warfare, our loss, say the destruction of New York, may mean very little gain to him. An enforceable disarmament agreement might be a favorable outcome for both sides; mutual thermonuclear destruction would be an unfavorable outcome for both. Therefore, we cannot always assume that the opponent chooses $z$ to minimize our "payoff," $E$. However, there are interesting circumstances in which it is reasonable for us to assume that our opponent will pick $z$ to minimize $E$. First, if it should happen to be the case, in some particular situation, that our gain is strictly his loss, in which case the interests of the two sides are directly opposed, then it will be reasonable to assume that he chooses $z$ to minimize $E$ since $E$ is a measure of his loss. This situation has been termed by game theorists a *constant sum game* because the sum of the gains and losses must be constant. Second, if we are very uncertain about his relative valuation of the different outcomes and if we have no strong reason for supposing that the interests of the two sides are not directly opposed, then it may be very reasonable for us to "play it safe" and to adopt as our criterion the outcome that follows when he does his worst to us.

[40] The basic treatise on the theory of games is John von Neumann and Oskar Morgenstern, *Theory of Games and Economic Behavior*, Princeton University Press, Princeton, New Jersey, 1944. A more manageable mathematical exposition is presented by J. C. C. McKinsey, *Introduction to the Theory of Games*, McGraw-Hill, New York, 1952. For a recent exposition from the point of view of its applications, see R. Duncan Luce and Howard Raiffa, *Games and Decisions*, Wiley, New York, 1958.

However, in this case, we may forego opportunities to do better if he does not do his worst to us in exchange for the guarantee not to do worse than a certain minimum.

If we assume that he does his worst to us in each case, we are adopting the *minimax* criterion. We arrange our choice so as to *minimize the maximum loss* our opponent can inflict upon us. The constant sum assumption might be appropriate in the planning of an air defense system but inappropriate in evaluating a disarmament scheme.

Suppose that we wish to minimaximize $E$, that is, to maximize $E$ on the assumption that our opponent is attempting to minimize it, and suppose that the payoff function to each side is concave, that marginal costs are constant, and that each side has a fixed budget.[41] In this case, $E$ is concave in $x$ and convex in $z$, and there will exist a point, known as a *saddle point*, which has the property that $E$ falls below its value at that point as the variables $x$ are changed, and rises above it as the variables $z$ are changed. That is, if $x^0$, $z^0$ is the saddle point, it is a maximum with respect to $x$, a minimum with respect to $z$, and

$$(7.2) \qquad E(x, z^0) \leqq E(x^0, z^0) \leqq E(x^0, z)$$

for all $x$ and $z$ satisfying the budget constraints of the two sides.

Let our budget constraint be

$$(7.3) \qquad B_x - \sum_{i=1}^{n} x_i p_{x_i} \geqq 0$$

and that of our opponent be

$$(7.4) \qquad B_z - \sum_{j=1}^{m} z_j p_{z_j} \geqq 0.$$

Then, the necessary and sufficient conditions for $x^0$ to maximize $E$ subject to $(7.3)$, $x^0 \geqq 0$ and $\lambda_x^0 \geqq 0$, and given $z$, are

$$(7.5) \qquad \begin{aligned} \frac{\partial E^0}{\partial x_i} - \lambda_x^0 p_{x_i} &\leqq 0, \qquad\qquad (i = 1, \ldots, n) \\ x_i^0 \left( \frac{\partial E^0}{\partial x_i} - \lambda_x^0 p_{x_i} \right) &= 0, \\ \lambda_x^0 (B_x - \sum_{i=1}^{n} x_i^0 p_{x_i}) &= 0. \end{aligned}$$

The necessary and sufficient conditions for $z^0$ to minimize $E$ subject to $(7.4)$, $z^0 \geqq 0$ and $\lambda_z^0 \geqq 0$, and given $x$, are

[41] That is, $E$ is a concave function of $x$, given $z$, and $-E$ is a concave function of $z$, given $x$.

$$\frac{\partial E^0}{\partial z_j} - \lambda_z^0 p_{z_i} \leqq 0, \qquad (j = 1, \ldots, m)$$

(7.6)
$$z_j^0 \left( \frac{\partial E^0}{\partial z_j} - \lambda_z^0 p_{z_i} \right) = 0,$$

$$\lambda_z^0 \left( B_z - \sum_{j=1}^{m} z_j^0 p_{z_i} \right) = 0.$$

If $x^0$ and $z^0$ satisfy these conditions simultaneously, $E(x^0, z^0)$ is a saddle point. Thus, to minimaximize $E$, we solve a maximum problem in the variables $x$ and a minimum problem in the variables $z$. If $x_i$ is used at all, then the marginal product of $x_i$ must be equal to its marginal imputed cost. If the opponent finds it optimal to use $z_j$ in a positive amount, $z_j$ must decrease the value of $E$, that is, $\partial E / \partial z_j$ must be negative, and its marginal product to the opponent, $-\partial E / \partial z_j$ must be equal to its marginal imputed cost.[42]

This is the simplest case in the theory of games. The interesting cases are generally more complicated. For example, the players may not face diminishing marginal returns. Our opponent may perceive that he will lose if both sides pursue minimax strategies, or that he may be able to do much better following a different strategy if we make a mistake which he considers likely, and he may decide to "take a chance" for a more favorable outcome.[43] We may have good reason to believe that the situation does not fit the constant sum model. There may be more than two "sides" in the game. The constant sum game between two players is the beginning rather than the end of the theory of games.

[42] See Kuhn and Tucker.

[43] For a discussion of this kind of possibility, see Daniel Ellsberg, "Theory of the Reluctant Duelist," *American Economic Review,* Vol. XLVI, No. 5, December 1956, pp. 909–923.

# BIBLIOGRAPHY

## GOVERNMENT PUBLICATIONS

*ARDC Program Management Procedures,* ARDC Manual No. 80–4, Headquarters, Air Research and Development Command, U.S. Air Force, Baltimore, September 1, 1956.

*Budget of the United States Government for the Fiscal Year Ending June 30, 1960,* U.S. Government Printing Office, Washington, 1959.

Commission on Organization of the Executive Branch of the Government (The Second Hoover Commission), *Task Force Report on Military Procurement,* U.S. Government Printing Office, Washington, 1955.

*Composite Report of the President's Committee to Study the United States Military Assistance Program* [The Draper Committee Report], Vols. I and II, U.S. Government Printing Office, Washington, 1959.

Council for Economic and Industry Research, Inc., *Foreign Assistance Activities of the Communist Bloc and Their Implications for the United States,* a study prepared at the request of the Special Committee to Study the Foreign Air Program, U.S. Senate, U.S. Government Printing Office, Washington, 1957.

*The Economic Report of the President,* together with a Report to the President, *The Annual Economic Review,* by the Council of Economic Advisers, U.S. Government Printing Office, Washington, 1952.

*Federal Expenditure Policy for Economic Growth and Stability,* Hearings before the Subcommittee on Fiscal Policy of the Joint Economic Committee, 85th Congress, 1st Session, U.S. Government Printing Office, Washington, 1958.

*Federal Expenditure Policy for Economic Growth and Stability,* papers submitted by panelists appearing before the Subcommittee on Fiscal Policy of the Joint Economic Committee, 85th Congress, 1st Session, U.S. Government Printing Office, Washington, 1957.

*Federal Tax Policy for Economic Growth and Stability,* papers submitted by panelists appearing before the Subcommittee on Tax Policy, Joint Committee on the Economic Report, 84th Congress, 1st Session, U.S. Government Printing Office, Washington, 1956.

*Inquiry into Satellite and Missile Programs,* Hearings before the Preparedness Investigating Subcommittee of the Committee on Armed Services, U.S. Senate, U.S. Government Printing Office, Washington, 1958.

*The Military Assistance Program of the United States,* two studies and a report prepared at the request of the Special Committee to Study the Foreign Aid Program, U.S. Senate, U.S. Government Printing Office, Washington, 1957.

*A Modern Concept of Manpower Management and Compensation for Personnel of the Uniformed Services* [The Cordiner Report], Defense Advisory Committee on Professional and Technical Compensation, U.S. Government Printing Office, Washington, 1957.

Novick, David, "Lead-Time in Modern Weapons," in Hearings before the Sub-committee of the Joint Economic Committee, Congress of the United States, 85th Congress, 1st Session, November 18–27, 1957, U.S. Government Printing Office, Washington, 1958, pp. 374–383.

President's Materials Policy Commission, *Resources for Freedom*, A Report to the President, Vol. II, U.S. Government Printing Office, Washington, 1952.

Rowen, Henry, *National Security and the American Economy in the 1960's*, Study Paper for the Joint Economic Committee, 86th Congress, 2d Session, U.S. Government Printing Office, Washington, 1960.

*Soviet Economic Growth: A Comparison with the United States*, A Study Prepared for the Subcommittee on Foreign Economic Policy of the Joint Economic Committee by the Legislative Reference Service of the Library of Congress, U.S. Government Printing Office, Washington, 1957.

U.S. Department of Commerce, *National Income Supplement to the Survey of Current Business*, prepared in the Office of Business Economics of the Department of Commerce, U.S. Government Printing Office, Washington, 1954.

U.S. House of Representatives, *Civil Defense*, Hearings before a Subcommittee of the Committee on Government Operations, 85th Congress, 2d Session, U.S. Government Printing Office, Washington, 1958.

—— *Department of Defense Appropriations for 1957, Procurement Policies and Practices of the Department of Defense*, Hearings before the Subcommittee of the Committee on Appropriations, 84th Congress, 2d Session, U.S. Government Printing Office, Washington, 1956.

—— *Department of Defense Appropriations for 1958*, Hearings before the Subcommittee of the Committee on Appropriations, 85th Congress, 1st Session, U.S. Government Printing Office, Washington, 1957.

—— *Department of Defense Appropriations for 1959, Overall Policy Statements*, Hearings before the Subcommittee of the Committee on Appropriations, 85th Congress, 2d Session, U.S. Government Printing Office, Washington, 1958.

—— *Military Construction Appropriations for 1958*, Hearings before the Subcommittee of the Committee on Appropriations, 85th Congress, 1st Session, U.S. Government Printing Office, Washington, 1957.

—— *Mutual Security Act of 1952*, Hearings before the Committee on Foreign Affairs, 82nd Congress, 2d Session, U.S. Government Printing Office, Washington, 1952.

—— *Study of Civil Works*, Part 2, Hearings before the Subcommittee to Study Civil Works of the Committee on Public Works, 82nd Congress, 2d Session, U.S. Government Printing Office, Washington, 1952.

U.S. Senate, *Airpower*, Report of the Subcommittee on the Air Force of the Committee on Armed Services, 84th Congress, 2d Session, U.S. Government Printing Office, Washington, 1957.

U.S. Senate, *Department of Defense Appropriations for 1957*, Hearings before the Subcommittee of the Committee on Appropriations, 84th Congress, 2d Session, U.S. Government Printing Office, Washington, 1956.

—— *Department of Defense Appropriations for 1958*, Hearings before the Subcommittee of the Committee on Appropriations, 85th Congress, 1st Session, U.S. Government Printing Office, Washington, 1957.

—— *Study of Airpower*, Hearings before the Subcommittee on the Air Force of the Committee on Armed Services, 84th Congress, 2d Session, U.S. Government Printing Office, Washington, 1956.

Washington Center of Foreign Policy Research, Johns Hopkins U., *Developments in Military Technology and Their Impact on United States Strategy and Foreign Policy,* Committee on Foreign Relations, U.S. Senate, 86th Congress, 1st Session, December 6, 1959.

Wood, Marshall K., and John D. Norton, *Post-Attack Resource Management,* A Report to OCDM by the National Planning Association, August, 1959 (available from Director of Operations Research, OCDM).


## OTHER BOOKS AND PAMPHLETS


Alchian, A. A., K. J. Arrow, and W. M. Capron, *An Economic Analysis of the Market for Scientists and Engineers,* The RAND Corporation, Research Memorandum RM-2190-RC, June 6, 1958.

Arrow, Kenneth J., *Social Choice and Individual Values,* John Wiley and Sons, New York, 1951.

—— and Leonid Hurwicz, *Decentralization and Computation in Resource Allocation,* Technical Report No. 56, O.N.R. Contract N6onr-25133, Department of Economics, Stanford University, June 5, 1958.

Asher, Harold, *Cost-Quantity Relationships in the Airframe Industry,* The RAND Corporation, Report R-291, July 1, 1956.

Baum, Warren C., *The French Economy and the State,* Princeton University Press, Princeton, N.J., 1958.

Becker, Abraham S., *Prices of Producers' Durables in the United States and the USSR in 1955,* The RAND Corporation, Research Memorandum RM-2432, August 15, 1959.

Bergson, Abram (ed.), *Soviet Economic Growth,* Row, Peterson and Company, White Plains, New York, 1953.

—— *Soviet National Income and Product in 1937,* Columbia University Press, New York, 1953.

Blackett, P. M. S., *Atomic Weapons and East-West Relations,* Cambridge University Press, Cambridge, England, 1956.

Blackman, J., A. Basch, S. Fabricant, M. Gainsbrugh, and E. Stein, *War and Defense Economics,* Rinehart and Company, New York, 1952.

Brodie, Bernard (ed.), *The Absolute Weapon: Atomic Power and World Order,* Harcourt, Brace and Company, New York, 1946.

—— *A Guide to Naval Strategy,* 4th ed. (Naval War College Edition), Princeton University Press, Princeton, N.J., 1958.

—— *Strategy in the Missile Age,* Princeton University Press, Princeton, N.J., 1959.

Burkhead, Jesse, *Government Budgeting,* John Wiley and Sons, New York, 1956.

*Capital Formation and Economic Growth,* A Conference of the Universities-National Bureau Committee for Economic Research, Princeton University Press, Princeton, N.J., 1955.

Chandler, L. V. and D. H. Wallace (eds.), *Economic Mobilization and Stabilization,* Henry Holt and Company, New York, 1951.

Coale, Ansley, J., *The Problem of Reducing Vulnerability to Atomic Bombs,* Princeton University Press, Princeton, N.J., 1947.

Colm, Gerhard, *Can We Afford Additional Programs for National Security?,* National Planning Association, Washington, October, 1953.

Committee for Economic Development, *Economic Growth in the United States, Its Past and Future,* A Statement on National Policy by the Research and Policy Committee, February, 1958.

—— *The Problem of National Security,* A Statement on National Policy by the Research and Policy Committee, July, 1958.

—— *Taxes and the Budget: A Program for Prosperity in a Free Economy,* A Statement on National Policy by the Research and Policy Committee, November, 1947.

Dinerstein, Herbert S., *War and the Soviet Union,* Frederick A. Praeger, New York, 1959.

Director, Aaron (ed.), *Defense, Controls and Inflation,* University of Chicago Press, Chicago, 1952.

Dorfman, Robert, Paul A. Samuelson, and Robert M. Solow, *Linear Programming and Economic Analysis,* McGraw-Hill Book Company, New York, 1958.

Douglas, Paul H., *Economy in the National Government,* University of Chicago Press, Chicago, 1952.

Eckstein, Otto, *Trends in Public Expenditures in the Next Decade,* A Supplementary Paper of the Committee for Economic Development, Committee For Economic Development, New York, April, 1959.

*Economic Survey of Asia and the Far East 1956,* United Nations, Bangkok, 1957.

Ellis, Howard S. (ed.), *A Survey of Contemporary Economics,* Blakiston Company, Philadelphia, 1948.

Fabricant, Solomon, *Economic Progress and Economic Change,* 34th Annual Report, National Bureau of Economic Research, New York, May, 1954.

Finletter, Thomas K., *Power and Policy,* Harcourt, Brace and Company, New York, 1954.

Friedman, Milton, *Essays in Positive Economics,* University of Chicago Press, Chicago, 1953.

Galbraith, J. K., *The Affluent Society,* Houghton Mifflin Company, Boston, 1958.

Garthoff, Raymond L., *Soviet Strategy in the Nuclear Age,* Frederick A. Praeger, New York, 1958.

—— *The Soviet Image of Future War,* Public Affairs Press, Washington, 1959.

Gavin, James M., *War and Peace in the Space Age,* Harper and Brothers, New York, 1958.

Gilbert, Milton, and associates, *Comparative National Products and Price Levels,* Organization for European Economic Cooperation, Paris, 1958.

—— and Irving B. Kravis, *An International Comparison of National Products and the Purchasing Power of Currencies,* Organization for European Economic Co-operation, Paris [no date, but probably published in 1954].

Great Britain, Minister of Defence, *Defence: Outline of Future Policy,* Cmd. 124, H.M.S.O., London, April, 1957.

Haley, Bernard F. (ed.), *A Survey of Contemporary Economics,* Vol. II, Richard D. Irwin, Homewood, Illinois, 1952.

Harris, Seymour E., *The Economics of Mobilization and Inflation,* W. W. Norton and Company, New York, 1951.

Hart, B. H. Liddell, *Strategy,* Frederick A. Praeger, New York, 1954.

Hirschman, Albert O., *National Power and the Structure of Foreign Trade,* University of California Press, Berkeley, California, 1945.

—— *The Strategy of Economic Development,* Yale University Press, New Haven, Connecticut, 1958.

Hitch, Charles J., *America's Economic Strength*, Oxford University Press, London, 1941.

Hodgman, Donald R., *Soviet Industrial Production, 1928–51*, Harvard University Press, Cambridge, Massachusetts, 1954.

Hoeffding, Oleg, and Nancy Nimitz, *Soviet National Income and Product*, The RAND Corporation, Research Memorandum RM-2101, April 6, 1959.

Hollister, William W., *China's Gross National Product and Social Accounts 1950–1957*, Free Press, Glencoe, Illinois, 1958.

Huntington, Samuel P., *The Soldier and the State*, Belknap Press of Harvard University, Cambridge, Massachusetts, 1957.

*International Financial Statistics*, International Monetary Fund, March, 1958.

*International Stability and Progress: United States Interests and Instruments*, The American Assembly, Columbia University, New York, June, 1957.

Ismay, Lord, *NATO, The First Five Years*, North Atlantic Treaty Organization, Paris, 1955.

Jewkes, John, David Sawers, and Richard Stillerman, *The Sources of Invention*, Macmillan and Company, London, 1958.

Kahn, Herman, *On Thermonuclear War*, Princeton University Press, Princeton, N.J., 1960.

——— and Irwin Mann, *Techniques of Systems Analysis*, The RAND Corporation, Research Memorandum RM-1829-1, rev., June, 1957.

Kaplan, Norman M., and William L. White, *A Comparison of 1950 Wholesale Prices in Soviet and American Industry*, The RAND Corporation, Research Memorandum RM-1443, May, 1, 1955.

Kaufmann, William W. (ed.), *Military Policy and National Security*, Princeton University Press, Princeton, N.J., 1956.

Kendrick, M. Slade, *A Century and a Half of Federal Expenditures*, Occasional Paper No. 48, National Bureau of Economic Research, New York, 1955.

Kintner, William, R., with Joseph I. Coffey and Raymond J. Albright, *Forging A New Sword*, Harper and Brothers, New York, 1958.

Kissinger, Henry A., *Nuclear Weapons and Foreign Policy*, Harper and Brothers, New York, 1957.

Knorr, Klaus, *The Crisis in U.S. Defense*, Memorandum No. 14, Series of the Center of International Studies, Princeton University, also published as Special Section of *The New Leader*, December 30, 1957, pp. 1–31.

——— *The War Potential of Nations*, Princeton University Press, Princeton, N.J., 1956.

Lerner, Abba P., "Design for a Streamlined War Economy," unpublished paper written at Amherst College, 1942.

——— *The Economics of Control*, Macmillan Company, New York, 1944.

Lewis, W. Arthur, *The Theory of Economic Growth*, George Allen and Unwin, London, 1955.

Lincoln, George A., *Economics of National Security*, 2nd ed., Prentice-Hall, New York, 1954.

Lindblom, Charles E., *Bargaining: The Hidden Hand in Government*, The RAND Corporation, Research Memorandum RM-1434-RC, 1955.

Little, I. M. D., *A Critique of Welfare Economics*, Clarendon Press, Oxford, 1950.

Luce, R. Duncan, and Howard Raiffa, *Games and Decisions*, John Wiley and Sons, New York, 1958.

March, James G. and Herbert A. Simon, *Organizations*, John Wiley and Sons, New York, 1958.

McKean, Roland N., *Efficiency in Government through Systems Analysis*, John Wiley and Sons, New York, 1958.

McKinsey, J. C. C., *Introduction to the Theory of Games*, McGraw-Hill Book Company, New York, 1952.

Meade, J. E., *The Theory of International Economic Policy*, Vol. II, *Trade and Welfare*, Oxford University Press, Oxford, 1955.

*The Mighty Force of Research* by the Editors of *Fortune*, McGraw-Hill Book Company, New York, 1956.

Millikan, Max F., and W. W. Rostow, *A Proposal, Key to an Effective Foreign Policy*, Harper and Brothers, New York, 1957.

Millis, Walter, *Arms and Men, A Study in American Military History*, G. P. Putnam's Sons, New York, 1956.

—— with Harvey C. Mansfield and Harold Stein, *Arms and the State, Civil-Military Elements in National Policy*, Twentieth Century Fund, New York, 1958.

Moore, Clarence A., "Agricultural Development in Brazil," unpublished TALA paper, No. 54-044, University of Chicago, September 29, 1954.

Morgenstern, Oskar, *The Question of National Defense*, Random House, New York, 1959.

Mosher, Frederick C., *Program Budgeting: Theory and Practice*, Public Administration Service, Chicago, 1954.

National Bureau of Economic Research, *A Critique of the United States Income and Product Accounts*, Studies in Income and Wealth, Vol. 22, Princeton University Press, Princeton, N.J., 1958.

National Planning Association, *The Nth Country Problem and Arms Control*, Planning Pamphlet No. 108, National Planning Association, Washington, January, 1960.

*NATO Letter*, North Atlantic Treaty Organization, Information Service, February, 1957, and January, 1958.

Nelson, Richard R., *The Economics of Parallel R and D Efforts: A Sequential-Decision Analysis*, The RAND Corporation, Research Memorandum RM-2482, November 12, 1959.

Novick, David, *Efficiency and Economy in Government Through New Budgeting and Accounting Procedures*, The RAND Corporation, Report R-254, February 1, 1954.

—— *Weapon-System Cost Methodology*, The RAND Corporation, Report R-287, February 1, 1956.

—— *Which Program Do We Mean in 'Program Budgeting'?*, The RAND Corporation, P-530, May 12, 1954.

—— M. Anshen, and W. C. Truppner, *Wartime Production Controls*, Columbia University Press, New York, 1949.

*On Limiting Atomic War*, Royal Institute of International Affairs, London, 1956.

Osgood, Robert E., *Limited War, The Challenge to American Strategy*, University of Chicago Press, Chicago, 1957.

Parkinson, C. Northcote, *Parkinson's Law: And Other Studies in Administration*, Houghton Mifflin Company, Boston, 1957.

Patterson, Gardner, and Edgar S. Furniss, Jr., *NATO, A Critical Appraisal*, A Report Prepared on the Basis of an International Conference Held at Princeton University, Department of Economics and Sociology, Princeton, N.J., 1957.

Pigou, A. C., *The Economics of Welfare*, 1st ed., Macmillan and Company, London, 1920.

Price, Don K., *Government and Science*, New York University Press, New York, 1954.

Ransom, Harry H., *Central Intelligence and National Security*, Harvard University Press, Cambridge, Massachusetts, 1958.

*Report on a Study of Non-Military Defense*, The RAND Corporation, Report R-322-RC, July 1, 1958.

Robbins, Lionel, *The Economic Problem in Peace and War*, Macmillan and Company, London, 1947.

Rockefeller Brothers Fund, Inc., *International Security — The Military Aspect*, Special Studies Report II, Doubleday Headline Publications, New York, 1958.

Rostow, W. W., *The Process of Economic Growth*, Clarendon Press, Oxford, 1953.

Samuelson, Paul A., *Economics*, 3d ed., McGraw-Hill Book Company, New York, 1955.

—— *Foundations of Economic Analysis*, Harvard University Press, Cambridge, Massachusetts, 1948.

Schelling, Thomas C., *International Economics*, Allyn and Bacon, Boston, 1958.

—— *The Strategy of Conflict*, Harvard University Press, Cambridge, Massachusetts, 1960.

Schlaifer, Robert, and S. D. Heron, *Development of Aircraft Engines and Fuels*, Graduate School of Business Administration, Harvard University, Boston, 1950.

Schlesinger, James R., *The Political Economy of National Security*, Frederick A. Praeger, New York, 1960.

Schultz, Theodore W., *The Economic Organization of Agriculture*, McGraw-Hill Book Company, New York, 1953.

—— *Redirecting Farm Policy*, Macmillan Company, New York, 1943.

Schurr, Sam H., and Jacob Marschak, *Economic Aspects of Atomic Power*, Princeton University Press, Princeton, N.J., 1950.

Scitovsky, Tibor, Edward S. Shaw, and Lorie Tarshis, *Mobilizing Resources for War*, McGraw-Hill Book Company, New York, 1951.

Shubik, Martin, *Strategy and Market Structure: Competition, Oligopoly, and the Theory of Games*, John Wiley and Sons, New York, 1959.

Shute, Nevil, *On the Beach*, William Morrow, New York, 1957.

Slessor, Sir John, *The Great Deterrent*, Frederick A. Praeger, New York, 1957.

Smithies, Arthur, *The Budgetary Process in the United States*, McGraw-Hill Book Company, New York, 1955.

Stigler, George J., *The Theory of Price*, Macmillan Company, New York, 1946.

Striner, Herbert E., Richard U. Sherman, Jr., Leon N. Karadbil, Alexander Sachs, Margaret H. Tupper, and Sidney G. Winter, Jr., *Defense Spending and the U.S. Economy*, ORO-SP-57, Vols. I and II, Operations Research Office, 1958.

Supreme Allied Commander, Europe, [SACEUR] *Second Annual Report*, Paris, 1953.

Turner, Gordon B. (ed.), *A History of Military Affairs Since the Eighteenth Century*, rev. ed., Harcourt, Brace and Company, New York, 1956.

Tybout, Richard A., *Government Contracting in Atomic Energy*, University of Michigan Press, Ann Arbor, Michigan, 1956.

Uzawa, Hirofumi, *Note on a Gradient Method*, Technical Report No. 36, O.N.R. Contract N6onr-25133, Department of Economics, Stanford University, October, 1956.

Von Neumann, John, and Oskar Morgenstern, *Theory of Games and Economic Behavior*, Princeton University Press, Princeton, N.J., 1947.

Washington Center of Foreign Policy Research, Johns Hopkins University, *Military Policy Papers,* Washington, December, 1958.

Whitin, Thomson M., *The Theory of Inventory Management,* Princeton University Press, Princeton, N.J., 1953.

Williams, John D., *The Compleat Strategyst,* McGraw-Hill Book Company, New York, 1954.

Wolf, Charles, Jr., *Foreign Aid: Theory and Practice in Southern Asia,* Princeton University Press, Princeton, N.J., 1960.

Wolfe, Philip, *The Simplex Method for Quadratic Programming,* The RAND Corporation, P-1205, October 25, 1957.

*World Economic Report, 1953–54,* United Nations, New York, 1955.

*World Economic Survey, 1956,* United Nations, New York, 1957.

## ARTICLES

Abramovitz, Moses, "Resource and Output Trends in the United States Since 1870," *American Economic Review, Papers and Proceedings,* May, 1956, pp. 5–23, reprinted by the National Bureau of Economic Research as Occasional Paper No. 52.

Alchian, Armen, "Uncertainty, Evolution, and Economic Theory," *Journal of Political Economy,* June, 1950, pp. 211–221.

Alsop, Joseph, "The New Balance of Power," *Encounter,* May, 1958, pp. 3–10.

Amster, Warren, "Design for Deterrence," *Bulletin of the Atomic Scientists,* May, 1956, pp. 164–165.

Arrow, Kenneth J., "Economic Welfare and the Allocation of Resources for Invention," The RAND Corporation, Paper P-1856, December 15, 1959.

———— and Leonid Hurwicz, "Gradient Methods for Constrained Maxima," *Operations Research,* April, 1957, pp. 258–265.

Baldwin, Hanson W., "Arms and the Atom — I," *New York Times,* May 14, 1957, p. 21.

———— "The Lessons of Oman . . . ," *New York Times,* August 15, 1957, p. 4.

Barnett, H. J., "The Changing Relations of Natural Resources to National Security," *Economic Geography,* July, 1958.

Baumol, W. J., and M. H. Peston, "More on the Multiplier Effects of a Balanced Budget," *American Economic Review,* March, 1955, pp. 140–148.

Breckner, Norman V., "Government Efficiency and the Military 'Buyer-Seller' Device," *Journal of Political Economy,* October, 1960, pp. 469–486.

Brodie, Bernard, "Unlimited Weapons and Limited War," *The Reporter,* November 18, 1954, pp. 16–21.

Brozen, Yale, "Business Leadership and Technological Change," *American Journal of Economics and Sociology,* October, 1954, pp. 13–30.

———— "The Economic Future of Research and Development," *Industrial Laboratories,* December, 1953, pp. 5–8.

———— "Invention, Innovation, and Imitation," *American Economic Review, Papers and Proceedings,* May, 1951, pp. 239–257.

Buchanan, James M., "The Pricing of Highway Services," *National Tax Journal,* June, 1952, pp. 97–106.

Clark, Colin, "Public Finance and Changes in the Value of Money," *Economic Journal,* December, 1945, pp. 371–389.

Colm, Gerhard, and Manuel Helzner, "General Economic Feasibility of National Security Programs," National Planning Association, March 20, 1957, published in *Federal Expenditure Policy for Economic Growth and Stability,* Hearings before the Subcommittee on Fiscal Policy of the Joint Economic Committee, 85th Congress, 1st Session, U.S. Government Printing Office, Washington, 1958.

Cooper, Gershon, "Taxation and Incentive in Mobilization," *Quarterly Journal of Economics,* February, 1952, pp. 43–66.

Davenport, John, "Arms and the Welfare State," *Yale Review,* Spring, 1958, pp. 335–346.

Davies, R. W., "Reports and Commentaries: Industrial Planning Reconsidered," *Soviet Studies,* April, 1957, pp. 426–435.

Devons, Ely, "The Aircraft Industry," in Duncan Burn (ed.), *The Structure of British Industry,* Vol. II, Cambridge University Press, Cambridge, England, 1958, pp. 45–92.

Earle, Edward M., "The Influence of Air Power Upon History," *Yale Review,* Summer, 1946, reprinted in Gordon B. Turner (ed.), *A History of Military Affairs Since the Eighteenth Century,* rev. ed., Harcourt, Brace and Company, New York, 1956.

Eckstein, Alexander, with the assistance of Y. C. Yin and Helen Yin, "Communist China's National Product in 1952," *Review of Economics and Statistics,* May, 1958, pp. 127–139.

Eisenhower, Dwight D., "The Chance for Peace," an address reprinted in *The Department of State Bulletin,* April 27, 1953, pp. 599–603.

Ellsberg, Daniel, "Theory of the Reluctant Duelist," *American Economic Review,* December, 1956, pp. 909–923.

Enke, Stephen, "Controlling Consumers in Future Wars," *Quarterly Journal of Economics,* November, 1958, pp. 558–573.

———— "An Economist Looks at Air Force Logistics," *Review of Economics and Statistics,* August, 1958, pp. 230–239.

———— "On Maximizing Profits," *American Economic Review,* September, 1951, pp. 556–578.

———— "Some Economic Aspects of Fissionable Material," *Quarterly Journal of Economics,* May, 1954, pp. 217–232.

Enthoven, Alain C., "An Economist's View of the Cordiner Recommendations," *Air Force,* January, 1958, pp. 38–41.

———— and Harry S. Rowen, "Defense Planning and Organization," *Public Finances: Needs, Sources, and Utilization,* A Conference of the Universities-National Bureau Committee for Economic Research, Princeton University Press, Princeton, N.J., 1961, pp. 365–417.

Farrell, M. J., "In Defense of Public-Utility Price Theory," *Oxford Economic Papers* (New Series), February, 1958, pp. 109–123.

Fisher, Gene H., "Weapon-System Cost Analysis," *Operations Research,* October, 1956, pp. 558–571.

Frank, Marguerite, and Philip Wolfe, "An Algorithm for Quadratic Programming," *Naval Research Logistics Quarterly,* March-June, 1956, pp. 95–110.

Friedman, Milton, "Foreign Economic Aid," *Yale Review,* Summer, 1958, pp. 500–516.

Galbraith, J. K., "The Illusion of National Security," Chapter XII of *The Affluent Society,* Houghton Mifflin Company, Boston, 1958, pp. 161–180.

Gallois, General Pierre M., "A French General Analyzes Nuclear-Age Strategy," *Réalités,* November, 1958, pp. 19–22, 70–72.

———— "Nuclear Aggression and National Suicide," *The Reporter,* September 18 1958, pp. 23–26.

Goldsmith, Raymond, "A Perpetual Inventory of National Wealth," *Studies in Income and Wealth,* Vol. 14, National Bureau of Economic Research, New York [no date].

Gordon, Lincoln, "Economic Aspects of Coalition Diplomacy — The NATO Experience," *International Organization,* Autumn, 1956, pp. 529–543.

———— "NATO in the Nuclear Age," *Yale Review,* Spring, 1959, pp. 321–335.

Griliches, Zvi, "Research Costs and Social Returns: Hybrid Corn and Related Innovations," *Journal of Political Economy,* October, 1958, pp. 419–431.

Haley, Bernard F., "Are Price Control and Rationing Necessary?", *American Economic Review, Papers and Proceedings,* May, 1950, pp. 199–208.

Heller, Walter W., "CED's Stabilizing Budget Policy after Ten Years," *American Economic Review,* September, 1957, pp. 634–651.

Hicks, U. K., "Direct Taxation and Economic Growth," *Oxford Economic Papers* (New Series), October, 1956, pp. 302–317.

Hirshleifer, Jack, "On The Theory of Optimal Investment Decision," *Journal of Political Economy,* August, 1958, pp. 329–352.

———— "War Damage Insurance," *Review of Economics and Statistics,* May, 1953, pp. 144–153.

Hitch, Charles J., "An Appreciation of Systems Analysis," *Journal of the Operations Research Society of America,* November, 1955, pp. 466–481.

———— "Economics and Military Operations Research," *Review of Economics and Statistics,* August, 1958, pp. 199–209.

———— "Suboptimization in Operations Problems," *Journal of the Operations Research Society of America,* May, 1953, pp. 87–99.

Hoag, Malcolm W., "Economic Problems of Alliance," *Journal of Political Economy,* December, 1957, pp. 522–534.

———— "Is 'Dual' Preparedness More Expensive?," *Bulletin of the Atomic Scientists,* February, 1957, pp. 48–51.

———— "NATO: Deterrent or Shield?," *Foreign Affairs,* January, 1958, p. 278–292.

———— "The Place of Limited War in NATO Strategy," in *NATO and American Security,* ed. Klaus Knorr, Princeton University Press, Princeton, N.J., 1959, pp. 98–126.

———— "Some Complexities in Military Planning," *World Politics,* July, 1959, pp. 553–576.

Hoeffding, Oleg, "Strategy and Economics: A Soviet View," *World Politics,* January, 1959, pp. 316–324, a review of the book by A. N. Lagovskii, *Strategiia i ekonomika,* Voennoe Izdatel'stvo Ministerstva Oborony Soiuza SSR, Moscow, 1957.

Kahn, Herman, "How Many Can Be Saved?," *Bulletin of the Atomic Scientists,* January, 1959, pp. 30–34.

Kalecki, M., "General Rationing," *Studies in War Economics,* Oxford University Institute of Statistics, Basil Blackwell, Oxford, 1947, pp. 137–141.

Kaplan, Norman M., and Eleanor S. Wainstein, "A Comparison of Soviet and American Retail Prices in 1950," *Journal of Political Economy,* December, 1956, pp. 470–491.

———— "A Note on Ruble-Dollar Comparisons," *Journal of Political Economy,* December, 1957, p. 543.

Katzenbach, Edward L., Jr., "The Military Lessons of Suez," *The Reporter,* November 29, 1956, pp. 11–13.

Kendrick, John W., "Productivity Trends: Capital and Labor," *Review of Economics and Statistics,* August, 1956, pp. 248–257, reprinted by the National Bureau of Economic Research as Occasional Paper No. 53.

Kennan, George F., "A Chance to Withdraw Our Troops in Europe," *Harper's Magazine,* February, 1958, pp. 34–41.

King, James E., Jr., "Arms and Man in the Nuclear-Rocket Age," *The New Republic,* September 1, 1958, pp. 16–19.

Kissinger, Henry A., "Strategy and Organization," *Foreign Affairs,* April, 1957, pp. 379–394.

Kittel, Charles, "The Nature and Development of Operations Research," *Science,* February 7, 1947, pp. 150–153.

Klein, Burton H., "A Radical Proposal for R. and D.," *Fortune,* May, 1958, pp. 112–113, 218, 222, 224, 226.

—— and William H. Meckling, "Application of Operations Research to Development Decisions," *Operations Research,* May-June, 1958, pp. 352–363.

Knorr, Klaus, "The Concept of Economic Potential for War," *World Politics,* October, 1957, pp. 49–62.

Kuhn, H. W., and A. W. Tucker, "Nonlinear Programming," *Proceedings of the Second Berkeley Symposium on Mathematical Statistics and Probability,* University of California Press, Berkeley, California, 1951, pp. 481–492.

Kuznets, Simon, "Quantitative Aspects of the Economic Growth of Nations," *Economic Development and Cultural Change,* October, 1956, pp. 1–94.

Leghorn, Richard S., "How the Arms Race Can Be Checked," *The Reporter,* March 6, 1958, pp. 16–20.

Levinson, Horace C., "Experiences in Commercial Operations Research," *Journal of the Operations Research Society of America,* August, 1953, pp. 220–239.

Lewis, Craig, "Air Force Tests Turboprop Reliability," *Aviation Week,* April 29, 1957, pp. 50–61.

Lipsey, R. G., and K. Lancaster, "The General Theory of Second Best," *Review of Economic Studies,* 1956–57, pp. 11–32.

Livingston, J. Sterling, "Decision Making in Weapons Development," *Harvard Business Review,* January-February, 1958, pp. 127–136.

Marshall, A. W., and W. H. Meckling, "Predictability of the Costs, Time, and Success of Development," The RAND Corporation, Paper P-1821, December 11, 1959.

Marshall, S. L. A., "How Ready Is Our Ready Reserve?," *The Reporter,* October 3, 1957, pp. 16–18.

—— "The War That Really Ended War," *The Reporter,* August 8, 1957, pp. 50–52.

McManus, Maurice, "Transformations in Economic Theories," *Review of Economic Studies,* February, 1958, pp. 97–108.

Mendershausen, Horst, "Economic Problems in Air Force Logistics," *American Economic Review,* September, 1958, pp. 632–648.

Moore, Clarence A., "Agricultural Development in Mexico," *Journal of Farm Economics,* February, 1955, pp. 72–80.

Nelson, Richard R., "The Link Between Science and Invention: The Case of the Transistor," The RAND Corporation, Paper P-1854-RC, December 15, 1959.

Nutter, G. Warren, "Industrial Growth in the Soviet Union," *American Economic Review, Papers and Proceedings,* May, 1958, pp. 398–411.

"Organizing for the Technological War," A Staff Study, *Air Force,* December, 1957, pp. 41–45, 48.

Rabinowitch, Eugene, "Living with H-Bombs," *Bulletin of the Atomic Scientists,* January, 1955, pp. 5–8.

Samuelson, Paul A., "Diagrammatic Exposition of a Theory of Public Expenditure," *Review of Economics and Statistics,* November, 1955, pp. 350–356.

———— "The Pure Theory of Public Expenditure," *Review of Economics and Statistics,* November, 1954, pp. 387–389.

Schelling, Thomas C., "Bargaining, Communication, and Limited War," *Journal of Conflict Resolution,* March, 1957, pp. 19–36.

———— "The Strategy of Conflict: Prospectus for a Reorientation of Game Theory," *Journal of Conflict Resolution,* September, 1958, pp. 203–264.

———— "Surprise Attack and Disarmament," in *NATO and American Security,* ed. Klaus Knorr, Princeton University Press, Princeton, N.J., 1959, pp. 176–208.

Schmookler, Jacob, "The Changing Efficiency of the American Economy: 1869–1938," *Review of Economics and Statistics,* August, 1952, pp. 214–231.

Schultz, Theodore W., "Latin-American Economic Policy Lessons," *American Economic Review, Papers and Proceedings,* May, 1956, pp. 425–432.

Schwartz, G. L., "Planning and Economic Privilege," *The Manchester School,* January, 1946, pp. 53–71.

Silberman, Charles E., and Sanford S. Parker, "The Economic Impact of Defense," *Fortune,* June, 1958, pp. 102–105, 215–216, 218.

Simon, Herbert A., "Theories of Decision-Making in Economics and Behavioral Science," *American Economic Review,* June, 1959, pp. 253–283.

Slichter, Sumner, "Thinking Ahead: On the Side of Inflation," *Harvard Business Review,* September-October, 1957, pp. 15 ff.

Smithies, Arthur, "Fiscal Aspects of Preparedness for War," *American Economic Review, Papers and Proceedings,* May, 1949, pp. 356–365.

Thomas, Clayton J., and Walter L. Deemer, Jr., "The Role of Operational Gaming in Operations Research," *Operations Research,* February, 1957, pp. 1–27.

Tintner, G., "The Theory of Choice under Subjective Risk and Uncertainty," *Econometrica,* July-October, 1941, pp. 298–304.

Tobin, James, "Defense, Dollars, and Doctrines," *Yale Review,* Spring, 1958, pp. 321–334.

Tucker, A. W., "Linear and Nonlinear Programming," *Operations Research,* April, 1957, pp. 244–257.

Wagner, Harvey M., "The Simplex Method for Beginners," *Operations Research,* March-April, 1958, pp. 190–199.

Wohlstetter, Albert, "The Delicate Balance of Terror," *Foreign Affairs,* January, 1959, pp. 211–234.

# INDEX

Since 1961 CHARLES J. HITCH has been Assistant Secretary of Defense (Comptroller) in the U.S. Department of Defense. Earlier he was Head of the Economics Division, The RAND Corporation (1948-1960). He served in the U.S. Army during World War II and as Chief of the Stabilization Controls Division, Office of War Mobilization and Reconversion (1945-1946). A Rhodes Scholar at Oxford University, he became a Fellow, Praelector, and Tutor at Queen's College, Oxford (1935-1948), and was General Editor of the *Oxford Economic Papers* (1941-1948).

Mr. Hitch has also served as President of the Operations Research Society of America; as Irving Fisher Research Professor, Yale University; as a consultant to the Ford Foundation, Committee for Economic Development, and various government agencies.


ROLAND N. McKEAN, Professor of Economics at the University of California, Los Angeles, was in the Economics Department at The RAND Corporation from 1951 to 1964. On a leave of absence during 1961-62, he studied American governmental and legal processes with the aid of a Social Science Research Council grant and, while holding a Fulbright award, was affiliated with the University of Glasgow. Earlier he taught economics at Vanderbilt University (1948-51), studied at the University of Chicago. He has served on various government panels and committees, and as a member of the Board of Editors of the *American Economic Review*.

*PUBLISHED RAND RESEARCH*

### COLUMBIA UNIVERSITY PRESS, NEW YORK, NEW YORK

*Soviet National Income and Product, 1940–48,* by Abram Bergson and Hans Heymann, Jr., 1954
*Soviet National Income and Product in 1928,* by Oleg Hoeffding, 1954
*Labor Productivity in Soviet and American Industry,* by Walter Galenson, 1955

### THE FREE PRESS, GLENCOE, ILLINOIS

*Psychosis and Civilization,* by Herbert Goldhamer and Andrew W. Marshall, 1949
*Soviet Military Doctrine,* by Raymond L. Garthoff, 1953
*A Study of Bolshevism,* by Nathan Leites, 1953
*Ritual of Liquidation: The Case of the Moscow Trials,* by Nathan Leites and Elsa Bernaut, 1954
*Two Studies in Soviet Controls: Communism and the Russian Peasant, and Moscow in Crisis,* by Herbert S. Dinerstein and Leon Gouré, 1955
*A Million Random Digits with 100,000 Normal Deviates,* by The RAND Corporation, 1955

### HARVARD UNIVERSITY PRESS, CAMBRIDGE, MASSACHUSETTS

*Smolensk under Soviet Rule,* by Merle Fainsod, 1958

### McGRAW-HILL BOOK COMPANY, INC., NEW YORK, NEW YORK

*The Operational Code of the Politburo,* by Nathan Leites, 1951
*Air War and Emotional Stress: Psychological Studies of Bombing and Civilian Defense,* by Irving L. Janis, 1951
*Soviet Attitudes toward Authority: An Interdisciplinary Approach to Problems of Soviet Character,* by Margaret Mead, 1951
*Mobilizing Resources for War: The Economic Alternatives,* by Tibor Scitovsky, Edward Shaw, and Lorie Tarshis, 1951
*The Organizational Weapon: A Study of Bolshevik Strategy and Tactics,* by Philip Selznick, 1952
*Introduction to the Theory of Games,* by J. C. C. McKinsey, 1952
*Weight-Strength Analysis of Aircraft Structures,* by F. R. Shanley, 1952
*The Compleat Strategyst: Being a Primer on the Theory of Games of Strategy,* by J. D. Williams, 1954
*Linear Programming and Economic Analysis,* by Robert Dorfman, Paul A. Samuelson, and Robert M. Solow, 1958
*Introduction to Matrix Analysis,* by Richard Bellman, 1960
*The Theory of Linear Economic Models,* by David Gale, 1960

## PUBLISHED RAND RESEARCH

### THE MICROCARD FOUNDATION, MADISON, WISCONSIN

*The First Six Million Prime Numbers,* by C. L. Baker and F. J. Gruenberger, 1959

### NORTH-HOLLAND PUBLISHING COMPANY, AMSTERDAM, HOLLAND

*A Time Series Analysis of Interindustry Demands,* by Kenneth J. Arrow and Marvin Hoffenberg, 1959

### FREDERICK A. PRAEGER, PUBLISHERS, NEW YORK, NEW YORK

*War and the Soviet Union: Nuclear Weapons and the Revolution in Soviet Military and Political Thinking,* by H. S. Dinerstein, 1959

### PRINCETON UNIVERSITY PRESS, PRINCETON, NEW JERSEY

*Approximations for Digital Computers,* by Cecil Hastings, Jr., 1955
*International Communication and Political Opinion: A Guide to the Literature,* by Bruce Lannes Smith and Chitra M. Smith, 1956
*Dynamic Programming,* by Richard Bellman, 1957
*The Berlin Blockade: A Study in Cold War Politics,* by W. Phillips Davison, 1958
*The French Economy and the State,* by Warren C. Baum, 1958
*Strategy in the Missile Age,* by Bernard Brodie, 1959
*Foreign Aid: Theory and Practice in Southern Asia,* by Charles Wolf, Jr., 1960

### PUBLIC AFFAIRS PRESS, WASHINGTON, D.C.

*The Rise of Khrushchev,* by Myron Rush, 1958
*Behind the Sputniks: A Survey of Soviet Space Science,* by F. J. Krieger, 1958

### RANDOM HOUSE, INC., NEW YORK, NEW YORK

*Space Handbook: Astronautics and Its Applications,* by Robert W. Buchheim and the Staff of The RAND Corporation, 1959

### ROW, PETERSON AND COMPANY, EVANSTON, ILLINOIS

*German Rearmament and Atomic War: The Views of German Military and Political Leaders,* by Hans Speier, 1957
*West German Leadership and Foreign Policy,* edited by Hans Speier and W. Phillips Davison, 1957
*The House without Windows: France Selects a President,* by Constantin Melnik and Nathan Leites, 1958
*Propaganda Analysis: A Study of Inferences Made from Nazi Propaganda in World War II,* by Alexander L. George, 1959

### STANFORD UNIVERSITY PRESS, STANFORD, CALIFORNIA

*Strategic Surrender: The Politics of Victory and Defeat,* by Paul Kecskemeti, 1958
*On the Game of Politics in France,* by Nathan Leites, 1959
*Atomic Energy in the Soviet Union,* by Arnold Kramish, 1959
*Marxism in Southeast Asia: A Study of Four Countries,* by Frank N. Trager, *et al.,* 1959

### JOHN WILEY & SONS, INC., NEW YORK, NEW YORK

*Efficiency in Government through Systems Analysis: With Emphasis on Water Resource Development,* by Roland N. McKean, 1958

# *Atheneum Paperbacks*

## THE NEW YORK TIMES BYLINE BOOKS

## THE ADAMS PAPERS

## ECONOMICS AND BUSINESS

## PHYSICAL SCIENCES AND MATHEMATICS

# *Atheneum Paperbacks*

# *Atheneum Paperbacks*

## HISTORY

## HISTORY—ASIA

# *Atheneum Paperbacks*

## STUDIES IN AMERICAN NEGRO LIFE

# *Atheneum Paperbacks*

# *Atheneum Paperbacks*

## POLITICAL SCIENCE